Mastering Q&A for Windows

Common Q&A Write Tool Bar Buttons

BUTTON	BUTTON NAME	EQUIVALENT COMMAND	SHORTCUT KEYS
	New	File ➤ New	Ctrl+N
	Open	File ➤ Open	Ctrl+O
	Save	File ➤ Save	Ctrl+S
	Cut	Edit ➤ Cut	Ctrl+X
	Copy	Edit ➤ Copy	Ctrl+C
	Paste	Edit ➤ Paste	Ctrl+V
	Undo/Redo	Edit ➤ Undo or Redo	Ctrl+Z
	Frame	Insert ➤ Frame	Alt+F7
	Create/Edit Envelope	Tools ➤ Create Envelope or Edit Envelope	N/A
	Spell Check	Tools ➤ Spelling	Ctrl+F2
	Print	File ➤ Print	Ctrl+P
	View at 25%	View ➤ Full Page (25%)	Ctrl+1
	View at 100%	View ➤ Normal (100%)	Ctrl+3
	Custom Scale	View ➤ Custom Scale	Ctrl+0
	Merge Field	Insert ➤ Merge Field	Ctrl+Shift+M
	Print Merge Document	File ➤ Print Merge	N/A
	Left Justification	Format ➤ Paragraph	Ctrl+F5
	Center Justification	Format ➤ Paragraph	Ctrl+F5
	Right Justification	Format ➤ Paragraph	Ctrl+F5
	Full Justification	Format ➤ Paragraph	Ctrl+F5
	Single Line Spacing	Format ➤ Paragraph	Ctrl+F5
	One-and-One-Half Line Spacing	Format ➤ Paragraph	Ctrl+F5
	Double Line Spacing	Format ➤ Paragraph	Ctrl+F5
	No Paragraph Spacing	Format ➤ Paragraph	Ctrl+F5
	Add Paragraph Spacing	Format ➤ Paragraph	Ctrl+F5
	Show/Hide	View ➤ Show Detail or Show Proof	Ctrl+W

For every kind of computer user, there is a SYBEX book.

All computer users learn in their own way. Some need straightforward and methodical explanations. Others are just too busy for this approach. But no matter what camp you fall into, SYBEX has a book that can help you get the most out of your computer and computer software while learning at your own pace.

Beginners generally want to start at the beginning. The **ABC's** series, with its step-by-step lessons in plain language, helps you build basic skills quickly. Or you might try our **Quick & Easy** series, the friendly, full-color guide.

The **Mastering** and **Understanding** series will tell you everything you need to know about a subject. They're perfect for intermediate and advanced computer users, yet they don't make the mistake of leaving beginners behind.

If you're a busy person and are already comfortable with computers, you can choose from two SYBEX series—**Up & Running** and **Running Start**. The **Up & Running** series gets you started in just 20 lessons. Or you can get two books in one, a step-by-step tutorial and an alphabetical reference, with our **Running Start** series.

Everyone who uses computer software can also use a computer software reference. SYBEX offers the gamut—from portable **Instant References** to comprehensive **Encyclopedias**, **Desktop References**, and **Bibles**.

SYBEX even offers special titles on subjects that don't neatly fit a category—like **Tips & Tricks**, the **Shareware Treasure Chests**, and a wide range of books for Macintosh computers and software.

SYBEX books are written by authors who are expert in their subjects. In fact, many make their living as professionals, consultants or teachers in the field of computer software. And their manuscripts are thoroughly reviewed by our technical and editorial staff for accuracy and ease-of-use.

So when you want answers about computers or any popular software package, just help yourself to SYBEX.

For a complete catalog of our publications, please write:

SYBEX Inc.
2021 Challenger Drive
Alameda, CA 94501
Tel: (510) 523-8233/(800) 227-2346 Telex: 336311
Fax: (510) 523-2373

SYBEX is committed to using natural resources wisely to preserve and improve our environment. As a leader in the computer book publishing industry, we are aware that over 40% of America's solid waste is paper. This is why we have been printing the text of books like this one on recycled paper since 1982.

This year our use of recycled paper will result in the saving of more than 15,300 trees. We will lower air pollution effluents by 54,000 pounds, save 6,300,000 gallons of water, and reduce landfill by 2,700 cubic yards.

In choosing a SYBEX book you are not only making a choice for the best in skills and information, you are also choosing to enhance the quality of life for all of us.

Mastering Q&A™ for Windows™

Sandra E. Eddy
Michael M. Swertfager

San Francisco • Paris • Düsseldorf • Soest

SYBEX®

Developmental Editor: David Peal
Project Editor: Kristen Vanberg-Wolff
Editor: Armin A. Brott
Technical Editor: Scott Howley
Book Designer: Suzanne Albertson
Production Artist: Lisa Jaffe
Screen Graphics: John Corrigan and Aldo X. Bermudez
Typesetters: Stephanie Hollier, Alissa Feinberg
Proofreader/Production Assistant: Stephen Kullmann
Indexer: Ted Laux
Cover Designer: Ingalls + Associates
Cover Photographer: Mark Johann

Library of Congress Card Number: 93-87025
ISBN: 0-7821-1397-4

To Delle

To my brother, Robert Swertfager,
and to the memory of Keasha

ACKNOWLEDGMENTS

ALTHOUGH the authors of a book are ultimately responsible for its contents, there are many others who play major roles in bringing everything together. We recognize all those people here.

We especially thank the people at SYBEX for all their help and support. Special thanks go to Developmental Editor David Peal and Project Editor Kris Vanberg-Wolff. For his care and attention to our words and pictures, thanks to Armin Brott.

For accuracy and care in reviewing every page, a special thank you to our Technical Editor, Scott Howley.

For their help and assistance, we acknowledge the people in the Software Quality Assurance and Technical Support departments at Symantec.

A very special thanks to the following Symantec employees: Paul Vallez, Carl Rivas, Mike Magsanay, and Cheryl Rubin Young.

For their continued encouragement, our families and friends.

For support and friendship: Keith Krohn, David Engelbrecht, David Wyllie, and Mark Williams.

Special thanks to my wonderful parents who support me in all that I do: Jack and Kelly Swertfager, and Steve and Barbara Perry.

For their special contributions—Indy, Toni, and Bart.

$\mathcal{C}$ontents AT A GLANCE

CONTENTS

CONTENTS

FOREWORD

MICHAEL Swertfager and Sandra Eddy have created a certified winner in their book, *Mastering Q&A for Windows*. The authors' extensive experience with Q&A and their unique ability to communicate in a friendly way, result in a book that goes well beyond other reference manuals and tutorials. This book is a perfect companion to the manuals included with our software.

I am confident in the authors because I know where they are coming from. Michael Swertfager worked at Symantec for several years as a Q&A software analyst. He'll help you figure out the best ways to use Q&A in solving all your business problems. Sandy Eddy is the author of a number of computer books, including a best-seller on Q&A for DOS. She succeeds in making every topic as simple as possible.

For years Q&A for DOS has been the most popular integrated database and word-processing program specially designed for business. This new Windows version now contains a full-featured, fully integrated word processor—Q&A Write. While our other Q&A programs are intended to work in concert, the database and word processor in Q&A for Windows allow for unparalleled integration. Even a complicated task such as sending a form letter to a large number of your customers at once is made simple. *Mastering Q&A for Windows* shows you how to fully exploit the benefits of Q&A for Windows.

The authors' approach in teaching Q&A is perfect for people learning the product as well as people who just need a good reference. Michael and Sandy rely heavily on step-by-step examples and explanations to cover important Q&A concepts and techniques. This "reader-friendly" writing style is one of the main reasons I'm so impressed with *Mastering Q&A for Windows*.

Michael and Sandy start by giving you a firm grounding in the Q&A Windows database. Then they show you how to use the exceptional features of Q&A for Windows to structure a database for maximum efficiency. In the end, you'll be able to manipulate the technical features of Q&A for Windows and, more importantly, you will understand the program well enough to use your creativity to save time and money.

From there, Michael and Sandy cover the new Q&A word processor—Q&A Write. In their coverage of the program, they show you how to create a variety of common business documents. You'll learn all the basic word processing skills you need to work with Q&A Write.

Finally, the authors cover the most important benefit of Q&A for Windows—connectivity. In *Mastering Q&A for Windows*, you'll see how you can make your business even more productive. You'll find out how to share data and applications between the Q&A word processor and database program. This will allow you to conduct large-scale marketing outreach to your customers, even import database reports into other documents.

Mastering Q&A for Windows, I believe, is your best bet for getting the most out of this revolutionary new program. By using this book, you *will* become more effective with Q&A. And you'll find yourself referring to the book time and again for as long as you use Q&A for Windows. Have fun!

Gordon Eubanks, Jr.
President & CEO
Symantec Corporation

INTRODUCTION

WELCOME to *Mastering Q&A for Windows*! Whether you are an experienced Q&A for DOS user who has very little Windows experience or an experienced Windows user who has never used Q&A, this book will help to answer all your questions—from creating your first database to finding out how to program in Q&A.

Who This Book Is For

This book is designed for people who have worked with Windows but are new to Q&A for Windows. If you are new to database management systems, be sure to read Chapter 1 and work along with the features, examples, and procedures in Chapter 2. In these chapters, you'll learn both the terminology and the basic building blocks of Q&A.

If you have used other database applications, including Q&A for DOS, it's still important to read Chapters 1 and 2 to find out how Q&A for Windows works.

Although *Mastering Q&A for Windows* assumes you have some knowledge of Windows, you can always refer to Appendix B for information about the Windows features that will help you run Q&A for Windows more efficiently.

How to Use This Book

This book is a combination of both reference and tutorial. From the beginning to the end of the book, you'll find useful tables, illustrations, sets of procedures to guide you through Q&A for Windows, explanations of both database and Q&A terms, and these special features:

Fast Tracks are brief summaries of features covered in the chapter. Use Fast Tracks to refresh your memory without reading background information and descriptions.

Notes emphasize important information about a topic.

Tips provide shortcuts and easy-to-use methods for performing functions.

Warnings inform you about potential problems and pitfalls.

About This Book

You can use this book along with your Q&A manuals to get a complete picture of every feature and function of both Q&A Database and Q&A Write. In fact, this book provides information that you won't find anywhere else.

Mastering Q&A for Windows is arranged in three parts:

Part One—Managing Information with Q&A for Windows

In the first part of the book, you'll learn about the elements of the application windows, how to start and end a work session, open a file, move around a file, preview and print a file, delete files, and get help. Part One shows you how to plan, design, and create a new database; define field types; view records; create, edit, and delete input forms; manage and re-design database files; customize database structure; enter, retrieve, and sort data; report on your data in several ways; use the Intelligent Assistant and the Scripting Assistant; write programming statements; and perform both mass updates and mass deletes.

Part Two—Creating Documents with the Q&A Word Processor

In the second part, you'll learn how to plan and create a document; check spelling, words, and document statistics; close, save, and print a document. This part also shows how to search and replace text and formats; add special characters; choose fonts, point size, and emphasis; format paragraphs, characters, and the entire document.

Part Three—Importing, Exporting, and Securing Data

Finally, in Part Three, you'll discover valuable information about how to import data to and export data from other Windows applications; perform mail merge; print envelopes; secure your database with users and groups of users; assign user IDs and passwords; and lock your database.

Appendices

At the back of the book are five appendices that provide detailed information about installing Q&A, using Windows, setting user preferences for both Q&A Database and Q&A Write; and using every one of the Q&A programming functions and commands.

Conventions Used in This Book

Mastering Q&A for Windows provides the following keyboard conventions, text conventions, and command syntax.

Keyboard Conventions

Windows applications such as Q&A for Windows support both the mouse and the keyboard. This book provides these keyboard conventions:

Single Keys

Press a single key (for example, ←, →, ↓, ↑, PgUp, PgDn, Del, Backspace, Spacebar, Home, and End) to instruct Q&A to perform an action. For example, you can press Enter to complete most commands, and you can press Esc to close a dialog box or menu without taking an action.

Key Combinations

Use a *key combination* (two or three keys pressed simultaneously) as a shortcut to execute commands or perform actions in Q&A for Windows and in other Windows applications. In this book, key combinations are shown as two or three keys, each separated by a plus sign (+). For example, the key combination used to open a file for both Q&A Database and Q&A Write is Ctrl+O, and the key combination used to exit Windows applications and Windows itself is Alt+F4. As you view Q&A menus, you'll notice that many, but not all, commands have key combinations.

To execute a key combination, press and hold down the first key, then press the next key or keys. For example, to display a dialog box from which you can open a file, press and hold down the Ctrl key, press O, and release both keys.

Issuing Menu Commands

You can also issue commands by pressing the underlined keys in menus and commands. (See Appendix B for information about using underlined letters within dialog boxes.)

To select a menu, press the Alt key. Then press the underlined letter for the menu you want. For example, to select the menu File, press Alt and then press F. Q&A opens the menu and displays commands, all with more underlined letters. To select a command from the menu, press the underlined letter in the desired command (for example, the O in Open). Press Esc to cancel the command or close the menu.

In this book, the menu-command selections are represented by this combination of text and symbol: File ➤ Open. This sequence tells you to choose File from the menu bar; then select the Open command from the displayed File menu.

Occasionally, you'll see a sequence consisting of a menu, a command, and a subcommand. For example, if you see Format ➤ Align Text ➤ Center, you'll choose Format from the menu bar, choose the Align command, which opens a cascading menu, and then choose the Center command.

Text Conventions

In this book, *italicized* text represents both variables (for example, a file name or value to be typed) and new terms.

This font:

    #10=IF @ERROR THEN @MSG("The XLOOKUP couldn't be found")

indicates programming statements that you type or emulate when creating your own statements.

Command Syntax

Commands and functions in this book use this syntax:

    command or abbreviation (*parameter1, parameter2, ...parameter3*)

where italics represent parameters that you enter. When typing a command or function, either type the full command or function *or* the abbreviation. Then type the parameters.

part one

Managing Information with Q&A for Windows

chapter

1

A Bird's-Eye View of Q&A

fast TRACK

● **A database**   6

is an organized collection of related information, such as a customer list or an inventory of video tapes or movies.

● **A database management system**   10

is the computer software, such as Q&A Database, with which you set up and organize database information.

● **A word processor**   12

is the computer software, such as Q&A Write, with which you produce documents (letters, pamphlets, proposals, reports, mailing labels).

● **A record**   10

is a set of information for one entity, such as one customer or one video tape.

● **A field**   10

is one piece of information in a record. A field contains a customer's last name or a video tape title.

● **An input form**   10

is a record layout into which you type data or from which you view the contents of a record. The ideal input form is designed so that data entry is both easy and efficient.

● **Spreadsheet view**   10

   is a viewing format that shows you several records at a time in
   a spreadsheet-like format.

● **Form view**   10

   is a viewing format that shows you one record at a time.

● **Intelligent Assistant (IA)**   11

   is a Q&A feature that is an English language query and retrieval
   tool.

● **A query**   11

   is an inquiry or question about a Q&A database. For example,
   you can ask the IA how many customers live in a particular
   town or ZIP code.

● **Scripts**   12

   are directions that tell Q&A to perform sets of instructions
   you use often.

● **Scripting Assistant**   12

   is a Q&A feature that allows you to write scripts.

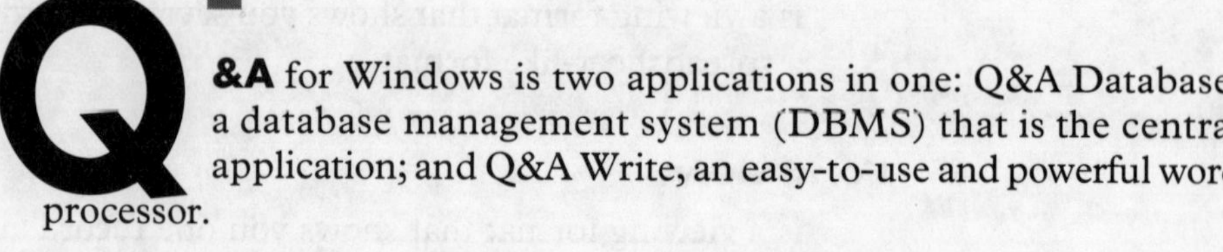

Q **&A** for Windows is two applications in one: Q&A Database, a database management system (DBMS) that is the central application; and Q&A Write, an easy-to-use and powerful word processor.

What's Special About Q&A?

Q&A Database allows you to plan, design, create, and manage *databases*, organized collections of related information. For example, you can keep track of your customers, their addresses, spending habits, all the items they have ever bought, and so on. Or, you can create an inventory of video tapes or the movies you have seen, including as much information as you desire for each movie—director, producer, actors and actresses; date of purchase and price; and even how you rate it. You can set up and manage (hence the name *database management system*) a computerized database to gather and report on almost any imaginable group of information.

Q&A Write, which works with Q&A Database but also works independently, has all the features of the most powerful Windows word processors. Q&A Write offers sophisticated formatting, advanced search and replace, a spell checker and thesaurus, and much more.

Because Q&A for Windows is a Windows-based application, if you know Windows, you'll notice that Q&A has the same "look and feel" as other Windows applications. Another benefit of running under Windows is that both applications can share data with each other and with other Windows applications. For example, you can copy a picture from Paintbrush into a Q&A file, or you can merge information—from a single letter to a long proposal—from Q&A Database into a Q&A Write document.

If you're a Q&A 4.0 for DOS veteran using a Windows application for the first time, you'll find the same familiar features. You'll be able to use the navigation keys with which you are familiar, retrieve specs, and sort specs—but they'll be much easier to use. You will also have the additional benefit of being able to use your current Q&A 4.0 databases. In fact, Q&A 4.0 and Q&A for Windows users can work side by side on the same databases. As you move from Q&A 4.0 to Q&A for Windows, this inter-operability between the two applications makes it easy to migrate.

What Can I Do with Q&A?

It's amazing how many types of databases people create with Q&A. Here are just a few of the possibilities:

The Customer Database The most frequently used Q&A database consists of information about different customers. With this database, you can:

- Print reports of customer names, addresses, and telephone numbers.
- Run mail merges for billing statements and letters.
- Create mailing labels to notify customers of special sales and events.

The Real Estate Tracking Database A real estate office has a database of unsold and sold properties. With this database, you can:

- Create printed reports of all properties not sold, including length of time on the market, and asking price.
- Create reports of all sold properties, including the time it took to sell, the selling price, and the difference between the asking price and selling price.
- Match a buyers database with the properties database using a function called XLOOKUP.

- Run mail merges of letters to prospective buyers about properties for sale.

- Retrieve specific groups of properties that meet certain criteria for prospective buyers.

The Meeting Agenda Database A company, department, or organization might use an agenda database with information about meetings and agendas. With this database, you can:

- Create a printed report of all those who attended one meeting or all meetings.

- Create a report of topics (including those carried over from the previous meetings) for each meeting.

- Create a report to summarize each meeting.

- Print the minutes of each meeting.

- Retrieve a list of meetings that met certain criteria. For example, you could retrieve a list of meetings during which raising members' dues were discussed.

- Run mail merges of letters to members.

- Create mailing labels to send pamphlets about special events.

The Survey Tracking Database A market research or polling firm may have a database that tracks entire surveys or individual questions. With this database, you can:

- Create a printed report of the number of people who answered a particular question in a certain way. (You can also add personal information about individuals to the report.)

- Calculate standard deviations (and other statistics) on the results of surveys.

- Create a mail merge to all people who took the survey or who responded in a certain way.

- Produce mailing labels for special mailings, such as advertising leaflets and supermarket coupons.

The Inventory Database A corporation, department, or non-profit agency could set up an inventory database. With this database, you can:

- Print inventory reports based on the entire inventory or categories of items. For example, you can age the inventory or find out how popular certain items are.

- Create a mail merge to send letters, payments, and requests for bids from vendors.

- Produce mailing labels to distributors.

You can even build a very elaborate inventory database. For example, you can get a bar-code reader and turn the computer with the database into a "cash register." You can then fully automate the "cash register" with scripts that will start retrieving records. Read the bar-code into the first field and watch it retrieve a purchased item. At this point, you can print the record, which will tell you anything you want to know about this item: an elaborate description, a warranty, costs, prices, and even a picture.

When an item is purchased, the database can record the number of items purchased and calculate the number of items remaining in inventory. Using this information, you can create a complete Just In Time (JIT) inventory system to manage your stock.

So you can see that your imagination is the only limitation when using Q&A. Now it's time to learn more about the important building blocks of the Q&A package.

Building Blocks

Now let's look a little more closely at Q&A Database and Q&A Write to see the major features that they have to offer. At the same time, we'll introduce you to a few of the terms that you'll see throughout this book. We will cover these same database terms in greater detail in Chapter 3.

Q&A Database is equipped with valuable tools: The Intelligent Assistant, the Scripting Assistant, and an extensive programming facility. Let's take a closer look at these components.

The Q&A Database

Using the Q&A Database, you can create, organize, and manipulate database files. Databases are groups of *records*—all the information about one person or thing, such as a customer or an inventory item. Records are made up of *fields*—one piece of information about a person or thing, such as a customer's last name or an inventory item's identification number. When you work with a database, you can type directly into an *input form* (a layout designed so that data entry is both easy and efficient) or import data from another application. Then you can arrange and format the data to produce reports, letters, mailing labels, and even applications to run a small business or corporate department. Figure 1.1 shows a sample record (and fields) in a table view called *Spreadsheet View*. Notice that each row is a different record and each column is a different field. Your other choice for viewing the contents of a database is to switch to the *Form View* (as shown in Figure 1.2), which enables you to see one record at a time.

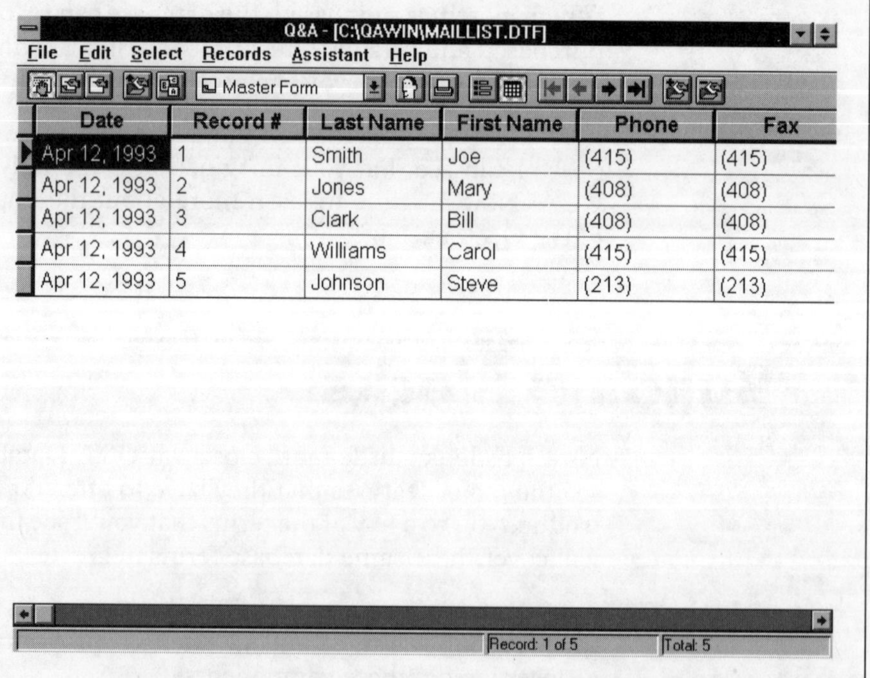

Date	Record #	Last Name	First Name	Phone	Fax
Apr 12, 1993	1	Smith	Joe	(415)	(415)
Apr 12, 1993	2	Jones	Mary	(408)	(408)
Apr 12, 1993	3	Clark	Bill	(408)	(408)
Apr 12, 1993	4	Williams	Carol	(415)	(415)
Apr 12, 1993	5	Johnson	Steve	(213)	(213)

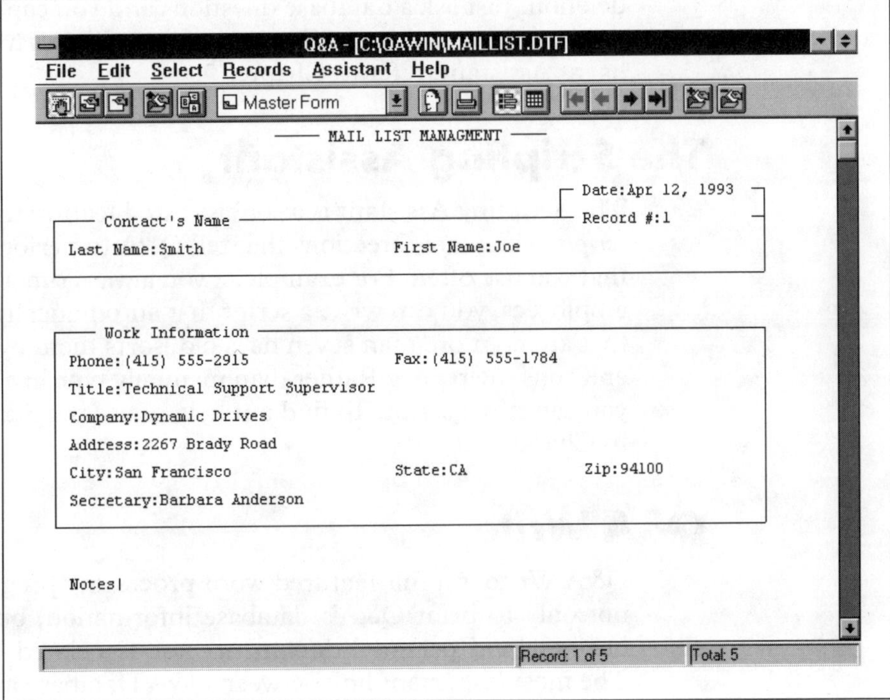

Even if you have been keeping a database for years, and even if the database is huge, you can easily redesign it as your needs change. Simply open the database and view the appropriate records, which you can then sort, edit, update, or delete.

The Intelligent Assistant

The Intelligent Assistant (IA) is an English language query and retrieval tool. A *query* is an inquiry or question. For example, if you want to ask the database how many customers live in a particular town or zip code, use the IA. You also can ask the IA to retrieve certain records from the database. For example, if you wish to send a special coupon to recent customers, you can tell the IA to retrieve records of customers who ordered in the last six months. On the other hand, if you run a catalog company and want to eliminate customers who have been inactive for the past two years, you can tell the IA to retrieve those records for a reminder letter or deletion. Just ask a database questions and you can create reports, search and sort data, and even fill in input forms. To learn about using the Intelligent Assistant, refer to Chapter 9.

The Scripting Assistant

The Scripting Assistant is a sophisticated feature that allows you to write *scripts*, which are directions that tell Q&A to perform sets of instructions that you use often. For example, if you always run a Friday report on new employees, you can write a script that automatically retrieves the records that are no more than seven days old, sorts them by the Last Name field, and runs the report. Rather than manually type in a series of instructions, you can run a script. To find out how to use the Scripting Assistant, refer to Chapter 10.

Q&A Write

Q&A Write is a full-featured word processing program that you can use not only to print Q&A's database information, but also to write other business and personal documents not associated with Q&A Database. The most important link between Q&A Database and Q&A Write is *mail merge*, which allows you to designate information to be merged from a database into a mail merge letter, label, or other document. Another method by which Windows applications such as Q&A Database and Q&A Write communicate is by using DDE (Dynamic Data Exchange). If files are linked, as you update data in one application (such as an Excel spreadsheet) the contents of a file in the other application (e.g., a Q&A Write newsletter) are also updated.

Other important Q&A Write features are:

- Character, paragraph, and document formatting
- Spell check and thesaurus
- Sophisticated search and replace
- Headers and footers
- Automatic save
- Multiple columns
- Styles and libraries of styles

- Graphic support, including Windows bitmaps, PCX, and TIFF

- Fax and mail support

- Outlining

- Recognition of other word processor formats

- Import files from and export files to other applications

- Frames

- Customized tool bar and preferences

For information about using Write, refer to Chapters 13, 14, and 15.

To Sum Up

This chapter introduced you to Q&A Database and Q&A Write. First, you discovered the advantages of using Q&A for Windows. Then we showed you how you might use Q&A for Windows for conventional as well as extraordinary purposes. To wind up the chapter, we introduced the special features of Q&A Write.

In Chapter 2, you'll take a whirlwind tour of Q&A. You'll learn how to start and exit both Windows and Q&A, and we'll introduce you to elements of the Q&A window and how to use them. You'll find out how to use the mouse, the keyboard, and Q&A's tool bar. So hold onto your hat and let's start the tour.

chapter

2

Getting Acquainted with Q&A

fast **TRACK**

● **To move around a record**   32

click on the arrows at either end of the horizontal scroll bar or vertical scroll bar, or drag the scroll box (i.e., the thumb) along the scroll bar; or press Alt and the arrow key that points in the direction in which you want to go; or press PgUp or PgDn.

● **To view a file as it will print**   33

Choose File ➤ Print Preview.

● **To print a record or retrieved records**   36

choose File ➤ Print, or press Ctrl+P. In the Print dialog box, select the range of pages, select the print resolution, or print to a file. Then click on OK or press Enter.

● **To delete a file**   38

switch to the Program Manager and double-click on the File Manager icon. Select the appropriate directory in the Tree pane, and search for the appropriate .DTF and .IDX files. Click on the first file to be deleted, press Ctrl, and click on the second file to be deleted. Press the Del key and respond to the prompts.

THE BEST way to learn how an application works is to jump right in, and that's just what we're going to do in this chapter. You'll experience how the pieces fit together, how Q&A looks, and how it acts. Then, once you have the big picture, in the rest of the book we'll show you how to unlock the power of Q&A in your own work.

Starting Windows

The first step is to start Windows. If Windows is not displayed on your computer screen, just type win at the DOS prompt and then press the Enter key. To learn about some of the other ways to start Windows, refer to Appendix B.

Starting a Q&A Session

Q&A for Windows

Q&A Write

After starting Windows, you can start either the Q&A Database or Q&A Write, by clicking on the appropriate icon. You'll then see either the Q&A Database window (Figure 2.1) or the Q&A Write window (Figure 2.2).

Before we explain the elements of the Q&A window, we'll open EMPLOYEE.DTF, one of the sample databases that is installed when you do a complete installation. This will allow you to see how the pieces of the window work.

The opening window for the Q&A Database with typical Windows application window elements.

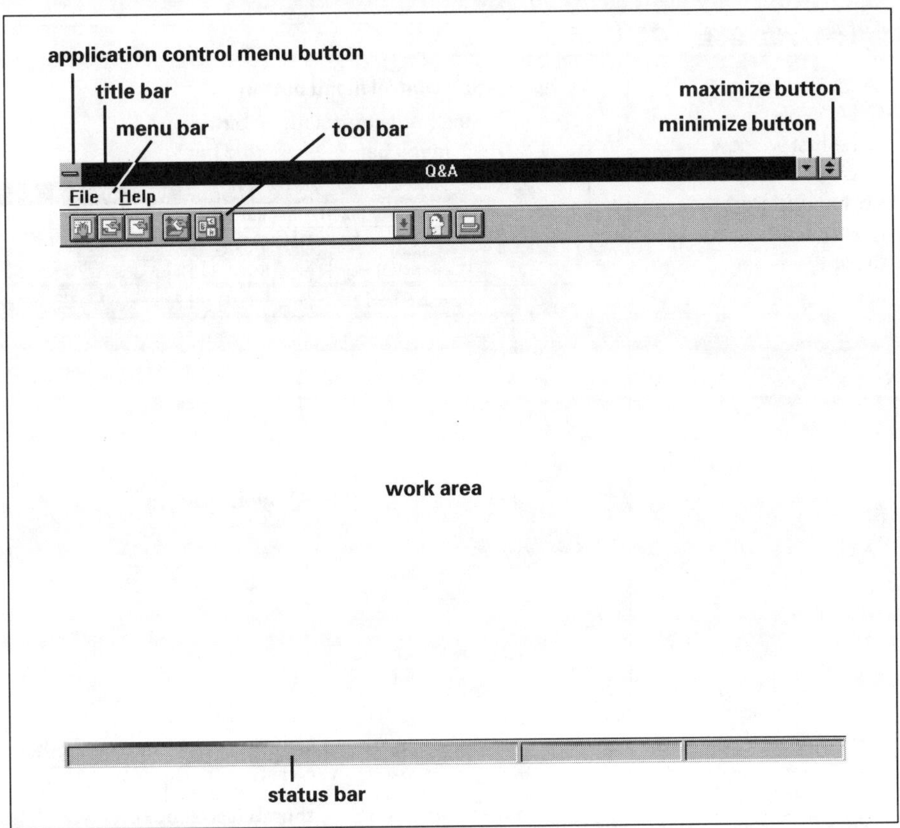

Opening a File

Opening a file in Q&A is very similar to opening a file in any other Windows application.

Unlike many Windows applications, you can have only one file open at a time in Q&A. In fact, whenever you open any new file, Q&A automatically closes the active file in the work area.

FIGURE 2.2

After you launch Q&A Write, this is the first window displayed. To get started, just start typing in the work area.

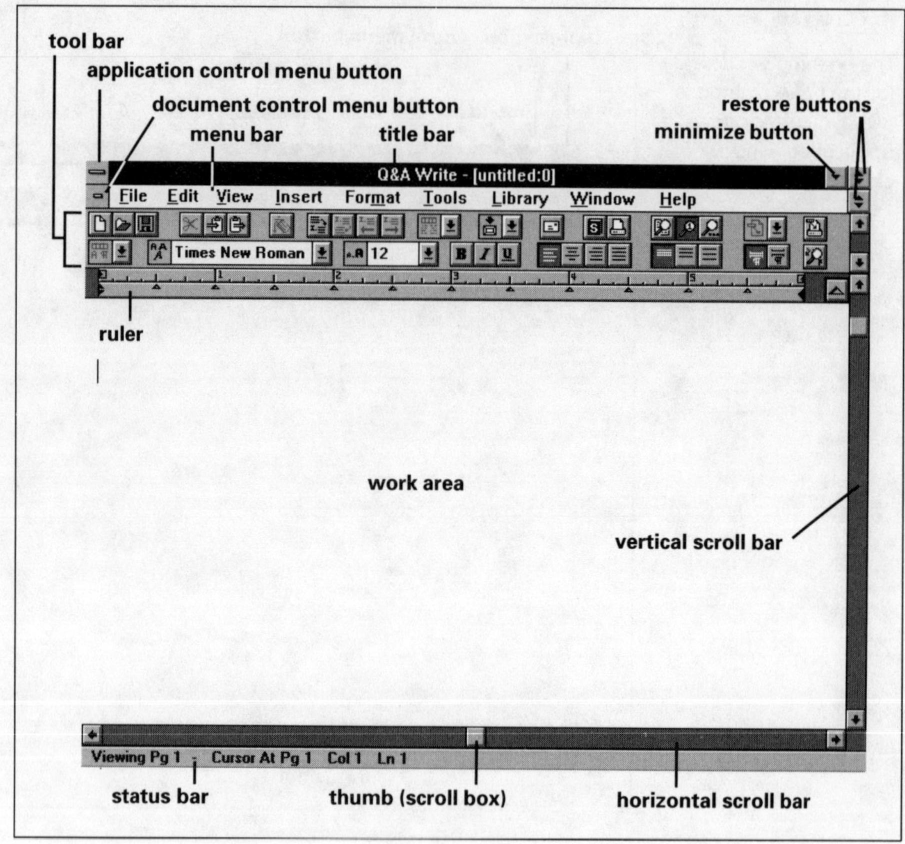

To open a file, follow these steps:

1. Either press the shortcut key combination Ctrl+O on the keyboard or choose File ➤ Open. Q&A displays the Open File dialog box (Figure 2.3). You use a dialog box to specify how you want to perform an action, such as (in this case) opening a specific file.

The EMPLOYEE.DTF database is located in the QAWIN subdirectory.

2. Double-click on EMPLOYEE.DTF. Q&A opens the file (see Figure 2.4) and you are on your way.

FIGURE 2.3

In Q&A's Open File dialog box, you can open a database that is located on a specific drive, in a particular directory.

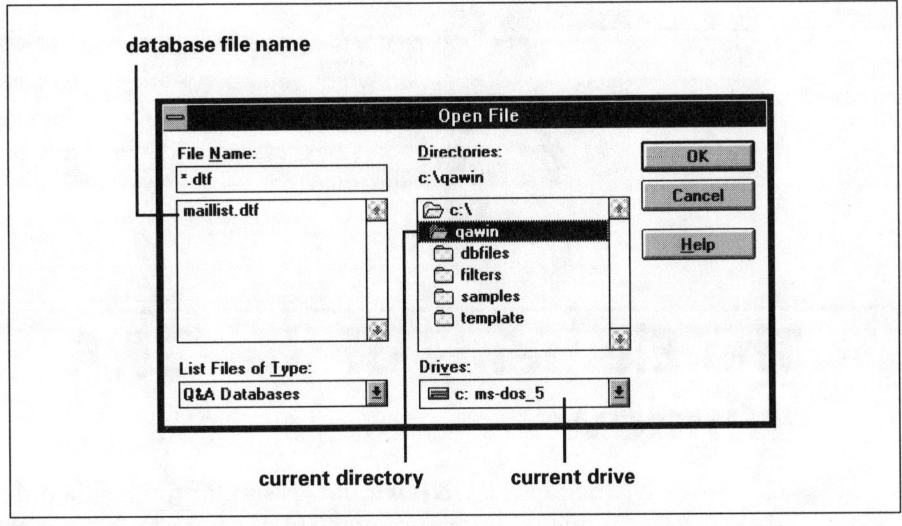

FIGURE 2.4

The first record in EMPLOYEE database shows both personal and business information about each employee.

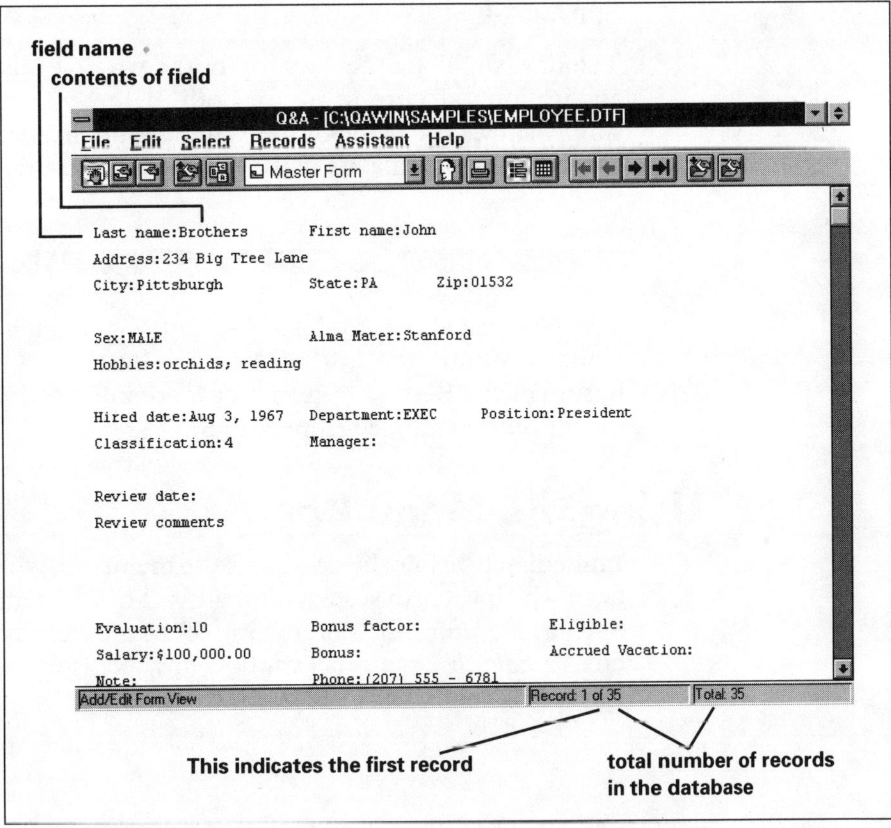

If the file that you wish to open is one of the last three on which you have worked, you can select it from the bottom of the open File menu. Either click on the file name or press the underlined number preceding the file name.

The Elements of the Q&A Window

Much of the Q&A window is similar to most Windows applications but a few elements are unique to Q&A. Let's look more closely at the Q&A window. For additional information about Windows application windows, see Appendix B.

The *title bar,* along the very top of the window, displays the name of the application, the current file, or both. Before you open a file, the title bar simply shows the name of the Windows application—in this case, Q&A. Once you open a file, its name is added to the title bar.

The title bar also contains small buttons at each end: the Application Control Menu button, the Minimize button, and either the Maximize button or the Restore button. For more information about what these title bar buttons do, see Appendix B.

Using the Menu Bar

Immediately below the title bar is the menu bar, which displays the menus from which you can select commands. These commands begin an action, open a *cascading menu,* branching off to the right or left, or open a dialog box. A *dialog box* is a small window in which you specify how you want to perform an action or change a setting.

<u>F</u>ile   <u>E</u>dit   <u>S</u>elect   <u>R</u>ecords   <u>A</u>ssistant   <u>H</u>elp

The menus you initially see on the opening Q&A Database window are <u>F</u>ile, from which you opened EMPLOYEE.DTF, <u>E</u>dit, and <u>H</u>elp. Once you open a file, Q&A displays a new menu bar, offering commands appropriate to working with database files. As you travel through various Q&A modes, you'll find that the menu bars change to fit the purpose of the mode. For more information about how Windows menus and commands work, see Appendix B.

Let's open a menu and look around. The <u>S</u>elect menu (Figure 2.5) allows you to view and work with different parts of a database. Let's choose <u>S</u>elect ➤ Design Input <u>F</u>orms to display a data input form (see Figure 2.6). *Input forms* are record layouts into which you enter data. The *Master Form* is the default input form for every database file. To find out how to select a new default input form, see Appendix C.

<table>
<tr><td>

</td><td>

<u>S</u>elect	
√ <u>A</u>dd/Edit	Ctrl+E
<u>D</u>esign Input <u>F</u>orms	Ctrl+M
<u>D</u>esign Reports/<u>L</u>abels	Ctrl+Y
<u>R</u>un Report...	
Database <u>S</u>tructure	
Mass <u>U</u>pdate	
M<u>a</u>ss Delete	
<u>L</u>oad Input Form...	Ctrl+L

</td></tr>
</table>

On the input form, you see field labels and *field boxes*—the boxes that show some or all the contents of the fields. Choose <u>S</u>elect ➤ Database <u>S</u>tructure to see how each field on the form is defined (see Figure 2.7). For example, you can see that the data type of a field is text or number. (In Chapter 3, you'll learn more about defining fields.) To return to the way that the database was first displayed, choose <u>S</u>elect ➤ <u>A</u>dd/Edit.

A sample input form with field names and the boxes that hold the values for fields. In the Design Input Forms work area, you can edit and enhance the field names and can drag fields and field names around until the input form is exactly as you desire.

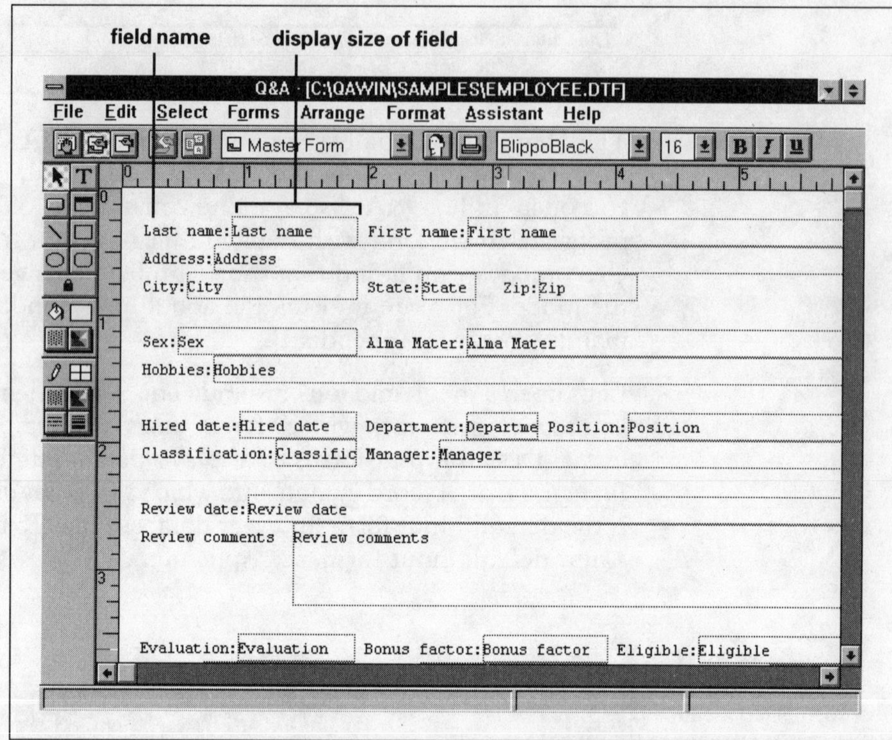

Now click on the <u>R</u>ecords menu (Figure 2.8). This menu offers you several ways to navigate through records. For example, if you are viewing the first record in your database, choose <u>R</u>ecords ➤ <u>N</u>ext Record to display the second record in the database, or <u>R</u>ecords ➤ <u>L</u>ast Record to go to the last record. To return to the first record, choose <u>R</u>ecords ➤ <u>F</u>irst Record.

Using the Tool Bar

Underneath the menu bar is the tool bar, which displays a series of buttons and drop-down boxes. When you click on a button or choose from a drop-down box, you tell Q&A to do something (such as open or print a file or display an input form) that would otherwise take a couple of steps using menus, commands, and dialog boxes. The buttons on each tool bar vary within Q&A Database and Q&A Write.

The Database Structure work area for the sample MAILLIST database. The field names are listed in the first column and the type of information in the field is in the second column.

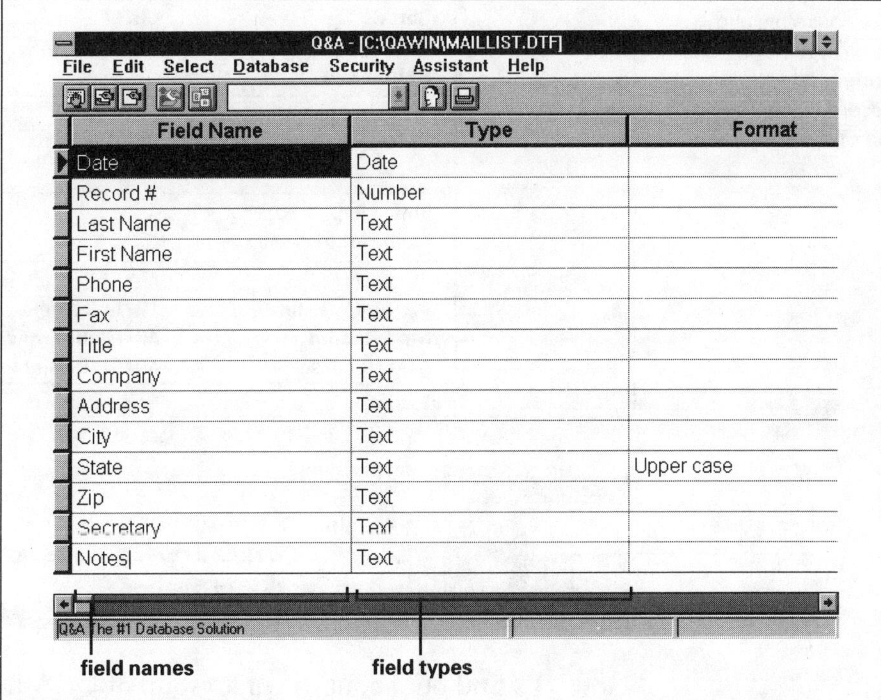

Let's take a closer look at the Q&A Database tool bar that you'll encounter whenever you create or edit a database. When we introduce you to other Q&A Database features (such as Print Preview and Design Input Forms) that provide special tool bar buttons, we'll show you how to use each set of buttons. (Q&A Write has a unique tool bar, which you can find out about in Chapter 12.) You can see whether buttons are related by how close they are to their neighbors. For example, the leftmost three buttons are linked; you can choose only one of the three at a time.

Records	
New Record	Ctrl+N
Duplicate Record	Ctrl+D
Delete Record	Ctrl+B
Revert Record	
Sort...	Ctrl+T
Retrieve	Ctrl+R
Retrieve All	
View as Spreadsheet	
Spreadsheet View Font...	Ctrl+F
Save Spreadsheet Layout	
Field Help...	
Field Restrictions...	
First Record	Alt+Shift+Left Arrow
Previous Record	Alt+Left Arrow
Next Record	Alt+Right Arrow
Last Record	Alt+Shift+Right Arrow

TIP

Click on any tool bar button with the right mouse button to view a short description in the status bar at the bottom-left side of the bar.

Now let's find out about the first group of Q&A Database tool bar buttons and list boxes. As you read, try clicking on buttons to see what happens. If a button looks dimmer than other buttons, it is not available for use now. For example, when you first open EMPLOYEE.DTF, Q&A displays the first record. This means that the tool bar buttons that enable you to go to the first record or to the prior record, are not active. If a button looks as if it is pressed down, it is selected and you don't have to click on it. For example, notice that the first button, Add/Edit, is pressed down. This means that you are viewing the database in Add/Edit mode and you can work with information in the database.

If you open the Select menu, you'll see that there is a check mark next to the first command, Add/Edit, which indicates that it is the active command. For every tool bar button, there is a counterpart menu command and quite often a shortcut key or key combination. Table 2.1 illustrates and describes each Q&A Database tool bar button and list box used when creating or editing a database file.

TABLE 2.1:   Q&A Database Tool Bar Buttons—Creating or Editing a Database

BUTTON	BUTTON OR LIST BOX NAME	DESCRIPTION	KEYBOARD EQUIVALENT	SHORTCUT KEYS
	Add/Edit	Enables you to work with (add, modify, or delete) information in a Q&A database.	Select ➤ Add/Edit	Ctrl+E
	Design Input Forms	Enables you to work with input forms for a Q&A database. (See Chapter 4.)	Select ➤ Design Input Forms	Ctrl+M
	Design Reports/ Labels	Enables you to work with reports and labels in a Q&A database. (See Chapter 9.)	Select ➤ Design Reports/Labels	Ctrl+Y
	Retrieve Records	Enables you to retrieve certain records from the open database. (See Chapter 8.)	Records ➤ Retrieve	Ctrl+R
	Sort Records	Enables you to specify the order in which records are retrieved. (See Chapter 8.)	Records ➤ Sort	Ctrl+T

TABLE 2.1: Q&A Database Tool Bar Buttons—Creating or Editing a Database (continued)

BUTTON	BUTTON OR LIST BOX NAME	DESCRIPTION	KEYBOARD EQUIVALENT	SHORTCUT KEYS
Master Form	Input Form	Allows you to select one of the input forms associated with the current database. (See Chapter 4.)	Select ➤ Load Input Form	Ctrl+L
	Intelligent Assistant	Enables you to use the IA.	Assistant ➤ Intelligent Assistant.	Ctrl+I
	Print	Allows you to print the current record or a group of selected records. (See this chapter.)	File ➤ Print	Ctrl+P
	Form View	Allows you to view records in the current database one by one. (See Chapter 3.)	Records ➤ View as Form	N/A
	Table View	Allows you to view records in the current database in a table or spreadsheet format--several records at a time. (See Chapter 3.)	Records ➤ View as Spreadsheet	N/A

TABLE 2.1: Q&A Database Tool Bar Buttons—Creating or Editing a Database (continued)

BUTTON	BUTTON OR LIST BOX NAME	DESCRIPTION	KEYBOARD EQUIVALENT	SHORTCUT KEYS
⏮	First Record	Displays the first record in the current database if you are not already viewing the first record. (See this chapter.)	<u>R</u>ecords ➤ <u>F</u>irst Record	Alt+Shift +←
◀	Previous Record	Displays the previous record in the current database if you are not already viewing the first record. (See this chapter.)	<u>R</u>ecords ➤ <u>P</u>revious Record	Alt+←
▶	Next Record	Displays the next record in the current database if you are not already viewing the last record. (See this chapter.)	<u>R</u>ecords ➤ Ne<u>x</u>t Record	Alt+→
⏭	Last Record	Displays the last record in the current database if you are not already viewing the last record. (See this chapter.)	<u>R</u>ecords ➤ <u>L</u>ast Record	Alt+Shift +→

TABLE 2.1: Q&A Database Tool Bar Buttons—Creating or Editing a Database (continued)

BUTTON	BUTTON OR LIST BOX NAME	DESCRIPTION	KEYBOARD EQUIVALENT	SHORTCUT KEYS
	New Record	Allows you to add a new record to the current database. (See Chapter 7.) Q&A automatically saves the database whenever you add a record.	Records ➤ New Record	Ctrl+N
	Delete Record	Allows you to delete the current record. (See Chapter 7.)	Records ➤ Delete Record	Ctrl+B

Try adding data in a few fields on a new record now and see how it feels. Click on the New Record button and type something in the first field. (To get from one field to the next, either press the Tab key, press Enter, or click in the field with your mouse.) Q&A saves each new record and updates the database file automatically. To delete the new record, just click on the Delete record button. You'll learn about the details of entering data in Chapter 7.

Try It Yourself: Using the Tool Bar

Try using some of these tool bar buttons:

- Click on the Design Input Forms button to see EMPLOYEE.DTF as you would edit its input form. Click on the Add/Edit button to return to the original window.

- Click on the arrow on the right side of the Input Forms drop-down list box to reveal the list of input forms you can use.

- Click on the Table View button to get your first glimpse of Table View (see Chapter 3). Click on the Form View button to return to the original window.

- Click on the Next Record button, the Last Record button, the Previous Record button, and the First Record button.

- Click on the New Record button and add some information to a couple of fields. Click on the Delete Record button to remove the record that you just added.

Using the Work Area

The largest part of the window is the appropriately named work area, in which you labor away at your database files and Write documents. If you have been working along with this chapter, you have already ventured into the work area.

Using the Status Bar

The status bar, at the bottom of the window, contains a variety of information, depending on the mode you are using. For example, if you select the Add/Edit button, the status bar contains the information shown in Figure 2.9: your current location in Q&A, the current file location, and the number of records in the current database.

In addition, if you select a menu command or a tool bar button, the status bar shows a brief description.

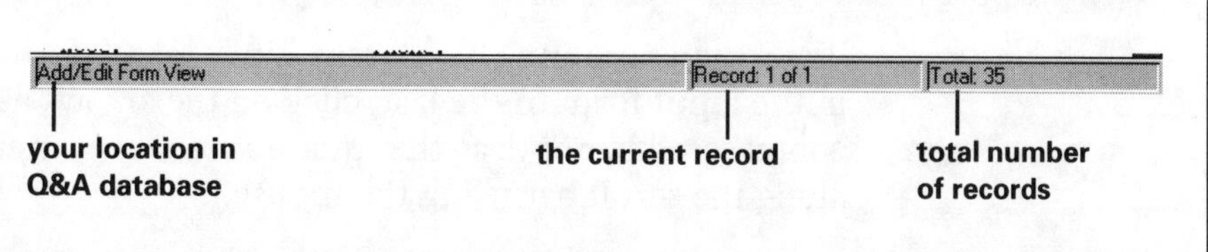

The Q&A Write status bar displays the current cursor location by page number, column number, and line number.

Moving Around a File

Now let's try moving around the EMPLOYEE database using the tool bar, the mouse, and the keyboard.

You've already seen how to use the four tool bar buttons dedicated to moving among records. Now click on the First Record, Previous Record, Next Record, and Last Record buttons to jump around the database. Remember that if a button looks dim, it is not currently available. For example, when you first opened EMPLOYEE, the current record was the first record. That meant that both the First Record button and Previous Record button were unavailable.

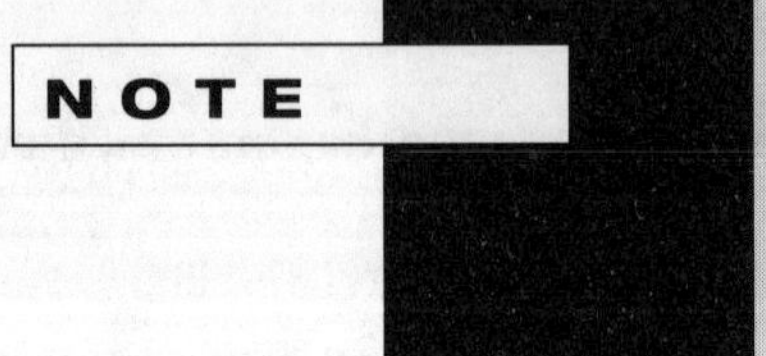

Try moving around the current input form. To move from the first field in the input form to the last, click on the arrows at either end of the horizontal scroll bar or drag the square *scroll box* (sometimes called the *thumb*) along the scroll bar using the mouse.

To move to the bottom of an input form, click on the arrow at the bottom of the vertical scroll bar. To move to the top, click on the arrow at the top. You can also drag the scroll box so that you can view the desired area of the record.

You can use the keyboard to move around the current record and to move among all the records in the database file. Table 2.2 lists Q&A Database navigation keys and key combinations. Try some of these keys to see for yourself how they work.

TABLE 2.2: Q&A Database Navigation Keys and Key Combinations

PRESS	TO MOVE TO
Alt+←	Previous record (unless you are currently viewing the first record)
Alt+→	Next record (unless you are currently viewing the last record)
Alt+Shift ←	First record
Alt+Shift →	Last record
PgDn, Ctrl+PgDn, or Shift+PgDn	Next page of the current record
PgUp, Ctrl+PgUp, or Shift+PgUp	Previous page of the current record

Viewing Records As They Will Print

Print Preview allows you to see what a record, input form, report, or mailing label will look like when it prints. So, if you spot boldface in a place in which the text should be underlined or a field that is not aligned the way it should be, you can edit before wasting paper.

You can view a record in several ways. You can look at either a single page or two facing pages. For example, if you need to compare facing pages (i.e., a set consisting of one even-numbered page and one odd numbered page) for placement of graphics, charts, and text, click on the Two Page button.

You can adjust the display to fit in the window so that the proportions of length to width are correct and the display is as large as possible. You can magnify or reduce the display by clicking on the Zoom In or Zoom Out button, respectively. Then click the resulting magnifying glass mouse pointer repeatedly within the document to display a document that is 25 percent, 50 percent, 75 percent, 100 percent, 200 percent, or 400 percent of the size of its Add/Edit screen display. To exit Zoom In mode, either click on the Fit in Window or Zoom Out buttons. To exit Zoom Out mode, either click on the Fit in Window or Zoom In buttons. If your record has more than one page, you can move to the previous or next page by clicking on the Previous Page or Next Page button.

Choose File ➤ Print Preview. Q&A displays a window (see Figure 2.10) in which the current page of the database is displayed.

A sample Print Preview window. In the default view, you will not see the text on the page, but you can zoom in to read it.

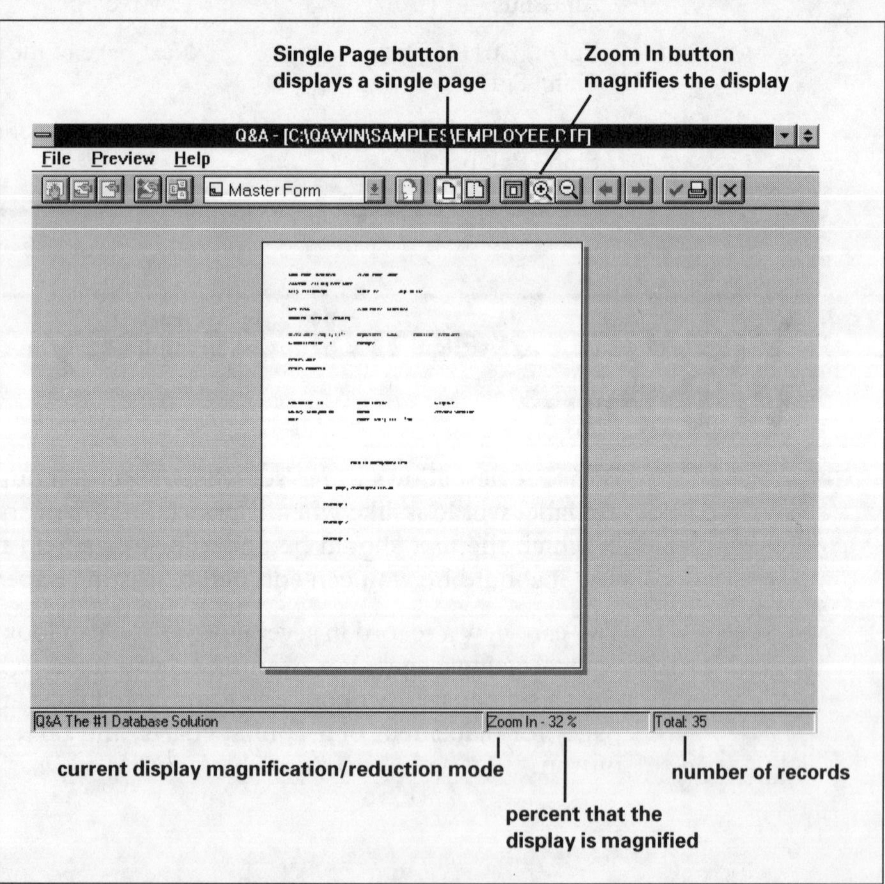

The Print Preview tool bar contains several unique buttons, which are listed in Table 2.3.

TABLE 2.3: Q&A Database Tool Bar Buttons—Print Preview

BUTTON	BUTTON OR LIST BOX NAME	DESCRIPTION	KEYBOARD EQUIVALENT	SHORTCUT KEYS
	Single Page	Displays a single page formatted as it will print. This is the default view.	Preview ➤ One Page	N/A
	Two Page	Displays two side-by-side pages formatted as they will print.	Preview ➤ Two Pages	N/A
	Fit in Window	Adjusts the size of the page (or pages) within the window. This is the default size.	Preview ➤ Reduce to Fit	N/A
	Zoom In	Magnifies the document display in several steps.	Preview ➤ Zoom In	N/A
	Zoom Out	Reduces the document display in several steps.	Preview ➤ Zoom Out	N/A
	Previous Page	Displays the previous page in the document.	Preview ➤ Previous Page	N/A
	Next Page	Displays the next page in the document.	Preview ➤ Next Page	N/A
	Print	Allows you to print the current records or a group of selected records.	File ➤ Print	Ctrl+P
	Exit	Closes Print Preview and returns to the previous window.	Preview ➤ Cancel Preview	Esc

Printing a Document

Once you have previewed the records you want to print and have made all the necessary corrections, you can print it. The paperless office is not here yet, so Q&A provides several convenient ways of printing a document:

- Click on the Print button on either the Print Preview window or the Add/Edit area.

- Choose File ➤ Print.

- Press Ctrl+P.

In response, Q&A displays the Print dialog box (Figure 2.11). This is the standard Windows printing dialog box with two differences:

- You can choose to print the current record or retrieved records.

- You can go to the Print Preview window.

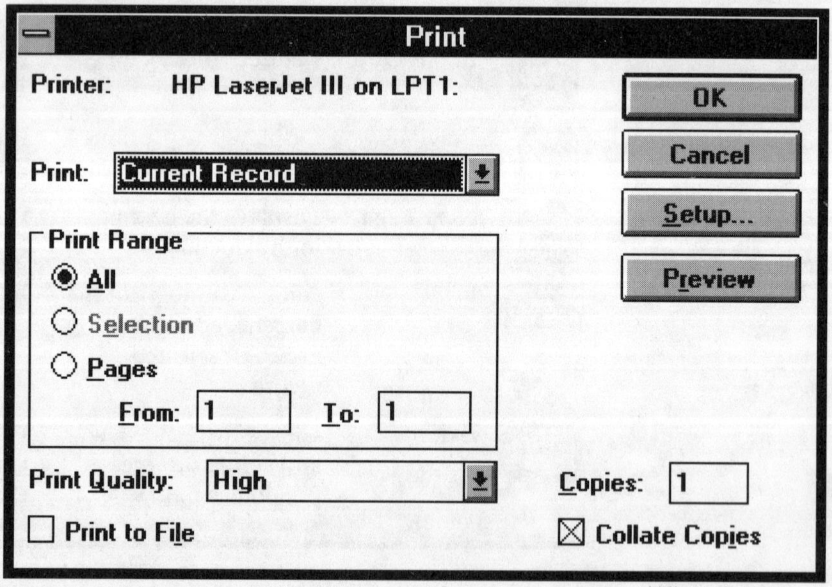

FIGURE 2.11

Q&A's Print dialog box, in which you set printing specifications and from which you print the current record or retrieved records

If you print from Print Preview, the standard Windows Print dialog box appears. This means that you can't print the current record or retrieved records as you can from the Add/Edit work area.

Before you actually print the current record or retrieved records, select options in the Print dialog box.

Print You can either print the current record (the default) or all the records that you have retrieved. Simply open the Print drop-down list box and select either Current Record or All Retrieved Records. When you choose All Retrieved Records, Q&A prints all the records located in the last retrieval you ran. Retrieving records is explained Chapter 8.

Print Range The Print Range group offers three radio buttons and two text boxes in which you can specify a range of pages to be printed. If you choose <u>A</u>ll (the default), you print the entire record or retrieved records. For records that extend for more than one page, you can select one or more particular pages for printing. Click on <u>P</u>ages to determine the starting page (by typing a value in the <u>F</u>rom box) and the last page (by typing a value in the <u>T</u>o box). S<u>e</u>lection, the middle choice in the Print Range group, is always dimmed (i.e., not available).

If you select the <u>P</u>ages option, and wish to start printing on the first page of the document, you don't have to fill in the <u>F</u>rom box; if you wish to end printing on the last page of the document, you don't have to fill in the <u>T</u>o box.

Print Quality To set the print quality or the resolution of the text and/or graphics, which depends on the type of printer you are using, choose High, Medium, Low, or Draft from the Print Quality drop-down list box. If you are printing a form that you have not finished designing and you want to print a rough draft, (perhaps you haven't added all those lines, ellipses, and pictures), the fastest way is to select Draft.

Print to File If no printer is attached to your computer, you can print to a file, which you can print later. To print to a file that you can share with others or print at a later time, check the Print to File check box.

Copies To print several copies of the current record or all retrieved records, just type the number of copies in the Copies text box. The default is 1.

Setup Button To change the default printer, select a printer from the list defined to your computer system, or set options specific to your printer, click on the Setup button. When the Print Setup dialog box appears, fill it in. For information about using the Print Setup dialog box, see your Windows documentation.

Preview Button To view the record as it will print, click on the Preview button. Q&A displays the record in Print Preview mode.

Collate Copies When printing multiple copies of a record, you can indicate how pages come out of the printer. If you check the Collate Copies text box, the printer collates pages (i.e., it prints all the pages in one copy before printing the first page of the next copy). If this text box is unchecked, the printer prints all the copies of the first page, all the copies of the second page, and so on.

Deleting Files

The easiest way to delete a file you no longer need is to use File Manager. However, before you remove any file, ask yourself if you'll ever need this file again. Anyway, if you still want to go ahead with the deletion, follow these steps:

1. Open the Task List dialog box (as shown in Figure 2.12) by pressing the Ctrl+Esc key combination.

2. Double-click on Program Manager. Windows displays the Program Manager on your desktop.

FIGURE 2.12

The Task List dialog box let's you switch to another active application, exit an active application, change the way active windows are arranged on your desktop, and arrange the icons at the bottom of your desktop.

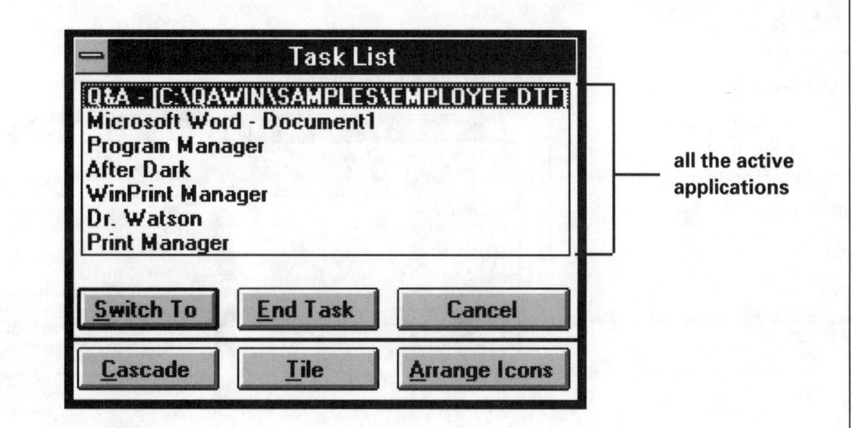

TIP

If you are only running a few applications at this time, an alternate way of getting to File Manager is to press Alt+Tab repeatedly until the Program Manager information box appears. When you release the Tab key, Windows displays the Program Manager on your desktop.

3. If needed, maximize the program group in which the File Manager icon is located so that you can find the icon.

4. Open File Manager by double-clicking on its icon.

5. In the Tree pane on the left side of the File Manager window (as shown in Figure 2.13), click on the icon that represents the directory in which your Q&A database files are located.

6. On the right side of the File Manager window in the Directory pane, search for the name of the database files to be deleted. You will find two files with the same file name: one file has a .DTF extension and the second file has an .IDX extension. The .DTF file contains your actual data. The .IDX file contains indexing information for that data. Click on the first file to be deleted and then, pressing Ctrl, click on the second file to add it to the selection list.

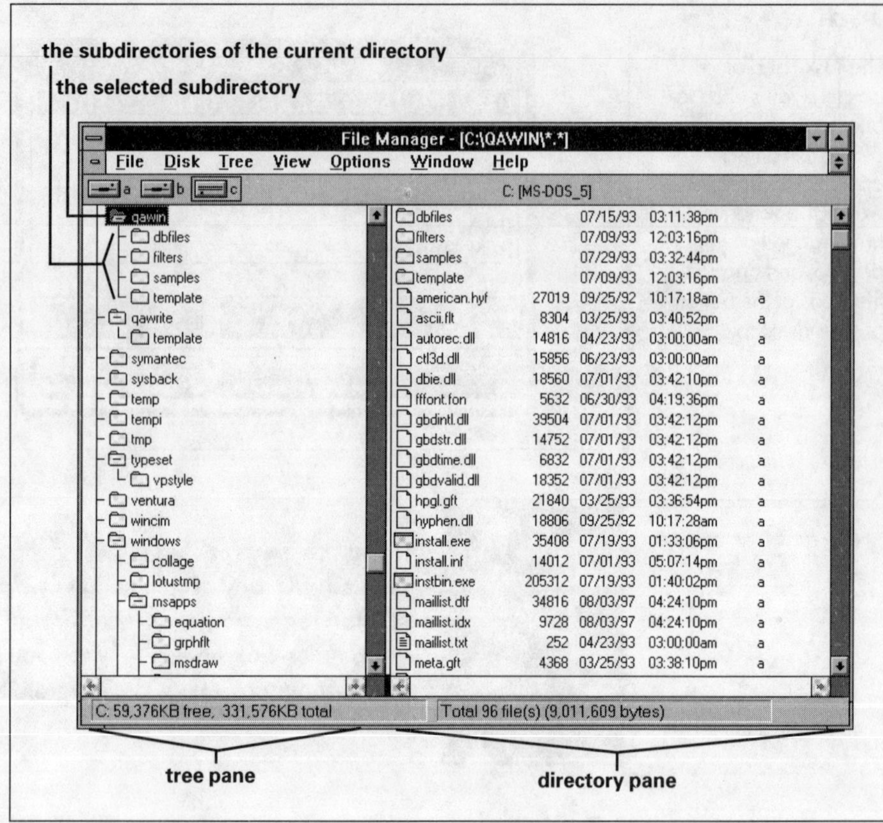

7. Delete the files by choosing File ➤ Delete or by pressing the Del key. Depending on your File Manager attributes, Windows displays one or two dialog boxes to which you must respond.

8. Close File Manager and resume your Q&A session.

To learn more about using File Manager and other Windows features, see Appendix B.

Getting Help

The Q&A help facility closely resembles the help facility for other Windows applications. If you have a question about a Q&A element or procedure, help is always available in several forms. On the menu bar, open the Help menu (see Figure 2.14) and you can choose from five commands.

- Contents provides a summary of help topics. You might be able to select how to's, commands, or a brief description of a topic.

- Selecting Search for Help On opens a dialog box that lists topics and functions about which you can learn more. Simply select a topic and click on the Show Topics button. When the help facility displays one or more related topics, select one and click on the Go To button. At this point, you will see one or more screens of helpful information.

- How to Use Help provides a "table of contents" about the Help facility itself.

- To view the Q&A tutorial, select Tutorial and follow the instructions.

- About Q&A provides information about Q&A—the version number and the copyright dates. This window also provides important information about your computer system's memory usage and CPU.

For a more complete description of Windows help, see Appendix B.

FIGURE 2.14

The open Q&A Help menu.

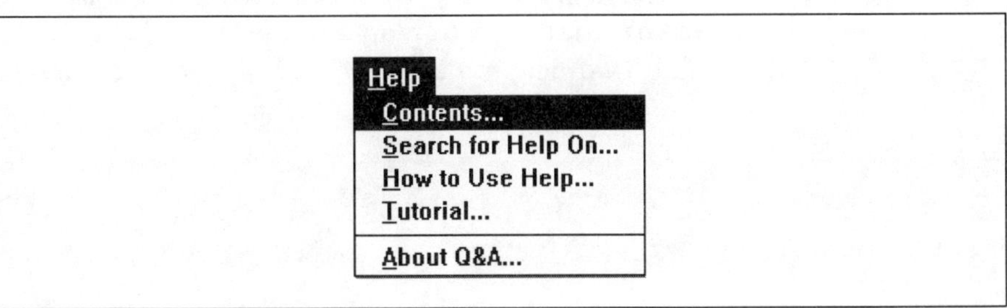

Ending a Q&A Work Session

To exit Q&A, choose File ➤ Exit, type the key combination Alt+F4, or double-click on the Application Control Menu button. Q&A will prompt you to save any unsaved work before you actually end the session.

Exiting Windows

To exit Windows, you can use the same steps: choose File ➤ Exit, type the key combination Alt+F4, or double-click on the Application Control Menu button. Windows prompts you to acknowledge whether you want to end your Windows session.

To Sum Up

In this chapter, you have learned many Q&A basics. You've seen what makes up the Q&A window and how to use each component. You've also learned how to start both Windows and Q&A. While in Q&A, you've found out how to open a database, move around in Q&A, delete a file, and finally how to exit both Q&A and Windows. We hope it's been an enjoyable trip.

In the next chapter, you'll learn about databases, acquire some important terms, and begin to plan and design a Q&A database. You'll learn above all how quick and easy it is to set up a Q&A database.

chapter

3

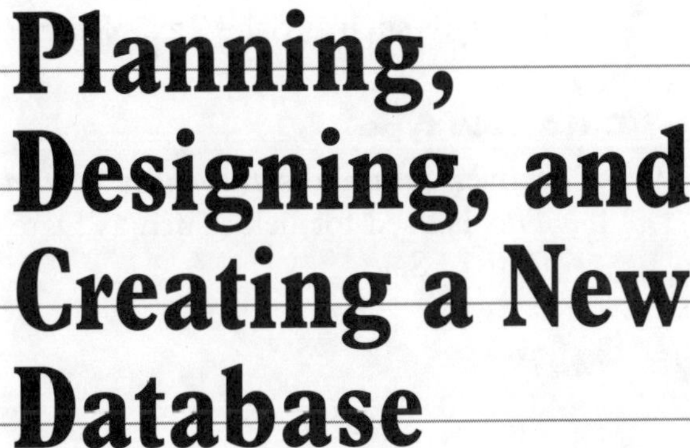

Planning, Designing, and Creating a New Database

NOW that you've had your whirlwind tour of Q&A for Windows, it's time to learn more about databases in general and the Q&A Database specifically. In this chapter, you'll learn more about the components of a database and how they relate to one another. Then you'll see how easy it is to build your first database, using either our sample or perhaps one of your own. In later chapters, you'll find out how to redesign a database either to improve it, grow with it, or to correct early mistakes. So don't worry about making any mistakes.

Learning about the Elements of a Database

Chapter 1 introduced several database terms. Now let's elaborate on these terms and learn some more about the components of a database.

Database

Let's start off with the most important term: a *database*. A database organizes your information in such a way that it can be sorted, retrieved, reported on, and used in other documents such as letters and mailing labels. A database needn't be electronic—just think of a file cabinet drawer loaded with all sorts of letters and documents. If each folder in the drawer is arranged in some sort of order, you'll be able to find the information you are looking for almost instantaneously. An electronic database gets rid of the problem of high stacks of disorderly correspondence and data reports piled on your desk, waiting to be filed. This helps you find a crucial document when your manager urgently needs it. Unlike a paper one, an electronic database allows several people to use the same data at the same time. Since Q&A is not a relational database, the fields are not linked to other databases—this makes Q&A less complex.

Field

A *field*, which is the smallest component of a database, is the area into which you type a single piece of information. Using our paper database analogy, a field is like one piece of information on a form or letter in the file drawer. For example, one field on an employment application includes the name of the college that an applicant attended and another field holds the applicant's first name.

Field Type

To describe the kind of information that is entered into a field and tell Q&A how it can use that information, assign a *field type*. For example, you can define a field entitled Date to contain only date entries. This might be useful if you want to calculate the difference between application data and hire date to track the time it takes for a prospective employee to become an actual employee. There are many different field types for the different kinds of data that you can enter into a field. You'll learn about the different field types later in this chapter.

Field Name

A *field name* is the label that you give to a field; it helps the person entering data to identify what kind of information the field contains. Returning to the file cabinet analogy, if you were filling out a job application, some typical field names might be University Attended and First Name. It's very clear that the applicant is expected to fill in the name of his or her alma mater and first name.

Record

A *record* contains a group of related fields which together describe some person or thing. A record might be a group of fields that, when taken together, define an employment application. You might set up your database so your records represent time cards, trip reports, and passport applications.

Input Form

In Q&A, an *input form* is a record layout that you (or somebody else) plans and designs. It consists of an arrangement of fields used to display or enter data. This provides a consistent form for information to be entered, making your records easier to read and compare. For the sake of your company image and for the comfort of those who fill them out, it's important to use well-designed forms.

Planning and Designing an Effective Database

It's time to get started with your first database. Our sample database, STAFF, contains 19 fields of employee information. In this chapter, you'll plan, design, and actually create this database (or one of your own, if you wish). In future chapters, you'll see how a database design evolves.

Before you type your first character, devote some time to planning and designing the database. Although Q&A makes it easy to fine-tune and re-design an existing database on the fly, it is a good idea to use pencil and paper to develop a good plan. All you have to do is write down the name of each field. After you learn about the specific field types in "Specifying Field Types," later in this chapter, you'll add the appropriate type next to each field name. It's not important, at this point, to decide on an input form design; we'll get to that later. You also don't have to worry about how wide a field is; Q&A takes care of that detail by automatically expanding a field's width if you type in too many characters. Figure 3.1 shows you what you are aiming for—an input form that has gone through all the stages of planning and design.

As you plan any database, review the following questions:

- What are the main reasons for creating this database? Will you create mailing labels, are you gathering information for reports, or both?

- What fields does this database need? When developing your list of fields, are you thinking about your company's or department's growth and plans for the future? For example, do you have room for several telephone number fields—for voice, fax, and modem?

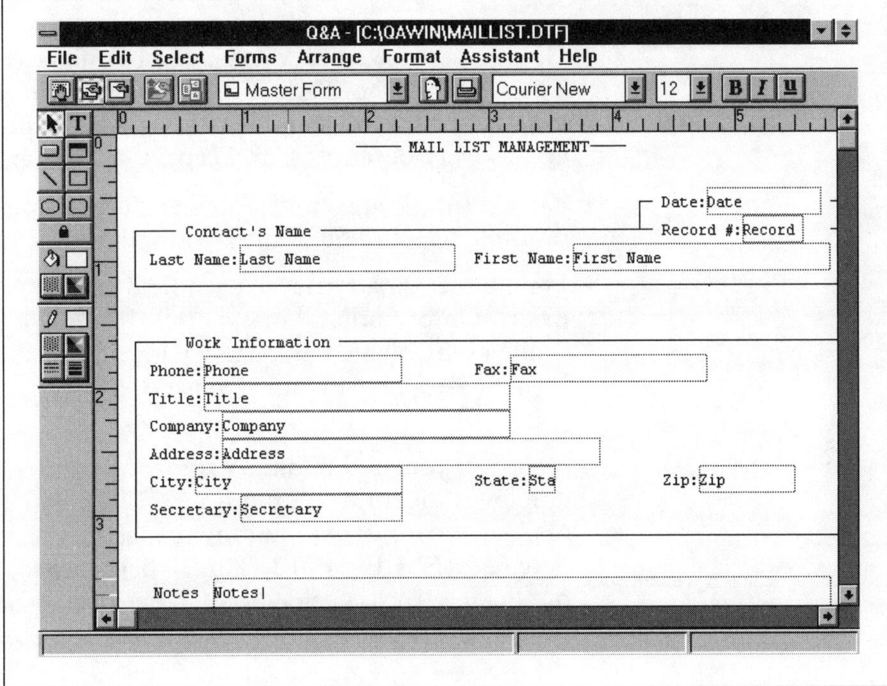

- Do you need to reserve space for new fields, or is it more practical to create a new database?

- Are the fields arranged so that data entry is easy? Are related fields grouped together?

- What information types should you assign to each field? What fields are used for calculations? for sorting? for indexes? (You'll learn about sorting in later chapters.)

- How many ways do you need to sort the information in the database? How many subsets of records do you wish to retrieve?

- Should the database include room for addresses outside your home country?

Here are some tips for creating flexible and efficient databases:

- Give a database an easy-to-remember name. For example, TRAVEL or even EMP_TRAV are excellent reminders that a database contains travel information. Field names like EMP_09AB are not very descriptive and can be confusing.

- Keep it simple and small! You can add complex computations and multiple pages of fields after you spend time learning Q&A.

- For simpler data retrieval, each field should contain only one piece of information. For example, instead of entering Ms. Sally Smile in the Name field, use separate fields for Title (Ms.), First Name (Sally), Last Name (Smile).

- It is a good idea to include a field with a unique identifier for each record. If you are building a company database, you can use the employee's identification number. But if you are compiling a list of clients, consider combining the last name with the year and date (e.g., SMIL950712). An ID field makes it more difficult to duplicate records accidentally. When you create the STAFF database, you'll see two built-in identifiers: the employee number and the key name.

To learn about designing input forms, see Chapter 4.

Creating a Q&A Database

After planning and designing your first database, you're probably anxious to actually create it. Well here's your opportunity! Start Q&A, if you haven't already done so, and then follow these simple steps:

1. In the Q&A window, choose <u>F</u>ile ➤ <u>N</u>ew. Q&A then opens the New File dialog box (see Figure 3.2).

The New File dialog box with the name of a new database already typed in. Note the subdirectory that will hold all database files. When there are many databases in the same subdirectory, create more subdirectories to hold databases by category.

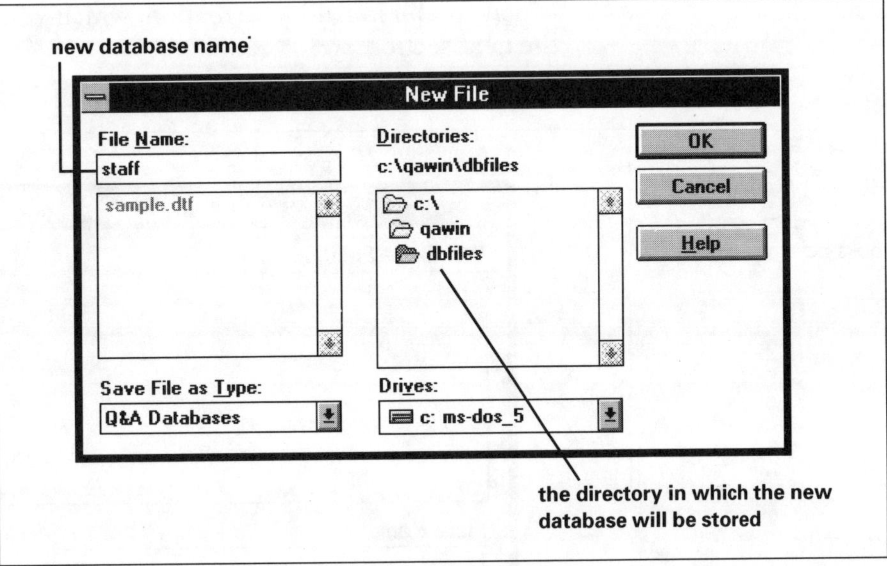

2. To store the new file in a different subdirectory from that shown in the <u>D</u>irectories box, select from the choices in the Directories box. To store the new file in a different drive from the drive named in the Dri<u>v</u>es drop-down box:

click on the arrow to the right of the box and select the appropriate drive identifier.

3. In the File <u>N</u>ame text box, type a unique filename (e.g., STAFF), which can be from one to eight characters in length.

4. Click on OK or press the Enter key. You don't have to type an extension after the filename; Q&A saves the database with a .DTF extension and also saves an index file with a .IDX extension. Q&A then opens the Add & Delete Fields dialog box (Figure 3.3) in

which you fill in field information, which you'll find out about in the next section.

The Add & Delete Fields dialog box as it looks before you add fields

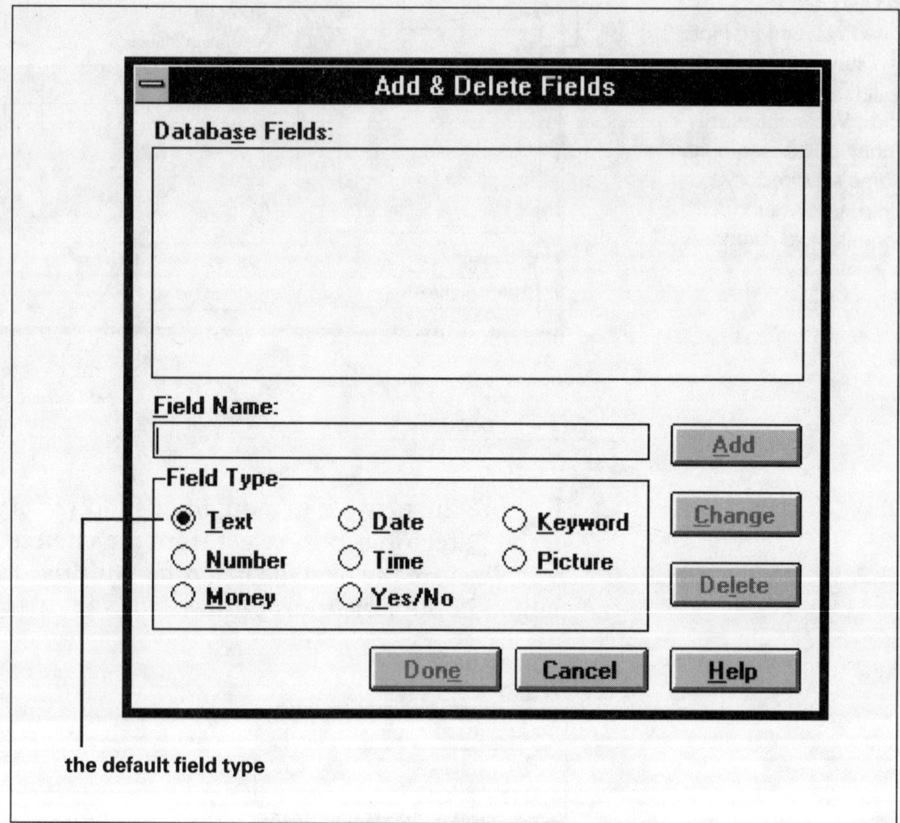

Selecting a Q&A Field Type

When you design a Q&A database, the two important pieces of information you'll provide for a field are its name and its type. Selecting the correct field type ensures the following:

- You'll see the contents of a field in a familiar format (e.g., a typical date field looks like Apr 17, 1998).

- You'll be able to calculate numbers when needed (e.g., to determine an employee's years of service or to compute a commission in dollars for a pay check).

- You can define a field so that it contains a graphic (e.g., to display your company logo on a report or mailing label).

Table 3.1 lists the Q&A field types and describes each.

TABLE 3.1: Q&A Field Types

FIELD TYPE	VALID INFORMATION
Text	Alphanumeric information, such as names, addresses, zip codes, telephone numbers, social security numbers
Number	Numeric information, such as percentages, quantities, units, discount rates, multipliers, bonus factors, and measures
Money	Currency information, for dollars and cents formatting
Date	Date information, for date formatting
Time	Time information, for time formatting
Yes/No	Answers to Yes/No, True/False, or 0/1
Keyword	Lists of alphanumeric information, separated by semi-colons
Picture	A picture, in .BMP or .WMF format, which can be imported from a Windows application or from the Clipboard

Text Field Type

The most common field type is text, which is the default field type for Q&A and which accepts any combination of characters: alphabetic, numeric, punctuation, or special symbols. Use this field type for any data that you either won't use for calculations or don't want Q&A to format as money, a date, or a time. Define fields that only *appear* to be numeric (and are not calculated) as text fields, such as social security numbers, ZIP codes, and telephone numbers. Fields like these often contain non-numeric characters, such as dashes (e.g., 10010-7855) and parentheses (e.g., (555)555-5555), ampersands, and alphabetic characters. Other examples of text fields are identification numbers, last name, address, city, and state. In the STAFF database, every field that does not fall into another field type category is a text type.

Number Field Type

The numeric field type is the all-purpose field type for numbers you want to perform calculations on or numerically sort, but cannot categorize as money, date, or time field types. Q&A does not accept non-numeric characters typed in a numeric field, except for negative signs, commas, and decimal points, which indicate negative numbers, numbers greater than 100, and numbers that are not integers, such as −10,901.34. However, typing commas into a number field is not necessary because Q&A removes or adds them depending on the format for that number field. Q&A does not accept leading zeroes in a number field—in fact, if you type a leading zero, Q&A removes it. For example, if you enter *0566.80*, Q&A records only *566.80*. (This is yet another reason why you shouldn't set values such as ZIP codes, Social Security numbers, and record identification numbers as number field types.) Examples of number fields are percentages, quantities, units, discount rates, multipliers, bonus factors, and measures. In the STAFF database, Commission, which is a percentage, is a numeric field. To change the default number format, use the Global Format Options dialog box, which you can find out about in Chapter 6.

Money Field Type

Choosing the money field type ensures that numbers typed in a field are converted to a currency format. If you type non-numeric characters in a money field, Q&A issues a reminder that you must type only numbers. The default money format contains the dollar sign and combinations of commas and periods. For example, if you type 7645123 in a money field that formats dollars and cents, Q&A converts the number to $76,451.23. To change the default money format or currency symbol, use the Global Format Options dialog box.

Q&A performs calculations in money fields. For example, you can compute a final price by adding the list price, sales tax, and shipping costs. In the STAFF database, Salary is a money field.

Date Field Type

Selecting the date field type ensures that appropriate numbers and characters typed in a field are converted to a date format. The default date format is the Windows short system format, which is set in the Windows control panel. For instance, you might have your short date format set as *mon, nn, yyyy* (where *mon* indicates the first three or more characters of a month, *nn* indicates the one- or two-digit date, and *yyyy* indicates the year in all four digits or as the last two digits). For example, if you type 4/17/98, 4-17-98, Apr 17, 98, or April 17, 1998 in a date field, Q&A converts the date to Apr 17, 1998. If you separate the numbers in a date with any other character except – or /, or do not follow the syntax, Q&A issues an error message. To change the default Windows date format, select the International icon in the Control Panel. For more Windows information, see Appendix B. To change the default date format from within Q&A, use the Global Format Options dialog box, which you'll learn about in Chapter 6.

When you type data into a date field, make sure that you type all components of the date. However, if you leave out the year in a date entry, Q&A automatically inserts the current year (which is taken from your computer's internal clock) in the date.

Q&A can use date fields in calculations. For example, you can have Q&A compute the number of years that an employee has worked for your company by subtracting the date of hire from today's date. You can also calculate someone's age by subtracting a birthday field from the current date. You can also use the date field type to retrieve ranges of dates. For example, if you operate a small business and you want to contact customers who bought from you during 1992, you can retrieve only 1992 records. In the STAFF database, Hire Date is a date field.

Time Field Type

The time field type ensures that Q&A formats numbers typed in the field as a time. Q&A issues a message if you type non-numeric characters (except for am, pm, a, or p) in a time field. The default time format is *nn:mm* am | pm (where *nn* indicates an hour from 1 to 12, *mm* indicates minutes from 00 to 59, am indicates the time period from midnight to noon, and pm indicates the time period from noon to midnight. To change the default 12-hour time format to 24-hour format (i.e., without the suffix am or pm), use the Global Format Options dialog box, which you can learn about in Chapter 6.

Q&A can perform calculations using data in time fields. For example, an employee can track his or her hours by having Q&A subtract a login time from a logout time.

Yes/No Field Type

You can use the Yes/No field type to answer questions to which the answer is Yes or No, True or False, or 1 or 0. For example, in the STAFF database, a Yes/No field shows whether an employee travels or not. Yes, Y, True, T, or 1 indicates that the employee travels; otherwise, the answer is No, N, False, F, or 0. Examples of questions for which a Yes/No field can hold the answer are:

Is it tax deductible?

Has a payment been made?

Has the bid been accepted?

Keyword Field Type

The very powerful keyword field allows you to have more than one entry (separated by semicolons) in a single field. One example of keywords used in fields are lists of employee interests. If your company wants to join a local softball league, it would be helpful to compile a list of employees who are interested in softball or baseball.

Use a keyword field to search for one item in a group of items. For example, if you list the product lines that an employee sells, you can search for a knowledgeable salesperson before sending him or her to a demanding client. You can also keep track of courses that employees complete successfully to identify those who have expertise in a particular area or those who are candidates for promotions. An example of an appropriate keyword field in the STAFF database is Projects, which contains a list of projects on which an employee has worked. If the Projects field contains up to three values, the Perry Proposal, the Brooks Proposal, and the Mason Contract, you can use the power of the keyword field to search for every employee who worked on the Brooks Proposal. During a search, every record that has the Brooks Proposal anywhere in that one field is retrieved. (If you tried this sort of search in a plain text field, you'd have to use wildcard characters, which are explained in Chapter 8.)

Picture Field Type

Q&A uses the picture field type to define a field in which a picture is stored. There is no picture field in the STAFF database, but there could be if you wanted to insert the company logo on reports, store employee pictures, or show photographs of real estate properties.

You can use two formats in Picture fields: bitmap images (with a .BMP extension); and Windows metafiles (with a .WMF extension). This means that you can insert these types of images into a picture field. Use Windows Clipboard copying and pasting to paste an image into a picture field. For more information about inserting images into picture fields, see Chapter 7.

You cannot redefine a picture field as another field type, and you cannot change any other field type to a picture field. Therefore, the only way that you can create a picture field is by adding it to your database either during creation or while editing. Q&A's picture fields do not use OLE (Object Linking and Embedding), which is a Windows feature that automatically updates a linked object in one application while editing it in its source application. You can use picture fields to hold pictures, photographs, graphs, charts, schematics, diagrams, and maps.

Structure of the Staff Database

The sample database STAFF.DTF contains 19 fields with all but the time and picture field types represented:

FIELD NAME	DESCRIPTION	FIELD TYPE
Emp No	Employee identification number	Text
Hire Date	Date employee started work	Date
First Name	Employee's first name	Text

FIELD NAME	DESCRIPTION	FIELD TYPE
Last Name	Employee's last name	Text
Address 1	First line of employee's street address	Text
Address 2	Second line of employee's street address (e.g., apartment number or post office box number)	Text
City	City or town in which the employee resides	Text
State	State in which the employee resides	Text
ZIP	ZIP code	Text
Key Name	The name by which the employee is identified to the network	Text
Network ID	The name of the network to which the employee is defined	Text
Department	The department to which the employee is assigned	Text
Title	The employee's job title or position	Text
Extension	The employee's telephone extension	Text
Salary	The employee's current gross salary	Money
Commission	A percentage of sales for which the employee is to some degree responsible. If an employee is not entitled to a commission, the value in this field is 0.	Number
Office Location	The office in which the employee is based (i.e., works in an assigned office)	Text

FIELD NAME	DESCRIPTION	FIELD TYPE
Travel	A yes or no answer to whether the employee travels for the company	Yes/No
Products	A list of products that an employee either sells, manufactures, trains, or supports, depending on whether the employee is a sales representative, a production worker, trainer, or technical representative.	Keyword
Photo	A picture of the Employee	Photo
Last Update Date	Contains the date the record was last updated	Date
Last Update Time	Contains the date the record was last updated	Time

Defining Field Names and Field Types

Now let's learn how to define fields using the Add & Delete Fields dialog box. As you build a database file, you should give each field a name that is both easy to remember and meaningful. Examples of good field names that will not be misunderstood are First Name, Last Name, City, and State. You can name a field with just one character or as many as 79—including spaces.

To define a field name (and therefore a field) in a database file, use the following steps:

1. In the Add & Delete Fields dialog box, which is displayed when you create a new database, type the first field name in the Field Name text box (see Figure 3.4).

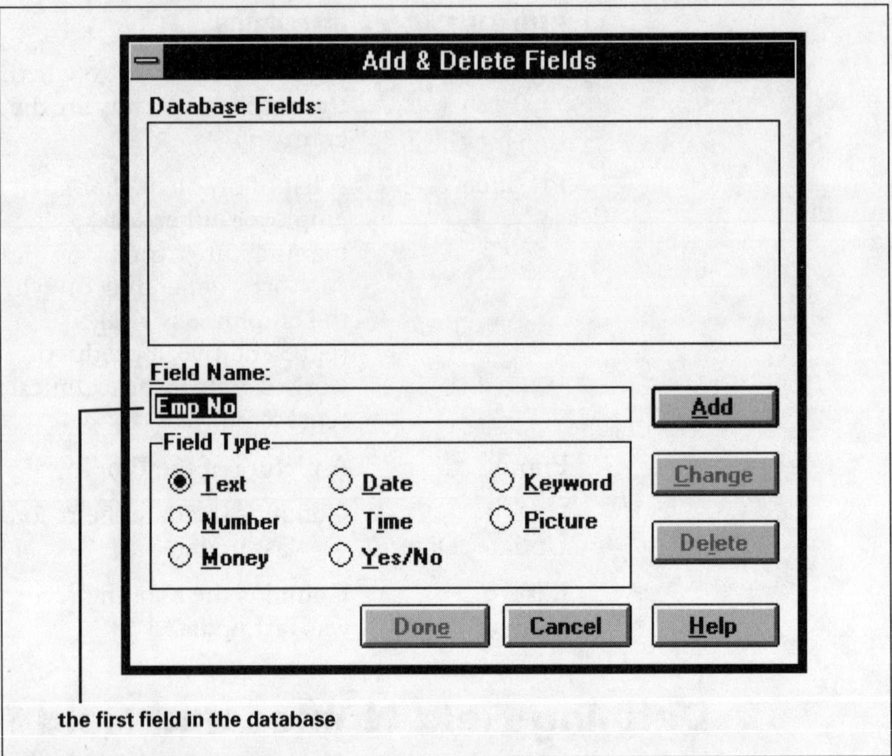

NOTE

Q&A for Windows has self-expanding fields. Field boxes start at a set size, but you can expand the field box (which shows a certain number of characters of information) in the Design Input Form Mode, which is covered in the next chapter.

2. Assign a field type by clicking on a radio button in the Field Type section (see Figure 3.5).

3. To add the field to the database, click on the Add button. The Add & Delete Fields dialog box changes to look like Figure 3.6. Q&A adds the name of the new field to the Database Fields box.

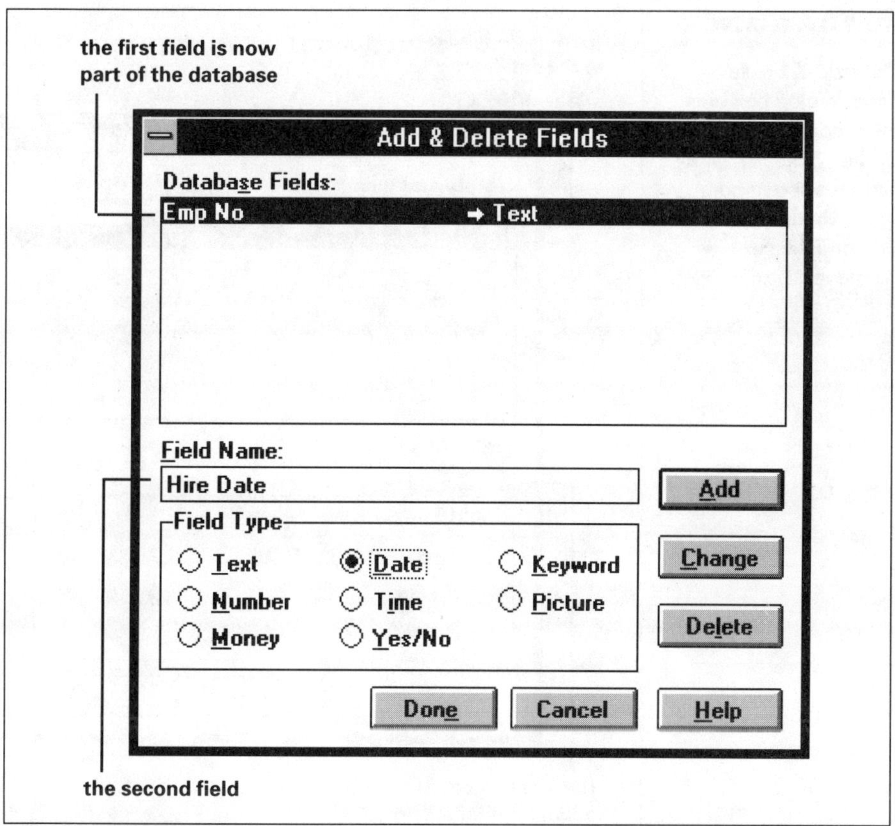

Adding a field with the same field type as the prior field is very easy. Because the name in the Field Name text box is highlighted, all you have to do is type the new field name, which automatically replaces the old field name, and press Enter, which adds the field to the database. You can use this method to add several fields very quickly.

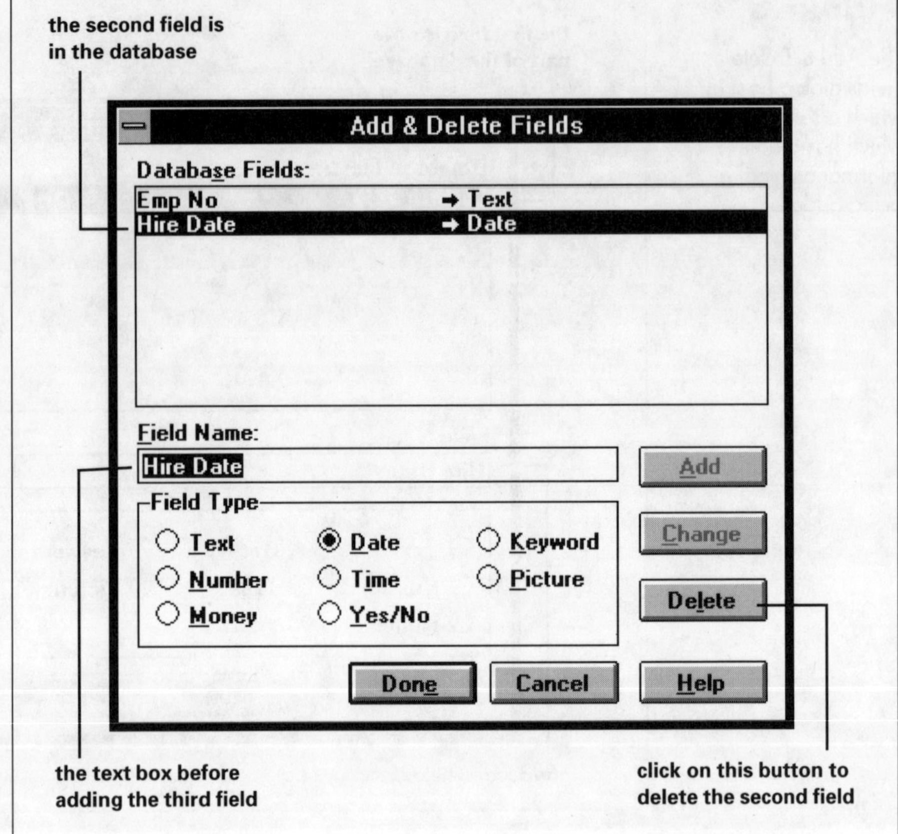

4. Repeat steps 1, 2, and 3 until you have added all the fields to the
new database. Figure 3.7 shows the Add & Delete Fields dialog
box with all the fields added to the STAFF database.

The Add & Delete Fields dialog box with the last fields in STAFF displayed in the Database Fields box.

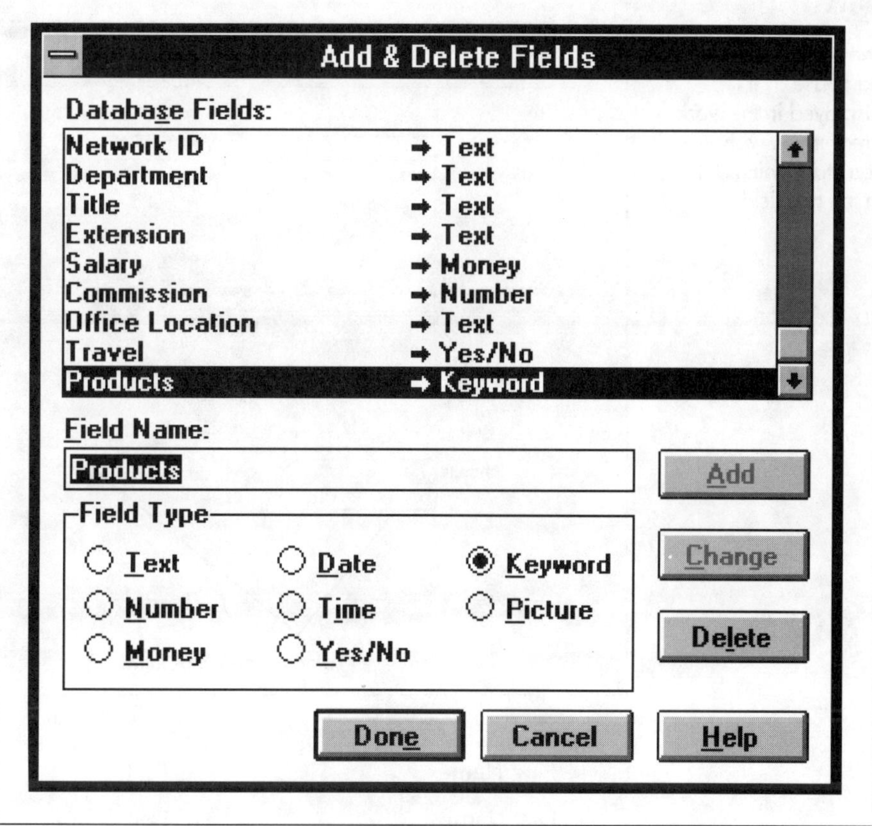

5. When the fields in the database are exactly as you want, click on Don*e* or press Enter. Q&A displays the database in the work area (see Figure 3.8).

Creating the Staff Database

Create your first database, STAFF, by choosing File ➤ New. In the File Name text box in the New File dialog box, type STAFF and either click on OK or press Enter. In the Add & Delete Fields dialog box, type the following fields with their appropriate field types:

Emp No	Text
Hire Date	Date

The new STAFF database as it is displayed in the work area. If you wish, you can start typing data in the first field.

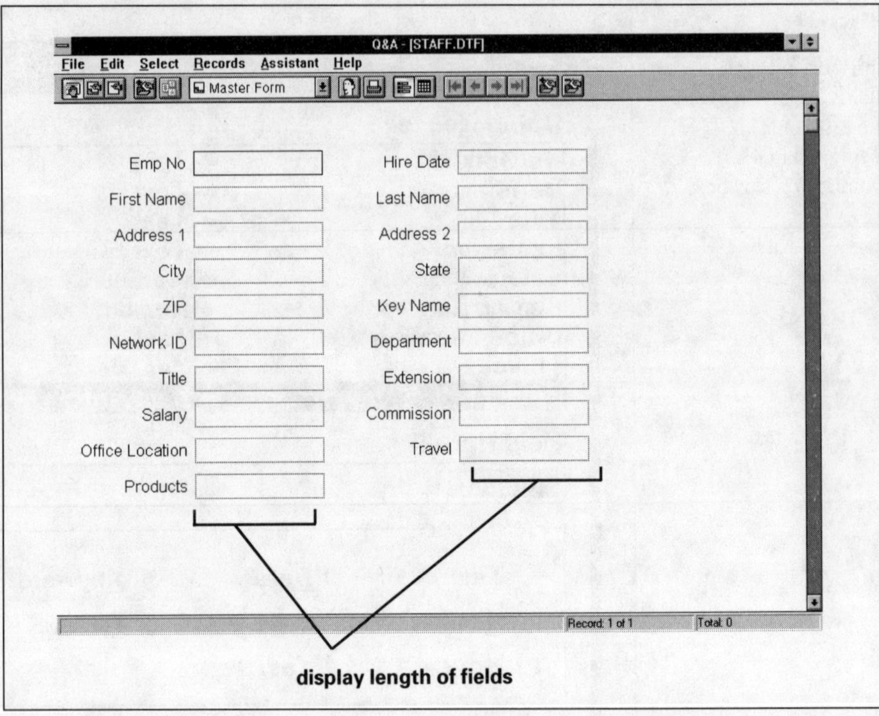

First Name	Text
Last Name	Text
Address 1	Text
Address 2	Text
City	Text
State	Text
ZIP	Text
Key Name	Text
Network ID	Text
Department	Text
Title	Text
Extension	Text
Salary	Money

Commission	<u>N</u>umber
Office Location	<u>T</u>ext
Travel	<u>Y</u>es/No
Products	<u>K</u>eyword
Photo	<u>P</u>icture
Last Update Date	<u>D</u>ate
Last Update Time	<u>T</u>ime

Viewing Records in a Database

Up to now (except for testing the toolbar buttons in Chapter 2), as you have viewed the Q&A sample database and created your first database, you have viewed one record at a time in Form view mode, which is the default.

Q&A also allows you to view records in a tabular or spreadsheet-like format, which is called Spreadsheet view. In Spreadsheet view, each row contains a complete record, and each column contains one field from several records.

The easiest way to switch between Form view (see Figure 3.8) and Spreadsheet view (see Figure 3.9) is to click on the appropriate button on the tool bar. Click on the Form view button to display the database record by record, and click on the Spreadsheet view button to display several records at a time.

You also can choose <u>R</u>ecords ➤ Vie<u>w</u> as Spreadsheet to switch to Spreadsheet view from Form view, or <u>R</u>ecords ➤ Vie<u>w</u> as Form to switch to Form view from Spreadsheet view. Note that Vie<u>w</u> as and Vie<u>w</u> as Form occupy the same line on the <u>R</u>ecords menu; Vie<u>w</u> as Spreadsheet is displayed only when you are in Form view, and Vie<u>w</u> as Form is displayed only when you are in Spreadsheet view.

When in Form view or Spreadsheet view, you can either browse through your data or edit it. When browsing, Q&A displays only your information. For instance, if you set up programming for your records, the programming statements are not executed as you browse through the records.

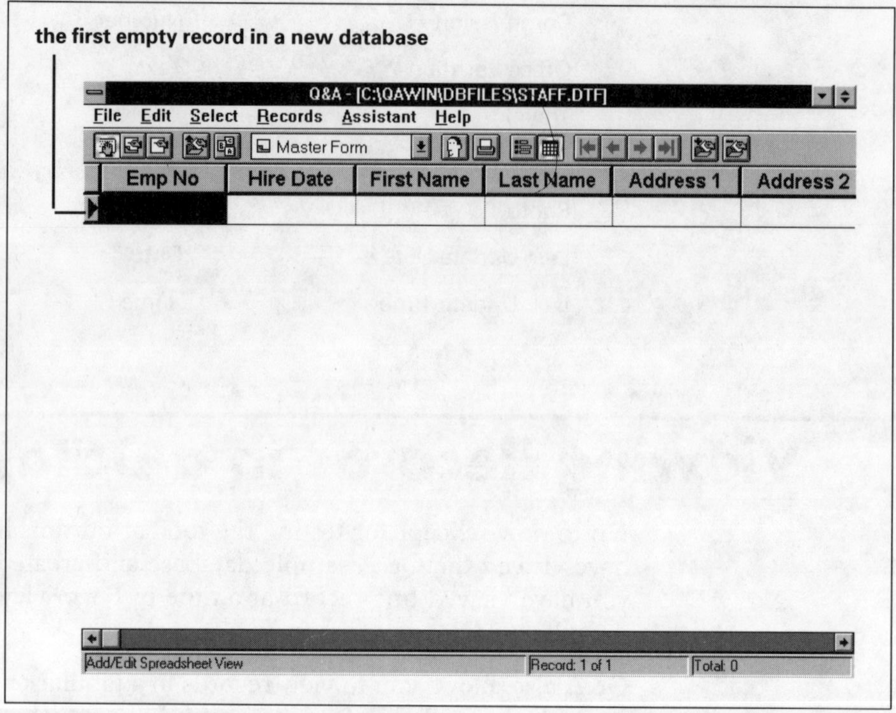

However, if you pass through your records while editing, the programming statements are executed. (Programming is explained in detail in Chapter 11.)

When your cursor is placed in any field (you've double clicked in it), you are editing information. However, if your cursor is not in any field (such as when you first open a database), you are browsing your data.

Table 3.2 lists the keys and key combinations that you can use to either move around the window or display specific parts of the window in either Form view or Spreadsheet view or both. To see a description of the function in Form view (or Spreadsheet view), look at the Form view Function column (or Spreadsheet view Function column). If Q&A does not support a key or key combination in a particular mode, you'll see an N/A in the appropriate column.

TABLE 3.2: Form View and Spreadsheet View Keys and Key Combinations

KEY OR KEY COMBINATION	FORM VIEW OR SPREADSHEET VIEW FUNCTION WHEN EDITING	SPREADSHEET VIEW FUNCTION WHEN BROWSING
Enter	Moves the ready-to-edit cursor to the next field	Moves the ready-to-edit cursor to the next field
Tab	Moves to the next field	Moves to the next field
Shift+Tab	Moves to the prior field	Moves to the prior field
→	Moves to the next character in the field	Moves to the next field
←	Moves to the prior character in the field	Moves to the prior field
↑	Moves to the line above, in that field	Moves to the same field of the prior record. If the cursor is already at the first record, the cursor does not move.
↓	Moves to the line below, in that field	Moves to the same field of the next record. If the cursor is already at the last record, the cursor does not move.
Home	Moves to the first character of that line	Displays the first screen of records
End	Moves to the last character of that line	Displays the last screen of records
PgUp	Scrolls down one page	Displays the prior screen of records
PgDn	Scrolls up one page	Displays the next screen of records
Alt+Shift←	Moves the cursor to the first record	Moves the cursor to the first record

TABLE 3.3: Form View and Spreadsheet View Keys and Key Combinations (continued)

KEY OR KEY COMBINATION	FORM VIEW OR SPREADSHEET VIEW FUNCTION WHEN EDITING	SPREADSHEET VIEW FUNCTION WHEN BROWSING
Alt+←	Moves the cursor to the prior record except if the cursor is already at the first record	Moves the cursor to the prior record except if the cursor is already at the first record
Alt+→	Moves the cursor to the next record except if the cursor is already at the last record	Moves the cursor to the next record except if the cursor is already at the last record
Alt+Shift+→	Moves the cursor to the last record	Moves the cursor to the last record

N O T E

Repeatedly pressing the navigation keys in Table 3.2 cycles through all the fields in a particular record. For example, if the last field is currently highlighted, pressing a key that moves the cursor to the next field moves the cursor to the first field. If the first field is currently highlighted, pressing a key that moves the cursor to the prior field moves the cursor to the last field in the record.

To view another record in either Form view or Spreadsheet view, either click on the arrows on the tool bar, press the keys and key combinations listed in Table 3.2, or choose Records ➤ First Record, Records ➤ Previous Record, Records ➤ Next Record, or Records ➤ Last Record.

To Sum Up

In this chapter, you learned more about database terms. You then planned, designed, and set up your first database. You found out about field types, switching between Form view and Spreadsheet view, and you discovered the shortcut keys and key combinations used in Form view and Spreadsheet view.

The next chapter tells you all you need to know (and more) about laying out and enhancing input forms, which put the best face on a database. Well-designed input forms help to put your company in the big leagues— for employees and customers alike.

chapter

4

Laying Out Your Database with Input Forms

AFTER creating a database and defining its fields and field types, you can start adding data. But it's best to find out about and experiment with an important intermediate step—designing and creating an input form. Forms ensure that you or your users enter information as accurately and quickly as possible.

Planning, Designing, and Creating an Input Form

Once you have created a database, you can start adding information into the Master Form, the ready-made default input form which always displays all of the fields in the database. However, Q&A lets you design and create customized input forms, which should make data input a more efficient (and pleasant) experience. Designing a new input form enhances the way that you type data into an input form and the way you view the data on an input form.

Figure 4.1 shows a STAFF database record on the Master Form. Since all fields are the same size, it's difficult to understand the contents of fields with many characters. For example, the Products field at the bottom of the input form shows a little over two keywords, which may not be sufficient. Notice that the input form is arranged in two columns of fields in the order in which you added them. In contrast, Figure 4.2 shows a record from the sample MAILLIST database using a custom form. This input form is arranged in groups of related fields. It is much easier to view and to fill in than the automatically generated Master Form.

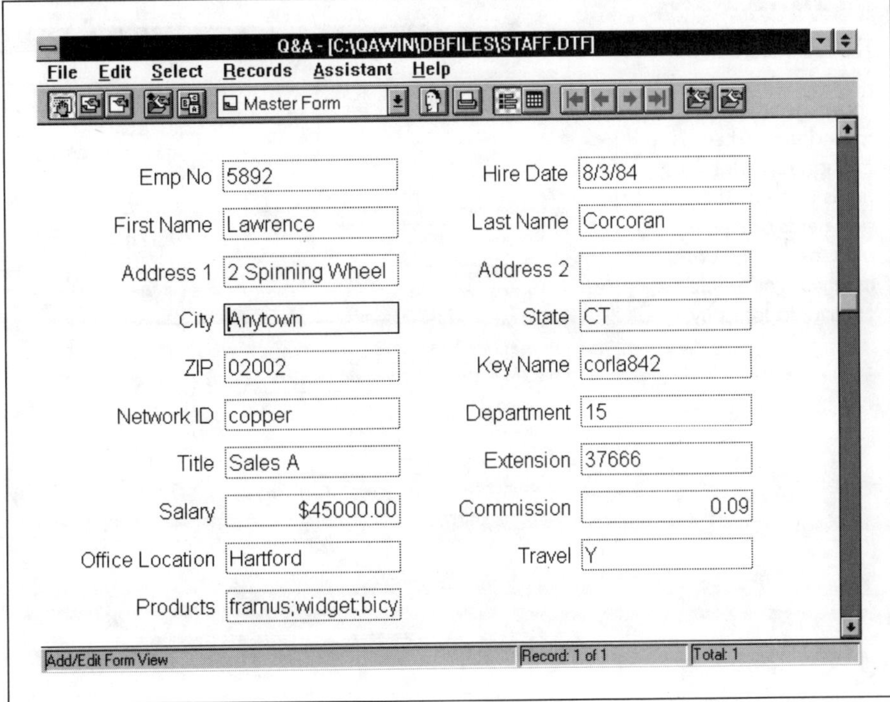

When you rearrange an input form, everything is broken into *objects*, which are items such as fields, field names, and any graphics you can add, such as boxes, pictures, lines, etc. You can select and move these objects around the screen until the input form is exactly the way you want it—with objects and groups of objects arranged logically and, at the same time, with plenty of *white space* (nontext, nongraphic parts of the input form).

In sketching out your own database design on paper, plan for easy data entry by spreading fields out (from the left margin to the right margin, and from the top of the screen to the bottom). Is there room for adding lines and boxes? Use white space, boxes, and lines to group similar or related fields and to separate dissimilar fields. Make sure that you leave enough room to add a new field to groups of related fields.

The Master Form always contains all the fields (up to 2045) in the database, and the default field boxes are always the same size. Q&A allows you to change the Master Form design. If you always plan on using the same input form for a database and if you know that you will always fill in every field, you can change the Master Form for the database. However, if you

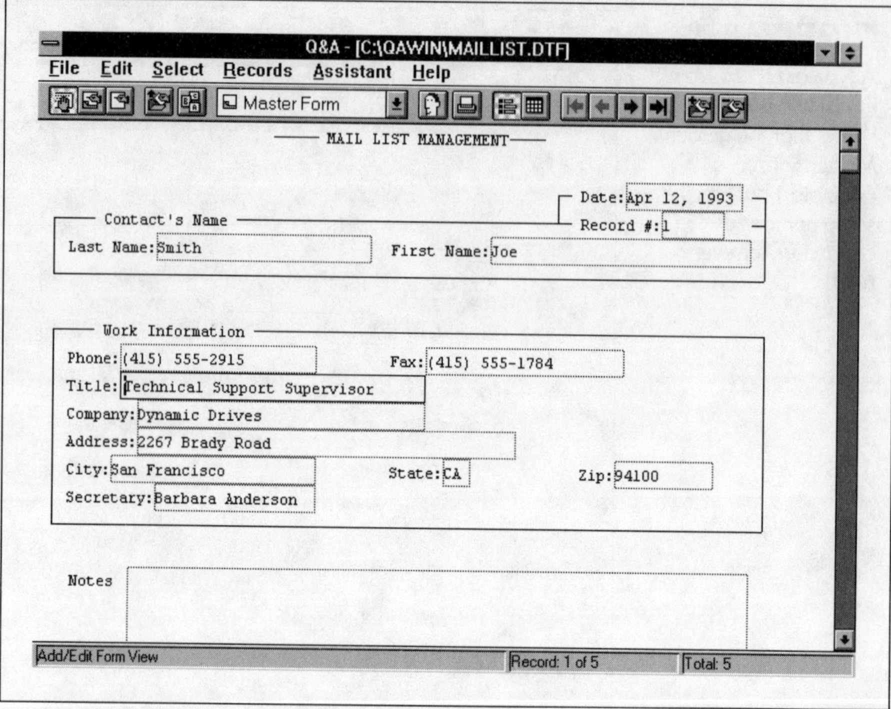

plan to retrieve several types of information from a database (for example, if you want to create special mailing labels or a unique report), create an input form for each type of retrieval. If you use one database to hold several types of data (say you just need names and addresses and no further information for certain individuals), create an input form with only the desired fields.

Creating a New Input Form

When you create a new input form, you'll do almost all your work in the New Input Form dialog box. First, you'll select the fields that you wish to have in the input form, and then you'll click on either the Add or Add All button. If you wish to remove any of your selections, you'll click on either the Remove or Remove All button. The buttons in the New Input

Form dialog box are:

A<u>d</u>d	Adds the fields that you have selected to the input form
Ad<u>d</u> All	Adds all the fields in the database to the input form
<u>R</u>emove	Removes selected fields from the input form
Re<u>m</u>ove All	Removes all fields from the input form

Windows-based applications, such as Q&A, let you select several consecutive fields or separate fields. To select multiple fields, click on a field. Then press and hold down the Shift key, and click on other fields. Q&A highlights all the fields selected. To select several non-contiguous fields, click on your first selection; then press and hold down the Ctrl key while clicking on fields to be added to your selection. Q&A highlights each new selection while keeping prior selected fields highlighted. You can select a combination of contiguous and non-contiguous fields by selecting the contiguous ones first, pressing the Shift key. Then press the Ctrl key and continue adding new fields to your selection.

To create a new input form for your new database, open the STAFF database (or the database with which you are working) and follow these steps:

1. Choose <u>S</u>elect ➤ Design Input <u>F</u>orms. Q&A displays the Design Input Forms work area with the Master Form (Figure 4.3). Notice that all fields are the same length and are displayed in two columns.

You can display the Design Input Forms work area by clicking on the Design Input Forms button on the tool bar (the second button from the left) or by pressing the Ctrl+M shortcut key combination.

2. To begin a new input form, choose F<u>o</u>rms ➤ <u>N</u>ew Input Form. Q&A displays the New Input Form dialog box (see Figure 4.4).

FIGURE 4.3

The Design Input Forms work area with the Master Form for the STAFF database displayed. This work area is fully equipped for editing and enhancing an input form.

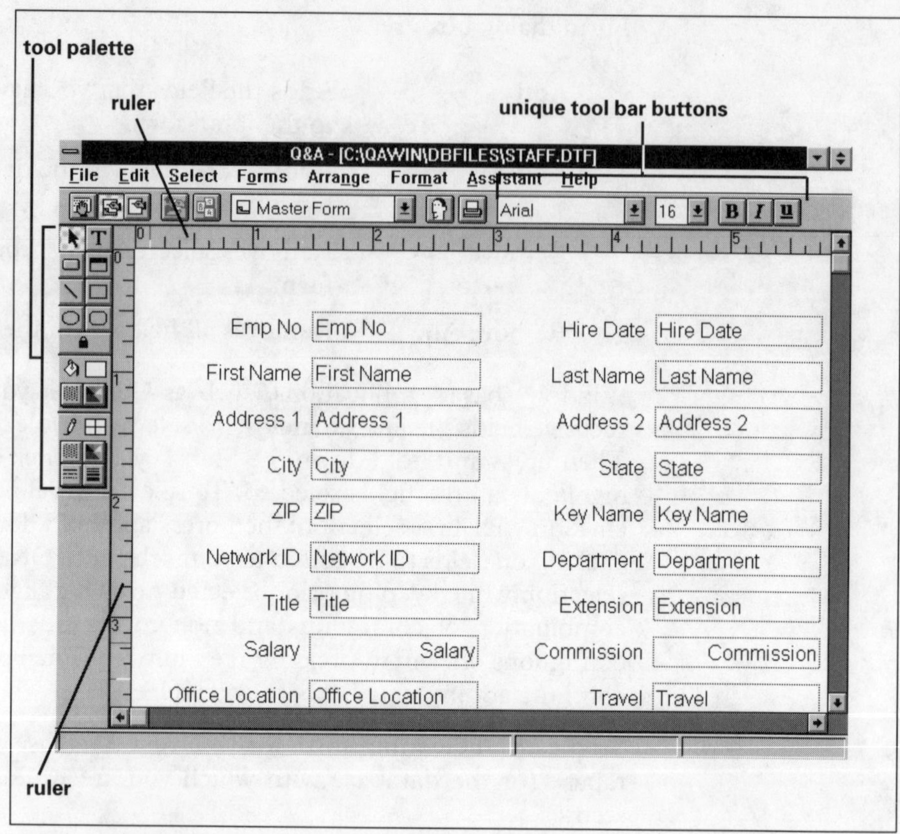

TIP

You can start a new input form by pressing the Ctrl+N shortcut key combination.

3. Select fields to be added to the input form.

TIP

To add all but a very few fields in the current database to the new input form, click on the A̲dd All button. Then remove fields you don't want.

FIGURE 4.4

The New Input Form dialog box in which you can lay out a custom input form for the current database

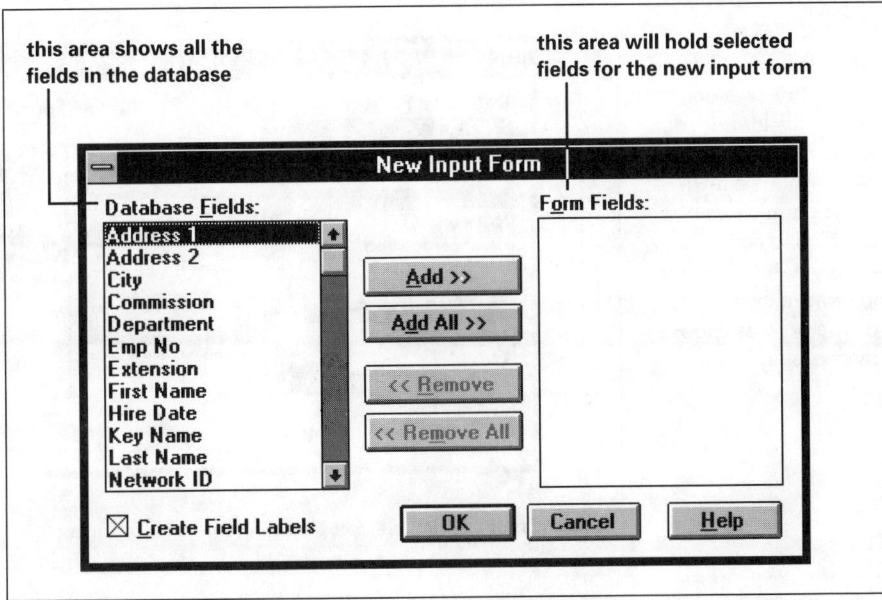

4. Click on the Add All (Figure 4.5) or Add button (Figure 4.6) to add all or selected fields to the input form.

FIGURE 4.5

The New Input Form dialog box with all fields added to an input form.

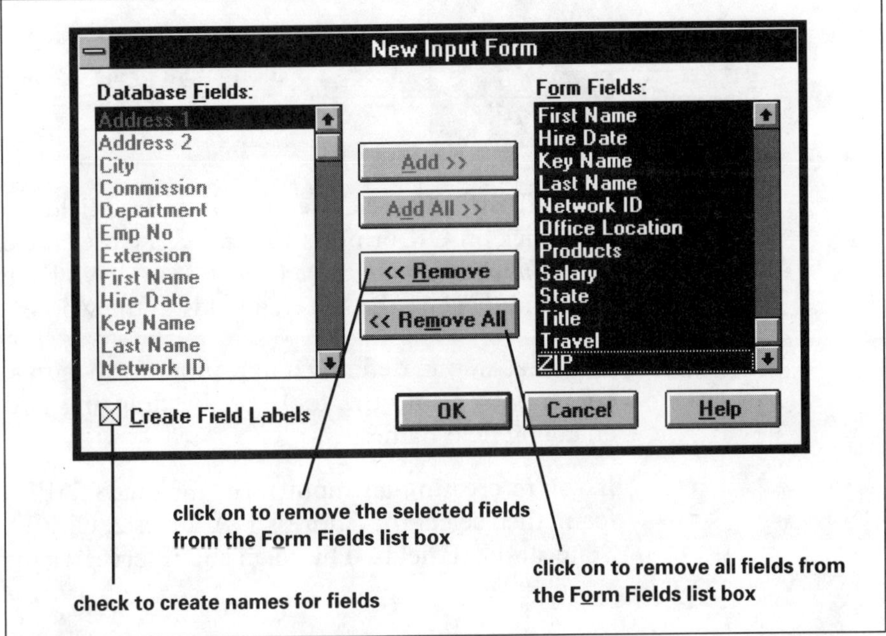

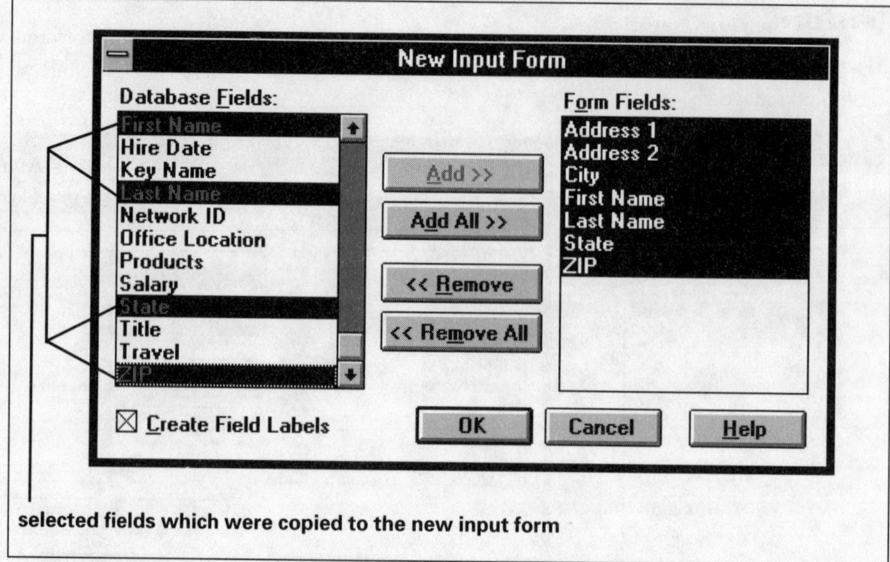

selected fields which were copied to the new input form

5. To remove fields from the input form one at a time, select the field and click on the Remove button. To remove all fields from the input form, click on the Remove All button.

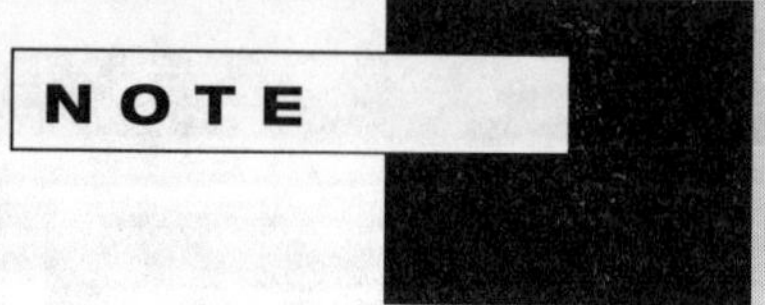

To add the field labels to each field, make sure that there is a check mark in the Create Field Labels check box. This is the default.

6. When you have added all the desired fields to the new input form, click on OK or press Enter. Q&A closes the dialog box, inserts *Untitled Form* in the leftmost drop-down list box in the tool bar, and displays the selected fields in the work area (see Figure 4.7).

The next step in defining a new input form is to save it and then edit its contents by using the tool bar, by dragging and sizing fields, and by changing field names.

If you're creating an input form for the STAFF database, open a new form, then select the Address 1, Address 2, City, First Name, Last Name, State, and ZIP fields. This form could serve as a mailing label input form.

FIGURE 4.7

The Design Input Forms work area with an untitled form displayed

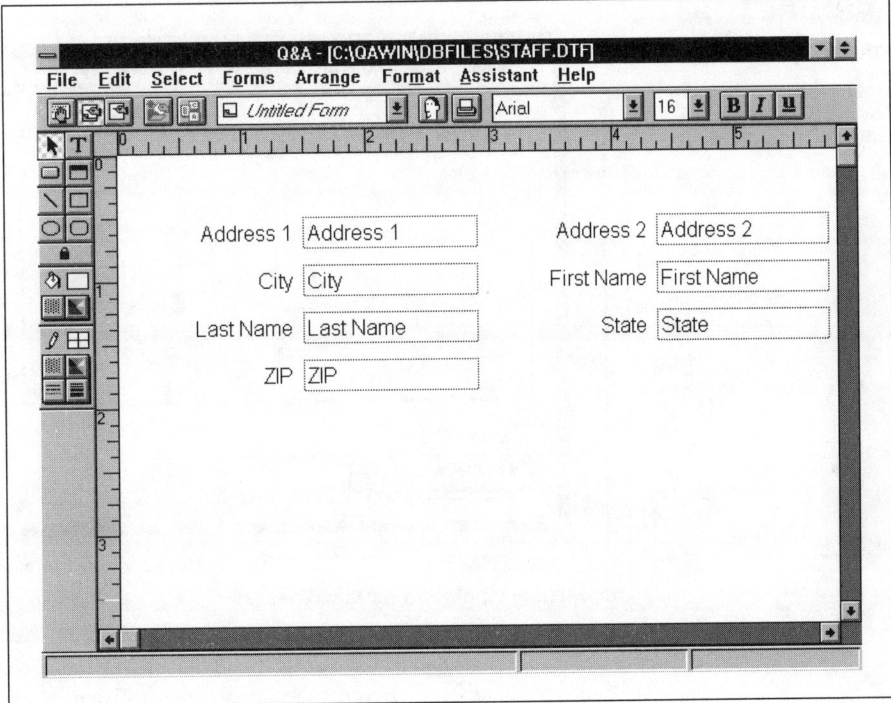

Saving an Input Form

Unlike a database file, which Q&A automatically saves whenever you change it, you *must* save a new input form. However, if you forget to save an input form, Q&A prompts you (Figure 4.8) before you move on to another part of your work session or manipulate another input form.

FIGURE 4.8

The information box with which Q&A prompts you to save an input form that has been changed

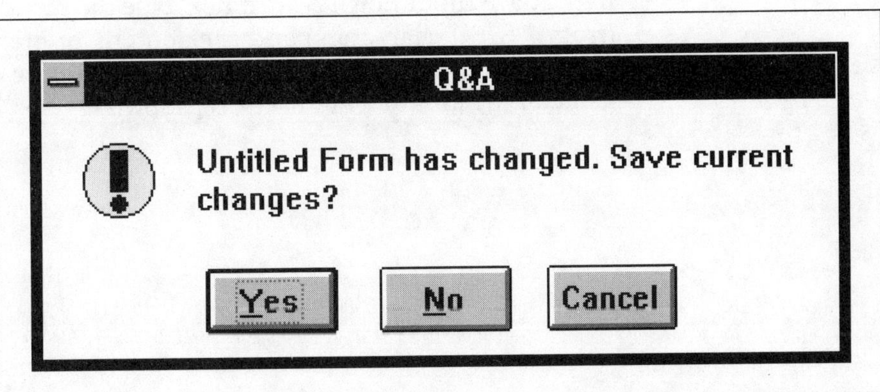

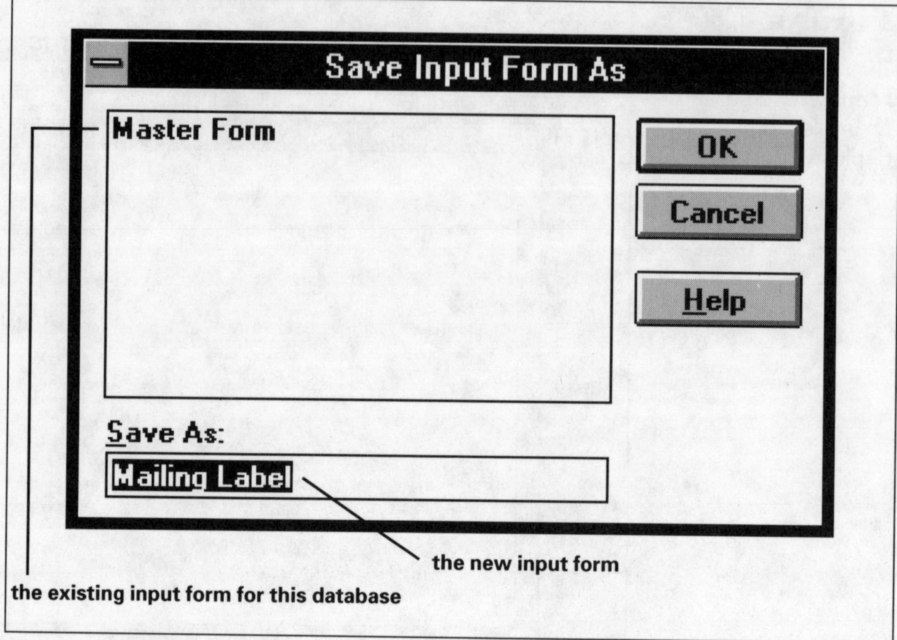

When you choose **F**orms ➤ **S**ave Input Form to save an input form for
the first time, you must give it a name using the Save Input Form As dialog box. When you choose **F**orms ➤ **S**ave Input Form to save an input
form that has already been saved, Q&A automatically saves the form
without opening a dialog box.

If you wish to save an input form under a different name or save it to a
different location, choose **F**orms ➤ Save Input Form **A**s, which displays
the Save Input Form As dialog box (Figure 4.9).

In the Save Input Form As text box, type the name of the new input form
(from 1 to 30 characters) and click on OK or press Enter. Q&A returns
to the Design Input Forms work area (see Figure 4.10) and displays the
name of the input form in the drop-down list box in the tool bar.

The named input form, which still waits for a new layout

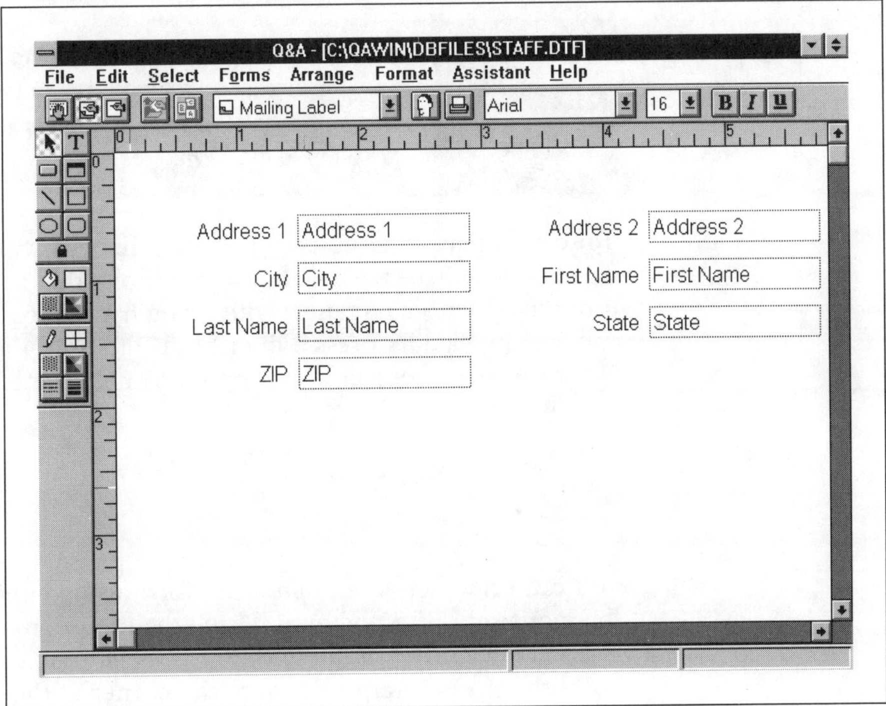

WARNING

If you choose F**o**rms ➤ **S**ave Input Form (or press Ctrl+S) to save a new version of an existing input form, you are telling Q&A to overwrite (erase) the prior version of the input form. Make sure that this is your intention. Otherwise, choose F**o**rms ➤ Save Input Form **A**s.

If you type the name of an input form that already is listed in the Save Input Form As dialog box, Q&A asks you whether you wish to overwrite this form. If you answer **Y**es, Q&A saves the new form and in effect erases the old form with the same name. If you answer **N**o, Q&A returns you to the dialog box without taking any action.

Selecting Objects in an Input Form

Before you modify input form objects, you must select them. You can select either a specific object or several objects at once.

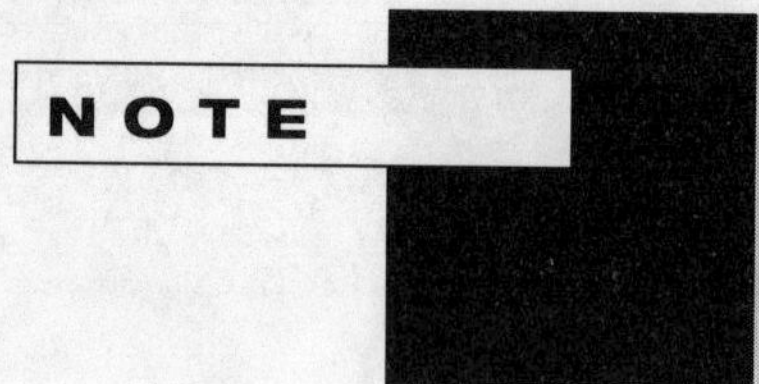

To select an object in the Design Input Forms area, make sure the selection tool looks as though it is pressed down. If it isn't, you might inadvertently edit text or add graphics to the form.

To select a particular object, click on it. Experiment by clicking on a field name. Then click on a field box. Q&A shows that a field is selected by surrounding it with a rectangle with sizing handles on the four corners. You can also repeatedly press Tab or Shift-Tab until the desired object is selected. When an object in the input form is selected, it looks like this:

You can select an area of an input form using either the mouse or both the mouse and the keyboard. Using the mouse, move the mouse pointer to a starting corner of the selection, press and hold down the mouse button, drag the pointer to the opposite corner of the selection, and release the mouse button to complete the selection. When selecting in this way, make sure you are using the selection arrow and that the mouse pointer is outside the boundary of an object; if you click within the boundary, you'll select a specific object. When you use this method, the selected area (before you release the mouse button) looks like this:

After you release the mouse button, the selected area looks like this:

For example, point to the intersection of the imaginary lines from the $^1/_2$ inch mark on both rulers, press and hold down the mouse button, and then drag diagonally past the right side of the First Name field box. Try it once or twice more to master the technique.

To use both the mouse and the keyboard to select several objects on an input form, click on the first object to be selected (e.g., every field name in the left column), then press the Shift key and continue to click on other objects, which can be in any other part of the form, until your selection is complete. To remove an object from the selection, simply click on it again before releasing the Shift key.

To select all the objects in the input form, choose Edit ➤ Select All.

To "unselect" one or multiple selected objects, either press the Esc key, click on another part of the input form, or click on the object a second time with the Shift key still down.

In the Master Form for the STAFF database, practice selecting the First Name field name by clicking on it. Then use the mouse to select the first three field names and field boxes in the input form. Finally, using the mouse and the Shift key, select all the field names in the right column of the input form.

Once you have selected an area of the input form, the next step is to apply the changes. Just follow the procedures in the following sections.

Sizing Objects on an Input Form

The default Master Form lets you see the same number of characters in a field box, regardless of the size of the field itself. Some fields can hold more characters than can be displayed, some less. For example, in a database used by an emergency medical station in a town with a Church Street and a Church Road, it's a good idea to be able to view the complete name so that an ambulance arrives at the right location as quickly as possible.

Before you arrange the field boxes in an input form, you can adjust their length and height if you think you'll make data entry easier and improve the final look of the input form. You can also modify the field boxes during and after changing the location of field boxes.

Re-sizing a field box is quite easy. First, you have to click on the field box to be changed. When Q&A activates the field box by displaying handles at its corners, move the mouse pointer to a corner, press and hold down the mouse button, and drag the clicked-on corner to its new location.

Tips for Arranging Fields and Other Objects

Here are some tips to help you more efficiently arrange fields and other objects in a custom form:

1. Before starting to move objects around the input form, turn the grid on. Select Format ➤ Rulers & Grid. Then in the Rulers & Grid dialog box, check the Show Grid text box.

2. While the Rulers & Grid dialog box is available, refine the grid by increasing the number in the Increments per Inch or Increments per Centimeter scroll/text box.

3. If you know that you will be increasing the length of a field in its final location, be sure to leave extra room on the input form. In fact, if the field will be quite long, don't drag another object to the same horizontal grid line.

4. If you know that you will shorten the length of a field, you can squeeze more objects in the same area and adjust the length later.

5. If an object is one of the last to be moved, temporarily drag it to an empty space, preferably at the bottom of the input form. This gets it out of the way, leaving you with more workspace.

6. Although it's very useful to group related objects, there is a disadvantage. Before you can add or remove room from an object in a group, you must ungroup. There is enough fine-tuning to each field and field name on an input form that grouping can be counterproductive. Therefore, it is good to do your grouping as one of your later steps. Grouping is discussed later in this chapter.

Figure 4.11 illustrates the rearranged STAFF Master Form.

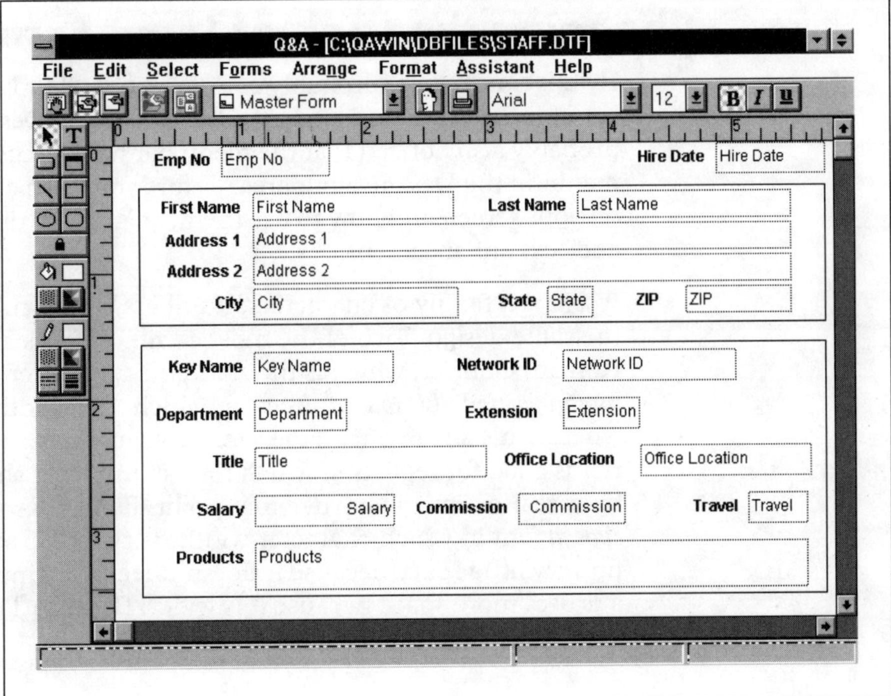

FIGURE 4.11

The STAFF Master Form. Notice that the field boxes are now varying widths.

Changing the Appearance of Text on an Input Form

Instead of formatting and enhancing the input form you've just created, select the Master Form and work on that. Simply open the input form drop-down list box on the button bar, and select Master Form. Q&A displays all the database fields in the work area. Now you can start formatting, but first here's some background information.

Q&A provides a great deal of flexibility as you design input form. After you add the desired fields to an input form, for example, you can enhance the text and move objects around the form using tool bar buttons, menu commands, and shortcut keys and key combinations. But before you can start editing, you have to select objects to edit.

Changing the Look of Input Form Text

By this time, you're probably curious about all those new buttons you can see in the tool bar and along the left side of the Design Input area. You've probably also noticed that the menu bar has changed; there are three new menus in the Design Input area. Before you learn about the new elements on your screen and how to use them, let's briefly discuss fonts, point size, and text enhancement.

A *font* is a family of characters, numbers, and symbols that are based on the same design. Two of the most common fonts are Courier and Times Roman. Courier, which is the standard typewriter font, is a *monospace* or *nonproportionally spaced* font in which the width of every character, whether it's an *i* or a *w*, is the same. Because it is a monospace font, Courier is good for reports in which rows of numbers should be aligned either by a real or imaginary decimal point. Times Roman is a *proportionally spaced* font in which character widths vary. For example, an *i* or a *1* takes up very little space because it doesn't need very much. However, an *m* or a *w* uses more space because it is wider. Because Times Roman is easy to read, it's a very popular newspaper font.

```
This is sample text set in the TrueType Courier New font. Notice how the
characters in all the lines match vertically.
wwww  iiii
```

This is a sample sentence set in the TrueType Times New Roman font. The characters in
all the lines do not match vertically.
wwww iiii

 There are two types of fonts of which you should be aware. TrueType fonts, designed specifically for the current Windows software, are true WYSIWYG (pronounced "wizzywig" and standing for What You See Is What You Get) fonts; the characters look the same printed as they do on your computer screen. In a list of Windows fonts, TrueType fonts are indicated by the TT symbol shown to the left. Printer fonts, which are built into your printer's processor, are indicated by the printer symbol. The number of printer fonts vary by the current printer. PostScript printers usually provide the most printer fonts, and dot matrix printers the least, with non-PostScript laser printers somewhere in between. For more information about fonts, see your Windows documentation or one of the many books devoted to typography.

A font includes sets of characters in various point sizes. A *point*, which is the measurement from the highest point of a character such as *d* to the lowest point of a character like *p*, is 1/72" high. Typical point sizes are 10 to 12 for standard text (with the smallest possible size for the fine print in a contract) and at least 14 to 16 for headings, but it's up to you to decide on the best point size and font. Increasing the point size for both printed and displayed text can increase readability, but decreasing the point size makes it easier to group related fields and to add plenty of white space between the groups.

In addition to point size, a font family typically contains sets of normal, boldface, italics, and bold italicized characters. When you learn about the Font dialog box a little later in this chapter, you'll find out about the additional enhancements of strikethrough and underline.

When experimenting with fonts, point sizes, and enhancements, try to avoid the ransom note look of having too many variations on an input form. It's best to restrict yourself to one or two fonts and a couple of point sizes.

There are two good ways to learn about text enhancement and layout: reading about it and doing it. You have just read a little about it; now let's experiment with the Master Form in your new database.

Changing to a New Font Using the Tool Bar

The tool bar provides both the easiest and fastest way to change the font for selected text. Table 4.1 describes the new tool bar buttons for the Design Input area.

To change a font, just follow these steps:

1. Select the text whose font you wish to change. For example, select the first field name, Emp No.

TABLE 4.1: Q&A Database Tool Bar Buttons—Design Input Form Area

BUTTON	BUTTON OR LIST BOX NAME	DESCRIPTION	EQUIVALENT COMMAND	SHORTCUT KEYS
Arial	Font	Click on the arrow to the right of the drop-down list box to choose a different font for selected text.	Format ➤ Font	Ctrl+F
16	Point Size	Click on the arrow to the right of the drop-down list box to choose a different point size for selected text.	Format ➤ Font	Ctrl+F
B	Bold	Click on to apply boldface or to remove boldface from selected text.	Format ➤ Font	Ctrl+F
I	Italic	Click on to italicize or remove italics from selected text.	Format ➤ Font	Ctrl+F
U	Underline	Click on to underline or remove an underline from selected text.	Format ➤ Font	Ctrl+F

2. Click on the font drop-down list box to open it. Both the closed and open boxes are shown below.

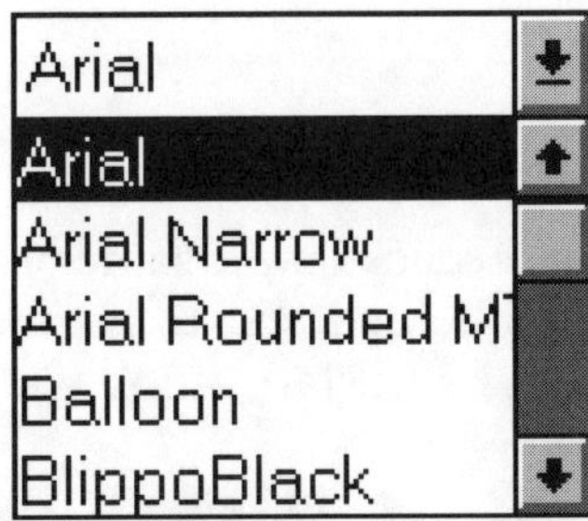

3. Using the scroll bar, browse through your choices of fonts in the open list box. (The font list includes all the fonts installed on your computer system. So if you have invested in several font software packages, the list will be quite long.) Arial is the current font; let's change to Times New Roman.

4. Click on the desired font to select it. Q&A closes the drop-down list box and applies the change to the selected text.

5. If you wish, repeat steps 1, 2, 3, and 4 for other selected field names.

Using the Tool Bar to Change the Point Size of Selected Text

In the same way that you change fonts, you can change point size with the tool bar. Select the text to be changed. (This time, experiment by selecting more than one field simultaneously.) Click on the point size drop-down list box to open it. Use the scroll bar to browse through the point sizes in the list box. Click on the desired point size (12 is a good size) to select it. Q&A closes the drop-down list box and applies the change.

Enhancing Selected Text with the Tool Bar

The last three Design Input Forms tool bar buttons allow you to choose any or all of these enhancements by clicking on the Bold, Underline, and Italics buttons. If a tool bar button looks as though it is pressed down, you have applied the enhancement. Just select the text to be enhanced and click on one, two, or three enhancement buttons on the tool bar. You can bold, italicize, or underline text, or perform any combination of these enhancements.

To undo an enhancement, click on the same button you used to apply it—clicking on bold returns bolded text to normal. Alternatively, you can press Edit ➤ Undo if it was the last action you performed.

A One-Step Approach to Formatting and Enhancing Text

You also can use the Font dialog box to format and enhance selected text in all the ways you just learned. The main advantage of using the Font dialog box is that you not only can apply or remove boldface, italics, and underlines, but also can select a new font or change the point size in just one dialog box. The Font dialog box also provides two additional enhancements: you can strike through text and change the color of text, which is an important addition to a screen display and to printed output (if you have a color printer attached to your computer system).

To change font or point size or to apply an enhancement to selected text, use the following set of procedures:

1. Select the text to be changed. For example, select all the field names on the input form.

2. Choose Format ➤ Font or press the shortcut key combination Ctrl+F. Q&A displays the Font dialog box (Figure 4.12).

3. Change the font or point size of the selected text, enhance it, and apply strikethrough or colors as desired.

TIP

One advantage of using the Font dialog box to change fonts and enhance text is that you can view the results before finalizing your choices. Just make a change and look at the display in the Sample box.

4. After completing your choices, click on OK or press Enter. Q&A closes the dialog box and applies the change.

The Font dialog box with which you can modify the look of input form text in one step. Just open the dialog box and choose from the five groups.

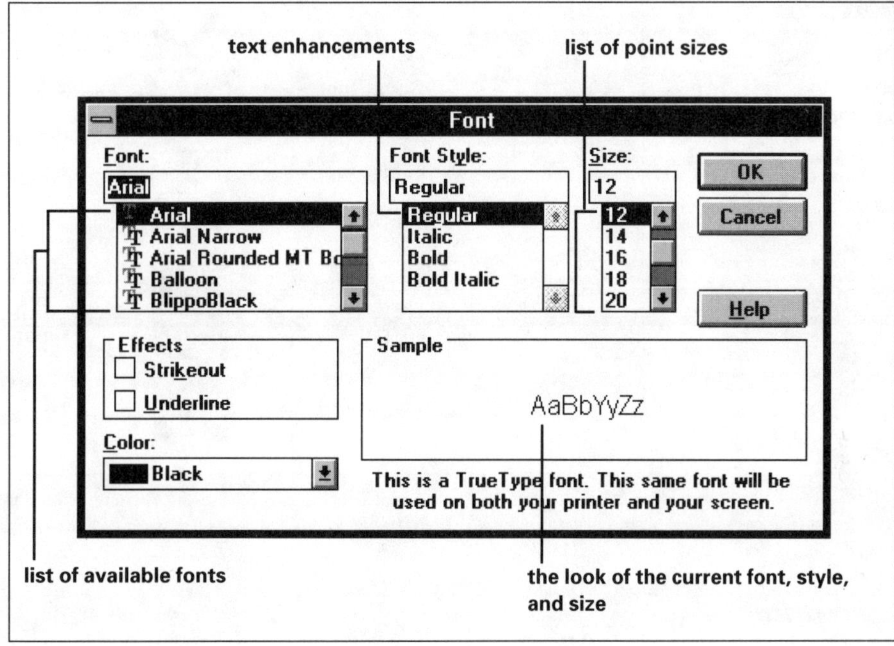

Modifying an Input Form Using the Tool Palette

One way to enhance the usefulness of an input form is to draw and change the color and patterns of lines and rectangles. To allow you to do this, Q&A provides an entire palette of tools in the Design Input Forms area. Before experimenting with the input form, let's find out about all the parts of the tool palette (see Figure 4.13). Table 4.2 illustrates, names, and describes each Tool Palette button.

Drawing in an Input Form

It's quite easy to emphasize groups of related objects on an input form; you can use the tools on the tool palette to draw lines, rectangles, and ellipses.

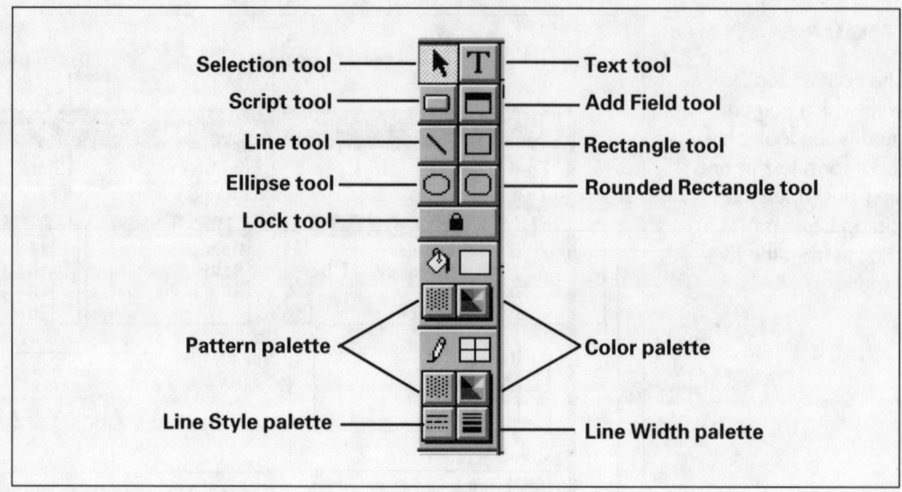

TABLE 4.2: Q&A Tool Palette Buttons and Mouse Pointers

BUTTON	NAME	DESCRIPTION
	Selection tool	Enables you to select objects on the input form for editing. This is the default button on the tool palette.
	Text tool	Allows you to edit or enhance text on the input form. Double-clicking on any input form text is another way of selecting the Text tool.
	Script tool	Draws a button to which you can attach a *script*, which automates regularly used sets of procedures (See Chapter 10).
	Add Field tool	Adds a field that is already defined to this database but not in the current input form. (You can't add a field to the Master Form because it already contains all the fields.)

TABLE 4.2: Q&A Tool Palette Buttons and Mouse Pointers (continued)

BUTTON	NAME	DESCRIPTION
	Line tool	A graphic object tool that allows you to draw a line anywhere on the input form.
	Rectangle tool	Draws a rectangle (or square if you press the Shift key) on an input form.
	Ellipse tool	Draws an ellipse (or circle if you press the Shift key) on an input form.
	Rounded rectangle tool	Draws a rounded rectangle (or rounded square if you press the Shift key) on an input form.
	Lock tool	Prevents Q&A from changing a tool you are using back into the selection tool. Click on both the Lock tool and the drawing tool and you'll be able to draw multiple objects without reverting to the Select tool.
	Pattern	In both the Fill Attributes and Line Attributes box, opens a palette from which you can choose a pattern for the inside of a box or a line.
	Color	In both the Fill Attributes and Line Attributes box, opens a palette from which you can choose a color for the inside of a box or a line.
	Line Style	Opens a palette from which you can choose a line style.
	Line Width	Opens a palette from which you can choose a line width.

Because Q&A is a Windows application, you can use other Windows applications to add pictures to an input form. For example, you can use Paintbrush to create a company logo, choose Edit ➤ Copy to copy it to the Clipboard, and then paste it into the Q&A input form by choosing Edit ➤ Paste.

Drawing any graphic on an input form requires almost the same set of procedures. Let's draw rectangles in the STAFF Master input form with the following steps:

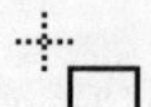

1. Click on the Rectangle tool. Q&A changes the look of the mouse pointer.

2. Move the mouse pointer to one corner of the rectangle you wish to draw. Then press, hold down, and drag the mouse pointer diagonally toward the opposite corner.

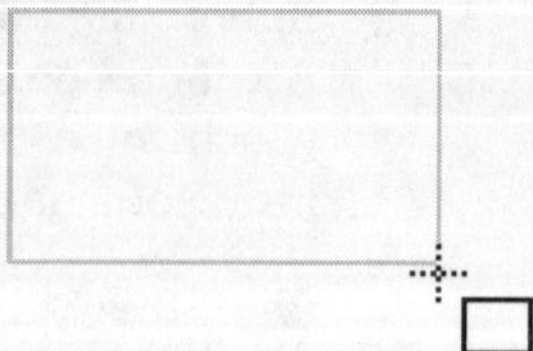

If you press and hold down the Shift key while dragging, you'll draw a square or change a rectangle into a square. Q&A ensures that all lines of the rectangle you are drawing are the same length.

3. Release the mouse button to add handles to the rectangle.

4. To change the shape of the rectangle, move the mouse pointer to a handle (it changes to a double-headed arrow).

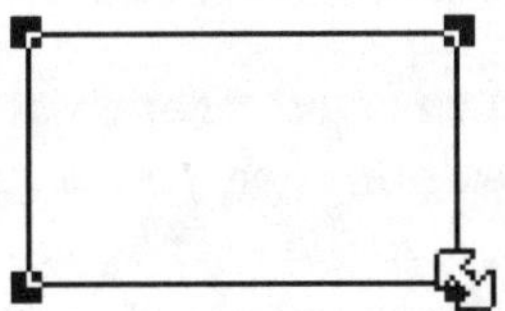

5. Press and hold down the mouse button, and drag the corner of the rectangle to a new position.

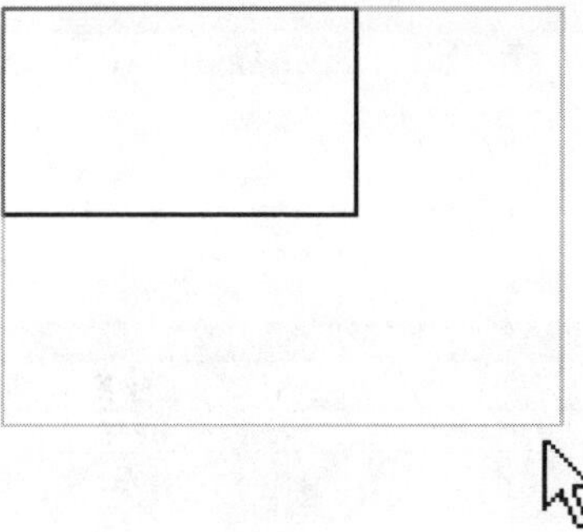

6. Release the mouse button, and Q&A places handles around the rectangle again.

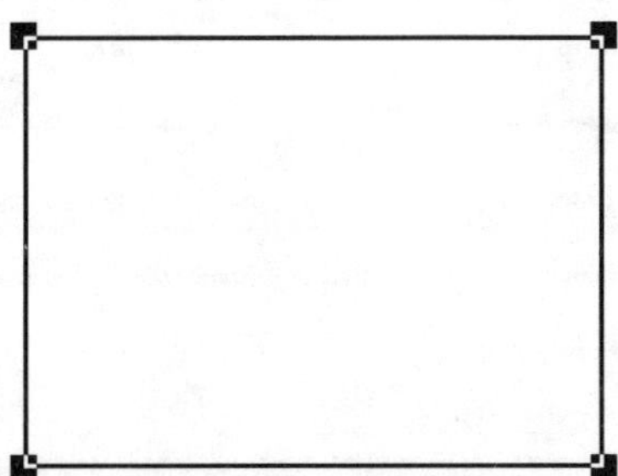

N O T E   To delete a rectangle, line, or ellipse, click on it to make it active (i.e., like any selected object, it has handles at the corners or ends). Then press the Delete key or the Backspace key.

TIP

If adding an object hides an object underneath it (e.g., all the fields and field names), choose Arrange ➤ Bring Forward, Arrange ➤ Bring to Front, Arrange ➤ Send Back, or Arrange ➤ Send to Back until the object appears. The shortcut key combination for Bring to Front is Ctrl+Shift+F, and for Send to Back is Ctrl+Shift+J. These options actually move objects to layers of the input form.

Figure 4.14 shows the STAFF Master Form with two rectangles.

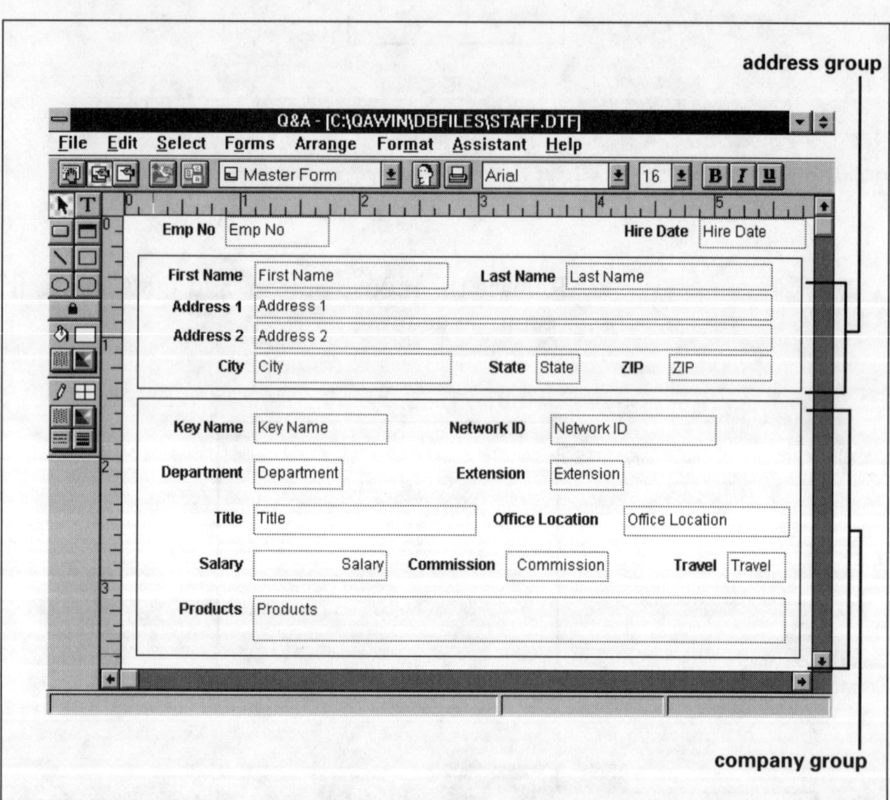

Enhancing a Drawing in an Input Form

For additional emphasis, you can add colors or patterns to a drawing in an input form. For example, you may wish to encourage a data entry clerk not to miss typing an employee identification number or a customer address by applying a *fill pattern* or *line pattern*. You apply a fill pattern to an enclosed shape, such as the rectangle surrounding a field or form, while you apply a line pattern to the line enclosing the shape. A *line style* is, for example, a dotted, hatched, or solid line. In working with line patterns and styles, be aware that:

- Line style only works on hairline and thin line (the first two choices in the line style box).

- Combining thin lines with line patterns is a good way of making interesting looking line styles and calling attention to messages or fields.

- Line patterns works best on thick lines.

To highlight address information in the STAFF database, you can use the following steps to add a pattern to the rectangle that you just drew:

1. Click on any side or corner of the rectangle enclosing the STAFF address information. Q&A shows you that the rectangle is active by adding handles.

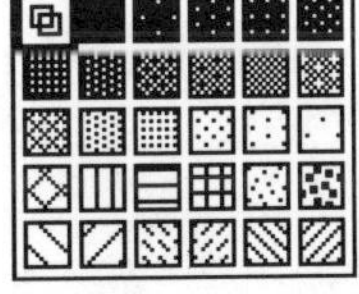

2. In the Fill Attributes box in the Tool palette, click on the Pattern button. Q&A opens a pattern palette. (You can close a palette without making a selection by either pressing the Esc key or by clicking off the palette.)

The double-square in the upper left corner of the box indicates that the selected object is *transparent*. This means that you can see objects located behind the transparent object that would ordinarily be hidden.

3. Click on a box in the pattern palette. Q&A closes the palette and applies the pattern.

4. In the Fill Attributes box in the Tool palette, click on the Color button. Q&A opens a color palette.

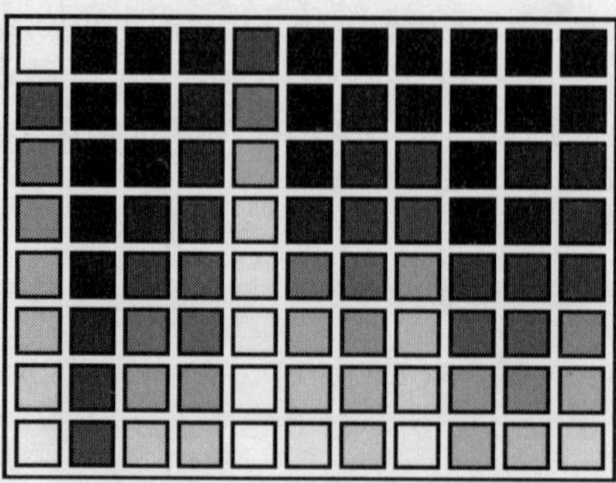

5. Click on a color from the palette. Q&A closes the palette, applies the color, and shows you the current pattern or color in the box in the upper right corner of the Fill Attributes box.

The number of available colors in the palette varies with the graphics modes or the graphics card you are using.

Figure 4.15 shows the STAFF Master Form with the name and address information enhanced by adding color.

Bringing and Sending Objects on an Input Form

You just learned how to add lines, rectangles, and ellipses to a form. As you found out, when you place one object over another, you lose sight of the object that's underneath. Q&A allows you to switch the order of objects from back to front and from front to back. In the STAFF input form, notice the rectangle around the name and address information (see Figures 4.13 and 4.14). Because the rectangle was added *after* the fields were arranged in related groups, it was placed on "top" of other objects, blocking out all the information underneath. In order to display the name, address, city, state, and ZIP fields and field names, the rectangle must be moved "in back of" the fields and field names.

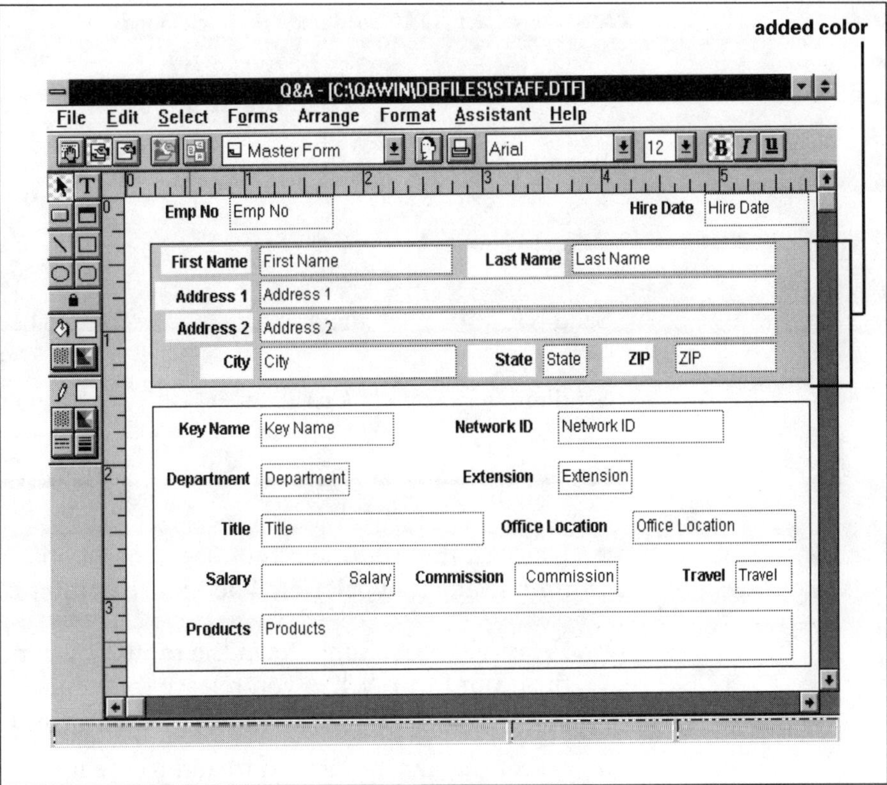

Q&A provides four Arrange menu commands that allow you to rearrange overlapping objects on an input form. Table 4.3 lists the bring and send commands, shortcut key combinations (if available), and descriptions.

Adding a Field to an Input Form

Adding a field to an input form is not the same as adding a new field to a database; it's adding a field already in the database but not included on the current input form. To learn how to add a field to an input form, change to the Mailing Label form that you created early in this chapter. (Remember that the Master Form, which you've been editing, always shows every field in the database.) To add a field to an input form, follow these steps:

1. Open the input form drop-down list box and select an input form. For the STAFF database, select Mailing Label.

TABLE 4.2: Q&A Send and Bring Commands

COMMAND	SHORTCUT KEY COMBINATION	MOVES AN OBJECT
Bring Forward	N/A	forward one layer of overlapping objects
Bring to Front	Ctrl+Shift+F	to the front of all overlapping objects
Send Back	N/A	backward one layer of overlapping objects
Send to Back	Ctrl+Shift+J	to the back of all overlapping objects

2. Click on the Add Field tool (the second button in the right column in the tool palette). The mouse pointer changes its shape.

3. Pressing and holding down the mouse button, draw a field box in the input form. When you release the mouse button, Q&A displays the New Field dialog box (as shown in Figure 4.16).

4. Select the name of a field to add to the input form and either click on OK or press Enter. Q&A adds the field to the input form in the location where you drew the field box.

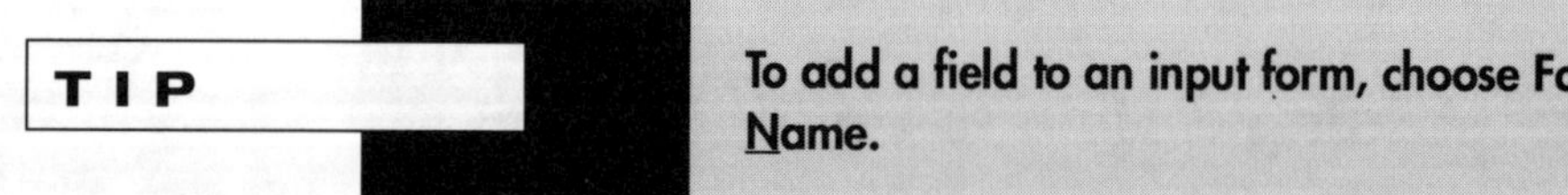

TIP   To add a field to an input form, choose Format ➤ Field Name.

Aligning Objects with the Rulers and the Grid

You have already moved objects around the input form, but there is no reason why you can't change or adjust the basic layout at any time. For example, if you are not satisfied with the look of the newly arranged input

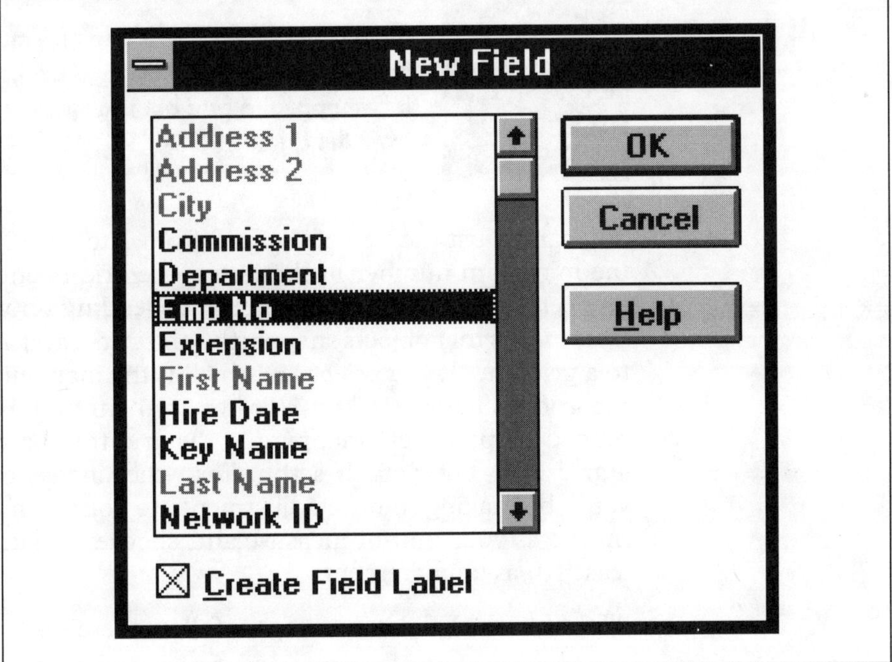

form, you may have to fine-tune the layout using the rulers and the *grid*—a web of parallel rows and columns that look like graph paper. You can turn the grid on and off. If it's on, you can choose to see or hide it.

When you move the mouse pointer around the work area, you'll notice that fine lines on the *rulers* also move. This shows that you can use the rulers to move objects to specific spots on the input form.

Q&A provides the grid for two reasons: for automatic alignment and control over proportions. You can have Q&A automatically align objects horizontally and vertically, and create logical and attractive layouts of fields and objects. When you use the grid, Q&A keeps the size of field boxes in relative proportion with other field boxes on the form. Not snapping to the grid gives you the freedom to adjust the dimensions of an object in any way you wish—which can be handy in placing individual objects (such as a logo) that require special treatment.

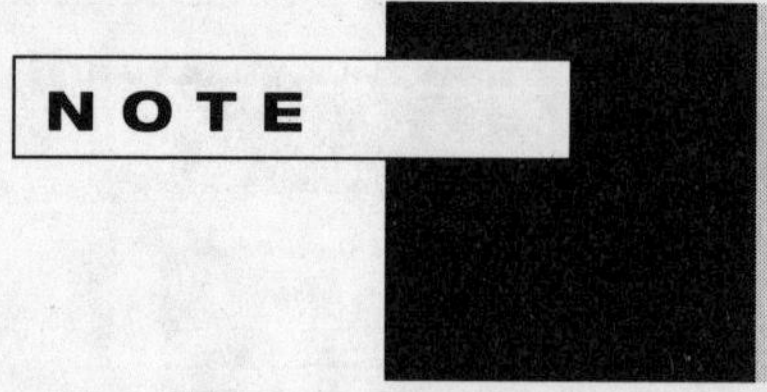

N O T E   If a line on a field box is one centimeter from the grid point when you select Snap to Grid, the line will act as if it is snapped to grid but is always one centimeter away from the grid.

You can adjust the size of the grid from 1 to 16. If you select 1, which is the minimum number in the range, the grid is one inch by one inch or one centimeter by one centimeter, depending on your unit of measure. This means that objects snapping to the grid travel a long distance to snap to a grid line. If you select 16, which is the maximum allowable number, the grid is either 1/16" by 1/16" or 1/16 cm by 1/16 cm, which is a very refined snap; objects snapping to the grid travel a very short distance to a grid line. The default setting for either inches or centimeters is 8. If you'll be making minute adjustments to your form objects, select centimeters as your unit of measure and choose a relatively high number (at least 10) as an increment.

With the STAFF database open, follow these instructions:

1. Choose Format ➤ Rulers & Grid. Q&A displays the Rulers & Grid dialog box as shown in Figure 4.17.

Q&A's Rulers & Grid dialog box with which you can adjust rulers and grid settings.

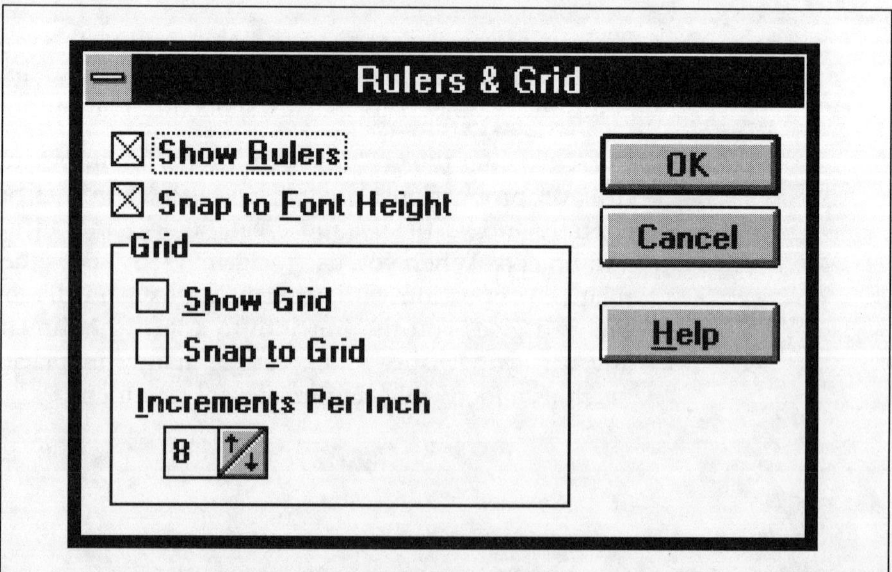

2. To hide (or reveal) the rulers, remove (or add) the checkmark in the Show Rulers check box. The default is to show the rulers.

3. To automatically adjust the height of a resized object to the point size of its font and therefore to display all the text in the object, check the Snap to Font Height check box. (An unchecked check box, which is the default, may result in partially hidden text within the boundaries of the object.)

N O T E

With this option selected when changing the height of the field box, keep in mind that the height is in multiples of the point size of the text in the field box. For example, if the text is 10 point, you can only resize the field box to fit one line of 10 point text, two lines of 10 point, and so on.

4. To display the grid, which makes it easier to size and align objects, place a check in the Show Grid check box. The default is an unchecked check box; the grid is not shown. Figure 4.18 shows you the STAFF Master Form with the grid turned on.

5. To cause the edge of an object to "stick to" (or "snap to") the points of a grid, check the Snap to Grid check box, the default.

6. To adjust the dimensions of the grid, you can either scroll through the numbers in the Increments per Inch or Increments per Centimeter (depending on your default unit of measure) scroll/text box, or you can type in a number from 1 to 16.

7. When you have selected all the desired settings, either click on the OK button or press Enter.

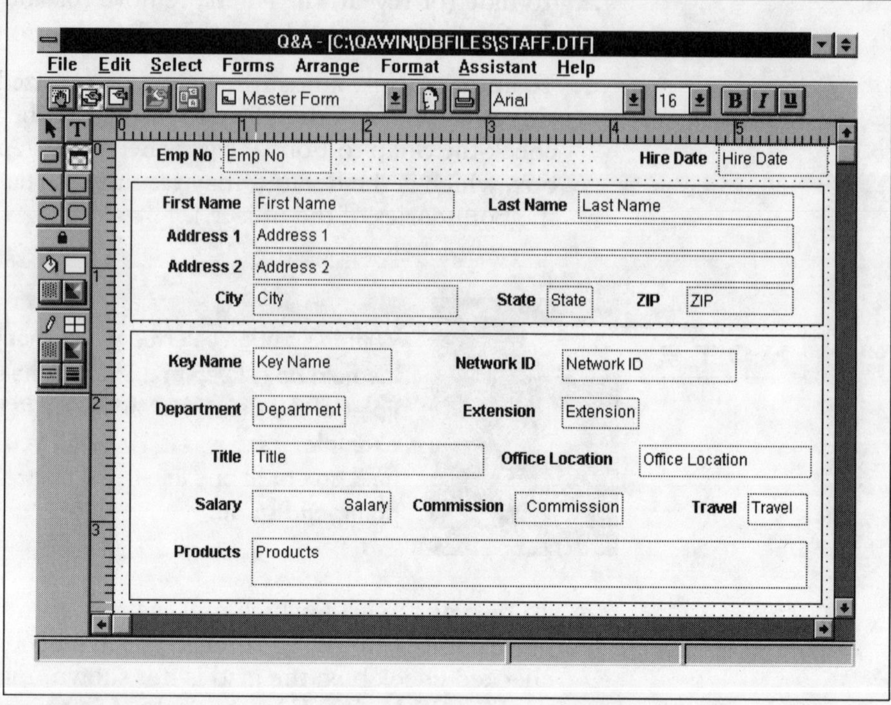

Aligning Objects on an Input Form

Imagine that you have to type data using a badly misaligned and poorly arranged form. Carefully aligning the form makes for easier, more efficient, and faster data entry. There are four ways that you can align objects in an input form:

Arrange ➤ Align to Grid	Aligns selected objects with the grid even if Snap to Grid is turned off
Arrange ➤ Align Objects	Aligns two or more selected objects using the values set in the Alignment dialog box
Arrange ➤ Alignment	Specifies horizontal and vertical settings that govern the alignment of two or more selected objects with one another

For<u>m</u>at ➤ <u>A</u>lign Text	Aligns text within the borders of an object (e.g., a field box)

If an *object* is one centimeter from the grid, and you select Snap <u>t</u>o Grid, the object will remain one centimeter away from the grid. However, if you select Align to G<u>r</u>id, Q&A snaps the object to the grid. If you have not selected an object, this command is dimmed (i.e., unavailable).

You can align all the objects in an input form to the grid simultaneously by choosing <u>E</u>dit ➤ Select <u>A</u>ll (or pressing the Ctrl+A shortcut key combination) and then choosing Arra<u>n</u>ge ➤ Align to G<u>r</u>id.

So far you probably used the default settings for aligning objects relative to each other. You can change these settings by choosing the Align<u>m</u>ent command. For example, if you select two objects—one narrow and one wide—that are in the same column, you can align the narrow object (e.g., in the STAFF Master Form, the field name City) against the left side, the right side, or from a center point of the wide object (e.g., the field name Address 2). If two objects—one higher than the other—that are in the same row are selected, you can align the shorter object against the top, bottom, or center of the higher object.

But before you start experimenting with the Align<u>m</u>ent command, reveal the grid by choosing For<u>m</u>at ➤ <u>R</u>ulers & Grid. In the Rulers & Grid dialog box, place a check mark in the <u>S</u>how Grid check box in the Grid group and either click on OK or press Enter. Then you can define your Q&A alignment criteria and align selected objects in the Design Input Forms area by using the following steps:

1. Choose Arra<u>n</u>ge ➤ Align<u>m</u>ent. Q&A displays the Alignment dialog box, as shown in Figure 4.19.

TIP

Press the Ctrl+Shift+K shortcut key combination to open the Alignment dialog box.

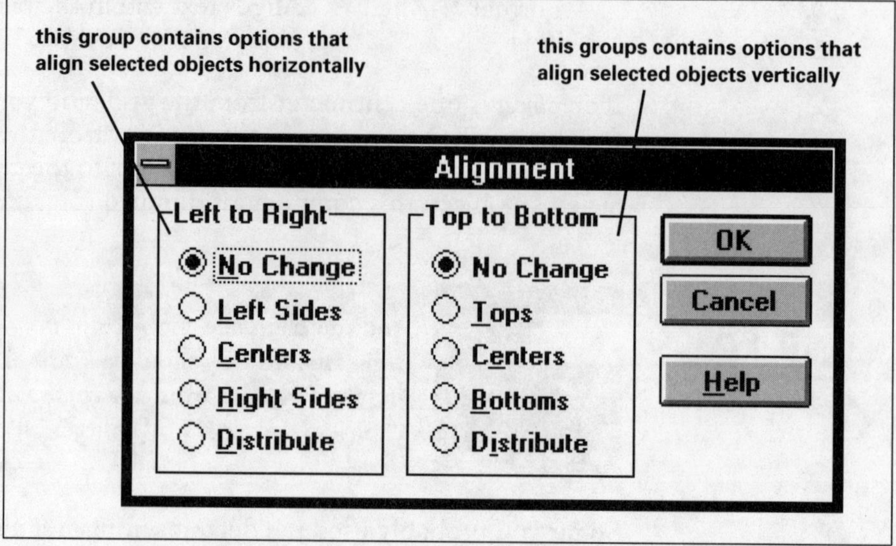

2. To control the horizontal alignment (moving between the left to right sides of the input form) of objects, click on a radio button on the left side of the dialog box. Use the horizontal alignment option to align objects, which are above or below each other. The radio buttons that control horizontal alignment are:

No Change
Keeps the current alignment of the selected objects.

Left Sides
Aligns all the selected objects with the left side of the object that stretches the farthest to the left. For example, if you click on Emp No (or the first field name in the left column) and drag it toward the left side of the input form, selecting Left Sides aligns all the selected objects to match the location of Emp No.

Centers
: Centers all the selected objects from an imaginary vertical middle point. For example, after aligning all the selected objects with the leftmost object (i.e., Emp No), choose <u>C</u>enters. All selected objects, including Emp No, are centered.

<u>R</u>ight Sides
: Aligns all the selected objects with the right side of the object that stretches the farthest to the right. For example, when centered, the right sides of several fields in the STAFF database are aligned very closely to the field box. If you select <u>R</u>ight Sides, all the shorter fields are close to their field boxes.

<u>D</u>istribute
: Places all the selected objects an equal distance apart along the horizontal axis. For example, if you select the two fields at the top of the input form (for STAFF, Emp No and Hire Date are the top fields), selecting <u>D</u>istribute places the field names and field boxes equally apart.

WARNING

Be careful about the objects you select for alignment. For example, if you choose one from the left column and another from the right, and then choose <u>L</u>eft Sides, the object from the right column moves on top of the object in the left column, obscuring it. You can correct this by selecting <u>E</u>dit ➤ <u>U</u>ndo (or by pressing Ctrl+Z).

3. To control the vertical alignment (moving between the top and the bottom of the input form) of objects, click on a radio button from the right side of the dialog box. Use the vertical alignment option to align objects that are side by side. The radio buttons that control vertical alignment are:

No Change
: Keeps the current alignment of the selected objects.

Tops
: Aligns all the selected objects with the top edge of the object that is the farthest toward the top of the input form. For example, if you move Emp No toward the top of the input form and then select both Emp No and Hire Date field names, choosing Tops moves Hire Date up to the level of Emp No.

Centers
: Centers all the selected objects from an imaginary horizontal middle point. For example, if you add the Emp No field box to the Emp No and Hire Date field names selection, choosing Centers moves Emp No and Hire Date field names down and the Emp No field box up so that all three selected objects are aligned.

Bottoms
: Aligns all the selected objects with the bottom edge of the object that is the farthest toward the bottom of the input form. For example, if you drag the bottom of the Emp No field box down to the next grid line and select both Emp No field name and Emp No field box, if you choose Bottoms, the Emp No field name moves down to align with the bottom of the field box.

Distribute   Places all the selected objects an equal
                      distance apart along the vertical axis.
                      For example, if you choose all the field
                      names in the left column and select
                      Distribute, all the field names are
                      distributed the same vertical distance
                      apart. If you have changed the point
                      size of the field names only, you will
                      find that field names and field boxes
                      are mismatched.

4. Either click on OK or press Enter. Q&A returns to the Design Input Forms area.

To align two or more selected objects using the values set in the Alignment dialog box, choose Arrange ➤ Align Objects, which allows you to avoid displaying the dialog box; you can align selected objects in fewer steps.

Press the Ctrl+K shortcut key combination to align two or more selected objects to the specifications in the Alignment dialog box.

You can align text within the borders of an object by choosing Format ➤ Align Text. When the cascading menu appears, just select the desired alignment: Default, which is normally left, Left, Center, or Right.

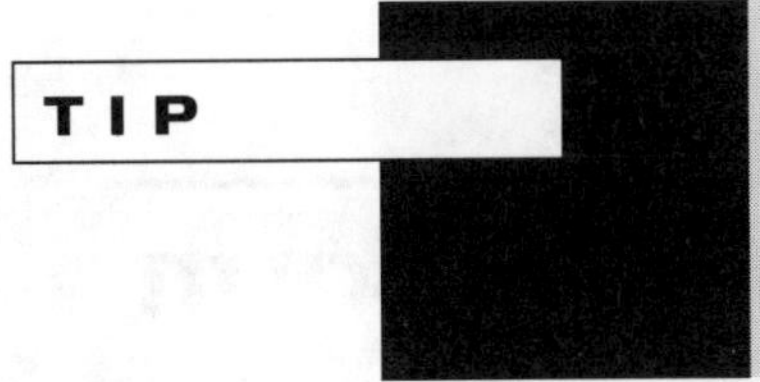

Press the Ctrl+Shift+L, Ctrl+Shift+C, or Ctrl+Shift+R shortcut key combination to align text within its boundaries, on the left side, in the center, or on the right side, respectively.

Grouping Objects on an Input Form

If two or more related objects, such as a field name and field, belong together on an input form, you can group them into a single object so that you can move them as one object. This means that you won't inadvertently leave an object behind. Another reason for grouping is to delete several objects simultaneously. All you have to do is group objects to be deleted and press Del or Backspace. However, be aware that once objects are grouped, the resulting object has one set of properties; if you have to adjust the size of an object in the group, you'll have to ungroup the object, adjust the alignment, and then group again.

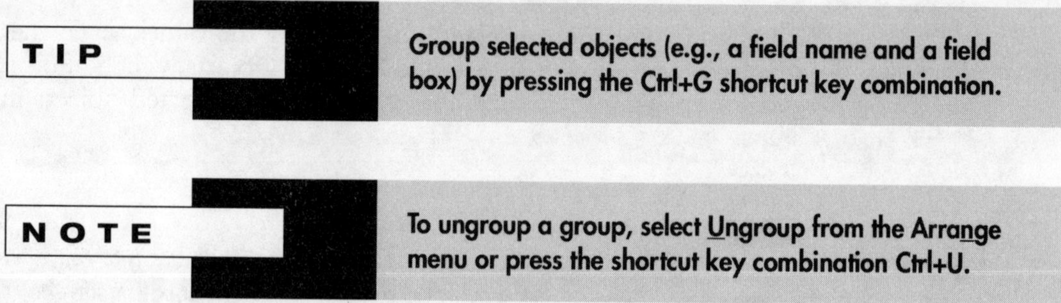

TIP

Group selected objects (e.g., a field name and a field box) by pressing the Ctrl+G shortcut key combination.

NOTE

To ungroup a group, select Ungroup from the Arrange menu or press the shortcut key combination Ctrl+U.

To create a group, select two or more objects, first ensuring that the individual objects are aligned exactly the way you want. Choose Arrange ➤ Group, and Q&A groups the selected objects. Note that the number and positions of the handles shows that the objects are grouped. If you haven't been successful, each selected object is surrounded by handles; if you have successfully made a group, the result is one object with one set of handles.

Designing Tab Order in a Form

Normally, as you press the Tab key in an input form, the cursor moves from field to field in a left to right, top to bottom pattern. In Q&A, you can change this order in any way you wish. Just choose Format ➤ Tab Order ➤ Show and click in the tab symbols in the order in which you want the cursor to move.

N O T E

You can have different tab orders for different input forms. Remember, though, that tab order is in Form view only.

When you show the tab order for a specific input form, tab symbols are superimposed over the fields on the input form. If the tab symbols are blank (Figure 4.20), the input form uses the default tab order. If there are numbers on the tab symbols (Figure 4.21), the cursor travels from 1 to 2 to 3, and so on. You can view and/or change tab order for the current input form by following these steps:

1. Choose Format ➤ Tab Order ➤ Show. Q&A overlays tab symbols on the Fields of the input form.

FIGURE 4.20

The input form with the default tab order; the tab symbols are blank.

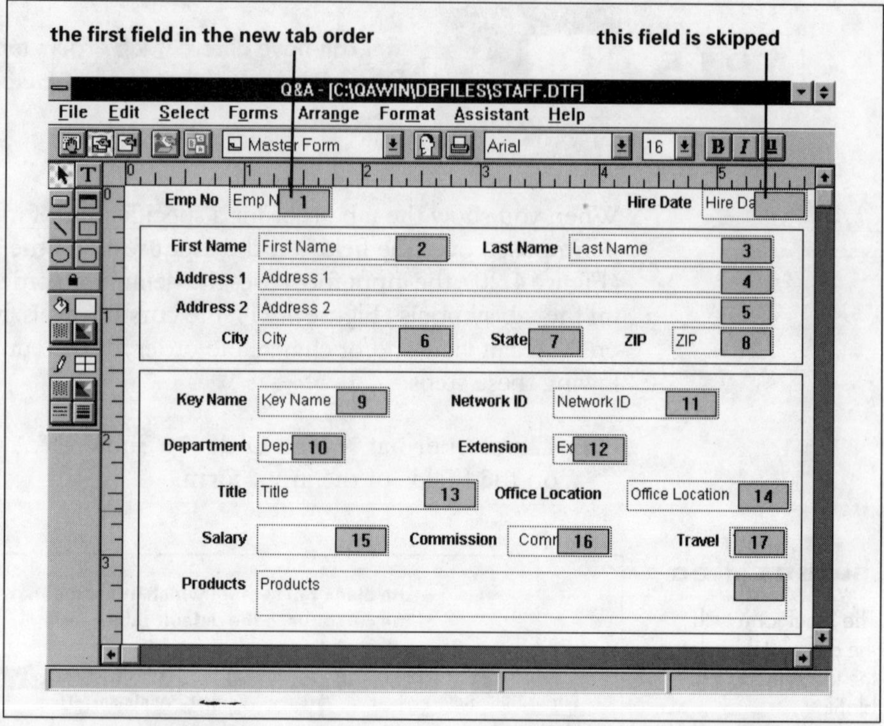

2. To specify a particular tab order, make sure that the Selection tool on the Tool Palette is selected; then click on the tab symbol representing the first field to which the cursor will move. Q&A shows 1 on the tab symbol.

3. Click on successive fields until all desired tab symbols display numbers (i.e., 2, 3, 4, and so on).

NOTE

If you accidentally assign the wrong tab order, the only way to reset the tab order is to choose Format ➤ Tab Order ➤ Clear All.

4. When you have clicked on all fields to which the cursor will move, choose Format ➤ Tab Order ➤ Hide.

When the tab order is hidden, it still exists— it is just invisible.

5. To explicitly save the new tab order, open the F<u>o</u>rms menu and choose <u>S</u>ave Input Form.

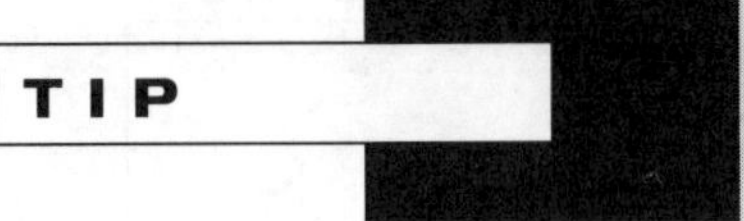

To save the new tab order, press Ctrl+S. In essence, you are saving the input form with the new tab order.

Viewing an Input Form for Data Entry

After you have finished formatting, enhancing, and moving objects around the input form, you should view it as a data entry person will, in Add/Edit form view (Figure 4.22). Either click on the Add/Edit button, the leftmost button on the tool bar, choose <u>S</u>elect ➤ <u>A</u>dd/Edit, or press the shortcut key combination Ctrl+E. You'll probably find that you need to make further adjustments on the input form in the Design Input Forms area.

Deleting an Input Form

When you decide to move to a better input form design or you change a database in such a way that an input form is obsolete, it's better to remove it than to keep it. This reduces the file size of your database, saving room on your hard drive. To remove an input form, follow these steps:

1. Make active the input form in the Design Input Forms area by selecting it from the drop-down list box on the tool bar.

2. Choose F<u>o</u>rms ➤ <u>D</u>elete Input Form. Q&A displays a message box that prompts you to confirm the deletion.

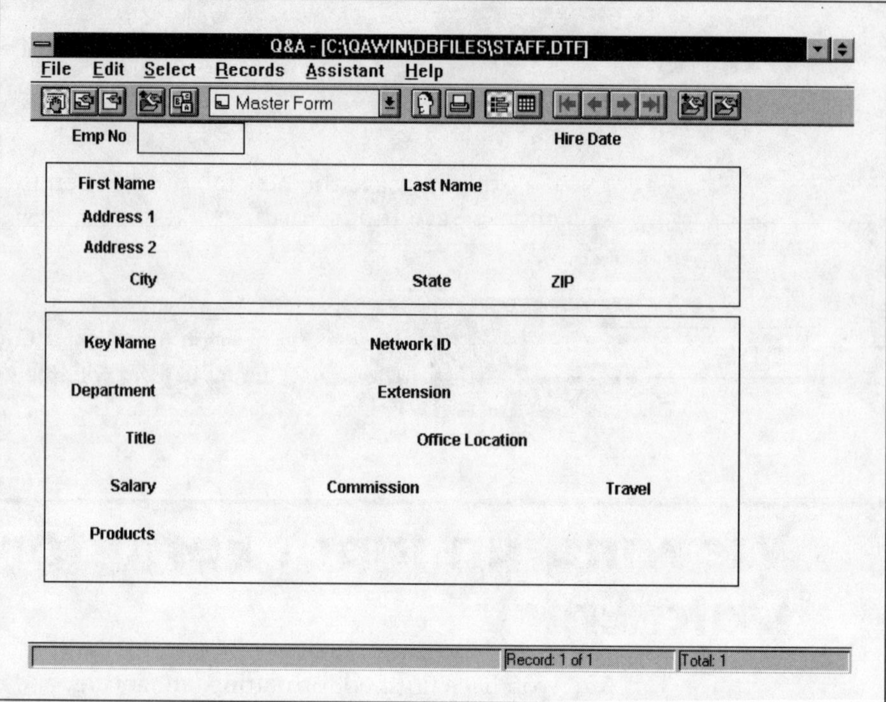

3. To delete the input form, click on <u>Y</u>es. If you change your mind, click on <u>N</u>o.

To Sum Up

In this chapter, you learned about planning, designing, creating, and viewing an input form; changing the look and location of objects on the input form; drawing on the input form; and deleting an input form.

In the next chapter, you'll find out about how to manage and redesign database files.

chapter

5

Managing and Redesigning Database Files

f *ast* **TRACK**

● **To copy a database design**   **120**

open the database to be copied, choose File ➤ Copy Database, check Copy the Design of this Database, and click on OK or press Enter. In the Copy To New dialog box, type the name of the new database, and either click on OK or press Enter.

● **To copy a database design and data**   **123**

open the database to be copied, choose File ➤ Copy Database, check Copy the Design of this Database and Copy Selected Records, and click on OK or press Enter. In the Copy To New dialog box, type the name of the new database, and either click on OK or press Enter. In the Copy Records dialog box, specify which fields are to be copied by using one of the four buttons in the center of the dialog box. Click on Copy.

● **To rename a database using Windows**   **128**

open File Manager and from the Tree pane, select the subdirectory in which the database is located. Select the .DTF file from the Directory pane. Choose File ➤ Rename, type the new name in the To text box, and either click on OK or press Enter. Repeat the same process to rename the .IDX file.

● **To recover a database**   **133**

choose File ➤ Recover with an empty work area. Type the file name in the File Name text box, either click on OK or press Enter, and click on Yes.

- ### To add a field to a database   136

  open the database to which you want to add a field, choose Select ➤ Database Structure, and choose Database ➤ Add &
  Delete Fields (or press Ctrl+N). In the Field Name text box,
  type the name of the new field, click on the field type radio
  button, click on Add, and click on Done.

- ### To delete a field from a database   137

  open the database from which you want to remove a field,
  choose Select ➤ Database Structure, and choose Database ➤
  Add & Delete Fields (or press Ctrl+N). In the Database
  Fields list box, select the field to be deleted, click on Delete,
  click on Done, and click on Yes.

- ### To change a field name   138

  open the database in which you want to change a field name,
  choose Select ➤ Database Structure, and choose Database ➤
  Add & Delete Fields (or press Ctrl+N). In the Database
  Fields list box, select the field to be changed, and edit the
  name, click on Change, and click on Done.

- ### To change a field type   139

  open the database in which you want to change a field type,
  choose Select ➤ Database Structure, and choose Database ➤
  Add & Delete Fields (or press Ctrl+N). In the Database
  Fields list box, select the field whose field type is to be
  changed, click on the appropriate field type radio button, click
  on Change, and click on Done.

O**NCE** you have planned, designed, and created an input form (or redesigned the Master Form) for a new database, it's a good idea to find out more about managing database files. Since no database is perfect—especially a new one—you should be prepared to redesign it. In this chapter, you'll learn about copying, renaming, backing up, and recovering a database as well as adding and deleting fields, and changing field names and field types.

Managing Database Files

When you manage a database, you not only add new records and edit existing records, but you may also perform many other tasks. For example, you may back up the database regularly, design and distribute new databases, ensure that obsolete records are eliminated, or handle the job of mass updates and deletions.

Making a Copy of a Database

At times, it may be easier to make a copy of a database and add new data rather than building a database from scratch. For example, you may have created an address book for vendors and now you want to use the same design for your customers database. All you need to do is copy the database design, edit the database fields, and enter completely new data. As another example, if your company opens a new branch and, as a result, is splitting its customer list, you can copy the database and its contents, and then delete the unneeded customer records from each database.

Q&A allows you to copy the design of a database without copying the data, or copy the design and some or all of the data. (If you copy the design and all the data, you end up, of course, with a duplicate of the database.) You can also copy some or all of the data into another database, but you must create the database file first. Q&A also allows you to copy Intelligent Assistant (IA) queries into the new database file. To learn more about the IA, see Chapter 10.

TIP

It's a good idea to have a plan for the location of your database files. You can store all your database files in one subdirectory. This is good if you don't have many files to track, or you can create subdirectories in which to store files by category. For example, the STAFF.DTF database (and other test files) are all located in the \dbfiles subdirectory, which was created by choosing File ➤ Create Directory in the Windows File Manager.

Copying a Database Design Without the Data

With Q&A, you can copy the design of a database while not copying its data. When you copy a database design, everything in it—reports, programming, layouts, and scripts—besides the data, is copied.

NOTE

Through Q&A's interoperability features, it is possible to have DOS IA and DOS reports saved with your Q&A for Windows database if the database has been created or used in Q&A for DOS. You have the option to copy these parts of the databse if they exist.

To make a copy of a database design only and not copy records from the source database to the new database, use the following steps:

1. Open the database from which you wish to copy. To do this, choose File ➤ Open, and select a file.

2. Choose File ➤ Copy Database. Q&A displays the Copy Database dialog box (Figure 5.1).

Q&A's Copy Database dialog box lets you copy a database design and gives you the option to copy selected records.

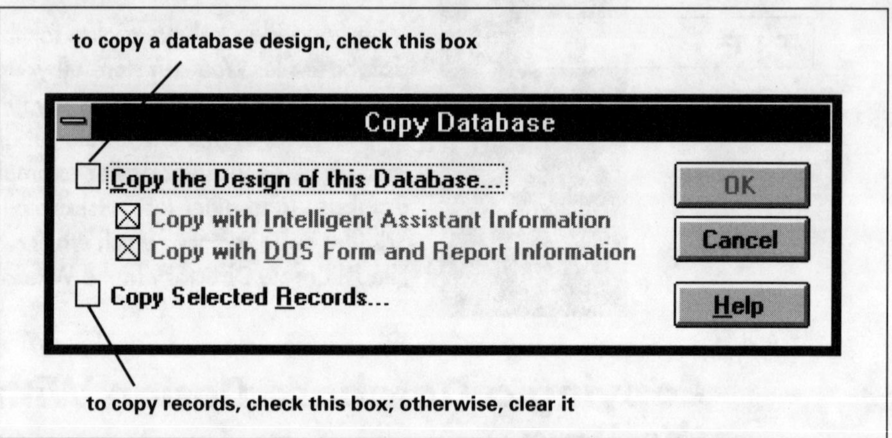

3. Check the Copy the Design of this Database check box.

4. If you have created DOS Intelligent Assistant information or DOS Form and Report information, check the Copy with Intelligent Assistant Information and/or Copy with DOS Form and Report Information check boxes, respectively.

5. Click on OK or press Enter. Q&A displays the Copy To New File dialog box (Figure 5.2).

6. Type the name of the new database (containing a .DTF extension) in the File Name text box and either click on OK or press Enter. Q&A copies the database design to the new database and returns to the source database.

At this point, if you wish to enter data in the new database, choose File ➤ Open to open the new database. Remember that when you open a database, Q&A automatically closes the current database.

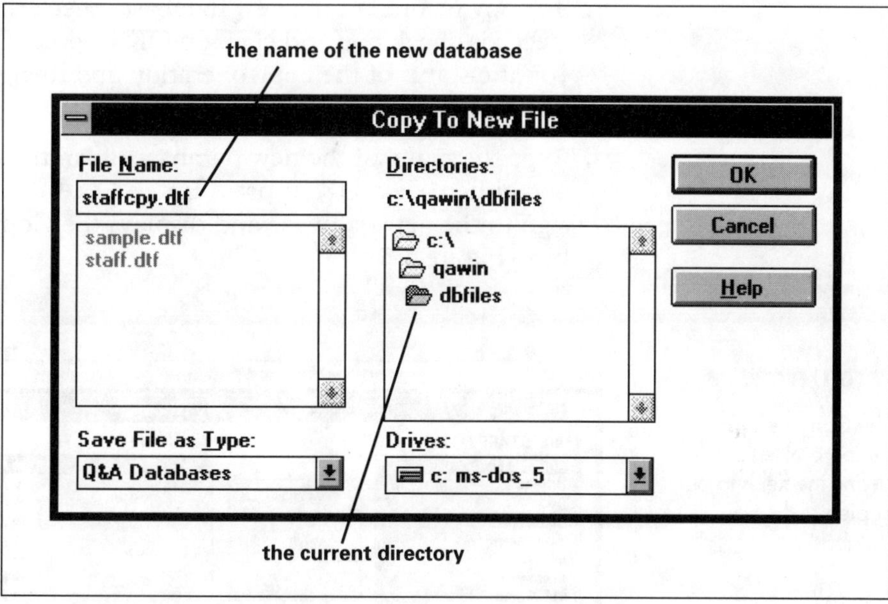

Copying a Database Design With Data

To make a copy of a database design *and* its data, use the following steps:

1. Open the database from which you wish to copy. To do this, choose File ➤ Open, and select a file.

2. Choose File ➤ Copy Database. Q&A displays the Copy Database dialog box (Figure 5.1).

3. To copy the design of the database, check the Copy the Design of this Database check box.

4. If you have created DOS Intelligent Assistant information, DOS Form and Report information, or both, check the Copy with the Intelligent Assistant, Copy with DOS Form and Report Information check boxes, or both. The Intelligent Assistant information and DOS Form and Report information is only created if the database was created or opened by Q&A for DOS.

5. To copy records to the new database, check the Copy Selected <u>R</u>ecords check box and click on OK or press Enter. Q&A shows you the status of the copy operation and then displays the Copy To New File dialog box (Figure 5.2).

6. Type the name of the new database file in the File Name text box and either select OK or press Enter. Q&A copies the database design to the new database and displays the Copy Records dialog box (Figure 5.3).

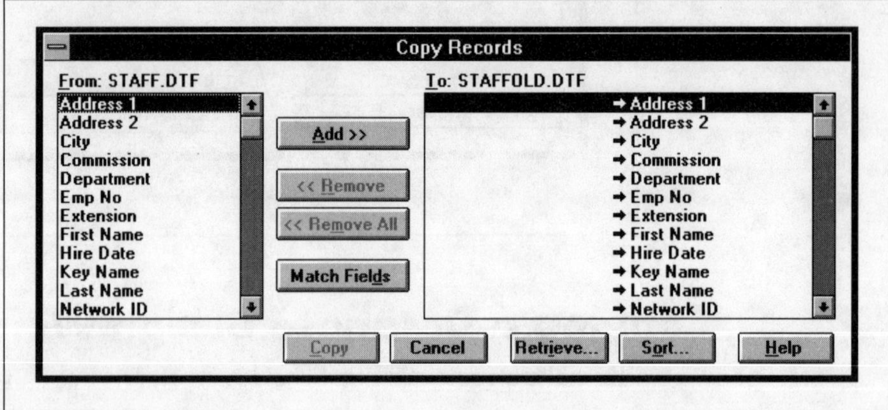

FIGURE 5.3

The Copy Records dialog box lets you define the fields to be copied to the new database.

Copying Records and Fields into a Copy of a Database

Once you have set the design to be copied into a new database (and if you have indicated that you plan to copy all or some of your field information or records to the new database), Q&A displays the Copy Records dialog box.

To copy all the fields into the new database:	Click on Match Fiel<u>d</u>s (Figure 5.4)
To tag a field to be copied into the new database:	Click on the field in the <u>F</u>rom: *database*.DTF list box and click on <u>A</u>dd (Figure 5.5)

The Copy Records dialog box with all the fields copied into the new database. Just click on the Match Fields button.

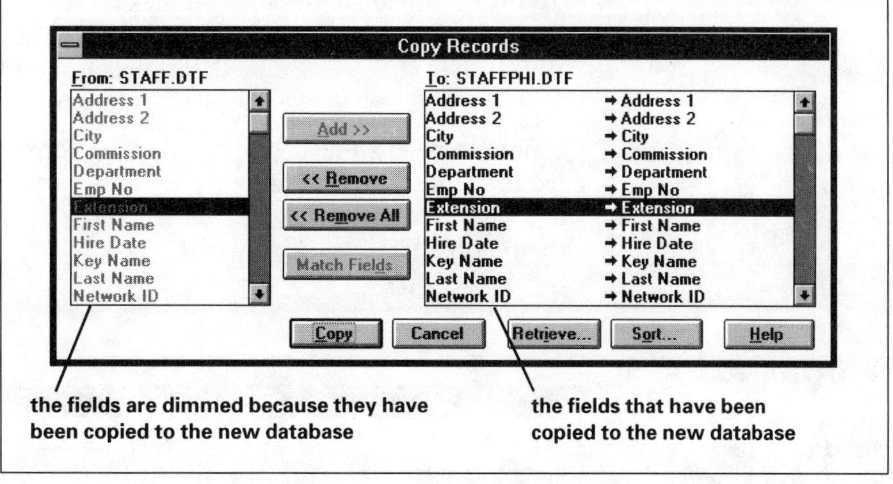

The Copy Records dialog box with one field being copied into the new database. Just select a field and click on Add.

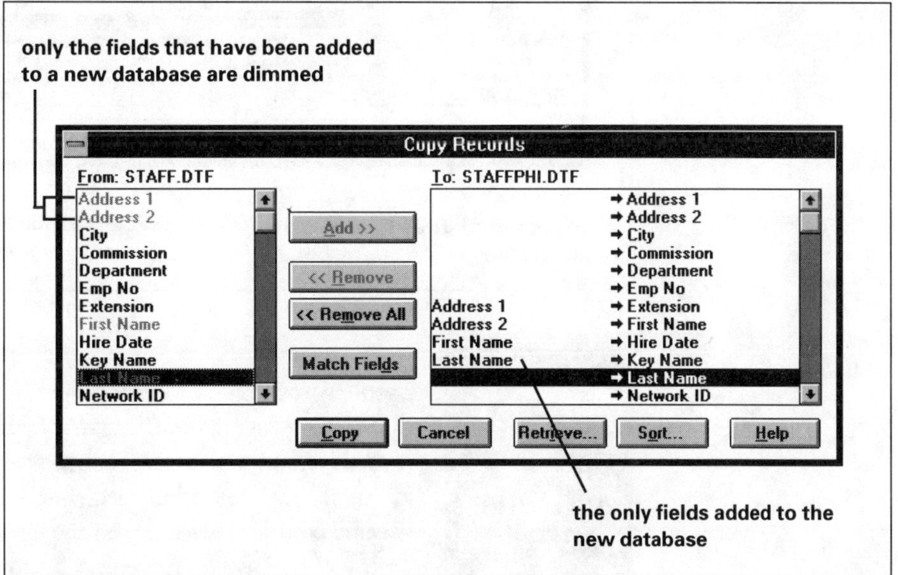

| To untag a field set to be copied: | Click on the field on the left side of the To: *database*.DTF list box and click on Remove (Figure 5.6) |
| If fields are set to be copied into the new database and you do not want them copied: | Click on Remove All button |

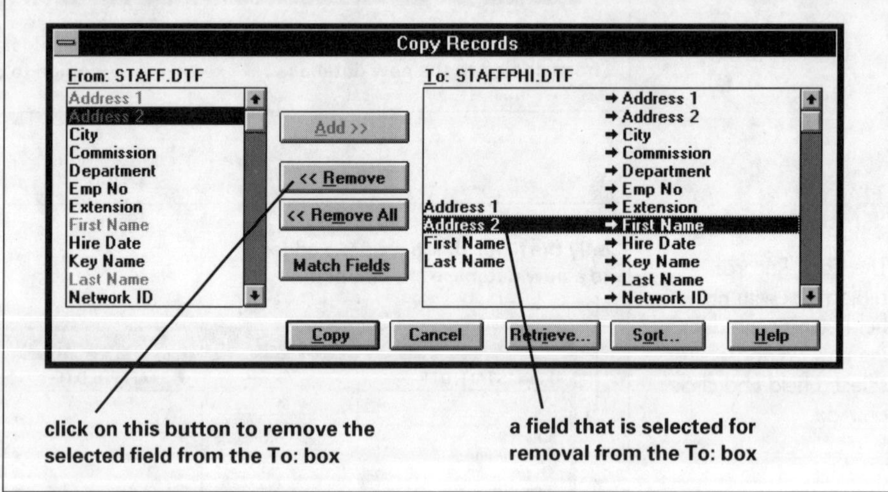

FIGURE 5.6

The Copy Records dialog box as one field is ready to be removed from the To: box. Just select a field and click on Remove.

NOTE

Because you will be learning the details about retrieving and sorting records in Chapter 8, you'll copy *all* the records from the source database to the new database in this section instead of retrieving records that meet specific criteria. However, on the Copy Record dialog box, you can use Retrieve and Sort buttons to specify specific records to copy and the order in which to copy them. If these buttons are not used in the copy process, all records are copied in the current saved order of the database.

Follow these steps to copy some or all fields and all records to a new database:

1. In the Copy Records dialog box, select the fields that you want to add to the new database. Either click on Match Fie<u>l</u>ds to select all fields or click on <u>A</u>dd to select some fields.

2. To copy all records, click on the <u>C</u>opy button. Q&A closes the Copy Records dialog box and shows you the status of the copy operation.

Renaming a Database

From time to time, you'll want to rename a database. Your company might adopt new naming standards or you might feel that the current name is inaccurate or difficult to remember. Unlike copying, when you rename a database, there will be only one database. When you copy a database, you have the original as well as the copy.

N O T E

Each database consists of two files: .DTF and .IDX. Normally, you only refer to the .DTF file because Q&A understands that it uses both the files together. However, when you are referring to a Q&A database while outside of the Q&A environment (say you're in Windows' File Manager or DOS), you need to refer to both files. The .DTF (database) file contains your data; the .IDX (index file) file contains things like programming and reports.

You can rename a database in Windows and in DOS. You'll learn both renaming methods in the following two sections.

Renaming a Database Using Windows

To rename a database, close it and either exit from or minimize Q&A. Then follow these steps:

File Manager

1. Press the Ctrl+Esc key combination to display the Windows Task List.

2. Select Program Manager to display the Program Manager window.

3. Double-click on the File Manager icon, which normally is in the Main Group. Windows displays the File Manager window (Figure 5.7).

The Windows File Manager window. You can use File Manager to manage files and disks (e.g., to copy or move files, to format and label disks, to rename files, and so on).

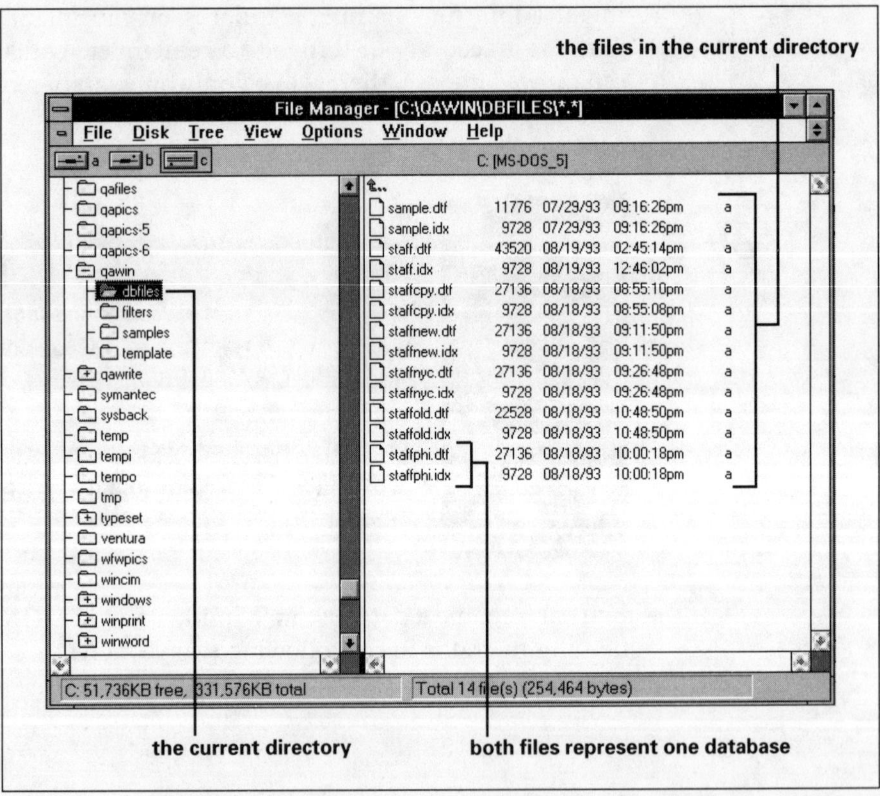

4. On the left side of the window, click on the icon representing
   the subdirectory in which the Q&A database file is stored. On the
   right side of the window, File Manager displays the files in the
   subdirectory.

TIP

If the icon representing the subdirectory is not displayed, double-click on the directory or subdirectory
that is the parent. (A *parent* is the next higher directory
in the path. For example, if your database files are
stored in C:\QAWIN\DBFILES, \QAWIN is the parent of
\DBFILES.) This shows you every branch off the parent
directory. Then you can click on the desired icon and
see its files in the directory pane.

5. Click on the .DTF file to be renamed, then choose File ➤ Rename. File Manager displays the Rename dialog box (Figure 5.8).

6. In the To: text box in the Rename dialog box, type the new file
   name. Make sure the new file name has the .DTF extension.
   Because you clicked on the file name (see step 5), the From text
   box already should be filled in with the current file name. Click
   on OK or press Enter. File Manager renames the file.

FIGURE 5.8

Use the Rename
dialog box to rename
the file in the From
text box to the new
name in the To: text
box.

WARNING Make sure that the file to be renamed is not in use. If it is, you will see the following message:

7. Click on the .IDX file to be renamed.

8. Repeat steps 5 and 6, ensuring that the file name for the .IDX file matches that of the .DTF file. However, this file needs an .IDX extension. When you are done, close File Manager by choosing File ➤ Exit.

9. Return to Q&A by opening the Task List and double-clicking on Q&A or by repeatedly pressing Alt+Tab until the Q&A information box appears.

For more information about using File Manager, see Appendix B.

Renaming a Database Using DOS

To rename a database in DOS, you must either exit Windows or double-click on the MS-DOS prompt. Then go to the proper directory by typing *CD dirname* (where *dirname* represents the name of the directory) at the C:\ prompt. Then at the C:\ prompt, type:

rename *oldfile*.dtf *newfile*.dtf

and press Enter. Then type:

rename *oldfile*.idx *newfile*.idx

where *oldfile* represents the current file name, and *newfile* represents the new file name.

If you got to DOS through the DOS icon, type Exit to return to Windows.

Creating a Backup Copy of a Database

You should back up all your files often to ensure that you don't have to spend any time redoing your work if you lose power or if your hardware konks out. You can copy files in Windows using almost the same steps as in renaming files (but you'll choose <u>C</u>opy instead of Re<u>n</u>ame). In DOS, you issue the Copy command using the same format that you used for renaming a database. When backing up your database files, remember to copy both the .DTF and .IDX files.

Although you can back up to a different part of your hard drive, it's better to copy the files onto floppy disks and store them in a safe place away from your office. In this way, if you experience a disaster in your office, the floppy disks will not be affected.

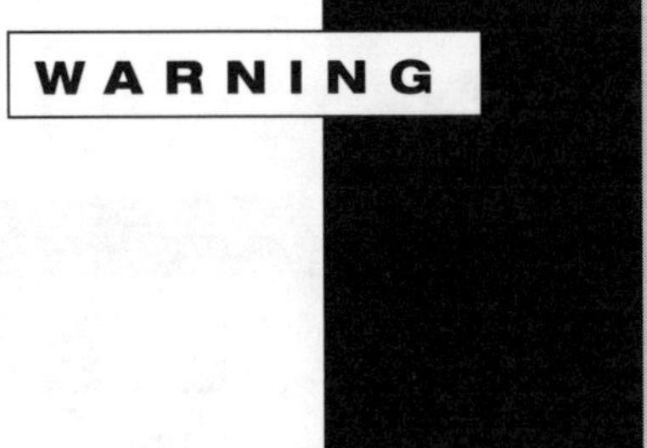

Now you'll learn how to back up files using both Windows and DOS.

Backing Up a Database Using Windows

To copy a database, close it and either exit from or minimize Q&A. Then use the following procedures:

1. Using Ctrl-Esc or Alt+Tab, select Program Manager. Windows displays the Program Manager window.

2. Double-click on the File Manager icon. Windows displays the File Manager window (Figure 5.7).

3. On the left side of the window, click on the icon representing the subdirectory in which the Q&A database file is stored. On the right side of the window, Q&A displays the files in the subdirectory.

4. Click on the .DTF file to be copied., and choose File ➤ Copy. File Manager displays the Copy dialog box (Figure 5.9).

TIP — Press the F8 shortcut key to display the Copy dialog box in which you can copy a file.

5. In the To text box, type the new file name including the .DTF extension. Because you clicked on the file name (see step 4), the From text box already should be filled in with the current file name. Click on OK or press Enter. File Manager copies the file and rearranges the file list.

6. Click on the .IDX file to be copied.

FIGURE 5.9

The Windows File Manager Copy dialog box with which you can copy a file to a disk or to another file.

7. Repeat steps 3,4, and 5, ensuring that the file name for the .IDX file matches that of the .DTF file with an .IDX extension. Then close File Manager by choosing File ➤ Exit.

8. Return to Q&A by opening the Task List and double-clicking on the miniaturized Q&A icon or by repeatedly pressing Alt+Tab until the Q&A information box appears.

For more information about using File Manager, see Appendix B.

Backing Up a Database Using DOS

To copy a database in DOS, you must either exit Windows or double-click on the MS-DOS prompt. Go to the proper directory by typing *CD dirname* and the name of the directory in which the database files are located. Then at the C:\ prompt, type:

copy *oldfile*.dtf *newfile*.dtf

and press Enter. Then type:

copy *oldfile*.idx *newfile*.idx

where *oldfile* represents the current file name, and *newfile* represents the new file name.

Recovering a Backed Up Database File

If your database files have been damaged for some reason—say you lost your electricity while copying a database—you can try to recover the information by using the Q&A Recover command. Although you should have a very recent backup copy of the database, before you start the recovery, back up both the .DTF and .IDX files again—to uniquely named backup files.

Q&A does not allow you to start the recovery operation with an open database. So, to close the database if one is open, follow these steps:

1. Choose File ➤ Recover. Q&A displays the Recover File dialog box (see Figure 5.10).

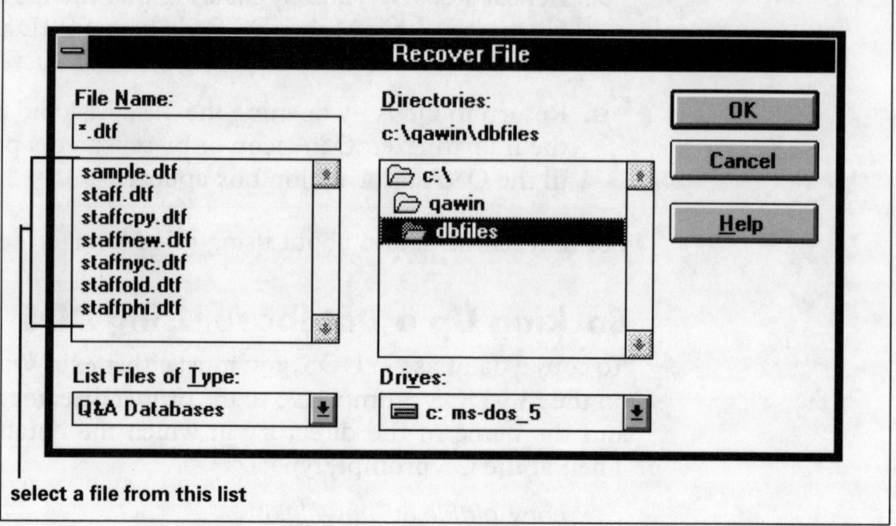

2. In the File **N**ame text box, either type or select the name of the
   file to be recovered from the list of files.

3. Either click on OK or press Enter. Q&A issues a message
   that prompts you to back up the database before continuing (Figure 5.11).

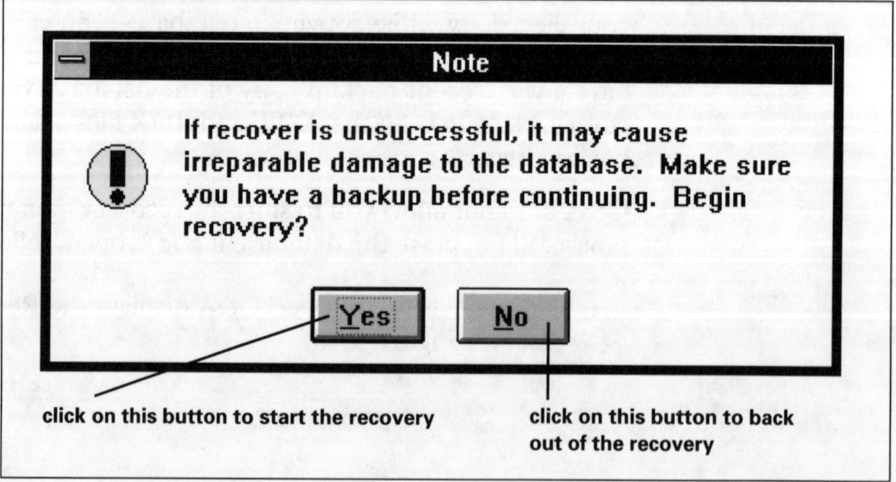

4. Click on <u>Y</u>es to recover the database. (Click on <u>N</u>o to stop the recovery process so that you can back up your database first.) Q&A shows you the status of the recovery and displays an information box (Figure 5.12) when the recovery is complete.

After recovering a database, Q&A signals that the recovery was successful.

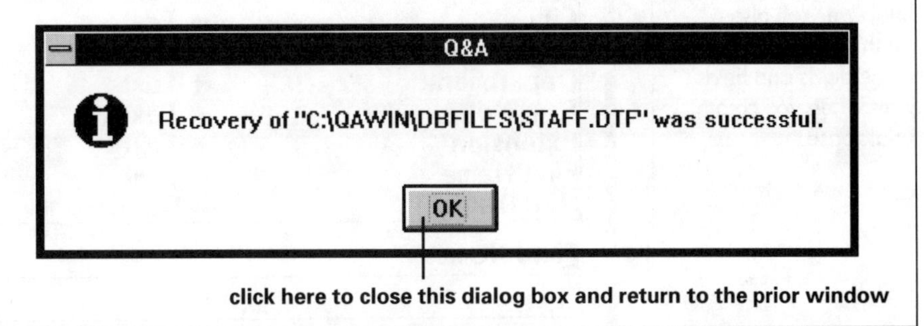

Redesigning the Contents of a Database

In Chapter 3, you learned how to define field names and field types, and in Chapter 4, you found out how to adjust the length of fields and how to move both field names and fields around an input form. At this point, you will learn how to add or delete a specific field and change a field's name or type.

You can add, delete, or change fields at any time. However, redesigning a database, especially changing attributes, is somewhat more dangerous if it contains data. Just to play it safe, back up both the .DTF and .IDX files before you make any changes. All three procedures use the Add & Delete Fields dialog box (see Figure 5.13). In Chapter 3, you first saw the Add & Delete Fields dialog box when you created your first database. When you were ready to define fields and field types, Q&A automatically opened it. Now you are explicitly opening the dialog box to change the same fields and field types that you defined two chapters ago. In the next chapter, you'll find out another way to change fields and field types in the Database Structure area.

The Add & Delete Fields dialog box in which you can add, delete, or change fields in the current database. You also use this dialog box to define fields and field types when you create a database.

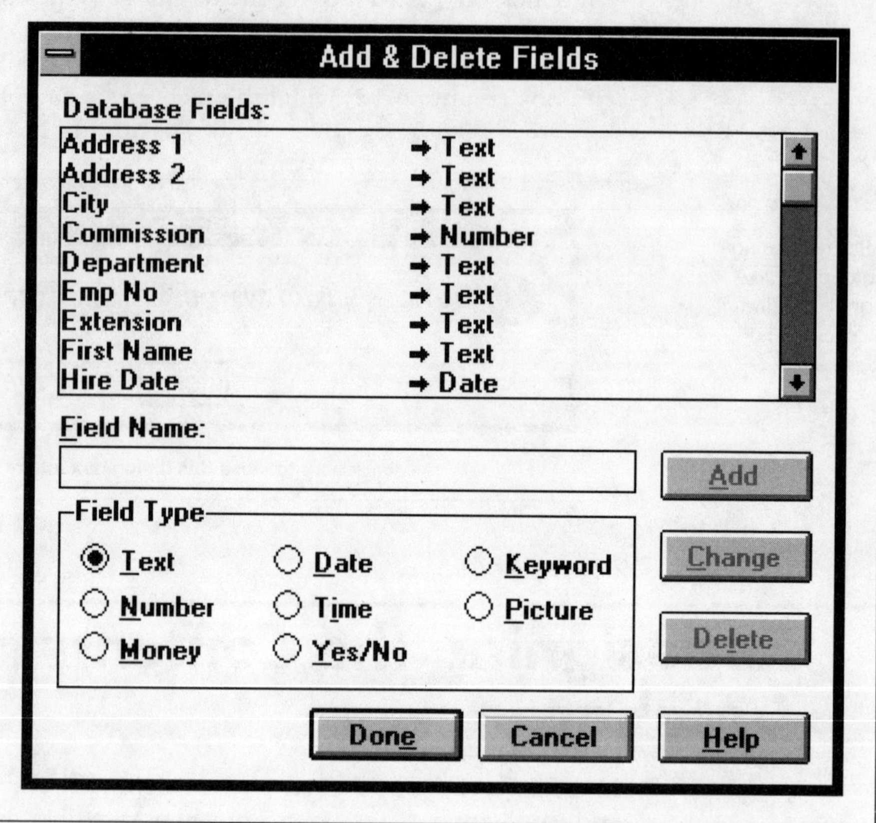

Adding a New Field

Adding a new field to a database is very easy to do. Once you start a database, you'll never truly be finished with creating it. For example, you may want to refine a database (such as STAFF.DTF) by adding fields in which you enter the last date and time that you accessed a particular record. With Q&A, you can embed pictures in a database, so you could include photos in your Employees database. To add a new field to a database, simply follow these steps:

1. Open the database in which you wish to add a field.

2. Choose Select ➤ Database Structure. Q&A displays the open database in the Database Structure area.

3. Choose Database ➤ Add & Delete Fields or press the Ctrl+N shortcut keys. Q&A displays the Add & Delete Fields dialog box (Figure 5.13).

4. In the Field Name text box, type the name of the new field.

5. Click on the radio button that indicates the field type for the new field.

6. Click on the Add button. Q&A adds the new field to the end of the list in the Database Fields list box.

7. To add more fields, repeat steps 4, 5, and 6.

8. If you have completed your work in the dialog box, click on the Done button. Q&A adds the new field to the database and closes the dialog box.

NOTE

After adding the field, Q&A adds it to the Master Form; however, other input forms won't have the field. For instructions on adding the new field to other input forms, see Chapter 4.

Deleting a Field

Deleting a field from a database allows you to remove the possibility of entering data you no longer need. However, deleting is completely destructive—meaning that once you remove the field, you can't reverse the action. If you decide to go ahead, the deletion procedure is very easy to do.

There are many reasons for deleting a field. For example, you might decide to split a personnel database into two files: one that contains confidential information only available to senior management and another that provides information to anyone who asks. In other databases, information that was once considered important may not be anymore. For example, if a company has rented automobiles from several car rental agencies, a field that lists the agency that an employee or department uses is important. However, if the company negotiates a contract with one agency for company-wide rentals, the field is unnecessary.

To delete a field from a database, follow these steps:

1. Open the database from which you wish to remove a field.

2. Choose Select ➤ Database Structure.

3. Choose Database ➤ Add & Delete Fields or press the Ctrl+N shortcut keys. Q&A displays the Add & Delete Fields dialog box.

4. In the Database Fields list box, click on the field to be deleted.

5. Click on Delete and then click on Done. Q&A displays a message that reminds you that data may be lost if you continue with the deletion.

6. To remove the field, click on Yes. Q&A deletes the field and closes the dialog box. (If you change your mind about deleting the field, click on No and then click on Cancel to "back out" of the dialog box and not delete the field.)

WARNING

Once you have deleted a field, the field and the data in it are gone forever (unless you have a backup from which you can restore the file to its previous condition).

Changing the Attributes of a Field

Q&A provides two ways to edit a field's *attributes*—its name and type. You'll learn one method in this chapter and the second in the next chapter. Because of the dynamic nature of companies, databases should be easy to change. For example, you readily want to change a field such as Travel, which is currently a Yes/No field in the STAFF database, to a text field in which an employee's extent of travel and required permissions could be spelled out. Or your company could decide to pay sales employees bonuses rather than commissions, which would entail changing both the field name and the field type.

Changing a Field Name

Until recently, database programs required one-word field names (e.g., ADDRESS_1 or FIRST_NAME). With Q&A you can make a field name more understandable by adding spaces or otherwise editing it for readability. To edit a field name, use the following steps:

1. Open the database in which you wish to change a field name.

2. Choose Select ➤ Database Structure.

3. Choose Database ➤ the Add & Delete Fields. Q&A displays the Add & Delete Fields dialog box.

4. In the Database Fields list box, click on the field to be changed. Q&A displays the name in the Field Name text box.

5. Edit the name in the Field Name text box.

6. Click on Change. Q&A changes the field name.

7. Click on Done to close the dialog box.

Changing a Field Type

It's quite common for a novice database developer to assign number field types to fields such as Employee No, ZIP, Extension, Social Security Number, and Telephone Number. As you learn Q&A, you'll find that although these fields may look like numbers, they will never be calculated and some of them contain nonnumeric characters. Fortunately, Q&A makes it very easy to change any early field type mistakes. Just follow these steps to change a field type.

1. Open the database in which you wish to change an information type.

2. Choose Select ➤ Database Structure.

3. Choose Database ➤ Add & Delete Fields. Q&A displays the Add & Delete Fields dialog box.

4. In the Database Fields list box, click on the field whose field type you wish to change. Q&A displays the name in the Field Name text box.

5. Click on the appropriate radio button in the Field Type group.

6. Click on Change. Q&A changes the field type.

7. Click on Done. Q&A closes the dialog box.

To Sum Up

In this chapter, you have learned about managing database files and editing field names and field types. You have discovered how to make a copy of a database and move records to the new database, how to rename a database, and how to copy a database. Then you found out about adding new fields, deleting unnecessary fields, and changing field names and field types.

In the next chapter, you'll learn about customizing your database structure. You'll review all the options that allow you to control the contents of fields: how to restrict values, set initial values, create a masking template, change global formats, and how to define custom help messages.

chapter

6

Customizing Your Database Structure

f a s t **TRACK**

● **To select columns for display in the Database Structure area**   **148**

select <u>D</u>atabase ➤ Show <u>C</u>olumns, check the columns to be displayed, and clear the columns to be hidden.

● **To change the order of the fields in the Database Structure area**   **149**

choose <u>D</u>atabase ➤ Sort <u>T</u>able. In the Sort Table dialog box, select one of these sorts: Creation Order, Field Name, Field Type, Field Index, and Field ID.

● **To change a field name or field type**   **153**

choose <u>D</u>atabase ➤ <u>E</u>dit Field Attributes ➤ <u>F</u>ield Name & Type or double-click in the Field Name or Field Type column in the Database Structure area. In the Edit Field Name & Type dialog box, highlight the field to be renamed, click inside the Field N<u>a</u>me box, type the preferred field name, and click on a radio button in the Field Type group.

● **To change the format of a field**   **161**

choose <u>D</u>atabase ➤ <u>E</u>dit Field Attributes ➤ F<u>o</u>rmat or double-click in the Format column in the Database Structure area. In the Edit Format dialog box, highlight the field to be changed, and select the desired options in the Format group.

● **To enter field restrictions**   **162**

choose <u>D</u>atabase ➤ <u>E</u>dit Field Attributes ➤ <u>R</u>estriction or double-click in the Restriction column in the Database Structure area. In the Edit Restriction dialog box, highlight the field to be changed, click inside the <u>R</u>estriction Formula box, and type the restriction.

To create a field mask   170

> choose <u>D</u>atabase ➤ <u>E</u>dit Field Attributes ➤ <u>M</u>asking or double-click in the Masking column in the Database Structure area. In the Edit Masking dialog box, highlight the text field to be masked, and either select the type of masking or type a mask in the <u>C</u>ustom text box.

To set an initial value   172

> choose <u>D</u>atabase ➤ <u>E</u>dit Field Attributes ➤ Initial <u>V</u>alue or double-click in the Initial Value column in the Database Structure area. In the Edit Initial Value dialog box, highlight the desired field, and either select the type of initial value or type an initial value in the <u>C</u>ustom text box.

To specify global options for a database   176

> choose <u>D</u>atabase ➤ <u>G</u>lobal Format Options, and select from the options in the Global Format Options dialog box.

To create a custom help message   178

> choose <u>D</u>atabase ➤ <u>E</u>dit Field Attributes ➤ Custom <u>H</u>elp or double-click in the Initial Value column in the Database Structure area. In the Edit Custom Help dialog box, highlight the desired field, click in the Custom Help text box, and type the help message.

WHILE any database program offers the ability to enter data, the more powerful database programs, like Q&A, allow you to customize your database structure to make it easier to use and to streamline efficiency. Q&A gives you this control in the Database Structure area (see Figure 6.1).

The Database Structure View

Working in the Database Structure area puts you in command of how Q&A translates, manipulates, and uses the data you enter.

The first thing you will notice when you switch to the Database Structure area is that all the field settings are grouped in a table with rows, columns, and *cells* (which are created by the intersection of a row and a column), just like a spreadsheet.

The columns in the Database Structure area represent attributes that you can change for any field—field name, type, format, restriction, index, initial values, custom help, programming, and masking. You'll learn about most of these attributes in this chapter. Double-clicking anywhere within a column opens a related dialog box that allows you to change these settings. For example, if you double-click on a cell in the Index column, the Index dialog box appears. Then you can add or edit Index information for the selected field.

The rows in the Database Structure area represent the fields in your database. For instance, the row with Zip in the Field Name column contains the Zip field's type, format, restriction, and so on. When you double-click within an intersection of a row and column, the dialog box for that column appears and the field for the row is highlighted. For example, if you

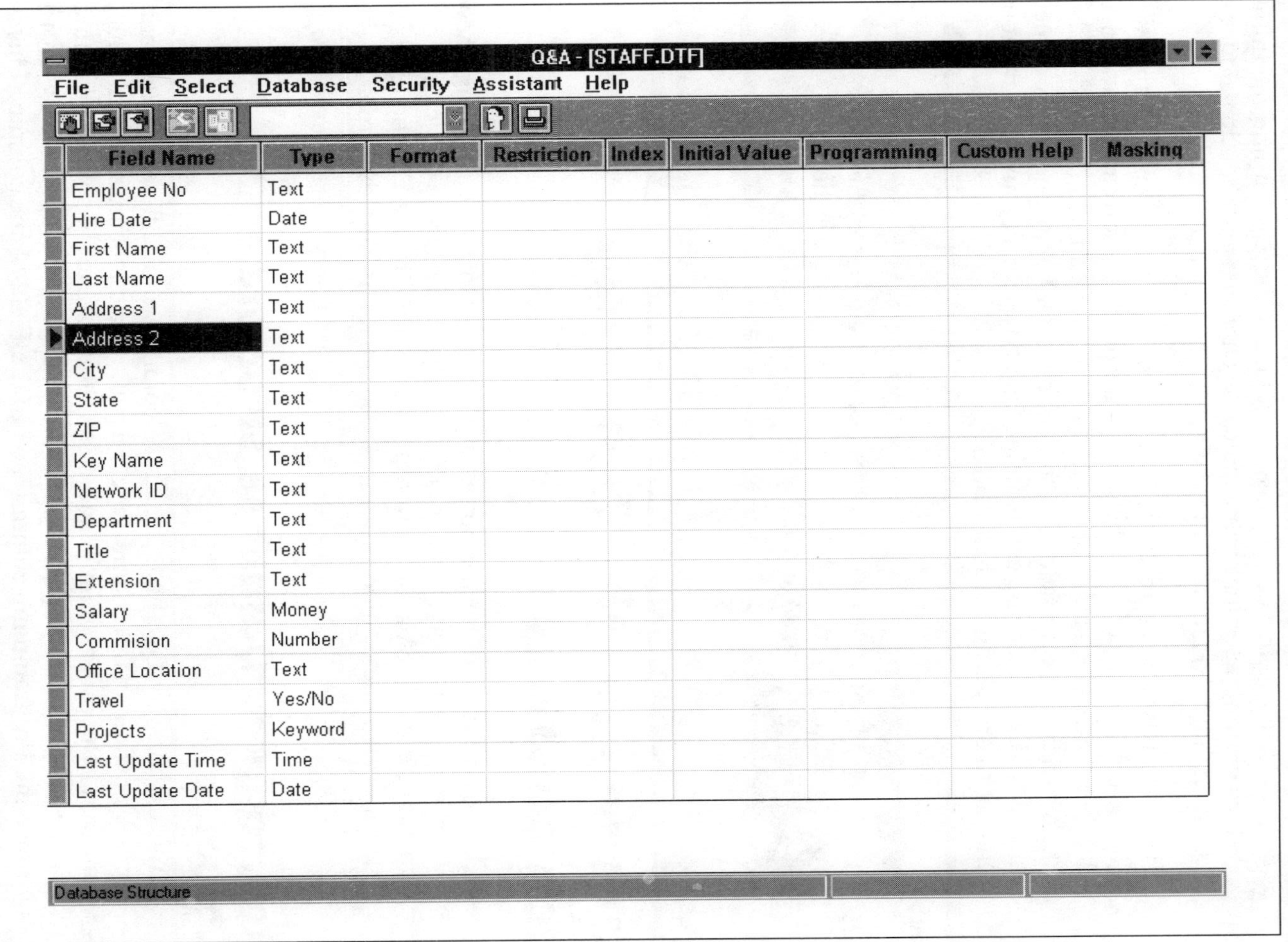

FIGURE 6.1

Part of the Database Structure view of STAFF.DTF. The name of each field appears in the first column, and the field type for each field appears in the second column.

double-click within a cell at the intersection of the Zip row and the Initial Value column, the Initial Value dialog box appears and the Zip field is already highlighted and ready to define or edit.

The Database Structure dialog boxes allow you to change the settings for all the fields. After altering the settings for one field, you can keep the dialog box open to change the same type of settings for other fields. This makes changing your fields an efficient process. For instance, if you open the Type dialog box, you can redefine field types for all your fields without having to open another dialog box.

The Database Structure area displays all the fields in the database, whether or not they are in the active input form.

Commanding the Database Structure Area

Before you start using the power of Database Structure to change how your database works, consider customizing the Database Structure area to your needs. Q&A allows you to rearrange the Database Structure columns, widen them, hide unwanted columns, and sort the order of the fields in the columns.

Rearranging Database Structure Columns

You can display Database Structure columns in a different order than Q&A's default of field name, type, format, restriction, index, initial value, custom help, programming, and mask. For instance, if you are planning to set up programming statements for your database, you may want to move the Programming column next to the Field Name column. This is useful because when programming you can reference fields by their names. As another example, if you change the Custom Help column often, you may want to move it as far left as possible. Then, when you enter the Database Structure area from Add/Edit or Input Design area, the column is immediately in view without having to use the horizontal scroll bar. To move a column to another location, use the following steps:

1. Open the database that you want to modify, and choose Select ➤ Database Structure. Q&A displays database field names and other attributes.

2. Move the mouse pointer to the column heading and press and hold down the left mouse button. (Because the mouse pointer is on a column heading, the cursor changes from an arrow to a miniature column with arrows on either side of it.)

3. Click on the column to select it.

4. Drag the column to its new location and release the mouse button. The column fits between the column you dropped it on and the preceding one.

N O T E   Choosing Edit ➤ Undo does not return a column to its original position after it is moved.

Changing the Width of a Column

Changing field widths can make restructuring your database much easier. It can be the difference between easily viewing programming statements at a glance and having to open a dialog box every time you want to check them. To change column width, follow these procedures:

1. Move the mouse pointer to the right edge of the desired column heading until the pointer changes to a double-sided arrow.

2. Click on the right edge of the column heading. Q&A selects and highlights the right border of that column.

3. Drag the right border to the desired width.

4. Release the mouse button. The right border of the column is now set in place.

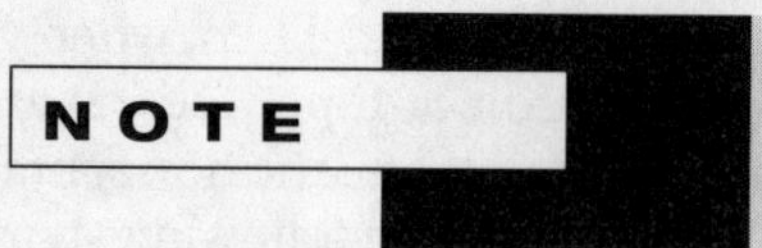

You cannot use Edit ➤ Undo to revert to a column's original width.

Revealing and Hiding Columns

Once you have widened columns to show all the characters in every field name, you may find yourself with a very wide Database Structure window that you must scroll through to work in all the columns. You can use the Show Columns dialog box (Figure 6.2) to display only the columns that you need to see. This makes it easier to view the complete Database Structure without a great deal of scrolling. Simply choose Database ➤ Show Columns. Then keep the check marks in the check boxes of fields to be displayed, and clear the check boxes of fields that you wish to hide. When you have made all your choices, either click on OK or press Enter.

FIGURE 6.2

The Show Columns dialog box allows you to either display or hide all the Database Structure columns except for Field Name.

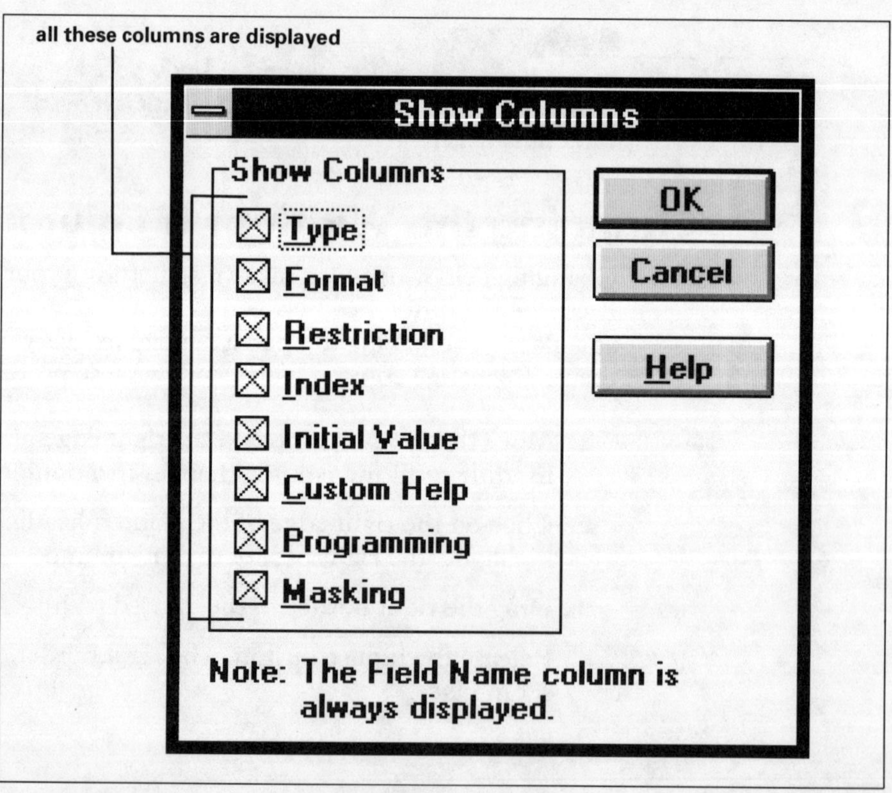

The Field Name column is not one of the eight choices in the Show Columns dialog box because it is always needed as a reference column for Database Structure.

Even if a column is hidden, you can change all the attributes of your fields. For example, if you hide the Format column, you can still choose Database ➤ Edit Field Attribute ➤ Format and change formatting settings for your fields in the Edit Format dialog box.

Changing the Order of Fields

Q&A allows you to set the order of the fields in the Database Structure area so that you can work more easily. When you choose a sort order, Q&A not only reorders your rows in the Database Structure area, but rearranges the field names in the Q&A dialog boxes. For instance, if you sort your fields by field name, when you open a dialog box such as the Edit Format dialog box, your fields will be listed in the same order in which they were sorted.

To change the order of fields, choose Database ➤ Sort Table. The Sort Table dialog box (Figure 6.3) appears, giving you the choice to sort by Creation Order, Field Name, Field Type, Field Index, or Field ID.

Now you will explore why and how to change your field order.

Sorting by Creation Order

Sorting by creation order rearranges the fields in the order in which they were created. The first field you added to this database becomes the first row of the Database Structure table, the second field you created is the second row of the table, and so on.

Sorting by Field Name

Sorting by field names rearranges rows in ascending alphabetical order (A-Z) by Field Name, in the first column of the Database Structure area.

Sorting by field name is an alphabetical (not numeric) sort. This means that as Q&A sorts, it only looks at one character at a time. It begins by

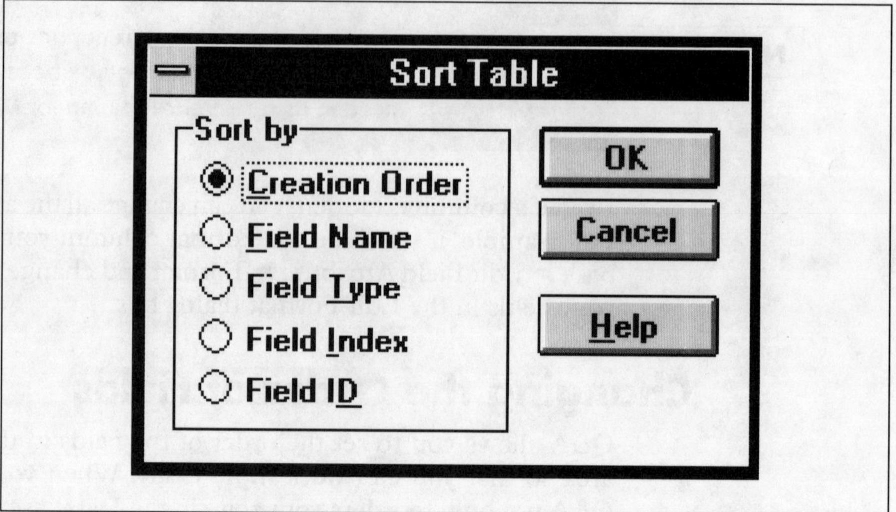

looking at the first character of every field and rearranges the fields. Then, it looks at the second character of every field, and rearranges them again, and so on. This type of sort puts a field named *100* before a field named *2* and both before a field named *ABC*. Numbers as field names are recognized as characters not numbers.

Sorting by Field Type

When sorting by field type, the rows of the Database Structure view are sorted by the contents of the Type column. Field types are sorted in ascending alphabetical order: date, keyword, money, number, picture, text, time, and Yes/No.

Sorting by field type is useful when changing the formats of more than one field with the same field type. For example, to restrict all money fields to allow only numbers greater than zero to be typed into them, sort fields by field type and then double-click within the Restriction column to open the Edit Restriction dialog box. Since you sorted by field type, all the money fields are grouped together in the dialog box, making it easy to select money fields to edit. You'll learn more about editing field restrictions later in this chapter.

Sorting by Index Number

Sorting by indexed fields sorts the rows in your database structure table by the Index column. (*Indexing* helps you to search more quickly by creating a special list of indexed fields rather than all fields in your database. For more information about indexing, see Chapter 11.) The index column is sorted in this order: Not Indexed, All Values, Existing Values, and Unique Values.

Although it is not first alphabetically, the Not Indexed option is listed first. Not Indexed fields display nothing in the index column of the Database Structure table and a blank value comes first in alphabetical order. If none of the fields are indexed when you select Sort by Index, Q&A sorts your fields by field name.

Sorting by Field ID

Sorting by Field ID is a powerful addition for those who use Q&A programming features. Sorting by Field ID, which, unlike Field Name, is a *numeric* sort, rearranges rows by the field ID you give the fields in their programming statements. This sort enables you to easily search through a sorted list of programming statements until you find a specific field ID.

To change the sort order of fields in the current database, follow these steps:

1. Making sure that you are in the Database Structure area, choose <u>D</u>atabase ➤ Sort <u>T</u>able. Q&A displays the Sort Table dialog box.

2. Select a sort type.

3. Click on OK or press Enter. Q&A sorts the fields.

N O T E

Sorts are executed only when they are selected from the Sort Table dialog box. For example, if you sort by field name, Q&A sorts your fields accordingly. If you then change a field name, Q&A changes the name of the field but does not reorder your fields to account for the altered field name. To reorder fields to adjust for the change, open the Sort Table dialog box and click on OK or press Enter.

Controlling Field Attributes

Now that you have found out about the Database Structure area, you can move to the next step. You can start changing database field *attributes*, the qualities that a field possesses such as its name and type.

As you have learned, you can open dialog boxes that change field attributes by double-clicking on any cell in the appropriate column. Another way to display these dialog boxes is to choose Database ➤ Edit Field Attributes (Figure 6.4).

All the field attribute dialog boxes except the Edit Field Name & Type dialog box contain a Clear All button. (Q&A doesn't allow you to remove field names in the Edit Field Name & Type dialog box.) Clicking on Clear All erases all the edit settings for all the fields in the Database Fields box. For example, if you click the Clear All button in the Edit Restrictions dialog box, Q&A deletes all the restriction settings for the database.

The Database menu and Edit Field Attribute cascading menu. You can open any field attribute dialog box by choosing from the cascading menu.

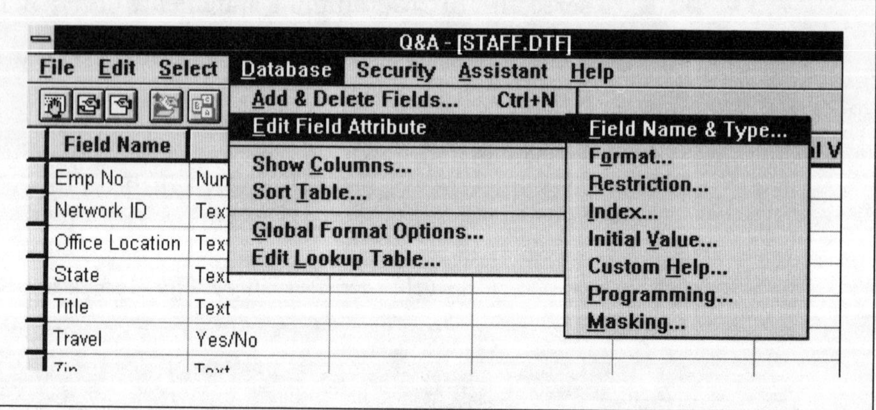

If you choose Clear All by mistake, the results can be disastrous. For example, you can erase all the formatting statements for all your fields. Fortunately, Q&A prompts you with a warning message before you can continue. If you do ignore the warning, you can still click on Cancel and you can recover all but the changes you made since you last opened the dialog box.

Changing Field Names and Type

If you use Q&A extensively, you will probably need to change field names and field types at some time. For example, if you define a telephone number field as a number type, you will probably want to change it to a text field so you will be able to use hyphens and parentheses. Or, you may decide to rename your telephone number field name to Work Phone. In either case, you need to know how to use the Edit Field Name & Type dialog box (Figure 6.5).

To change the field name of one of your fields, do the following:

1. Choose Database ➤ Edit Field Attributes ➤ Field Name & Type. (You can also double-click in any cell in the Field Name or Type columns in the Database Structure area.) Q&A displays the Edit Field Name & Type dialog box.

2. In the Database Fields box, click on the field to be edited. (If the field name is not in the Database Fields list box, scroll to it.) Q&A displays the selected field name in the Field Name box and marks the field type in the Field Type group.

3. Click inside the Field Name box and type a new field name, if needed.

4. Choose a different field type for the selected field, if needed.

5. To change the name of another field, select the field and repeat step 3. This saves the changes that you have just made to the first field selected. Repeat these steps to change other fields.

6. Once you have finished editing, click on OK or press the Enter key. To ignore all the changes you have made, click on the Cancel button or press the Esc key.

The Edit Field Name & Type dialog box, in which you can change field names and field types. However, you cannot delete field names using this dialog box.

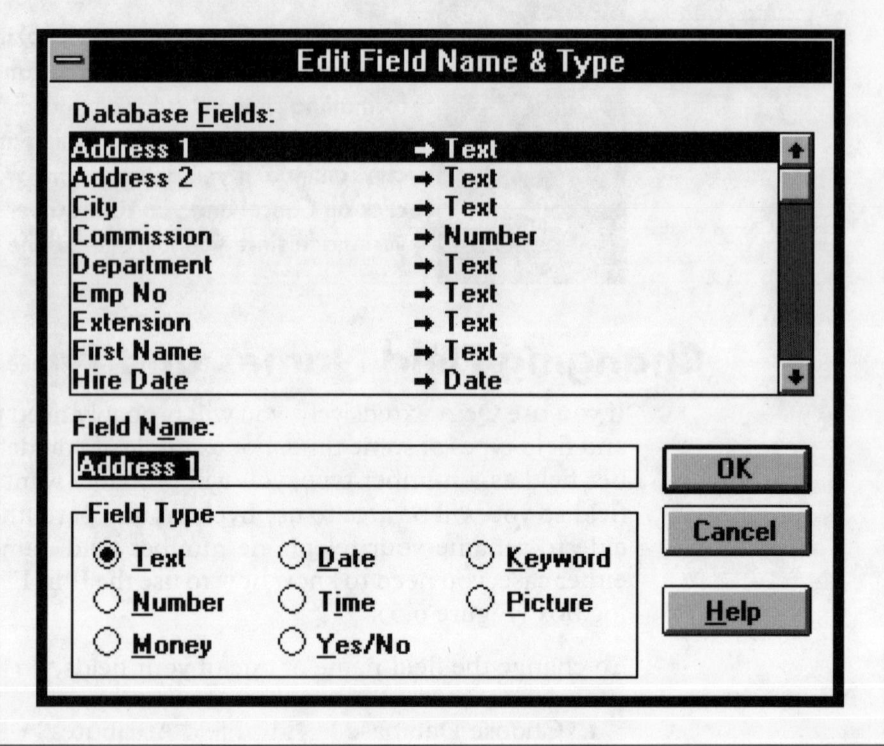

The term field name is used loosely when referring to a field. Each field has both a field name and a field label. The field name is the way that Q&A recognizes and references a field. A field label is how you and others refer to the field (it's the typed name next to the box on the form). When you create a field, Q&A defines the field name and you define the field label by typing it in the Field Name box in the Add & Delete Fields dialog box. For example, in the STAFF database, one field is named *Emp No*. At that point, both the field label and field name are *Emp No*. However, don't assume that the two will always be the same. If you change a field name in Q&A's Edit Field Name & Type dialog box, the field name is changed, but the field label remains the original name. This is apparent when you change a field name in the Edit Field Name & Type dialog box. The change appears in the Database Fields box in all the Edit dialog boxes. However, you will not see a change of the field label in the input form in Add/Edit mode or in the Design Input Forms work area.

To quickly change a field label, go to the Design Input Forms area, double-click on the field title in the Master Form, and make your changes.

Formatting Fields

After you have edited field names, field labels, and field types, as desired, make sure that when you enter data, the field contents look appropriate. Q&A provides you with great flexibility in displaying the contents of fields in the proper format. The options vary from field type to field type. For example, you can make sure that number fields contain commas in the right places, that money fields are preceded by the proper currency symbol, and that certain text, yes/no, and keyword fields can display data in only uppercase characters.

Since the contents of a picture field are completely graphical, Q&A cannot make any format changes to this field.

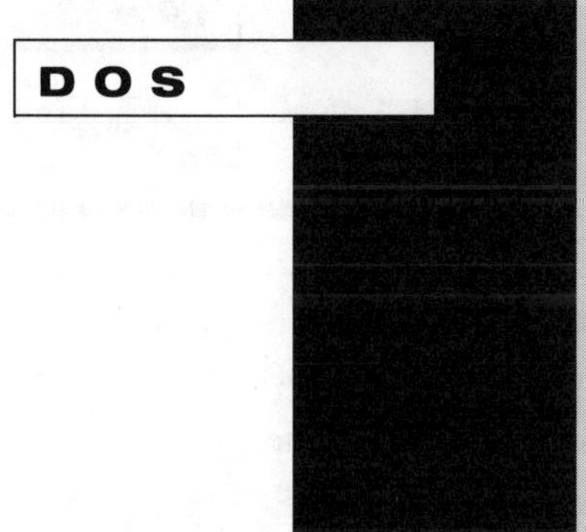

If you are familiar with Q&A for DOS, don't let the word *format* confuse you. In Q&A for DOS, you can change the field type and the format settings in a screen called Format Spec. In Q&A for Windows, you change the field type in the Edit Field Name & Type dialog box and not in the Edit Format dialog box. Q&A for Windows has incorporated the options that allow you to change field name and field type options in the Edit Field Name & Type dialog box because they are often used together.

In the Edit Format dialog box, the Database Fields box always contains the same fields from the current database. However, the format box changes depending on the type of field selected in the Database Fields box. Now you'll learn about the options that are provided in the six different format groups in the Edit Format dialog box.

Formatting Text, Y/N, and Keyword Fields

The Text Format group (Figure 6.6) provides uppercase and lowercase options for formatting text, Yes/No, and keyword field types.

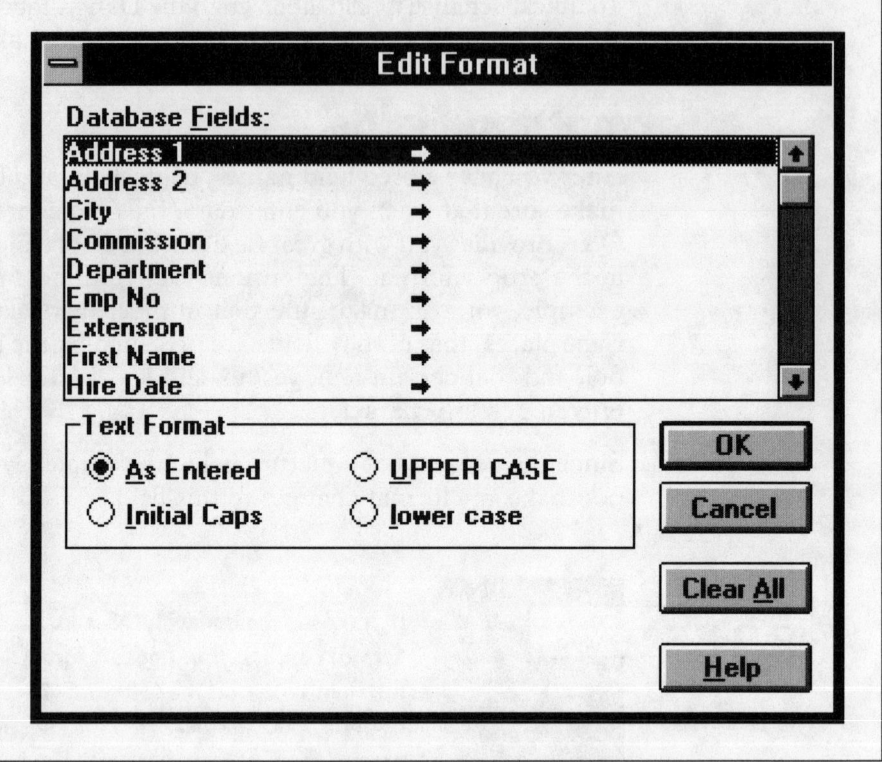

As Entered	Click on this radio button to keep text formatted in the same combination of uppercase and lowercase in which you typed it. This is Q&A default mode.
Initial Caps	Click on this radio button to change the initial character of every word to uppercase. For example, *symantec incorporated* becomes *Symantec Incorporated*.
UPPER CASE	Click on this radio button to transform all text to uppercase. For example, *Q&A for Windows* becomes *Q&A FOR WINDOWS*.

lower case   Click on this radio button to change
                              all text to lowercase. For example,
                              Q&A for Windows becomes *q&a for
                              windows.*

Displaying Time Field Formats

The Time Format group (Figure 6.7) displays your current time format.
To change time formats, choose <u>D</u>atabase ➤ <u>G</u>lobal Format Options, and
select options in the Global Formatting Options dialog box. (You'll learn
about changing global format options later in this chapter.)

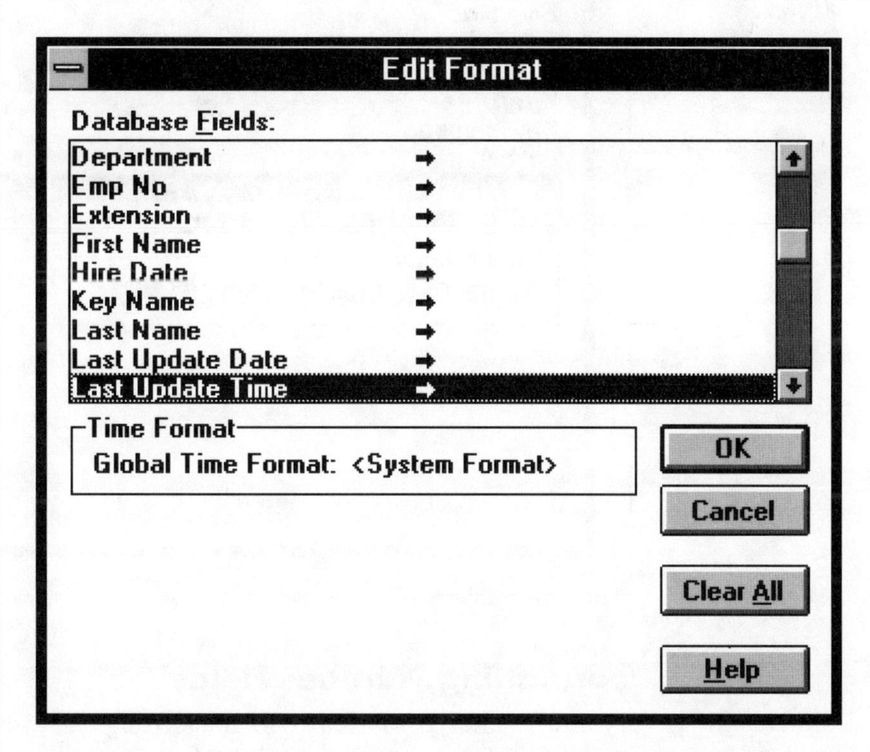

Displaying Date Field Formats

The Date Format group (Figure 6.8) displays your current date format. To change date formats, choose Database ➤ Global Format Options, and select options in the Global Formatting Options dialog box. You'll learn about changing global format options later in this chapter.

The Edit Format dialog box with the Date Format group, which shows the current date format

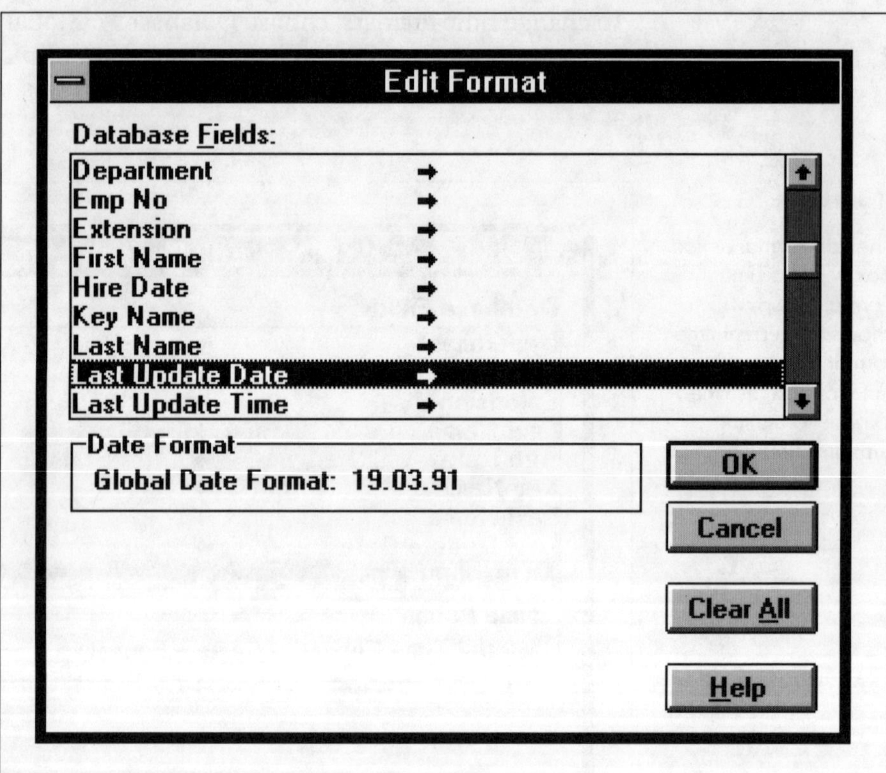

Formatting Number Fields

Number field types have two format settings that you can alter: the Thousands Separator and the number of decimal digits. Figure 6.9 shows the Edit Format dialog box with the Number Format group.

When you click on the Use Thousands Separator check box, Q&A automatically inserts commas to separate the thousands from the hundreds and the millions from the thousands. For example, if you type

The Edit Format dialog box as it looks when editing a number field

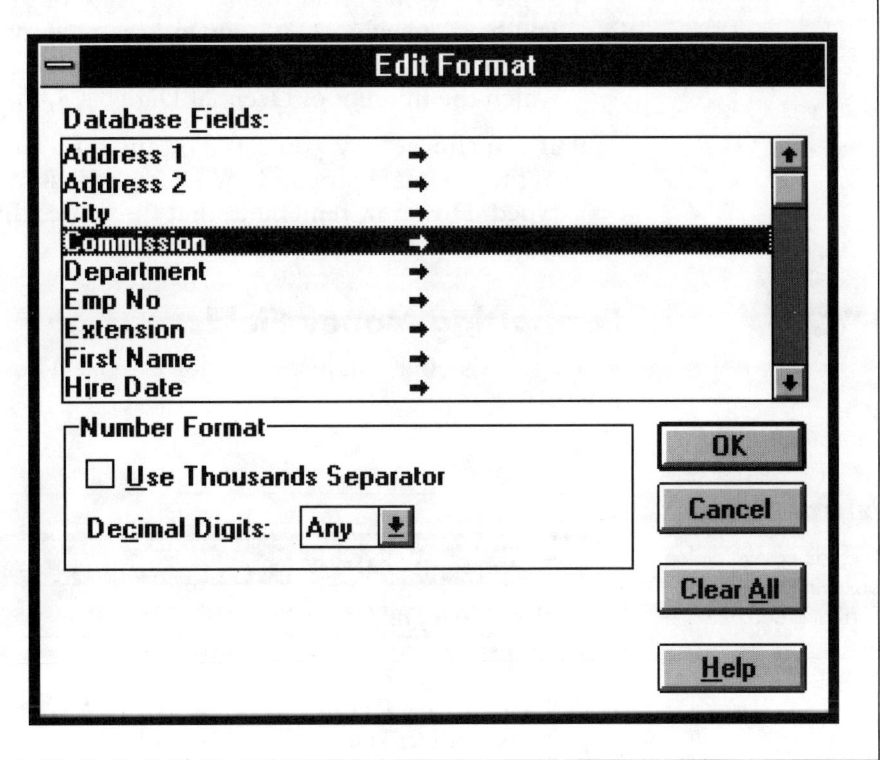

6567840.98 into a number field with Use Thousands Separator option checked, the result is 6,567,840.98. All fields entered prior to choosing Use Thousands Separator also have commas automatically inserted.

You can also select the number of digits (from 0 to 7 or Any) to the right of a decimal point in number fields. When you set a number of Decimal Digits, Q&A displays the value in that field with that many digits to the right of the decimal point.

- If the value has more digits to the right of the decimal point than you have specified, Q&A rounds the extra digits up and displays the rounded amount. For example, if you type the value 715.39 in a field in which the number of Decimal Digits is 1, the result is 715.4.

- If the value has fewer digits to the right of the decimal point than you have specified, Q&A appends extra zeros to the end of the number. For example, if you type the value 17.2 in a field in which the number of Decimal Digits is 3, the result is 17.200.

- If you choose Any, you can type any number of digits to the right of the decimal point and the results will always be exactly as you typed. However, remember that the values that Q&A displays are limited by the size of the field box.

Formatting Money Fields

Money fields offer you just one choice—Use Thousands Separator (Figure 6.10).

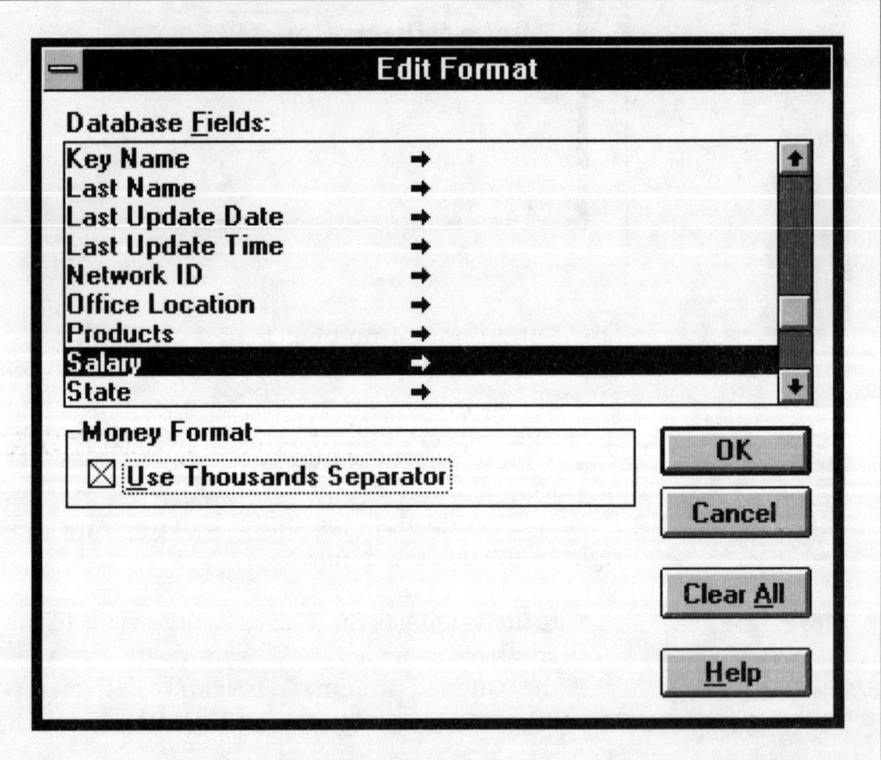

Picture type fields are dimmed in the Database Fields box because format options are not available for picture fields.

Changing Field Formats

You have just learned the basics of formatting various field types. Now let's apply them by following these steps:

1. In the Database Structure area, choose Database ➤ Edit Field Attribute ➤ Format. Q&A displays the Edit Format dialog box.

To quickly open the Edit Format dialog box, double-click in the Format column in the Database Structure area.

2. In the Database Fields box, choose the field to be changed.

3. Select the options you desire in the format group for the selected field type. Q&A displays the selected formats on the right side of the Database Fields box.

4. Repeat steps 2 and 3 until you have applied all the formats you desire. Whenever you select a new field to change, Q&A saves the changes that you just made.

5. Click on OK or press Enter when you have completed all your changes.

Specifying Restrictions

Using field restrictions, Q&A can limit the data entered in a field to a range, a list of items, or a number of characters. When you restrict the contents of fields, you limit the data-entry by specifying a correct value or range of values for a field. For example, imagine that someone in your department is going to enter the salaries of your employees into a database. If you know that the maximum salary in your department is $70,000 and that the minimum salary is $17,000, you can restrict the salary field to accept only values between 17,000 and 70,000. This helps to prevent data entry mistakes, such as adding an extra zero or two.

To set restrictions, use the Edit Restriction dialog box (Figure 6.11).

To enter a restriction for a field, use these steps:

1. While in the Database Structure area, double-click in the Restriction column in the Database Structure area or choose Database ➤ Edit Field Attributes ➤ Restriction. Q&A displays the Edit Restriction dialog box.

2. In the Database Fields box, choose a field in which you want to specify a restriction.

3. Click inside the Restriction Formula box.

FIGURE 6.11

Edit Restriction dialog box

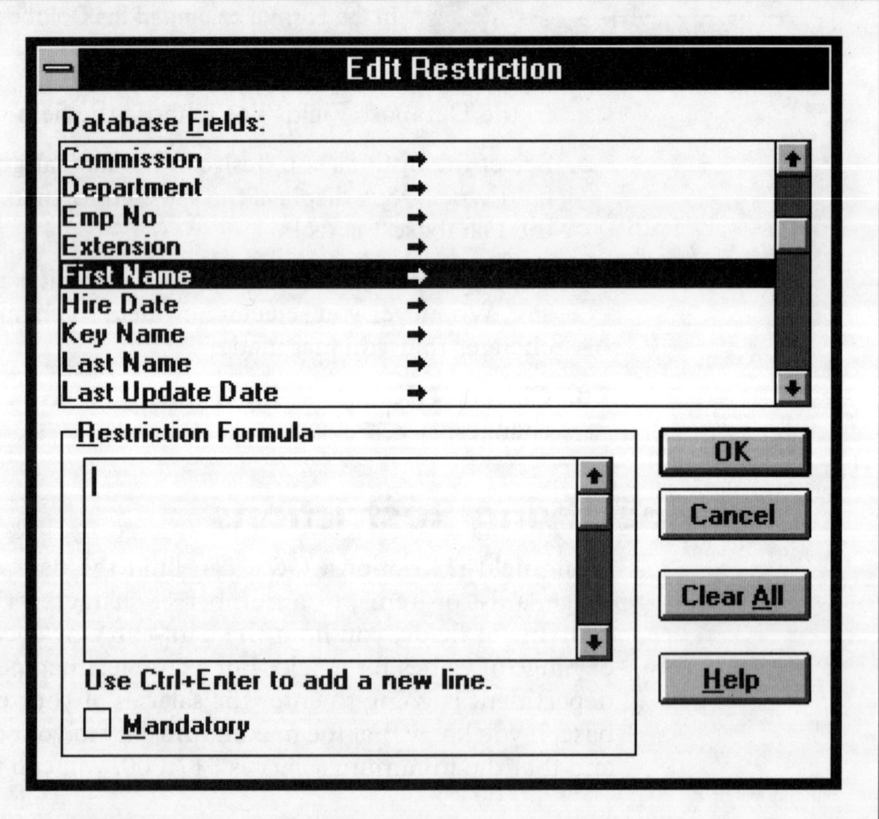

4. Type a restriction using the codes described in Tables 6.1 through 6.4.

5. Repeat steps 2, 3, and 4 until you have assigned all the restrictions you desire.

6. Choose OK or press Enter to accept your entries and save the changes.

To enter a restriction formula, you need to specify a code that both suits your needs and is allowed for the field type. You can restrict all field types but picture fields.

All field types except the picture field type allow restrictions that require exact matches. Exact match restrictions are listed in Table 6.1.

TABLE 6.1: Q&A Exact Match Restrictions

RESTRICTION (WITH X AND Y VARIABLES)	DESCRIPTION	EXAMPLE OF RESTRICTION	EXAMPLES OF VALID INPUT
X	Equal to X	Symantec	Symantec
$/X$	Not equal to X	Symantec	IBM
=	Empty	=	
/=	Not empty	/=	Symantec, IBM, Synoptics, Apple
$X;Y$	Equal to X or Y	Symantec; IBM	Symantec, IBM

All fields but picture and Yes/No fields allow restrictions that are limited to a range of data. Table 6.2 lists range restrictions.

TABLE 6.2: Q&A Range Restrictions

RESTRICTION (WITH X AND Y VARIABLES)	DESCRIPTION	EXAMPLE OF RESTRICTION	EXAMPLES OF VALID INPUT
$>X$	greater than X	>30	40, 10000
$>=X$	greater than or equal to X	$>=30$	30, 40, 10000
$<X$	less than X	<50	40, 0, -1400
$<=X$	less than or equal to X	$<=50$	50, 40, 0, -1400
$>X..<Y$	greater than X and less than Y	$>20..<50$	30, 40
$>X;<Y$	greater than X or less than Y	$>50;<30$	60, 1000, 20, 0, -700

When you need to ensure that the text in either a keyword or text field contains certain characters, use character restrictions. For example, Table 6.3 lists character restrictions.

TABLE 6.3: Q&A Character Restrictions

RESTRICTION (WITH X AND Y VARIABLES)	DESCRIPTION	EXAMPLE OF RESTRICTION	EXAMPLES OF VALID INPUT
$X..$	Begins with X	S..	Symantec
$..X$	Ends with X	..M	IBM
$X..Y$	Begins with X and ends with Y	S..C	Symantec
$..X..$	Includes X	..pp..	Apple
$X..Y..Z$	Begins with X, includes Y, and ends with Z	S..y..c	Symantec
?	Any one character	?	S
??	Any two characters	??	Sy
\x	Literal restriction (restricted to the character following the backslash)	\=	=

You can use two special time and date programming commands to restrict the values in time and date fields, respectively. Table 6.4 lists these special restrictions.

TABLE 6.4: Q&A Special Restrictions

RESTRICTION (WITH *X* AND *Y* VARIABLES)	DESCRIPTION	EXAMPLE OF RESTRICTION	EXAMPLES OF VALID INPUT	VALID FIELD TYPE
={@DATE}	equals todays date	={@DATE}	01/01/96	date fields only
={@TIME}	equals the current time	={@TIME}	6:42 AM	time fields only

You can use the @DATE and @TIME statements with combinations of greater than, less than, and equal to symbols. The @DATE and @TIME commands must be enclosed in braces ({}). For example, if you wish to restrict a date field to a value greater than or equal to today's date, use this statement: >={@DATE}. So if today's date were June 10, 1996, you could only enter dates greater than or equal to June 10, 1996.

N O T E

In the Restriction Formula box, you can write complete programming statements to restrict values in fields. For more information about restriction programming, see Chapter 11.

Checking or clearing the <u>M</u>andatory box at the bottom of the Edit Restriction dialog box determines whether you or a user *must* enter data in a field. If you do not check <u>M</u>andatory, when you type a value that does not meet the restrictions specified for the field, Q&A issues a prompt (Figure 6.12) to which you must respond. If you check the <u>M</u>andatory box, when you type a value that does not meet the restrictions, Q&A issues a message (Figure 6.13) and does not allow you to continue to the next field without entering a valid value.

FIGURE 6.12

This invalid entry prompt indicates that you entered a value which is not valid. However, you are given the option to have that invalid entry accepted by clicking Yes.

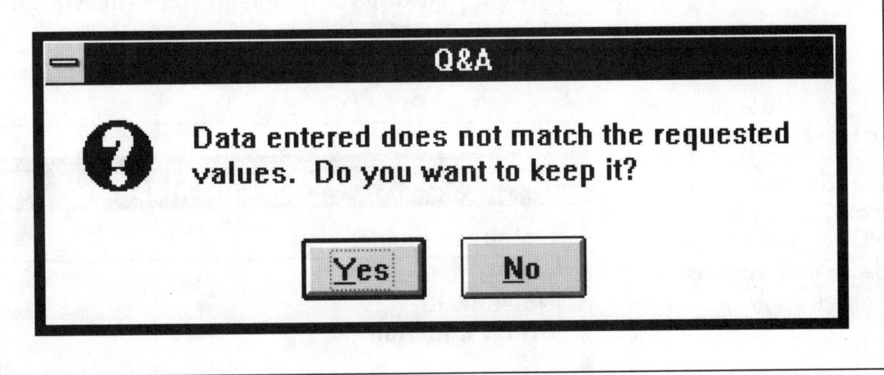

FIGURE 6.13

This invalid entry prompt informs you that the entered value is not valid for this field. Since it is a mandatory field, you will not be able to exit until you input a valid entry.

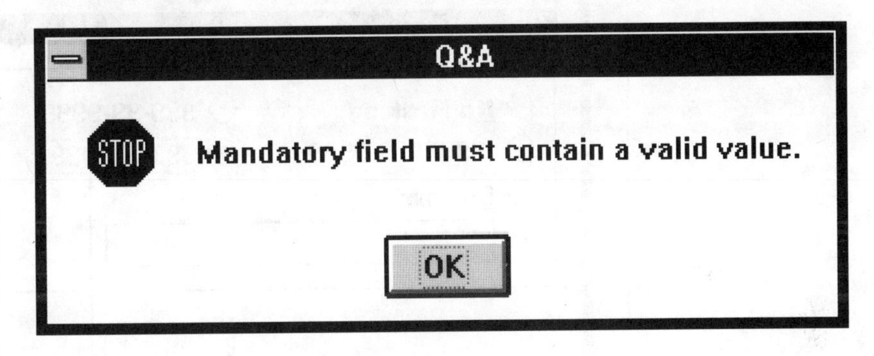

Creating a Field Mask

For more efficient data entry for text fields, such as telephone numbers, social security numbers, and zip codes, Q&A allows you to create *field masks*, which format the data that you or a user enters. Field masks automatically insert characters for you so that you can type data more quickly and read it more easily. For example, you can set up telephone number fields so that all you need to type are the numbers. If you type the number 5555555555, Q&A automatically formats the result as *(555)555-5555.* Thus, you can save time when you enter many telephone numbers, reduce errors, and increase the consistency of formatting in reports.

Specify field masking templates in the Edit Masking dialog box (see Figure 6.14).

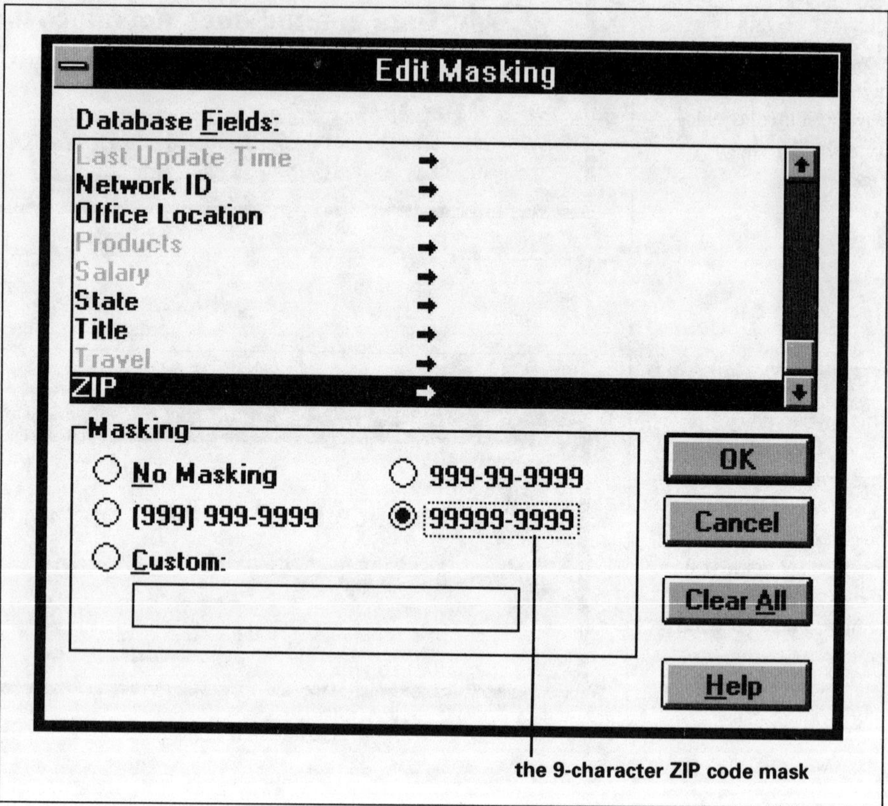

D O S   In Q&A for DOS, field masks were referred to as *field templates.*

In the Masking group in the Edit Masking dialog box, you can choose from:

<u>N</u>o Masking	This is the default. Q&A does not alter the data typed into the field.
(999) 999-9999	Template for American phone numbers
999-99-9999	Template for social security numbers
99999-9999	Template for zip codes
<u>C</u>ustom:	Create your own template

You can use any characters in a masking template. If the template you want does not already appear in the Masking group, you can define it in the <u>C</u>ustom text box. For example, for a record identifier, you could define the field mask ####@@@, which would allow you to type four numbers followed by three alphabetic characters. Table 6.5 lists the codes that are available for a custom masking template.

TABLE 6.5: Custom Masking Codes

CODE	DESCRIPTION
@	Use as a placeholder for any alphabetic character.
# or 9	Use as a placeholder for any number.
$	Use as a placeholder for any alphabetic character, number, or symbol.
!	Use this character at the beginning of your custom template to disable the Override Field Mask option from the Edit menu and force the person entering to use the template.

When you use masking templates, the template itself is not actually saved with the data entered but is only generated whenever you view the data. For example, if you enter the number 5555555555 using the (999) 999-9999 mask, Q&A internally saves the data just as you entered it. However, when you view that record, Q&A applies the mask to your entry and displays (555) 555-5555. Keep this in mind when exporting data. If you don't specify that Q&A include the field masks when exporting, your data will export *without* the template. However, the report and mail merge processes *do* automatically include field masks.

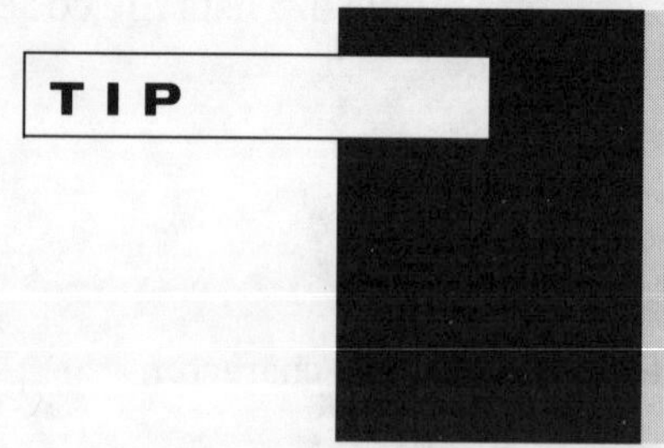

If your custom template could be difficult to understand, use a help box or the @MSG programming command to aid in data entry. You'll find out how to create a help box later in this chapter. To learn about programming in Q&A, see Chapter 11, and for specific information on using @MSG, see Appendix D.

To create a field mask, follow these steps:

1. In the Database Structure area, choose <u>D</u>atabase ➤ <u>E</u>dit Field Attribute ➤ <u>M</u>asking.

To open the Edit Masking dialog box, double-click in the Masking column in the Database Structure area.

2. Select the field in which you want to create your mask. Only text fields can have masks.

3. Select the type of masking you prefer in the Masking box or enter your own in the <u>C</u>ustom text box. If you decide to enter a custom mask, use the codes in Table 6.5.

4. Repeat steps 2 and 3, until you have finished assigning masks to your database.

5. Choose OK or press Enter to return to the Database Structure area and save your changes.

Setting Initial Values

Q&A allows you to enter data automatically in a field when you add a record. For example, you can instruct Q&A to automatically put the current date into a Date Contacted field. If you add a record for every new contact, Q&A can enter today's date for you. This ensures that the date is accurate (if your computer system date is accurate) and also saves you data entry time. All fields but picture fields accept initial values (except for those noted in the following list). You can select from these initial values in the Edit Initial Value dialog box (Figure 6.15).

INITIAL VALUE	RESULTS
No Initial Value	There is no initial value in the selected field. This is the default.
Custom	Whatever you type in this text box is the initial valuc.
Current Date	This places the system date, which is based on the computer's internal clock, in the selected field.
Current Time	This places the system time, which is based on the computer's internal clock, in the selected field. Use this initial value only with time fields.
Number	This initial value is a *counter* (a number that is incremented by one each time it is used). The first record that you add has 1 in the selected field, the second record has 2, and so on. For more information about the number counter, see the @NUMBER command in Appendix D.

The Edit Initial Value dialog box in which you can set initial values for fields in a database

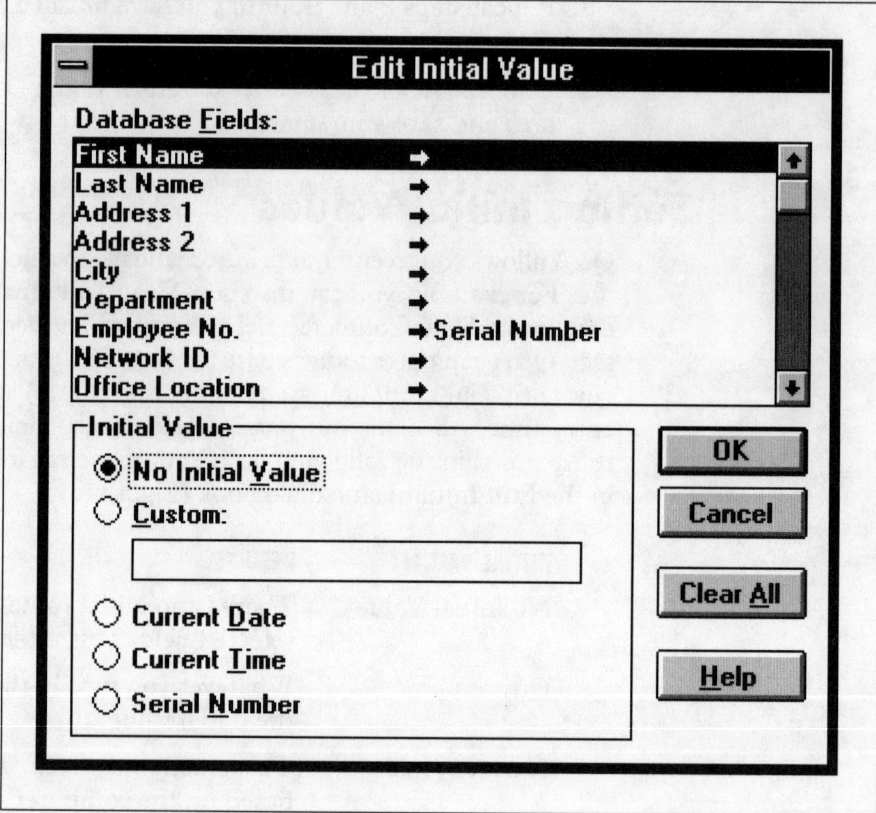

To create initial values, use these steps:

1. In the Database Structure area, choose Database ➤ Edit Field Attributes ➤ Initial Value or double-click in the Initial Value column in the Database Structure area. Q&A displays the Edit Initial Value dialog box.

2. Click on an initial value radio button or type any initial value in the Custom text box.

3. Repeat step 2 until you have assigned all the desired initial values.

4. Choose OK or press Enter to return to the Database Structure area and save your changes.

Changing Global Formats

Using the Global Formatting Options dialog box (see Figure 6.16), you can control a variety of formats for Date, Time, Money, and Number fields. For example, you can change the way that dates, time, and currency are displayed. As the title of this dialog box indicates, all changes in the Global Formatting Options dialog box affect your database globally. For example, if you change how time fields are displayed, all time fields in the current database are changed accordingly.

N O T E   The Global Option settings do not affect how the data is stored; they only affect how it is displayed.

FIGURE 6.16

The Global Formatting Options dialog box

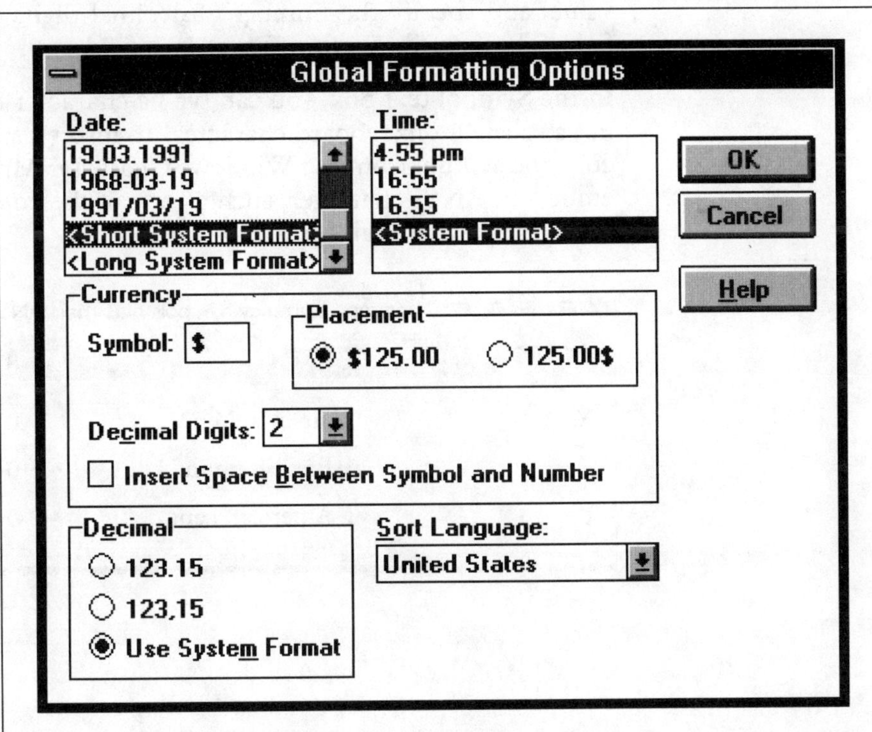

You can choose from five sets of format options: date, time, currency, decimal, and sort language.

Changing Date and Time Formats

You can change formats for date and time fields by choosing options from the Date list box and the Time list box. Simply click on a selection and either choose OK or press Enter.

The default setting for date fields is the <Short System Format>, which is the date format set in the Windows Control Panel. The default setting for time fields is <System Format>, which is the Windows time format.

Changing Formats for Money Fields

The currency group in the Global Formatting Options dialog box allows you to change the symbol used to indicate currency, change the location of the currency symbol, add a space between the currency symbol and the value, and specify the number of decimal digits to display in a money field. These settings only affect money fields.

In the Symbol text box, you can type a character from your keyboard or use a special nonkeyboard character. To insert a special character, either copy the symbol from the Windows Character Map (see Appendix B) or embed an ANSI character, such as one of the commonly used currency symbols shown in Table 6.6.

TABLE 6.6: Common Currency Symbols and Their ANSI Codes

SYMBOL	NAME	ANSI CODE
¥	Japanese Yen	0165
£	English pound	0163
¢	American cent	0162

To use a special currency symbol in Q&A, follow these steps:

1. Click inside the Symbol text box.

2. Press the NumLock key to activate the numeric keypad.

3. Hold down the Alt key and type the ANSI number that represents the currency symbol you desire on the numeric keypad.

4. Release the Alt key. Your character appears in the Symbol text box.

5. Press the NumLock key to deactivate the numeric keypad.

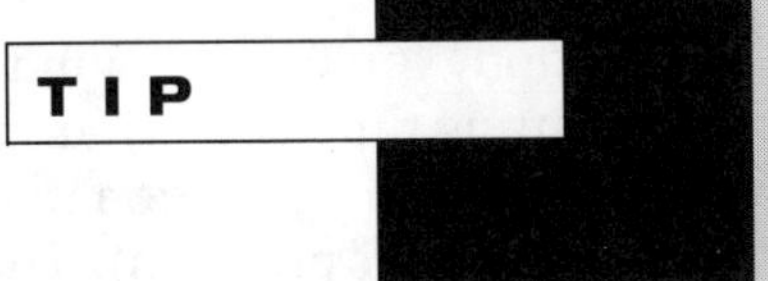

TIP

You can also use this procedure to embed ANSI characters in your database fields. You might use this to inert the registered rademark or copyright symbols.

In the Placement group, you can change the location of the currency symbol from the beginning of a money field to the end of a currency field. Choose $125.00, the default, to place the symbol in front of the currency value, or choose 125.00$ to place the symbol after the value.

The Decimal Digits drop-down list box allows you to set the number of digits that follow the decimal point in a currency value. You can select values from 0 to 7.

NOTE

When you choose the number of decimal digits to be displayed in the Global Formatting Options dialog box, you are affecting the format of *all* the currency fields in the database. In contrast, when you select the number of decimal digits to be displayed in the Edit Format dialog box, you are specifying the format of a particular number field.

You can check the Insert Space Between Symbol and Number box to put a space between the value and the currency symbol. This works for both symbols that precede and those that follow the currency value.

Changing the Display of Decimal Points

The decimal group enables you to choose how the decimal point is displayed: as a comma, a period, or the system format controlled by the Windows Control Panel. This setting only affects number fields.

Selecting the Language That Controls Sorting

Since Windows is an international application, you can set Windows to use different international settings for formatting times, dates, currencies, and other values. One of these settings is the Language option in the International section of the Control Panel (a Windows program). The Language option lets you specify the language that you use in Windows. Since different languages use different characters, what is a correctly sorted order of records in English might be wrong in Spanish. (*Sorting* records means ordering them alphabetically or numerically, in ascending or descending order.) Therefore, Q&A allows you to sort data by using different language rules. To sort data appropriately for your Windows language, choose from the Sort Language drop-down list box. The default is United States.

Setting Global Options for a Database

Now that you understand all the options provided in the Global Formatting Options dialog box, you can set global options for your database by following these steps:

1. In the Database Structure area, choose Database ➤ Global Format Options. Q&A displays the Global Formatting Options dialog box.

2. Choose all the settings you prefer.

3. Choose OK or press Enter.

Defining Custom Help

You can define custom help messages that can help someone enter data for a record. For example, in the STAFF database, in the Products keyword field, you might want to show a complete list of all the keywords used thus far in the field. This will prevent the keyword list from growing as people think of new synonyms for existing keywords. Define custom help messages in the Edit Custom Help dialog box (Figure 6.17).

FIGURE 6.17

The Edit Custom Help dialog box in which you can define custom help text for the selected field

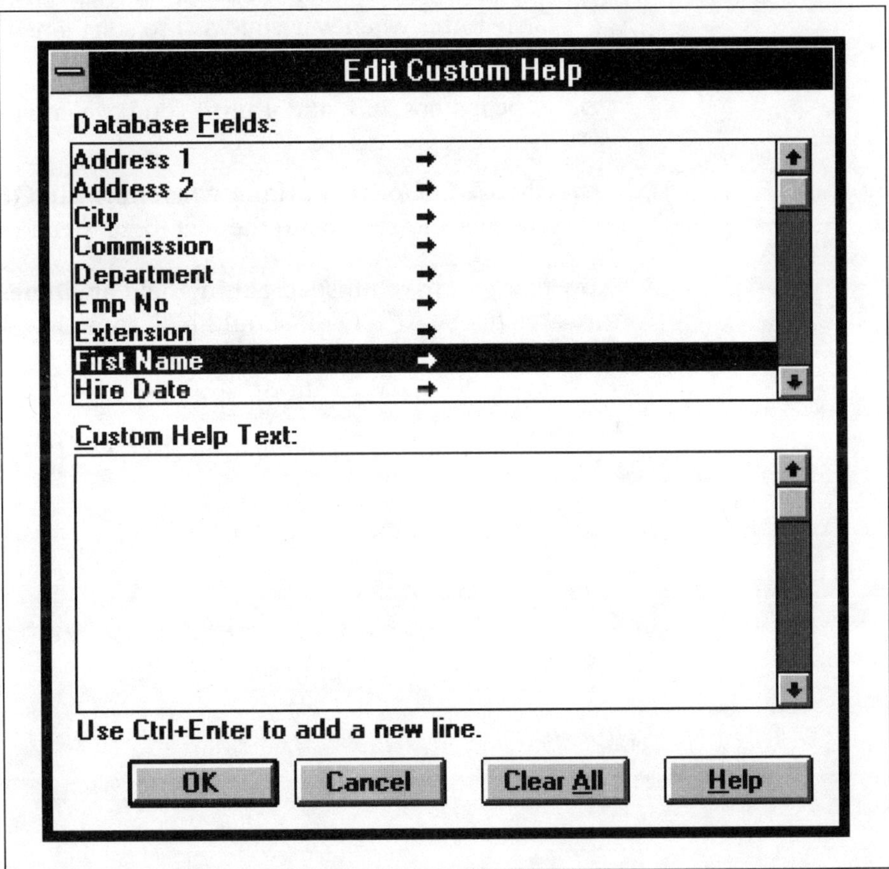

To create a custom help dialog box, follow these steps:

1. In the Database Structure area, choose Database ➤ Edit Field Attribute ➤ Custom Help or double-click in any cell in the Custom Help column. Q&A displays the Edit Custom Help dialog box.

2. In the Database Fields box, choose the field for which you want to define custom help.

3. Click on the Custom Help Text box.

4. Type the custom help message you want displayed, pressing Ctrl+Enter whenever you wish to start a new line. If you press Enter, the dialog box closes.

5. Repeat steps 2, 3, and 4 until you have created all the custom help messages you desire.

6. Choose OK or press Enter when finished. Q&A saves your changes and returns to the Database Structure area.

Now that you have finished editing field attributes, the Database Structure area for STAFF.DTF should look something like Figure 6.18.

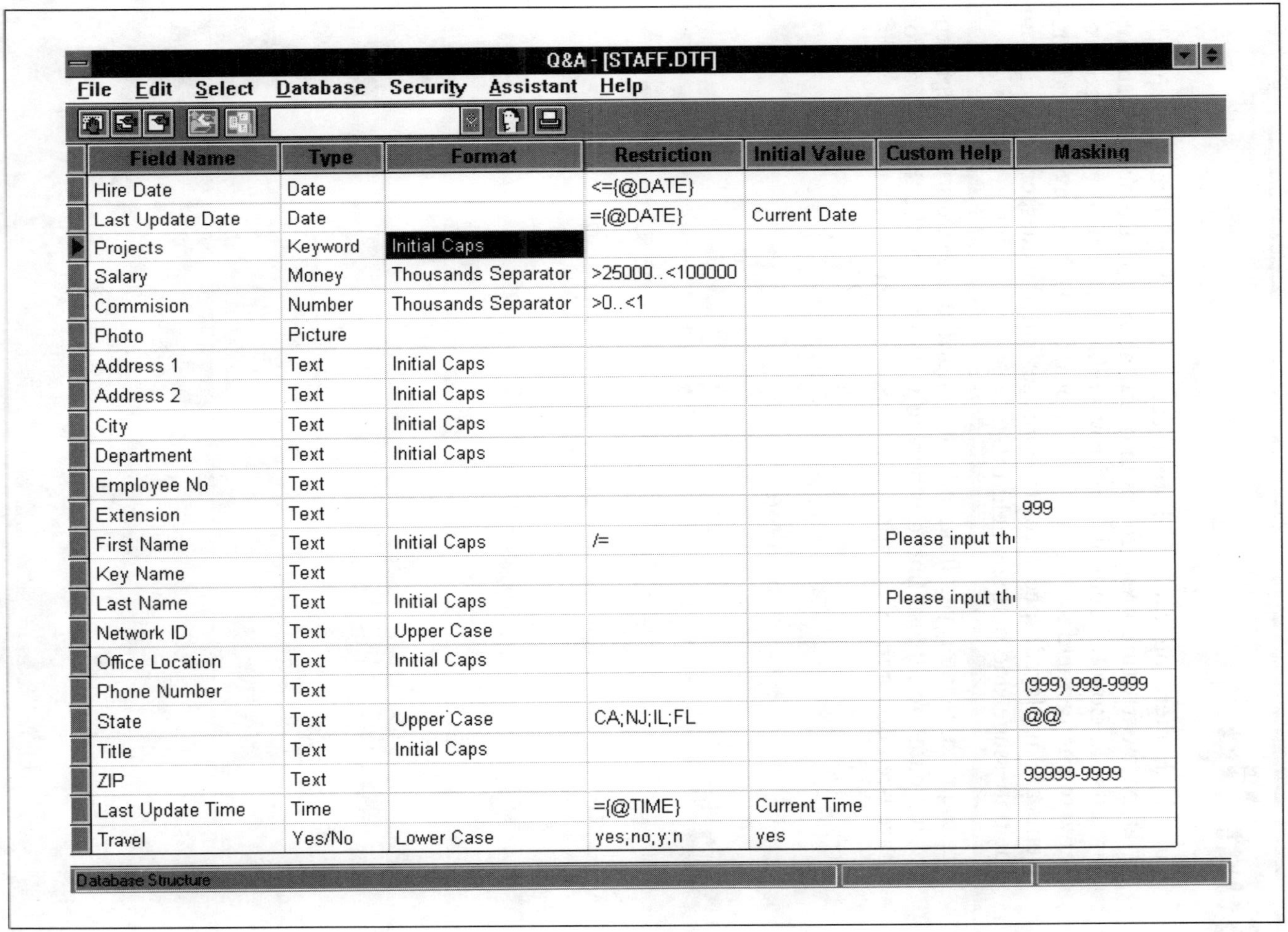

Q&A - [STAFF.DTF]

File Edit Select Database Security Assistant Help

Field Name	Type	Format	Restriction	Initial Value	Custom Help	Masking
Hire Date	Date		<={@DATE}			
Last Update Date	Date		={@DATE}	Current Date		
Projects	Keyword	Initial Caps				
Salary	Money	Thousands Separator	>25000..<100000			
Commision	Number	Thousands Separator	>0..<1			
Photo	Picture					
Address 1	Text	Initial Caps				
Address 2	Text	Initial Caps				
City	Text	Initial Caps				
Department	Text	Initial Caps				
Employee No	Text					
Extension	Text					999
First Name	Text	Initial Caps	/=		Please input th	
Key Name	Text					
Last Name	Text	Initial Caps			Please input th	
Network ID	Text	Upper Case				
Office Location	Text	Initial Caps				
Phone Number	Text					(999) 999-9999
State	Text	Upper Case	CA;NJ;IL;FL			@@
Title	Text	Initial Caps				
ZIP	Text					99999-9999
Last Update Time	Time		={@TIME}	Current Time		
Travel	Yes/No	Lower Case	yes;no;y;n	yes		

Database Structure

FIGURE 6.18

STAFF.DTF after editing field attributes

To Sum Up

In this chapter, you learned all about customizing your database using the Database Structure area. You found out about the Database Structure area itself—how the columns and rows relate—and then you discovered how to change field names and field types, format the way the field contents are displayed, specify restrictions, set initial values, create a custom help message, and define a field mask.

In the next chapter, you'll put all your knowledge to work and begin entering data. You'll also find out how to view some of the things that you have been doing in this chapter while entering data.

chapter

7

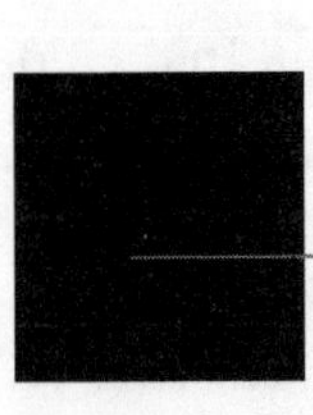

Entering
Data

W**HEN** working with Q&A, you can retrieve records, create reports, design input forms, and change a database's structure. Most of the time, however, you'll be entering data—either by adding new records or by editing already existing records—in Add/Edit mode. In this chapter, you'll find out all about entering data—from preparation to the different types of fields and special methods by which you can save time.

Displaying Records in Add/Edit Mode

As you have learned, records in Add/Edit mode are displayed in two different ways: in Form view (Q&A's default view), or in Spreadsheet view. Form view displays the fields in various locations in the work area. Spreadsheet view displays your fields and records in columns and rows, respectively, in a spreadsheet format. Regardless of the view, you can enter data in the same way. The only difference between the two views is the layout of fields and records.

To choose between the two views, click on either the Form view icon or the Spreadsheet view icon. Another way to switch between the two different views is to choose <u>R</u>ecords ➤ Vie<u>w</u> As Spreadsheet or <u>R</u>ecords ➤ Vie<u>w</u> As Form, depending on whether you are in Form view or Spreadsheet view. For an example, in the STAFF database, switch between Form view and Spreadsheet view to see how you would enter data in each.

Displaying a Database in Form View

When in Form view, you can display your fields in any location in the work area using input forms. Remember that you can move the fields and alter their fonts and field box sizes through the Design Input Forms mode, discussed in Chapter 4. In Form view, you can also choose the input form you desire from the drop-down list box in the middle of the tool bar, by choosing Select ➤ Load Input Form, or by pressing Ctrl+L. Figure 7.1 displays Q&A in Form view mode with the Master Form selected as the current input form.

The STAFF.DTF form in Form view. There is only one record on display.

Displaying a Database in Spreadsheet View

Spreadsheet view displays your fields as columns in a table. Each record of the database is displayed as a row of the table. Since Spreadsheet view can display more than one record at a time, it offers a more complete view of your database than Form view, which can only display one. Figure 7.2 shows the Master Form in Spreadsheet view.

Although Spreadsheet view does not display graphics in the background work area, it can display pictures in picture fields. Since the fields in Spreadsheet view are so small, pictures are sized accordingly. When you move to another type of field, the word *picture* appears in the picture field instead of an actual picture.

FIGURE 7.2

The STAFF.DTF Master Form in Spreadsheet view. There are several records on display at once.

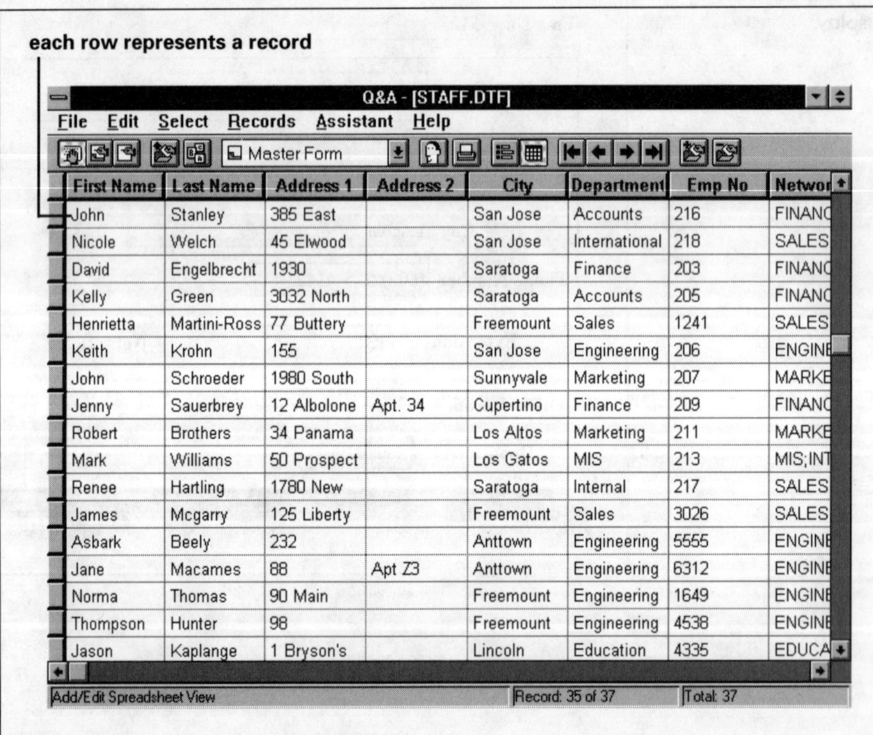

First Name	Last Name	Address 1	Address 2	City	Department	Emp No	Networ
John	Stanley	385 East		San Jose	Accounts	216	FINANC
Nicole	Welch	45 Elwood		San Jose	International	218	SALES
David	Engelbrecht	1930		Saratoga	Finance	203	FINANC
Kelly	Green	3032 North		Saratoga	Accounts	205	FINANC
Henrietta	Martini-Ross	77 Buttery		Freemount	Sales	1241	SALES
Keith	Krohn	155		San Jose	Engineering	206	ENGINE
John	Schroeder	1980 South		Sunnyvale	Marketing	207	MARKE
Jenny	Sauerbrey	12 Albolone	Apt. 34	Cupertino	Finance	209	FINANC
Robert	Brothers	34 Panama		Los Altos	Marketing	211	MARKE
Mark	Williams	50 Prospect		Los Gatos	MIS	213	MIS;INT
Renee	Hartling	1780 New		Saratoga	Internal	217	SALES
James	Mcgarry	125 Liberty		Freemount	Sales	3026	SALES
Asbark	Beely	232		Anttown	Engineering	5555	ENGINE
Jane	Macames	88	Apt Z3	Anttown	Engineering	6312	ENGINE
Norma	Thomas	90 Main		Freemount	Engineering	1649	ENGINE
Thompson	Hunter	98		Freemount	Engineering	4538	ENGINE
Jason	Kaplange	1 Bryson's		Lincoln	Education	4335	EDUCA

Spreadsheet view was called Table view in Q&A for DOS. Note that the processes in Q&A for DOS Table view are very similar to those in Spreadsheet view. For example, if you have checked Use Q&A DOS Key commands as a preference, pressing Alt+F6 brings you to Spreadsheet view as it brought you to the Table view in Q&A for DOS.

In both Form view and Spreadsheet view, you can select input forms. Just select the input form you desire by opening the drop-down list box in the middle of the tool bar, by choosing Select ➤ Load Input Forms, or by pressing Ctrl+L.

Editing Columns and Changing the Font in Spreadsheet View

You can make it easier to enter data in Spreadsheet view by moving and adjusting the width of columns and by changing the font. For example, if your fields are arranged alphabetically, you can change their order so you can type all address information together and then type all company information.

Moving Columns in Spreadsheet View

As in Database Structure area, Q&A allows you to rearrange the columns in Spreadsheet view. This means that you can position the columns in the database to work best with your needs. For instance, if you are entering data into your database from a form that lists an applicant's name in Last Name, First Name, and Middle Name order, you can arrange your columns in that order for quicker data entry.

To move a column in Spreadsheet view, follow these steps.

1. Move the mouse pointer to the column heading. The mouse pointer changes to a miniature column with arrows pointing to the left and to the right.

2. Click on the column to select it and drag the column to its new location. When you release the mouse button, the column fits between the column you dropped it on and the preceding one.

For example, you can arrange STAFF.DTF columns in Spreadsheet view in an order in which you can easily enter data. From left to right, order your columns as First Name, Last Name, Address 1, Address 2, City, State, Zip, and Phone Number. Put all other columns to the right in any order.

Changing the Width of a Column

If you cannot see the data in a field, or if the field is too wide, you can adjust the width of the column by performing the following steps:

1. Move the mouse pointer over the right edge of the desired column heading. This changes the pointer to a double-sided arrow.

2. Click on the right edge of the column to select and highlight the right border of the field to the left.

3. Drag the right border to the desired width and release the mouse button.

Changing the Spreadsheet View Font

The font formats that you create for your input forms are not displayed in Spreadsheet view, so Q&A provides a separate option to change the fonts in this view. To change the fonts, follow these steps:

1. Either choose Records ➤ Spreadsheet View Font or press Ctrl+F to open the Font dialog box. (For more information about the Font dialog box, see Chapter 4.)

2. Choose the desired font setting.

3. Click OK or press Enter.

The font settings that you choose affect all the columns and rows in Spreadsheet view for this database. For example, if you change STAFF.DTF to New Times Roman and a 10 point size, you might be able to fit more information on one screen, and if you change the color for text, you might make it easier to view.

Saving Spreadsheet Layouts

All the layout changes in Spreadsheet view are lost unless you explicitly save them before going to a different mode or input form. To save your spreadsheet layout changes for this input form, simply choose Records ➤ Save Spreadsheet Layout. If you use several input forms for this database, you can change and save different layouts for each.

Adding Records to a Database

You can add records in both Form view and Spreadsheet view by using the following steps:

1. Click on the Add button on the tool bar, choose Records ➤ New Record, or press Ctrl+N. This puts Q&A in Add mode, placing your cursor in the first field of a new record.

2. Add the appropriate data in the new record.

3. To add another new record, click on the Add button, choose Records ➤ New Record, or if you checked the Use DOS Key Commands option in the Preferences dialog box, press F10. (Pressing F10 just allows you to add another record once you are in Add mode; it does *not* put you in Add mode.)

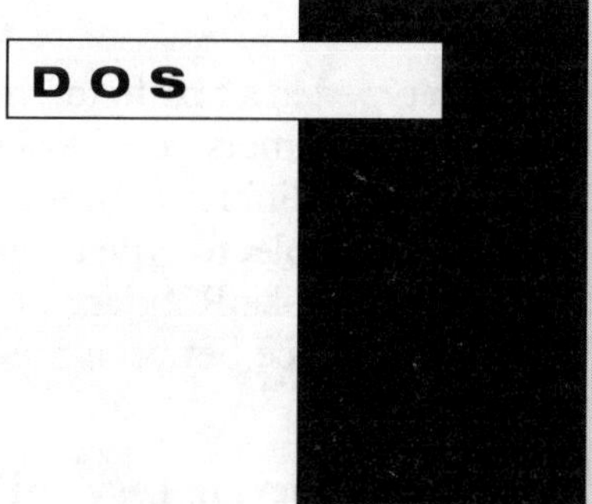

When adding or editing records in Q&A for DOS, you need to press F10 to save your additions or changes. If you exit Add mode without doing so, you lose the new information. Fortunately, with Q&A for Windows, you don't need to press F10. Whenever you change to a different mode or start to add another record, Q&A automatically saves your changes or additions up to that point.

If you added a record or you are in the process of adding a record, you can delete it by clicking on the Delete key on the tool bar or by choosing Records ➤ Delete Record.

Entering Data into Different Types of Fields

When you enter data into different types of fields, the data is accepted differently. For instance, if you type a number with a leading zero in a number field, Q&A removes the leading zero. For example, this changes an entered value of 056.1 to 56.1. However, if you type a number with a leading zero in a text field, the leading zero remains. For example, if you type 02139 in the ZIP field, which is a text field, Q&A will not remove the leading zero.

Now let's look at the effects of data entry in the various field types. As you read this section, practice entering data in the STAFF database.

Text Fields

Unless you have programming statements or field attributes set for a field, data entered in a text field is not altered in any way. For instance, you can type text, numbers, and dates into a text field and the data is not changed from the way in which you entered it. However, these entries are no longer considered dates, times, and numbers and will probably not retrieve, sort, or calculate properly. For example, if you add the numbers 20 and 11 in text fields, the result is 2011 because adding text fields just appends one value to the other. However, if you set specific field attributes (for example, you set initial capitalization in Chapter 6) for a field, you can type data any way you wish, but Q&A will format it as you have defined.

Keyword Fields

In the same way that data is unchanged when typed in a text field, the data in a keyword field does not change (except for formats you have specified). To use a keyword field effectively, type the different values in the field and separate them with semicolons. For example, to type the names Mike, Rob, and Jack in a keyword field, type either Mike;Rob;Jack or Mike; Rob; Jack. It doesn't matter whether you add a space between the semicolon and the next value or not.

However, there is a major difference between retrieving keyword fields and text fields. You can retrieve multiple entries or individual entries from a keyword field. For instance, if a keyword field contains the values Mike, Rob, and Jack, you can retrieve individual entries (for example, Rob) by typing just Rob in that field. This differs from a text field in which you need to type ..Rob.. to perform the same search. For more information about keyword field retrieves, see Chapter 8.

Yes/No Fields

Yes/No fields allow you to only use a few affirmative and negative entries: Yes, No, Y, N, True, False, T, F, 1, and 0. Any other entries will return an invalid entry prompt. However, you can restrict entries further in the Database Structure area. For example, in STAFF.DTF, the Travel Yes/No field only allows values of yes, no, y, and n. Q&A prompts you to type the proper value if you enter any other value in the Travel field.

Number Fields

You can type only numeric values in a number field. Remember that Q&A removes leading zeros from numbers. You do not need to enter decimal points or comma separators in your values. You can specify thousands place separators and decimal digit restrictions in the Edit Format dialog box in Database Structure view, and you can use the Global Formating Options dialog box to set the number of decimal digits. For example, in the STAFF database, Commission is a number with three digits. If you type a value in this field, Q&A formats it with three decimal digits. For more information about these dialog boxes, see Chapter 6.

Money Fields

Typing values in money fields is no different than typing values in number fields. You don't need to type commas, decimal points, or currency symbols, but it does no harm to do so. Remember that Q&A controls all the settings for commas, decimal points, and currency symbols in the Edit Format and Global Formating Options dialog boxes described in Chapter 6.

Time Fields

When you type a time (or have Q&A automatically enter a time) in a time field, Q&A automatically converts your data to the time format set in the Global Formating Options dialog box. You can type a time value in either military (for example, 1700) or standard (5:00 p.m.) format. If you type a time in standard format and do not follow it with either a.m. or p.m., Q&A defaults to a.m.

Date Fields

You can type a value in a date field using any combination of these formats:

MONTH	DAY	YEAR
Jan	01	1995
January	1	95
01	1	95

Picture Fields

Picture fields can only contain graphical images—either Bitmap images (.BMP) or Windows Meta File images (.WMF)—pasted from the Windows Clipboard.

To place a picture in a picture field, first copy it into the Clipboard by selecting the picture in the application you want to copy it from and then either choosing Edit ➤ Copy or pressing Ctrl+C. Then move the mouse pointer into the picture field of your Q&A database and either choose Edit ➤ Paste or press Ctrl+V. When the image is pasted into the picture field, Q&A sizes the image to the width and height of the field. For instance, if the image is about two inches tall and you paste it into a picture field that is one inch tall, your picture is shrunk to about half the height. The same resizing occurs if the field is too big for the picture. If the same image is placed into a field that is twice its height, the image is expanded to match the size of the field.

To create and place a picture in a picture field, follow these steps:

1. Either press Ctrl+Esc or Alt+Tab to switch to the Windows Program Manager.

2. Launch the Paintbrush program, which, by default, is in the Accessories group.

3. Draw a picture.

4. Use the Scissors tool to cut out the picture.

5. Choose Edit ➤ Copy or press Ctrl+C to copy the selected image to the clipboard.

6. Switch back to Q&A using either Alt+Tab or Ctrl+Esc.

7. Switch to Form view or Spreadsheet view by clicking on the Form view button or by choosing <u>R</u>ecords ➤ Vie<u>w</u> As Form.

8. Click on the picture field (for example, in the STAFF database, the Photo field). If you are in Spreadsheet view, double-click on the picture field.

9. Choose <u>E</u>dit ➤ <u>P</u>aste or press Ctrl+V. Your picture appears in the picture field.

Q&A's Auto Expanding Fields

Often it is necessary to type more in a field than the field box seems able to contain. Fortunately, Q&A automatically expands field boxes to contain all the data that you type. Whenever the typed data approaches the right edge of the field box, Q&A expands the field in height to allow more typing room.

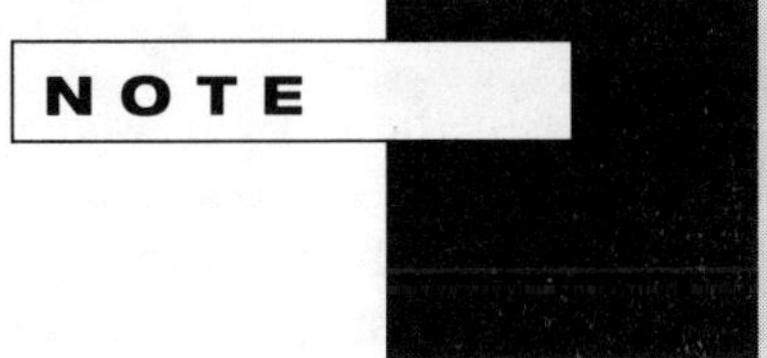

NOTE If you have specified an exact match restriction for a field (as described in Chapter 6), the field does not expand. Instead, your entry scrolls to the right as you type.

Navigating Through Q&A's Records

If you just added more than one record or you retrieved multiple records, you can navigate through them using the record navigation buttons on the tool bar, navigation options in your <u>R</u>ecords menu, or special key combinations (see Table 7.1).

Browsing

When you are in Add/Edit mode, you are can either *edit* your records or *browse* through them. When you initially open a database, all your records are retrieved for you in a browse mode. Being in browse mode is great for moving around your fields and records—especially in Spreadsheet view—but you can't type values into a field. When browsing through fields and records, your programming statements are not executed. This saves you the time of waiting for Q&A to complete computations.

TABLE 7.1: Navigating through Records Using Tool Bar Buttons, Menu Selections, and Key Combinations

YOUR NEED	TOOL BAR BUTTON	MENU ITEM ➤ RECORDS	KEY COMBINATIONS	DOS KEYS
Go to the previous record		Previous Record	Alt+Left Arrow	F9
Go to the next record		Next Record	Alt+Right Arrow	F10
Go to the first record		First Record	Alt+Shift+ Left Arrow	
Go to the last record		Last Record	Alt+Shift Right Arrow	

You can tell whether you are in browse or edit mode by how the active field (or cell) looks. When you are browsing through records in Spreadsheet view, the active cell is completely filled in (when editing, however, the active cell is only highlighted). Also, while browsing in Form view, the field cursor is not visible. It *is* visible, however, when editing.

To change from browse mode to edit mode while in Spreadsheet view, double-click in a cell. If you're in Form view, just click once. To return to browse mode, click once on a different cell of the Spreadsheet view or click on the background (not the field) on the Form view.

N O T E

Pictures in picture fields are not displayed in Spreadsheet view unless that particular cell is active and you are in edit mode.

Navigating Through Q&A's Fields

To navigate through Q&A's fields in both Spreadsheet view and Form view, use the Tab key. Pressing Tab will bring you to the next field in your record's tab order. Pressing Shift+Tab will move your cursor to the previous field. By default, the tab order begins with the first field in the upper-left corner of the record. The order continues in sequence with the next field to the right. When there are no more fields to the right of the cursor, the tab order continues with the left-most field on the line below. The tab order can be altered, as explained in Chapter 4.

You can also navigate through your fields by simply clicking in the field.

Navigating Within a Field

When you are entering data, using navigation routines can save you time and effort. This is especially true if you are entering a lot of data. Table 7.2 gives you a listing of the different navigation routines you can exercise within a field.

Q&A also offers a variety of routines (displayed in Table 7.2) to help you quickly and efficiently select your text.

TABLE 7.2: Navigating and Selecting Items within Your Fields Using These Key Combinations

MOVING YOUR CURSOR POSITION	KEY COMBINATIONS	SELECTING TEXT	KEY COMBINATION
Move to the begining of the line	Home	Select everything to the begining of the line	Shift+Home
Move to the begining of the field	Ctrl+Home	Select everything to the begining of the field	Shift+Ctrl +Home
Move to the end of the line	End	Select everything to the end of the line	Shift+End

TABLE 7.2: Navigating and Selecting Items within Your Fields Using These Key Combinations (continued)

MOVING YOUR CURSOR POSITION	KEY COMBINATIONS	SELECTING TEXT	KEY COMBINATION
Move to the end of the field	Ctrl+End	Select everything to the end of the field	Shift+Ctrl +End
Move one character to the left	Left Arrow	Select one character to the left	Shift+Left Arrow
Move one character to the right	Right Arrow	Select one character to the right	Shift+Right Arrow
Move one word to the left	Ctrl+LeftArrow	Select one word to the left	Shift+Ctrl+Lef tArrow
Move one word to the right	Ctrl+Right Arrow	Select one word to the right	Shift+Ctrl +Right Arrow
Move to the next line above	Up Arrow	Select everything up to the next line	Shift Up Arrow
Move to the line below	Down Arrow	Select everything down to the line below	Shift Down Arrow

Entering Data into Restricted Fields

When you type data in a restricted field (something you learned to do in Chapter 6), you'll notice that if the data does not follow the restrictions, Q&A issues a prompt as you leave the field. Normally, the prompt informs you that your entry has not met the restrictions and asks if you want to continue accepting the value. However, if you have set the restriction to mandatory, Q&A does not allow you to continue.

If a field is set with an exact match restriction, a downward-pointing arrow appears on the right side of the field box when your cursor enters it. Clicking on this arrow displays a list of the restrictions for this field. Click the scroll bars to display the previous or next restriction from which to choose (Figure 7.3).

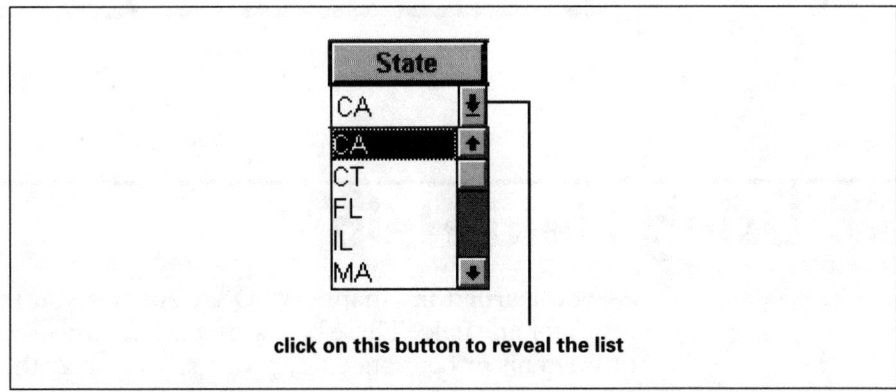

To see a field's restrictions, choose <u>R</u>ecords ➤ Field Restri<u>c</u>tions, which displays the Field Restriction dialog box (Figure 7.4). If the restriction is an exact match restriction, you can select the entry you want for that field. For more information about restrictions and to view the specific restrictions set for the STAFF database, see Chapter 6.

Field restrictions, which are displayed by selecting <u>R</u>ecords ➤ Field Restri<u>c</u>tions

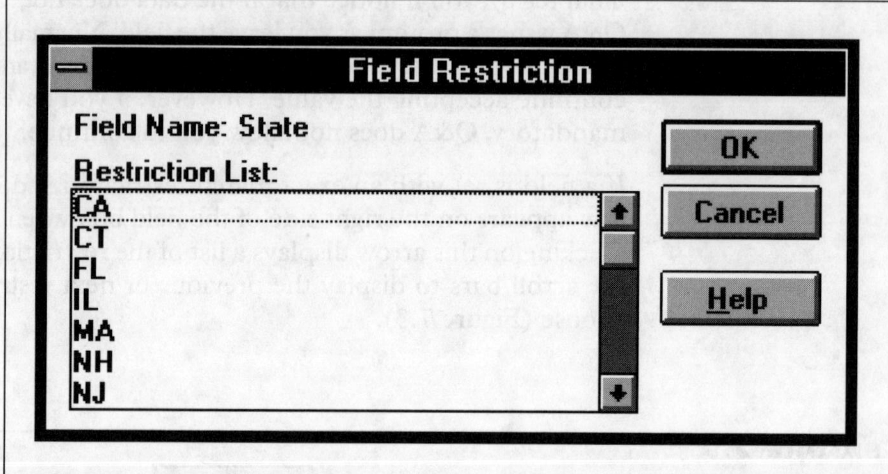

Using Field Help

As you learned in Chapter 6, Q&A enables you to create custom help boxes for any field. These boxes are particularly useful for coaching a user through his or her data entry process. To display the custom help box for a particular field, move the mouse pointer to the desired field and select <u>R</u>ecords ➤ Field <u>H</u>elp.

When a custom help box is displayed for a specific field, you don't need to close the help box to enter data. The custom help box will open as you click on a field to enter data and will stay open until you choose Close.

Therefore, as you move your cursor from one field to another, the help messages for each field are displayed in the help box. If there is no custom help, the box will be empty.

TIP

If the user opens the Field Help dialog box at the beginning of data entry and leaves it open, he or she can create a running instruction guide to coach him or her through a difficult data entry process. For example, when a user gets to a field called SS#, a prompt such as Enter the Social Security number for this employee might appear. Then when the user tabs to the next field, Salary Range, the help box displays Enter the employee's salary for the last year. Of course the easiest way to ensure that the user understands the meaning of a field is to name the field properly (rather than SS#, use Social Security Number).

DOS

In Q&A for DOS, a user needed to set the help screen to enter data in a field while the box remained open. In Q&A for Windows, this is not necessary. When a field help box appears in Q&A for Windows, you can either close it or leave it open.

You can display the custom help box automatically with the @HELP command. For more information, see Appendix D.

Entering Data into a Field Mask

As you learned in Chapter 6, to help data entry, Q&A allows you to create *field masks,* which serve as templates that rearrange the data that you enter in a field (for example, the Phone No. field in STAFF.DTF). When data is typed into a masked field, you can enter only the characters that are not already displayed. For instance, if a field contains a mask that looks like ( )   –   , just type the digits that are needed to complete the phone number (for example, if you type the number 5555555555, Q&A displays it as (555) 555-5555. Masks also limit you to a certain number of characters. For instance, the phone number mask in STAFF.DTF only accepts ten numbers.

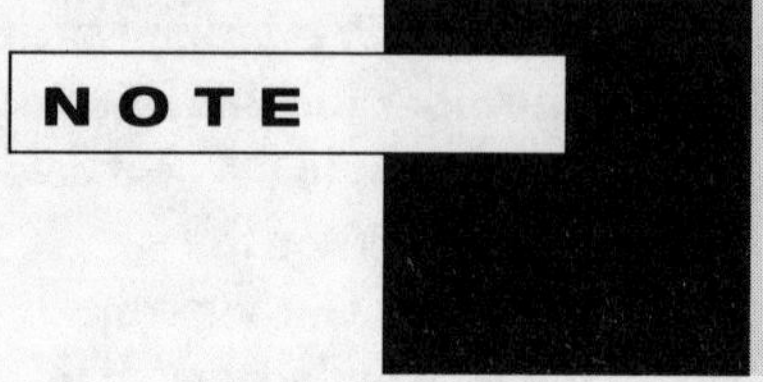

If you wish to enter data without the restrictions and modifications of a field mask, choose Edit ➤ Override Field Mask. This allows you to enter data into the masked field as if it didn't contain a mask.

Copying the Contents of the Prior Field into the Current Field

The Ditto feature enables you to copy the contents of a field from the prior record to the current record in Add mode only. Just choose Edit ➤ Paste Special ➤ Last Record or press Ctrl+Shift+L. Q&A places the contents of the current field from the previous record into the current field in the current record. For instance, if the previous record contains the first name of Mark and the First Name of this record should also contain Mark, add the record. When you choose From Last Record in the First Name field, Q&A copies Mark from the previous record to this record.

To use the Ditto feature, follow these steps:

1. Type information in a record and add the record by pressing Ctrl+N.

2. Start adding a new record and go to the First Name field.

3. Choose <u>E</u>dit ➤ Paste <u>S</u>pecial ➤ <u>L</u>ast Record. Q&A copies the first name from the previous record into the current record.

N O T E   You can automatically ditto information using the @DITTO command. For more information, see Appendix D.

Duplicating the Last Record in the Current Record

While the Ditto feature lets you duplicate the contents of a field, the <u>Rec</u>ords ➤ <u>D</u>uplicate Record duplicates a whole record. When you use this function, Q&A copies the contents of the last active record into the current record. For example, if you are viewing a record and you choose <u>Rec</u>ords ➤ <u>N</u>ew Record, Q&A displays a blank record into which you can enter data. Select <u>Rec</u>ords ➤ <u>D</u>uplicate Record or press Ctrl+D and the data from the record you were viewing is entered into your current record. This is a fast way to create a new record containing almost identical information. For example, you might be entering the names of new freshmen in a college database. Rather than retype the dormitory name and address, duplicate the record and edit the names, room numbers, and telephone numbers.

If, when viewing your last record, you were using an input form with more fields displayed than the input form you are using when you choose <u>Du</u>plicate Record, the contents of all the fields are still placed in the new record, although you are not able to see the data in the current input form. To create a duplicate record, follow these steps:

1. Add a record by filling in more than one field and pressing Ctrl+N.

2. Choose <u>R</u>ecords ➤ <u>D</u>uplicate Record or press Ctrl+D when in any field to create a duplicate record.

Pasting the Current Date and Time

Q&A enables you to paste the current date and time through the Paste Special command. To paste the current date in a field, choose <u>E</u>dit ➤ Paste <u>S</u>pecial ➤ Current <u>D</u>ate or press Ctrl+Shift+D. To paste the current time in a field, choose <u>E</u>dit ➤ Paste <u>S</u>pecial ➤ Current <u>T</u>ime or press Ctrl+Shift+T.

Reverting a Record

When you change a record and realize that you have made a mistake, you can revert to the last saved version of this record by choosing <u>R</u>ecords ➤ Re<u>v</u>ert Record.

To Sum Up

In this chapter, you learned all about entering data into your databases in either Form view or Spreadsheet view. You also learned how entering data in different types of fields with specific attributes affects the way that the data appears. Then you found out about the different ways to navigate through records and fields, and even *within* fields. You also discovered how to duplicate information in fields and records. Lastly, you learned how to use special paste options.

In the next chapter, you will learn about *retrieves*. You'll also find out about using keyword searches and the Options dialog box.

To get the most out of the next chapter, enter a few records in your sample database. Because you will retrieve records that meet certain criteria (for example, all records from one city or one state), vary the values in each record.

chapter

8

Retrieving
Data

LIKE any good filing system, Q&A can search for and update the records already entered into a database. With Q&A, you can easily select the specific records you want to retrieve for viewing, printing, or editing. The Q&A retrieval process is both easy and powerful. If understood and used properly, the retrieve capabilities in Q&A put you in complete control of selecting and editing your records.

The Q&A retrieve process allows you to specify particular records to be viewed or edited or both. For example, let's say that for tax purposes you need to find all employees who have worked for you for more than six years, or those that have a salary from $33,400 to $61,200. With a paper filing system, this task probably requires searching through each record— a lengthy process if you have many employees. However, using Q&A, the retrieve is immediate.

Retrieving Records from a Database

When you want to get a specific set of records to view, print, or edit, you need to run a *retrieve*, which is a set of criteria by which you define the records to be retrieved. When you run a retrieve, Q&A puts you in Add/Edit mode and gets the records you specified, an *answer set*. To retrieve an answer set of records, follow these steps:

1. When in Add/Edit mode, click on the Retrieve button, choose <u>Re</u>cords ➤ <u>R</u>etrieve or press Ctrl+R. If you have checked <u>U</u>se Q&A DOS Key commands as a preference, press F7. This puts you in Retrieve mode.

2. If any retrieve specifications remain from the last retrieve, choose Retrieve ➤ New Retrieval, press Ctrl+N, or press F3.

3. Type the retrieve criteria you want into the fields.

4. To retrieve the records that contain the specified retrieve criteria, choose Retrieve ➤ Run This Retrieve, or press F10.

In the status bar, you can see how many records were retrieved, how many total records, and the number of the current record. For example, Figure 8.1 shows the status bar when the third record of an answer set of six records in a 37-record database is displayed. You can also retrieve all the records in your database (for example, to print them all). To retrieve all your records, leave all the fields blank when you command Q&A to retrieve your records. Another quick way to retrieve all of your records, is to choose Records ➤ Retrieve All when you are in the Add/Edit mode.

FIGURE 8.1

The status bar

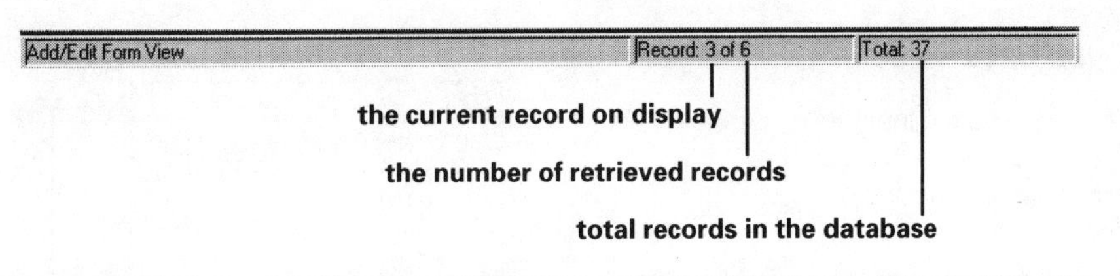

TIP

When retrieving records, normally you view the work area in Form view. However, it is possible to view retrieved records in Spreadsheet view. If you are in Spreadsheet view when you switch to Retrieve view, the records that you retrieve are displayed in Spreadsheet view. Since you can see more than one record at a time in Spreadsheet view, using this view to display your retrieved records is often more efficient than using Form view.

 To cancel a retrieve, click on the cancel retrieve toolbar button, choose Retrieve ➤ Cancel Retrieve, or press Esc. Q&A returns to Add/Edit mode with the same records you originally retrieved. For instance, if you are in the Add/Edit mode with five records retrieved and you click on the Retrieve button, you will go to Retrieve mode. If you exit from Retrieve mode, you return to Add/Edit mode with the original five-record answer set.

Using Different Input Forms with Retrieves

As in Add/Edit mode, you can use any input form in Retrieve mode. Simply select it from the input form drop-down list box (Figure 8.2), choose Select ➤ Load Input Form, or press Ctrl+L. Whether you select an input form in either Retrieve view or Add/Edit mode, that input form remains until you load another.

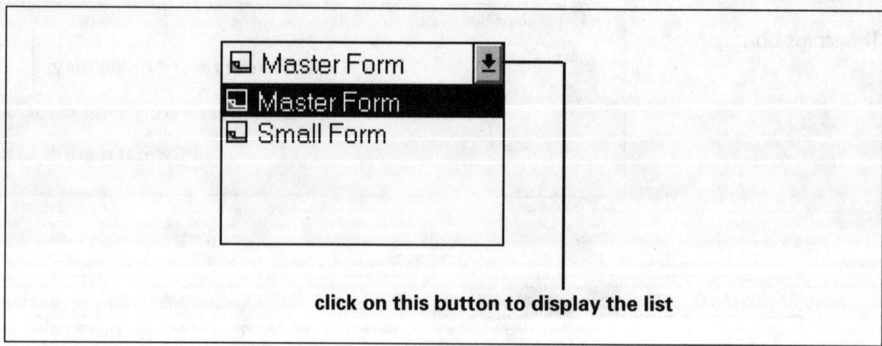

FIGURE 8.2

You can use the input form drop-down list box to load your input form.

About the Retrieve Menu

When you change from Add/Edit mode to Retrieve view, the Records menu becomes the Retrieve menu (Figure 8.3).

Creating a Retrieve Specification

Now that you have a general understanding of retrieves, let's learn how to use them. The criteria you put in fields while in the Retrieve mode make up the retrieve specification, also called a *retrieve spec*. The retrieve spec is essentially the sum of all search criteria that you specified in the

FIGURE 8.3

The Retrieve menu replaces the Records menu when changing to Retrieve view.

fields. Q&A selects the records in your answer set by retrieving all the records that meet your conditions of the retrieve spec. A retrieve spec can contain multiple conditions for one or more fields. For the moment, you'll concentrate on how to create one condition per retrieve spec. However, by the end of this chapter you will know how to specify multiple conditions for multiple fields.

Setting a Condition for a Retrieve

Requesting certain records in Q&A works in the same way that you might request a set of records from a filing cabinet. For instance, you might ask someone to get all Steve's files by asking, "Get all the records where the NAME field contains Steve." This same sentence structure applies to Q&A's retrieve capabilities. The request, "Get all the records where the NAME field is Steve," is simply:

    NAME=Steve

The verbal request is in essence the same as the typed retrieve condition but with all the unnecessary words removed. Since the purpose of the retrieve spec is to get all the records that match its conditions, the phrase "Get all the records where the" is dropped from the retrieve condition because it is understood to always exist. The word NAME is the label of the field, signifying the subject of the condition to follow. The phrase "is Steve" is represented by the =Steve, which is the retrieve condition that must be matched to have a record included in the answer set.

Retrieve specs are not case-sensitive. Therefore, if you are searching for any records with the value Nicole in a field, you can enter the retrieve spec as nicole, Nicole, NICOLE, or any other combination of uppercase and lowercase.

Understanding Field Types in Retrieves

Different field types act differently in retrieves. For example, a text field type cannot perform some retrieve tasks that a keyword field type can perform.

Retrieving Text Fields

Text field types are the most straightforward of the field types. The information you type in a text field for a retrieve is the information that Q&A retrieves.

Retrieving Keyword Fields

Remember that Q&A keyword fields were created to allow you more power in retrieving text values. Keyword fields, as explained in Chapter 3, can contain multiple entries separated by semicolons. Q&A recognizes these separate entries as separate values. Keyword fields, therefore, have different and more powerful retrieve options.

In keyword fields, you can search for a value that is one of multiple values in a field. For instance, if a keyword field contains Barbara;Steve;Rob;Mike, you can retrieve that record by entering the following as your retrieve spec:

    Barbara

The record is retrieved because Barbara is one of the values in the keyword field. You can also retrieve that record by entering:

    Mike;Jack

While Jack is not one of the values in the keyword field, Mike is. The retrieve spec Mike;Jack, when used in a keyword field, translates to retrieve the records in which Jack or Mike is a value in that field.

Retrieving Yes/No Fields

Yes/No fields only retrieve two kinds of values: affirmative values and negative values. All affirmative values in a retrieve spec are viewed in the same way. For example, if you use the condition Y or any other affirmative value as your retrieve spec, Q&A retrieves records that have the values Yes, Y, True, T, or 1 in that field. The Y retrieve spec translates to retrieve the records where the value in the field is affirmative. The negative values in Yes/No fields work in the same way.

Retrieving Number Fields

Defining retrieve specs for number fields is also straightforward. Just type a number into a number field and Q&A retrieves only the record that contains that value. Unlike retrieving text in a masked field, Q&A allows you to optionally enter commas and decimal points in retrieve specs for number fields. For example, to retrieve the records with the value of 17,000.00, type either of these retrieve specs:

    17,000.00
    17000

Retrieving Money Fields

Money fields function in Retrieve view like number fields. The information that you specify in the retrieve spec is the information that Q&A retrieves. When using money fields, you have the option to use commas, decimal points, and currency symbols in the retrieve spec. For example, to retrieve records with the value of $17,000.00, enter either of these retrieve specs:

    $17,000.00
    17000

Retrieving Date Fields

When entering dates into a retrieve spec, you can use any acceptable date format. For example, the following retrieve specs will retrieve records with the date of January 1, 1995:

01/01/95
January 1, 1995

Retrieving Time Fields

If you are entering a retrieve condition into a time field, you can enter time in either military or standard format. The following retrieve specs retrieve records with the value of 5:00 p.m.:

17:00
5:00 p.m.

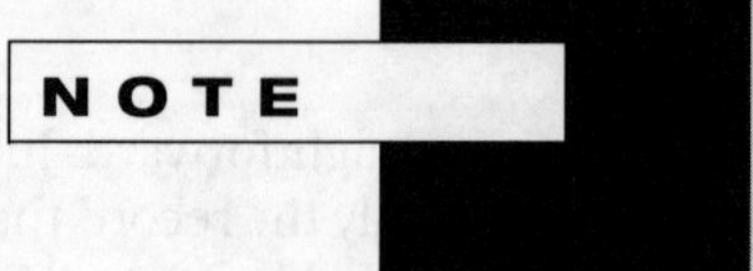

You cannot retrieve the contents of picture fields. In fact, you cannot move the cursor to a picture field when in Retrieve view.

Retrieving Exact Matches

Exact match retrieves, which are the simplest and most commonly used type of retrieve spec, retrieve records that exactly match the conditions entered in the retrieve spec. An example of an exact match retrieve is the condition =Barbara. Since exact match retrieves are so common, Q&A gives you the opportunity to shorten the retrieve condition by not requiring you to type in the equal sign. For instance, the exact match retrieve condition =Barbara can be entered as Barbara.

Table 8.1 lists exact match retrieves for different types of fields.

TABLE 8.1: Exact Match Retrieves for Different Field Types

OPERATION	ACTION
Exact Match Retrieves (Except Picture Fields)	
Blank	All records
=X	Equal to X
X	Equal to X
/X	Not equal to X

TABLE 8.1: Exact Match Retrieves for Different Field Types (continued)

OPERATION	ACTION
=	Empty
/=	Not empty
X;Y;Z	X or Y or Z
Range Retrieves (Except Pictures Fields)	
>X	Greater than X
<X	Less than X
>=X	Greater than or equal to X
<=X	Less than or equal to X
Character Retrieves (Text and Keyword Only)	
..	Any group of characters
X..	Begins with X
..X	Ends with X
..X..	Contains X
X..Y	Begins with X and ends with Y
X..Y..Z	Begins with X, contains Y and ends with Z
..X..Y..Z..	Contains X, Y, and Z in that order
?	Any single character
??	Any two characters
\	Finds the literal character following (i.e. \? finds a question mark)
Special Use Retrieves (Except Picture Fields)	
..	Values of the correct field type
Values of the incorrect field type	]
Highest n values	MAXn

TABLE 8.1: Exact Match Retrieves for Different Field Types (continued)

OPERATION	ACTION
Lowest n values	MINn
Sounds Like Retrieves (Text and Keyword Only)	
~X	Sounds Like X

Retrieving Ranges of Information

Range retrieves allow you to retrieve records that contain values that fall within a range specified in the retrieve spec. For instance, you can retrieve records of employees who earn between $25,000 and $33,000.

Range retrieves let you use the greater than, less than, greater than or equal to, and less than or equal to operators (>,<,>=,<=).

Table 8.2 lists operators for specifying range retrieves.

TABLE 8.2: Range Retrieve Operators

OPERATION	ACTION
$>X$	Retrieves the records with fields containing values that are greater than X
$<X$	Retrieves the records with fields containing values that are less than X
$>=X$	Retrieves the records with fields containing values that are greater than or equal to X
$<=X$	Retrieves the records with fields containing values that are less than or equal to X

When retrieving ranges of text values, Q&A retrieves text as it is placed alphabetically in the range. For instance, the record that contains the name Steve is included in the retrieved records if the retrieve spec is created to search for all the names that are greater than M. This is because Steve comes after M in alphabetical order. Values beginning with M (such as Michael, Mitch, and Michelle) are also included.

In range retrieves, you use upper and lower bounds to control the contents of the answer set to be retrieved. For instance, if you want to retrieve all the records with values from $10,000 to $30,000, $10,000 is your lower boundary, the lowest value that your range allows, and $30,000 is your upper boundary, the highest that your range allows.

When defining a range with upper and lower boundaries, type the lower boundary, followed by two periods, and then the upper boundary. The following example retrieves any numbers between 50 and 100.

    >50..<100

Q&A also allows you to use the greater than or equal to and less than or equal to operators (>=, <=). Using the retrieve spec below, Q&A retrieves the values that are greater than or equal to 50 and less than or equal to 100.

    >=50..<=100

Table 8.3 lists examples of range retrieve specifications as they are used for different field types.

TABLE 8.3: Examples of Range Retrieves for Different Field Types

FIELD TYPE	RETRIEVE	ACTION
Text	>=B..<C	Retrieves the records in which the field contains values greater than or equal to the letter B and less than the letter C.
Keyword	>Tea	Retrieves the records in which any of the field's values are greater than the value Tea.

TABLE 8.3: Examples of Range Retrieves for Different Field Types (continued)

FIELD TYPE	RETRIEVE	ACTION
Y/N	>N	Retrieves the records in which the value is greater than negative, which is all the affirmative values (Yes, Y, True, T, 1). All the negative values are less than the affirmative values.
Number	<100	Retrieves the records in which the field contains a value less than 100
Money	>170..<=200	Retrieves the records in which the field contains money values greater than 170 and less than or equal to 200
Date	>01/01/95..<2/17/96	Retrieves the records in which the field contains a date later than January 1, 1995, and earlier than February 17, 1996.
Time	>5:15 pm	Retrieves the records in which the field contains a time after 5:15 pm until midnight. Since time is only a 24-hour cycle, time retrieves are limited to the hours 12:00 am to 11:59 pm.

Retrieving Information Based on Characters

Someday you might want to retrieve some important information from a database, but you only remember the first few letters of the contents of the field that you want to find. Fortunately, Q&A's character retrieve abilities give you the power to find such records. Character retrieves allow you to find records that contain a string of characters or even a specific character. You can only use character retrieves for text and keyword fields.

Variable Length Character Retrieves

To use variable length character retrieves, replace the characters that you do not know or that you want Q&A to ignore with two dots (..). The dots act as a *wildcard*, which allows any number of characters to reside in that position. For example, to retrieve records for all employees whose last names begin with the letter S, type:

    S..

You can also use the same type of logic to retrieve records that end with a certain string. For example, to retrieve all records for employees with last names ending with *son*, type:

    ..son

You can also search for a string located anywhere in a field. For example, to find records with the word *deductible* anywhere in the selected field, type:

    ..deductible..

You can also search for a pattern or order of text in a field. For example, to find the records in which the field contains a value that begins with the letter *s*, contains the letter *e*, and ends with the letter *r*, type the following retrieve spec:

    s..e..r

This will retrieve values such as Swertfager.

Fixed Length Character Retrieves

When you need to use a character retrieve, you can use the question mark wildcard character to restrict the retrieved information to a certain number of characters. For instance, to retrieve the five-digit zip codes that begin with 95, type:

    95???

The three question marks restrict the retrieve to records that have zip codes beginning with 95 followed by any three characters. If the zip code has fewer than or more than five characters, the record is not retrieved.

Literal Character Retrieves

The use of the question mark, two dots, and the tilde (~), which is explained later in this chapter, as retrieve operations seems to remove them from the characters for which you can search. Fortunately, Q&A allows you to use a literal character symbol. This symbol indicates that the character that follows it is a character for which Q&A will search. For instance, to find the records with only a question mark (?) in the selected field, type:

    \?

You can use this literal character with the other character retrieve operators. For instance, the following retrieve spec retrieves all the records that have a question mark anywhere in the field:

    ..\?..

Special Use Retrieves

Q&A also gives you a variety of special retrieve operations that do not fall under the preceding categories.

Sounds Similar Retrieves

Text and keyword fields also have a special retrieve operator that retrieves values that sound like your retrieve spec. Just type a tilde (~) in front of what you think the value sounds like. For instance, if you want to retrieve all records with fields that contain names that sound like Swerts (for example, Schwartz or Swarts), type the following in the retrieve spec:

    ~Swerts

Maximum and Minimum Retrieves

To find the records having the largest or the smallest values in a certain field, use the Max or Min functions. To retrieve the largest (or smallest) values in a field, type Max (or Min) followed by the number of records you want to find. For instance, to find the records with the three largest salaries, type this retrieve spec:

    Max3

Another example is the search for the first ten people, alphabetically, in a database. For such a request, type this retrieve spec:

    Min10

If you only want to retrieve one record when using the Min and Max retrieves, you don't have to type the number 1. For example, to retrieve the largest value in a field, all you have to do is type the following: Max. In a date field, Min retrieves the earliest date; Max retrieves the latest date.

Correct Field Type Retrieves

It is possible to have data in a field that is not of the correct field type. For instance, a date field may contain a nondate entry, like Not Available or Not Applicable. In these cases, Q&A allows you to retrieve every record that contains appropriate data for all but picture fields. To retrieve all records that have data that matches its field type, type the following retrieve spec in the selected field:

The two main reasons for having data in your fields that are not of the correct format are: (1) If you import data into your database from an external file, Q&A doesn't prompt you if the data does not match the field type. Instead Q&A enters the data as it is. This relieves you of the time and hassle of clicking through the thousands of possible prompts that you might get when importing large amounts of data. (2) There are times when someone deliberately enters information that doesn't match its field type. For example, if you decide to include subcontractors in the employee database so that mailings go to both types of people, you might type None in the Hire Date field.

In Q&A for Windows, this type of retrieve is referred to as a Correctly Formatted retrieve. However, in Q&A for DOS, field type settings are controlled from the Format Spec screen. To clarify, in this book, this type of retrieve is known as a Correct Field Type retrieve.

Nonstandard Value Retrieves

You can also search for data that is not the correct field type. Just type the data preceded by a right bracket (]). For example, to search for the word none in a time field, type the following retrieve spec:

    ]none

The right bracket instructs Q&A to search through the records as if the particular field is a text field.

You can use the nonstandard retrieve feature to search for records that contain a date entry of a particular month or day. For example, to find all records with a January date, type the following retrieve spec:]19??/01/??. This retrieve spec will produce a subset containing records with dates like 01/05/95, 01/28/93, and 01/01/99.

Q&A reads dates and times that are preceded by the] character in Q&A's internal format. Q&A's internal format of a date is YYYY/MM/DD (for example, 1995/01/28). Q&A's internal format of a time is HH:MM in a military format (for example, 23:05).

Not Value Retrieves

So far in this chapter you have identified retrieve information by specifying what you want. Sometimes it is easier to retrieve records by specifying the records you *don't* want. For example, you may want to retrieve all the records except the ones with the dates 01/01/94 and 10/25/95. You can tell Q&A to retrieve all the records except the ones preceded by the not symbol, a slash (/). For instance, to retrieve all the records except for the ones that contain Bob, type:

    /Bob

The not symbol works for all field types except picture fields.

Entering More Than One Condition in a Retrieve Spec

Up to this point, you have just entered one retrieve spec at a time. In real life, you will probably need to retrieve a subset of records based on retrieve conditions in more than one field. For instance, you can retrieve all the records that have a value less than $30,000 in the salary field and a value less than .05 in the commission field. Q&A allows you to do this by typing the two different retrieve conditions in their appropriate fields; type <30000 in the salary field and <.05 in the commission field.

Using the Retrieve Options

Q&A gives you even more power to control your retrieves through the Options dialog box, as seen in Figure 8.4.

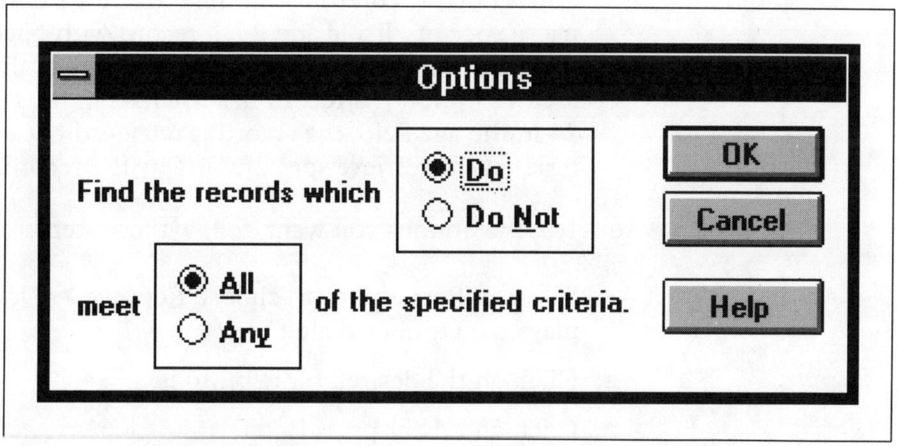

FIGURE 8.4

You can use the Options dialog box to retrieve records based on whether or not certain criteria are met.

The Options dialog box controls how Q&A uses your retrieve specs. In the Options dialog box, you see a sentence that is completed through either of two sets of two radio buttons. You can make four different choices in the Options dialog box:

- You can find the records that *Do* meet *All* the specified criteria. This means that for a record to be retrieved, it must meet the criteria of all the conditions specified in the retrieve spec. For example, if you typed Nicole in the first name field and 23 in the age field of the retrieve spec, a record with Nicole and 19 is not retrieved because not all the criteria are met.

- You can find the records that *Do* meet *Any* of the specified criteria. This means that for a record to be retrieved, it must meet the criteria of any of the conditions that you specified in the retrieve spec. For example, the record with Nicole and 23 and the record with Nicole and 19 are both retrieved because at least one of the criteria is met.

- You can find the records that *Do Not* meet *All* the specified criteria. This means that for a record to be retrieved, it must not meet the criteria of at least one of the conditions on the retrieve spec. Again using our example, a record with the first name field as Nicole and the age field as 19 is retrieved because at least one of the criteria on the retrieve spec is not met.

- Find the records that *Do Not* meet *Any* of the specified criteria. This means that for a record to be retrieved, it cannot meet the criteria of any condition on the retrieve spec. Based on the retrieve spec of Nicole and 23, a record with Nicole and 19 is not retrieved because at least one of the criteria in the retrieve spec is met. However, if a record has Michael in the first name field and 24 in the age field, the record is retrieved because none of the criteria on the retrieve spec are met by the record.

To select the options you want, follow these steps:

1. While in Retrieval view, choose Retrieve ➤ Options. Q&A displays the Options dialog box.

2. Click on the desired radio buttons.

3. Click on OK or press Enter.

Retrieving Based on Multiple Field Conditions

Q&A allows you to enter multiple retrieve conditions in a field. All you need to do is separate each condition with a semicolon. There are two types of multiple criteria retrieves: multiple Or conditions and multiple And conditions.

Multiple Or Conditions in a Field

With multiple Or conditions, Q&A retrieves the records that contain any of the values in the condition. For example, to retrieve any records with the zip codes 95070, 95112, or 95128, type each zip code, separating each with a semicolon. To retrieve the records that contain these three zip codes, type the following retrieve spec:

    95070;95112;95128

Multiple And Conditions in a Field

Using the ampersand symbol (&) preceding multiple conditions in a field makes it necessary for all the conditions to exist in the field for the record to be retrieved. For example, to retrieve all zip codes that begin with the numbers 95 *except* 95070, use the following retrieve spec:

    &95..;/95070

Using the Not Symbol with Multiple Conditions in a Field

When using the not symbol with multiple Or conditions in a field, every subsequent criteria following a condition using the not symbol is also considered negative. For example, the retrieve spec:

    95070;95112;95128

translates to retrieve the records in which the zip code field is not equal to 95070, 95112, or 95128.

However, if you use the not symbol with multiple And conditions in a field, only the conditions preceded by the not symbol are considered negative. For example, the retrieve spec:

    &/95070;9..

retrieves the records in which the zip code field is not equal to 95070 and the value begins with the number 9.

NOTE

For even more ways to retrieve records, Q&A allows you to make retrieve specs using programming functions. To learn how to create a retrieve spec with programming statements, see Chapter 12.

Creating Retrieves with the Retrieve Helper

The Retrieve Helper is a second way of entering criteria into a retrieve spec. The Retrieve Helper does not offer any more functions beyond those offered when you enter criteria directly in a retrieve spec. However, you may decide that the Retrieve Helper is an easier way to create retrieve specs, which contain combinations of field names and function types. To use the Retrieve Helper to create a retrieve spec using a combination of field names and function types, follow these steps:

1. Move the cursor to the field in which you want to enter the retrieve spec.

2. Choose Retrieve ➤ Helper or press Ctrl+H. Q&A displays the Helper dialog box (Figure 8.5).

3. If the Formula list box contains a value from another retrieve spec, delete the value.

4. To add a field name into the formula, click the Field Names radio button. Q&A displays a list of field names in the list box in the Elements group. Then double-click on a field name to insert it into the formula.

5. To insert a symbol or function into the formula, click on the Function Type radio button. Q&A displays a list of symbols and functions in the list in the Elements group. Then double-click on a function or symbol to insert it into the formula.

6. Repeat steps 2 and 3 in the order in which you wish to insert field names and symbols or functions until the formula is complete.

The Helper dialog box lets you build a formula one step at a time.

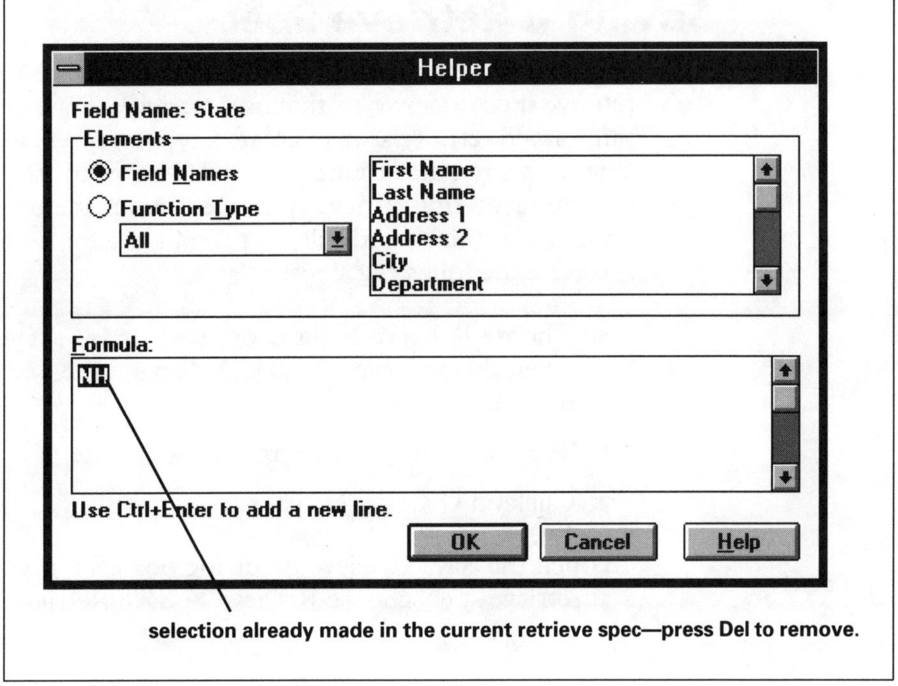

7. Click on OK or press Enter.

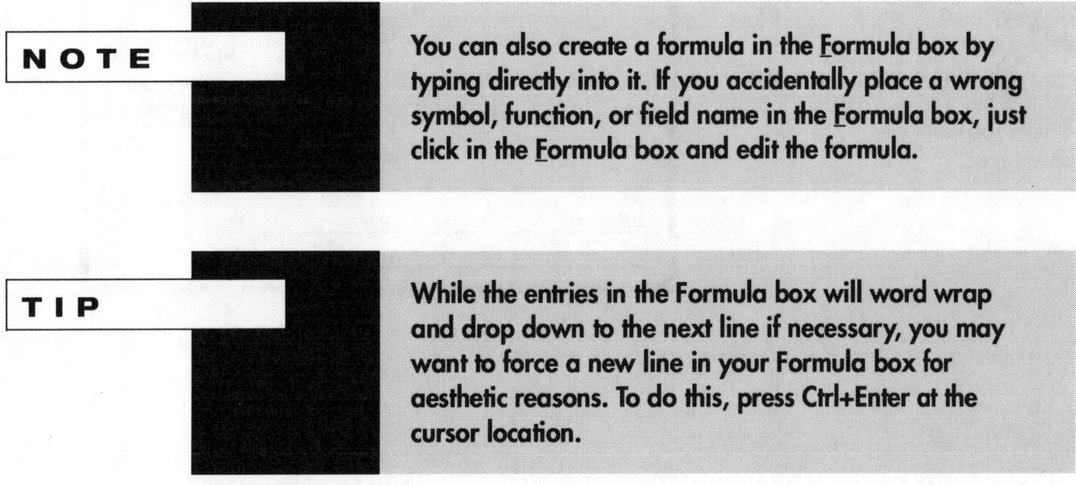

You can also create a formula in the Formula box by typing directly into it. If you accidentally place a wrong symbol, function, or field name in the Formula box, just click in the Formula box and edit the formula.

While the entries in the Formula box will word wrap and drop down to the next line if necessary, you may want to force a new line in your Formula box for aesthetic reasons. To do this, press Ctrl+Enter at the cursor location.

Saving a Retrieve Spec

Q&A lets you save your retrieve specs for later use. You can use these saved retrieve specs in any view that uses retrieves. For example, you can use the same saved retrieve spec to create a report, a mail merge, to print mailing labels, or any other routine that allows you to use retrieves. If you have already saved this retrieve spec, Q&A saves the updated retrieve criteria under its last name and will not prompt you for a name. To save a retrieve spec, use the following steps:

1. Choose Retrieve ➤ Save. or press Crtl+S. If you have not yet saved this retrieve spec, Q&A displays the Save Retrieve As dialog box (see Figure 8.6).

2. Type the name of the retrieve spec in the Save As text box.

3. Click on OK or press Enter.

To open the Save Retrieve As dialog box even if you have already saved that retrieve spec, choose Retrieve ➤ Save Retrieve As.

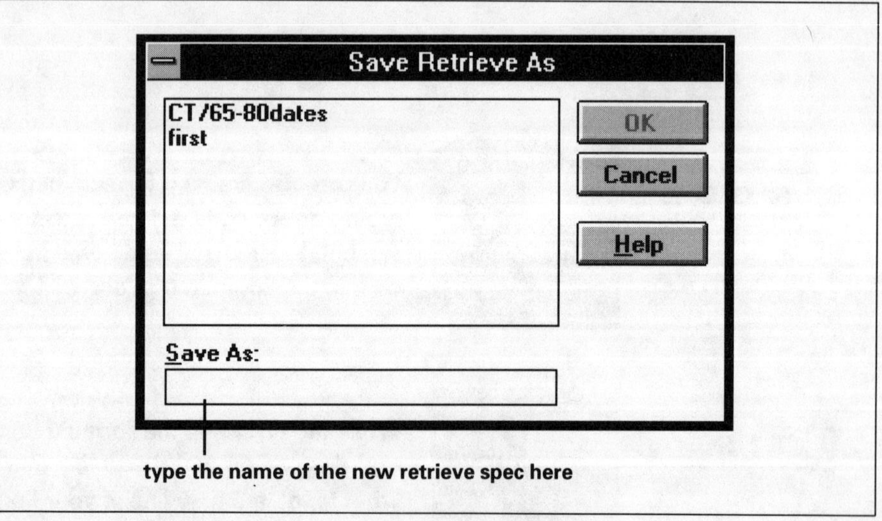

The Save Retrieve As dialog box displays all the currently saved retrieve specs in the large box. If you save your retrieve with an already existing name, Q&A prompts you with a dialog box that allows you to replace the already saved retrieve spec with the new one.

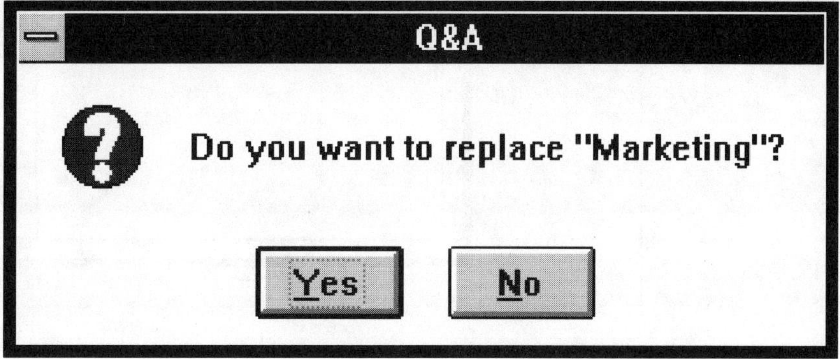

Loading a Retrieve Spec

You can load any saved retrieve spec even if the retrieve spec was created for use in another view. For example, if you created and saved a retrieve spec when designing a columnar report, you can still use that same spec when retrieving information for Add/Edit mode. To load a retrieve spec, use these steps:

1. Choose <u>R</u>etrieve ➤ <u>L</u>oad Retrieve, or select the saved retrieve spec from the drop-down list box.

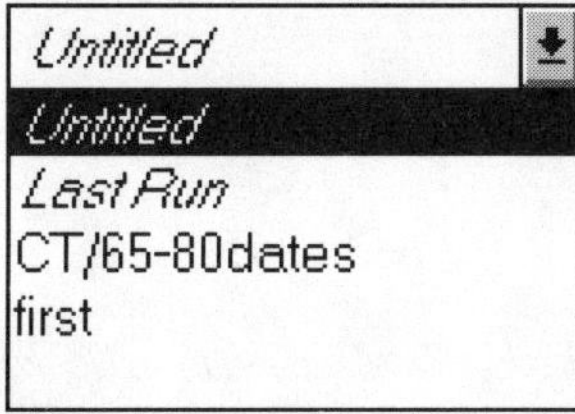

2. In the Load Retrieve dialog box (Figure 8.7), choose the desired retrieve spec.

3. Click on OK or press Enter.

The Load Retrieve dialog box. Select any of the listed retrieve specs.

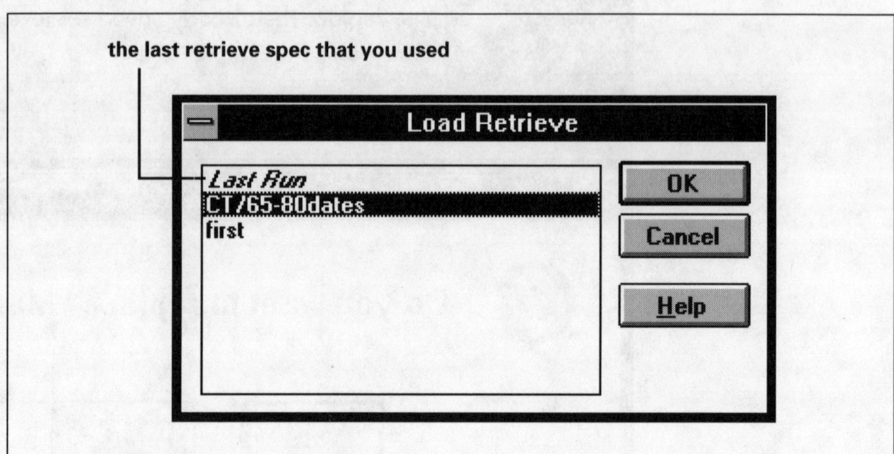

The Last Run option on the list of saved retrieve specs loads the last retrieve spec used.

Deleting a Retrieve Spec

To delete a saved retrieve spec, use these steps:

1. Load the retrieve spec you want to delete.

2. Choose Retrieve ➤ Delete Retrieve. This displays an information box.

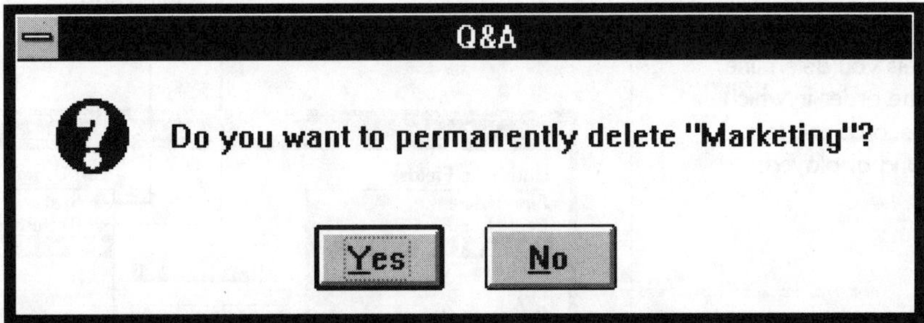

3. Click on <u>Y</u>es to delete the selected retrieve spec. Click on <u>N</u>o to close the information box without deleting the spec.

Sorting Records

Now that you know all about retrieving records, you will learn how to display records in a sorted order. For example, when retrieving records, Q&A can arrange the records in various orders depending on the field type. Text, keyword, and Yes/No fields are sorted in alphabetical order; number and money fields are sorted in numeric order; and dates and times are sorted in chronological order. You cannot sort picture fields. All the sorting capabilities are controlled from within the Sort dialog box (Figure 8.8). To display the Sort dialog box in Add/Edit mode, choose <u>R</u>ecords ➤ Sor<u>t</u> or press Ctrl+T.

Creating a Sort Specification

A Sort spec instructs Q&A how to arrange records when they are retrieved. You can make a sort spec simple, complex or anything in between. A simple sort spec sorts your records by one field. In the case of a simple sort spec, Q&A just reorders the records based on that field. However, a complex sort spec, which sorts your records based on more than one field, first sorts your records by the first sort field and then by the secondary sort, third sort, and so on. If some of the sorted records in the first sort have identical values, Q&A reorders those records by the secondary sort, and so on. For an example, let's take a hypothetical database with two fields: First Name and Last Name, and three records: John Williams,

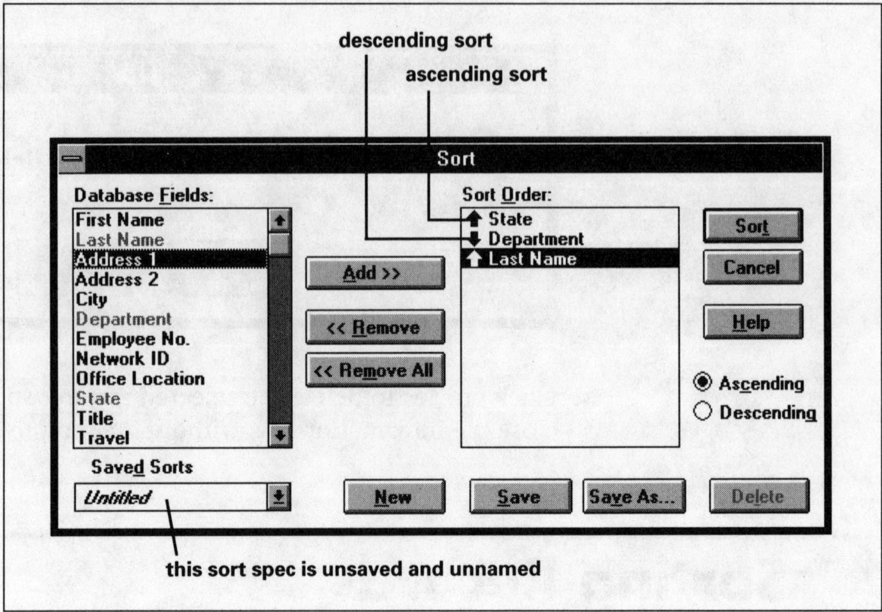

Chris Peaks, and John Steinbach. For this database, all records will be retrieved and sorted using an ascending sort first in the First Name field and then in the Last Name field. Q&A first sorts the fields by first name, producing the answer set of Chris Peaks, John Williams, and John Steinbach. Q&A then sorts those records in which the first name field is the same for more than one record (that is, the John Williams and John Steinbach records). Finally, Q&A sorts these records by last name producing the sorted answer set Chris Peaks, John Steinbach, and John Williams.

When you run a sort, it doesn't matter whether the current input form shows all fields in the database. Even if your input form shows very few records, Q&A makes all fields available to you during a sort.

While Q&A allows you to use ascending sorts (abcdefg... and 1234567...), you can also select a descending sort (zyxwvut... and 987654...).

To create a sort spec, follow these steps:

1. Choose Retrieve ➤ Sort or press Ctrl+T. Q&A opens the Sort dialog box.

2. In the Database Fields box, click on the field by which you want to sort and click on Add. Q&A places the selected field in the Sort Order box.

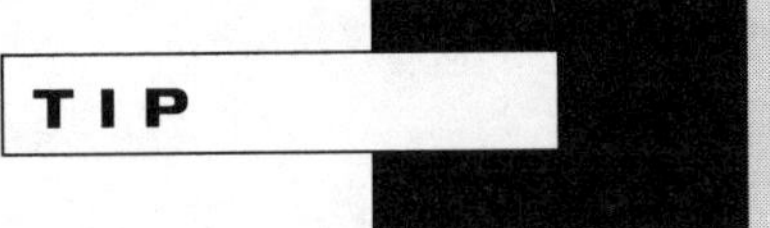

A quick way to add a field to the Sort Order list is to double-click on it in the Database Fields box.

3. To run a descending sort, while a field is highlighted in the Sort Order box, click on the Descending radio button. Otherwise Q&A defaults to an ascending sort.

4. Repeat steps 2 and 3 until you have finished creating the sort spec.

5. Click on OK or press Enter to accept your sort spec and return to the retrieve spec.

The up arrows and down arrows preceding the field names in the Sort Order box indicate whether those field sorts are ascending or descending sorts, respectively.

If you place the wrong field in the Sort Order box, you can remove it by highlighting that field and clicking on the Remove button. To delete all the fields in the Sort Order dialog box and start over, click on the Remove All button.

Running a sort spec often takes longer than most processes in Q&A. Therefore, when you execute a routine with a sort spec attached, Q&A displays a dialog box showing the progress of the procedure.

NOTE

The length of time it takes Q&A to sort a database depends on the number of fields sorted, the number of indexed fields being sorted (indexed fields are explained in Chapter 9), and whether you are running a retrieve at the same time.

Saving a Sort Spec

You can save the sort specs that you create for later use. In just the same way as saved retrieve specs, you can use saved sort specs in all views that use sorts. If you have already saved and named this sort spec, just click on the Save button; Q&A saves the updated sort criteria under its original name. To save and name a sort spec, in the Sort dialog box, follow these steps:

1. Click on the Save button. Q&A displays the Save Sort As dialog box (Figure 8.9).

2. Type the name of the sort spec in the Save As: box and click on OK or press Enter.

FIGURE 8.9

The Save Sort As dialog box, which looks just like the Save Retrieve As dialog box.

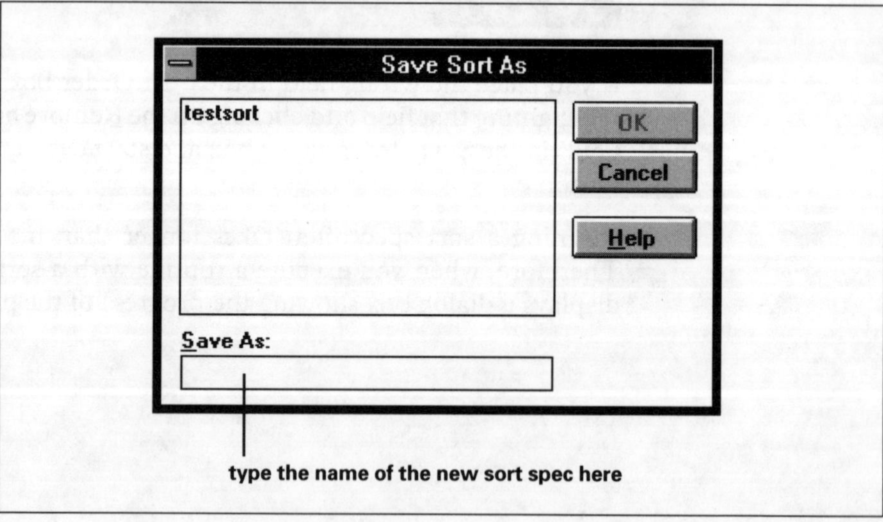

To open the Sort As dialog box even if you have already saved that sort spec, in the Sort dialog box, click on the Sa<u>v</u>e As button instead of the <u>S</u>ave button.

N O T E

The Save Sort As dialog box displays the names of all the currently saved sort specs. If you try to save your sort spec using an already existing name, Q&A prompts you to replace the already saved sort spec. This prompt is similar to the prompt you get when replacing a saved retrieve spec.

Using a Saved Sort Spec

You can use any saved sort spec even if it was created for use in an another view. To use a saved sort spec, select it from the Save<u>d</u> Sorts pull-down menu (Figure 8.10). The Last Run option in the Save<u>d</u> Sorts pull-down menu loads the last sort spec used.

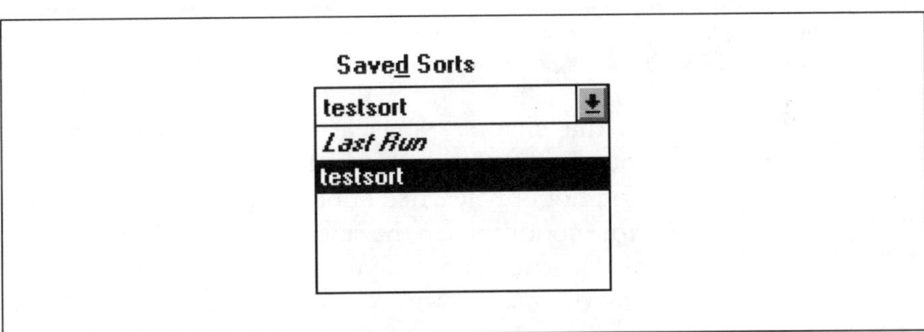

Deleting a Sort Spec

To delete a saved sort spec, use these steps:

1. Click on the saved sort spec to be deleted from the Save<u>d</u> Sorts pull-down menu. All of the sorted fields appear in the Sort Order box.

2. Click on the De<u>l</u>ete button. Q&A asks you to confirm the deletion.

3. To delete the sort spec, click on <u>Y</u>es; to escape the deletion process, click on <u>N</u>o.

NOTE

When a Q&A database is created, Q&A reserves a block of your disk space to save the records that are to be created. When you add a record, Q&A saves it within the nearest 64-byte block of free space. This process of saving records increases Q&A's speed. However, saving the records in this way prevents Q&A from saving them in a sorted order. When you retrieve records with a sort, they are sorted temporarily only for your immediate viewing and use. However, the next time you retrieve records, they will be unsorted unless you run another sort spec. To save records in a sorted order, copy both the database design and selected records using the procedures described in Chapter 5.

To Sum Up

In this chapter, you learned all about retrieves and retrieve specs. You found out about exact match, range, character, and special retrieves. You not only learned about single conditions but also how to create multiple conditions in the retrieve spec and multiple conditions per field. You also learned about keyword field retrieves and the retrieve helper. Finally, you discovered how to save, load, and delete retrieve specs.

The second topic explained in this chapter was Q&A's sorting capabilities. You found out how to create, save, load and delete sort specs.

In the next chapter, you will discover the power of Q&A's report capabilities for columnar, freeform, and table reports.

chapter

9

Reporting with Q&A

To add fields to a Freeform report   **283**

use the Add Field tool in the tool palette to draw a field box. Select the field to be added. If you want to add a derived column or summary field, click the appropriate button and choose its settings. Click on OK.

To add parts to a Freeform report   **284**

choose Format ➤ Define Parts. Click on New. Click on the part to be added. If you are creating a summary part, select the appropriate fields and settings to create the break. Click on OK.

To create a Label report   **295**

If you are in Add/Edit mode, choose Select ➤ Design Reports/Labels, press Ctrl+Y, or press the Report button on the tool bar. Select the New Label radio button and click on OK. If you are in a report mode, choose Reports ➤ New ➤ Label. In the New Label dialog box, select the desired fields, select the Label Type, and click on OK.

To assign an object to slide   **298**

select the objects you want to slide. Choose Arrange ➤ Slide Objects. To slide the objects to the left, check the Slide Left check box. To slide the objects up, check the Slide Up to Fill check box. Choose either the All Above radio button or the Directly Above radio button. Click on OK.

NOW that you understand how to enter, retrieve, and sort your data, you'll find out how to display that information in *reports* for viewing and analyzing. Q&A's report features give you the power to perform calculations that you are not able to do in Add/Edit mode.

With reports, you can gather data from your database fields and print it in an organized format. In addition, you can add graphics and special summary calculations, thus allowing you to produce an impressive and informative report.

In this chapter, you'll learn almost everything there is to know about Q&A reports. You'll see how to attach a retrieve spec to a report and how to save, load, delete, and print any type of report.

Q&A Reports

In Q&A, there are three types of reports: Columnar, Freeform, and Label.

- The **Columnar report** (Figure 9.1) allows you to easily build columns of information from your database. The columns are made up of the fields that you choose to display in the report. The rows are different records in the database. As in Spreadsheet view, this format provides an easy-to-understand presentation of your data.

- The **Freeform report** (Figure 9.2) enables you to place your fields in any location on the screen or page. This is particularly useful for reports that need to match a certain format.

- The **Label report** (Figure 9.3) lets you arrange the information from your database and print it on mailing labels.

The Columnar report displays your fields in columns and your records in rows.

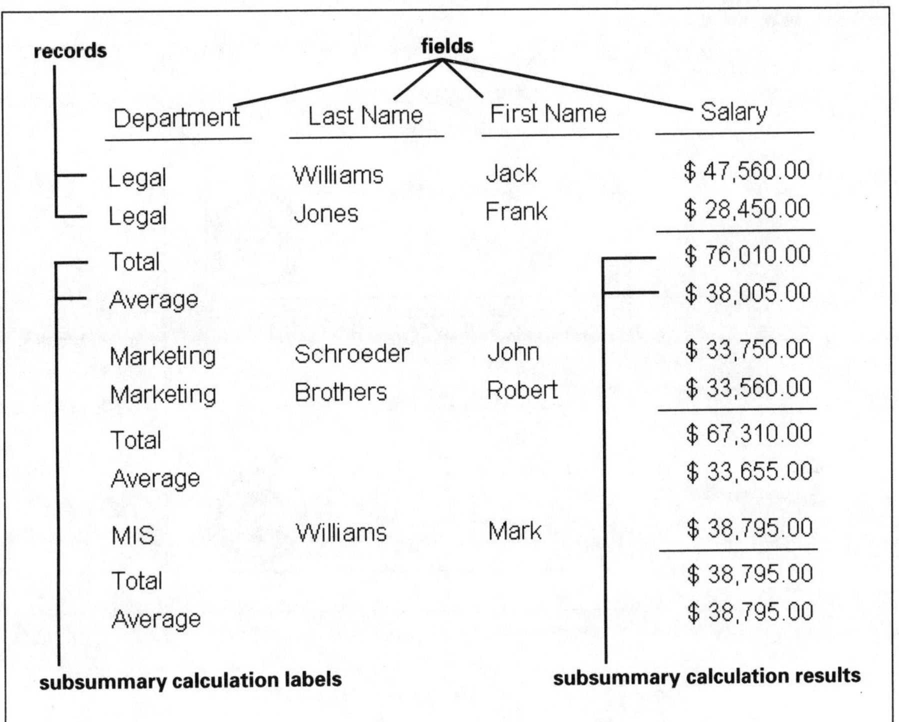

The Freeform report

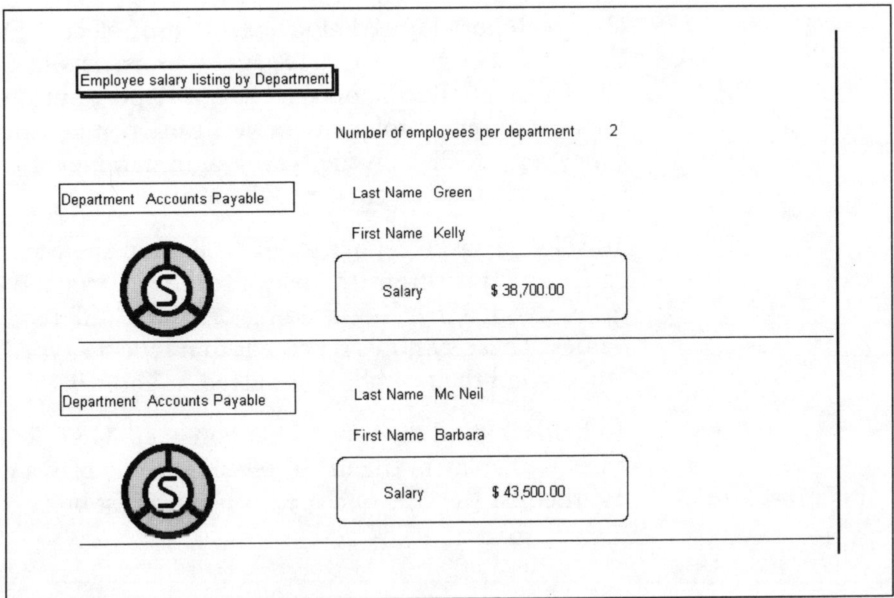

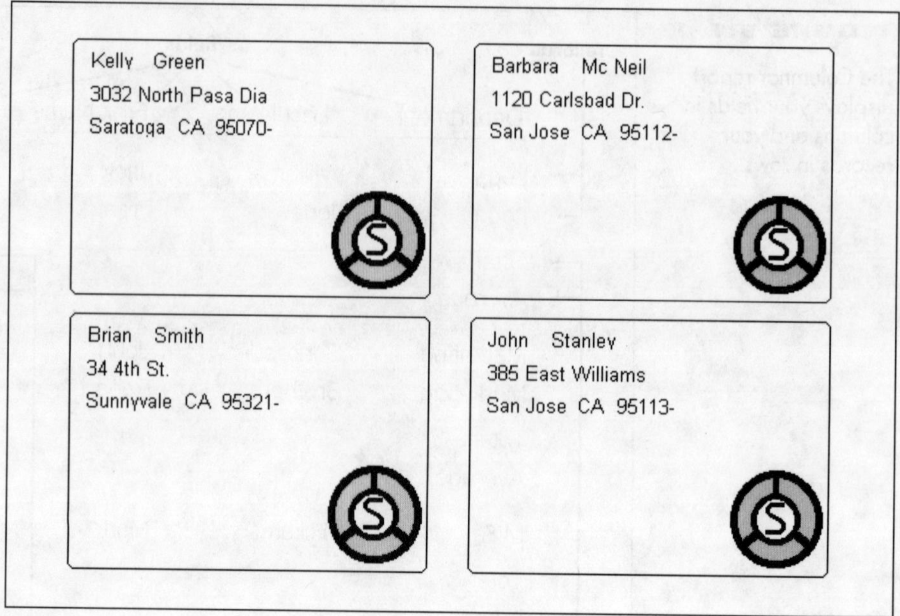

Designing a Report

Before you can create a report (in any mode other than report mode), you must use the Design Report/Label dialog box (Figure 9.4). To open the Design Report/Label dialog box, choose Select ➤ Design Reports/Labels. You can also get to the Design Report/Label dialog box by pressing Ctrl+Y or by clicking on the Design Report button. Then you can select the type of report to create or you can open an existing report. To create a new report, click on the New Columnar, New Freeform, or New Label radio button. Then click on OK or press Enter.

To select a saved report to edit, click on the Saved radio button. Then choose a report from the list of saved reports and click on OK or press Enter. Notice that the saved reports have different symbols next to their names. These symbols represent that report's type. The different types of reports and their symbols are listed in Table 9.1.

To help you find the report that you need, Q&A lets you select the report types to display in the list of reports. To display a certain type of report, use the List Reports of Type drop-down list box.

FIGURE 9.4

The Design
Report/Label dialog
box

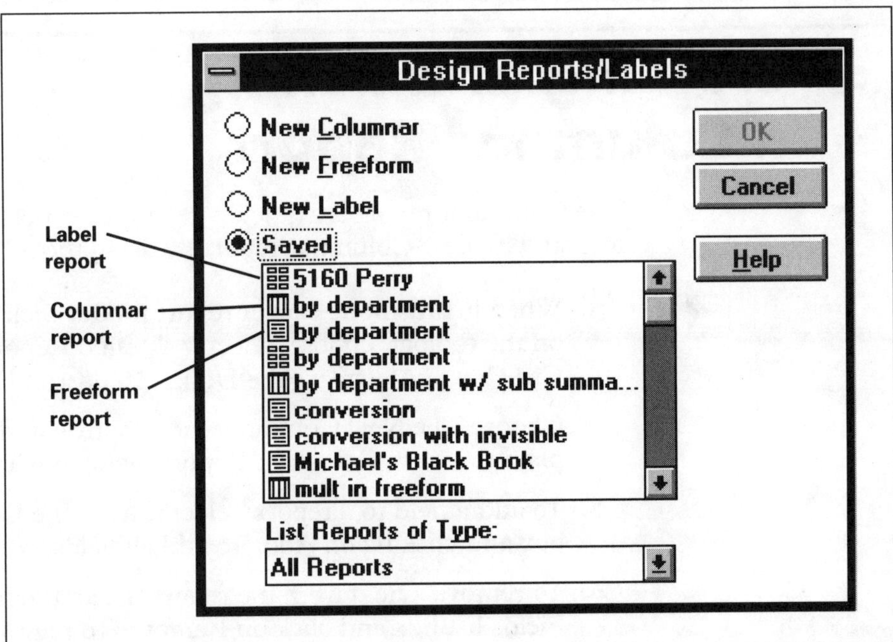

TABLE 9.1: Q&A Report Symbols

SYMBOL	TYPE OF REPORT
	Columnar report
	Freeform report
	Label report
	DOS Columnar report

Through Q&A's interoperability capabilities, you can access Q&A DOS databases with Q&A for Windows. The Columnar reports of those databases can be opened, altered, and printed from Q&A for Windows.

Creating and Editing a Columnar Report

The Columnar report is a quickly-generated report in an understandable format. Create a Columnar report by using the following steps:

1. When in any mode except report mode, click on the report icon on the toolbar, choose Select ➤ Design Reports/Labels, or press Ctrl+Y. Q&A displays the Design Report/Labels dialog box.

2. Choose The New Columnar radio button and click OK. This displays the New Columnar Report dialog box (Figure 9.5).

3. To add a field to a report, select it from the Database Fields list box and clicking on Add. To add all fields, click on Add All.

4. To remove a field from the report, select the field in the Report Fields list box and click on Remove. To remove all your fields, click on Remove All.

New Columnar Report dialog box

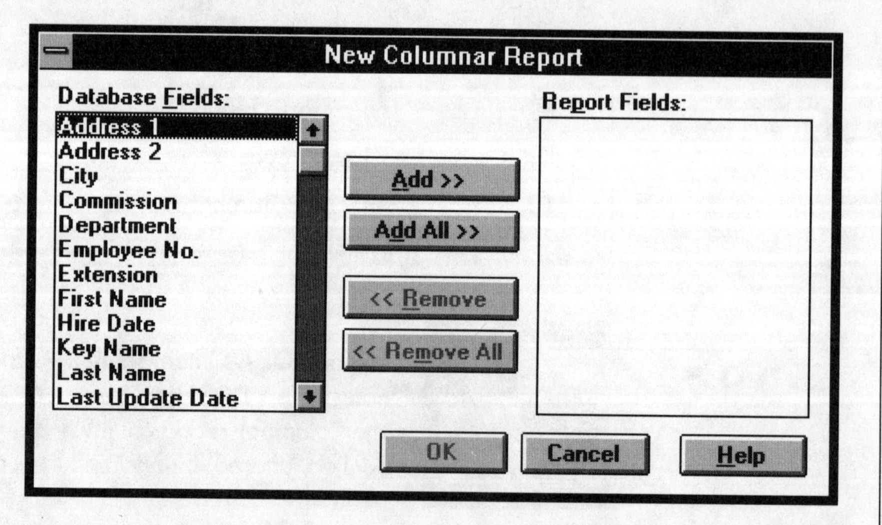

5. When you are done, click on OK or press Enter. Q&A displays the Columnar Report layout with the report created from the fields you specified.

The Columnar Report Layout

The Columnar Report layout (Figure 9.6) displays your fields as columns. In this screen, you specify how you want your fields and records displayed on the printed report. The rows are the different attributes used to create a Columnar report: Heading, Field ID, Sort, Alignment, Format, Width, Options, Breaks, Subsummaries, and Grand Summaries.

FIGURE 9.6

An example of Columnar report layout

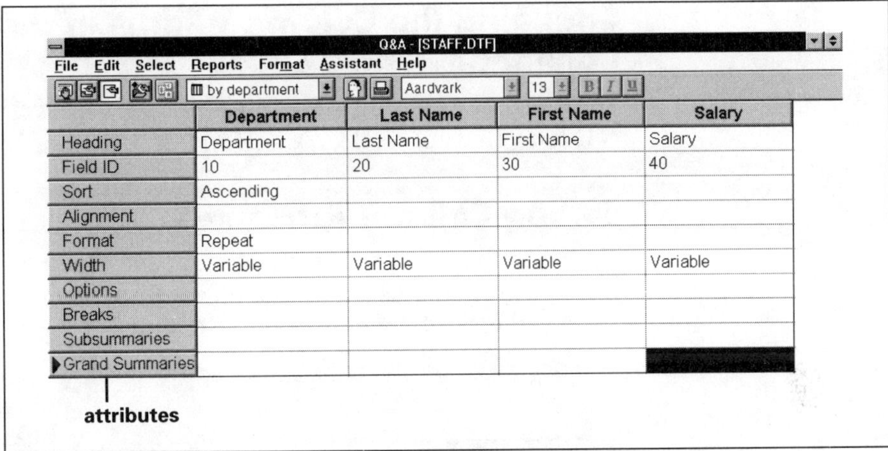

	Department	Last Name	First Name	Salary
Heading	Department	Last Name	First Name	Salary
Field ID	10	20	30	40
Sort	Ascending			
Alignment				
Format	Repeat			
Width	Variable	Variable	Variable	Variable
Options				
Breaks				
Subsummaries				
Grand Summaries				

For the Columnar report layout (as in Spreadsheet and Database Structure views), the columns and rows form a table of cells. Each of these cells is selectable. If you double-click in a cell, the corresponding attribute's dialog box is opened and adjusted for the field in that column. For instance, if you double-click in the cell that forms the intersection of the Format attribute and the Last Name field, Q&A opens the Format dialog box with the settings for the Last Name field already selected.

Moving Columns within the Columnar Report Layout

As in Spreadsheet view and Database Structure view, you can arrange the columns as you desire in Columnar report layout. Just click and drag the column to the location at which you want it to reside. This is the way that you arrange the columns for your printed report. For example, the first column in the Columnar report layout is the first column in your printout.

In Q&A for DOS, your column order is determined by Field ID. If you are familiar with Q&A for DOS, don't confuse it with the way that Q&A for Windows arranges its columns.

Changing the Column Widths in the Columnar Report Layout

To change the column width, move the cursor over the right border of the column you want to alter. Click and drag the border to the desired width.

Setting Column Attributes

To customize and present the data in the Columnar report, Q&A allows you to set attributes for all the columns of the report. The attributes are displayed in the left column of the Columnar report layout. Note that any attributes you set for a field are displayed in the cells of your report layout.

You can access all attribute dialog boxes through the Format menu or by double-clicking in a cell.

Assigning Field IDs

So that you can reference your fields through derived columns (explained later in this chapter), Q&A assigns Field ID numbers to your fields. Q&A assigns these Field IDs to the columns in the order in which the fields are created. The fields in the report are assigned Field ID numbers that are in multiples of 10. For instance, the first field you added is numbered 10, and the second field has a Field ID of 20, and so on. Fields added after the Columnar report layout is already designed are assigned Field ID numbers in multiples of five.

Through the Field ID dialog box (Figure 9.7), you can change the Field ID assigned to each column. To assign a different Field ID to a column, choose Format ➤ Field ID. This displays the Field ID dialog box. Click on the up or down arrows next to the Field ID box to select the new number to represent that column. You can also click inside the Field ID box and type the desired column number. Notice that when you scroll through the available numbers, the numbers already used for other columns are skipped.

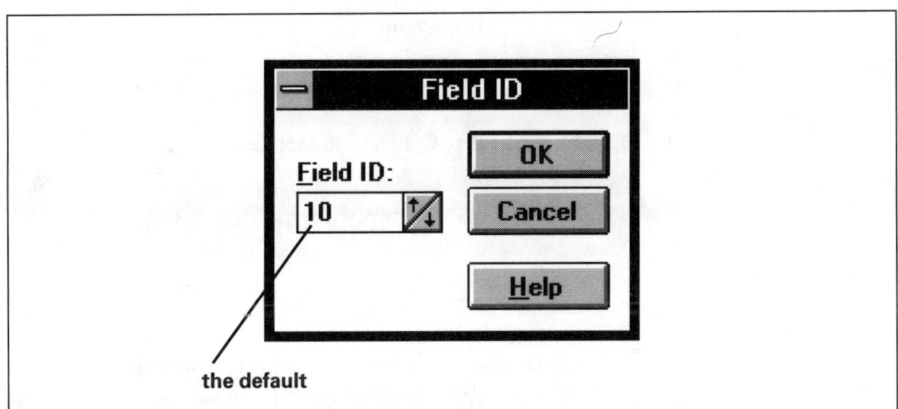

If you assign new Field IDs to your fields, it is good to assign numbers that allow space for later assignments. For example, rather than assigning 1, 2, 3, 4, which doesn't allow for any intermediate numbers, assign 10, 20, 30, 40, and so on.

Sorting the Contents of a Column

Through the Sort dialog box (Figure 9.8), Q&A enables you to sort a column in various ways. Table 9.2 lists the different sorts available to Q&A's Columnar report generator.

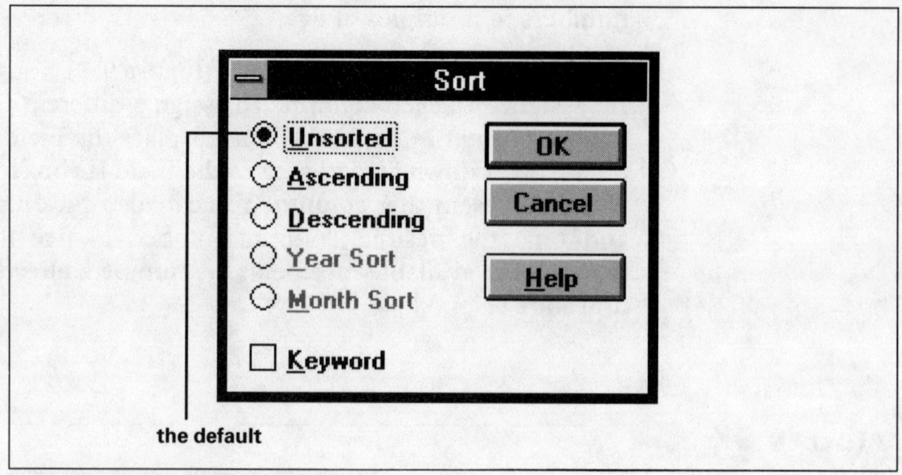

TABLE 9.2: Columnar Report Sort Options

SORT	DESCRIPTION	FIELD TYPES USED WITH
Unsorted	The data in this column will not be sorted.	All field types
Ascending	This is a standard ascending sort (abcde… or 123456…).	All field types except for picture
Descending	This is a standard descending sort (zyxwvu… or 987654…).	All field types except for picture
Year	This sorts your column in a chronological ascending order by year (12/13/93 9/16/93 1/16/94 2/03/95…). Months and days are ignored when using this sort.	Date fields only
Month	This sorts your column in a chronological ascending order by month and year. The month sort actually orders the column first by year then by month, causing a month sort within a chronological order of years (9/16/93 12/13/93 1/16/94 2/03/95…). Days are ignored when using this sort.	Date fields only

In addition to these five sorts, Q&A allows you to use the values in a keyword field as the basis for the sort. Keyword fields work in conjunction with the <u>A</u>scending and <u>D</u>escending sort types. If you select <u>U</u>nsorted, <u>Y</u>ear, or <u>M</u>onth, Q&A does not group the columnar report by keyword values.

N O T E

Keyword sorts only work as the first field in a columnar report. Remember that for a keyword field to recognize its contents as separate values, the values must be entered into the field separated by semicolons.

Figure 9.9 displays various records in Spreadsheet view. Notice the Sport field, which is a keyword field with multiple entries (some of which are the same), and the Name field, a text field. Figure 9.10 shows you how the records in Figure 9.9 are displayed in a Columnar report with a

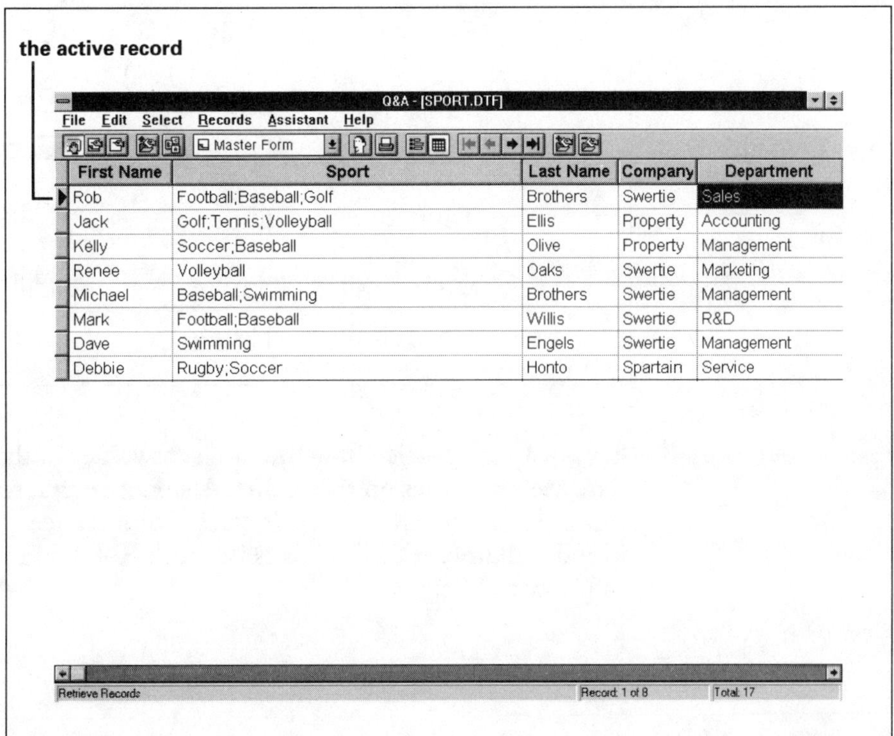

First Name	Sport	Last Name	Company	Department
Rob	Football;Baseball;Golf	Brothers	Swertie	Sales
Jack	Golf;Tennis;Volleyball	Ellis	Property	Accounting
Kelly	Soccer;Baseball	Olive	Property	Management
Renee	Volleyball	Oaks	Swertie	Marketing
Michael	Baseball;Swimming	Brothers	Swertie	Management
Mark	Football;Baseball	Willis	Swertie	R&D
Dave	Swimming	Engels	Swertie	Management
Debbie	Rugby;Soccer	Honto	Spartain	Service

Sport	First Name	Last Name
Baseball	Michael	Brothers
Baseball	Rob	Brothers
Baseball	Mark	Willis
Baseball	Kelly	Olive
Football	Rob	Brothers
Football	Mark	Willis
Golf	Jack	Ellis
Golf	Rob	Brothers
Rugby	Debbie	Honto
Soccer	Debbie	Honto
Soccer	Kelly	Olive
Swimming	Michael	Brothers
Swimming	Dave	Engels
Tennis	Jack	Ellis
Volleyball	Jack	Ellis
Volleyball	Renee	Oaks

keyword sort. Notice how the different values in the keyword field designate the categories on the report. Also notice that some of the records are repeated under different categories. For instance, you see the name Rob in more than one field. This is because Rob had more than one value in the keyword field.

To create a sort in a column, follow these steps:

1. Select the column in which you want to create the sort by clicking in any cell in that column. Choose For<u>m</u>at ➤ Sor<u>t</u>, press Ctrl+T, or double-click in the Sort row of that column.

2. Click on the desired sort radio button.

3. Check the check box labeled Keyword if you want the report grouped by keyword values.

4. Click on OK or press Enter.

Aligning the Contents of a Column

The alignment attribute determines where to place the data within the borders of a column in the printed report. To change the alignment of a column, highlight a cell in the column and choose For<u>m</u>at ➤ <u>A</u>lignment. When Q&A displays the Alignment dialog box (Figure 9.11), choose the desired alignment by clicking on a radio button. The <u>D</u>efault button aligns the column according to its field type. Text, keyword, Yes/No, date, time, and picture fields align on the left side of the column. Money and number fields align on the right side of the column. You can select <u>L</u>eft, <u>C</u>enter, or <u>R</u>ight to force alignment.

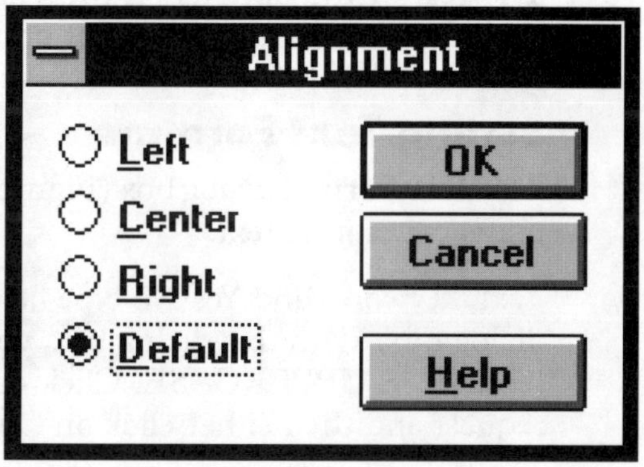

FIGURE 9.11

The Alignment dialog box lets you select <u>L</u>eft, <u>C</u>enter, <u>R</u>ight, or <u>D</u>efault column alignments.

Formatting the Contents of a Column

Format attributes allow you to set special options that apply to the columns based on their field types. These format options affect only the column of the report in which it is used. To set these formats, select a cell in the column to be altered and choose Format ➤ Format. When Q&A displays the Format dialog box, make your changes and click on OK. You'll see examples of all Format dialog boxes shortly.

All the Format dialog boxes allow you to specify Do Not Print this Field. If you check the Do Not Print this Field box, Q&A makes that column invisible (that is, it does not appear in the report). However, the column still exists in the report. For instance, if your first field is arranged by an ascending sort and the Do Not Print this Field box is checked, the report is still organized by the first field's ascending order although the first field is not visible.

All the Format dialog boxes except the columns containing picture fields provide the option Print Repeated Values When Sorted. If you check this box, Q&A prints the repeated values in the column. For instance, if you have more than one record containing Sales in the Department field and your first column in a Columnar report is the Department field, all the Sales are listed one on top of each other in a sorted field (see Figure 9.12). However, if you leave the Print Repeated Values When Sorted check box unchecked, the values are not repeated (see Figure 9.13).

The rest of the options on the Format dialog boxes vary by field type. Let's find out about the format options for each field type.

Setting Text Formats

The Text Format dialog box (Figure 9.14) lets you change formats for columns containing text.

Text, keyword, and Yes/No type fields use the options in the Text Format dialog box. With this dialog box, you can display your data either As entered or in UPPERCASE. Click on the radio button that matches your request and then either click on OK or press Enter.

Department	Last Name	First Name	Salary
Legal	Williams	Jack	$ 47,560.00
Legal	Jones	Frank	$ 28,450.00
Marketing	Schroeder	John	$ 33,750.00
Marketing	Brothers	Robert	$ 33,560.00
MIS	Williams	Mark	$ 38,795.00
Production	Newman	Nina	$ 25,675.00
Production	Dong	Milton	$ 23,600.00
Production	Lethryn	Beryl	$ 66,750.00
Production	Slattery	James	$ 28,990.00
Production	Werz	Waldo	$ 22,575.00
Sales	Lynch	James	$ 45,000.00
Sales	Martini-Ross	Henrietta	$ 35,000.00
Sales	Brennan	Bebe	$ 82,095.00
Sales	Mcgarry	James	$ 84,350.00
Sales	Corcoran	Lawrence	$ 45,000.00

Setting Number Formats

The Number Format dialog box (Figure 9.15) is the dialog box used
when formatting number columns.

You can select either the default format or create a custom format for the
column. If you select the Use Default Format Settings radio button, Q&A
uses the default attributes set in Database Structure view (see Chapter 6).
When you select Custom Format, you can use the thousands separator,
decimal digits, specify a currency format, or any combination of the three.
Remember that the thousands separator inserts commas or periods into
numbers to separate the thousands from the hundreds. Whether Q&A
uses a period or a comma depends on how you set Global Formatting Options in Database Structures view. The Number of Decimal Digits option
sets the number of digits that follow the decimal point. The option of Format as Money field attaches a currency symbol to your number.

Department	Last Name	First Name	Salary
Legal	Williams	Jack	$ 47,560.00
	Jones	Frank	$ 28,450.00
Marketing	Schroeder	John	$ 33,750.00
	Brothers	Robert	$ 33,560.00
MIS	Williams	Mark	$ 38,795.00
Production	Newman	Nina	$ 25,675.00
	Dong	Milton	$ 23,600.00
	Lethryn	Beryl	$ 66,750.00
	Slattery	James	$ 28,990.00
	Werz	Waldo	$ 22,575.00
Sales	Lynch	James	$ 45,000.00
	Martini-Ross	Henrietta	$ 35,000.00
	Brennan	Bebe	$ 82,095.00
	Mcgarry	James	$ 84,350.00
	Corcoran	Lawrence	$ 45,000.00

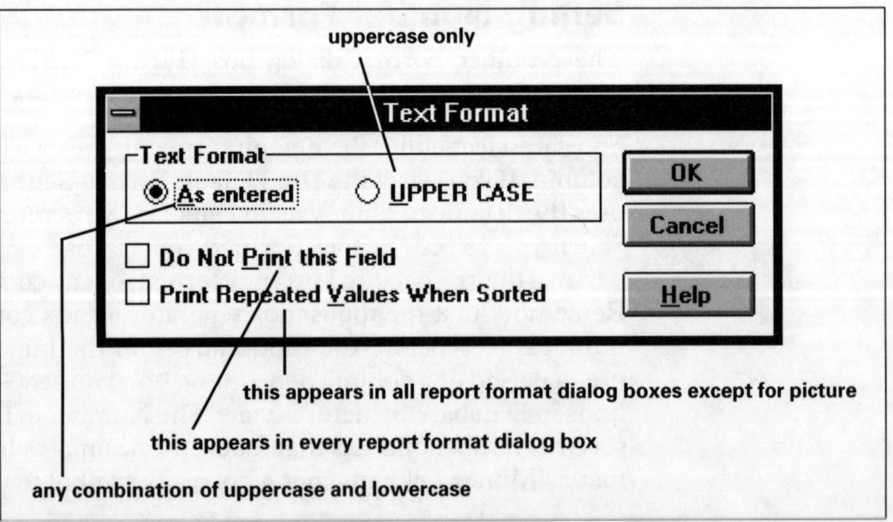

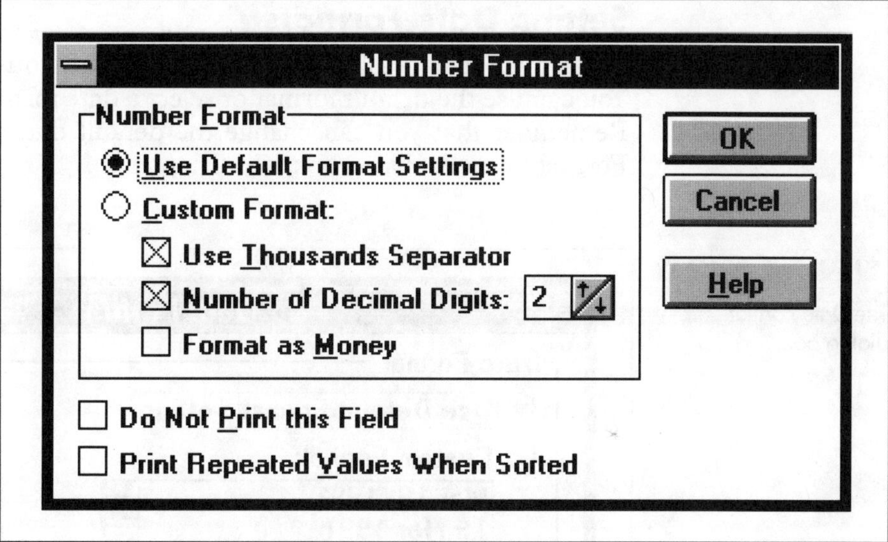

Setting Money Formats

The Money Format dialog box (Figure 9.16) lets you format money columns. The choices are the same as those for number fields.

Setting Date Formats

The Date Format dialog box (Figure 9.17) lets you format date columns. You can use the default format or select a date format from the scroll list. Remember that you can change the default date format in the Global Format Options dialog box (see Chapter 6).

The Date Format
dialog box

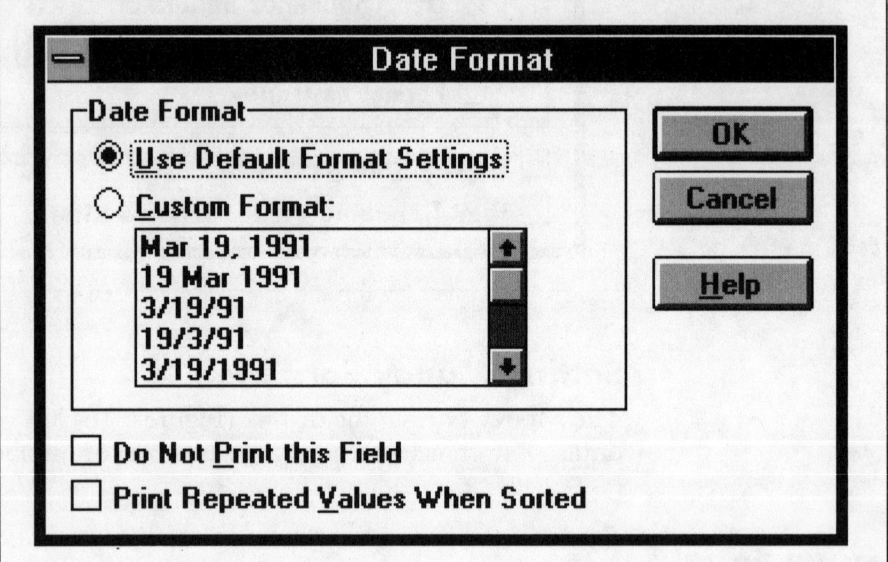

Setting Time Formats

The Time Format dialog box (Figure 9.18) lets you change formats for columns containing time fields. You can use the default time format or select a new time format. Remember that you can specify the default time format in the Global Formatting Options dialog box (see Chapter 6).

Setting Picture Formats

The Picture Format dialog box (Figure 9.19) lets you change alignment and size formats for columns containing picture fields. When Q&A uses a picture field in a Columnar report, Q&A creates a frame in which to place the graphic. To align the picture horizontally within the frame, choose from the Horizontal Alignment group: Left, Center, or Right. To

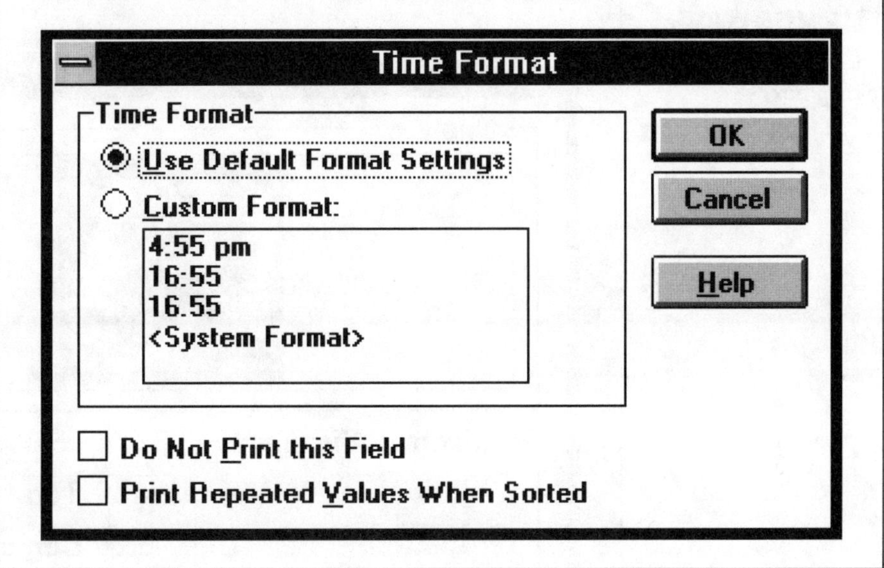

align the picture vertically, choose from the Vertical Alignment group: Top, Center, or Bottom.

You can size the picture in your report selecting one of three different settings: Keep Its Original Size, Scale to Fit (Maintain Proportions), and Scale to Fit Frame.

When you choose Keep Its Original Size, Q&A inserts the picture in its original size.

N O T E

Keep in mind that picture size might be different from the size of the graphic in Add/Edit view. As you learned in Chapter 6, if you create a very large graphic and paste it into a Q&A field, Q&A sizes it proportionally to fit within the field's boundaries. However, in a Columnar report, if you create a column with that picture field and select Keep Its Original Size, the graphic is presented in its original size.

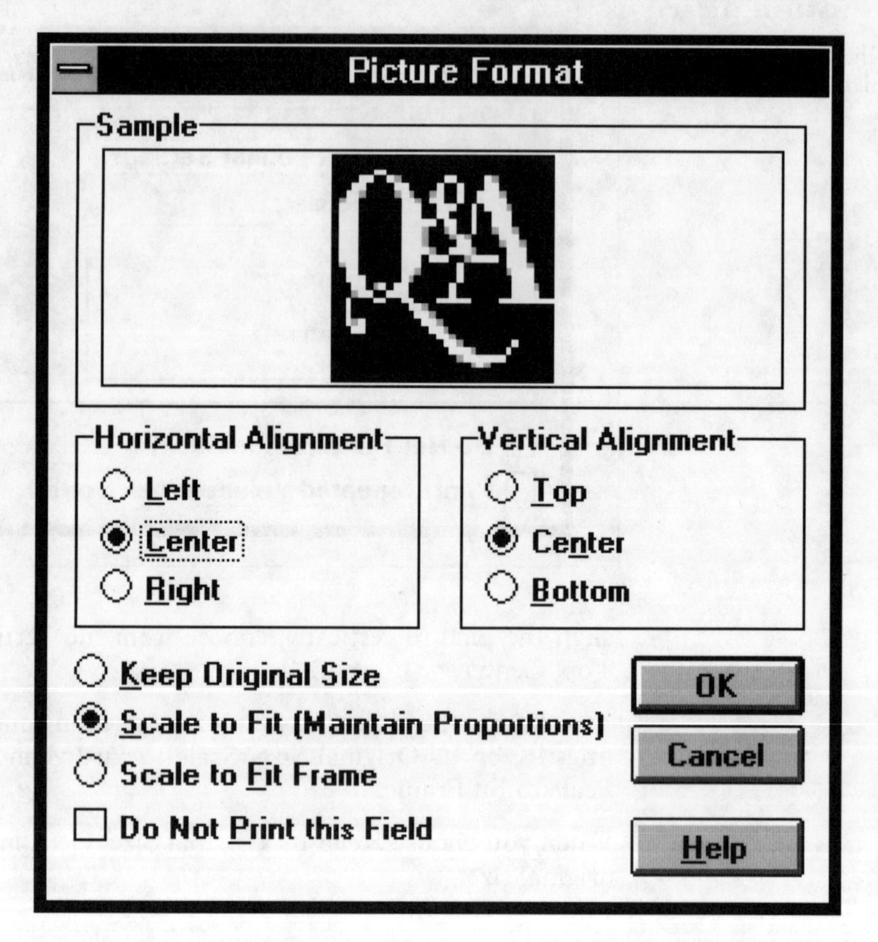

When you choose Scale to Fit (Maintain Proportions), Q&A presents the picture scaled to fit within the frame, which is determined by the width of the column, and keeps its original proportions. For instance, if the width of a picture is twice its height, and the picture is shrunk to fit on the report, the width of the picture will still be twice its height.

If you choose Scale to Fit Frame, the picture expands or reduces horizontally and vertically to fit to the exact size of the frame. Because proportions are not maintained, the picture can be distorted. For instance, if the graphic is expanded an inch in height, the width may not expand at all, creating a stretched image. When you select this option, horizontal and vertical alignment is meaningless since all sides of the graphic touch the borders of the frame.

To choose the correct format, you can look at the Sample box, which shows how certain settings affect the picture before you click on OK or press Enter.

Specifying the Width of a Printed Column

You can specify widths of printed columns by using the Width dialog box (Figure 9.20), which allows you to set the width of report columns in three ways. Simply choose Format ➤ Width or double-click in a cell in the Width row.

You can choose Same as Table to set the width of the printed report column to the same width as the column in the report layout. Then, if you select Same as Table and widen the column in the report layout, the column is printed with the new width. If you widen or narrow the column in the table, the width reading in the Width dialog box changes accordingly.

Choosing the Variable radio button allows Q&A to set the width of the column to any size it needs. This is the default width setting for all columns, except for the columns containing pictures. To determine the width of variable width columns, Q&A sums the widths of all the other columns.

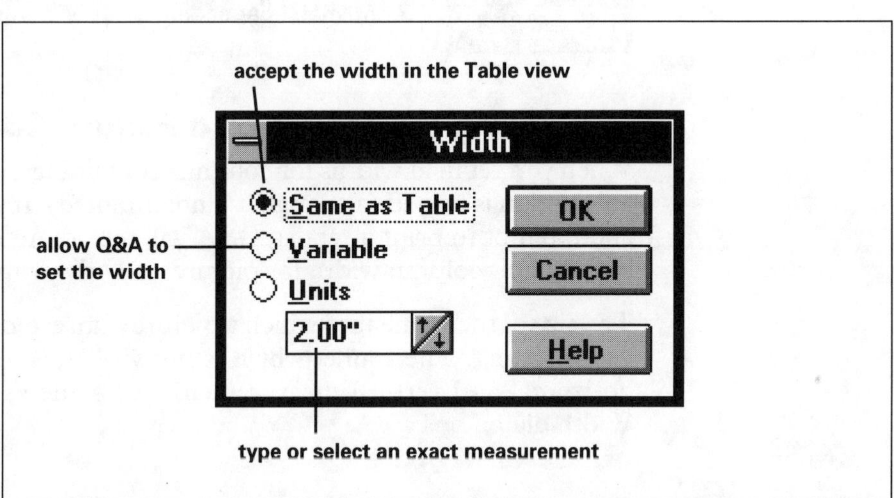

REPORTING WITH Q&A

It then compares this sum with the printable area of the paper (within the left and right margins). Then Q&A determines if there is enough room to print the columns across a single page without condensing the data too tightly. If there isn't enough room, Q&A splits the columns across multiple pages.

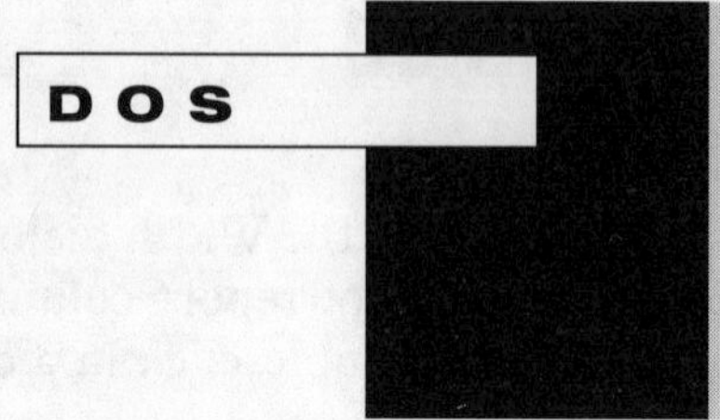

For Q&A for DOS users, remember that you saw the message Report TOO WIDE for the specified page **when your report did not fit across one page. In Q&A for Windows, you are not advised when the report has been split.**

When you specify <u>U</u>nits, Q&A assigns the width of the column to the number in the <u>U</u>nits text/list box. You can change the width by either typing or selecting a value from 0.10" to 20".

In Q&A for DOS, the width of a column was in characters rather than in inches or centimeters. In Q&A for Windows, however, because of the frequent use of proportionally spaced fonts in which the width of characters vary, Q&A specifies the width in inches or centimeters, depending on your default unit of measure.

Specifying the Width of a Picture Column

When you set field widths for columns containing picture fields, the <u>V</u>ariable option is invalid (although it is not dimmed). If you select this option, and attempt to print a report, Q&A will tell you to change your settings. The default column width for pictures is <u>U</u>nits with a two-inch width.

The size of the frame into which a picture is inserted is determined by the width setting. The frame, which is not visible, is a square with both its horizontal and vertical measurements the same as the width set in the Width dialog box.

Breaking Columns

When you sort a column, Q&A arranges field contents by groups. Let's consider a two-column report with the first report column sorted in an ascending order (Figure 9.21). When Q&A sorts the first column, it arranges the records by the contents of the fields. While Q&A sorts the column in order, it marks where the contents of the field change. These marks, called *column breaks,* identify the report's groups. When the data in the first field changes Q&A inserts a blank line, which illustrates the location of the column break. Even if you remove the blank lines, the column breaks still exist. These breaks tell Q&A to execute special procedures such as performing subcalculations, or inserting a page break.

To open the Breaks dialog box (Figure 9.22), either choose Format ➤ Breaks or double-click in a cell in the Breaks column. In the dialog box, you can specify other breaks: First Letter Changes, Year Changes, Month Changes, and Day Changes. If you leave this dialog box empty, every time a value changes in any way, the breaks occur. However, if you select an option, it becomes the basis of the column breaks.

FIGURE 9.21

A report with breaks occurring when the field values change. Notice the breaks between Accounts Payable, Accounts Receivable, and Education.

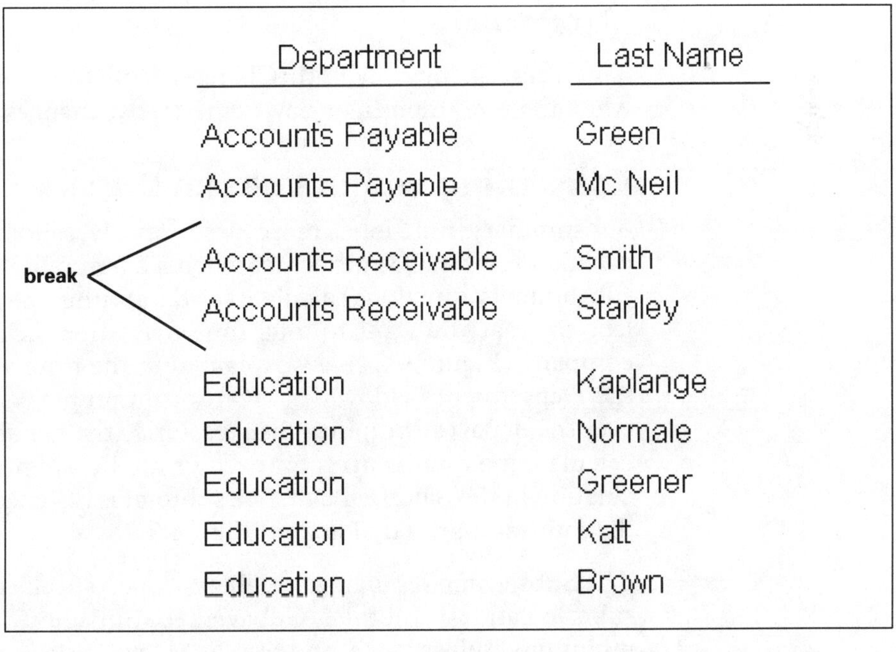

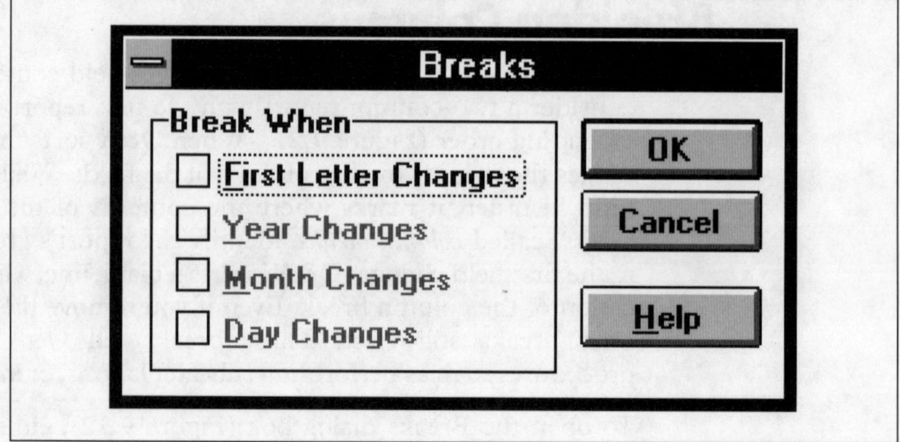

The First Letter Changes option forces a column break when the first character of that column changes. For instance, if you have sorted a list of names in that column with the First Letter option checked, the names are broken into alphabetical groups. All the names that begin with the letter A are grouped together. Then all the names that begin with letter B are listed, and so on. Figure 9.23 shows a report with a First Letter Changes break.

The Year Changes, Month Changes, and Day Changes trigger breaks when the year, month, or day, respectively, changes in the column.

Calculating within Column Breaks

Subsummary functions, more descriptively called subcalculations, are calculations that Q&A executes when a column break occurs. In essence, subsummary functions calculate the data within the groups. For example, let's say that you want to total the salaries for each department of your company (Figure 9.24). As explained in the prior section, you'll sort by the Department field, which creates column breaks (and groups) whenever the department name changes. Once the departments are grouped, calculate the total salaries for each group by assigning a totaling subcalculation in the Salaries field. The subtotal is assigned to the field through the Subsummaries dialog box (Figure 9.25).

The Subsummaries dialog box allows you to specify one of seven different subcalculations: Subtotal, Subaverage, Subcount, Submaximum, Subminimum, Subvariance, and Sub Std Dev (or substandard deviation). To

FIGURE 9.23

The First Letter Changes break issues a break whenever the contents of a field starts with a new character. There is no break between Accounts Payable and Accounts Receivable or between Education and Engineering.

Department	Last Name
Accounts Payable	Green
Accounts Payable	Mc Neil
Accounts Receivable	Smith
Accounts Receivable	Stanley
Education	Kaplange
Education	Normale
Education	Greener
Education	Katt
Education	Brown
Engineering	Hunter
Engineering	Macames
Engineering	Ryan
Engineering	Thomas
Engineering	Beely
Engineering	Simms
Engineering	Krohn
Engineering	Smith

(The label **break** with a line points to the gap between the Accounts Receivable and Education rows.)

assign a subcalculation to a column, choose Format ➤ Subsummaries or double-click in a cell in the Subsummaries row. When Q&A displays the Subsummaries dialog box, choose as many subcalculations from the Calculations box as you wish for the selected column.

Subsummary functions are usually executed with money and number field types. However, you can use subsummary functions for all field types because all have some sort of numeric value. Text and keyword field types are normally viewed as just character entries. If you type a number in a text or keyword field, it is not recognized as a number but as one or more characters. However, for reports, Q&A interprets number entries in a text or

A subtotal of the Salary field with a break on the Department field

Department	Last Name	First Name	Salary
Accounts Payable	Green	Kelly	$ 38,700.00
Accounts Payable	Mc Neil	Barbara	$ 43,500.00
Total			$ 82,200.00
Accounts Receivable	Smith	Brian	$ 27,560.00
Accounts Receivable	Stanley	John	$ 27,000.00
Total			$ 54,560.00
Education	Kaplange	Jason	$ 32,545.00
Education	Normale	Todd	$ 39,450.00
Education	Greener	Grazia	$ 39,425.00
Education	Katt	Stimpson	$ 42,500.00
Education	Brown	Charles	$ 39,450.00
Total			$ 193,370.00

The Subsummaries dialog box allows you to set a variety of subcalculations for a column.

keyword field as numeric values rather than as characters. This works only if the whole column contains numbers.

You also can use Yes/No fields in subsummary functions. When an affirmative value (such as Yes, Y, True, T, or 1) is in a column, it is considered to be the number 1. If a negative value (such as No, N, False, F, or 0) is used in a column, it is regarded as the number 0.

Dates are also viewed as numbers by the Q&A report generator. A date is equal to the number of days from January 1 in the year 0000 to that date. For example, the value for January 1, 1995, is 728294 (or 1995 years times 365 days a year plus various extra days for leap years).

Times are also viewed as number values. Q&A internally looks at a time as the number of minutes from midnight. Therefore, the time 1:00 a.m. is 60. This makes it possible to use time field types by subsummary functions.

Here are the subsummary functions and their definitions.

Subtotal	Allows you to total the values in each group. (This is the function used to produce the departmental salary totals shown in Figure 9.24.)
Subaverage	Displays the average of the values in the group. This function takes the sum of the values in the subaverage column and divides it by the number of entries in that column's group.
Subcount	Allows you to count the number of entries in the group. For example, if only five fields out of a seven-record grouping contain values, a subcount returns the number 5.
Submaximum	Returns the largest value in the group.
Subminimum	Gives you the smallest value in the group.
Subvariance	Returns the variance of the values in the group. (For more information about variances and how they work, see @VAR in Appendix D.)
Sub Std Dev	Displays the standard deviation of the values in the group. (For more information about standard deviations and how they work, see @STD in Appendix D.)

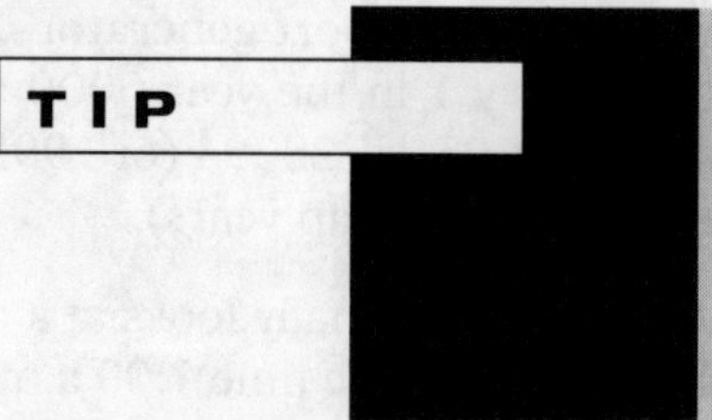

Using the Subtotal with Yes/No fields is a great way to tally the number of yes entries in a column. Since a yes is viewed as a 1 and no is viewed as a 0, subtotalling a yes/no column shows only the number of yes values in that group.

You can specify fonts used for summary functions by clicking on the font buttons on the right side of the dialog box. Pressing the Label Font button allows you to change the way subsummary labels appear. For example, you can alter the font used to print the word Total for Subtotals. Selecting the Data Font button allows you to change the way the summary data is presented.

Calculating an Entire Column

Grand Summaries functions work the same as Subsummaries functions. However, grand summaries return values for the whole column rather than just within the groups inside the columns. Q&A displays the resulting grand summary values for any type of field at the end of the report underneath the applicable column. Figure 9.26 displays a Grand Summary Total for a salary field.

To add a grand summary to a column, choose Format ➤ Grand Summaries or double-click in a cell in the Grand Summaries row. Q&A displays the Grand Summaries dialog box (Figure 9.27).

As you add summary functions, such as Subtotal or Total, to a column, they are listed in the Columnar report layout as new rows underneath the Subsummaries row or the Grand Summary row. This gives you a better view of summary functions assigned to each column (Figure 9.28).

Selecting Other Column Options

To select special options for your columns, choose Format ➤ Options or double-click in a cell in the Options row. Q&A displays the Options dialog box (Figure 9.29) in which you can check or clear three check boxes for the selected column: Truncate (Do Not Wrap), Cancel Subcalculations, and Page Break on Break. You can use the Options dialog box for all field types except picture fields.

Department	Last Name	First Name	Salary
Engineering	Beely	Asbark	$ 55,985.00
Engineering	Thomas	Norma	$ 56,035.00
Finance	Engelbrecht	David	$ 73,210.00
Finance	Sauerbrey	Jenny	$ 45,850.00
Legal	Williams	Jack	$ 47,560.00
Production	Lethryn	Beryl	$ 66,750.00
Sales	Mcgarry	James	$ 84,350.00
Sales	Brennan	Bebe	$ 82,095.00
Sales	Lynch	James	$ 45,000.00
Sales	Corcoran	Lawrence	$ 45,000.00
Total			$ 601,835.00

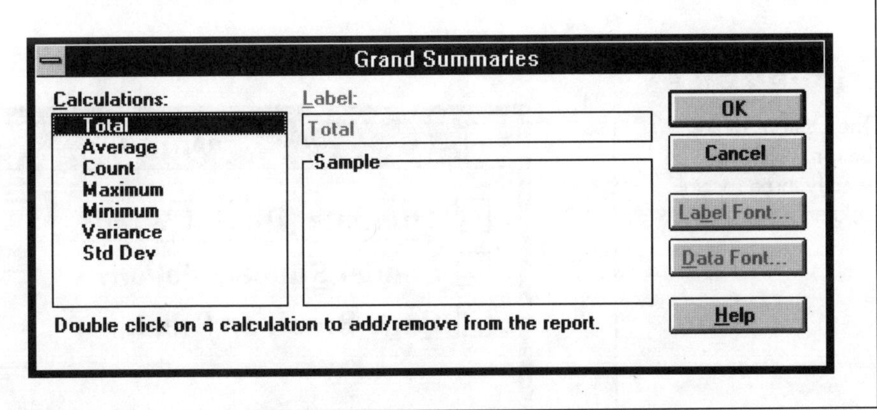

Truncate (Do Not Wrap) tells Q&A to truncate any characters that don't fit within the width of the selected column. For instance, if you have a valuc in a ficld that normally word wraps because the value is too wide to fit in the column, the characters or words that are normally wrapped to the next line are not printed at all.

A Subtotal, Subaverage, Total, and Average are assigned to the Salary column. Notice how the different summary functions create additional rows.

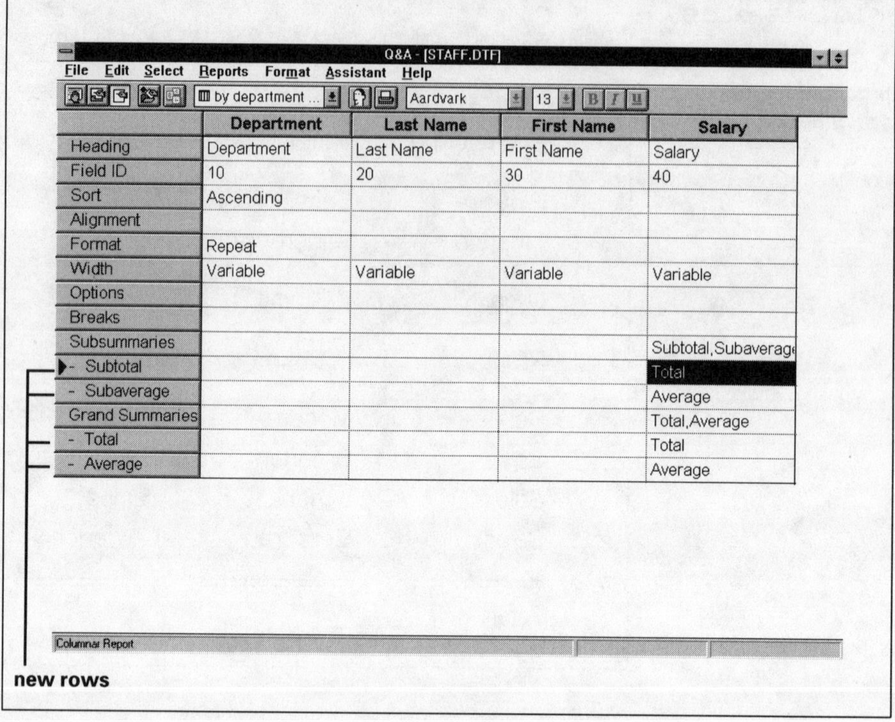

	Department	Last Name	First Name	Salary
Heading	Department	Last Name	First Name	Salary
Field ID	10	20	30	40
Sort	Ascending			
Alignment				
Format	Repeat			
Width	Variable	Variable	Variable	Variable
Options				
Breaks				
Subsummaries				Subtotal,Subaverage
▶ - Subtotal				Total
- Subaverage				Average
Grand Summaries				Total,Average
- Total				Total
- Average				Average

Columnar Report

The Options dialog box in which you can specify three special column options

Cancel <u>S</u>ubcalculations prevents the column break sort that creates subcalculations for the selected column. For example, let's say that you are working on a three-column report. The first column is a sorted column of companies, the second is a sorted column of departments in the companies, and the third is a subtotaled expense column. How do you get just the subtotal of expenses for each company? Because of the sorts in the company and department column, column breaks are issued to the report every time the department or the company values changes. This tells Q&A to subtotal on every department and company—something that can look like a big mess. Fortunately, if you choose Cancel <u>S</u>ubcalculation for the department column, only the sort in the company column issues a column break that subcalculates. The end result is a report sorted in the first two columns with a subtotal break down of expenses for each company (Figure 9.30).

Specifying Cancel Subcalculations can produce a report with the first two columns sorted and subtotals based on only one column.

Company	Department	Salaries	Last Name	First Name
Property Financial Group	Accounting	$56430.00	Ellis	Jack
	Contracts	$32040.00	Rhodes	Jason
	Management	$46340.00	Olive	Kelly
	Marketing	$34250.00	Day	Jenny
Total		$169060.00		
Spartain Legal Services	Contracts	$39430.00	Sesena	John
	Management	$38710.00	Frys	Keith
	Marketing	$34200.00	Bowman	Jenny
	Service	$38130.00	Honto	Debbie
Total		$150470.00		
Swertie Consulting	Accounting	$41320.00	Hajimoto	Rose
		$41280.00	Coax	Michael
	Management	$42650.00	Engels	Dave
		$65400.00	Brothers	Michael
	Marketing	$32870.00	Oaks	Renee
		$37200.00	Williams	Dave
	R&D	$43500.00	Willis	Mark
	Sales	$43780.00	Brothers	Rob
		$34810.00	Peachi	Nicole
Total		$382810.00		

Page Break on Break instructs Q&A to insert a page break when a column break occurs. This means that when a new grouping begins and a column break is issued, a new page begins. The report continues from the top of that page. This way you can have each grouping of data and subcalculations on separate pages.

Inserting Headers and Footers

In Columnar reports, you can create *headers* and *footers* by choosing Reports ➤ View Header/Footer. The header, (an area at the top of each report page) and footer (an area at the bottom) contain information that you want to appear on every page (for example, the date, your name, report name, page number, or your company name). For instance, at the top of the pages of this book, you can see the page number and chapter you're reading.

To create a header or footer, choose Reports ➤ View Header/Footer. This displays a special window (Figure 9.31) in which you can insert text, graphics, and special values for both the header and footer.

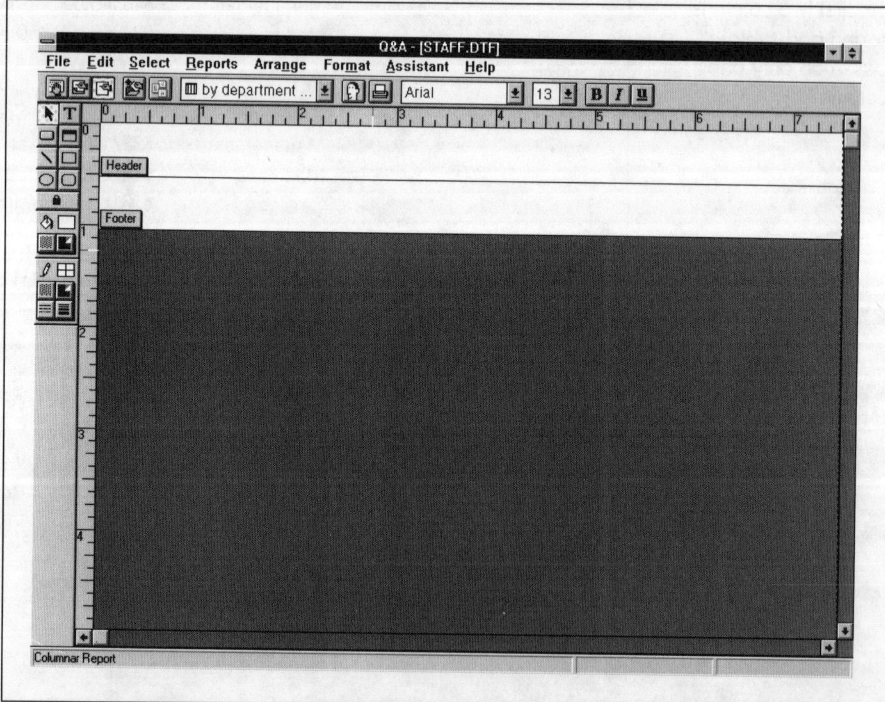

In this window, you will recognize the tool box palette that you used when you created input forms (see Chapter 4). With two exceptions, all the tools work exactly the same way they did in Chapter 4: you cannot place fields or buttons in the header or footer.

The header and footer work areas in the window allow you to create and customize the information to be displayed. Draw pictures or type text into the header work area above the box labeled Header. Create footers in the work area between the Footer label and the Header label. When you are done creating your header or footer, choose Reports ➤ View Columns.

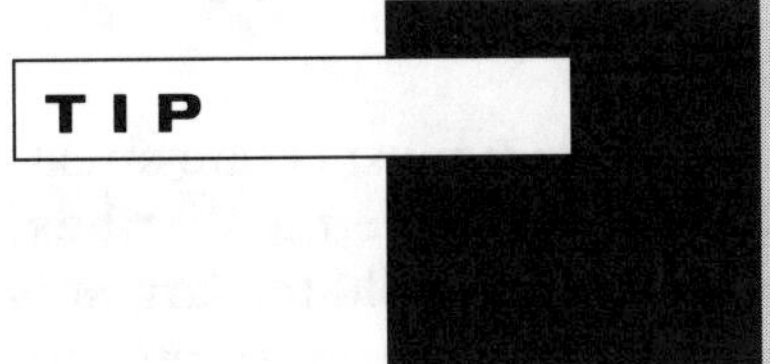

To increase your work area for the header or footer, drag the labeled boxes up or down. In addition, if the window is not already maximized, click on the maximize button on the right side of the title bar.

Pasting Special Values into a Header or Footer

Quite often, you'll need to insert the current date, current time, or page number in a header or footer. Q&A enables you to add these values to your reports by choosing Edit ➤ Paste Special and selecting a special symbol or stamp. When you print the report, Q&A replaces the stamp with updated information. Q&A's special paste values applicable to reports are:

Current Date	Stamps the current date from your computer system. This date is never updated.
Current Time	Stamps the current time from your computer system. This time is never updated.
Date Symbol	Stamps a placeholder that contains the current date from your computer system. Whenever you print this report, the date is updated, inserting the date the report is printed.

Time Symbol	Stamps a placeholder that contains the current time from your computer system. Whenever you print this report, the time is updated, inserting the time the report is printed.
Page Number Symbol	Stamps a placeholder that contains the number of the current page. Whenever you print this report, Q&A keeps the page number of the current page updated. Therefore, if you add or remove records, Q&A will print the correct number of pages in the report.

To create a stamp in the header or footer, you must create a text box in which the stamp can be placed. When you create the text box in the header or footer, make sure it is large enough to hold the largest possible value that you might stamp in it. For instance, if you stamp September 12, 1996, and the box is too small, some of your data will not be printed.

TIP

You can also type normal text in the text box. For example, you can type the word Page and then stamp the Page Number Symbol. This produces Page 1 on the first page.

To paste a special value in the header or footer, use these steps:

1. Choose <u>R</u>eports ➤ <u>V</u>iew Header/Footer to change to Header/Footer view.

2. Select the text tool (the button with the T) from the tool palette.

3. Create a text box in either the header or footer by clicking and dragging. A blinking cursor appears in the newly created text box.

4. Choose <u>E</u>dit ➤ Paste <u>S</u>pecial. Q&A displays a submenu of choices from which you can choose to paste into the text box.

5. Choose the value that you want to paste.

6. When you have completed the header or footer, choose <u>R</u>eports ➤ <u>V</u>iew Columns.

Adding New Columns

You can add any type of field as a column in a report. To add a new column to your Columnar report, follow these steps:

1. Making sure you are in the Columnar report layout, choose **Re**ports ➤ Add **C**olumns. Q&A displays the Add Columns dialog box (Figure 9.32).

2. Select any fields to be added to the report. (You can add a range of fields by pressing and holding down the Shift key and clicking on desired fields. You can select noncontiguous fields by pressing and holding down the Ctrl key and clicking on desired fields.)

3. Click on OK or press Enter. Q&A closes the dialog box and returns to the Columnar report layout.

TIP

You can only add a field as a column once. However, there is a way to get around this: you can add a derived column, which produces exactly the same effect. Derived columns are discussed in the following section.

FIGURE 9.32

You can define any field in your database as a column in a Columnar report.

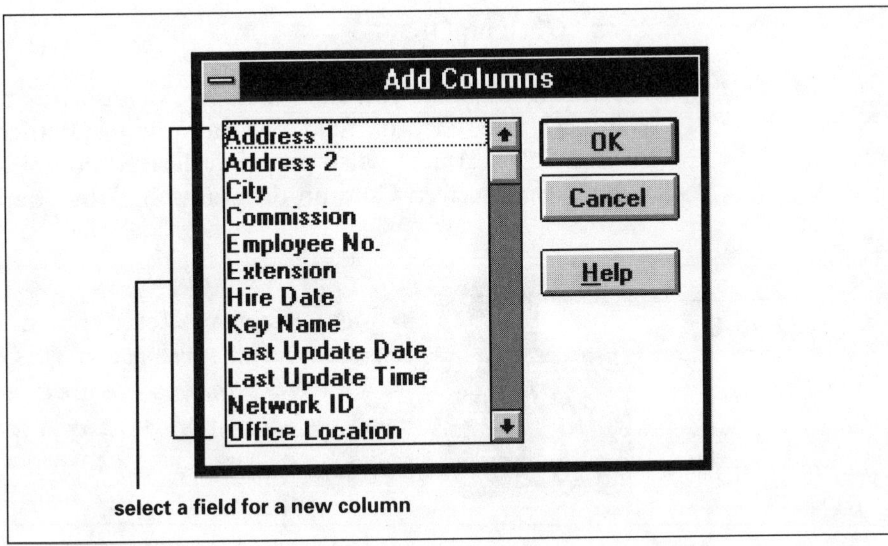

select a field for a new column

Adding Derived Columns

Q&A allows you to add *derived columns* to a Columnar report. Derived columns can contain the contents of another column, contents of fields not in your report, calculations, or calculations involving other columns or fields. Figure 9.33 displays an example of a derived column, Commission, which multiplies the Commission Rate by the Sales. Create a derived column by following these steps:

Last Name	First Name	Commision Rate	Sales	Commision
Brothers	Rob	0.07	$107066.00	$7,494.62
Sesena	John	0.068	$245080.00	$16,665.44
Rhodes	Jason	0.071	$198500.00	$14,093.50
Peachi	Nicole	0.065	$285040.00	$18,527.60

1. Choose <u>R</u>eports ➤ Add Derived Col<u>u</u>mn or press Ctrl+H. Q&A displays the Derived Field dialog box (Figure 9.34), which works identically to the Retrieve Helper dialog box you learned about in Chapter 8.

2. In the Form<u>u</u>la box, create the formula to compute the results to be placed in the Derived column.

3. Click on OK.

The formulas that you enter into the Form<u>u</u>la box can be simple field references like City or field programming statements like Commission Rate*Sales. You can also program derived columns. For more information, see "Derived Column Programming" in Chapter 11.

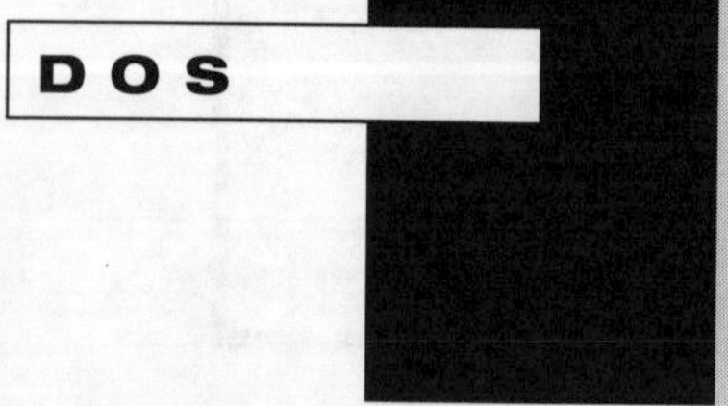

In Q&A for DOS, you could only calculate derived columns from other columns of the Columnar report. In Q&A for Windows, you can use any field from your database in your Derived Column Formula box, whether or not it is a column.

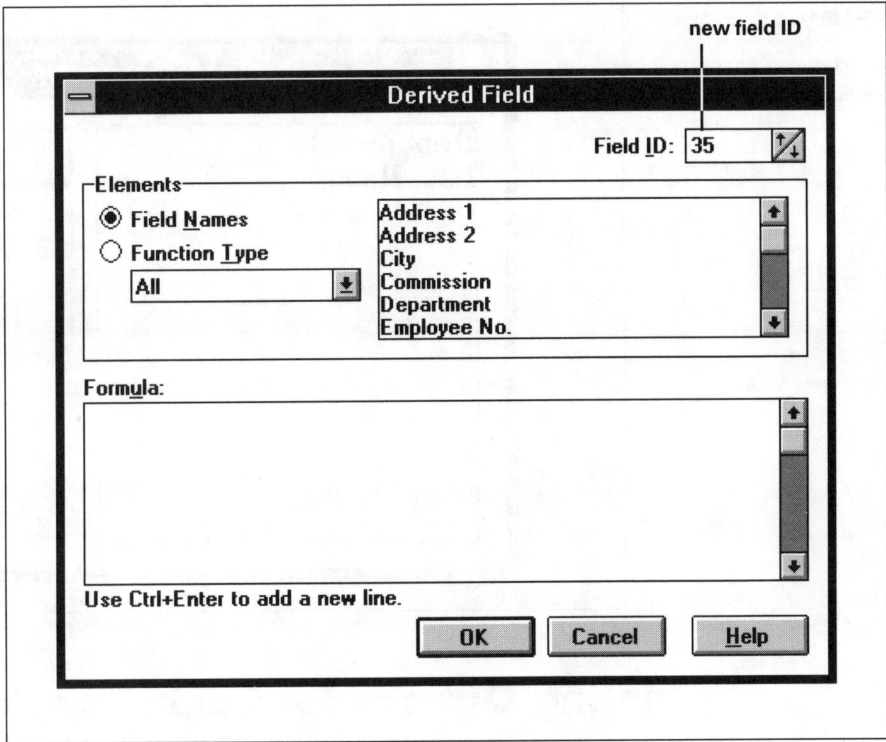

There is one difference between the Derived Field dialog box and other Helper dialog boxes such as Retrieve Helper. The Add Derived Column dialog box has a Field ID box, which contains the reference number with which you can refer to this derived column in derived column programming.

After typing the derived fields formula and returning to the report layout, you will notice that the formula is displayed in the Field ID row along with that column's field ID.

Deleting Columns

To revise your columnar report by deleting columns, choose Reports ➤ Delete Columns. Q&A displays the Delete Columns dialog box (Figure 9.35). Choose the columns to be deleted and click on OK or press Enter.

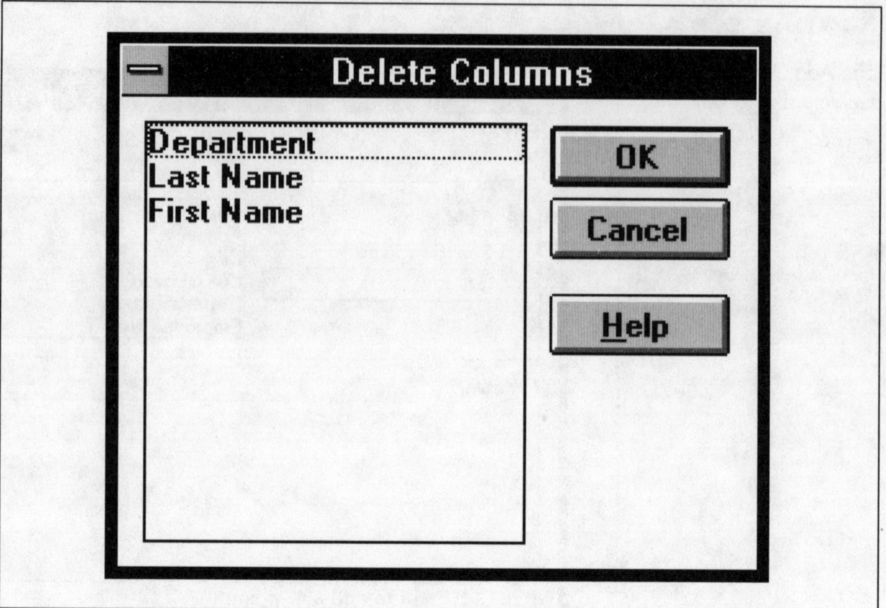

Printing Options for Columnar Reports

You can control how Q&A prints data in Columnar reports through the Report Print Options dialog box (Figure 9.36). Just choose Reports ➤ Report Print Options and then select from these options in the Report Print Options dialog box:

Print Blanks as Zeros

Q&A substitutes a zero for all blank values in money and number fields. Keep in mind that these zeros may affect Subsummaries and Grand Summaries. For instance, the subaverage of two fields, one that is 28 and the other blank, will produce 28. However, if you select Print Blanks as Zeros, the Subaverage will return 14. The default is an unchecked check box.

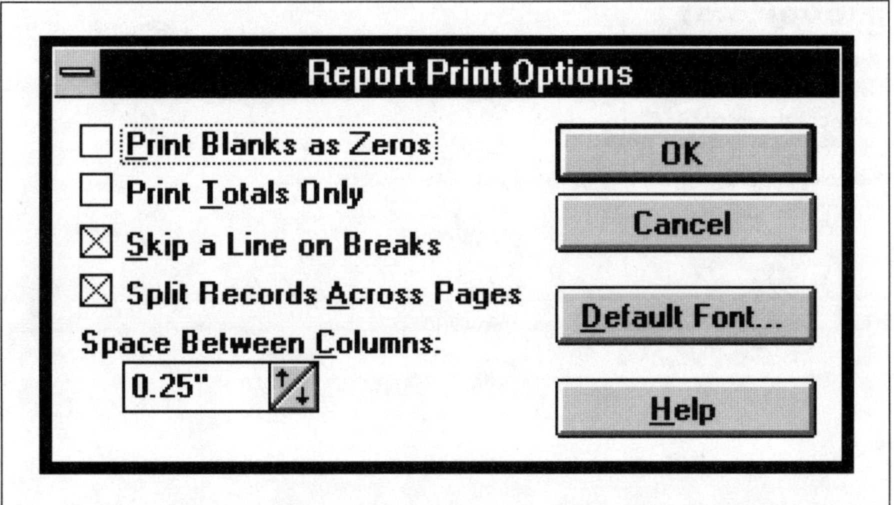

Print Totals Only	Q&A prints the Subsummaries and Grand Summaries and not the column data (Figure 9.37). The header, footer, names of groups, and column headings are printed. The default is an unchecked check box.
Skip a Line on Breaks	Q&A places a blank line between each group. If a column break occurs, Q&A skips a line before printing any more information. This often makes the report easier to read. The default is a checked check box.
Split Records Across Pages	Q&A allows you to break a record so it will print on more than one page. If you clear this check box, Q&A attempts to print the record on a single page. The default is a checked check box.

A Columnar report with the Print Totals Only check box selected. Notice that the column data is absent.

Department	Last Name	First Name	Salary
Legal			
Total			$ 76,010.00
Average			$ 38,005.00
Marketing			
Total			$ 67,310.00
Average			$ 33,655.00
MIS			
Total			$ 38,795.00
Average			$ 38,795.00
Production			
Total			$ 167,590.00
Average			$ 33,518.00
Sales			
Total			$ 291,445.00
Average			$ 58,289.00
Total			$ 641,150.00
Average			$ 42,743.33

Space Between Columns	Select a value from 0" to 20" to specify the space between the columns. Use this option to make a report easier to read. The default space between columns is 0.20".

Default Font

Click on this button to open the Font dialog box in which you can select fonts, font style, size, effects, and color for this report. The default settings affect everything in the report, including the data, the column headings, the summary data, and summary labels. However, if you have formatted an individual item, that setting overrides the default you set with this button.

Saving a Columnar Report as a Freeform Report

A Freeform report is probably the most difficult type of report to create—simply because of its flexibility. As a shortcut, you can save a Columnar report as a Freeform report. This transfers all the options that you specified when creating the Columnar report. You can then reorganize the report any way you want. This whole process can save you a great deal of time because you won't have to create a Freeform report from scratch. To save a Columnar report as a Freeform report, choose Reports ➤ Save As Freeform. Just specify the report name and click on OK or press Enter.

Q&A handles Freeform report fields as objects that you can move around at will. When you initially create a Columnar report, however, Q&A recognizes the fields only as stationary field references. When you print or run a report, Q&A converts the fields into objects. Therefore, before you save a Columnar report as a Freeform report, print or run your report. Previewing a report also converts your fields into objects.

Save your Columnar report before converting it to a Freeform report. If you switch to the Freeform report without saving, the Columnar report is lost. Therefore, if you think you may use your Columnar report someday, save it before converting it.

Creating and Editing a Freeform Report

Unlike Columnar reports, Freeform reports are not limited to placing fields in columns; you can place fields in almost any location on the page.

Freeform reports and Columnar reports also differ in the following ways:

- The layouts are displayed differently.

- You may use different routines to perform the same process in each type of report.

- Freeform reports can contain graphics in the work area and in picture fields. Columnar reports can only print graphics from a picture field.

- Freeform reports can have headers and footers that contain two separate pieces of information: those for the first page and those for the remaining pages.

To create a Freeform report, follow these steps:

1. To change to report mode, choose Select ➤ Design Reports/Labels, press Ctrl+Y, or click on the Report button on the tool bar.

2. Choose New Freeform and click on OK. Q&A displays the New Freeform Report dialog box (Figure 9.38).

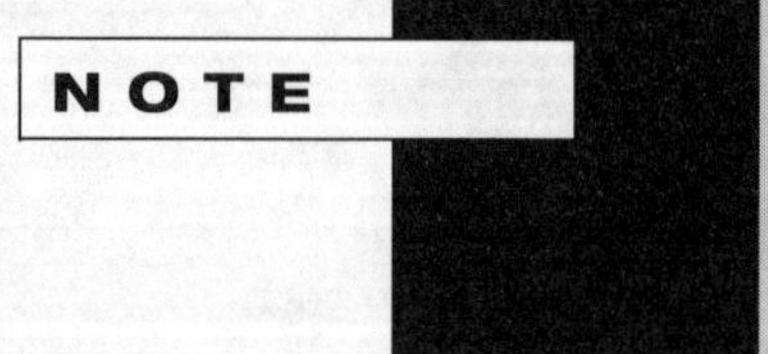

NOTE If you are creating a Freeform report while you are already in a report mode, (Columnar report or Label), choose Reports ➤ New ➤ Freeform Report. Q&A displays the New Freeform Report dialog box.

3. Choose the fields you want on your Freeform report by selecting one or more fields and clicking on Add. To add all the fields to the report, click on Add All.

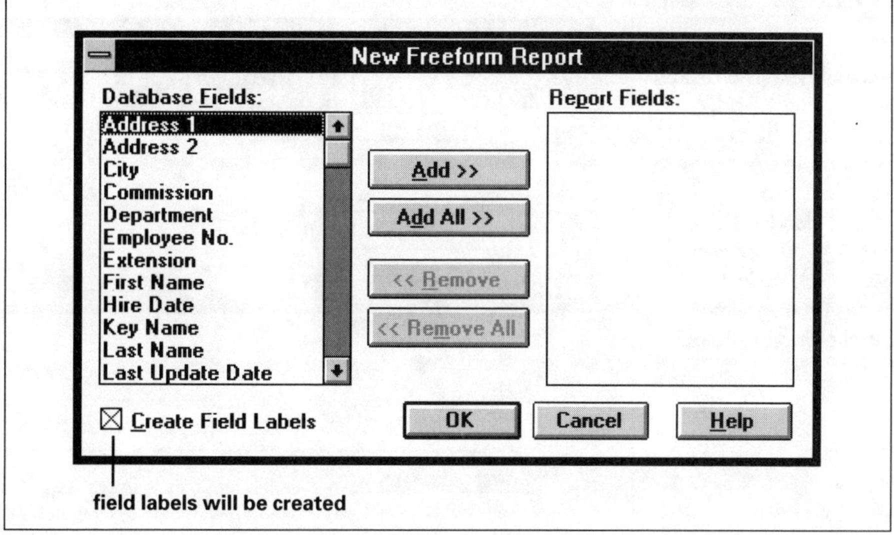

4. Click on OK or press Enter. Q&A displays your Freeform report layout.

The Freeform Report Layout

The Freeform report places its objects in work areas such as the Header/Footer view described earlier. However, instead of the report being broken into two work areas as in Header/Footer view, the Freeform report is broken into as many work areas as there are sections. For instance, if your Freeform report has the default three sections: header, body, and footer, your report has three work areas labeled Header, Body, and Footer (Figure 9.39). Sections, or parts, are discussed later in this chapter.

The header, body, and footer are the basis of all Freeform reports. The header and footer parts of the Freeform reports are almost the same as the header and footer of Columnar reports. However, in Freeform reports, headers and footers can contain fields.

When a field is printed in a header or footer, Q&A must identify the specific record that is to be used as the field value. The body of the report can have five records per page. However, the fields in the header or footer can contain only one value in each. If you place a field in the header, Q&A uses the values from the first record of that page of the report. For fields placed

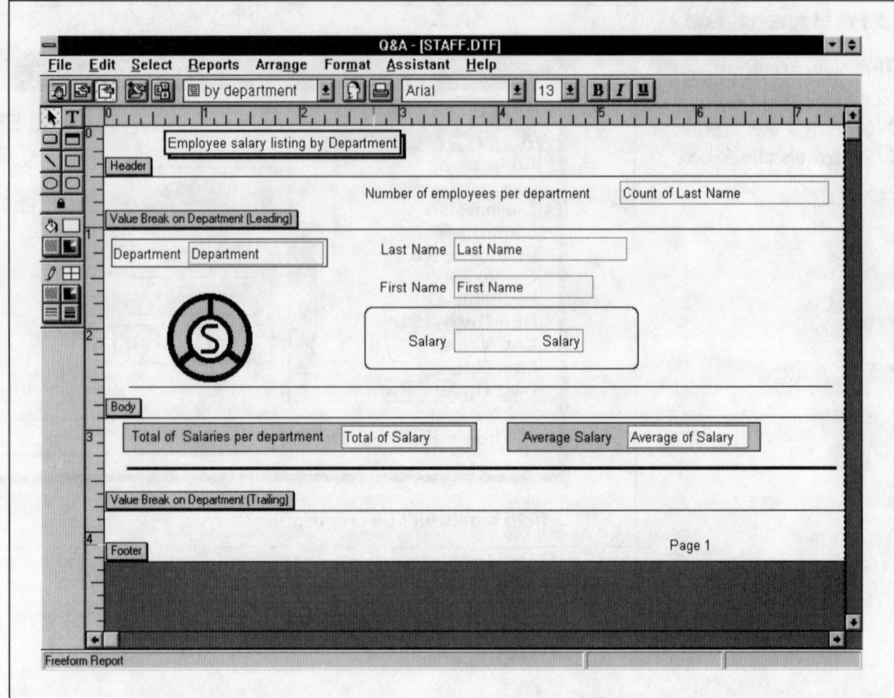

in the footer, Q&A uses the values from the last record of that page of the report.

Your field data is placed in the body of the report. Create fields in this work area using the Field tool (the second button from the top on the right side of the tool palette). For detailed information about the tool palette, see Chapter 4.

Using Parts and Work Areas

The Freeform layout consists of *parts* and *work areas*. Parts are the sections in the layout that make up the printed report. The work areas are the areas within the parts in which you can add fields or text, or create graphics. The parts (for example, Header, Body, and Footer) in your layout are identified by the *part handles*, which are the gray boxes that sit on top of the lines indicating each section. For instance, the gray box entitled Body in Figure 9.39 is a part handle.

When you create the design of your Freeform report, you will need to use the tool palette (which was described in Chapter 4). All the tools (except the script button, which is not usable in reports) operate in the same way in the Freeform reports layout as they do with input forms.

Adding Fields

To add a field to a report, select the Add Field Tool from the tool palette. Create a box by clicking and dragging the tool at any location within the work area. As you finish creating the field box, the New Field dialog box appears (Figure 9.40). In this dialog box, you can choose the field to be placed in your report, the Field ID, the type of field, (standard field, Derived field, Summary field) and whether Q&A should create a label for the field. Select the desired field, choose the settings that you want, and click on OK or press Enter.

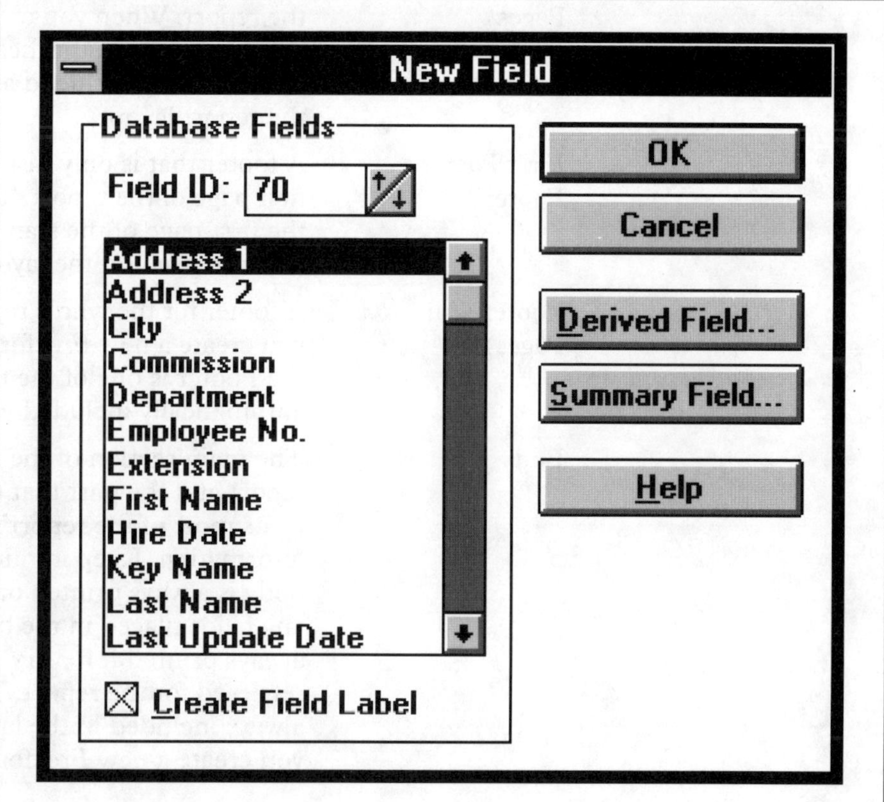

> To delete a field and its label, select both using the pointer and the Shift key. Then press the Del or Backspace keys.

Adding Parts

You can add the following parts (other than the Header, Body, and Footer) to a Freeform report:

First Page Header	A header that only appears on the first page of the report. When you use this type of header, it causes the contents of the standard header to be omitted from the first page.
Header (All Pages)	A header that appears on all pages of the report. When you create a Freeform report, this header is automatically included as a part in the report layout.
First Page Footer	A footer that is only displayed on the first page of the report. This overrides the first page of the standard footer if it is also used on the layout.
Footer (All Pages)	A footer for the whole report. When you create a new Freeform report, the Footer is one of the three Parts automatically included in the layout.
Body	The main section of the Freeform report and the part that typically hosts most of the report's information. Keep in mind that the body is always printed on the report; any fields placed in the body are always printed for every record retrieved for the report. This part is always included in the layout when you create a new Freeform report.

Leading Grand Summary	A part that contains grand summary calculations and which is always located before the body.
Trailing Grand Summary	A part that contains grand summary calculations. However, since it is the Trailing Grand Summary, the part is located after the Body.
Leading Break on	A part that contains subsummary fields and is located before the body. Unlike other parts, you can have multiple Leading Break on and Trailing Break on sections. Each type of break calculates the fields within its section to the specifications set in the Part Definition dialog box. Since you might want to have more subcalculations dependent on different breaks, you can define multiple break on sections. For instance, you might have a Leading Break on section set to calculate its fields when the contents of the Department field change. You might also have another Leading Break on section set to calculate its fields when the contents of the Last Name field changes.
Trailing Break on	A part that contains subsummary fields and which is located after the body part. Your Freeform layout can have multiple Trailing Break ons.

To add a part to your report, use these steps:

1. Choose Reports ➤ Define Parts. Q&A displays the Define Parts dialog box (Figure 9.41)

2. Click on New. Q&A displays the Part Definition dialog box (Figure 9.42).

The Define Parts dialog box

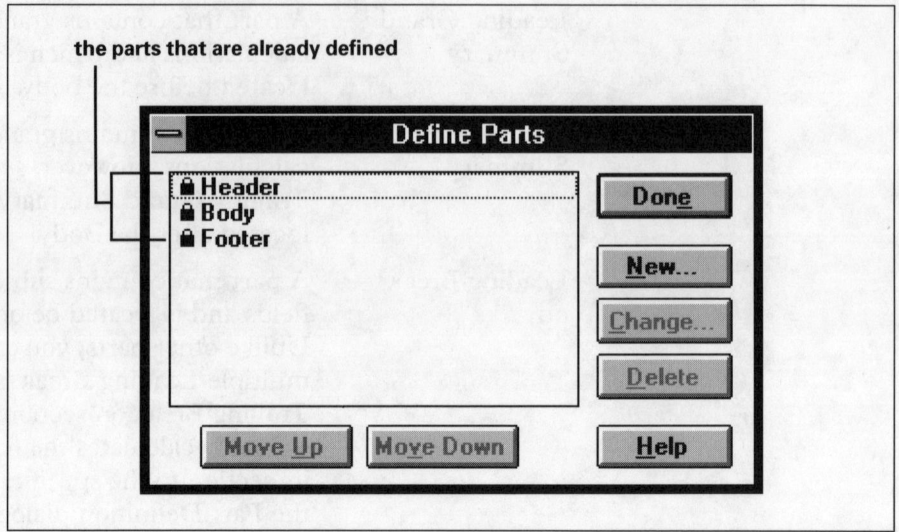

The Part Definition dialog box. Trailing Break on Department is checked, which makes the other options unavailable.

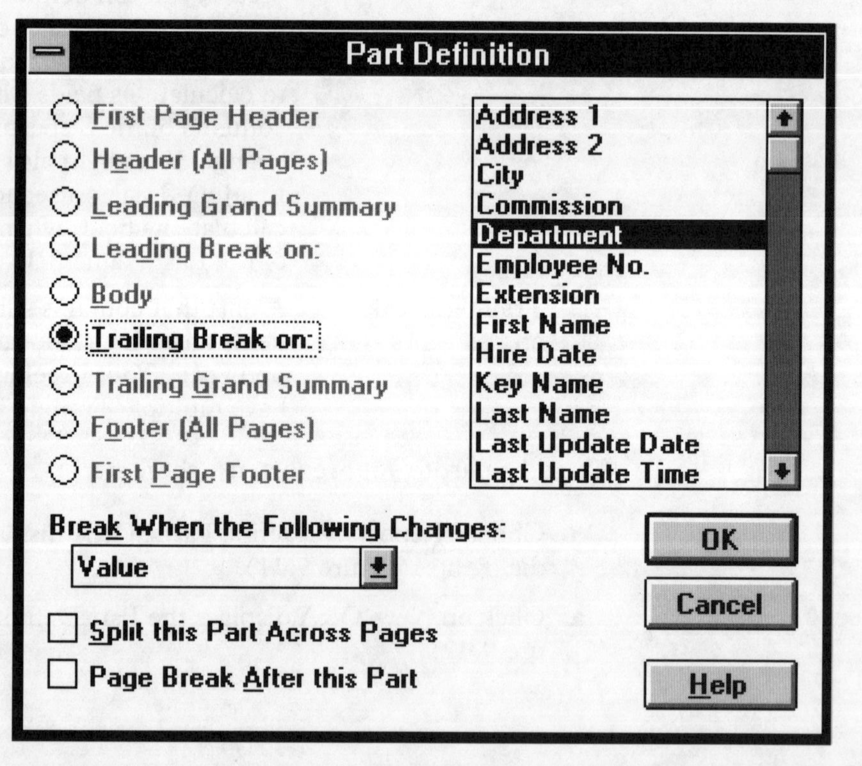

3. Click on the radio button for the selected part from the list on the left side of the dialog box. If a part is not available, it is because that part already exists in the Freeform layout. You can only use Leading Break on and Trailing Break on parts more than once.

4. If you are creating a subsummary part, make a selection from the Break When the Following Changes drop-down list and from the list of fields on the right side of the dialog box.

5. Click on OK or press Enter.

When you add a part to your Freeform report, the part is added to your layout.

Adding Subsummary Parts

Subsummary calculations are organized somewhat differently in Freeform reports. In Columnar reports, Q&A performs subcalculations whenever the groups in the preceding columns change. In Freeform reports, however, all the fields in the subsummary part are calculated when the groups change. For example, a subsummary part labeled Value Break on Department calculates all of the subsummary fields within its section when the value in Department changes. If the value in Department doesn't change the whole subsummary part, Value Break on Department is not printed in the report.

When you create a subsummary part in the Part Definition dialog box, you need to specify when you want Q&A to display that section (in essence when the break for that section occurs). To create a break for a subsummary part, use the Break When the Following Changes drop-down list box. Then from the right side of the dialog box, select the field that Q&A monitors for the change. Using the Break When the Following Changes list box, you can set Q&A to create breaks when the field value or the first character of the field value changes. When you use a date field to determine the break, you can set the break to occur when the day, month, or year changes.

Each part handle on the Freeform report layout contains a title describing its section. When you define a subsummary part, Q&A displays its settings in its part handle. For example, the First Character Break on First Name (Trailing) part handle means that the section defines a trailing break that breaks when the first character changes in the First Name field.

Adding Summary Fields to Parts

Now that you are familiar with summary parts, you can learn how to create summary fields to place into those parts. To add a subsummary field, create a summary field in a subsummary part. To add a grand summary field, create a summary field in a Grand Summary part. To create a summary field in a part, follow these steps:

1. Select the field tool (the second from the top in the right column of buttons) from the tool palette.

2. Create a field in the appropriate part of your layout by clicking and dragging the pointer to form a field box. When you release the mouse button, Q&A displays the New Field dialog box.

3. Click on the Summary Field button. Q&A opens the Summary Field dialog box (Figure 9.43).

4. Choose a Summary Type and a field to calculate.

5. Click on OK or press Enter.

While the Summary Field dialog box is open, you can change the label of the summary calculation by clicking in the <u>L</u>abel box and editing your changes. The summary types listed in the Summary Field dialog box are the same functions that were discussed earlier this chapter.

Adding Derived Fields

You can have derived fields in Freeform reports. (Remember that in Columnar reports, they are called derived columns.) To add a derived field, use these steps:

1. Select the field tool (the second from the top in the right column of buttons) from the tool palette.

2. Create a field in the appropriate part of your layout. After creating a field box, Q&A displays the New Field dialog box.

3. Click on the <u>D</u>erived Field button. Q&A displays the Add Derived Field dialog box (Figure 9.44).

FIGURE 9.44

The Add Derived Field dialog box

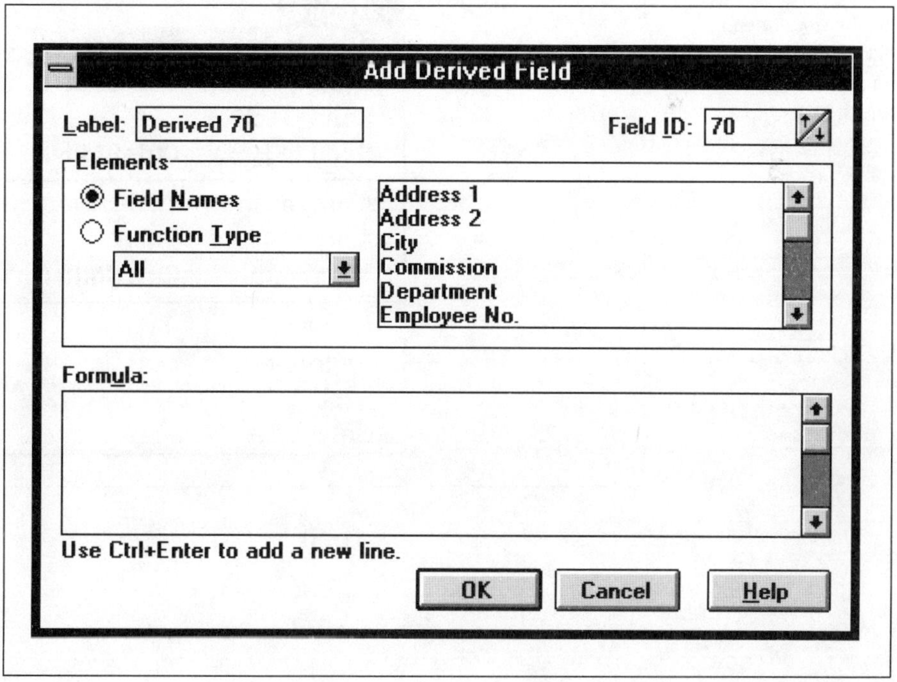

4. Create the formulas for your derived field in the Formula box. For information about derived field programming, see Chapter 11.

5. If you desire, you can change your field ID and field label.

6. Click on OK or press Enter.

Arranging Objects

When you select commands from the Arrange menu (Figure 9.45), Q&A helps to create an aesthetically pleasing layout of fields and other objects in a Freeform report. The Arrange menu serves three purposes: it allows you to send selected objects to different levels of the layout, it lets you align objects to each other, and it enables you to group and lock objects. If you are not familiar with these options, see Chapter 4.

You can also choose Format ➤ Rulers & Grid to display and use rulers, grids, or both.

FIGURE 9.45

The Arrange menu allows you to change the position of an object.

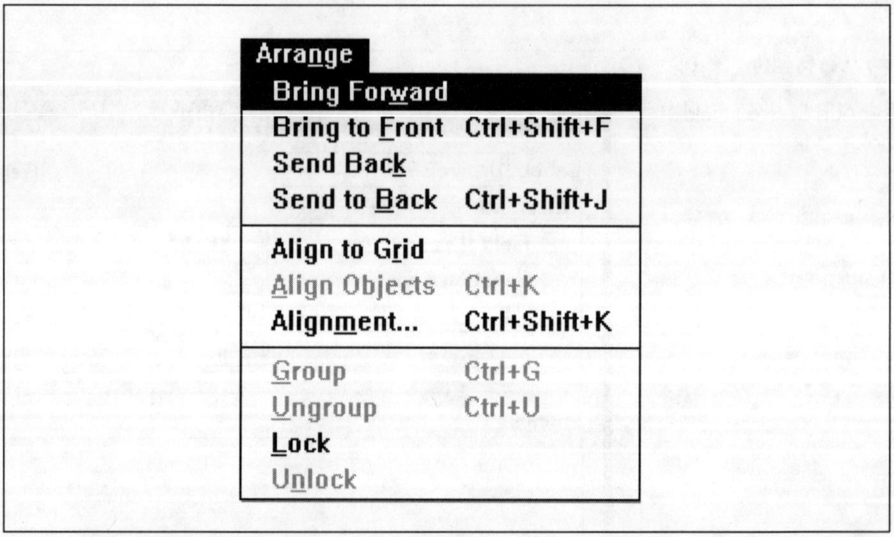

Formatting Fields

The commands on the Format menu deal mainly with how Q&A displays data. Notice that much of the Format menu lists format options for each field type. To use these options, select the field for which you want to change the formatting and choose the appropriate field type from the Format menu. Q&A then displays the format dialog box of the field type that you selected. These format dialog boxes are the same as those with which you formatted the Columnar report explained earlier in this chapter.

When you change the formats of derived fields and summary fields, Q&A selects the appropriate dialog box for the field type used in that summary field or derived field. For example, if a derived field performs a calculation involving numbers and a number field, it uses the Number Format dialog box. If a summary field performs a calculation based on a date field, it uses the Date Format dialog box.

Changing a Field

If you decide to change a field name or definition, you can choose Format ➤ Field Name & ID, which displays dialog boxes based on the different Freeform report fields: database fields, summary fields, and derived fields.

If you choose Format ➤ Field Name & ID when a database field is selected, Q&A displays the Field Name & ID dialog box (Figure 9.46). Through this dialog box, you can change the ID of the field or the database field that the field box references.

If a summary field is selected when you choose Format ➤ Field Name & ID, the Summary Field dialog box, discussed earlier in this chapter, appears. However, if a derived field is selected when you choose Format ➤ Field Name & ID, the Derived Field dialog box appears.

Changing Fonts and Alignment

You can choose Format ➤ Font to change the font of the currently selected field. When you choose this option, Q&A displays the Font dialog box (Figure 9.47). If you don't select a field when you change the font, Q&A uses that font setting for the fields and text objects you create in the future.

The Field Name & ID
dialog box

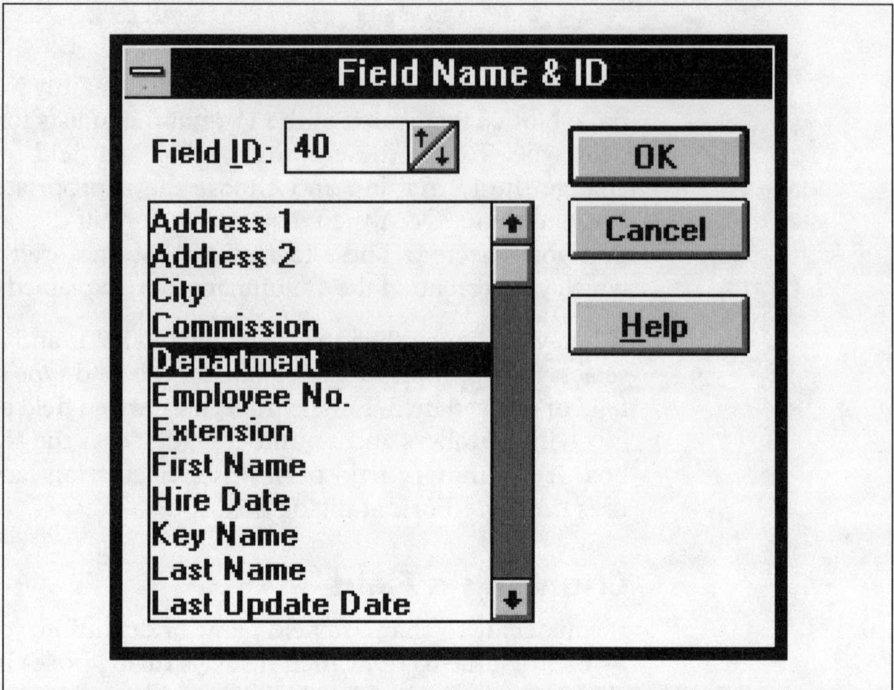

The Font dialog box

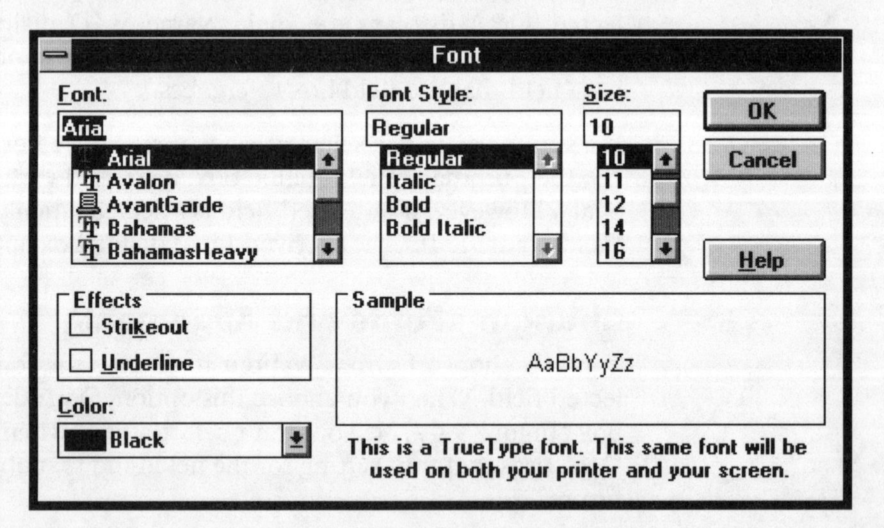

You can align the text inside fields and text boxes by selecting a field or text box and then choosing For_m_at ➤ Align Text. Q&A then displays a submenu of options from which you can select:

OPTION	COMMAND	RESULT
_D_efault	N/A	Aligns contents using the default for this field type (fields that display text are aligned to the left margin and fields that display numbers and money are aligned to the right margin)
_L_eft	Ctrl+ Shift+L	aligns contents on the left margins
_C_enter	Ctrl+ Shift+C	centers contents between the left and right margins
_R_ight	Ctrl+ Shift+R	aligns contents on the right margin

Pasting Special Values

When you create a text box using the text tool, you can use the special paste options from the _E_dit menu. You learned about pasting special values earlier in this chapter.

Moving Parts

You have already learned how to define parts. You can also move parts so that they are in a different order on your layout. To move the parts, choose _R_eports ➤ Define _P_arts. Q&A then displays the Define Parts dialog box. The parts in the box are listed in the order in which they are arranged on your layout. Notice that the parts have symbols before their names.

Here are the symbols you might see in the Define Parts dialog box:

▲   Indicates that this part cannot be moved.

▪   Indicates that this part can be moved ahead of the part above it.

▼   Indicates that this part can be moved under the part below it.

♦   Indicates that this part can be moved either ahead of the part above it or under the part below it.

> **N O T E** Only the Body and Break on parts can be moved.

Highlight the part to be moved and click on the Move Up or Move Down buttons to rearrange the list. When you are done click on Done.

Changing the Height of a Part

You may need to make more room in a certain section of your layout from time to time. Fortunately, Q&A lets you enlarge these sections by dragging part handles. For example, to enlarge the work area of a part, click on its part handle. Then drag the label to the desired height.

Deleting a Part

When you redesign a report, you may find that you wish to delete a part you created. To delete the part and all the objects inside it, Choose Reports ➤ Define Parts. Select the part to be deleted, click on the Delete button, and then click on Done.

Attaching Sorts to a Freeform Report

Q&A lets you attach a sort to your Freeform report so that your records are printed in the order you desire. Attaching a sort to a report is the same as attaching a sort to a retrieval (see Chapter 8). However, don't forget that the fields you use as breaks in your subsummary parts also need to be sorted. In this way, Q&A can group your records together so that they break properly.

There are activities that are common to all three Q&A reports. To find out how to attach a retrieve spec to a Freeform report, and to load, save, delete, and print a Freeform report, see the "Universal Functions for All Reports" section at the end of this chapter.

Creating and Editing a Label Report

The third type of Q&A report is a powerful and flexible report generator that prints on labels. While you can use this option for many purposes, it is most commonly used to create mailing labels.

Q&A allows you to select from a list of over 110 types of labels for both pin-fed (tractor-fed) printers and sheet-fed printers (ink jets, bubble jets, and lasers.) Most of the label definitions, or label types, are listed with the Avery product code number for your convenience. Therefore, if you need to print a certain type of label, you simply purchase the labels with the proper product code. You are then ready to create labels and print.

Label reports, unlike Columnar and Freeform reports, do not use derived fields or summary calculations. However, many of the other options that you have learned about for Columnar and Freeform reports are available in the Label report generator. Since you already know how to use these options, this section mentions them only briefly and focuses primarily on the unique Label report generator features.

Creating a Label report begins in the New Label dialog box (Figure 9.48). In this dialog box, you specify fields for the Label report and select the type of label. There are two ways to access the New Label dialog box: through Add/Edit view and through Report view.

If you are in Add/Edit view, choose Select ➤ Design Reports/Labels, press Ctrl+Y, or click on the Report button on the toolbar. In the Design Reports/Labels dialog box, click on the New Label radio button and either

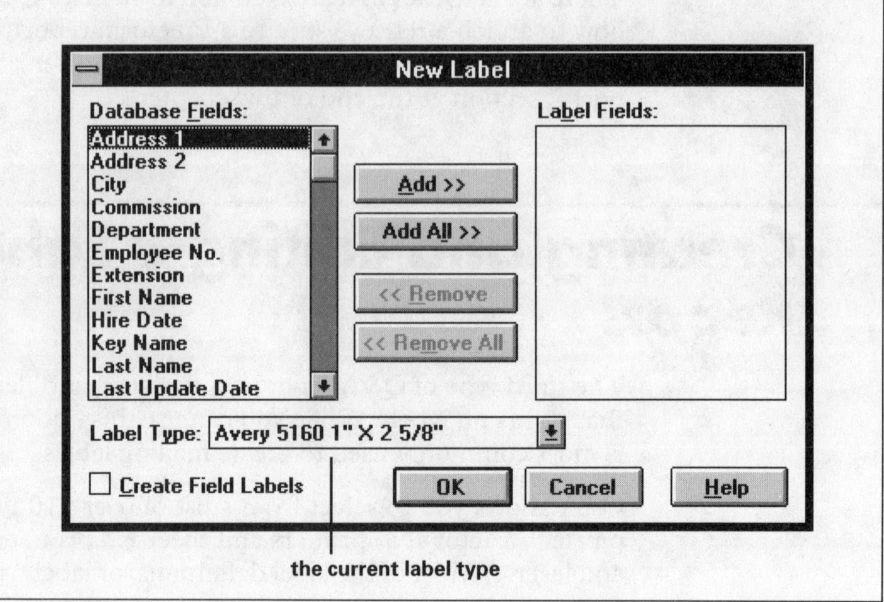

click on OK or press Enter. If you are in report view, choose Reports ➤ New ➤ Label. Q&A displays the New Label dialog box. To create a new Label report, follow these steps:

1. From the New Label dialog box, select fields in the Database Fields list box and click on the Add button. To select all the fields in this database, click on the Add All button. Q&A lists the selected fields in the Label Fields box.

2. If you want to create field labels with the fields you add, check the Create Field Labels check box.

3. From the Label Type drop-down list box, select the desired label. (You can select Custom Type from the bottom of the list and specify your own label dimensions. Choosing Custom Type brings you to the Label Size dialog box described later in this chapter.)

4. Click on OK or press Enter. Q&A closes the dialog box and displays a label in the work area (Figure 9.49).

The fields on the label are objects that you can manipulate in the same way as objects in a Freeform report or Input Form.

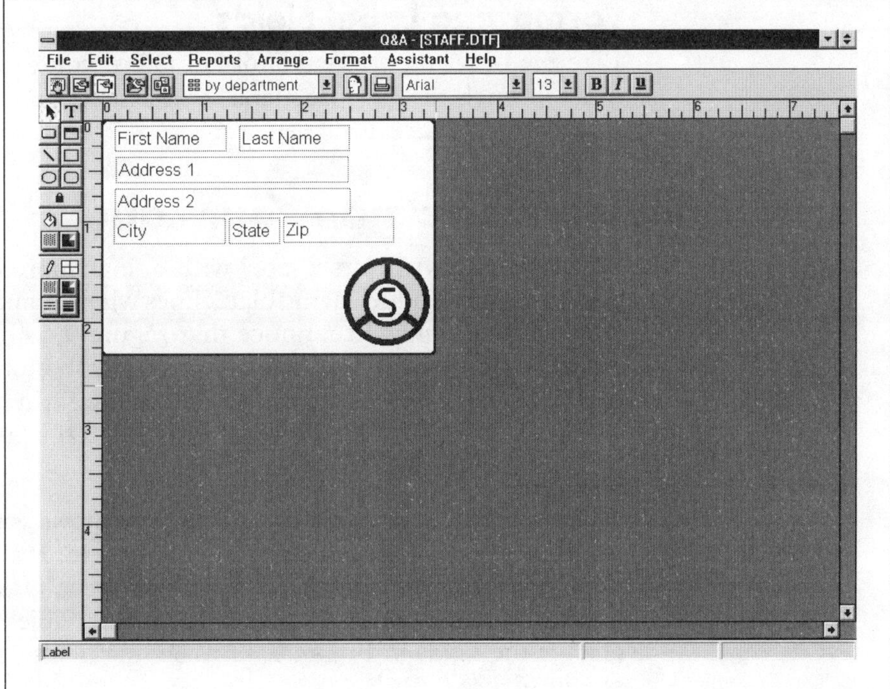

The Label Report Layout

The Label Report layout displays a single label in the work area. The objects you create in that work area are incorporated into every label you print. For example, if you create a label that has an address field in a rectangle, that rectangle will appear on every label that you print along with the fields that you specified from the current database.

Adding Fields to a Label

To add fields to labels, click on the field tool (the second button from the top in the second column) in the tool palette, and draw a field box. When you release the mouse button after drawing the field box, Q&A displays the New Field dialog box. Choose the field you want on your label and click on OK.

Formatting Label Fields

Like the other report generators in Q&A, you can change the field formats through the Format menu. You can assign and use formats just as you did for the Freeform reports.

Sliding Objects on Your Label

Sometimes Q&A prints a label with one or more blank fields. This can sometimes look odd, leaving blank lines where empty fields are located on your label. For instance, notice that Figure 9.49 has two address fields. Address 2 only contains the apartment number or post office box number. If a record doesn't contain Address 2 information, the printed label will have a blank line between Address 1 and the line containing the City, State, and Zip (see Figure 9.50).

To adjust for occurrences like this, Q&A allows you to slide objects into the empty areas in which there is a blank field. If a field is empty and the object next to it is assigned as a sliding object, Q&A deletes the space in which the field resides and slides the sliding object into its place. If you change the fields in Figure 9.49 to sliding fields, the label looks like the one in Figure 9.51.

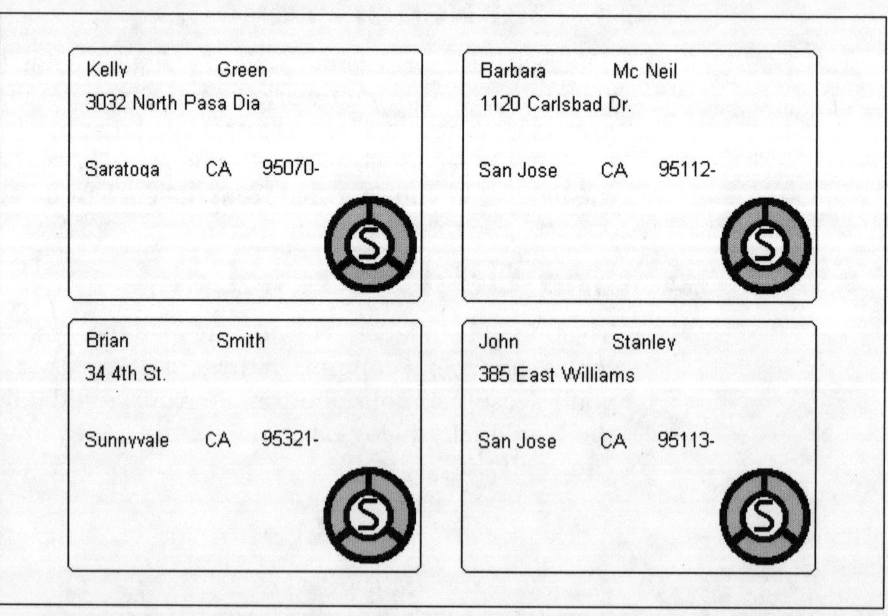

FIGURE 9.50

If the Address 2 field is empty, Q&A inserts a blank line on the label.

The printed label in Figure 9.50 as it looks with sliding fields

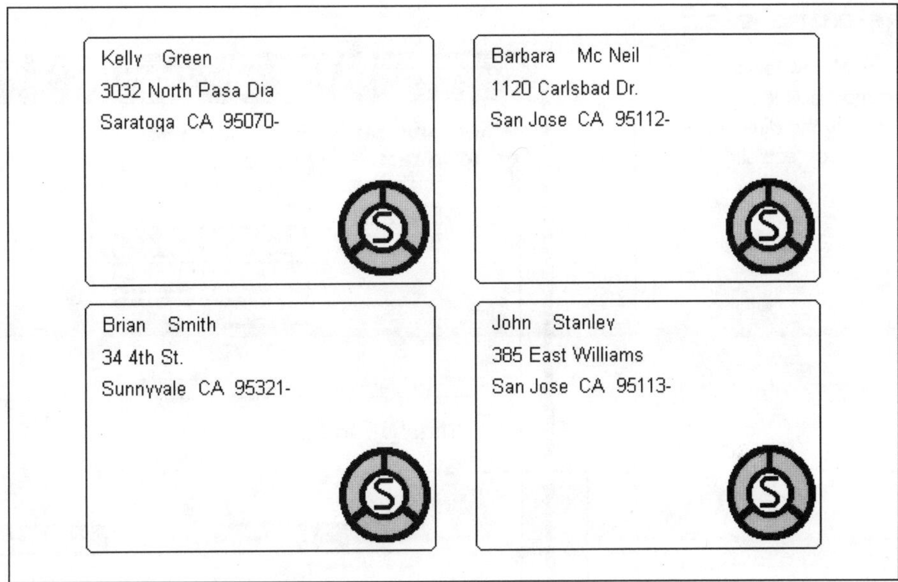

Just select an object and choose Arrange ➤ Slide Objects. Then click on the Slide Left or Slide Up to Fill check boxes in the Slide Objects dialog box (Figure 9.52) to specify the direction in which the slide objects will slide, if needed. Click on the All Above button (the default) to slide the object as far up as the whole row of objects can go, or click on the Directly Above button instructs Q&A to move each field as far up as each field can go.

To assign an object as a sliding object, use these steps:

1. Select the objects (for example, fields) to be assigned as sliding objects. (You can click on an object or select it using the select tool on the tool palette.) Often selecting all of the objects on the label works best.

2. Choose Arrange ➤ Slide Objects. Q&A opens the Slide Objects dialog box.

3. To slide the objects to the left, check the Slide Left box.

4. To slide the objects up, check the Slide Up to Fill box. Choose either the All Above or the Directly Above radio button.

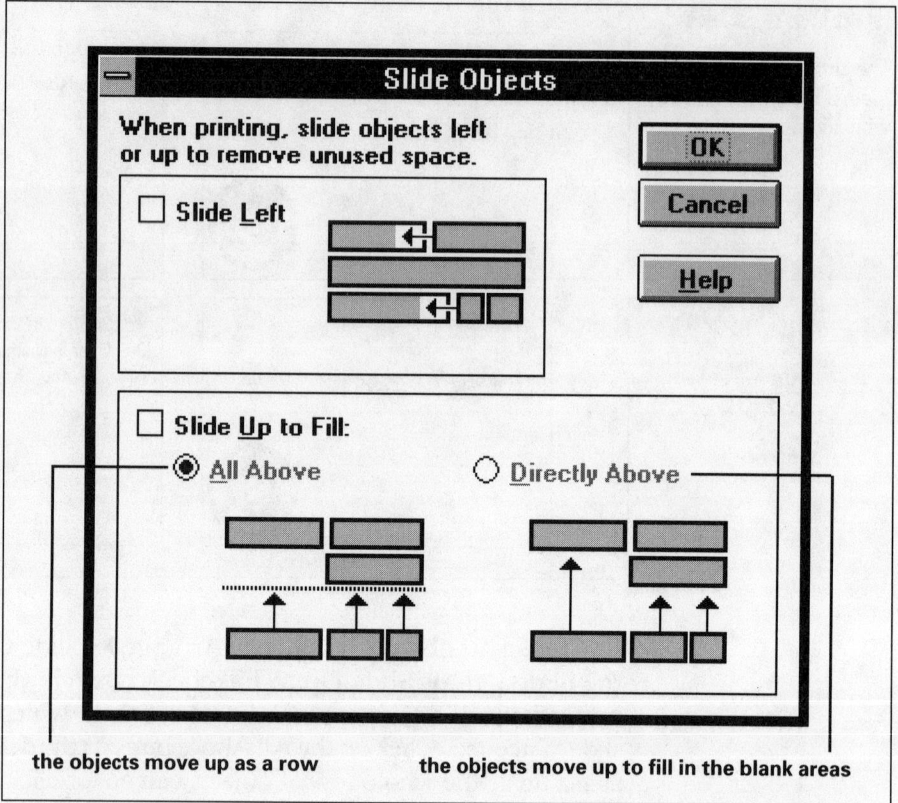

NOTE   You can check both the Slide **L**eft and Slide **U**p to Fill check boxes.

5. Click on OK. Q&A returns to the work area.

Showing Sliding Objects

Q&A allows you to see the objects that are assigned to slide while viewing the Label Report layout. Choose **R**eports ➤ **S**how Sliding Objects. This displays the sliding objects with arrows that show the direction in which they slide (Figure 9.53). If an object slides up, the field box contains an arrow pointing up. If an object slides to the left, its field box contains an arrow pointing to the left.

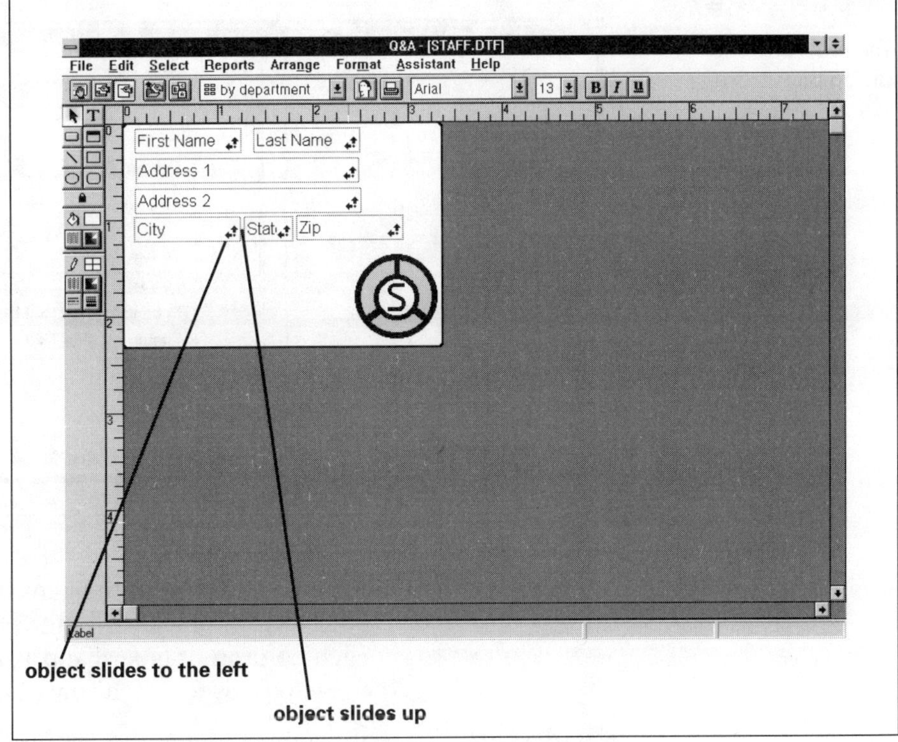

To hide the sliding objects indicators, choose Reports ➤ Hide Sliding Objects, which takes the place of the Show Sliding Objects command.

Changing the Size of a Label

If you want to use a different premanufactured label or a custom sized label, you can choose Report ➤ Label Size. Q&A then displays the Label Size dialog box (Figure 9.54) in which you can choose a label type from the Label Type drop-down list box.

Notice that the different groups on the right half of the dialog box reflect the settings for that label type.

Label Size   Specifies the width and height of each individual label.

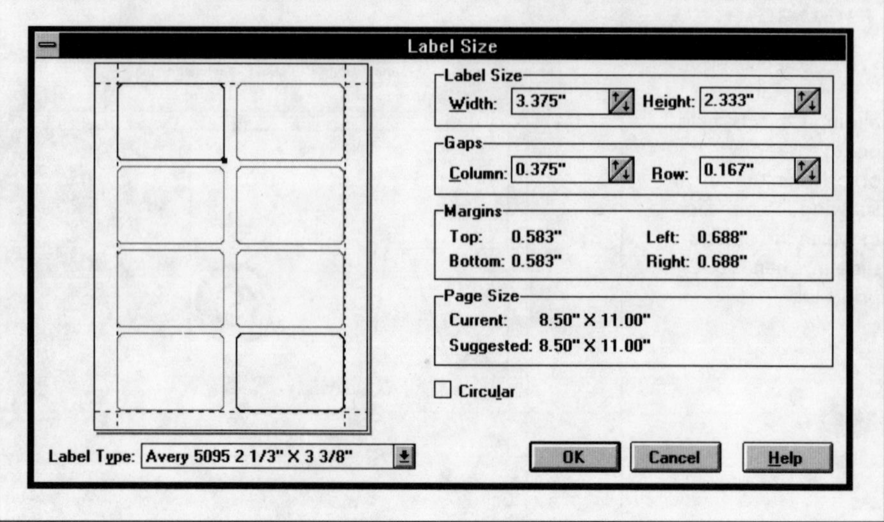

Gaps	Specifies the size of the gaps between labels. Column specifies the gap between each column of labels, and Row specifies the gap between each row of labels.
Margins	Indicates the margins set for the paper on which the labels are to be printed.
Page Size	Indicates the Current and Suggested paper size. The Current size is based on the paper dimensions set when you choose File ➤ Page Setup. The Suggested size is the size you need for the current label type.

Q&A allows you to change the size of the labels and the size of the gaps on the label sheet. If you look closely at the image of the label sheet on the left side of the dialog box, you will notice that the first and last labels have bold edges. Dragging the lower right corner of the first label changes the height and width of your labels. If you click anywhere on the last label, you can drag it to different positions, which changes the size of the column and row gaps. As you drag the label down, notice that the row gaps between labels increase. As you drag the last label to the right, the column gaps widen. Notice that as you change the label through the label sheet image the settings on the right half of the dialog box change appropriately.

N O T E

If you want to change the labels from rounded rectangles to circular or oval labels with the same height and width, check the Circular check box.

When you change the label sheet in the Label Size dialog box, the label type changes to Custom Type.

Managing Label Types

While the Label Size dialog box allows you to choose other label types and create new label sheets for immediate use, the Manage Label Types dialog box (Figure 9.55) lets you do the same and also add, change, and delete Label Types. To create a new label sheet, follow these steps:

1. Open the Manage Label Types dialog box by choosing Reports ➤ Manage Label Types.

2. Click on the New button. Q&A displays a new label sheet image.

3. Specify your settings through the controls on the right and the label images on the left.

The Manage Label Types dialog box lets you perform a multitude of activities related to Label reports.

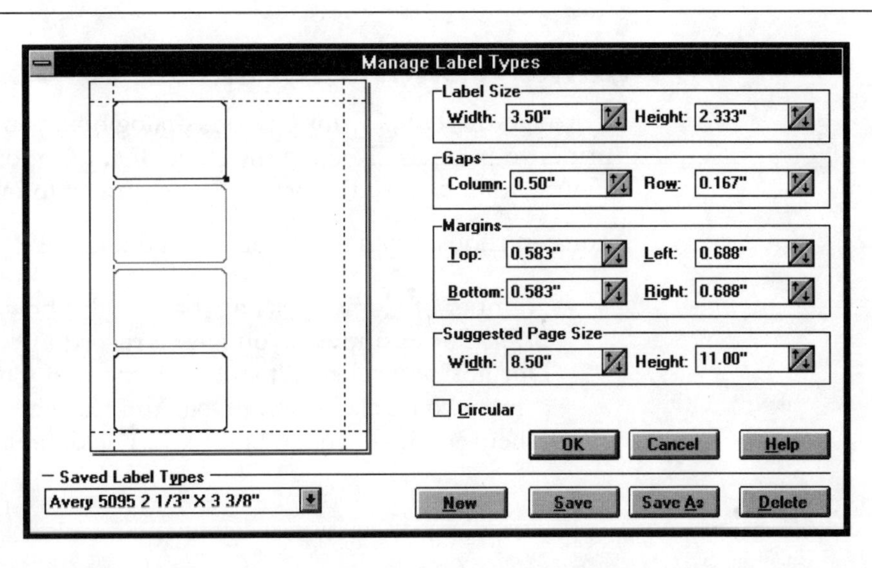

4. Click on Save _A_s. Q&A displays the Save Label Type dialog box.

5. Name the label that you created.

6. Click on OK. Q&A returns to the Manage Label Types dialog box.

If you created and saved a label that you do not want, you can delete it by following these steps:

1. If necessary, open the Manage Label Types dialog box by choosing _R_eports ➤ _M_anage Label Types.

2. Choose the label to be deleted through the Saved Label Types drop-down list box in the Manage Label Types dialog box.

3. Click on the _D_elete button.

4. Click on _Y_es when asked to confirm the deletion.

N O T E

Be careful when working in the Manage Label Types dialog box. It is easy to change or delete the label types that Q&A provides for you. Once you alter or delete a label type which is set precisely for a specific label, there is no way to reinstall those settings.

Printing Options for Label Reports

Through the Label Print Options dialog box, you can control how Q&A prints your labels. To open the Label Print Options dialog box shown in Figure 9.56, choose _R_eports ➤ Label _P_rint Options.

You can choose from these options in the Label Print Options dialog box.

- Number of _C_opies per Label tells Q&A how many of each label to print. For example, if you have a record in your database for John Doe and you selected two for Number of _C_opies Per Label, Q&A prints two labels for John Doe. You also get two labels for all the other records in your answer set. The default is 1.

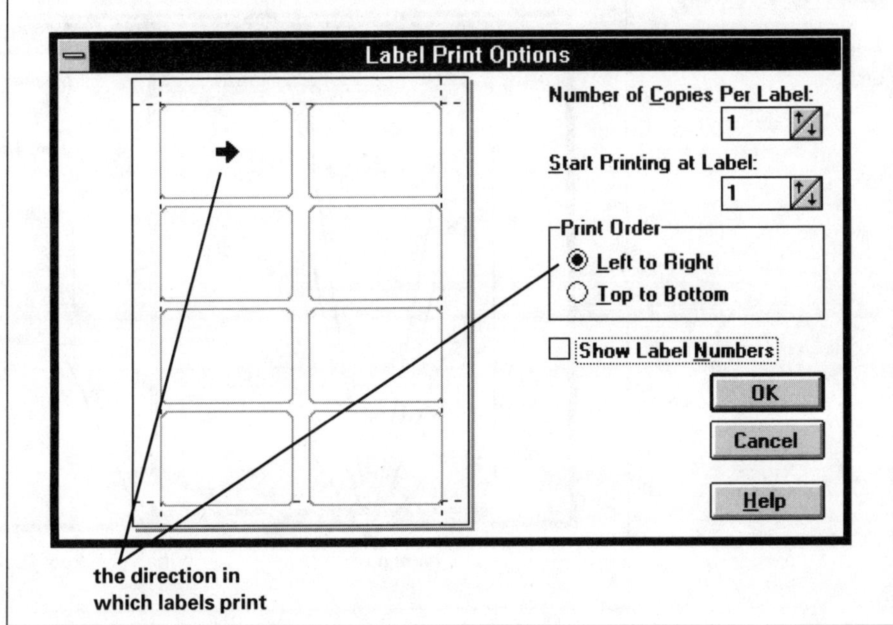

- Start Printing at Label instructs Q&A to start printing on a different label in the printing order. If you type a 4 in this text box, the first label that Q&A prints is the fourth label. If you plan to use this option, it is useful to have the Show Label Numbers check box checked. This way the label sheet image displays where Q&A will actually begin printing the labels.

- The options in the Print Order group instruct Q&A to print either Left to Right or Top to Bottom. Figure 9.57 displays an example of a Left to Right print order. Figure 9.58 displays a Top to Bottom print order. For these figures, the Show Label Numbers check box was checked to indicate the print order.

- The Show Label Numbers check box displays the print order of the labels on the label sheet.

A left to right print order

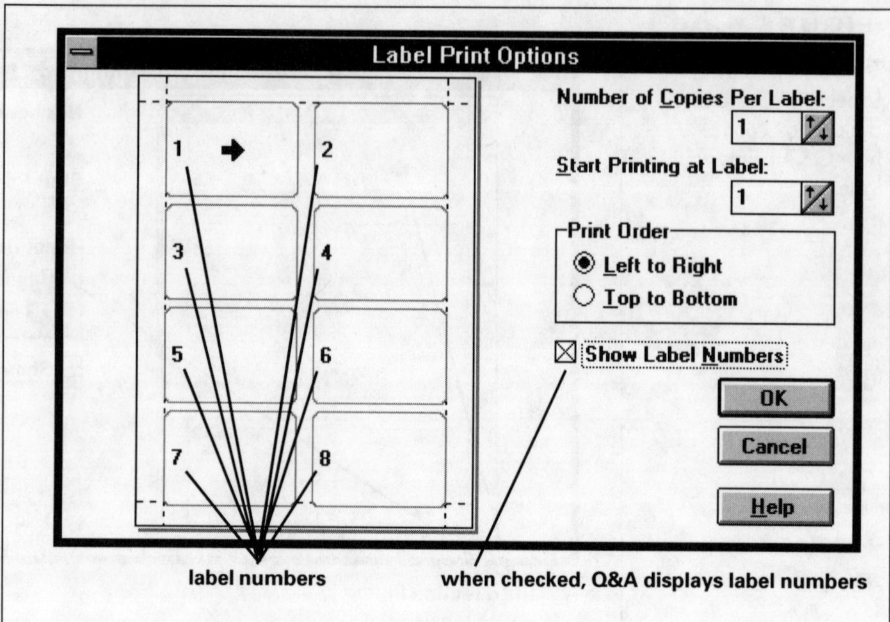

A top to bottom print order

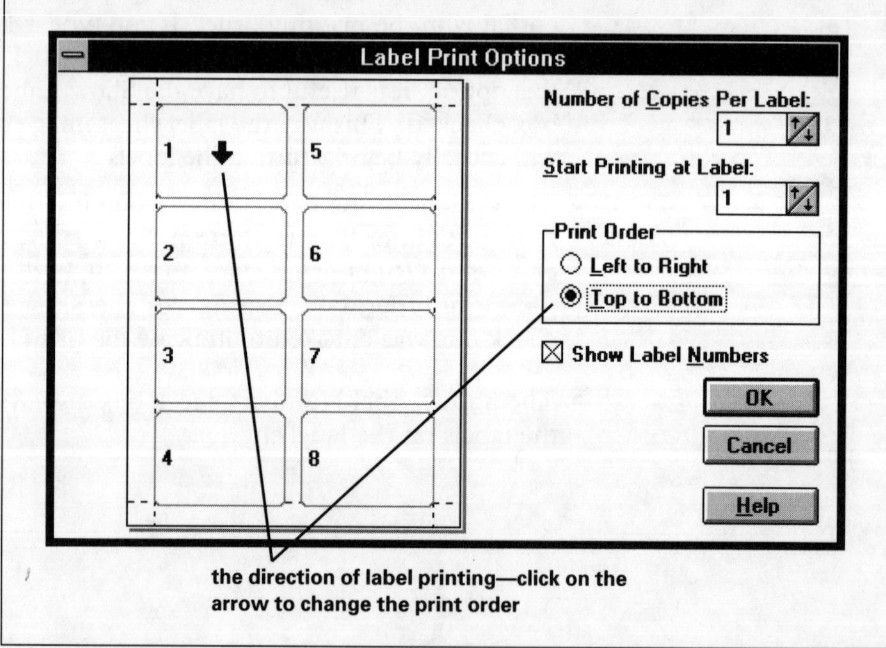

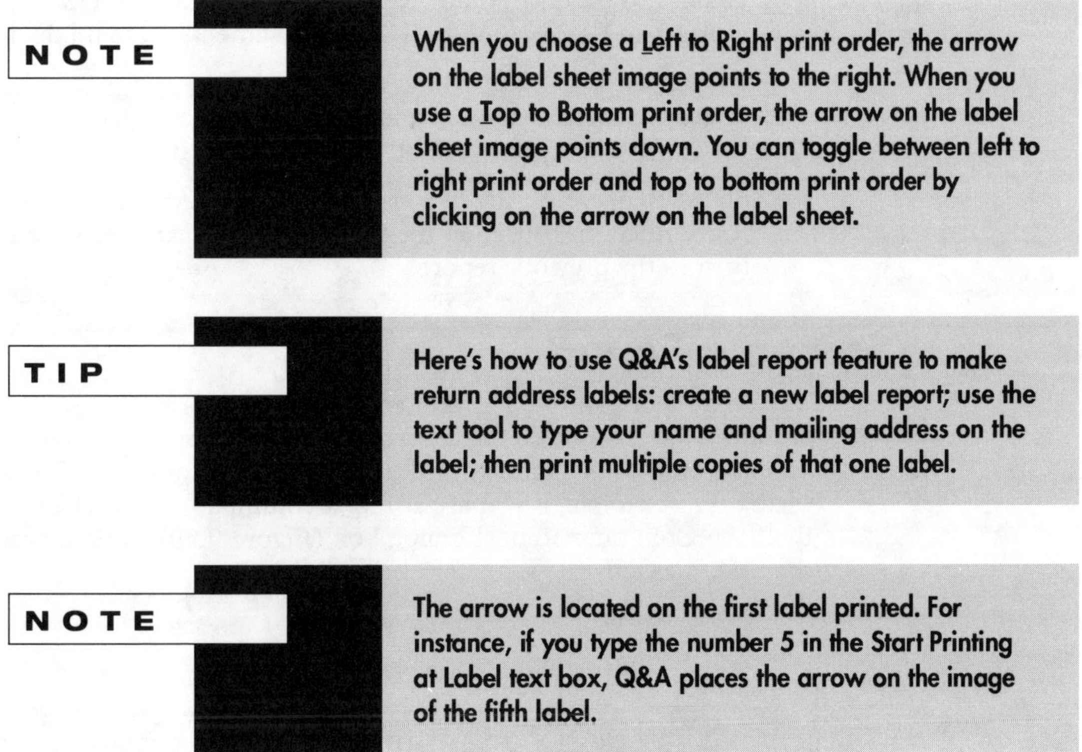

NOTE When you choose a Left to Right print order, the arrow on the label sheet image points to the right. When you use a Top to Bottom print order, the arrow on the label sheet image points down. You can toggle between left to right print order and top to bottom print order by clicking on the arrow on the label sheet.

TIP Here's how to use Q&A's label report feature to make return address labels: create a new label report; use the text tool to type your name and mailing address on the label; then print multiple copies of that one label.

NOTE The arrow is located on the first label printed. For instance, if you type the number 5 in the Start Printing at Label text box, Q&A places the arrow on the image of the fifth label.

Universal Functions for All Report Modes

Retrieving, saving, loading, deleting, and printing reports are almost identical for all three report modes. Now let's learn about these routines.

Attaching a Retrieve Spec

Q&A lets you attach retrieve specs to your reports. When you attach a retrieve spec, you are instructing Q&A to use it to create the answer sets used in the reports. You can either create a new retrieve spec or use a saved one.

1. Choose <u>R</u>eports ➤ Attach <u>R</u>etrieve or press Ctrl+R. Q&A changes to Retrieve mode. This is the same Retrieve mode described in Chapter 8.

2. Create your retrieve spec or load a saved retrieve spec. You can use retrieve specs saved in other modes in report mode.

3. Select <u>R</u>etrieve ➤ Attach This <u>R</u>etrieve or click on the Attach Retrieve Records button on the tool bar to use that retrieval and return to the previous report.

Saving a Report

To save a report, choose <u>R</u>eports ➤ <u>S</u>ave or <u>R</u>eports ➤ Save <u>A</u>s. If it is the first time you have saved the report or you choose Save <u>A</u>s, Q&A displays the Save Report dialog box for the particular type of report that you are saving. For example, if you are saving a columnar report, Q&A displays the Save Columnar Report dialog box (Figure 9.59), which, except for the title, is exactly the same for every type of report.

FIGURE 9.59

The Save Columnar Report As dialog box

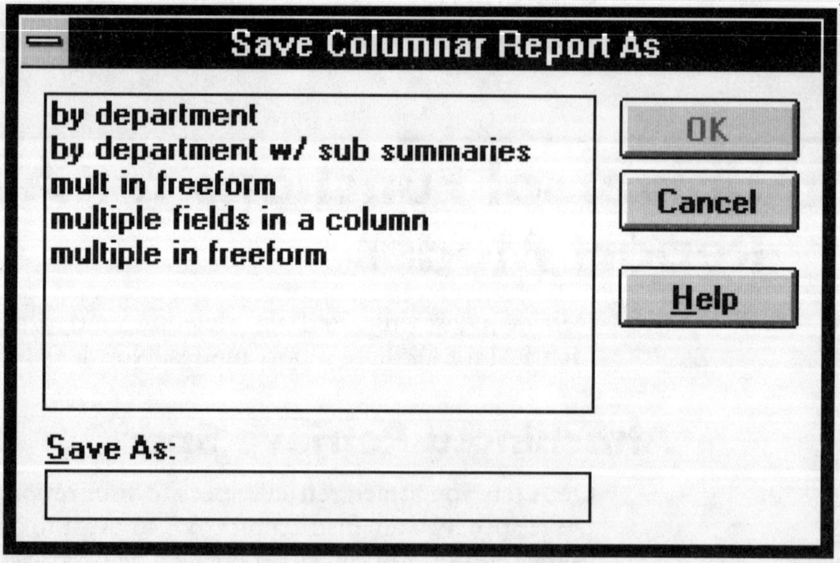

Type the name you want to save the report as in the Save As text box and click on OK. This saves your report and returns you to the report mode.

Loading a Report

To load a report, choose Reports ➤ Load Report/Label or press Ctrl+L. Q&A displays the Load Report/Label dialog box (Figure 9.60). Select the report to be loaded and click on OK. If you have not saved the report you are working in, Q&A asks you if you want to save the report before loading another.

If you know the type of report you want to load, you can narrow the search by selecting a report type from the List Report of Type drop-down list box.

While in any report mode, a quick way to load a report is to select it from the drop-down list box on your tool bar. This list box displays the name of the current report. Just select the report you want from the list and Q&A loads it.

The Load
Report/Label
dialog box

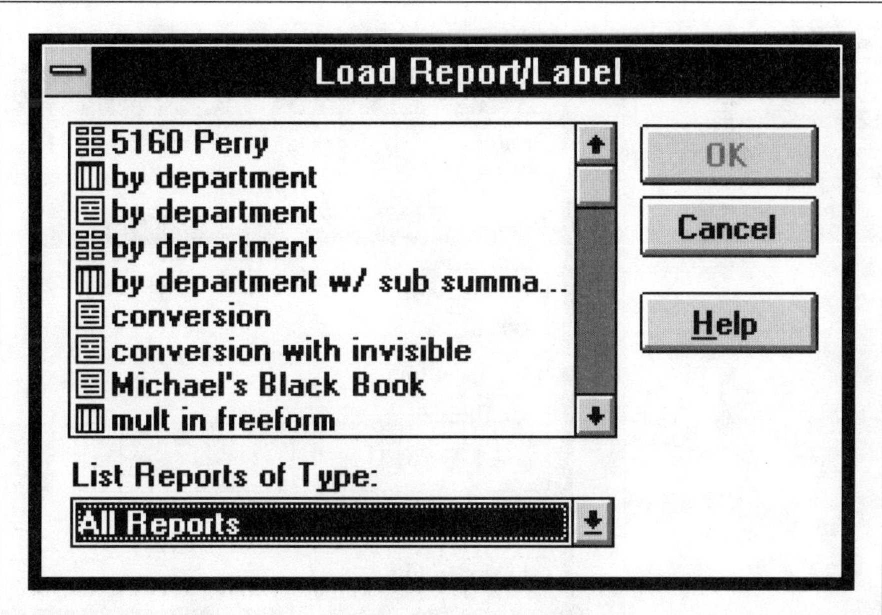

Deleting a Report

When you use this option, Q&A deletes the current report. To delete a report, choose Reports ➤ Delete Report. After you confirm the deletion, Q&A displays the Design Reports/Labels dialog box so that you can load a different report or create a new one.

Printing a Report

To print a report while in a print mode, choose File ➤ Print or choose the printer icon from the tool bar. This displays the Print dialog box (Figure 9.61). This familiar dialog box is almost identical for all report modes. The only difference between them is the Print drop-down list box, which displays different items to print depending on the type of report you are printing. To use the Print list box, choose the item you want to print from the list box and continue with the printing process.

- In Columnar reports, you can print the Columnar report, Columnar table layout, or the Columnar Header/Footer layout.

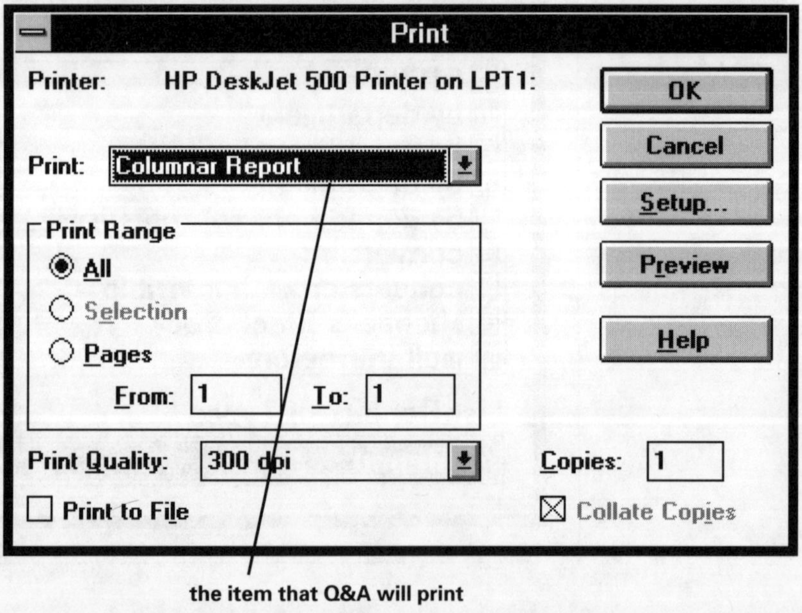

FIGURE 9.61

The Print dialog box. Note that the document that is set to be printed is a Columnar report.

- In Freeform reports, you can print the Freeform report or the Freeform Layout.

- In Label reports, you can print the Label report or the Label layout.

Running a Report

Running a report is a quick way of printing your report. This process prints your report without pausing at the normal printing dialog boxes. To run a report, choose Select ➤ Run Report. In the Run Report dialog box (Figure 9.62), select the report that you want to print and the retrieve spec to attach. Then click on OK. Note that you do not need to be in report mode to run a report.

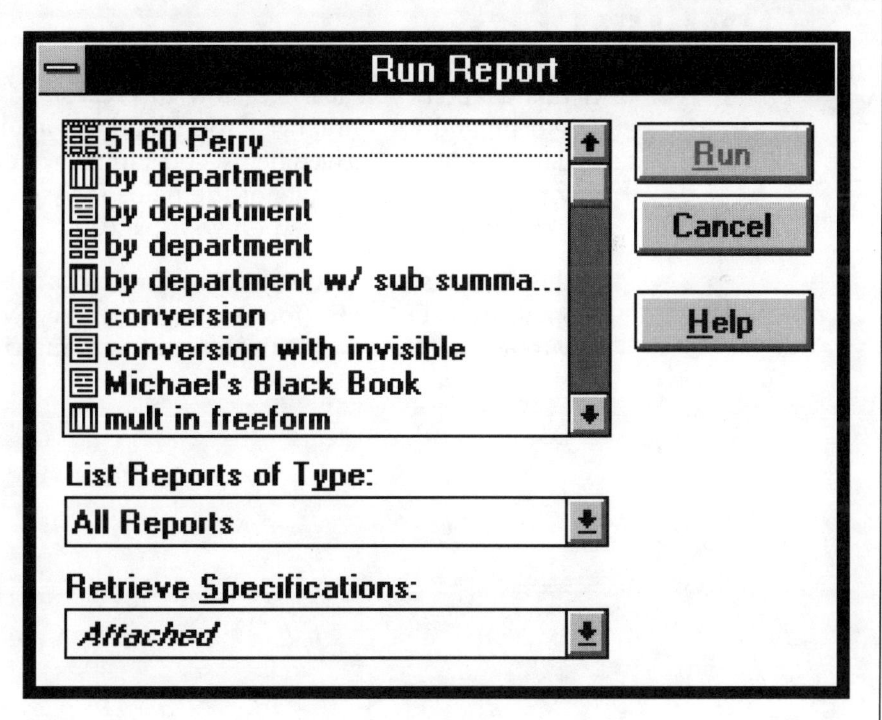

Using Print Preview

It is useful to use Print Preview to check how your layouts will look on paper before printing. The image that you see can illustrate the changes that you need to make. This saves you resources—from time waiting for the printer to print and paper that you might waste.

Except for the Windows printer drivers, Q&A uses the same files to create a page preview as it does to print a report. Through the preview option, Q&A determines how to create your report using your specified layout. Q&A then uses your preferences, options, and page setup to determine how the report will look when it is finally printed. Q&A then displays the image on the screen.

To Sum Up

In this chapter, you learned how to create and customize Columnar, Freeform, and Label reports. You found out about the details of setting up database fields, derived fields, and summary fields. You also discovered how to change the formats of the fields for your reports and to control how the reports are printed on your page.

In the next chapter, you will learn how to use the Intelligent Assistant, also known as D.A.V.E. (for Do Anything Very Well). You will also learn how to use the Scripting Assistant to set up multi-line scripts.

chapter

10

Your Q&A
Assistant

fast TRACK

⬤ **To save a script** 333

> click on the S̲ave button, type the name of the script in the S̲ave As text box, and either click on OK or press Enter.

⬤ **To delete a script** 339

> select it from the Saved Scripts drop-down list box and then click on the D̲elete button.

⬤ **To clear the current script and start a new one** 339

> click on the N̲ew button.

⬤ **To add a script to the A̲ssistant Menu** 341

> choose A̲ssistant ➤ M̲anage Assistant Menu. Select the desired script from the Sav̲ed Scripts box, click on A̲dd, and click on Don̲e.

⬤ **To run a script from the A̲ssistant menu** 342

> choose A̲ssistant and either click on the script option or press the number preceding the entry.

⬤ **To delete one script from the A̲ssistant menu** 342

> choose A̲ssistant ➤ M̲anage Assistant Menu, select the script to be removed, click on R̲emove, and click on Don̲e.

⬤ **To remove all scripts from the A̲ssistant menu** 342

> click on Rem̲ove All and click on Don̲e.

NOW that you have a good background in Q&A Database, you have an opportunity to learn about two timesavers: DAVE (Do Anything Very Easily) the Intelligent Assistant (IA); and DAVE the Scripting Assistant. Both Assistants allow you to build queries (which add records), produce reports, calculate, retrieve and sort—in short, everything that you have already learned about but in a more automated way. The difference between the two is that the IA runs just one query at a time, while the Scripting Assistant can run a series of several queries, somewhat like a macro. Both Assistants use the Query Guide, which enables you to build queries from phrases that appear in a phrase window. As you become more expert in using the Assistants, you can type your own queries.

Automating Your Work with the Intelligent Assistant (IA)

The IA serves three purposes: to automate your work; to help you learn about how Q&A works; and to perform data management operations using English-like sentences. For example, you can build a retrieval specification, run it to see if it works, and when it does, you can look at the retrieval spec to see how the IA built it. IA queries can be extremely powerful; for example, the IA can build both retrieval and sort specs from the same query.

The best way to learn about IA is to use it. Simply choose Assistant ➤ Intelligent Assistant, press Ctrl+I, or click on the IA button on the tool bar to get started. All the work you do in the IA is performed in one dialog box—the DAVE the Intelligent Assistant dialog box (see Figure 10.1).

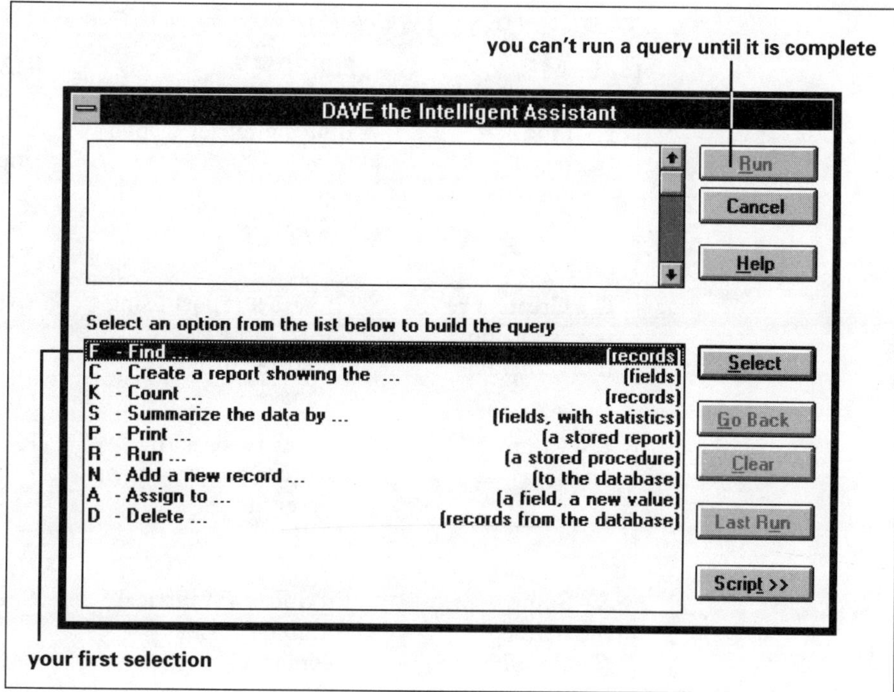

You can select Query Guide phrases by selecting them from the Phrase Window or by using the keyboard. If you are just beginning to use the IA, you'll want to select phrases to build queries. In fact, you may continue to use the Query Guide long after you know Q&A inside and out.

Building a Query with the Query Guide

After displaying the DAVE the Intelligent Assistant dialog box, select the first phrase in the query. Table 10.1 lists the choices in the first Phrase Window.

Select the first phrase and click on Select or press Enter. The IA displays your selection in the Query Window and succeeding phrases in the Phrase Window. Continue to add to the query by selecting phrases and clicking on Select. If you wish to backtrack by one phrase selection, click on Go Back. To clear the query and start all over, click on Clear. To switch to the

TABLE 10.1: The Opening Phrases for an IA Query

PHRASE	PURPOSE	NEXT WINDOW
F - Find... (records)	Builds a retrieval spec	S - and show using [input] form
		R - the records where
		A - ALL the records
C - Create a report showing the... (fields)	Creates a report using one or more fields from the current database	Select a field
K - Count... (records)	Counts records that meet certain criteria or all records	R - the records where
		A - ALL the records
S - Summarize the data by... (fields, with statistics)	Produces a statistical summary (Total, Average, Count, Maximum, Minimum, Variance, and Standard Deviation) for selected fields	Select a field (group)
P - Print... (a stored report)	Print an existing report or label	C - the Columnar Report
		D - the DOS Columnar Report
		F - the Freeform Report
		M - the Label
R - Run... (a stored procedure)	Runs an existing report, label, spec, or script	C - the Columnar Report
		D - the DOS Columnar Report

TABLE 10.1: The Opening Phrases for an IA Query (continued)

PHRASE	PURPOSE	NEXT WINDOW
R - Run... (a stored procedure) (continued)		F - the Freeform Report
		L - the Label
		R - the Retrieve Specification
		U - the Update Specification
		E - the Export Specification
		S - the script
N - Add a new record... (to the database)	Adds a new record to the current database	W - with (a field having a value)
		. - (to create an empty record)
A - Assign to... (a field, a new value)	Select a field in which you want to assign a text value or programming statement	V - the value
		E - the expression (programming statement)
D - Delete... (records from the database)	Delete all or selected records from the database	R - the records where
		A - ALL the records

Scripting Assistant, click on Script. (Once you do that, the Scripting Assistant takes over the query and you cannot return to the IA.) As you build a query, notice that phrases ending with an ellipsis (…) indicate that you will make at least another selection after this one; a phrase ending with a period indicates the end of a query. Table 10.2 lists the most common intermediate phrases, descriptions of each, and the beginning phrase from which they branch.

TABLE 10.2: The Most Common Intermediate Phrases for an IA Query

PHRASE	PURPOSE	BRANCHES FROM
& - and the (field)	Adds an AND field to the query	Create a report showing the *field name* from the records where *field name constraint1*
& - and by	Adds another field name to the query	Summarize the data by *field name*
/ - or the (field)	Adds an OR field to the query	Create a report showing the *field name* from the records where *field name constraint1*
= - is	Equals	Count | Find | Delete the records where money | date | number | text *field name*
> - is greater than	Is greater than	Count | Find | Delete the records where money | number *field name*
< - is less than	Is less than	Count | Find | Delete the records where money | number *field name*
A - after (a word)	Is after	Create a report showing the *field name* from the records where *field name* appears alphabetically
A - ALL the records	Performs the query on all the records in the current database	Find | Count | Delete

TABLE 10.2: The Most Common Intermediate Phrases for an IA Query (continued)

PHRASE	PURPOSE	BRANCHES FROM
A - appears alphabetically (before/after/ first/last)	Compares the value for its alphabetical order against a value in another position in the database	Count | Find | Delete the records where text | keyword *field name*
A - average (and grandaverage)	Calculates the average and grand average	Summarize the data by Yes/No field showing the
A - average	Calculates the average	Summarize the data by any field showing the
A - is after (a date)	Tests whether the selected date falls after a specific date	Count | Find | Delete the records where date | time | text | time *field name*
A - showing all statistics for	Shows all statistics for a selected field	Summarize the data by *field name*
B - begins with (a character sequence)	Tests whether any records contain the selected field beginning with these characters	Count | Find | Delete the records where text | keyword *field name*
B - is before (a date)	Tests whether the selected date falls before a specific date	Count | Find | Delete the records where date | time | text *field name*
B - before (a word)	Is before	Create a report showing the *field name* from the records where *field name* appears alphabetically
C - contains (a character sequence)	Tests whether any records contain the selected field with these characters	Count | Find | Delete the records where text | keyword *field name*

TABLE 10.2: The Most Common Intermediate Phrases for an IA Query (continued)

PHRASE	PURPOSE	BRANCHES FROM
C - count (without subcount)	Counts the number of records without producing any subtotals	Create a report showing the field name with grand
C - counts (number of records)	Counts the number of selected records	Summarize the data by any field showing the
C - is correctly formatted	Tests for a valid format for this field type	Count|Find|Delete the records where Yes/No|money|date|time|text|number *field name*
C - the Columnar Report	Displays or prints a saved columnar report	Print, Run
D - sorted by decreasing (values from the field)	Sorts the selected fields in descending order	Count|Find|Delete ALL the records
D - standard deviations	Calculates the standard deviation for a selected field	Summarize the data by any field showing the
D - the DOS Columnar Report	Displays or prints a saved DOS columnar report	Print, Run
E - ends with (a character sequence)	Tests whether any records contain the selected field ending with these characters	Count|Find|Delete the records where text|keyword *field name*
E - is empty (blank)	Tests whether any records contain the selected field with no value	Count|Find|Delete the records where Yes/No|money|date|time|text|number *field name*

TABLE 10.2: The Most Common Intermediate Phrases for an IA Query (continued)

PHRASE	PURPOSE	BRANCHES FROM
E - the Export Specification	Runs the specific Export Specification	Run
E - the expression (programming statement)	Assigns a programming statement to a field name	Assign to *field name*
F - from (records)	Selects certain records	Create a report showing the
F - is FALSE (NO)	Tests whether any records contain the selected Yes/No field with a negative value	Count | Find | Delete the records where Yes/No field name
F - the Freeform Report	Displays or prints a saved freeform report	Print, Run
F - first (before all other values)	Is the first	Create a report showing the *field name* from the records where *field name* appears alphabetically
G - is among the (earliest or latest)	Tests whether any records contain selected fields that are among the earliest or latest added	Count | Find | Delete the records where date | time | text field name
G - is among the (highest or lowest)	Tests whether any records contain selected fields that are among the highest or lowest	Count | Find | Delete the records where money | number field name
G - among the (first or last)	Is among the values	Create a report showing the *field name* from the records where *field name* appears alphabetically

YOUR Q&A ASSISTANT

TABLE 10.2: The Most Common Intermediate Phrases for an IA Query (continued)

PHRASE	PURPOSE	BRANCHES FROM
G – maximums (greatest value)	Finds the maximum value	Summarize the data by any field showing the
G – with grand (record count or Maximum, minimum, etc.)	Counts all the records in the database	Create a report showing the
I – is (blank or correctly formatted)	Finds records with selected fields that are either empty or correctly formatted, depending on the next phrase selected	Count | Find | Delete the records where text | keyword *field name*
K – includes	Includes a value	Count | Find | Delete the records where keyword *field name*
L – the Label	Runs the selected labels	Run
L – minimums (least value)	Displays the minimum value	Summarize the data by any field showing the
L – is at least	Performs on the records in which the value in the selected field is at least a specific value	Count | Find | Delete the records where money | number *field name*
L – last (after all other values)	Is the last	Create a report showing the *field name* from the records where *field name* appears alphabetically
M – is at most	Perform on the records in which the value in the selected field is a specific value at the most	Count | Find | Delete the records where money | number *field name*

TABLE 10.2: The Most Common Intermediate Phrases for an IA Query (continued)

PHRASE	PURPOSE	BRANCHES FROM
M - matches (a character sequence)	Tests whether any records contain the selected field matching these characters	Count | Find | Delete the records where (text | keyword *field name*)
L - the Label	Displays or prints a saved mailing label	Print
N - does not (one of the above)	Tests for a negative value in combination with another phrase	Count | Find | Delete the records where text | keyword *field name*
N - is not (one of the above)	Tests for a negative value in combination with another phrase	Count | Find | Delete the records where Yes/No | money | date | time | text | number *field name*
R - the records where	Tests for records that meet the following conditions	Find, Count, Delete
R - the Retrieve Specification	Runs a retrieval using a specific retrieve spec	Run
S - and show using form (input form)	Displays the selected records using a specific input form	Find
S - matches the SOUNDEX pattern (a letter sequence)	Retrieves records with fields that sound like a character string	Count | Find | Delete the records where text | keyword *field names* – sorted by (values from the field)
missing item?	Sorts the selected fields in ascending order	Count | Find | Delete ALL the records
S - the script	Runs a saved script	Run
S - with sub (and grand)	Calculates a subtotal and a grand total	Create a report showing the

TABLE 10.2: The Most Common Intermediate Phrases for an IA Query (continued)

PHRASE	PURPOSE	BRANCHES FROM
T – is TRUE (YES)	Tests whether any records contain the selected Yes/No field with a positive value	Count | Find | Delete the records where Yes/No *field name*
T – totals	Totals	Summarize the data by any field showing the
U – the Update Specification	Runs the saved Update Specification	Run
V – the value	Gives a specific value	Assign to *field name*
V – variances	Gives a statistical variance	Summarize the data by any field showing the
V – includes the keywords	Includes all the keywords	Count | Find | Delete the records where keyword *field name*
W – with (a field having a value)	Includes a field which has a specific value	Add a new record
X – is the (earliest or latest)	Tests whether any records contain selected fields that are either the earliest or latest	Count | Find | Delete the records where date | time | text *field name*
X – is the (greatest or least)	Tests whether any records contain selected fields that are either the earliest or latest	Count | Find | Delete the records where money | number *field name*

After completing the query (Figure 10.2), click on the <u>R</u>un button. The IA runs the query and displays the results (Figure 10.3). If, after running the request, the IA doesn't find any records that match the query, it displays the input form with no records retrieved. In the status bar of the input form, Q&A informs you that no records were selected. (Figure 10.4).

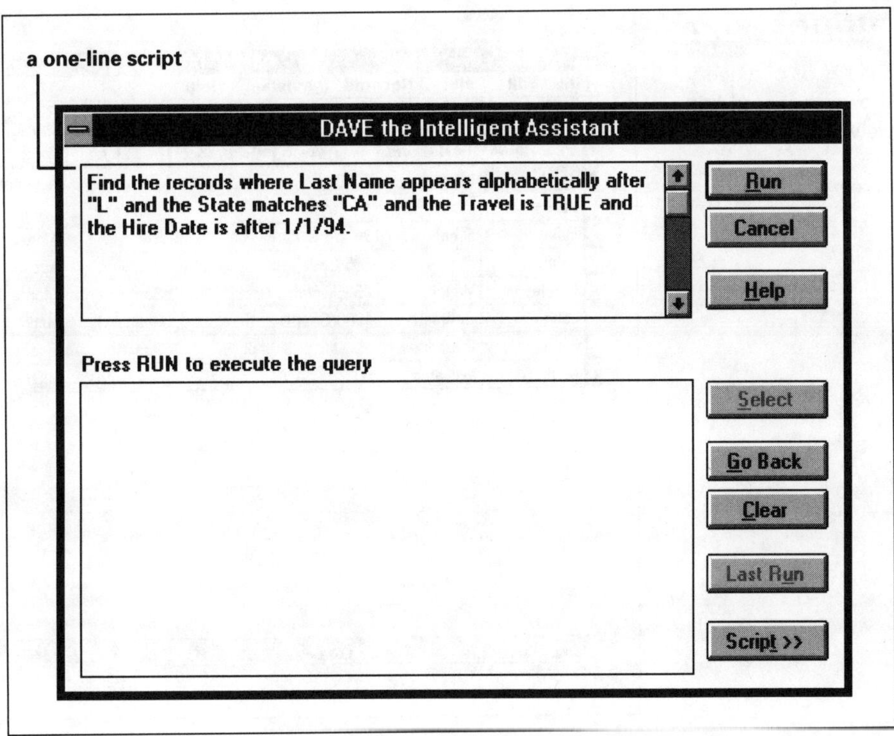

To see the actual Retrieve spec that you have just "written," choose
Records ➤ Retrieve or press Ctrl+R. Q&A displays the unsaved Retrieve
spec (Figure 10.5). To save it for future use, choose Retrieve ➤ Save
Retrieve or press Ctrl+S. If you have added a Sort spec to your query, you
can view that by choosing Records ➤ Sort or pressing Ctrl+T. Q&A displays the Sort dialog box (Figure 10.6) with the sort field in the Sort Order box.

You can use the IA for almost any Q&A task. Then you can see how the
IA did the job and you can save some of those specs without doing the
real work yourself.

To build a query for the current database, follow these steps:

1. Choose Assistant ➤ Intelligent Assistant or press Ctrl+I. Q&A displays the DAVE the Intelligent Assistant dialog box.

The results of a query shown in Spreadsheet view

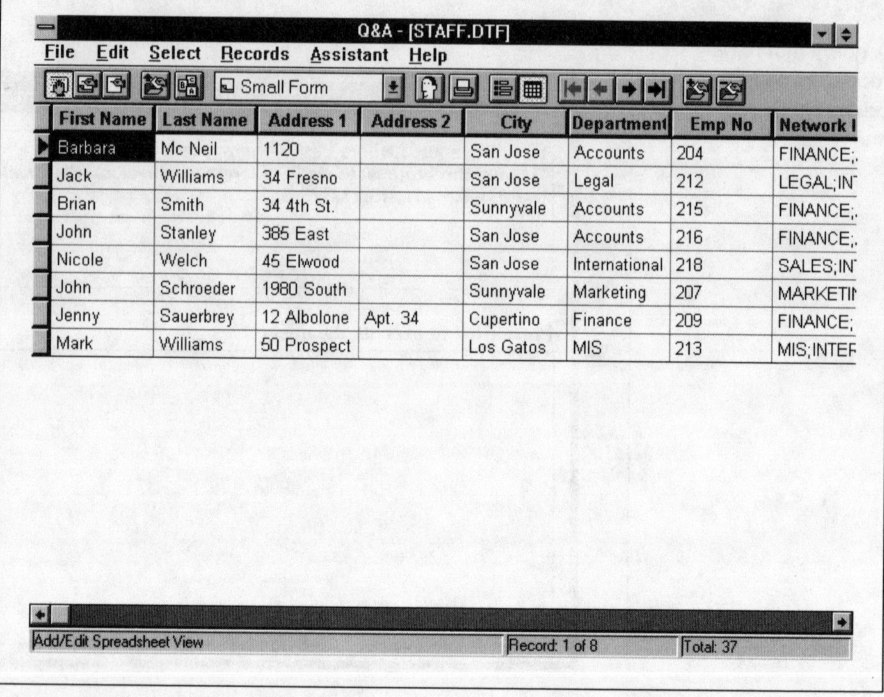

The results of a query that found no matching records

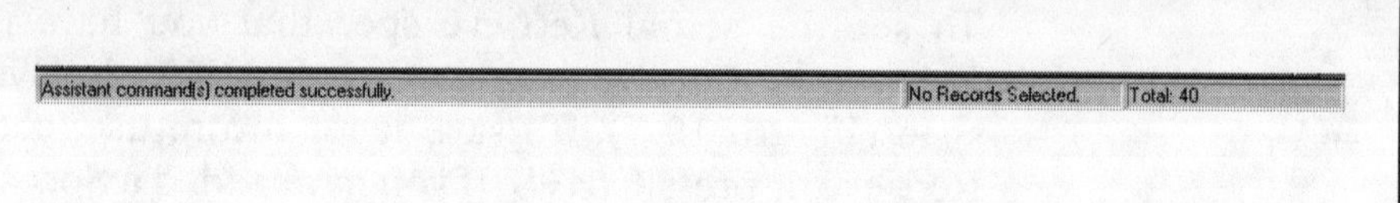

2. Select a starting phrase from the Query Window and press <u>S</u>elect to add it to the Query Window (Figure 10.7). Q&A adds another group of phrases to the Query Window, which vary depending on your starting phrase.

3. Select another phrase and press <u>S</u>elect (Figure 10.8). Q&A adds another group of phrases to the Query Window.

4. Repeat step 3 until you have added all the desired criteria to the query (Figures 10.9, 10.10, 10.11, 10.12, and 10.13).

5. Select a phrase ending with a period (Figure 10.14) to end the query sentence (Figure 10.15).

FIGURE 10.5

The Retrieve spec
resulting from the
query shown in
Figure 10.2

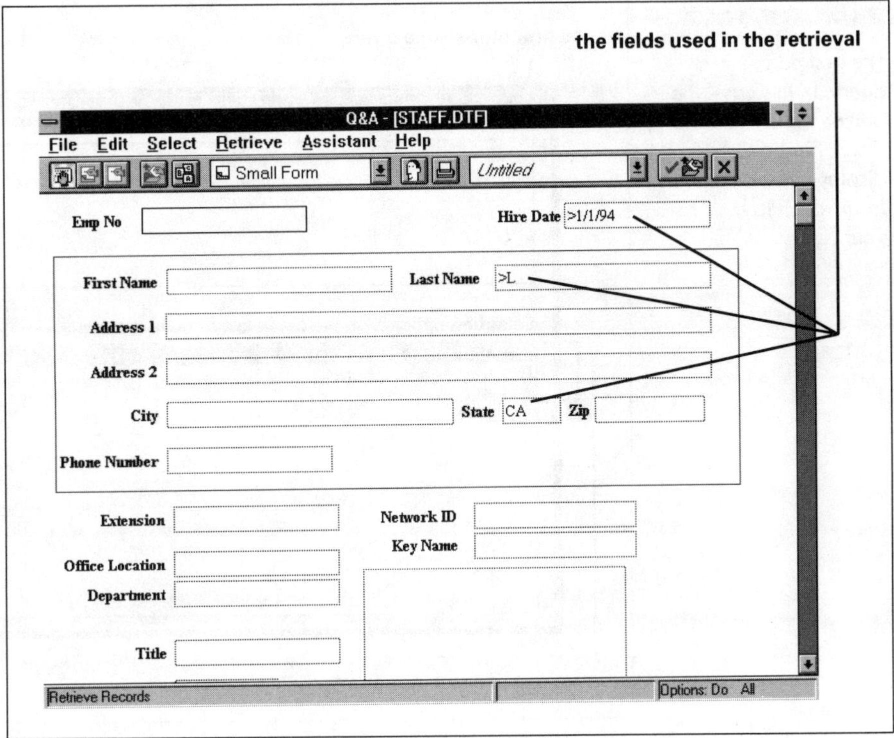

the fields used in the retrieval

FIGURE 10.6

The Sort dialog box

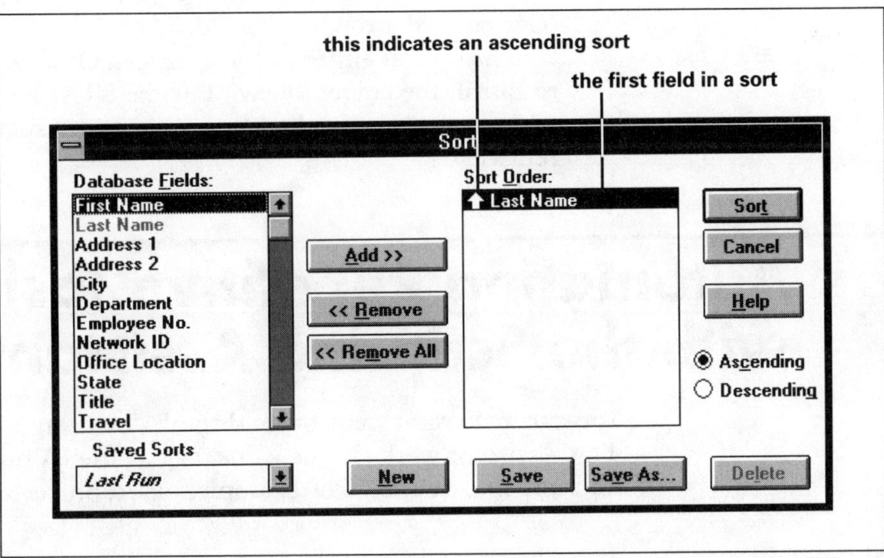

this indicates an ascending sort

the first field in a sort

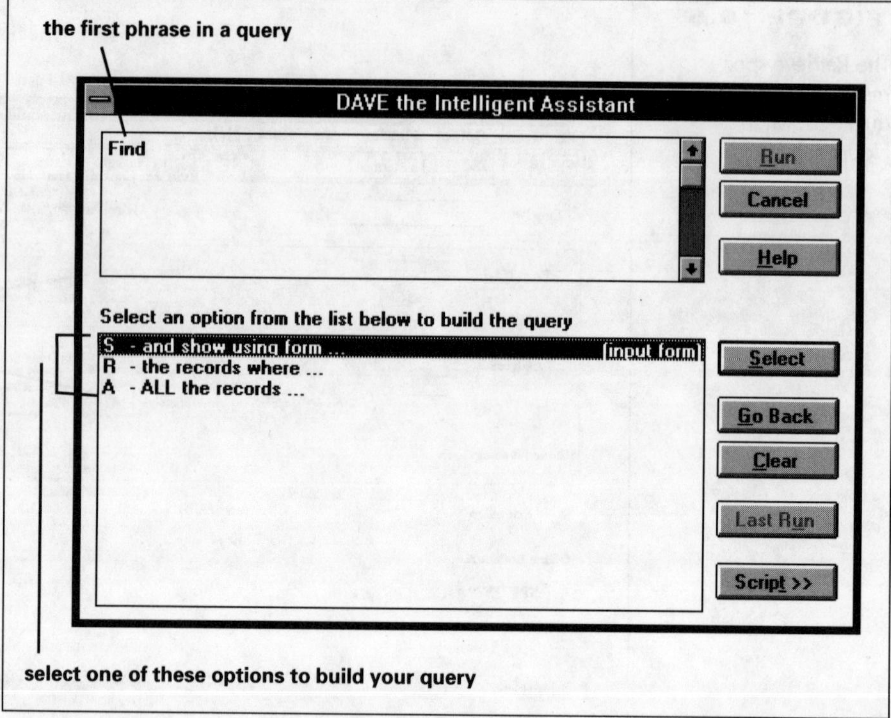

6. Click on <u>R</u>un to run the query. Q&A displays the results. If you have created a report, Q&A displays it in Print Preview view from which you can either print or cancel. Otherwise, Q&A displays the results in the current view. (For the STAFF database, Q&A found 12 records that matched the query and displayed them in the current view.)

Automating Repetitive Tasks with the Scripting Assistant

You can go several steps beyond the IA by using the Scripting Assistant. This Assistant works in the same way as the IA but allows you to create multiple-line queries. For example, based on certain criteria, you might

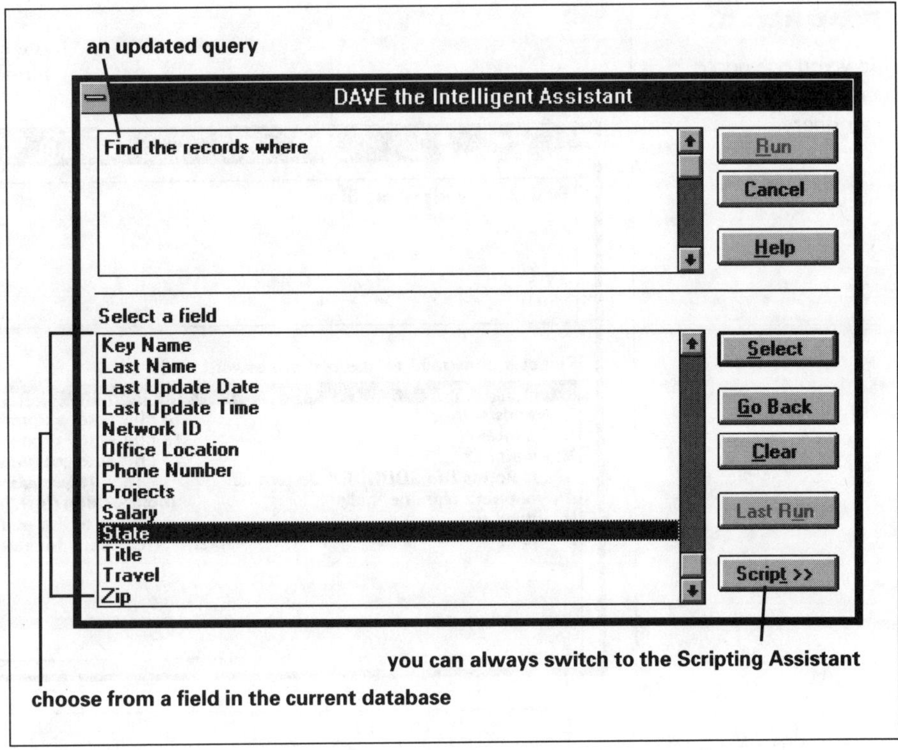

need to delete obsolete records once a month. You might run a monthly report on accrued vacation time or sick time. If you need to run a series of inventory reports every Friday, you can run the same script consisting of queries that build each report.

Using the Scripting Assistant, you can add a script to the <u>A</u>ssistant menu and run it by simply selecting it. If you use macros in your other Windows applications, you'll use the Scripting Assistant in much the same way.

TIP

A good way to test the individual lines in a script is to build each line as a query using the IA. Then run it, rebuild it (if needed), click on the Scrip<u>t</u> button to change to the Scripting Assistant, and save it as a script.

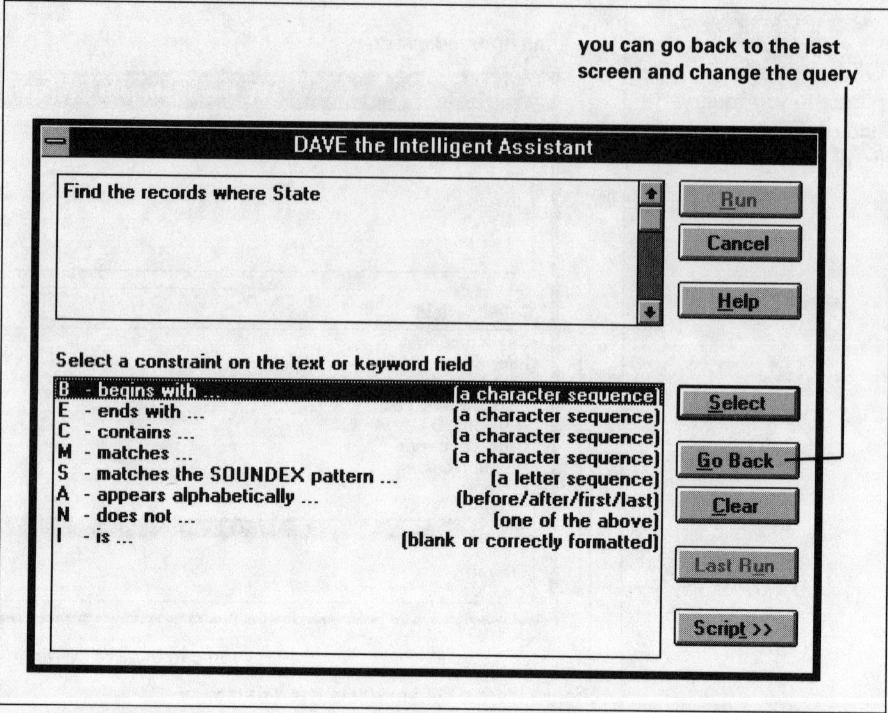

Writing a Script with the Scripting Assistant

As you have already learned in this chapter, you can access the Scripting Assistant from within the DAVE the Intelligent Assistant dialog box. You can also choose Assistant ➤ Scripting Assistant or press Ctrl+J to display the DAVE the Scripting Assistant dialog box (Figure 10.16).

The DAVE the Scripting Assistant dialog box looks very much like the DAVE the Intelligent Assistant dialog box. However, there are more phrases in the Phrase Window and there are more buttons. Table 10.3 lists the opening phrases in the dialog box.

You'll create a script in just the same way that you created a query using the IA. However, when using the Scripting Assistant, you can create multiple-line scripts that you can save rather than single-line queries that have

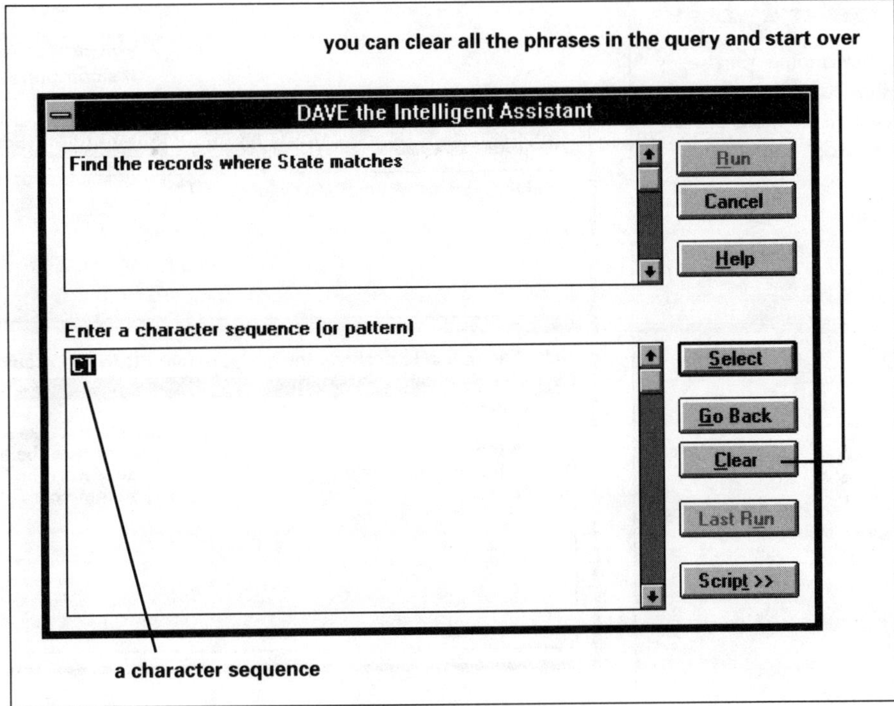

to be saved as specific retrieve specs or sort specs. For example, you can create a series of reports of your company's up-to-date telephone extensions. Simply create a script for each office and run the whole script once every month or so. Figure 10.17 shows the DAVE the Scripting Assistant dialog box with a two-line script. The Scripting Assistant regards each query as a line, even though it may actually go on for several lines.

To add a new line between the two existing lines, just move the mouse pointer to the location in which you wish to insert the line and click on the Insert Line button. To delete a line, select it and click on the Delete Line button.

You can save a script by clicking on the Save button. Q&A displays the Save Intelligent Script As dialog box (see Figure 10.18). Type the name of the script in the Save As text box and either click on OK or press Enter. Q&A saves the script and displays its name in the Saved Scripts drop-down list box.

FIGURE 10.11

Start another phrase that can constrain the search for matching records.

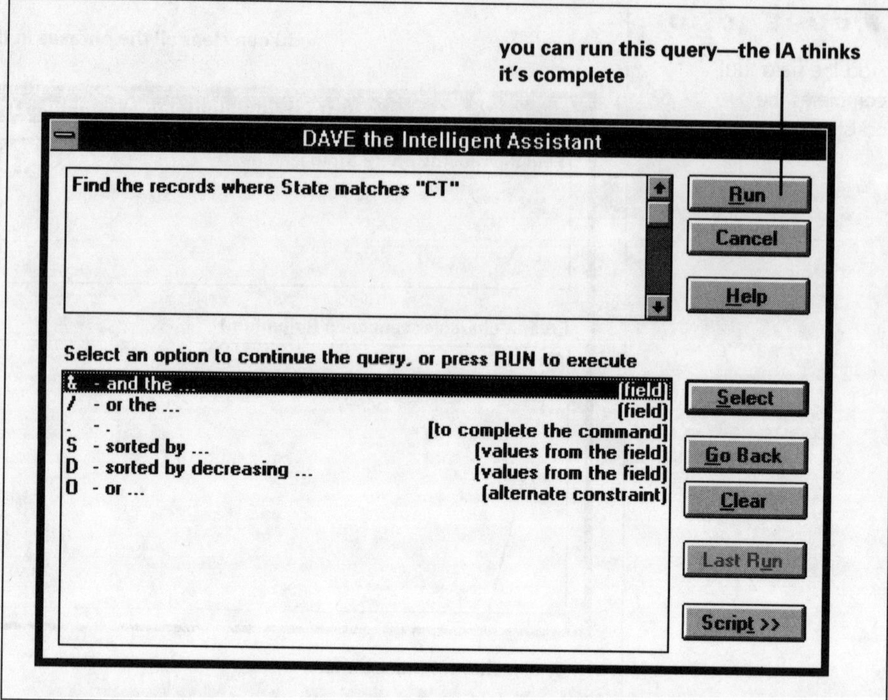

FIGURE 10.12

Add another constraining phrase to the query.

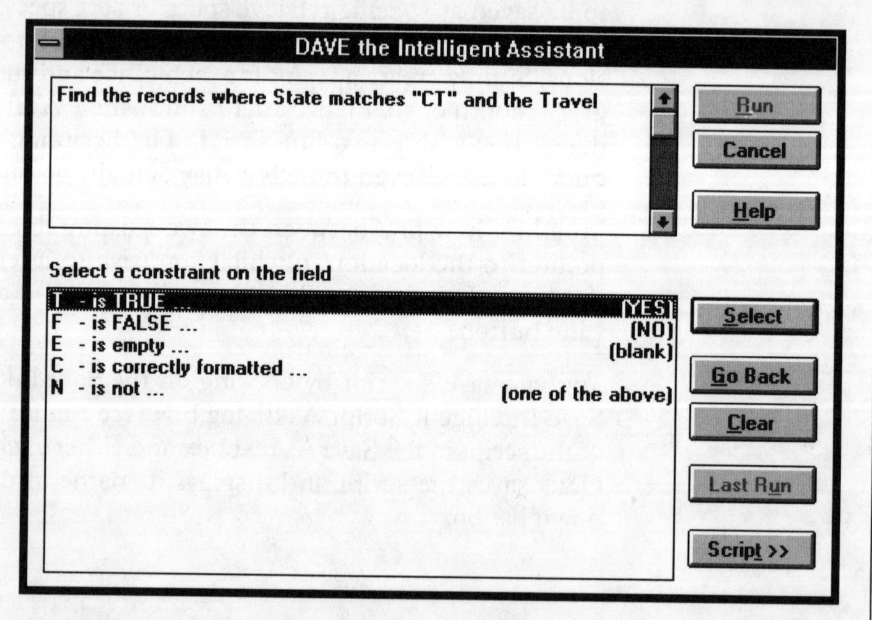

FIGURE 10.13

Closing in on the end of the phrase, sort the results of Q&A's search.

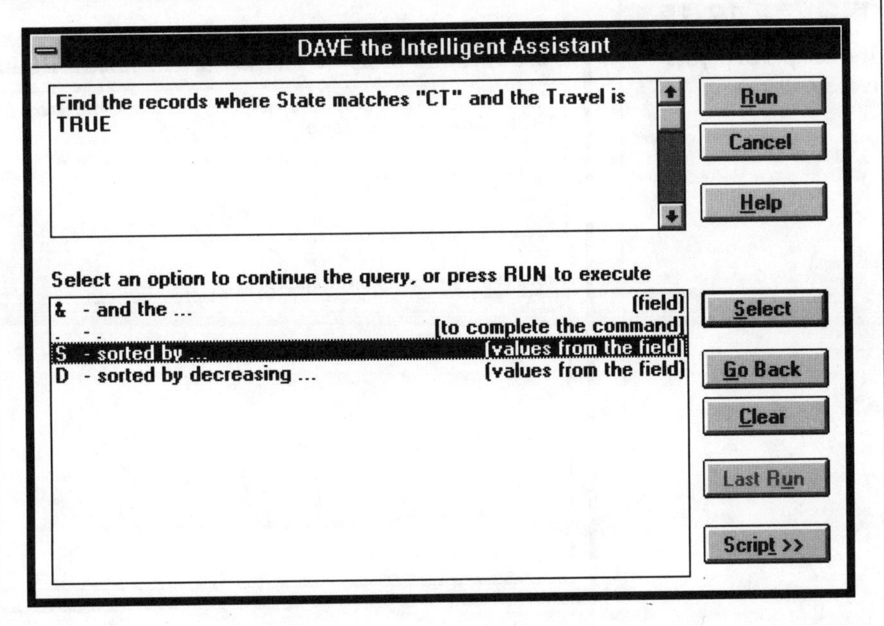

FIGURE 10.14

Finish the phrase by selecting a period.

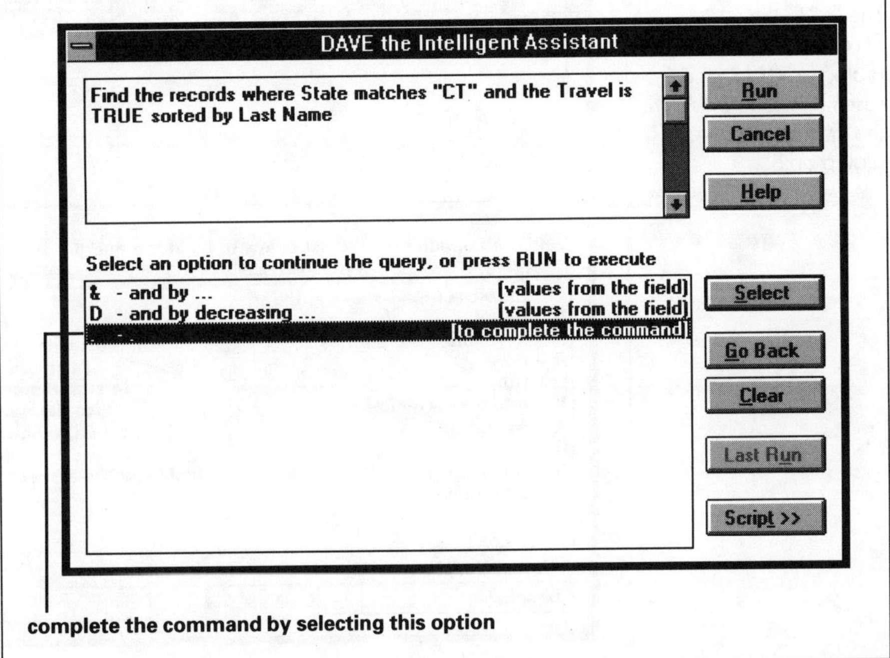

FIGURE 10.15

The completed phrase is ready to run.

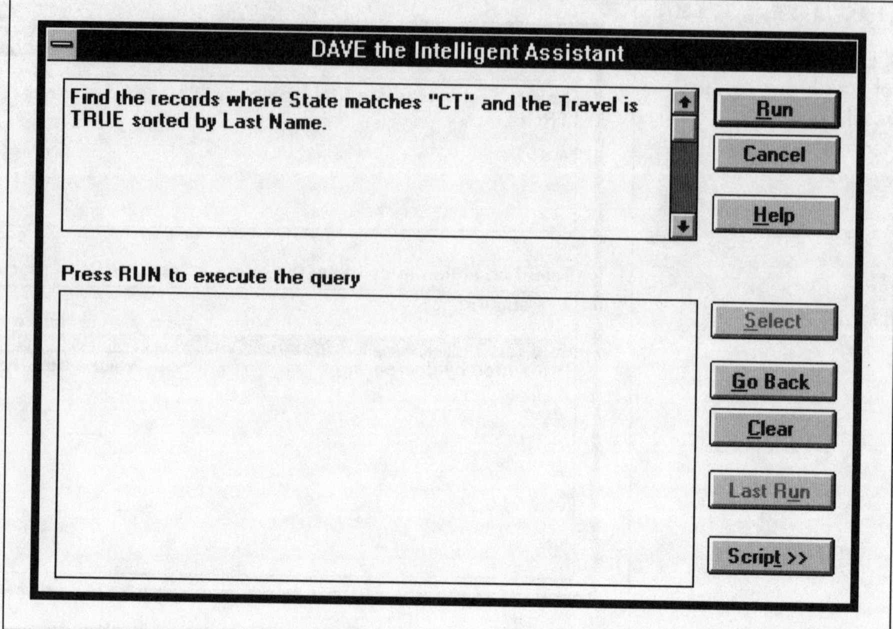

FIGURE 10.16

The DAVE the Scripting Assistant dialog box. Note the resemblance to DAVE the Intelligent Assistant dialog box.

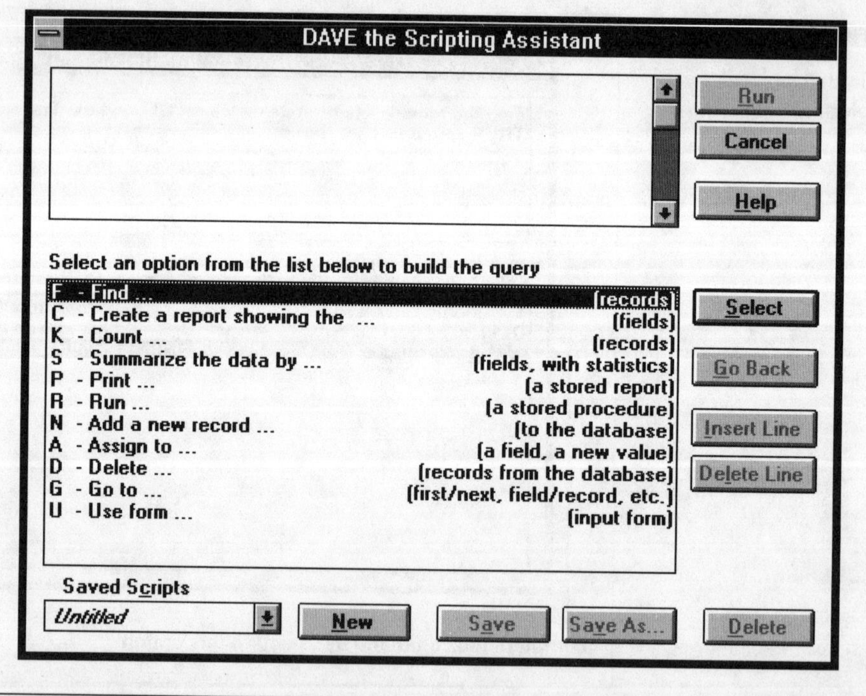

TABLE 10.3: The Opening Phrases for a Scripting Assistant Query (continued)

PHRASE	PURPOSE	NEXT WINDOW
F - Find... (records)	Builds a retrieval spec	S - and show using form (input form)
		R - the records where
		A - ALL the records
C - Create a report showing the... (fields)	Creates a report using one or more fields from the current database	Select a field
K - Count... (records)	Counts records that meet certain criteria or all records	R - the records where
		A - ALL the records
S - Summarize the data by... (fields, with statistics)	Produces a statistical summary (Total, Average, Count, Maximum, Minimum, Variance, and Standard Deviation) for selected fields	Select a field (group)
P - Print... (a stored report)	Prints an existing report or label	C - the Columnar Report
		D - the DOS Columnar Report
		F - the Freeform Report
		L - the Label
R - Run... (a stored procedure)	Runs an existing report, label, spec, or script	C - the Columnar Report
		D - the DOS Columnar Report
		F - the Freeform Report

TABLE 10.3: The Opening Phrases for a Scripting Assistant Query (continued)

PHRASE	PURPOSE	NEXT WINDOW
R - Run... (a stored procedure)		L - the Label
		R - the Retrieve Specification
		U - the Update Specification
		E - the Export Specification
		S - the script
N - Add a new record... (to the database)	Adds a new record to the current database	W - with (a field having a value)
		. - (to create an empty record)
A - Assign to... (a field, a new value)	Selects a field in which you want to assign a text value or programming statement	V - the value
		E - the expression (programming statement)
D - Delete... (records from the database)	Deletes all or selected records from the database	R - the records where
		A - ALL the records
		C - the current record (in view)
G - Go to (first/next, field/record, etc.)	Goes to a field or a record	1 - the first (field/record)
		L - the last (field/record)

TABLE 10.3: The Opening Phrases for a Scripting Assistant Query (continued)

PHRASE	PURPOSE	NEXT WINDOW
G - Go to (first/next, field/ record, etc.)		P - the previous (field/record)
		N - the next (field/record)
		F - field (name)
		R - record (number)
U - Use form (in-put form)	Uses one of the input forms for the current database	Master Form
		Form Name

To delete a script, load it by selecting it from the Saved Scripts drop-down list box. Click on the <u>D</u>elete button. To clear the current script from the DAVE the Scripting Assistant dialog box and start a new script, click on the <u>N</u>ew button. However, if you haven't saved the current script, when you clear it, it is gone forever.

To build a query for the current database, follow these steps:

1. Choose <u>A</u>ssistant ➤ <u>S</u>cripting Assistant or press Ctrl+J. Q&A displays the DAVE the Scripting Assistant dialog box.

2. Select a starting phrase from the Query Window and press <u>S</u>elect to add it to the Query Window. Q&A adds another group of phrases to the Query Window, depending on your choice.

3. Select another phrase and press <u>S</u>elect. Q&A adds another group of phrases to the Query Window.

4. Repeat step 3 until you have added all the desired criteria to the query.

5. Select a phrase that ends the line.

6. Save the script even before you finish building it by clicking on the <u>S</u>ave button. Q&A displays the Save Intelligent Script As dialog box.

FIGURE 10.17

This script will produce a report for each office location.

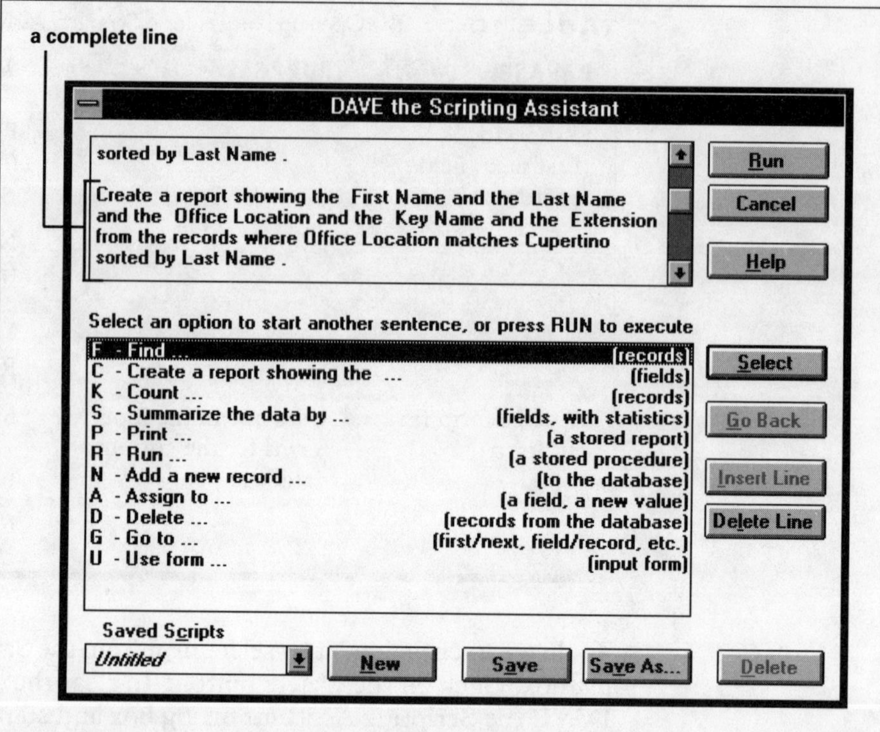

FIGURE 10.18

The Save Intelligent Script As dialog box

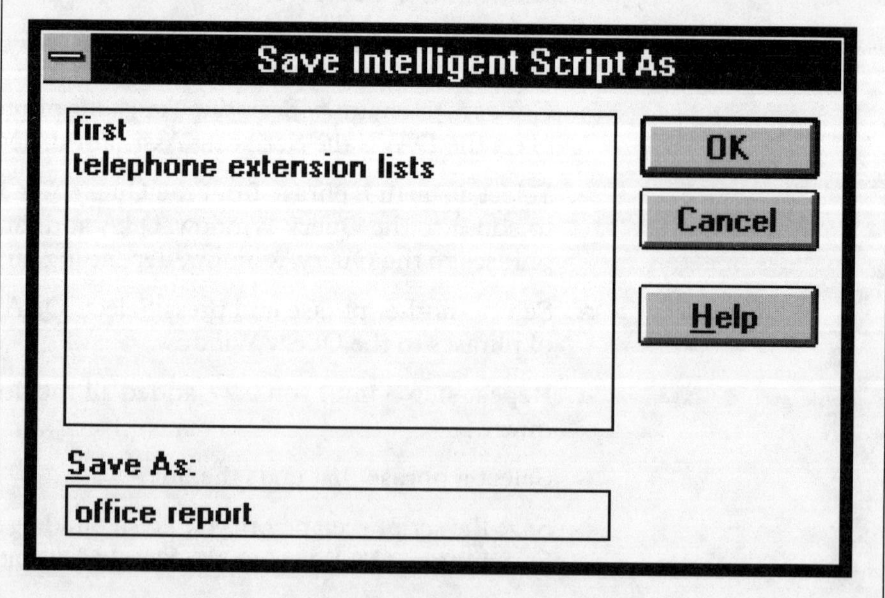

7. Type the name of the script in the <u>S</u>ave As text box and either click on OK or press Enter. Q&A saves the script and displays its name in the Saved S<u>c</u>ripts drop-down list box.

8. After completing the script, click on <u>R</u>un. Q&A runs the first line in the script, displays the results, runs the next line, displays the results, and so on. So if the results of the first script are incorrect, you'll find out. Although you can't stop Q&A from running the rest of the script, you'll be able to answer to No to any prompt that might delete records.

Adding a Script to the <u>A</u>ssistant Menu

Once you have created, tested, and edited a script so it is just the way you want it, you can add it to the <u>A</u>ssistant menu. There is room for just 10 scripts on the menu, so make sure that you choose only those you use regularly. Then when you want to run a script, just select it from the menu rather than opening the DAVE the Scripting Assistant dialog box.

To add a script to the <u>A</u>ssistant menu, choose Assistant ➤ <u>M</u>anage Assistant Menu. Q&A then opens the Manage Assistant Menu dialog box (Figure 10.19). Just select the desired script from the Sa<u>v</u>ed Scripts box and add it to the Menu <u>S</u>cripts box by clicking on the <u>A</u>dd button. Then

FIGURE 10.19

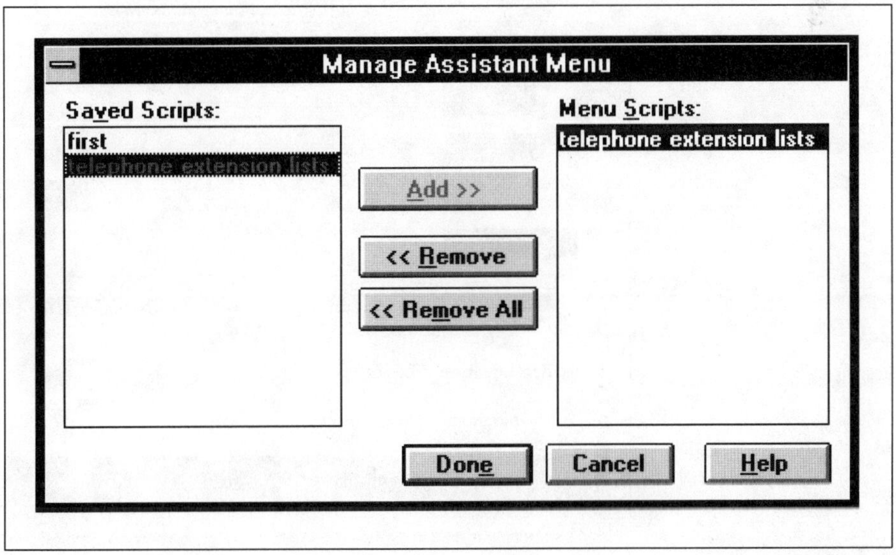

The Manage Assistant Menu dialog box in which you add scripts to and remove scripts from the <u>A</u>ssistant menu

click on Do_ne_. Q&A adds the script to the bottom of the _A_ssistant menu (Figure 10.20).

To run a script that has been added to the _A_ssistant menu, choose Assistant and either click on the script option or press the number preceding the entry.

It's as easy to delete a script from the _A_ssistant menu as it is to add it. Simply choose _A_ssistant ➤ _M_anage Assistant Menu. In the Menu _S_cripts box in the Manage Assistant Menu dialog box, select the script to be removed and click on _R_emove. (If this is the only entry in the box or if you wish to remove all entries, click on Re_m_ove All.) Then click on Do_ne_. Q&A closes the dialog box and removes the script entry from the _A_ssistant menu.

Adding Script Buttons

Once you have created scripts for your database, you can add *script buttons*. A script button is a button that you can place on your input forms

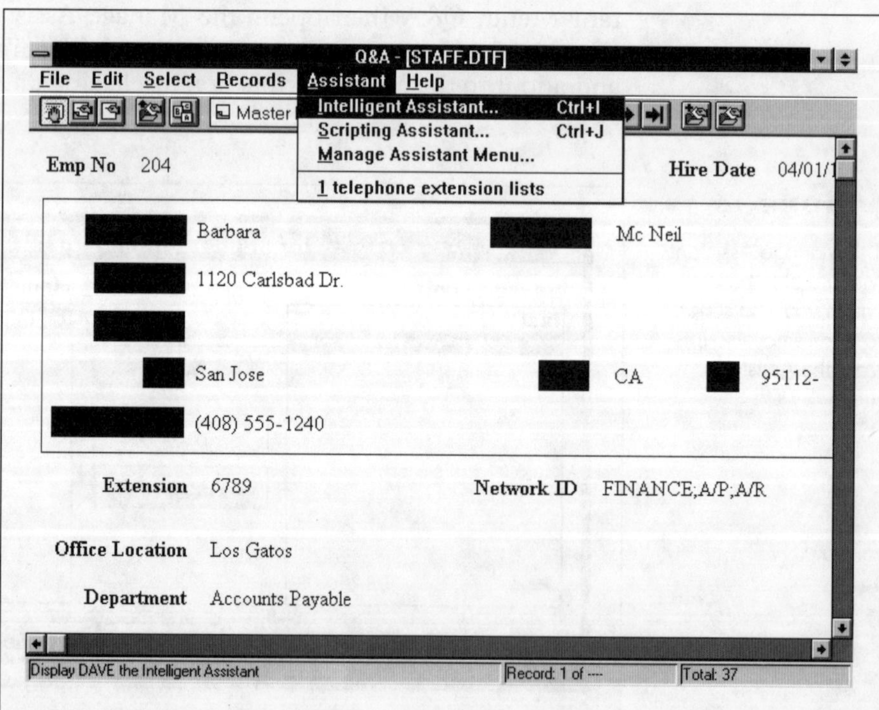

FIGURE 10.20

The open Assistant menu showing one script at the bottom

which executes a script when clicked. Figure 10.21 displays the STAFF database with two script buttons added to its Master Form.

To add script buttons to your database, do the following:

1. Choose Select ➤ Design Input Forms, or press Ctrl+M. This takes you to the Design Input Form mode where you can add your script buttons.

2. From the input form pull down list box, select the input form on which you want to add the button. You can also load your input form by choosing Form ➤ Load Input Form or pressing Ctrl+L.

3. Choose the Script Button tool from the tool palette. Notice that the pointer changes shape.

STAFF.DTF with Engineering and Sales script buttons added to the Master Form

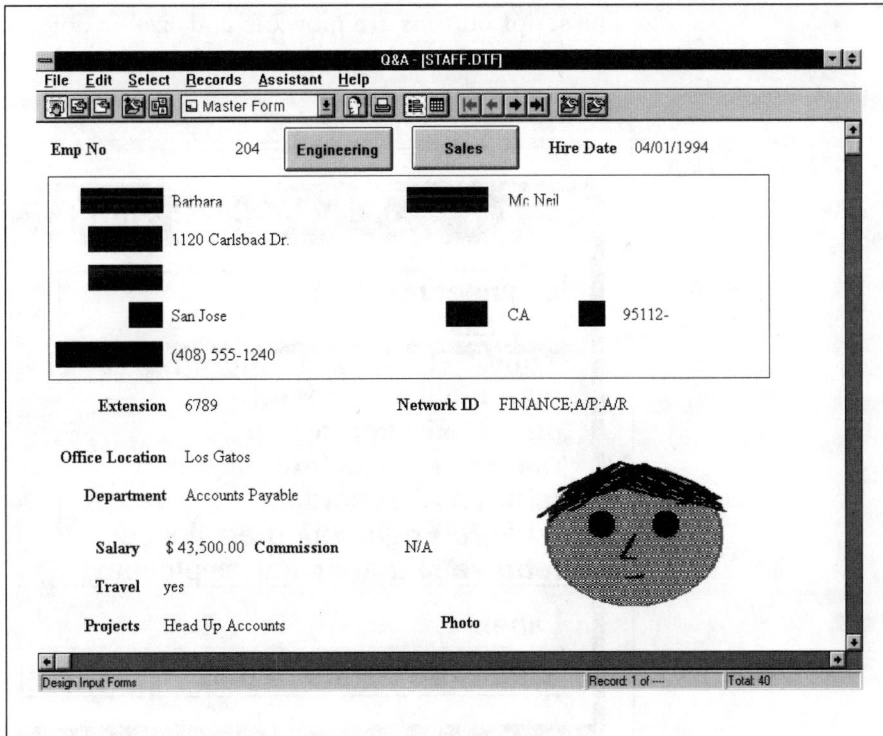

4. Click the pointer where you want the button to begin. Drag the mouse to the location where you want the button to end. When you release the mouse button, you will notice that Q&A creates a rectangular button in that location. Q&A then prompts you with the Attach Script dialog box (Figure 10.22). This box lists all of the scripts in your database.

5. From the larger list box, click on a script to attach to the newly created button. Notice, when you click on the script to attach to the button, the name of the script is placed in the Label box.

6. Through the Label box, alter the script label to what you want it to appear as on the script button.

7. Click OK or press enter. The name from the Label box appears on the button you created.

The script buttons are movable and sizable objects. However, their fonts or colors can't be changed.

FIGURE 10.22

The Attach Script dialog box

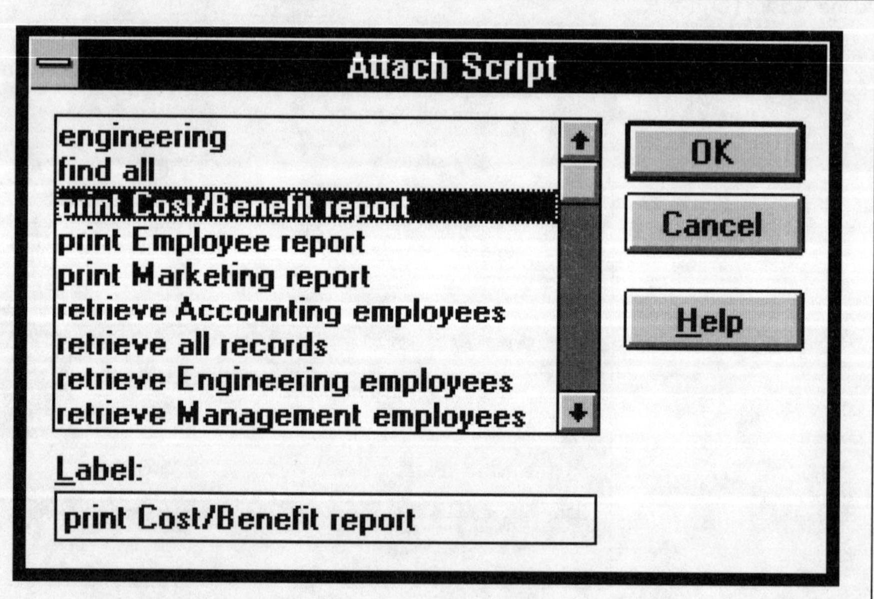

To Sum Up

In this chapter, you found out how easy it is to use the Intelligent Assistant to create queries, and the Scripting Assistant to set up multi-line scripts. You discovered that you can use both these assistants to learn Q&A and to build retrieve specs and to create reports.

In the next chapter, you'll be introduced to Q&A programming. First you'll find out about the types of programming Q&A offers. Then you'll create programming statements—by yourself and with the aid of the Program Helper. Finally, you'll learn how to perform mass updates and mass deletions.

chapter

11

Programming
with Q&A

To create a derived programming statement   376

you need to be in Columnar or Freeform report mode. Type the statements in the Formula box in either the Add Derived Column dialog box or Add Derive Field dialog box.

To create a navigation programming statement   380

choose Select ➤ Design Input Forms. Choose Format ➤ Field Navigation ➤ Edit Programming. Type your programming statements in the Formula box. Click on OK.

To create a programming statement for a mass update   383

choose Select ➤ Mass Update. Choose Update ➤ Helper or press Ctrl+H while the cursor is in the field for which you want to create the programming statement. Create the programming statement in the Formula box. Click OK.

To run a mass update   386

from Mass Update mode, choose Update ➤ Run This Mass Update or click on the Run Mass Update button on the tool bar. Then confirm the update.

To perform a mass delete   389

choose Select ➤ Mass Delete, select the deletion criteria, and choose Delete ➤ Run This Mass Delete or press the delete button on the tool bar.

THROUGHOUT the previous chapters, you learned how to use Q&A's database features to add, manipulate, and present data in the database. This chapter explains how to use Q&A's powerful programming abilities. The programming feature allows you to set Q&A to automatically perform calculations and tasks using the data in your database. Through programming, you can command Q&A to:

- Automatically calculate data using programming functions. You can calculate your future loan payments, total accounts receivable, or the commissions earned.

- Retrieve and use data from other databases and tables. You can find tax multipliers based on your tax bracket, automatically retrieve cities and states based on your zip code entry, or automatically fill in a client's record from the data in a different database.

- Move the cursor through a record based on the data that you entered in previous fields. This means that you can skip fields that are irrelevant or non-applicable. For example, your database might ask the client's marital status and spouse's name. You can program Q&A to skip the Spouse's Name field if the marital status is single.

Q&A Programming Types

You can use programming in many ways and in different modes. Q&A provides the following programming types:

Form programming	Manipulates data in Add/Edit mode. Form programming is the most common type of programming.
Navigation programming	Moves your cursor about your form for easier data entry in Add/Edit mode.
Retrieval programming	Retrieves records based on complex requests.
Derived programming	Calculates or uses functions in derived fields and derived columns in your reports.
Restrict programming	Creates powerful restrictions.
Write programming	Calculates or controls the data that is merged into write documents from a Q&A database. For information about Write programming and mail merge, see Chapter 16.

As you will learn—first with form programming and then with all the other programming types—all programming types work in about the same way. Once you learn how to use form programming, you'll discover different methods and restrictions that apply to the other programming types.

Form Programming

Form programming allows you to perform calculations and routines in the Add/Edit mode using any programming function listed in Appendix D. *Functions* are predefined expressions that perform a calculation or execute a routine. *Statements*, which can contain one or more functions or logical operations, instruct Q&A to perform specific tasks.

About the Edit Programming Dialog Box

You will do all your form programming in the Edit Programming dialog box (Figure 11.1), which consists of three groups: Database Fields, Elements, and Formula.

Database Fields	Lists all the fields in the current database. Select the field in which you want to write programming statements.
Elements	Provides the components to create your programming statement.

- Click on the Field Names radio button to list the field names in the scroll box.

- Click on the Function Type radio button to list the different types of functions or logical operators you can perform. These functions are also listed in the scroll box. The drop-down list box lets you choose the types of function in the list box. You can choose All (the default) or categories of functions.

Formula	The box in which you build your programming statements.

You can create formulas in two ways:

- Double-click on a function or field name to paste it in the Formula box. In this way you can construct a formula piece by piece.

Use the Edit
Programming dialog
box to add form
programming
statements to your
database.

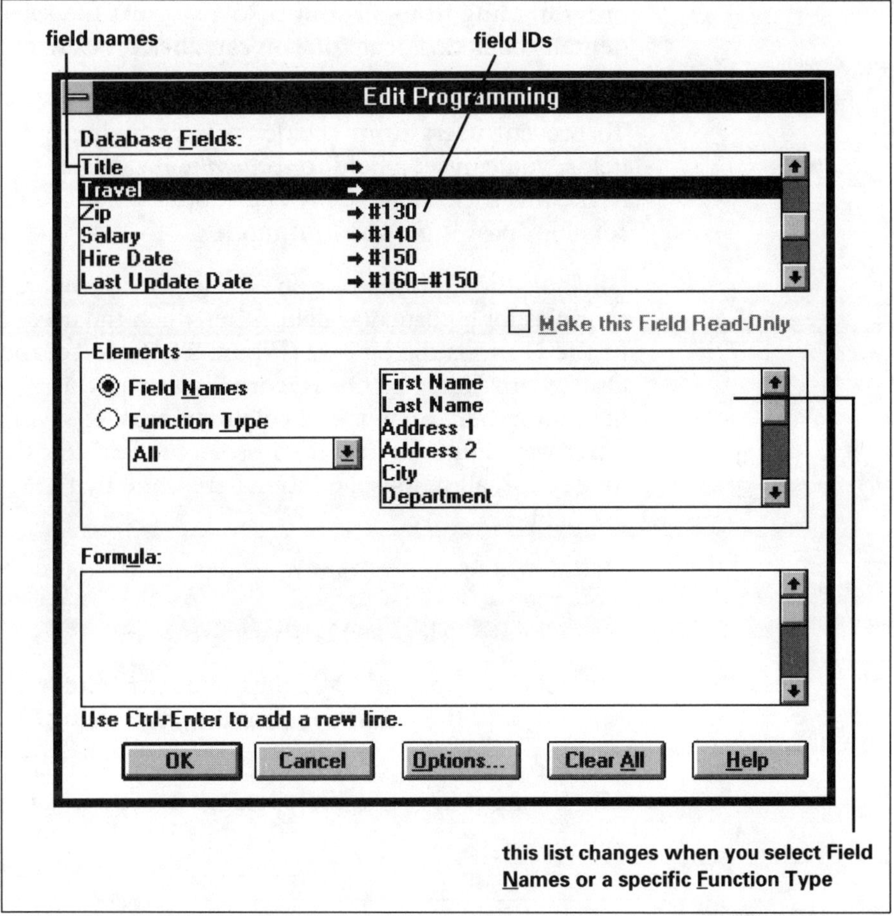

This is the best way of creating formulas if you are not familiar
with programming or would prefer to have a list of items from
which you can choose.

- You can click inside the Formula box and type your programming
  statement. The standard Windows editing functions (such as copying, cutting, and pasting) are available.

When working with the Edit Programming dialog box (also called the
Program Helper), you can clear all the form programming formulas for
your fields by clicking the Clear All button. Note that this clears the form

programming from all your fields, not just the selected field. If you accidentally click on Clear All, you can click on Cancel to close the dialog box without saving any changes.

To prevent users from accidentally changing field values for calculated fields, you can set a field to *read only*. Just select the field and click on the Make this Field Read-Only check box. When a field is read only, the cursor skips past it in Add/Edit mode.

Click on the Options button to specify whether Q&A executes the field formulas for a particular field either when the user enters or exits a record. In the Options dialog box (Figure 11.2), select the field from either the On Record Entry or On Record Exit drop-down list box. If you select a field for either entry or exit calculations, Q&A will not calculate it in any other way. For instance, if you select a field to calculate when you enter the record, all of its calculations are done by the time your cursor enters the field.

To define a form programming statement, follow these steps:

1. Choose Select ➤ Database Structure.

2. Choose Database ➤ Edit Field Attribute ➤ Programming. Q&A displays the Edit Programming dialog box.

3. Create your programming statement in the Formula box by either typing it in or double-clicking on elements to build a statement.

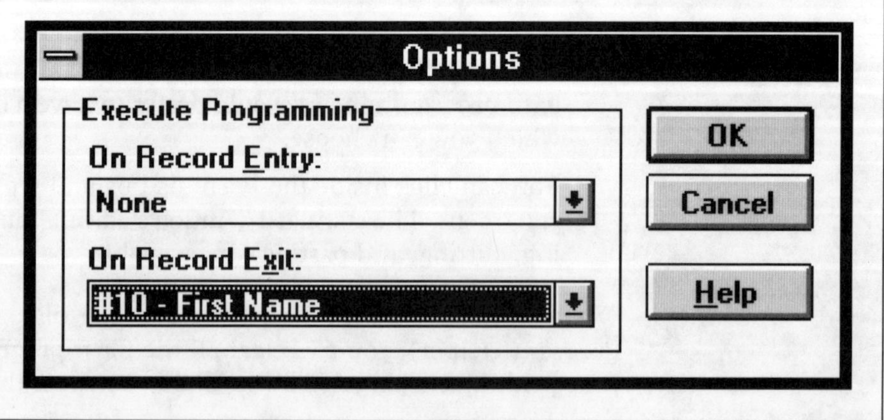

4. Click on the Options button to open the Options dialog box. Set the fields you want calculated when entering or leaving the record.

5. Click OK or press Enter.

Understanding the Structure of a Programming Statement

A programming statement is one or many commands used to instruct Q&A to perform a certain routine or calculation (such as retrieving a number from a field and multiplying it by 7). Form programming statements (Figure 11.3) are made up of four parts: a designator, a field ID, an equal sign or a colon, and an expression.

FIGURE 11.3

A form programming statement

```
        field ID    expression
         ┌─┴─┐      ┌──┴──┐
        >#10=#30*7
         │          │
     designator   equal sign or colon
```

The greater than sign is the *designator*, which indicates when Q&A should perform the programming statement. The #10 is the *field ID*, which assigns a number to that field so that it can be referenced by other programming statements. The equal sign or colon designates whether the value resulting from the statement is placed in that field or possibly in another field. The *expression* specifies the commands that you instruct Q&A to perform.

Designating the Time of Calculation

You can instruct Q&A to execute form programming statements at various times when in Add/Edit mode. One of the many ways to control the time of execution is through the statement designator. The designator can be one of three types: on entry (<), on exit(>), or on calculation.

The *on entry* designator (<) instructs Q&A to execute the programming statement for a field only when your cursor enters the field. This is called on-field-entry (OFE). Q&A performs the following programming statement when the cursor enters the field for which it is written.

```
<#10=#30*7
```

The *on exit* designator (>) instructs Q&A to execute the programming statement for a field when your cursor leaves it. This is called on-field-exit (OFX).

```
>#10=#30*7
```

On calculation means that Q&A calculates the statement when the record is calculated. Also referred to as main programming, on calculation statements are the most commonly used type of programming statement. Main programming statements are not preceded by any characters.

```
#10=#30*7
```

Using Field IDs in Programming Statements

The purpose of field IDs is to give Q&A field reference numbers for the fields in your database and to inform Q&A of the order in which to calculate the programming statements. If you need to refer to a field when using the Edit Programming dialog box, you can use the field ID number.

```
#20=#30
```

The preceding programming statement actually does two things. First it identifies that field as field #20 so that other programming statements can refer to it. Secondly, it sets that field equal to the value in field #30. In the programming statement, the value in field #30 is placed into field #20. Therefore, if field #30 contains the value Jack, field #20 will also contain the value Jack.

N O T E

Field IDs can be different in different programming modes. For example, although the First Name field has a field ID of #10 in the Edit Programming dialog box, the same field might have a field ID of #75 in the Helper dialog box, used for navigation programming. Therefore, you never need to worry how the field IDs are assigned in other programming dialog boxes.

Using the Colon or Equal Sign in Programming Statements

When entering a programming statement, you can either place a colon or an equal sign between the field ID and the programming expression. If you use an equal sign, the value from an expression is placed in that field. If you use a colon, the value from an expression can be placed in another field.

For example, the following expression copies the value of field #5 into field #10.

    #10=#5

However, if you use a colon after the field ID you can place the returned value in another field. The following programming statement tells Q&A to place the value of field #5 into field #15.

    #10:#15=#5

Since programming statements that begin with equal signs return values to that same field, they cannot use functions that do not return values or have an option to return the value to another field. These types of functions are commonly referred to as commands. Field programming statements beginning with equal signs cannot use the following: IF THEN statements, CLEAR, LOOKUP, LOOKUPR, XLOOKUP, XLOOKUPR, GOSUB, RETURN, STOP, and GOTO. But note that statements beginning with the equal sign can use @LOOKUP, @LOOKUPR, @XLOOKUP, and @XLOOKUPR.

Using Programming Expressions in Programming Statements

Programming expressions are the backbones of programming statements. The expressions tell Q&A the routines to perform or the calculations to make. These expressions can consist of simple calculations of numbers, calculations of fields, usage of functions and commands, or a combination of these routines. Table 11.1 lists examples of different expressions.

TABLE 11.1: Examples of Programming Expressions

TYPE OF EXPRESSION	PROGRAMMING EXAMPLE	EXPLANATION
Calculation of numbers	#10=5*6	The contents of field #10 equals 5 times 6
Calculation of fields	#10=#15-#20	The contents of field #10 equals the contents of field #15 minus the contents of field #20
Using a function or command	#10=@ABS(#20)	The contents of field #10 equals the absolute value of the number in field #20.
Combination of calculations	#10=#15+6+@ABS(#20)	The contents of field #10 equals the addition of the value in field #15 plus 6 plus the absolute value of the number in field #20.

Using Operators in Programming Statements

An operator is a mathematical symbol used to calculate values. For instance, the plus sign is used to add two values. Q&A supports the operators listed in Table 11.2. For this table, the value of field #15 is 3, and the value of field #20 is 15.

TABLE 11.2: Using Operators in Q&A

OPERATOR	PURPOSE	EXAMPLE	RESULT
+	addition	#10=#20+#15	#10=18
-	subtraction	#10=#20-#15	#10=12
*	multiplication	#10=#20*#15	#10=45
/	division	#10=#20/#15	#10=5

You can use these operators for multiplying, dividing, adding, and subtracting both numbers and fields—even nonnumeric fields. This means you can use fields as variables, and you can add days to dates, minutes to times, words to text (appending them), and other useful calculations.

How Does Q&A Determine the Order of Precedence?

The results of a calculation often depend on the order in which the elements are computed. For example, what does the statement #10=3+5*(20/4) equal? Does it equal 40, which is the result when 3 plus 5 is multiplied by 20 and then divided by 4. Or is the result 28, which is 20 divided by 4 times 5 plus 3. The answer is 28 because Q&A uses a specific calculation order as it computes a statement from left to right. Table 11.3 lists operators in their order of precedence.

TABLE 11.3: Q&A's Order of Precedence

ORDER	OPERATOR	DESCRIPTION
First	( )	Values in parentheses
Second	*	Multiplication
	/	Division
Third	+	Addition
	-	Subtraction

TABLE 11.3: Q&A's Order of Precedence (continued)

ORDER	OPERATOR	DESCRIPTION
Fourth	=	Equal to
	<>	Not equal to
	<	Less than
	>	Greater than
	<=	Less than or equal to
	>=	Greater than or equal to
Fifth	NOT	Reverses the values being compared
Sixth	AND	Both values being compared are true
	OR	One value being compared is true

Using Functions in Programming Statements

Functions request that Q&A perform a routine or calculation using data from a field and then return the resulting value to the field. Since functions return a value that must be placed in a field, they are set equal to a field ID. For example, if you want Q&A to display the square root of a value, the resulting value is placed in a field for viewing.

```
#10=@SQRT(#20)
```

This programming statement instructs Q&A to place the square root of the value in field #20 into field #10. In other words, the value of #10 is equal to the square root of the value in field #20.

All functions, which are listed in Appendix D, are preceded by the @ character. In contrast, commands, which are described in the next section, are not preceded by any special character.

Using Commands in Programming Statements

A command, like a function, performs a routine or calculation. However, commands do not return values. Therefore, you enter commands differently in the Formula box. When you enter a command, it is not assigned to a field like a function would be. For example, the following command clears or erases the value in field #20:

```
#10:CLEAR(#20)
```

Think of a command as telling Q&A to do something rather than asking for a value. Also, note that you normally only use commands in Form and Programming Mass Update programming.

Performing Calculations with Functions

Traditionally, we multiply, divide, add, and subtract numbers to or from other numbers. However, in Q&A we can also multiply, divide, add, and subtract functions with other functions. Since functions return values, you can use them as values in computations. For example, the following programming statement makes the contents of field #10 equal to the absolute value of field #15 times the square root of field #20.

```
#10=@ABS(#15)*@SQRT(#20)
```

Embedding Functions in Other Functions or Commands

You can also embed functions into other functions or commands. Programming with embedded functions can produce very powerful programming statements. To embed a function into a command or another function, replace a value with the function. For instance, you can replace #15 with the integer of #15 (The integer function, @INT, produces a whole number). This changes:

```
#10=@ABS(#15)
```

to

```
#10=@ABS(@INT(#15))
```

Now instead of taking the absolute value of field #15, the statement takes the absolute value of the integer of field #15.

When using this type of statement, make sure that the returned value of the embedded function is in the same format as the external function. For instance, the statement #10=@ABS(@CHR(#15)) does not work because @CHR(#15) returns a text character and @ABS calculates only numbers.

Understanding Programming Statements

Sometimes it is difficult to understand or to create a programming statement. A technique that often allows you to understand what a programming statement actually does is to reduce the programming to its calculated values and to calculate the finished product. For instance, the programming statement #10=@SQRT(@ABS(#15)+5) might seem a little complex. However, if you analyze the formula one step at a time substituting reasonable values for field IDs, the formula is rather simple. For example, take the innermost function and calculate it, hypothetically assigning #15 as –20. First concentrate on @ABS(#15), which is the absolute value of field #15. The absolute value of –20 is 20. Now we add 20 and 5, which results in 25. Now the formula is really @SQRT(25). This translates to the square root of 25, which is 5. On paper these calculations would look like this:

Step 1	#10=@SQRT(@ABS(#15)+5)
Step 2	#10=@SQRT(@ABS(-20)+5)
Step 3	#10=@SQRT(20+5)
Step 4	#10=@SQRT(25)
Step 5	#10=5

Defining Multiple Statements for a Field

To define more than one statement for a specific field, simply put semicolons between each statement.

```
#10:#40=#50*6;#30=#35+10
```

The preceding formula contains two statements. The first sets field #40 to the value in field #50 multiplied by 6. The second sets field #30 to the value in field #35 plus 10.

Testing Conditions with IF THEN Statements

A very useful type of programming statement is the conditional statement, more often referred to as the IF THEN statement. IF THEN statements allow you to execute a programming expression only if a certain condition is met. For example, to compute a tax for all nonperishable goods sold, you would use a conditional statement telling Q&A to add tax to the price if it is a nonperishable item. In essence, you would tell Q&A, "IF an item is not perishable, THEN add tax."

Construct IF THEN programming statements as you would a normal sentence. First, state the condition that must be met, and then tell Q&A what to do if the condition is true or if it exists. For instance, in the Formula box, enter a request "IF field #10 is equal to 'Non Perishable', THEN field #20 equals field #15 times .08" using this statement:

```
#5:IF #10="Non Perishable" THEN #20=#15*.08
```

You can use functions in IF THEN statements, too. The following programming statement tells Q&A to place the current date (@DATE), into field #20 when the value in field #10 is greater than 5.

```
#10:IF #10>5 THEN #20=@DATE
```

IF THEN programming statements begin with the field ID and a colon rather than an equal sign. The reason for using a colon is that an IF THEN statement is not a function, field ID, or number. An IF THEN statement performs commands and functions, which place values into fields. Since different fields can receive the values from IF THEN statements, these conditional statements must use the colon at the beginning.

Conditional statements perform complete statements. When a conditional statement is true or exists, a programming statement—not just an expression or formula—follows. The programming statement contains a field ID, an equal sign, and an expression.

```
#10:IF #20<#50 THEN #20=@DATE
```

PROGRAMMING WITH Q&A

Note the programming statement following THEN. The executed result of the programming statement, #20=@DATE, has a field ID (#20), an equal sign (=), and an expression (@DATE), which is a function. This statement, #20=@DATE, could stand on its own.

IF THEN programming statements can use logical operators for comparison purposes only. Table 11.4 names and describes these operators and gives an example and explanation of each.

TABLE 11.4: Q&A Comparison Operators

OPERATOR	PURPOSE	EXAMPLE	TRANSLATION
=	equal to	#10: If #10=5 THEN #15= "no transaction"	If field #10 is equal to 5, then the value of field #15 is "no transaction"
>	greater than	#10: If #10>5 THEN #20="sell"	If field #10 is greater than 5, then the value of field #20 is "sell"
<	less than	#10: If #10<5 THEN #20="buy"	If field #10 is less than 5, then the value of field #20 is "buy"
>=	greater than or equal to	#10: If #10>=6 THEN #20="sell"	If field #10 is greater than or equal to 6, then the value of field #20 is "sell"
<=	less than or equal to	#10: If #10<=4 THEN #20="buy"	If field #10 is less than or equal to 4, then the value of field #20 is "buy"
<>	not equal to	#10: If #10<>5 THEN #15="transaction"	If field #10 is not equal to 5, then the value of field #15 is "transaction"

Testing Conditions with IF THEN ELSE Statements

The only difference between IF THEN and IF THEN ELSE statements is that IF THEN ELSE statements allow you to tell Q&A what to do if the condition is not met. In the following example:

#5:IF #10="Nonperishable" THEN #20=#15*.08 ELSE #20="Not Taxed"

the programming statement multiplies field #15 by .08 and places the value into field #20 if field #10 contains the word "Nonperishable." If field #10 does not contain "Nonperishable", the ELSE statement places the value "Not taxed" in field #20.

Using Complex Conditions in IF THEN Statements

Q&A allows you to use AND and OR conjunctions to create complex conditions in IF THEN statements. For example, you can use two conditions in an IF THEN statement to determine if a certain procedure is to be performed.

#10: IF #20=5 AND #30=8 THEN #10=@DATE

This programming statement places the current date (@DATE) in field #10 if field #20 equals 5 *and* field #30 equals 8.

#10: IF #20=5 OR #30=8 THEN #10=@DATE

The preceding programming statement places the current date (@DATE) in field #10 if field #20 equals 5 *or* field #30 equals 8.

When you place a second condition in a programming statement, you must type the whole condition. #10: IF #15>12 AND #15<100 THEN #10=#15. See how #15 is repeated in both conditions.

You can use AND and OR conjunctions several times in a statement. The following statement places the value "FIFO" into field #10 if the value in field #15 is greater than 12 and less than 100 and the value in field #20 is "OK."

    #10:IF #15>12 AND #15<100 AND #20="OK" THEN #10="FIFO"

You can also use AND and OR conjunctions in the same programming statement. For example:

    #10:IF #15>12 AND #15<100 OR #20="OK" THEN #10="FIFO"

places "FIFO" into field #10 when the value of field #15 is greater than 12 and less than 100 *or* the value in field #20 is "OK."

Executing Multiple IF THEN Calculations with BEGIN and END

As you know, when an IF THEN statement is true, Q&A performs a routine or calculation. To perform more than one calculation or routine, you do not use the AND and OR conjunctions. However, you can have IF THEN programming statements perform these multiple routines using BEGIN and END. Just type BEGIN after THEN to mark where the multiple statements begin. After you have typed the last statement to be executed when the IF THEN is found to be true, type END. The following formula performs the multiple statements between BEGIN and END when the value of field #20 is 6. Notice that there is a semicolon between each statement.

    #10: IF #20=6 THEN BEGIN #45=6;#55="taxed";CLEAR (#30) END

You can use BEGIN and END in IF THEN ELSE statements to perform multiple statements. The following formula places the value 6 in field #45 if field #20=6. However if field #20 does not contain the value 6, Q&A performs the statements between BEGIN and END.

    #10: IF #20=6 THEN #45=5 ELSE BEGIN #45=6;#55="taxed";CLEAR
    (#30) END

To conserve space you can use braces ({}) instead of BEGIN and END. For instance, instead of:

    #10: IF #20=6 THEN BEGIN #45=6;#55="taxed";CLEAR (#30) END

you can type:

    #10: IF #20=6 THEN { #45=6;#55="taxed";CLEAR (#30) }

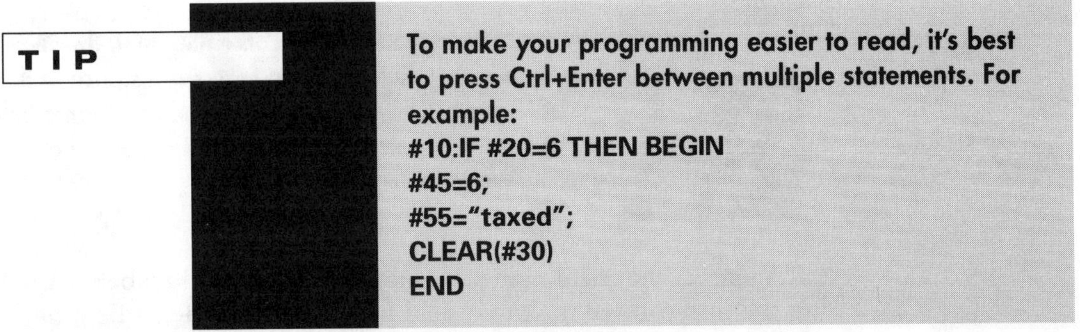

Using Field Names as References

While using field IDs is often convenient, it is not necessary. You can use field names to reference fields in programming statements. As a matter of fact, some programming modes don't use field IDs, thereby forcing you to use field names to reference fields. To refer to a field using a field name, just type the field name instead of the field ID:

    #10:First Name=""

The preceding statement places blanks in the First Name field.

You cannot use field names to replace the initial field ID of a form programming formula. For example, Q&A *does not accept* the following programming formula as a complete statement.

    Full Name=First Name + Last Name

However, if you precede the statement with a field ID, Q&A accepts it:

    #10:Full Name=First Name + Last Name

This programming statement appends First Name and Last Name and places the result in the Full Name field.

> **NOTE**
>
> When Q&A appends fields containing text, the second field immediately follows the first. For instance, if the First Name field contains "Mark" and Last Name field contains "Williams," the Full Name field will contain "MarkWilliams."

Remember that field names are not the same as field labels. A field label is the title you see next to a field in Add/Edit mode. A field name is the internal reference name that Q&A gives a field. To view the field names for your fields, look at the values inside the field boxes when in the Design Input Form mode.

Automatic vs. Manual Calculation

As explained earlier, when a programming formula is not preceded by a greater than sign (>) or a less than sign (<), the formula is calculated when Q&A computes the main programming for the record. These field programming formulas are known as main or *on calculation* programming formulas. You can instruct Q&A to calculate the main programming formulas based on your manual request (manual calculation) or whenever data changes in any field (automatic calculation). Regardless of the calculation mode you select, Q&A only calculates the main programming fields; programming statements that are set to calculate on exit or on entry of a field or record are not calculated. For instance, on field entry formulas that begin with a greater than sign are not calculated in either automatic or manual calculation modes.

When you select automatic calculation, Q&A calculates your record whenever you change the data in any field in the record. For example, if you change the contents of a field and press Enter, Tab, or click your mouse, Q&A calculates all the main programming fields.

When you select manual calculation, Q&A calculates your record only when you press the F8 key or choose Edit ➤ Calculate Now.

> **NOTE**
>
> Q&A calculates the form programming statements in the order of the lowest field ID to the highest field ID.

You can choose between manual and automatic calculation modes by following these steps:

1. While in Add/Edit mode, choose Edit ➤ Calculation Options. Q&A displays the Calculation Options dialog box (Figure 11.4).

2. Click on either Automatic or Manual from the Mode group.

3. Click OK or press Enter.

FIGURE 11.4

The Calculation Options dialog box

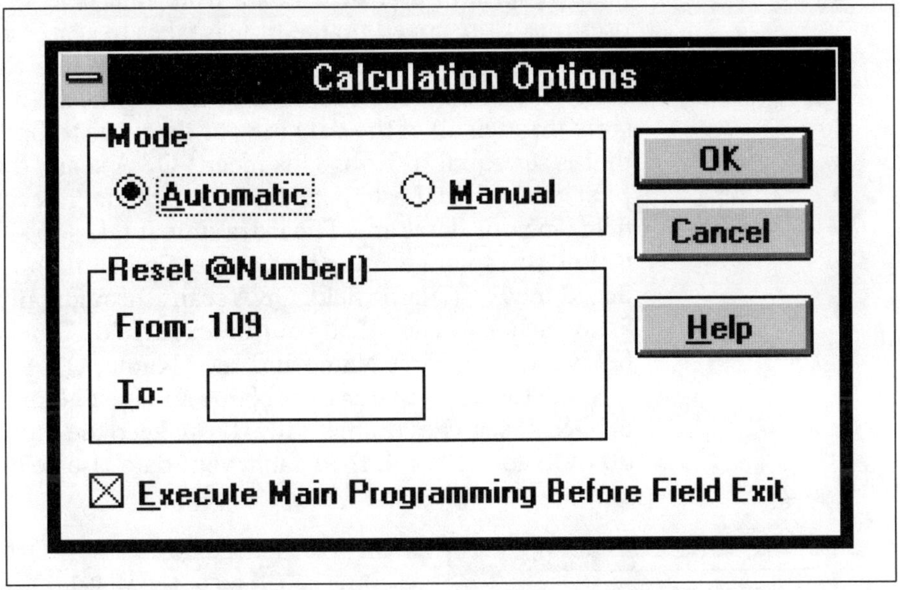

Executing Main Programming Before Exiting a Field

Imagine while in Add/Edit mode, that you exit an *on exit* calculated field to which you just added information. Q&A is set to calculate the programming statements for that field because it contains an *on exit* programming statement. Q&A is also set to calculate all the main programming fields because you just changed the contents of a field. Which calculation does Q&A perform first? To specify the order in which programming statements are performed, choose Edit ➤ Calculation Options. When Q&A displays the Calculation Options dialog box, either check or clear the Execute Main Programming Before Field Exit check box. If this check box is checked, Q&A executes the main programming statements first. If you clear this check box, Q&A executes the on exit programming statements first.

Indexing Your Database

Just as the index at the back of this book helps you find what you are looking for quickly, Q&A gives you the ability to index your database. An index is an internal list of your fields' data. Indexing a field in your database places copies of that field's data from that field in a different file. Q&A uses this list to speed up the time it takes to search for data. For instance, if you use a retrieve spec to search for the name Rob in the First Name field of a database, without the First Name field being indexed, Q&A sorts through all of the data in your database to find the First Name field that is set equal to Rob. This means Q&A scans through the data in the First Name field, Last Name field, Date field, Project field, and all the other fields in your database. The extra time it takes to sift through these fields is time you spend waiting for Q&A to find something. However, if you indexed the First Name field, Q&A scans through only the data in the index list, which is the list of all your indexed fields. Therefore, if you have two fields indexed, First Name and Last Name, Q&A will only need to scan through the data in your First Name and Last Name fields. This can speed up Q&A's searches dramatically. Try to keep the number of fields you index down to about 3 or 4. By default, your database fields are not indexed.

N O T E   The list created by indexing fields is placed in the .IDX file of your database. IDX is an abbreviation of INDEX.

To index a field do the following:

1. Go to the Database Structures view by choosing <u>S</u>elect ➤ Database <u>S</u>tructure.

2. Choose <u>D</u>atabase ➤ <u>E</u>dit Field Attribute ➤ <u>I</u>ndex. This brings you to the Edit Index dialog box (Figure 11.5).

3. Choose the field you want to index.

4. Select the type of indexing you want to use. Indexing types are explained below.

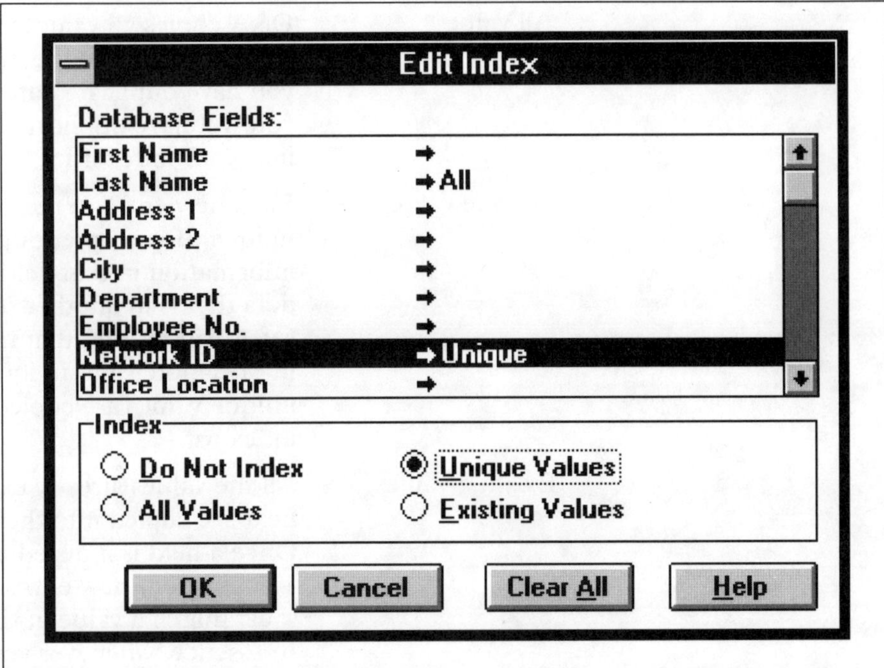

FIGURE 11.5

The Edit Index dialog box

5. Repeat steps 3 and 4 until you have specified all the fields you want to index.

6. Click OK or press Enter.

NOTE All fields that you use as reference fields in XLOOKUP programming statements need to be indexed. This is explained in greater detail in Appendix D.

You can choose from the following four types of indexing options:

Do Not Index — The data in the field is not indexed; none of the values from that field is copied into the index list.

All Values
Q&A copies all values from an indexed field into the index list. If you have duplicate data in that field, you will have duplicate data copied into your index list.

Unique Values
Each new entry in the field must be unique. If you enter duplicate information in that field (the same data that is in another record), then Q&A will tell you that the information is not unique. The unique values are copied into the index list.

Existing Values
All the values already existing in the field are copied into the index list. Once a field is indexed as Existing Values, every new entry in that field must match a value in the index list. In essence, whenever you add or edit data in that field of your database, it must already exist on other records. For instance, if you enter the value "CA" in the State field, Q&A checks the index list to see if a matching value of CA can be found in other records.

NOTE

Use the unique value index option to help with data entry on values that should never be repeated. For instance, you can index a Social Security field as Unique Values. This is useful because all Social Security Numbers are unique. Therefore, if you enter a Social Security Number that is the same as someone else's in your database, Q&A will prompt saying that the value is not unique if that field is indexed as Unique Values.

Retrieval Programming

When creating a retrieve spec, you may need to harness more power to create the answer set you need. That is why Q&A allows you to tap into Q&A's programming functions. For example, to retrieve all the records with a Hire Date within the past week, you can use retrieval programming.

To perform Retrieve spec programming, you must be in Retrieve mode. Either click on the Retrieve button in the tool bar, choose Records ➤ Retrieve, or press Ctrl+R. Then choose Retrieve ➤ Helper or press Ctrl+H to display the Helper dialog box (Figure 11.6), which is similar to other programming mode dialog boxes you'll read about later in this chapter.

Like all programming dialog boxes, the Helper dialog box contains a Formula box in which you enter the formula for a field and the Elements group from which you select field names or function types.

FIGURE 11.6

Use the Helper dialog box to create retrieve spec programming statements.

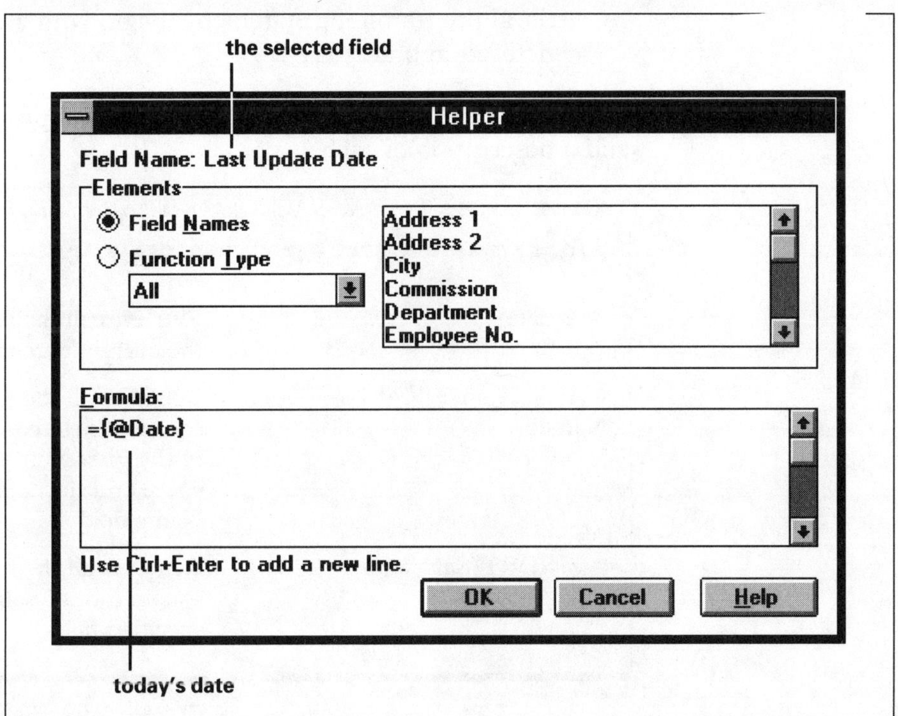

To create a retrieve spec programming statement, use the following steps:

1. In Retrieval mode, move the cursor to the field in which you want to add a retrieval programming statement.

2. Choose Retrieve ➤ Helper. Q&A displays the Helper dialog box.

3. Build the programming statement one piece at a time by double-clicking on items in the Elements box. You can also create your programming statement by typing directly in the Formula box.

4. Click OK or press Enter.

Retrieve spec programming differs from form programming in these ways:

- Since Retrieval programming is not used for altering data, it can only use functions. Therefore, you can't use commands or IF THEN statements. However, you can use TEXT to create conditional programming statements (see Appendix D).

- Retrieval programming does not use field IDs. Therefore, the Retrieval programming statements begin with an equal sign and are enclosed in braces ({}).

Table 11.5 contains examples of valid retrieval programming statements and a description of each.

TABLE 11.5: Examples of Valid Retrieval Programming Statements

PROGRAMMING STATEMENT	DESCRIPTION
={@date}	Retrieves all the records containing the current date in the specified field
={First Name+" "+Last Name}	Retrieves all the records if the specified field contains the contents of the First Name field followed by a space and the contents of the Last Name field
={@SQRT(Salary)}	Retrieves all the records in which the square root of Salary is in the specified field

As in Q&A for DOS, you can type the programming statements directly into the fields of the retrieve spec. It's not necessary to use the Helper dialog box to build or enter a retrieve programming statement.

Restrict Programming

From time to time, you may need the power of the programming functions to restrict data entry in records. You can create programming formulas in the Edit Restriction dialog box (Figure 11.7). The formulas in the Edit Restriction dialog box are subject to the same restrictions as the

FIGURE 11.7

The Edit Restriction dialog box, in which you can type a restriction formula for a selected field.

formulas for Retrieval programming and also follow the same format. Table 11.6 shows some examples of restriction programming statements:

TABLE 11.6: Examples of Valid Restriction Programming Statements

PROGRAMMING STATEMENT	DESCRIPTION
={@date}	Restricts entries in the specified field to the current date
={@XLOOKUP(Staff.dtf, Last Name,"Last Name","First Name"}	Restricts entries in the specified field to the contents of the First Name fields in the Staff database

Derived Column Programming

Many reports require specially calculated values. That is why Q&A enables you to create programming statements for derived columns in Columnar reports and derived fields in Freeform reports.

The programming statements for derived columns and derived fields are entered into the Formula boxes of the Derived Field dialog box (Figure 11.8) and the Add Derived Field dialog box (Figure 11.9).

Enter derived programming statements in the Formula box without a leading field ID. However, since Q&A automatically assigns field IDs to both derived columns and derived fields, you can refer to them by their field IDs. Since Q&A does not use derived programming for altering data, only Functions are allowed. Therefore, you can't use commands and IF THEN statements. Table 11.7 provides examples of formulas typed into the Formula box of the Derived Field dialog box.

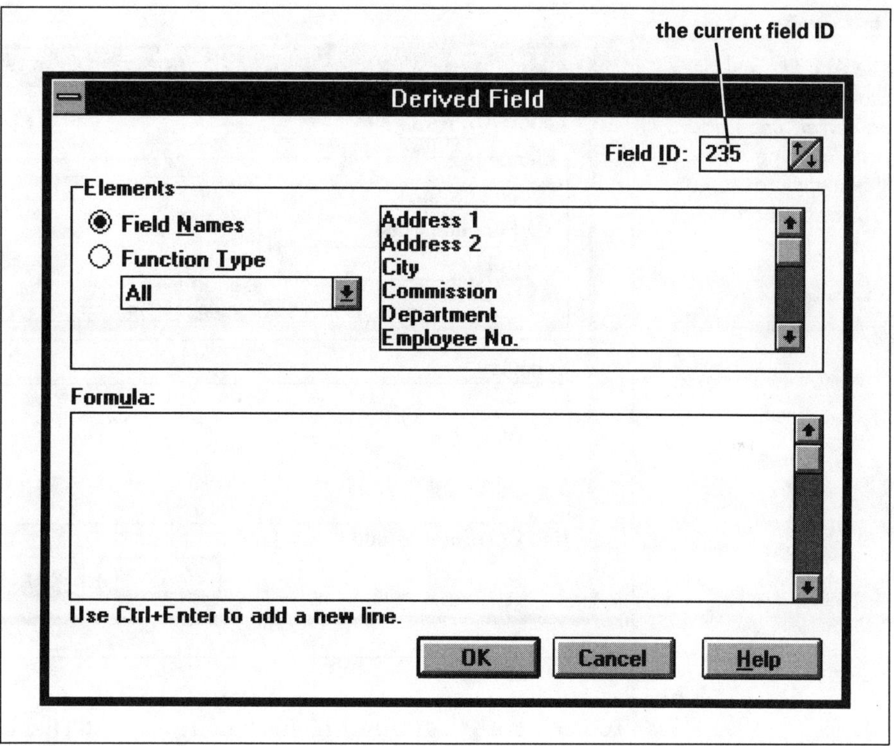

TABLE 11.7: Examples of Valid Derived Programming Statements

PROGRAMMING STATEMENT	DESCRIPTION
@date	Places the current date in a derived column
@XLOOKUP(Staff.dtf, Last Name,"Last Name","First Name"}	Finds and returns the first name of a person based on the Last Name field matched in the Staff database
@TEXT(#25>15,"Too High")	Returns the words Too High when the value in field or column #25 is greater than 15

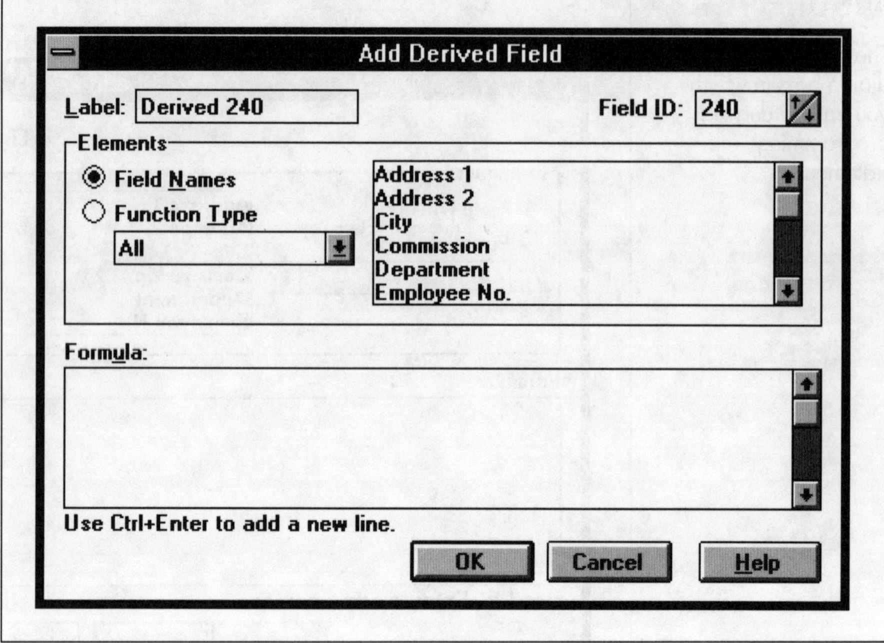

To create a programming statement for a derived column, follow these steps while in a Columnar report:

1. Choose Reports ➤ Add Derived Columns. Q&A displays the Add Derived Column dialog box.

2. Create the formulas for your derived column in the Formula box and either click on OK or press Enter.

To create a programming statement for a derived field, follow these steps in a Freeform report:

1. Select the field tool (the second from the top in the right column of buttons) from the tool palette.

2. Create a field in the appropriate part of your layout. After creating a field box, Q&A displays the New Field dialog box.

3. Click on the Derived Field button. Q&A displays the Add Derived Field dialog box.

4. Create the formulas for your derived field in the Formula box and either click on OK or press Enter.

For detailed information about Q&A reports, see Chapter 9.

Navigation Programming

Navigation programming is used in conjunction with form programming. While the tab order set for your database also controls the movement of the cursor from field to field, navigation programming provides more power using functions and special navigation commands.

Since the purpose of navigation programming is to control the travel of the cursor when it leaves a field, all navigation programming statements begin with *on field* exit symbols (>) or *on field* entry symbols (<).

The statements following the *on field exit* or *on field entry* symbols can start with a field ID so that you can refer to that field later.

    >#10: GOTO #20

or

    <#10: GOTO #20

This programming statement instructs Q&A to move the cursor to field #20 when it leaves field #10. However, the field ID is not necessary since you are already in the field from which you will go to the designated field. However, remember that you can use a programming statement containing the current field ID to refer to that field later. The following statement instructs Q&A to move the cursor to field #20 when it leaves this field:

    >GOTO #20

There is even more power available through navigation programming formulas. The following statement, for example, instructs Q&A to go to field #30 when field #20 is less than thirty days from today:

    >#10:IF #20<(@DATE+30) THEN GOTO #30

Navigation programming can use all the standard functions of Q&A. This, in combination with being able to use IF THEN statements, makes navigation programming very flexible and powerful. Table 11.8 describes the special commands that Q&A provides for navigation programming.

TABLE 11.8: Q&A Navigation Programming Commands

COMMAND	MOVES THE CURSOR TO:
GOTO n	Field ID n
CNEXT	The next field in sequence of left to right and from top to bottom. This overrides the tab order sequence.
CPREV	The previous field in sequence of right to left and from bottom to top. This overrides the tab order sequence.
CHOME	The first field of the record. This overrides the tab order sequence.
CEND	The last field of the record.
PGDN	The first field on the next page.
PGUP	The first field of the previous page.

To create a navigation programming spec, follow these steps:

1. Click on the Design Input Forms button on the tool bar, choose <u>S</u>elect ➤ Design Input <u>F</u>orms, or press Ctrl+M.

2. Choose For<u>m</u>at ➤ Field Na<u>v</u>igation ➤ <u>E</u>dit Programming or press Ctrl+H. Q&A displays the Edit Navigation Programming dialog box (Figure 11.10). Notice that this dialog box is basically the same as the Edit Programming Dialog box for form programming.

3. Create your formulas and either click on OK or press Enter.

The Edit Navigation Programming dialog box also allows you to run a field navigation programming statement upon opening a record. You can set this by clicking on the <u>O</u>ptions button. In the Options dialog box (Figure 11.11), type the field ID of the programming statement to be run when the record opens. Then either click on OK or press Enter.

The Edit Navigation
Programming
dialog box

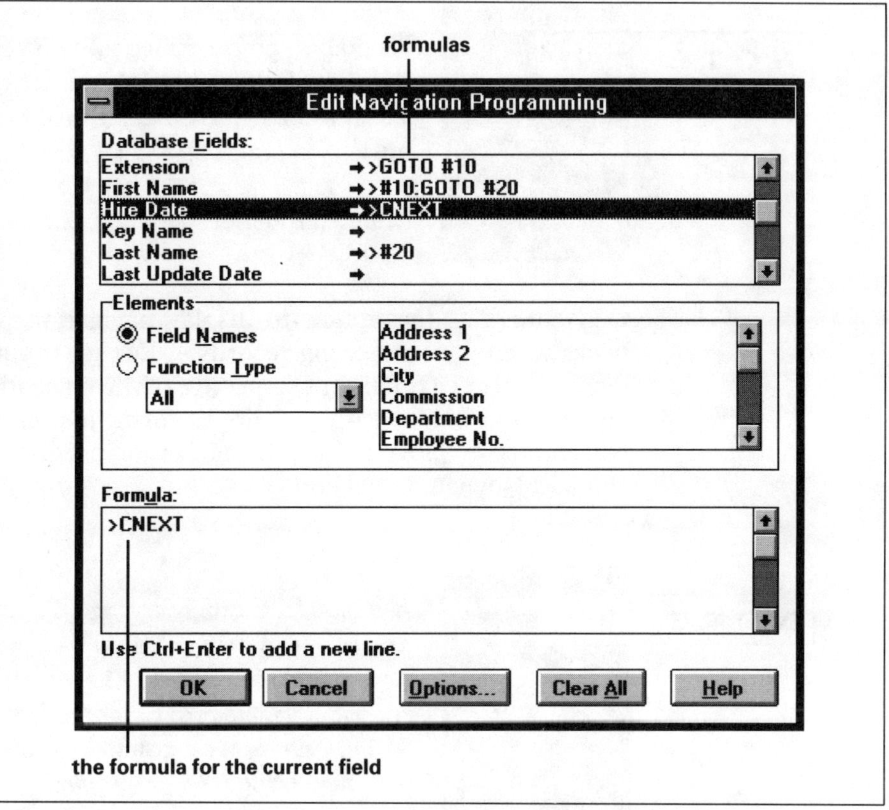

The Options dialog
box, which allows you
to run navigation
programming when
entering a record

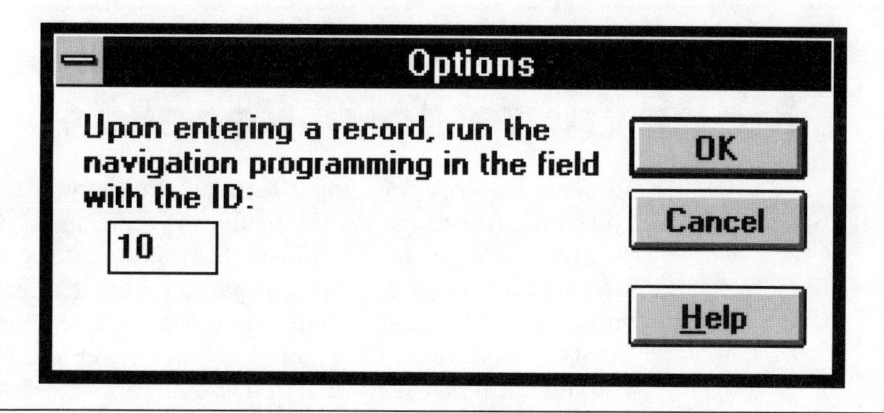

Navigation programming takes precedence over the tab order. For instance, if the tab order specifies that the cursor should proceed to the field to the right and the navigation programming instructs Q&A to move the cursor to the field to the left, the cursor moves to the field to the left.

Q&A provides the option to display navigation programming in field boxes when you're viewing records in Design Input Form view. This allows you to get a different perspective of the navigation programming and how it will operate with your input form. Just choose Format ➤ Field Navigation ➤ Show. To hide the navigation programming, choose Format ➤ Field Navigation➤ Hide.

Although form programming and navigation programming both influence the data entry process in Add/Edit mode, the field ID numbers are not related. For example, the field ID for the First Name field may be #10 in your form programming statements but #20 in your field navigation programming statements.

Using Mass Update to Manipulate Your Records

While form programming affects all the records that you will create or edit in the future, mass update allows you to manipulate the records that you have already added. Through mass update, you can retrieve an answer set and create programming statements to affect those records. Then you can run the mass update and Q&A will use your programming statements to update all the records in the answer set. For instance, if one of your customers just got married and changed her last name from Stevens to Hajimoto, you can use mass update to search through all your records and make the change. To replace all the occurrences of Stevens in the Notes field, type this in the field:

    #10=@REPLACE (#10, "Stevens", "Hajimoto")

Setting Up a Mass Update

Mass update programming is almost identical to form programming. Mass update formulas use field ID numbers, IF THEN statements, all of the formulas and commands, and can contain multiple statements per formula. However, a Mass Update formula cannot begin with a greater than or less than symbol. When running a mass update, you never switch between fields using the Tab or Enter key, so *on field entry* and *on field exit* programming statements don't work.

    #10=@ABS(#5)

This statement is a valid programming statement in Mass Update.

To create a mass update, use these steps:

1. Choose <u>S</u>elect ➤ Mass <u>U</u>pdate. Q&A displays Mass Update view (Figure 11.12), which looks very similar to a form in Add/Edit mode.

2. Move the cursor to the field in which you want to create a programming statement; then choose <u>U</u>pdate ➤ <u>H</u>elper or press Ctrl+H. Q&A displays the Helper dialog box (Figure 11.13).

3. Create your programming statement in the <u>F</u>ormula box.

4. Click on OK or press Enter.

5. If you want to attach a retrieve spec, choose <u>U</u>pdate ➤ Attach <u>Re</u>trieve. Select the desired retrieve spec and click on OK.

6. If you want to attach a sort, choose Update ➤ Attach Sor<u>t</u>. Either create or load a sort. Click on OK or press Enter.

FIGURE 11.12

Use Mass Update to create programming statements to alter the records already created in your database.

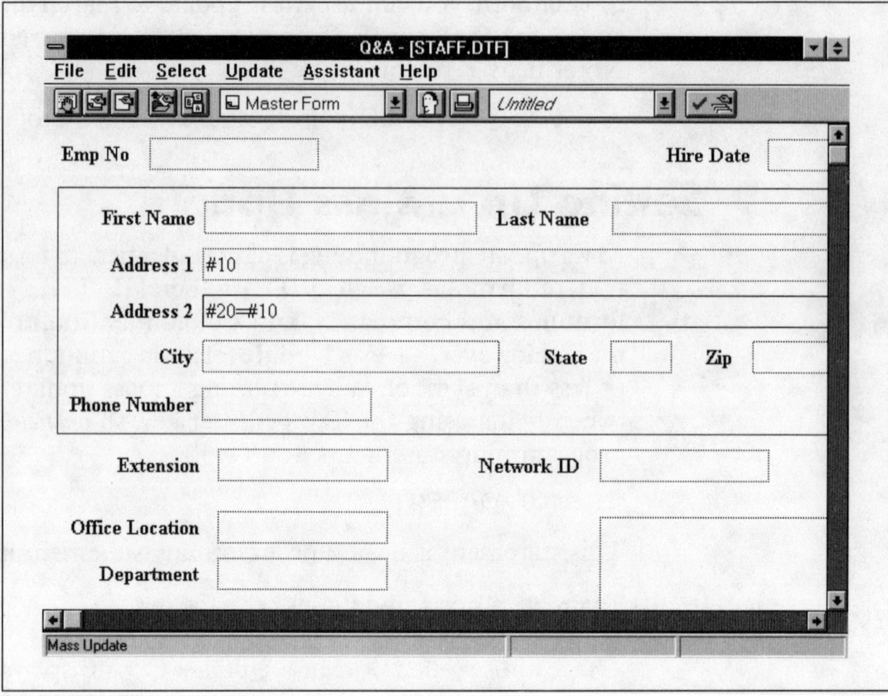

FIGURE 11.13

This Helper dialog box is used to create the programming for the Mass Update spec.

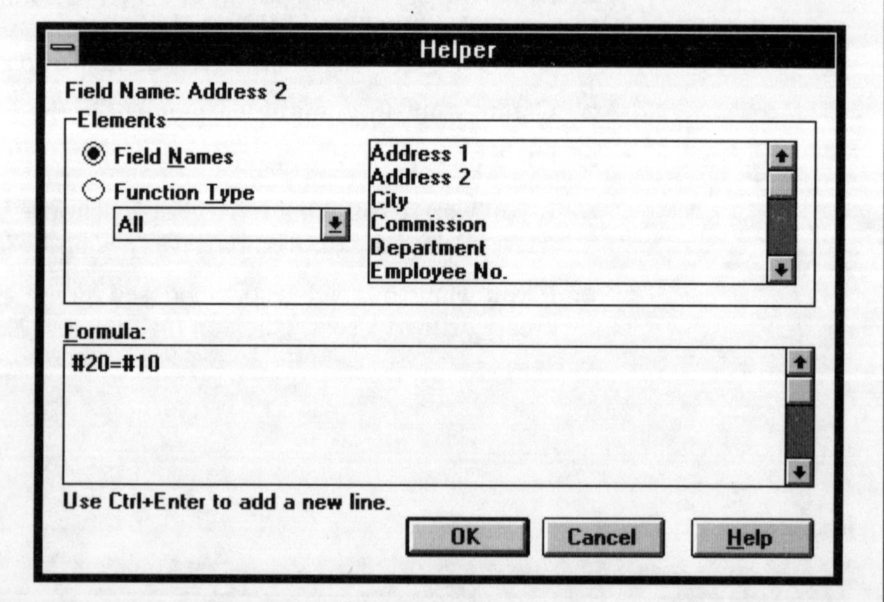

When you run a mass update, Q&A allows you to use the statements that you created in the Edit Programming dialog box. To use these statements, choose Update ➤ Options. In the Options dialog box (Figure 11.14), check the check boxes that contain the types of calculation statements to be executed from the Edit Programming dialog box. You can choose from Record Entry Statements, Main Programming Statements, and Record Exit Statements. When you choose an option, Q&A displays an indicator on the right side of the status bar. The options, descriptions, and their status bar indicators are:

Record Entry Statements	Executes all the on entry programming statements	ORE
Main Programming Statements	Executes all the main programming statements that you created in the Edit Programming dialog box	MAIN
Record Exit Statements	Executes all the on exit programming statements	ORX

Running a Mass Update

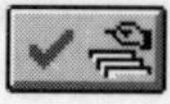

To run a mass update, choose Update ➤ Run This Mass Update or click on the Run Mass Update button on the tool bar. When running a mass update, Q&A scans the database to retrieve the answer set that you specified. Q&A then displays an information box (Figure 11.15). If you choose No, Q&A updates all the records in the answer set and return to Mass Update view. If you choose Yes, Q&A shows you the first record of the answer set and another information box (Figure 11.16). Your choices are:

Update Record	Q&A updates the record and displays the next record and the same information box
Do Not Update	Q&A does not update the record but displays the next record and the same information box
Update All	Q&A updates the remaining records in the answer set and returns to Mass Update view

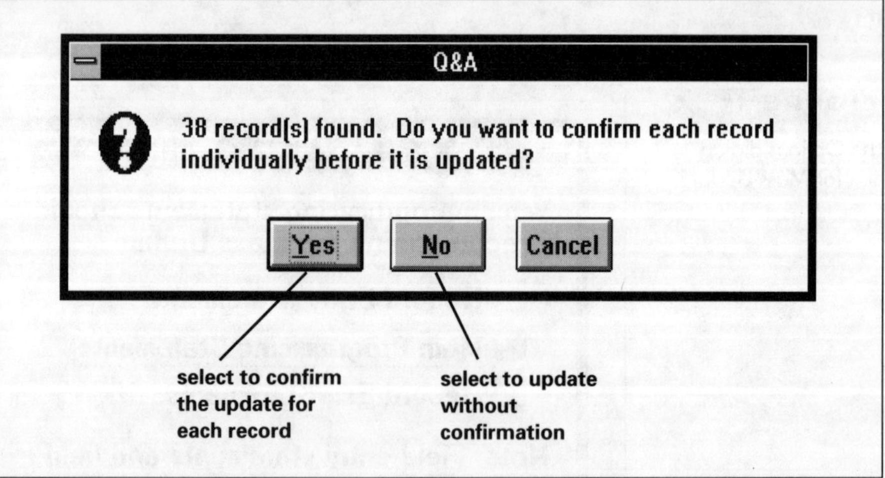

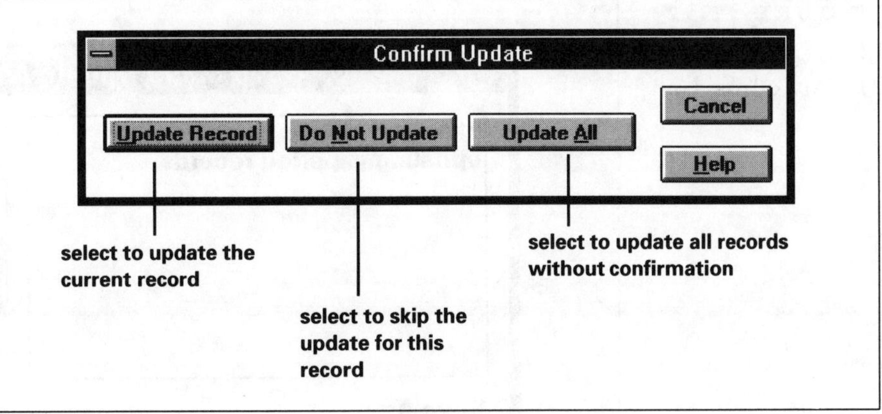

Saving, Loading, and Deleting Mass Update Specs

When you create programming for a mass update, the programming, attached retrievals, and attached sorts are part of that mass update spec. As with all other Q&A specs, you can save, load, and delete Mass Update specs, and the processes that you use are no different than saving, loading, and deleting Columnar reports, Freeform reports, and Retrieve specs. To save a Mass Update spec, choose Update ➤ Save Mass Update or Update ➤ Save Mass Update As. In the Save As text box in the Save Mass Update As dialog box (Figure 11.17), type a spec name. Then either click on OK or press Enter.

To load a Mass Update spec, choose Update ➤ Load Mass Update. Q&A displays the Load Mass Update dialog box (Figure 11.18). Select the desired Mass Update spec and click on OK. As a shortcut, you can select a saved Mass Update spec from the drop-down list box on the tool bar.

To delete a Mass Update spec, load the Mass Update spec to be deleted and choose Update ➤ Delete Mass Update.

The Save Mass
Update As dialog box

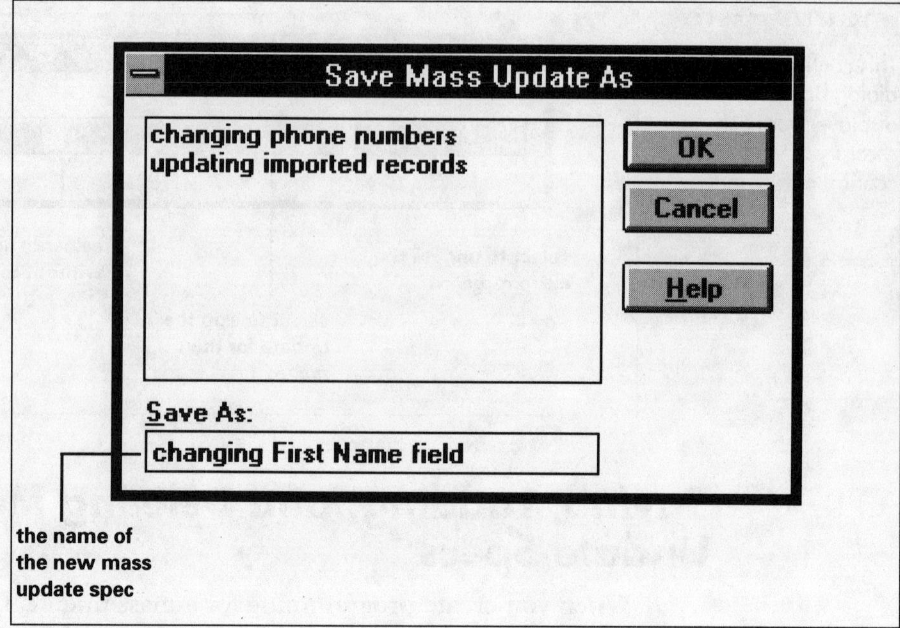

the name of
the new mass
update spec

The Load Mass
Update dialog box

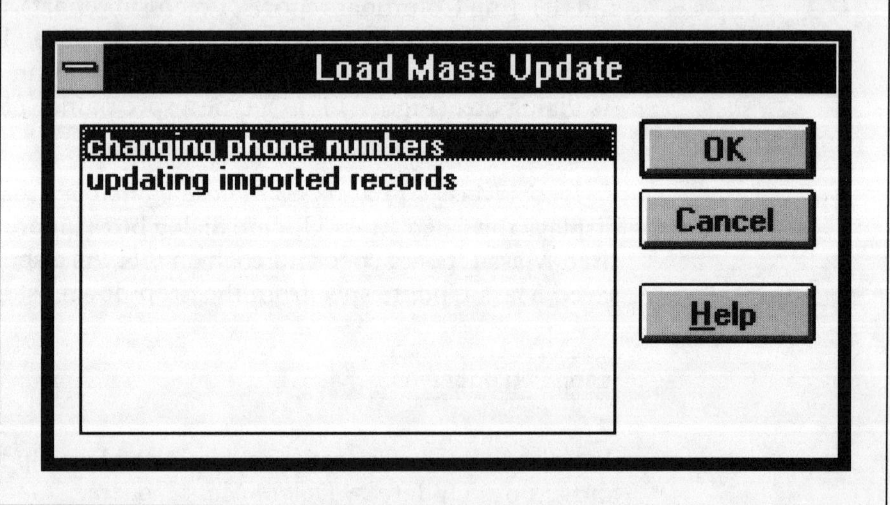

Deleting Many Records Simultaneously with Mass Delete

A mass delete is a way to delete selected, even all, records in your database. A mass delete is in essence a retrieval that deletes the records in the answer set rather than displaying them. Every menu item and tool bar button works the same as in Retrieval mode, and all retrieval functions are available in mass delete. However, you do not have the option of sorting your records through mass update.

In Add/Edit mode, choose Select ➤ Mass Delete to display the current database in Mass Delete mode. Select the deletion criteria and then choose Delete ➤ Run This Mass Delete or press the delete button on the tool bar. Before you can delete any records, Q&A prompts you with an information box (Figure 11.19), which asks you to confirm the mass delete.

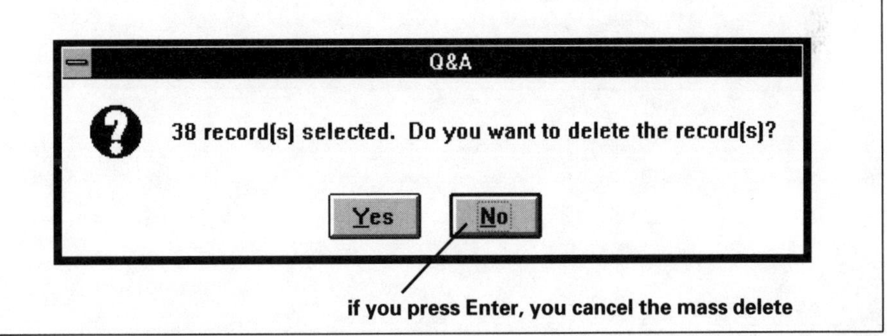

Once a record is deleted, there is no way to get those records back—unless you have a back-up of your database.

To Sum Up

In this chapter, you learned all about Q&A database programming. You found out about the structure of programming statements and how to create form, retrieval, restrict, derived, write, navigation, and mass update programming statements. You learned how to use IF THEN statements, multiple statements per formula, AND and OR conjunctions, BEGIN and END, and to perform complex statements with functions.

In the next chapter, you'll start learning how to plan and create your first document using Q&A Write. You'll learn about file handling, text manipulation, the spell checker, thesaurus, and document statistics. You'll also learn how to close, save, and print documents.

Creating Documents with the Q&A Word Processor

12

Planning and Creating Your First Document

● **To start Q&A Write** 397

from within the Q&A Database, choose File ➤ Q&A Write or press Ctrl+W, or click on the Q&A Write for Windows icon in the Symantec program group.

● **To open a Q&A Write document** 398

either press the shortcut key combination Ctrl+O or choose File ➤ Open. Either double-click on a file in the filename list box or type a file name in the text box.

● **To undo an action** 421

immediately choose Edit ➤ Undo or press Ctrl+Z.

● **To reverse the last Undo command** 421

choose Edit ➤ Redo or press Ctrl+Z.

● **To repeat the last action** 421

choose Edit ➤ Repeat or press F4.

● **To check your spelling** 422

choose Tools ➤ Spelling, press Ctrl+F2, or click on the Spell Checker tool bar button. Then click on Start.

● **To use the thesaurus** 426

select a word and choose Tools ➤ Thesaurus or press Ctrl+Shift+F2.

● **To check document statistics**   **428**

> choose File ➤ Statistics.

● **To save a document**   **428**

> choose File ➤ Save (or press Ctrl+S), choose File ➤ Save As
> (or press F12), or click on the Save button on the tool bar. If
> you are saving a new document, type a file name, and click on
> OK or press Enter.

● **To automatically save documents as you work**   **431**

> choose File ➤ Preferences ➤ File, place a check mark in the
> Auto Save Documents check box, and select a Frequency
> from 1 to 60 minutes.

● **To view a document as it will print**   **432**

> choose File ➤ Print Preview.

● **To print a document**   **433**

> choose File ➤ Print or press Ctrl+P, select the desired op-
> tions, and either click on OK or press Enter.

● **To exit Q&A Write**   **435**

> choose File ➤ Exit, type Alt+F4, or double-click on the Ap-
> plication Control Menu button.

IN the previous chapters, you found out almost all there is to know about the Q&A Database application. Now we'll introduce you to the other application in the Q&A package. In this and in the next chapter, you'll get a quick tour of Q&A Write, which is a standalone word processor that works side-by-side with the Q&A Database. When you have read and worked through both chapters, you'll have a good working knowledge of Q&A Write.

Getting Started with Q&A Write

Q&A Write is a sophisticated yet easy-to-use word processor. You can use Q&A Write to create letters, memoranda, and proposals—ranging from one page to many pages. You can also use Q&A Write to print envelopes and merge data from database files into your documents.

You or your company can use Q&A Write to build a collection of form letters that gather information from your databases for many uses—from holiday greetings to requests for payment—and then automate their printing and that of the accompanying envelopes.

Q&A Write's features include:

- Search and replace text and/or formats

- Customizable toolbar

- Setting custom preferences@n/blist bull =
  WYSIWYG word processing (what you see on the screen is what you get as a printed document)

- A complete help facility

- Zooming

- Print preview

- Page layout

- Spellchecking

- A thesaurus

- Multiple columns

- Automatic save

- Mail merge

- Envelope creation

- Outlines

- Object Linking and Embedding (OLE)

- Embedding graphics in several common formats

- Frames for tables, pictures, and text

- Import of files formatted in other programs

- Saving your files in other formats

Starting Q&A Write

There are two locations from which you can start Q&A Write: from within the Q&A Database, you can choose File ➤ Q&A Write or press Ctrl+W, or you can click on the Q&A Write for Windows icon in the Symantec program group. You'll see the Q&A Write window as shown in Figure 12.1.

FIGURE 12.1

To create your first document, just start typing in the work area.

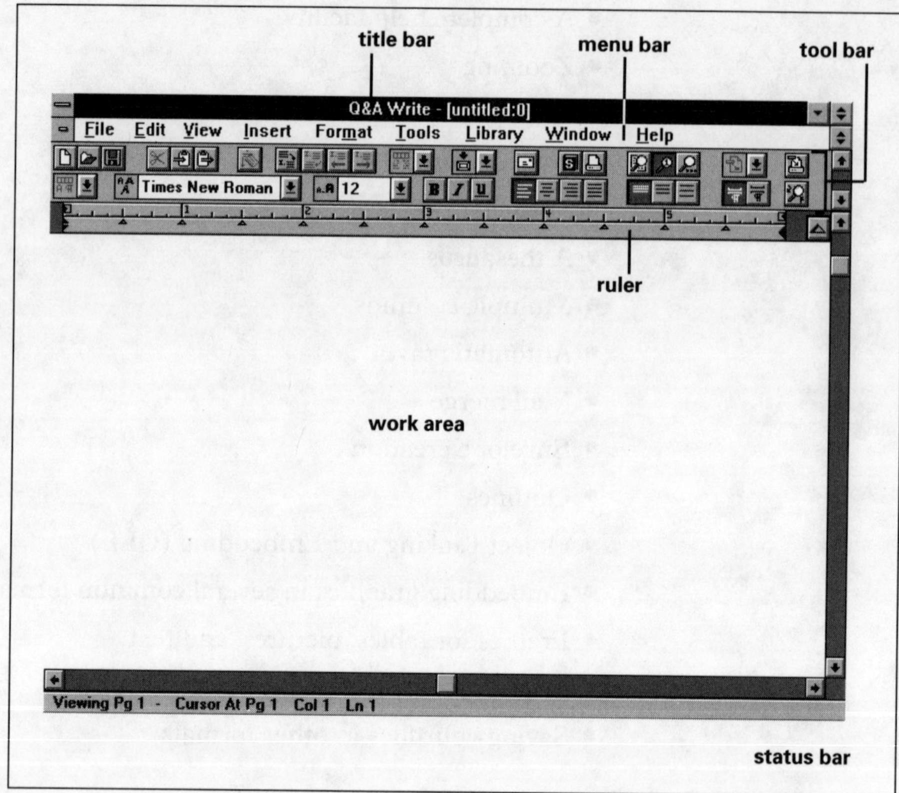

Opening a Q&A Write Document

Opening a file in Q&A Write is exactly the same as opening a Q&A Database file. However, where you can only open one database at a time in the Q&A Database, you can have up to eight Q&A Write documents open at a time. To open a Q&A Write document, follow these steps:

1. Either press the shortcut key combination Ctrl+O on the keyboard or choose File ➤ Open. Q&A displays the Open File dialog box (Figure 12.2).

In Q&A's Open File dialog box, you can open a document or template that is located on a specific drive, in a particular directory.

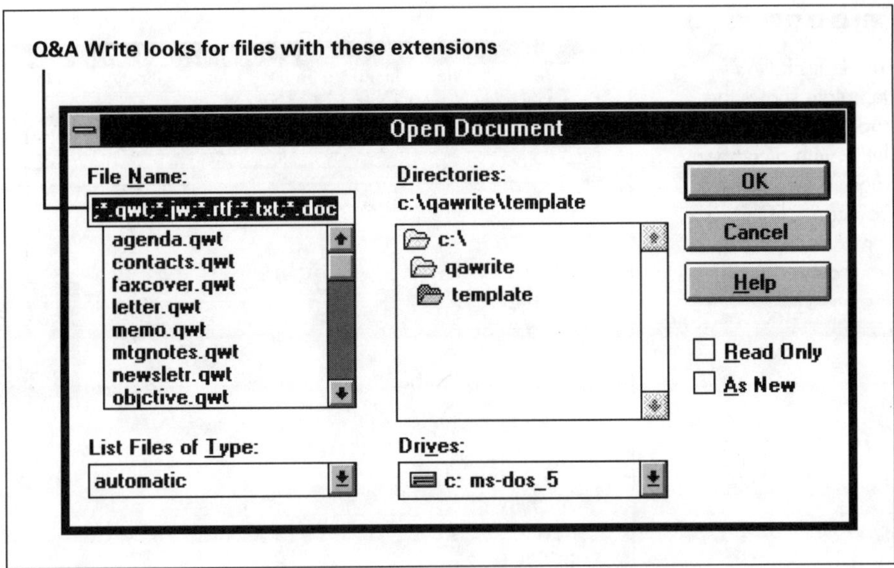

Before you learn about the details of the Q&A Write window, open LET-TER.QWT, one of the sample Q&A *templates* (a group of formatted documents on which you can base your own documents). For information about templates, see your Q&A Write documentation.

2. The LETTER.QWT template is located in the TEMPLATE sub-directory. To display the list of files in TEMPLATE, double-click on the icon next to *template* in the Directories list box.

3. Double-click on LETTER.QWT. Q&A opens the file (see Figure 12.3) and you can start working on your first Q&A Write document.

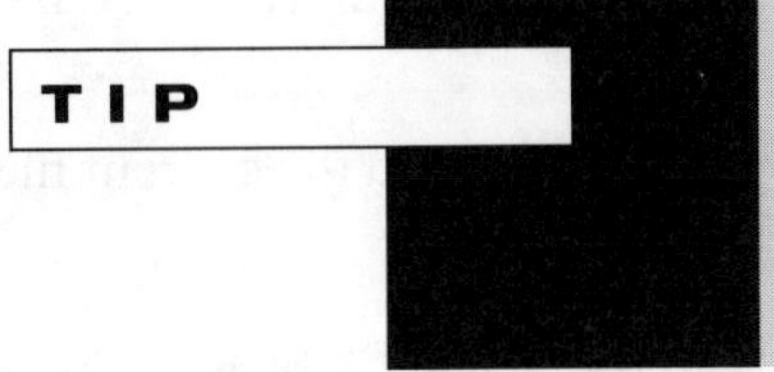

If the file that you wish to open is one of the last four on which you have worked, you can select it from the bottom of the open File menu. Either click on the file name or press the underlined number preceding the file name.

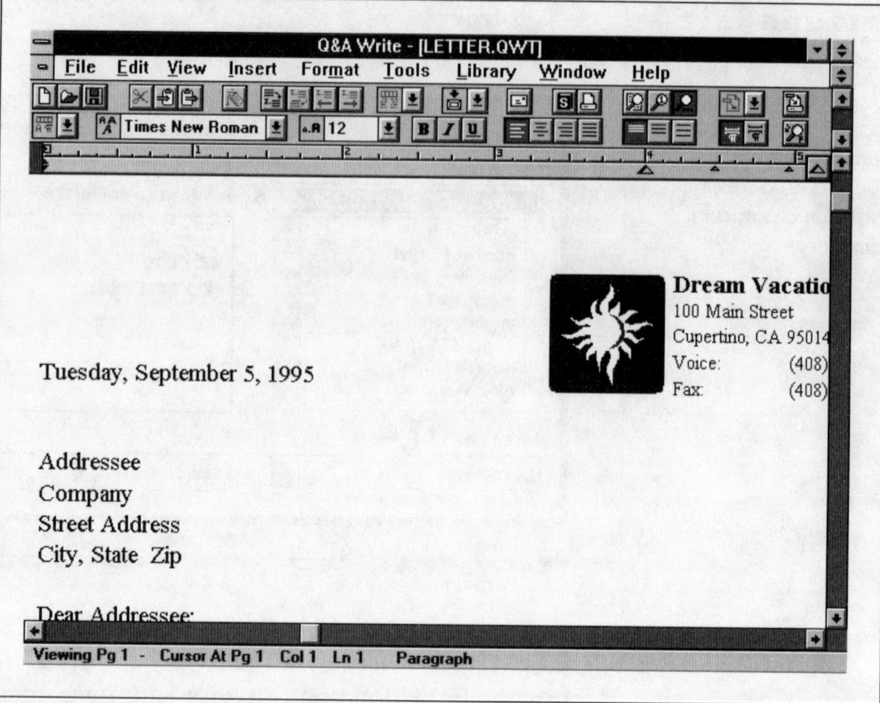

The Elements of the Q&A Window

Because much of the Q&A Write window is similar to the Q&A Database window, which was described thoroughly in Chapter 2, you'll receive a shorter explanation of each element. However, when an element is unique to Q&A Write, you'll be given an opportunity to learn all the details.

The *title bar* displays the name of the application and the current file (only if you have opened a file).

The title bar also contains the Application Control Menu button (which controls the application window), the Minimize button, and either the

Maximize button or the Restore button. For more information about these title bar buttons, see Appendix B.

Using the Menu Bar

Immediately below the title bar is the menu bar, which displays the menus from which you can select commands. The Q&A Write menu bar also provides a Document Control Menu button, which controls the window in which the current document appears, and either the Maximize button or the Restore button, which controls the size of the current document window.

The menus that you initially see upon opening a Q&A Write document window are the standard Windows menus File, Edit, Window, and Help, and several menus that are unique to Q&A Write. After you open documents and then close them all, the menu bar only includes File, Window, and Help. To reveal the full menu bar again, just open a new or saved document.

Using the Tool Bar

Underneath the menu bar is the double-row tool bar, which displays a series of buttons and drop-down boxes.

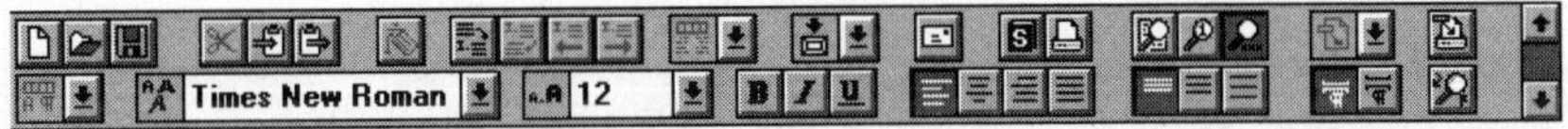

Let's take a closer look at each button and drop-down list box on the Q&A Write toolbar. When you learn about other Q&A Write features (such as Print Preview) that provide their own tool bar buttons, we'll show you how to use each set of buttons.

T I P   Click and hold down the right mouse button on any tool bar button to view a short description in the status bar.

Now let's find out about the Q&A Write tool bar buttons and list boxes at the top of the document window. As you learn about each element of the tool bar, click on the button or drop-down list box to see what it does to your document. Remember that if a button looks dimmer than other buttons, it is not available for use now. If a button looks darker than surrounding buttons and seems to be pressed down, it is already active and you don't have to click on it. For example, notice on the tool bar presented earlier that three buttons on the right side of the second row of buttons appear to be pressed down. This means that you are viewing the document left-aligned, single-spaced, and there is no space above the current paragraph. These are defaults for Q&A Write documents.

As in the Q&A Database, each tool bar button and drop-down list box has its counterpart menu command and, many times, a shortcut key or key combination. Table 12.1 illustrates and describes each Q&A Write tool bar button and list box used when creating or editing a document.

TABLE 12.1: Q&A Write Tool Bar Buttons—Creating or Editing a Document

BUTTON	BUTTON OR LIST BOX NAME	DESCRIPTION	EQUIVALENT COMMAND	SHORTCUT KEYS
	New	Opens a new, empty default document.	File ➤ New	Ctrl+N
	Open	Opens an existing document.	File ➤ Open	Ctrl+O
	Save	Saves the current document.	File ➤ Save	Ctrl+S
	Cut	Cuts a selection from the document and places it in the Clipboard.	Edit ➤ Cut	Ctrl+X
	Copy	Copies a selection from the document and places it in the Clipboard.	Edit ➤ Copy	Ctrl+C
	Paste	Pastes a selection from the Clipboard into the document.	Edit ➤ Paste	Ctrl+V
	Undo/ Redo	Reverses the last deletion, action, undo, or redo.	Edit ➤ Undo or Redo	Ctrl+Z

TABLE 12.1: Q&A Write Tool Bar Buttons—Creating or Editing a Document (continued)

BUTTON	BUTTON OR LIST BOX NAME	DESCRIPTION	EQUIVALENT COMMAND	SHORTCUT KEYS
	Convert to Outline mode	Changes the selected paragraph from normal text to part of an outline.	Edit ➤ Outline ➤ Add To	Ctrl+Shift+A
	Convert from Outline mode	Changes the selected paragraph from part of an outline to normal text.	Edit ➤ Outline ➤ Remove From	Ctrl+Shift+R
	Demote	Demotes the selected paragraph one level down in the outline.	Edit ➤ Outline ➤ Demote	Ctrl+Shift+>
	Promote	Promotes the selected paragraph one level up in the outline.	Edit ➤ Outline ➤ Promote	Ctrl+Shift+<
	Open Library	Displays the Open Library dialog box from which you can select a library to apply to the current document.	Library ➤ Open	N/A
	Frame	Inserts a frame that you select at the insertion point.	Insert ➤ Frame	Alt+F7
	Create/ Edit Envelope	Displays a window in which you can create an envelope or an existing envelope, which you can edit.	Tools ➤ Create Envelope or Edit Envelope	N/A
	Spell Check	Checks the spelling in the current document.	Tools ➤ Spelling	Ctrl+F2
	Print	Prints the current document.	File ➤ Print	Ctrl+P
	View at 25%	View the current document at 25 percent of its normal size.	View ➤ Full Page (25%)	Ctrl+1

TABLE 12.1: Q&A Write Tool Bar Buttons—Creating or Editing a Document (continued)

BUTTON	BUTTON OR LIST BOX NAME	DESCRIPTION	EQUIVALENT COMMAND	SHORTCUT KEYS
	View at 100%	View the current document at its normal size.	View ➤ Normal (100%)	Ctrl+3
	Custom Scale	Displays the current document at a scale (from 25 to 200 percent) that you set in the Custom View dialog box.	View ➤ Custom Scale	Ctrl+0
	Merge Field	Inserts a merge field from a database file or a merge list.	Insert ➤ Merge Field	Ctrl+ Shift+M
	Print Merge Document	Prints a merge document.	File ➤ Print Merge	N/A
	Apply Format	Applies a style format from the library to the selection.	Library ➤ Style	N/A
Century Schoolbook	Font	Selects a font to apply to the selected text.	Format ➤ Character	Ctrl+F3
12	Font Size	Selects a font size to apply to the selected text.	Format ➤ Character	Ctrl+F3
B	Bold	Applies boldface to or removes boldface from the selected text.	Format ➤ Character	Ctrl+F3
I	Italic	Applies italics to or removes italics from the selected text.	Format ➤ Character	Ctrl+F3
U	Underline	Underlines or removes an underline from the selected text.	Format ➤ Character	Ctrl+F3
	Left Justification	Aligns the selected paragraphs to the left margin.	Format ➤ Paragraph	Ctrl+F5

TABLE 12.1: Q&A Write Tool Bar Buttons—Creating or Editing a Document (continued)

BUTTON	BUTTON OR LIST BOX NAME	DESCRIPTION	EQUIVALENT COMMAND	SHORTCUT KEYS
	Center Justification	Aligns the selected paragraphs on either side of an invisible center point.	Format ➤ Paragraph	Ctrl+F5
	Right Justification	Aligns the selected paragraphs to the right margin.	Format ➤ Paragraph	Ctrl+F5
	Full Justification	Aligns the selected paragraphs from the left margin to the right margin.	Format ➤ Paragraph	Ctrl+F5
	Single Line Spacing	Applies single spacing to the selected lines.	Format ➤ Paragraph	Ctrl+F5
	One-and-One-Half Line Spacing	Applies one-and-one-half spacing to the selected lines.	Format ➤ Paragraph	Ctrl+F5
	Double Line Spacing	Applies double spacing to the selected lines.	Format ➤ Paragraph	Ctrl+F5
	No Paragraph Spacing	Does not add any space above the selected paragraphs.	Format ➤ Paragraph	Ctrl+F5
	Add Paragraph Spacing	Adds a half line of space above each of the selected paragraphs.	Format ➤ Paragraph	Ctrl+F5
	Show/Hide	Shows or hides nonprinting symbols (such as new lines, tab symbols, frames, and so on).	View ➤ Show Detail or Show Proof	Ctrl+W

To type a word with a special format such as bold, italics, or underline, select that button and type the word. To stop using the format, click the button again.

Try changing some of the formats or cutting and pasting in the open document. If you have used any other Windows word processors, you'll find that many of the tool bar buttons and actions are identical to those in Q&A Write.

Using the Ruler

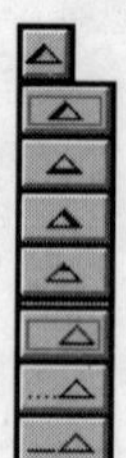

The ruler (Figure 12.4) provides a shortcut way to change margins, indents, and tab settings for the current document. To change these settings, move the mouse pointer to one of the markers on the ruler and drag it to a new location. Table 13.3 in Chapter 13 illustrates and describes each of the tab markers. You'll also learn more about setting and changing margins, indents, and tab settings using the ruler, the menu bar, and shortcut keys later in this chapter and in Chapter 13.

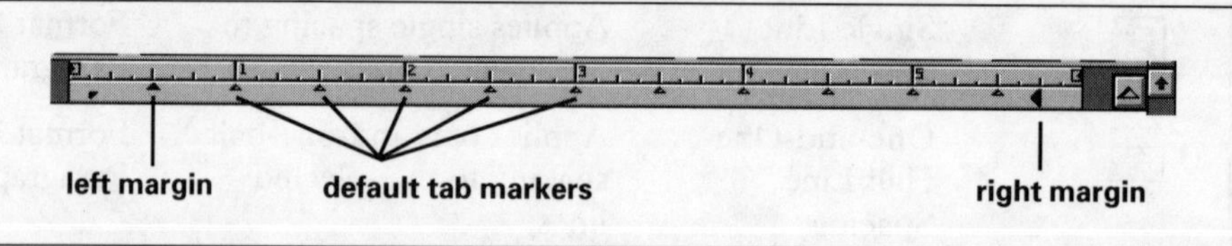

Using the Work Area

The largest part of the Q&A document window is the work area in which the current document resides. If you have been experimenting with the tool bar buttons, you have already seen the effects on the document in the work area.

Using the Status Bar

The status bar, at the bottom of the window, tells you exactly where you are in the document. For example, the status bar shown in Figure 12.5 contains three sections of information. From left to right, the status bar displays the following information:

- The page that you are viewing in Q&A Write

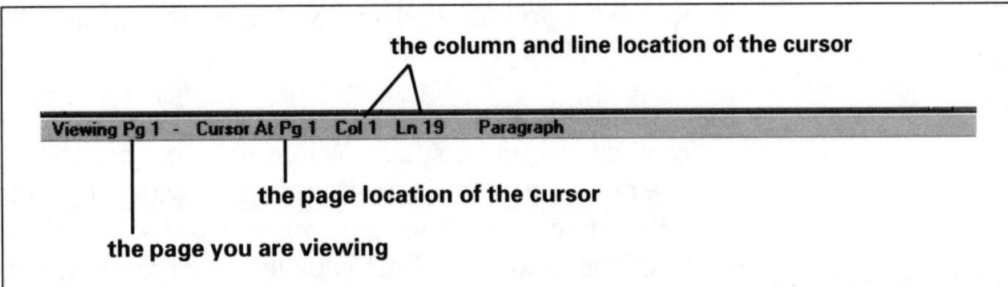

FIGURE 12.5

The Q&A Write status bar, provides information about where you are in the document.

- The current cursor location—page number, column number, and line number. The cursor can be in a different location than on the page that you're viewing.

- The part of the document on which the cursor resides. For example, the word *Paragraph* does not mean that the cursor is sitting in a paragraph; it indicates that the cursor is on a paragraph marker at the end of a paragraph.

Other information on the status bar can be very helpful. If you click and hold down the right mouse button on a tool bar button, the status bar shows a brief description of the button's function. In addition, if you open a menu and highlight a command by pressing the ↓ or ↑, the status bar provides an explanation of the command.

Before going on to the rest of this chapter, close the document in the work area to clear it. Choose File ➤ Close or press F3. When Q&A Write prompts you to save the changes, answer No. You don't want to save any changes that you might have made to the document.

Creating a Document

To create a document, choose File ➤ New or Ctrl+N. Then just start typing in the empty work area. By pressing the spacebar, you can move the cursor anywhere in the work area and start typing, but to quickly move the cursor to a specific location on the current line, press the Tab key. The default left margin is at 0 and default tab stops are set for every half inch. To move the cursor from the left margin to the tab at the two-inch mark, press the Tab key four times. If you choose View ➤ Show Detail or pressed Ctrl+W, you can see that Q&A places a tab mark at every location at which you press Tab. To move back toward the left margin, use the Backspace key.

As you type, the cursor position on the screen changes with each additional character or space. When text reaches the end of a line, the cursor does not stop at the right margin and wait for you to press Enter. Instead, Q&A Write senses the right margin and starts placing text at the left margin of the next line. This is called *word wrap*. If you make a mistake, you can press the Backspace key to erase the previous character or press the Del key to erase the character to the right of the cursor.

To start a new paragraph, press Enter. To remain in the same paragraph but start a new line, press Shift+Enter. If you chose <u>V</u>iew ➤ <u>S</u>how Detail or pressed Ctrl+W, Q&A places a paragraph mark or new line mark at the location at which you pressed Enter or Shift+Enter. Figure 12.6 shows a document early in the creation process.

FIGURE 12.6

A document consisting of one short paragraph and a header, which shows the embedded date and time and some text

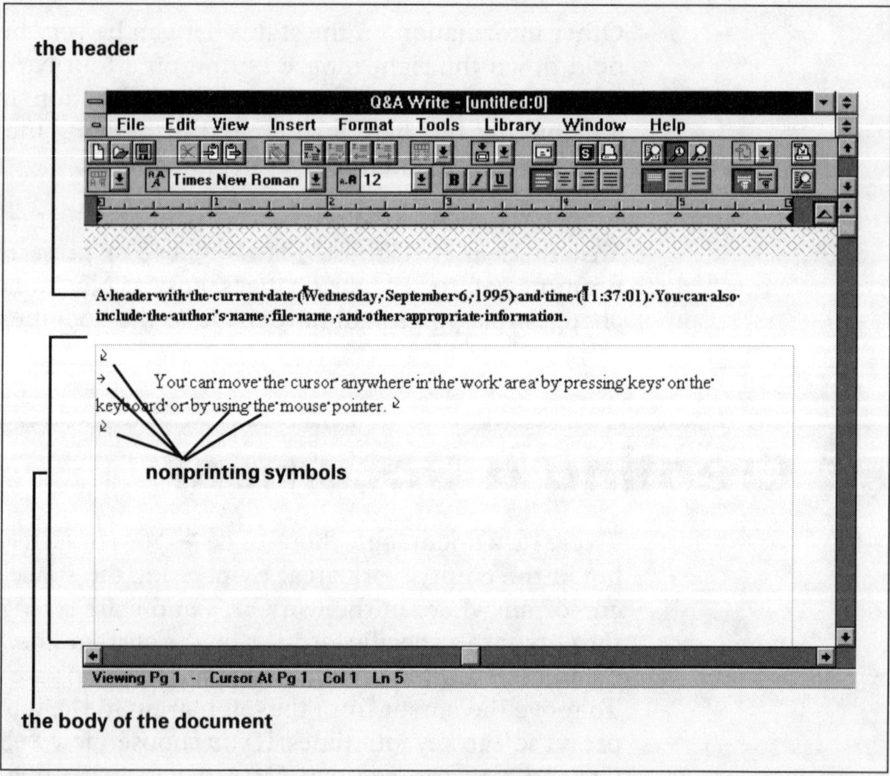

Overtype vs. Insert Modes

Q&A Write starts in *insert mode*, in which the text that you type is inserted in front of the old text. As you type in insert mode, the old text moves to the right and wraps to the next line. Press the Ins key to change to *overtype mode*, in which each character or space that you type replaces a character or space of old text. Press Ins to return to insert mode. When you switch between modes, notice that the cursor changes shape from a blinking vertical line (insert mode) to a blinking vertical rectangle (overtype).

Moving Around a Document

You can move around your document by using keys and key combinations, the mouse, and the Go To command. See Table 12.2 for a list of cursor movement keys and key combinations.

TABLE 12.2: Q&A Write Cursor Movement Keys and Key Combinations

PRESS	TO MOVE TO
←	The previous character on the current line
→	The next character on the current line
↓	The next line at the same column position, or the end of the line if there is a line break
↑	The previous line at the same column position
Ctrl+←	The previous word on the current line
Ctrl+→	The next word on the current line
Ctrl+↓	The start of the next paragraph
Ctrl+↑	The start of the previous paragraph
Ctrl+PgDn	The beginning of the next page
Ctrl+PgUp	The beginning of the previous page
PgDn	The bottom of the screen
PgUp	The top of the screen

TABLE 12.2: Q&A Write Cursor Movement Keys and Key Combinations (continued)

PRESS	TO MOVE TO
Home	The beginning of the current line
End	The end of the current line
Ctrl+Home	The beginning of the current document
Ctrl+End	The end of the current document
Ctrl+Shift+P	A specific page

Use the mouse to move around a document by clicking on either the vertical or horizontal scroll bar. Movement through the scroll bars is explained thoroughly in Chapter 2.

Manipulating Text

Typing text into an empty work area is just the beginning of the document creation process. Q&A Write lets you use the mouse, the menu bar, and keys and key combinations to edit, find text or formats, define page layout and paragraph formats, specify fonts and font sizes, print, and more. In this way, you can select the method with which you are most comfortable and go ahead with that. Most beginners choose a method that they are used to, but as they gain knowledge, they start selecting faster methods. For example, to start out, you can use the mouse to open a menu and choose a command. Later, you might change to a shortcut key combination to do the same thing. Table 12.3 contains a list of shortcut keys and key combinations and for each, a brief description, its counterpart command, and the chapter of this book in which you'll find a detailed explanation.

TABLE 12.3: Q&A Write Editing Keys and Key Combinations

KEY OR KEY COMBINATION	DESCRIPTION	EQUIVALENT COMMAND	CHAPTER
Alt+F4	Exits from Q&A Write.	File ➤ Exit	13
Alt+F7	Inserts a frame at the cursor location.	Insert ➤ Frame	15
Alt+F8	Inserts a section break at the cursor location.	Insert ➤ Section	14
Alt+F9	Inserts another file into this document.	Insert ➤ File	14
Ctrl+-	Inserts a hard hyphen at the cursor location.	Insert ➤ Special ➤ Hard Hyphen	14
Ctrl+<	Expands (reveals) the hidden levels in the outline.	Edit ➤ Outline ➤ Expand	15
Ctrl+>	Collapses (hides) all the lower levels in the outline.	Edit ➤ Outline ➤ Collapse	15
Ctrl+0	Shows the current document at a scale (from 25 to 200 percent) that you set in the Custom View dialog box.	View ➤ Custom Scale	14
Ctrl+1	Shows the current document at one-quarter its normal size.	View ➤ Full Page (25%)	14
Ctrl+2	Shows the current document at one-half its normal size.	View ➤ Reduced (50%)	14

TABLE 12.3: Q&A Write Editing Keys and Key Combinations (continued)

KEY OR KEY COMBINATION	DESCRIPTION	EQUIVALENT COMMAND	CHAPTER
Ctrl+3	Shows the current document at its normal size.	View ➤ Normal (100%)	14
Ctrl+4	Shows the current document at twice its normal size.	View ➤ Enlarged (200%)	14
Ctrl+5	Selects the entire document.	Edit ➤ Select ➤ All	13
Ctrl+A	Labels or removes the label from the selected paragraphs in the outline.	Edit ➤ Outline ➤ Label	15
Ctrl+C	Copies a selection from the document and places it in the Clipboard.	Edit ➤ Copy	13
Ctrl+End	Goes to the bottom of the document.	Edit ➤ Go To ➤ Document End	13
Ctrl+Enter	Inserts a page break at the cursor location.	Insert ➤ Break ➤ Page	14
Ctrl+F2	Checks the spelling in the current document.	Tools ➤ Spelling	13
Ctrl+F3	Formats the selected characters.	Format ➤ Character	14
Ctrl+F5	Formats the selected paragraphs.	Format ➤ Paragraph	14

TABLE 12.3: Q&A Write Editing Keys and Key Combinations (continued)

KEY OR KEY COMBINATION	DESCRIPTION	EQUIVALENT COMMAND	CHAPTER
Ctrl+F7	Replaces the search string with the replace string.	Edit ➤ Replace	14
Ctrl+F8	Formats the current section.	Format ➤ Section Layout	14
Ctrl+F9	Sets margins, tab stops, and the hyphen hot zone for the current document.	Format ➤ Page Setup	14
Ctrl+H	Finds a format and optionally replaces it with another format.	Edit ➤ Find & Replace Formats	14
Ctrl+Home	Goes to the top of the document.	Edit ➤ Go To ➤ Document Start	13
Ctrl+Ins	Copies a selection from the document and places it in the Clipboard.	Edit ➤ Copy	13
Ctrl+N	Opens a new document. The documents already open still exist in the background.	File ➤ New	13
Ctrl+O	Opens an existing document.	File ➤ Open	13
Ctrl+P	Prints the current document.	File ➤ Print	13

TABLE 12.3: Q&A Write Editing Keys and Key Combinations (continued)

KEY OR KEY COMBINATION	DESCRIPTION	EQUIVALENT COMMAND	CHAPTER
Ctrl+S	Saves the current document.	File ➤ Save	13
Ctrl+Shift+-	Inserts a soft hyphen at the cursor location.	Insert ➤ Special ➤ Page	14
Ctrl+Shift+<	Promotes the current paragraph in the outline.	Edit ➤ Outline ➤ Promote	15
Ctrl+Shift+>	Demotes the current paragraph in the outline.	Edit ➤ Outline ➤ Demote	15
Ctrl+Shift+A	Changes the selected paragraphs from normal text to part of an outline.	Edit ➤ Outline ➤ Add To	15
Ctrl+Shift+E	Reveals or hides the ruler.	View ➤ Ruler	14
Ctrl+Shift+End	Selects from the cursor position to the bottom of the document.	Edit ➤ Select ➤ To Document End	13
Ctrl+Shift+Enter	Inserts a column break at the cursor location.	Insert ➤ Break ➤ Column	14
Ctrl+Shift+F	Changes the location of the selected frame.	Format ➤ Frame ➤ Placement	15
Ctrl+Shift+F2	Checks a word for synonyms.	Tools ➤ Thesaurus	13
Ctrl+Shift+F5	Pastes a style format into the document.	Edit ➤ Paste Format ➤ Style Format	15

TABLE 12.3: Q&A Write Editing Keys and Key Combinations (continued)

KEY OR KEY COMBINATION	DESCRIPTION	EQUIVALENT COMMAND	CHAPTER
Ctrl+Shift+F8	Pastes a section format into the document.	Edit ➤ Paste Format ➤ Section Format	15
Ctrl+Shift+F9	Pastes a page setup format into the document.	Edit ➤ Paste Format ➤ Page Setup Format	15
Ctrl+Shift+H	Reveals or hides the paragraph bar in the left margin.	View ➤ Paragraph Bar	13
Ctrl+Shift+Home	Selects from the cursor position to the top of the document.	Edit ➤ Select ➤ To Document Start	13
Ctrl+Shift+L	Changes the selected text to lowercase.	Tools ➤ Lowercase	14
Ctrl+Shift+M	Inserts a merge field at the cursor location.	Insert ➤ Merge Field	18
Ctrl+Shift+O	Opens a frame.	Format ➤ Frame ➤ Open	15
Ctrl+Shift+P	Goes to a specific page.	Edit ➤ Go To ➤ Page	13
Ctrl+Shift+R	Changes the selected paragraph from part of an outline to normal text.	Edit ➤ Outline ➤ Remove From	15
Ctrl+Shift+S	Applies uppercase to the first letters of the selected sentences.	Tools ➤ Capitalize Sentences	14

TABLE 12.3: Q&A Write Editing Keys and Key Combinations (continued)

KEY OR KEY COMBINATION	DESCRIPTION	EQUIVALENT COMMAND	CHAPTER
Ctrl+Shift+U	Changes the selected text to uppercase.	Tools ➤ Uppercase	14
Ctrl+Shift+W	Applies uppercase to the first letters of the selected text.	Tools ➤ Capitalize Words	14
Ctrl+spacebar	Inserts a hard space at the cursor location.	Insert ➤ Special ➤ Hard Space	14
Ctrl+T	Opens a document template.	File ➤ Open Template	15
Ctrl+V	Pastes a selection from the Clipboard into the document.	Edit ➤ Paste	13
Ctrl+W	Shows or hides nonprinting symbols (such as new lines, tab symbols, frames, and so on).	View ➤ Show Detail or Show Proof	14
Ctrl+X	Cuts a selection from the document and places it in the Clipboard.	Edit ➤ Cut	13
Ctrl+Z	Reverses the last deletion, action, undo, or redo.	Edit ➤ Undo or Redo	13
F1	Displays the help index.	Help ➤ Help Index	2
F3	Closes the current document.	File ➤ Close	13

TABLE 12.3: Q&A Write Editing Keys and Key Combinations (continued)

KEY OR KEY COMBINATION	DESCRIPTION	EQUIVALENT COMMAND	CHAPTER
F4	Repeats the last action, if possible.	Edit ➤ Repeat	13
F5	Expands all the paragraphs in the outline.	Edit ➤ Outline ➤ Expand All	15
F7	Finds the next occurrence of the current search string.	Edit ➤ Find Again	14
F12	Saves the current document using another name or on another drive or directory	File ➤ Save As	13
Shift+Del	Cuts a selection from the document and places it in the Clipboard.	Edit ➤ Cut	13
Shift+Enter	Inserts a line break at the cursor location.	Insert ➤ Break ➤ Line	14
Shift+F7	Finds a search string.	Edit ➤ Find	14
Shift+Ins	Pastes a selection from the Clipboard into the document.	Edit ➤ Paste	13

Selecting Text

Before performing any operation on text already entered in your document, you must first select it. For example, to enhance an important word with boldface or a different font, select it and then apply the text emphasis. In the next chapter, you'll learn how to format paragraphs, sections, and the entire document, but the principle remains the same: you must select the text before you change the format. Tables 12.4 and 12.5 describe the keystrokes and mouse actions, respectively, used to select blocks of text of various sizes.

TABLE 12.4: Q&A Write Keyboard Selection Keys and Key Combinations

KEY OR KEY COMBINATION	ADDED TO THE SELECTION
Shift+→	The next character
Shift+←	The previous character
Shift+↓	The characters from the current cursor location to the location immediately below the current cursor location
Shift+↑	The characters from the current cursor location to the location immediately above the current cursor location
Shift+End	The characters from the current cursor location to the end of the current line
Shift+Home	The characters from the current cursor location to the beginning of the current line
Shift+PgDn	The characters from the current cursor location to the bottom of the screen
Shift+PgUp	The characters from the current cursor location to the top of the screen
Shift+Ctrl+End	The characters from the current cursor location to the end of the document

TABLE 12.4: Q&A Write Keyboard Selection Keys and Key Combinations (continued)

KEY OR KEY COMBINATION	ADDED TO THE SELECTION
Shift+Ctrl+Home	The characters from the current cursor location to the beginning of the document to the selection
Ctrl+5 (numeric keypad)	The entire document

TABLE 12.5: Q&A Write Mouse Selection Techniques

TO SELECT:	INSTRUCTIONS
A word	Move the mouse pointer anywhere within the word and click two times.
A sentence	Move the mouse pointer anywhere within the sentence and click three times.
A paragraph	Move the mouse pointer anywhere within the paragraph and click four times.
A range	Move the beginning of the selection, click, press and hold down the Shift key, move the mouse pointer to the end of the selection, and click. This is a good way of selecting a long range. Otherwise, clicking and dragging works fine.

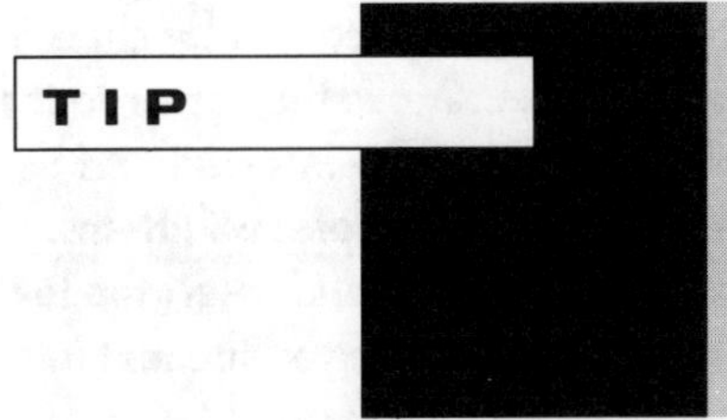

TIP

To "unselect" blocks of text using the keyboard, simply press the opposite key or key combination. For example, if you have added the next character to the selection by pressing Shift+→, just press Shift+← to remove the character from the selection.

Deleting Text

You can either delete a character permanently or cut it from the document and place it in the Clipboard for later use. To permanently delete a character, press either the Del or Backspace key. To delete the character to the left of the cursor, press Backspace; to delete the character to the right of the cursor, press Del. To delete a block of text, select it and then press either Backspace or Del.

If you plan to use deleted text in another place in the document, in another document, or even in a different Windows application, place it in the Windows Clipboard. Just select the text and then choose Edit ➤ Cut or press Ctrl+X or Shift+Del.

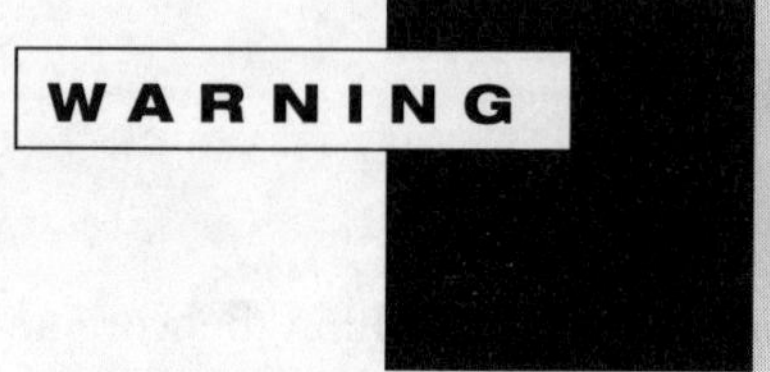

WARNING

Be aware that cutting text to the Clipboard can be potentially destructive. Whenever you copy or cut text to the Clipboard, what was already there is replaced (and therefore deleted) by the new selection.

Inserting Text

To insert (or paste) the contents of the Clipboard in a Q&A Write document or another Windows word processor or application, move the mouse pointer to the place where you wish to insert; then choose Edit ➤ Paste, or press Ctrl+V, or Shift+Ins.

TIP

If you want to insert the same text in several places in your document (for example, to add a very long and complicated technical phrase), type that text anywhere in your document. Select it and then copy it by choosing Edit ➤ Copy or pressing Ctrl+C. Move the cursor to the first location at which the text is to be inserted and choose Edit ➤ Paste, press Ctrl+V, or press Shift+Ins. Move the cursor to the next location and insert the text again. Repeat this until you have inserted the text in every desired location.

Copying Text

There is no need to delete text in order to insert it in another location. If you wish to keep selected text in its original location and insert copies elsewhere (for example, in the preceding tip), choose Edit ➤ Copy, or press Ctrl+C or Ctrl+Ins.

Undoing and Redoing Actions

If you have just completed a destructive action (for example, you deleted selected text and suddenly have realized that you made a big mistake), you can reverse the action immediately (if you haven't performed any other action in between), by choosing Edit ➤ Undo or pressing Ctrl+Z. Undo works primarily with Edit menu commands. For example, if you wish to undo formatting, either click on the appropriate tool bar button or choose the appropriate menu command.

Using the Redo command simply reverses the last Undo command. Let's say that you have reconsidered and now want to delete the text that you just restored. If you have not performed any other action, choose Edit ➤ Redo (which replaces the Undo command immediately after you have issued it) or press Ctrl+Z to undo the Undo. At this point, Q&A Write replaces Redo with Undo on the Edit menu. You can continue to go back and forth with these two commands until you have decided for sure the action to take.

Repeating the Last Action

A close relative to the Redo command is the Repeat command. You can use this command to quickly format words in the same way, to cut or copy a series of selections, to find or replace, to check spelling, and so on. Perform some action and then choose Edit ➤ Repeat or press F4 to repeat the action to either the same word or selection. For example, you can format a word and then remove the format by selecting the Repeat command again. Or you can apply a format such as boldface to a word, move the mouse pointer to another word, select it, and select Repeat. If the Repeat command is not available after a particular action, Q&A Write changes the command to Can't Repeat and dims it, thereby making it unavailable.

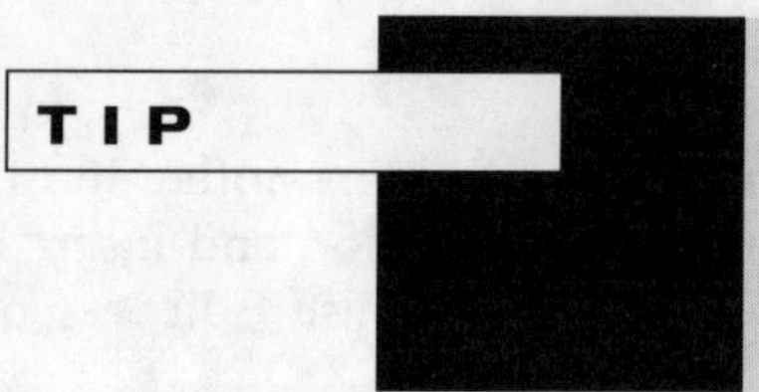

To reformat all the headings in a document, change the format of the first heading in the document, then move through the rest of the document, selecting headings and choosing the Repeat command.

Checking Spelling and Words

Once you have created and edited a document, or if you need help in deciding how to spell a word, you can use the Q&A Write spell checker. If you find yourself using the same word over and over, you can use the thesaurus to find synonyms.

Validating Your Spelling

Although Q&A Write provides its own dictionary, you can create your own dictionaries which contain words such as company and product names, surnames, programming commands, technical terms, and so on. When you check the words in the current document, the spell checker uses the main dictionary (USENG.NDX) and, if you have added it, one user dictionary, either USER.SPL, which is the default, or a dictionary you have created. Before you start your first spell check, it's a good idea to add a user dictionary so you can save words right away.

To check an entire document, move the cursor to the first character in the document and click on the Spell Checker button in the tool bar. To check a single word, highlight it. Then start the spell checker by either choosing Tools ➤ Spelling, pressing Ctrl+F2, or clicking on the Spell Checker button in the tool bar. In the Spelling dialog box (Figure 12.7), click on the Start button to start checking.

If you have selected a word, the spell checker checks only that word and then stops. However, when checking the entire document, the spell checker evaluates each word, comparing it against the main dictionary and the user dictionary (if one is active). When it finds a word not listed in either dictionary, it highlights it in the document, displays it in the Found text box, and lists optional replacement words in the list box (Figure 12.8).

FIGURE 12.7

The Spelling
dialog box

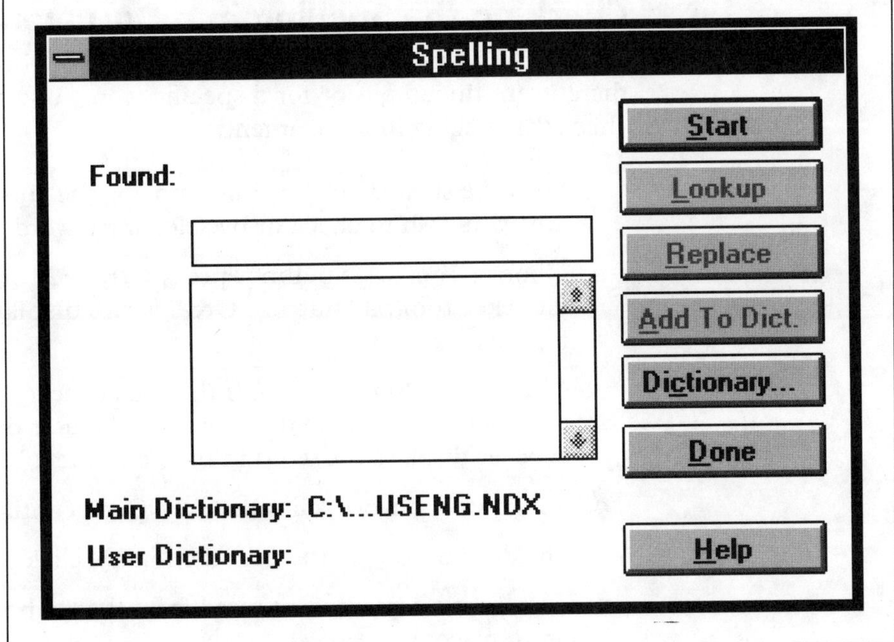

FIGURE 12.8

The Spelling dialog
box now contains a
misspelled word and
suggestions for
replacements.

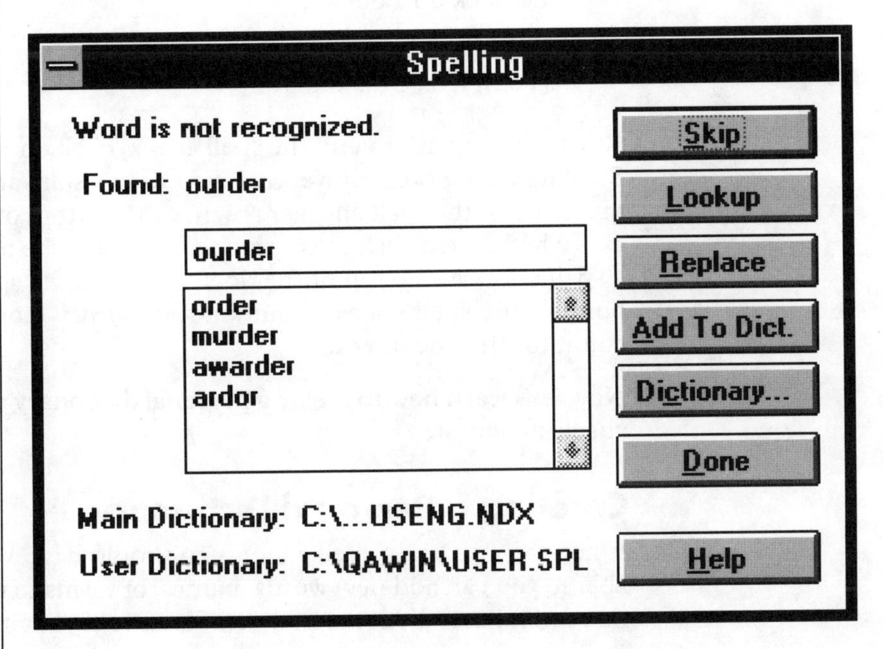

Checking the Spelling in a Document

After adding a personal dictionary, you can run the spell checker against the current document or for a specific word. Use the following steps to check the spelling in a document.

1. Start the spell check by either moving the cursor to the top of the area you wish to check or by selecting a word to be checked.

2. Choose Tools ➤ Spelling, press Ctrl+F2, or click on the Spell Checker tool bar button. Q&A Write displays the Spelling dialog box.

3. Click on the Start button. If the spell checker finds a word that is not in either the main dictionary or the user dictionary, the spell checker displays the word in the Found text box.

4. To ignore the word, click on Skip. Q&A continues the spellcheck.

5. To add the word to the user dictionary, click on Add To Dict.

6. To accept a replacement word from the list box, select it and click on Replace.

7. To try a replacement word not on the list, type it in the text box and click on Lookup.

8. Any time you wish to end the spell check or when the spell check is complete, click on Done.

Any time you wish to end the spell check, click on Done. Q&A closes the Spelling dialog box. However, if you didn't start at the top of the document, and if the spell checker reaches the bottom of the document, Q&A asks whether you wish to continue checking at the top. If you have started a spell check at the top of the document and the spell check reaches the bottom, the spell checker announces that it is done and shows a word count for the document.

Now let's learn how to create a personal dictionary and how to run a spell check step by step.

Creating a Personal Dictionary

Whenever you run a spell check, you should have a user dictionary available so you can add new words, names, or terms to it. In fact, you can define several user dictionaries—one for each of your interests. For example, if you write engineering books and articles, you can create a dictionary to which you can add engineering terms and company names. If your hobby is rejuvenating old cars, you can create another user dictionary to which you can add the names of old automobile models and parts. You can create or edit your user dictionary during a spell check or without going through the spell check process.

N O T E

Q&A allows you to change the main dictionary. For information, see the *Q&A Write User's Manual*.

To add a user dictionary, use these steps:

1. Choose <u>T</u>ools ➤ <u>S</u>pelling, press Ctrl+F2, or click on the Spell Checker tool bar button. Q&A Write then displays the Spelling dialog box.

2. Click on the Di<u>c</u>tionary button. Q&A displays the Spelling Dictionaries dialog box (Figure 12.9).

FIGURE 12.9

The Spelling Dictionaries dialog box lets you specify the type of dictionary to be added or replaced as well as add words to the personal dictionary.

3. Click on the Underline button. Q&A displays the Change User Spelling Dictionary dialog box (Figure 12.10).

4. Either select the default user dictionary, USER.SPL, or define your own by typing its name in the File Name text box. Then either click on OK or press Enter. Q&A automatically adds the .SPL extension to the file name.

5. Click on the Done button.

6. If you have completed the spell check, click on the Done button again. Otherwise, click on the Start button to continue checking your document.

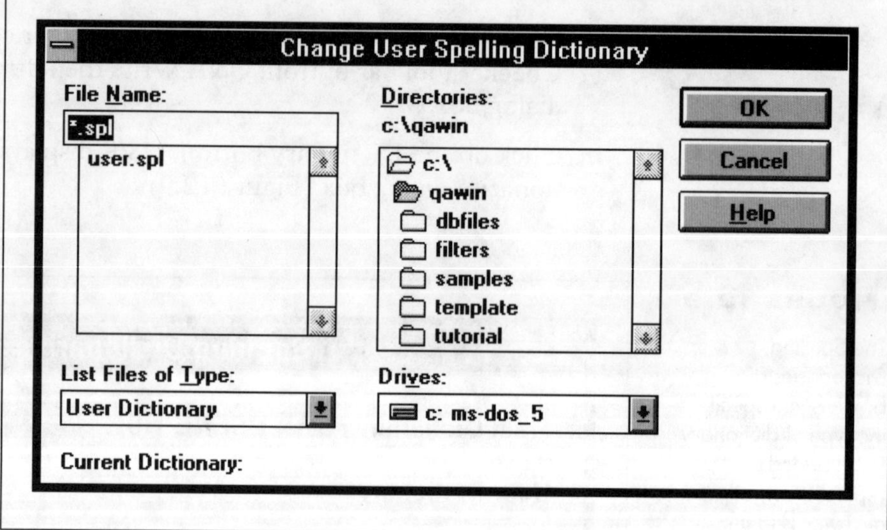

FIGURE 12.10

The Change User Spelling Dictionary dialog box allows you to select the USER.SPL user dictionary or to define another user dictionary.

Choosing the Right Words with the Thesaurus

When you find that you are overusing the same word, or a particular word just doesn't fit the meaning that you are trying to convey, use the thesaurus.

To display a list of synonyms for a selected word, move the cursor to the word and choose Tools ➤ Thesaurus or press Ctrl+Shift+F2. Q&A displays the Thesaurus dialog box (Figure 12.11).

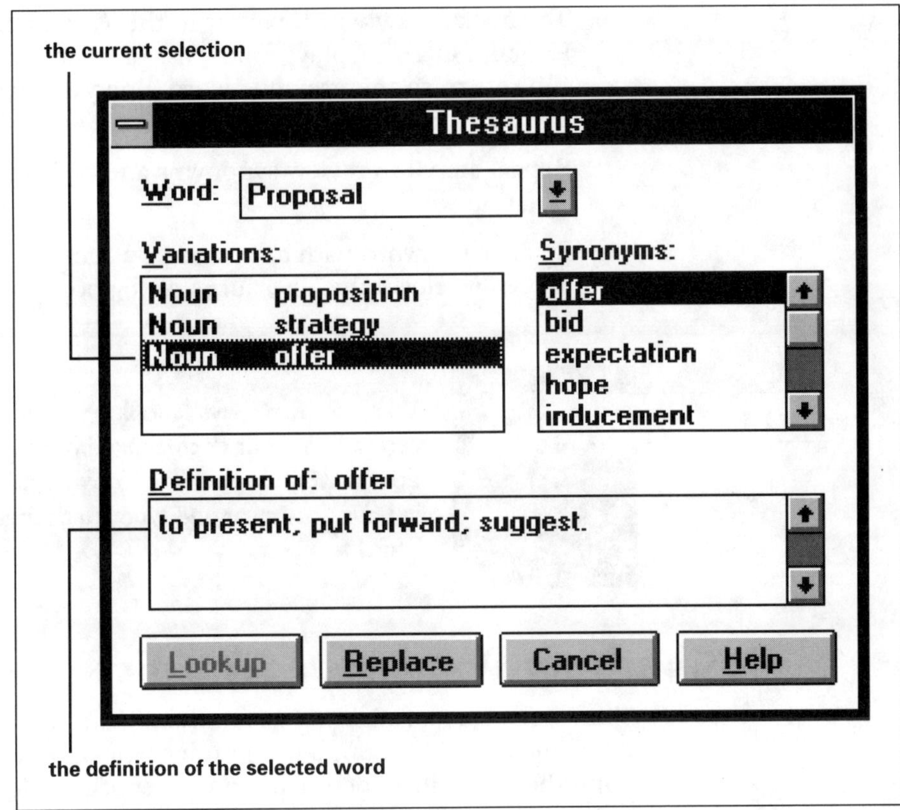

If the thesaurus contains a list of synonyms for the word, they appear in the <u>V</u>ariations list box along with the part of speech. Synonyms for the selected variation are listed in the <u>S</u>ynonyms box. (If the thesaurus does not have any synonyms for the word, the <u>V</u>ariations and <u>S</u>ynonyms boxes remain empty.) To use the thesaurus, follow these steps:

1. Select a word in the current document and choose <u>T</u>ools ➤ <u>T</u>hesaurus or press Ctrl+Shift+F2. Q&A displays the Thesaurus dialog box with a list of variations for the word.

2. Select a variation word. Q&A displays a list of its synonyms in the <u>S</u>ynonyms box.

3. Repeat step 2 to review synonyms and definitions for particular variation words.

4. To check a new word, type it in the Word text box and click on Lookup. Q&A displays a new list of variations and synonyms. (To return to the previous word, open the drop-down list box and select it.)

5. Repeat step 2 to review synonyms and definitions for particular variation words.

6. Replace the word with a variation by clicking on the Replace button. Q&A closes the Thesaurus dialog box.

TIP

There are two ways to look up a particular word not currently in your document: either type it in your document and select it, or look up a word that appears in your document and type the desired word in the Word text box.

Checking Document Statistics

Many managers, professors, teachers, and editors require you to hand in a document that contains a minimum or maximum number of words. To count the words in a document and to get other information, choose File ➤ Statistics. Q&A displays the Document Statistics dialog box (Figure 12.12). Click on OK or press Enter to close the dialog box after your review.

Saving a Document

Once you have created and edited a document—even though you may not be finished working on it—you should save it by choosing File ➤ Save (or pressing Ctrl+S), choosing File ➤ Save As (or pressing F12), or clicking on the Save button on the tool bar. If you are saving a new document, Q&A opens the Save Document dialog box (Figure 12.13), in which you can type a file name, or select a directory, drive, or file format. Then click on OK or press Enter.

The Document Statistics dialog box which provides a great deal of information about the current document.

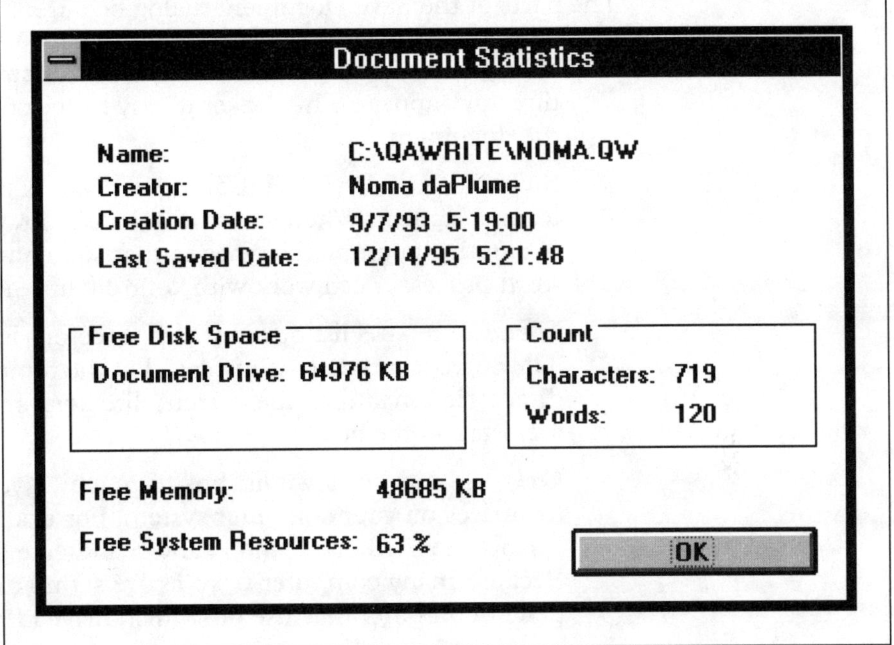

In the Save Document dialog box, you can name a file and indicate the drive and directory in which the file will be located.

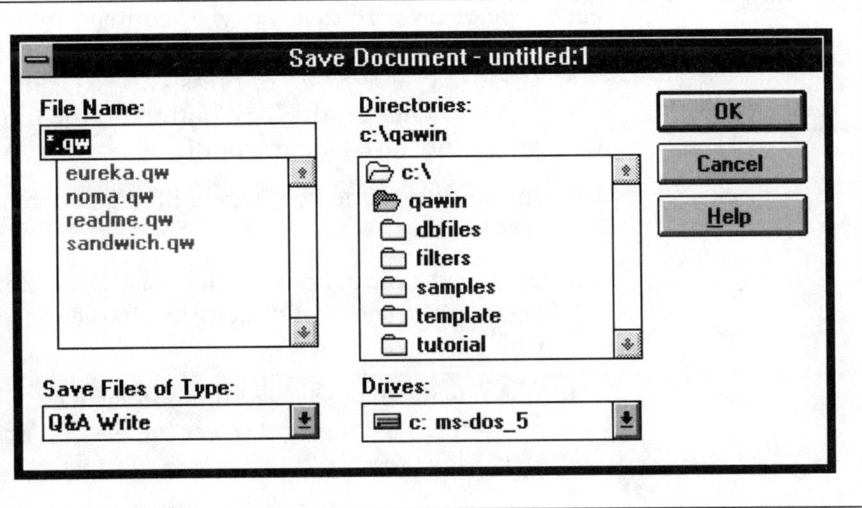

The parts of the Save Document dialog box are:

File Name—A list box in which all the documents in the current directory appear. This makes it easy to select a unique name for the document.

Save Files of Type—A drop-down list box in which all the file formats appear. When you save a document, you can convert it to one of the common file types so that someone using a different word processor can work with your document.

Directories—A list box in which directory information appears. The current directory is displayed at the top of this box, and other directories, including the current directory and the root directory, are listed in the box.

Drives—A drop-down list box from which you can select from all the drives on your computer system. For example, c: typically represents the hard drive, and a: and b: indicate floppy disk drives. Because many computer systems are set up differently, your particular computer may use other disk-drive identifiers.

Although you issue the same commands to save a new, unnamed document and an existing, named document, Q&A Write acts differently for each type of save. To save a new document, follow these steps:

1. Choose File ➤ Save (or press Ctrl+S), File ➤ Save As (or press F12), or click on the Save button on the tool bar. Q&A Write opens the Save Document dialog box.

2. In the File Name box, type a file name from one to eight characters long.

3. To save the file in another directory, in the Directories box, double-click on the series of directories that lead from the root directory to the desired directory.

4. If you want the file saved to another drive, click in the Drives drop-down list box and select the desired drive. Then repeat step 3 if necessary.

5. Select OK or press Enter. Q&A Write returns to the document and displays its new name in the title bar.

To save an existing document, choose <u>F</u>ile ➤ <u>S</u>ave (or press Ctrl+S), <u>F</u>ile ➤ Save <u>A</u>s (or press F12), or click on the Save button on the tool bar. Q&A Write automatically saves the document without displaying any dialog boxes.

Q&A Write also offers a way to automatically save the current document every few minutes. The most important reason for activating the Auto Save feature is to avoid having to reconstruct a document if you suddenly lose electrical power or accidentally turn off your computer without using the normal exit procedures. To select Auto Save, choose <u>F</u>ile ➤ <u>P</u>references ➤ <u>F</u>ile. In the File Preferences dialog box (Figure 12.14), place a check mark in the <u>A</u>uto Save Documents check box, and select a <u>F</u>requency from 1 to 60 minutes.

This is only one of the many ways with which you can customize your copy of Q&A Write. You'll learn more about setting preferences in Appendix C.

FIGURE 12.14

The File Preferences dialog box

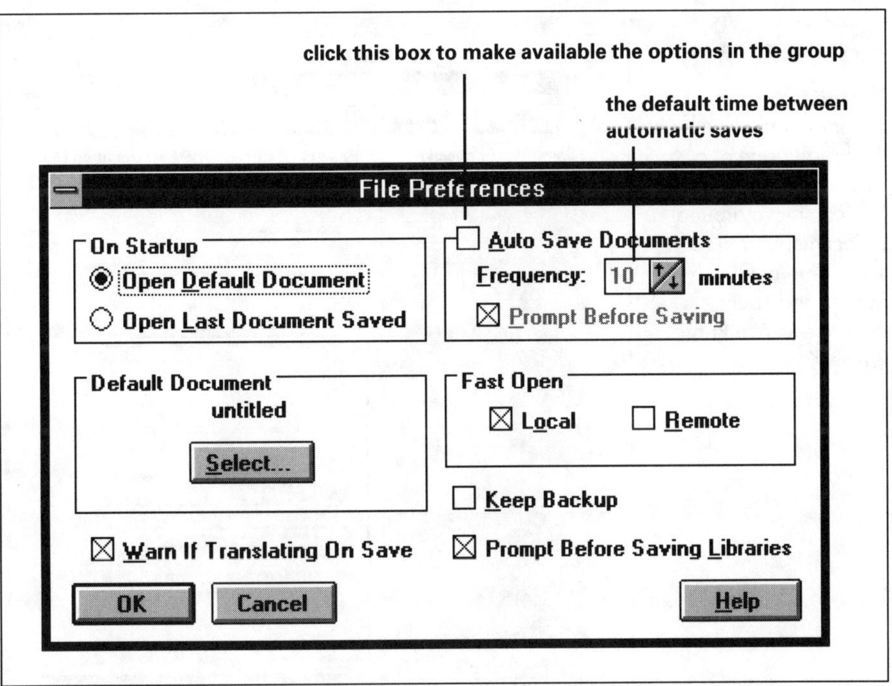

Viewing a Document as It Will Print

Before you print a document, it's a good idea to preview it on screen. This allows you to spot errors and avoid wasting paper. To preview a document, choose File ➤ Print Preview. Q&A displays the first page of your document (Figure 12.15).

The parts of the Print Preview window are:

Prev Page—Click on this button to see the previous page unless this is a one-page document or you are viewing the first page.

Next Page—Click on this button to see the next page unless this is a one-page document or you are viewing the last page.

FIGURE 12.15

The Q&A Write Print Preview window with the fourth page of a document on display. You can move around a document, print, show from one to six pages, and change the page size in Print Preview.

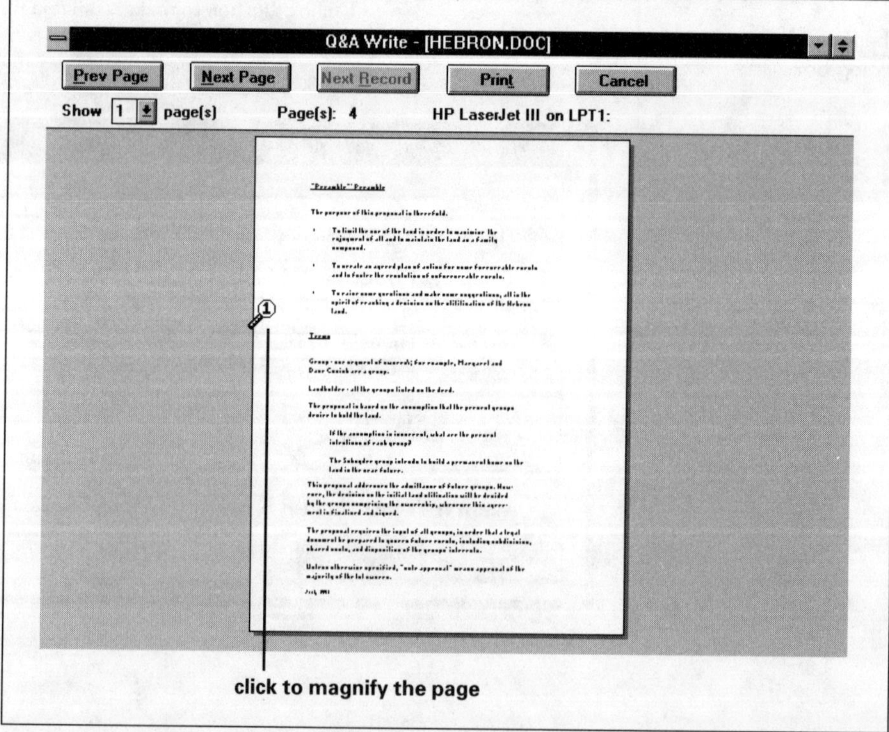

click to magnify the page

Next Record—Click on this button to view the next record in a database.

Print—Click on this button to print the document. (Q&A Write does not display the Print dialog box.)

Show page(s)—Shows 1, 2, 4, or 6 pages at the same time.

Page(s)—Displays the current page number.

  As a default, the Print Preview window fits the page in the window in proportion to its true length and width. In this size, you can't read any of the text. However, you can read, but not edit, the document by clicking the mouse button when the pointer looks like a magnifying glass enclosing a *1*. To return to the smaller view, click the mouse button again. (Notice that the magnifying glass looks different.)

Printing a Document

You can print your document any time while you're creating it—even before you save it. Choose File ➤ Print or press Ctrl+P, and Q&A Write displays the Print dialog box (Figure 12.16).

The parts of the Print dialog box are:

Current Printer—Q&A Write displays the name of the current default printer. You can change the default printer by choosing File ➤ Print Setup.

Copies—In this box, type or select a value from 1 (the default) to 999.

Pages—In this group, You have three choices:

- You can select All to print all pages.

- You can type or select the first page in the From box, and you can type or select the last page in the To box.

- If an envelope is associated with the document, click in the Envelope Only radio button to print without also printing the document.

Reverse Order—In this check box, place a check mark to print from the last page to the first page.

FIGURE 12.16

Q&A Write's Print dialog box.

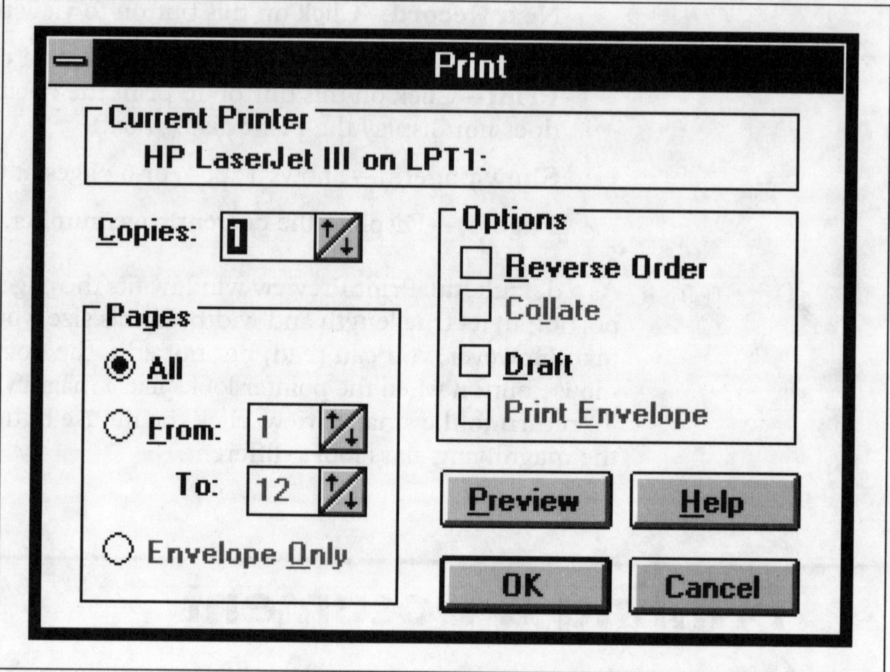

Collate—In this check box, place a check mark to print multiple copies from the first page to the last, or clear the box to print all the copies of the first page, all the copies of the second page, and so on.

Draft—In this check box, place a check mark to print a rough draft, which is not completely formatted. This often speeds up the printing process.

Print Envelope—In this check box, place a check mark to print the envelope that is associated with this document.

Preview—Click on this button to display this document as it will print.

To print the current document, use these steps:

1. Choose File ➤ Print or press Ctrl+P. Q&A Write displays the Print dialog box (Figure 12.16).

2. Select from the options in the dialog box. Then click on OK or press Enter.

Exiting Q&A Write

To exit Q&A Write, choose <u>F</u>ile ➤ E<u>x</u>it, type the key combination Alt+F4, or double-click on the Application Control Menu button. Write will prompt you to save any unsaved work before you actually end the session. If you started Q&A Write from the Program Manager, you'll return to the Program Manager. However, if you started Q&A Write from within the Q&A Database, you'll return to the Q&A Database.

To Sum Up

In this chapter, you got started with Q&A Write. You learned how to start it and how to exit. In between, you found out about the document window and its elements, how to create a document, how to move around a page and the whole document, and how to manipulate text. Then you found out about checking the spelling in your document, using the thesaurus to replace one word with another, and getting statistics about your document. Finally, you learned how to save and print your document.

In the next chapter, you'll learn more about fine-tuning your document—including formatting text; inserting new text, special symbols; formatting and aligning paragraphs; and laying out a document page by page.

13

Editing
Documents

To specify headers or footers   **463**

choose <u>V</u>iew ➤ Hea<u>d</u>er or <u>V</u>iew ➤ Foo<u>t</u>er. Type or stamp information in the pane and then click on Close.

To insert a page break   **466**

choose <u>I</u>nsert ➤ <u>B</u>reak ➤ <u>P</u>age or press Ctrl+Enter.

To change margins   **467**

choose For<u>m</u>at ➤ Page Setup or press Ctrl+F9. In the <u>D</u>efault Tab Stops text/list box, either type or select a value.

To find text   **470**

choose <u>E</u>dit ➤ <u>F</u>ind or press Shift+F7, fill in the Find dialog box, and click on the Find button.

To find the next occurrence of a search string   **473**

either choose <u>E</u>dit ➤ Find Aga<u>i</u>n or press F7.

To replace all occurrences of a search string   **475**

choose <u>E</u>dit ➤ Rep<u>l</u>ace or press Ctrl+F7, fill in the Find & Replace dialog box, and click on the Replace <u>A</u>ll button.

To find and optionally replace a search string   **479**

click on the Fin<u>d</u> & Replace button. Then either click on <u>Re</u>place & Continue, Skip & <u>C</u>ontinue, or Replace <u>A</u>ll. Finally, click on <u>D</u>one.

THE LAST chapter was just the beginning of the document creation process. In this chapter, you'll learn about the finer points of editing a document and find out about formatting a document—from individual words, lines, sentences, and paragraphs to the document as a whole. You'll review what you have previously learned about fonts and point sizes, applying emphasis, formatting and aligning paragraphs, and laying out a document page by page. Figure 13.1 shows you a sandwich shop menu in which all the text has been entered but isn't formatted yet. As you read through this chapter, you'll see how the menu changes as different formats and enhancements are applied.

An unformatted menu for a sandwich shop

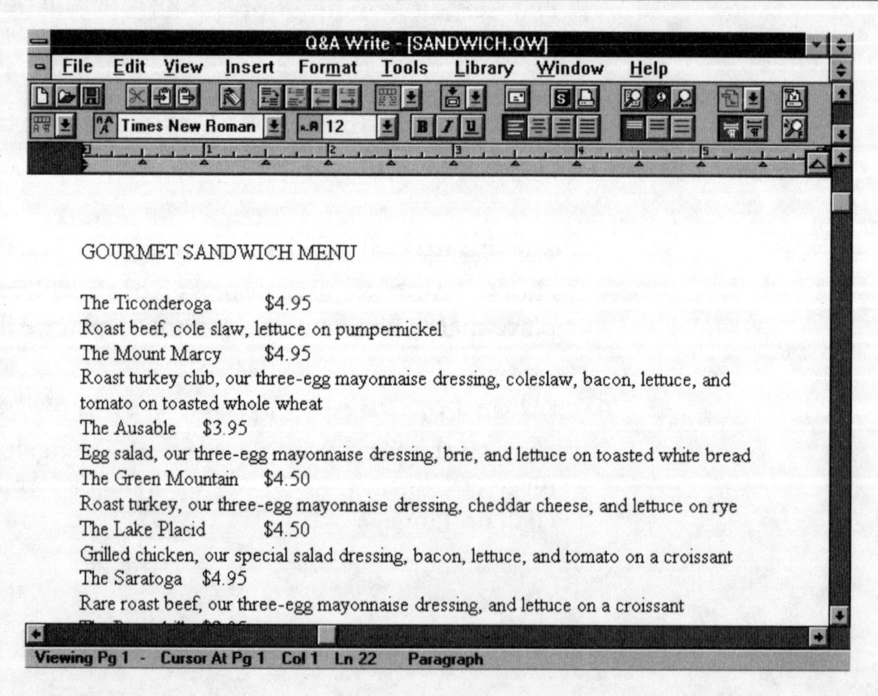

Editing a Document

Typing in the text of a document, naming it, and saving it is only the first step. If you expect to use your document for a long time, you'll have to adjust it in many ways: you'll add symbols and graphics, you'll enhance text, you'll change fonts and point size, and much more. Before you start editing, you might want to make a couple of adjustments in the document window. Let's find out how to change the size of a page in the window and how to show nonprinting symbols. Then we can start formatting our document.

Magnifying or Reducing a Document

Sometimes in order to see the details of a page or, conversely, to see the page as a whole, you may want to adjust its size on the computer screen. Table 13.1 lists the views that Q&A Write offers and shows you the toolbar buttons, menu commands, and shortcut keys that you can use to change your view of a document. To change the view of your document, click on a toolbar button, choose a command from the View menu, or press a shortcut key combination. With one exception, Q&A Write automatically changes the size of a page on the screen. If you click on the Custom Scale toolbar button, choose View ➤ Custom Scale, or press Ctrl+0, the Custom View dialog box (Figure 13.2) appears. You can select any percentage from 25 to 200.

TABLE 13.1: Q&A Write Document Reduction and Magnification Commands

VIEW PERCENTAGE	TOOL BAR BUTTON	MENU COMMAND	SHORTCUT KEY COMBINATION	DESCRIPTION
200%	N/A	View ➤ Enlarged	Ctrl+4	View a page at twice its normal size.
100%		View ➤ Normal	Ctrl+3	View a page at its normal size. This is the default.
50%	N/A	View ➤ Reduced	Ctrl+2	View a page at half its normal size.

TABLE 13.1: Q&A Write Document Reduction and Magnification Commands (continued)

VIEW PERCENTAGE	TOOL BAR BUTTON	MENU COMMAND	SHORTCUT KEY COMBINATION	DESCRIPTION
25%		View ➤ Full Page	Ctrl+1	View a page at one-quarter its normal size.
25%-200%		View ➤ Custom Scale	Ctrl+0	View a page at a custom size (from 25% to 200%). The default is 100%.

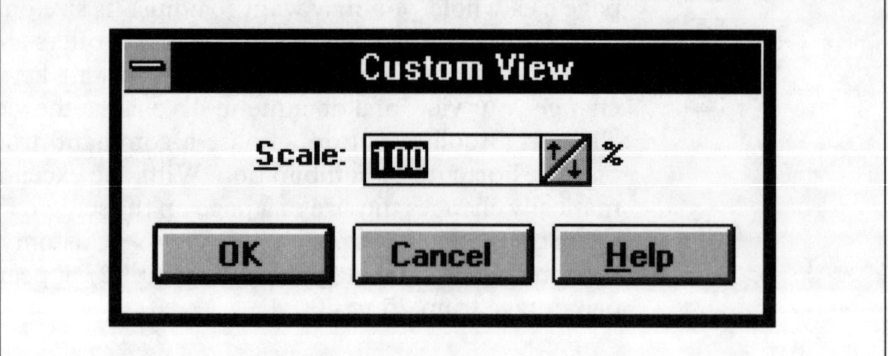

FIGURE 13.2

The Custom View dialog box

Viewing Nonprinting Symbols

When you want to check the number of spaces between words or sentences, or make sure that you have inserted a line mark rather than a paragraph mark, you can view the nonprinting symbols that can help you to evaluate. To display or hide nonprinting symbols, such as the new line mark, the paragraph mark, spaces, tab marks, frames, the edges of pages, and so on, either click on the Show/Hide button on the tool bar, choose View ➤ Show Detail or Show Proof, or press the Ctrl+W shortcut key combination. Table 13.2 shows some common Q&A Write nonprinting symbols.

TABLE 13.2: Q&A Write Nonprinting Symbols

SYMBOL	OBJECT
⑊	New Line
⑊	Paragraph
↳	Hard Page Break
→	Tab
	Frame
	Outside the edge of the paper
	The top right corner of a page

Adding Special Characters to a Document

At some point, you may need to put special characters or symbols, which do not appear on your keyboard, into a Q&A Write document. For example, you can insert the copyright and trademark symbols either by using Windows Character Map application (see Appendix B) or Q&A Write.

Because each computer and printer setup is unique, refer to your computer's, printer's, or video card's reference manual for the ANSI or ASCII chart to use. To insert a nonprinting symbol in a Q&A Write document, follow these steps:

1. Move the cursor to the location at which you wish to embed the special symbol.

2. Press the NumLock key to activate the numeric keypad.

3. Hold down the Alt key.

4. On the numeric keypad, type the ANSI number that represents the desired symbol.

5. Release the Alt key. Your character appears in the document.

6. Press the NumLock key to inactivate the numeric keypad.

WARNING

Be careful when experimenting with literal characters. If you do not refer to a chart related to your computer system, you may get strange results (for example, odd page breaks and the cursor skipping randomly from one part of the document to another).

Inserting a Document in Another Document

Let's say that you always insert a disclaimer at the bottom of the first page of a document, or you have stored your letterhead in a separate file, which you insert at the top of every new letter. Q&A Write provides a simple way to insert a document within the current document. Choose Insert ➤ File or press Alt+F9. When Q&A Write displays the File Insert dialog box (Figure 13.3), choose the desired file, and either click on OK or press Enter.

The File Insert
dialog box

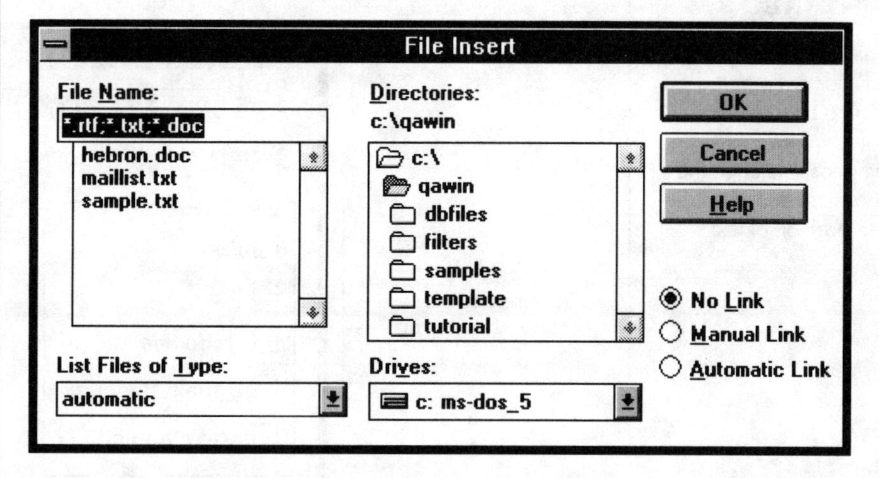

Formatting Text

In Chapter 4, you learned all about fonts and point sizes and how to change them using the tool bar, menu commands, and keyboard shortcuts. You also learned about applying emphasis. Since text emphasis works the same way for both the Q&A Database and Q&A Write, there is no need to review the basics here. However, the Q&A Write Character Format dialog box (Figure 13.4) provides a few extra options that the Q&A Database Font dialog box (Figure 13.5) didn't. In addition to the font styles and effects offered for the Q&A Database, Q&A Write allows you to double-underline selected text. You can also change the position of text—on the *baseline* the imaginary line on which most characters rest, above the baseline (by choosing Superscript), and below the baseline (by choosing Subscript). This can be used for typing math or chemical formats and footnotes.

Figure 13.6 shows the sample sandwich shop menu with boldface and italics added. Now let's learn how to format paragraphs in several ways.

FIGURE 13.4

The Q&A Write Character Format dialog box lets you select a new font, an emphasis, change the font size, and change the position of text.

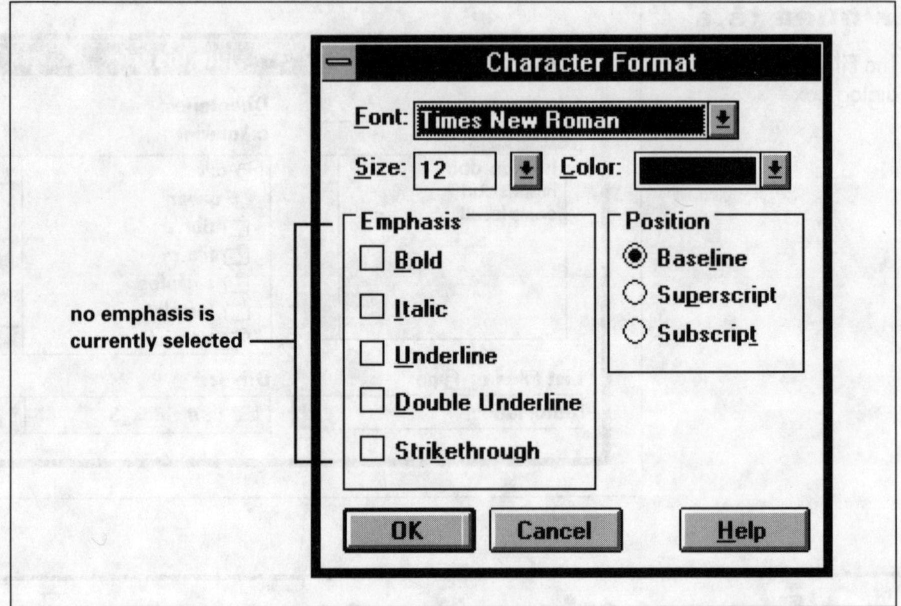

FIGURE 13.5

The Q&A Database Font dialog box lets you select a new font, a font style, change the font size, apply effects, and change the color of text.

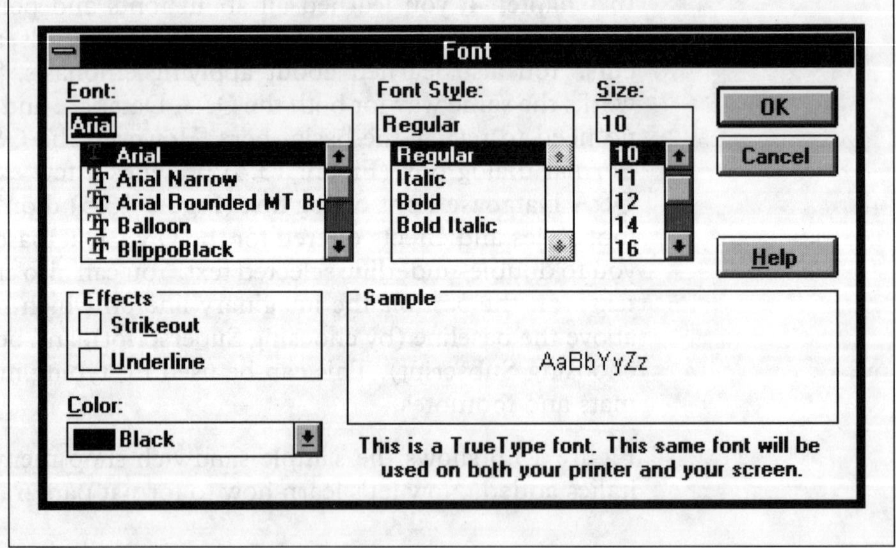

FIGURE 13.6

The sandwich shop menu with some character formats applied

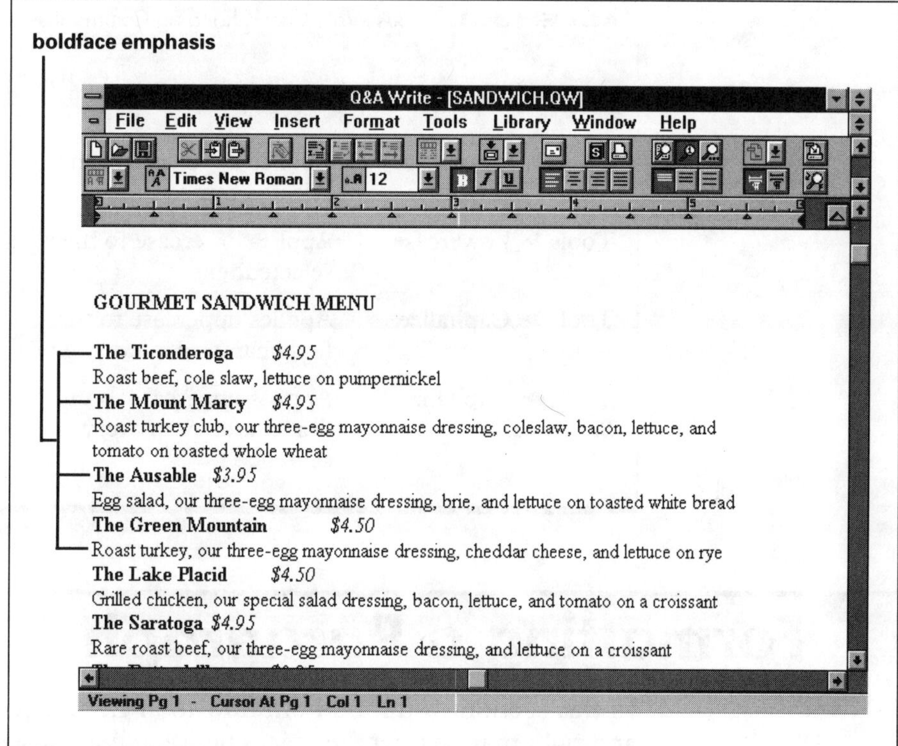

Applying Uppercase, Lowercase, and Initial Capitals

Q&A Write allows you to change the case of selected text rather than retyping it character by character (but not numbers and special symbols). For example, if you wish to change a headline from mixed case to uppercase, just choose the Tools ➤ Uppercase command or press Ctrl+Shift+U. For other related commands, see Table 13.3.

TABLE 13.3: Q&A Write Case-Changing Commands

MENU COMMAND	DESCRIPTION	SHORTCUT KEY COMBINATION
Tools ➤ Uppercase	Applies uppercase to the selected text	Ctrl+Shift+U
Tools ➤ Lowercase	Applies lowercase to the selected text	Ctrl+Shift+L
Tools ➤ Capitalize Words	Applies uppercase to the first character in every word	Ctrl+Shift+W
Tools ➤ Capitalize Sentences	Applies uppercase to the first character in every sentence	Ctrl+Shift+S

Formatting a Paragraph

In this section, you'll find out how to align paragraphs between the left and right margins, set the spaces between lines, insert spaces before paragraphs, and indent paragraphs. Q&A Write allows you to apply paragraph formats by clicking on tool bar buttons (see Table 12.1 in the previous Chapter), using the ruler, choosing Format ➤ Paragraph, or pressing Ctrl+F5. In the last two cases, Q&A Write opens the Paragraph Format dialog box (Figure 13.7). You'll learn how to set margins for an entire document later in this chapter.

The Q&A Write
Paragraph Format
dialog box

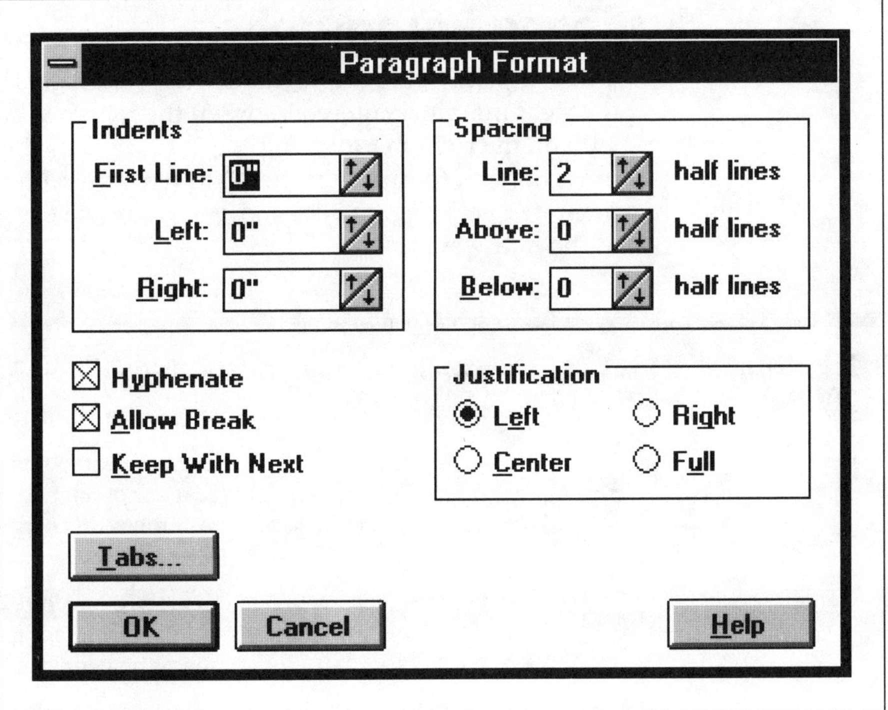

NOTE

Q&A Write provides the paragraph bar, which you normally use in outline mode. (For information about creating and working with outline, see your Q&A Write documentation.) You can also use the paragraph bar to select paragraphs. Choose View ➤ Paragraph Bar or press Ctrl+Shift+H to activate the paragraph bar. Q&A Write displays the bar in the left margin. To select a paragraph, move the mouse pointer to the paragraph bar. When the pointer changes to an arrow that points up and toward the right, click on the mouse button and Q&A Write selects the entire paragraph. Without the paragraph bar, to make a selection, you would have to move the mouse pointer to the left margin and quadruple-click.

Justifying Paragraphs

You can justify paragraph text so that it is aligned with either the left or the right margin, centered between the margins, or aligned with both the left and the right margins. Table 13.4 describes the four paragraph alignment options (notice that each tool bar icon represents the type of alignment it issues). Figure 13.8 shows you sample paragraphs aligned in each of the four ways.

TABLE 13.4: Q&A Write Paragraph Alignment Options

ALIGNMENT OPTION	TOOL BAR BUTTON	SHORTCUT KEY COMBINATION	DESCRIPTION
Left		Ctrl+L	Aligns selected text with the left margin. Text is not aligned (that is, it is jagged) with the right margin. This is the Q&A Write default.
Center		Ctrl+E	Centers selected text between the margins from an imaginary line running down the center of the document.
Right		Ctrl+R	Aligns selected text with the right margin. Text is not aligned (that is, it is jagged) with the left margin.
Full		Ctrl+J	Aligns selected text with both the left and right margins. Extra spaces are inserted, where needed, between words.

The advantage of choosing Format ➤ Paragraph to justify selected paragraphs is that you can remain in the Format Paragraph dialog box to change other paragraph formats. To justify selected paragraphs, using the menu bar, follow these steps:

1. Choose Format ➤ Paragraph or press Ctrl+F5. Q&A Write opens the Format Paragraph dialog box.

2. In the Justification group, select Left, Center, Right, or Full. Click on OK or press Enter. Q&A Write closes the dialog box and changes the justification of the selected paragraph.

Four sample paragraphs showing each of the four types of paragraph alignment. Notice that you can see nonprinting symbols.

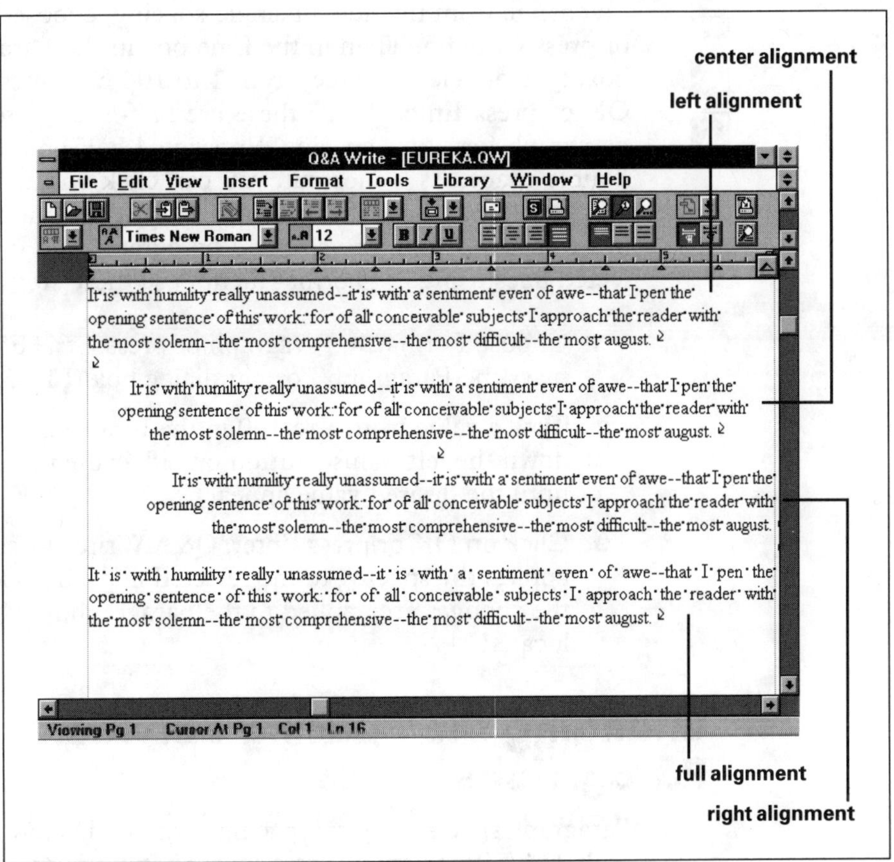

Changing the Spacing Between Lines

To subtly extend the length of a one-page document, or to make sure that each line stands out in a technical paper with superscripts and subscripts, consider adjusting the spacing between the lines within a paragraph. Although most letters, memoranda, and business reports are single-spaced, most manuscripts and term papers are double-spaced. Two common examples of line spacing are business letters, which are normally single-spaced (the Q&A Write default), and term papers, which are usually double-spaced. Don't confuse line spacing with paragraph spacing, which adjusts spacing before and after paragraphs and which is covered in the next section.

To change from the default single-spacing, choose Format ➤ Paragraph or press Ctrl+F5. Then in the Line box in the Paragraph Format dialog box, type or select a value (from 1 to 100 half-lines), and either click on OK or press Enter. Since these are half-lines, entering *2* will format a paragraph for single spacing. Entering 4 half-lines sets the paragraph to double-space. As a shortcut, you can click on the Single Line Spacing, One-and-One-Half Line Spacing, or Double Line Spacing tool bar button to apply spacing to selected paragraphs. To change spacing for selected lines using the Format menu, use these steps:

1. Choose Format ➤ Paragraph or press Ctrl+F5. Q&A Write displays the Paragraph Format dialog box (Figure 13.7).

2. Type a value from 1 to 100 in the Line box, or press and hold down the left mouse button on either the up or the down arrow until the desired value appears.

3. Click on OK or press Enter. Q&A Write closes the dialog box and applies the spacing to the selected lines. If no lines are selected, the changes are applied to the paragraph in which your cursor is located.

Changing the Spacing Between Paragraphs

Paragraph spacing adjusts spacing above and below a paragraph. As a default, Q&A Write has no extra spaces between paragraphs. However, consider using spaces to emphasis certain paragraphs in a document and to separate paragraphs in letters. For example, in our sample sandwich menu, you'll see how to add an extra space before each heading to separate each sandwich entry (Figure 13.9).

You can choose Format➤ Paragraph or press Ctrl+F5 to open the Paragraph Format dialog box in which you can set values (from 1 to 100 half lines) for Above and Below. As a shortcut, you can click on the No Paragraph Spacing or Add Paragraph Spacing tool bar button to apply spacing

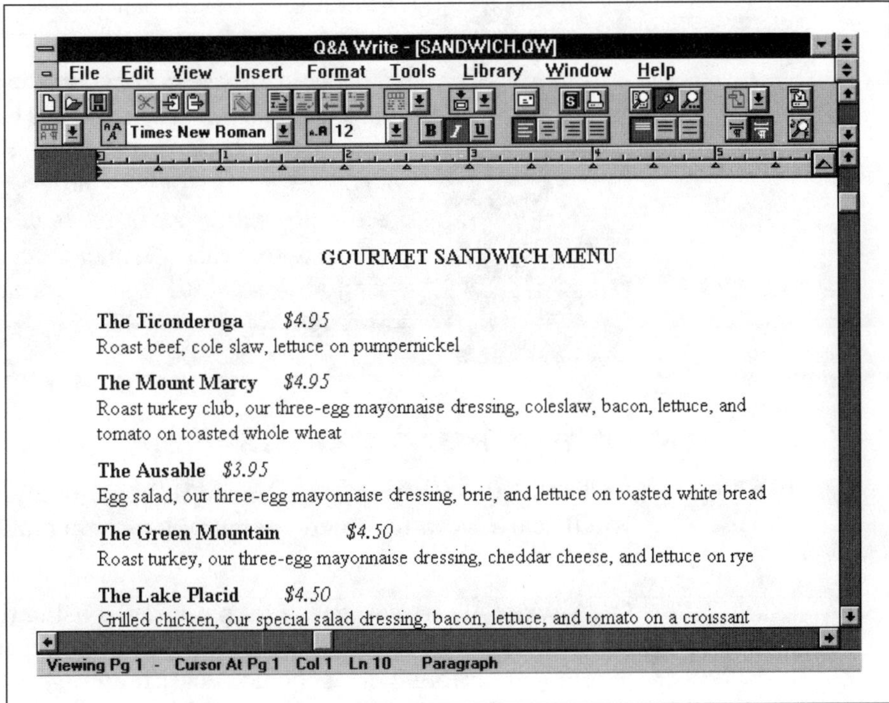

to selected paragraphs. To adjust paragraph spacing, follow these steps:

1. Choose Format ➤ Paragraph or press Ctrl+F5. Q&A Write displays the Paragraph Format dialog box (Figure 13.7).

2. Type a value from 1 to 100 in the Above box. Or press and hold down the left mouse button on either the up or the down arrow until the desired value appears.

3. Enter a value in the Below box in the same way.

4. Click on OK or press Enter. Q&A Write closes the dialog box and applies the spacing to the selected paragraphs.

It's better to choose just one type of paragraph spacing but not both to have better control over your entire document. For example, if you use both A**bo**ve and **B**elow, there may be times when one paragraph ends with an extra space or two and the next paragraph is preceded by extra space. This results in too much space between paragraphs. Another inadvertent result of mixing A**bo**ve and **B**elow is no space at all between paragraphs.

Indenting Paragraphs

Earlier in this chapter, you learned about justifying paragraphs. Now you'll learn how to indent paragraphs—either as a whole or just the first line.

Q&A Write allows you to indent paragraphs using the Paragraph Format dialog box or by dragging markers within the ruler. Use the dialog box to indent paragraphs with specific measurements; use the ruler to indent more quickly but less exactly. Q&A Write allows you to use these types of indents:

First-line indent Indents the first line of a paragraph away from the left margin but aligns the remaining lines with the left margin. Traditional business letters and reports are typical examples of the first-line indent.

Hanging indent Starts the first line of a paragraph with the left margin but moves the remaining lines away from the left margin. Bulleted lists and numbered lists are examples of hanging indents.

Block indent Indents all the lines of a paragraph from either or both margin.

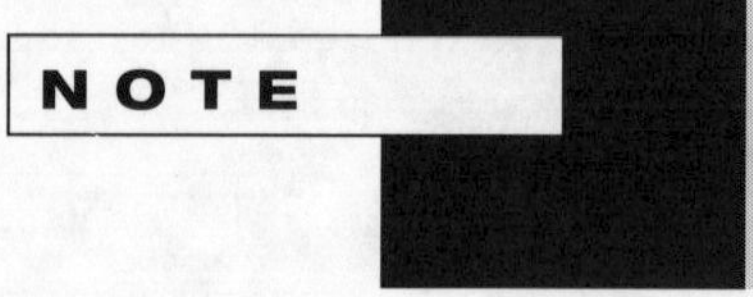

You can also create first-line paragraph indents by pressing the Tab key. Setting tab positions is covered later in this chapter.

Indenting Paragraphs with the Ruler

The quickest way to indent paragraphs and lines within paragraphs is by using the left and right margin markers on the ruler, shown in Figures 13.10, 13.11, and 13.12. There are two left margin markers on the ruler: the top marker is the first-line indent marker, and the bottom pointer is the left margin marker. Figure 13.13 shows our menu with block indents applied to the sandwich descriptions.

- To create first-line indents, drag the top left margin marker.

- To create a hanging indent, drag both the first-line and left margin markers to point where you want the lines indented. Then drag the first-line marker to the left.

- To create a block indent, drag the bottom left margin marker. Both the first-line and the left margin marker move together when you drag the bottom marker.

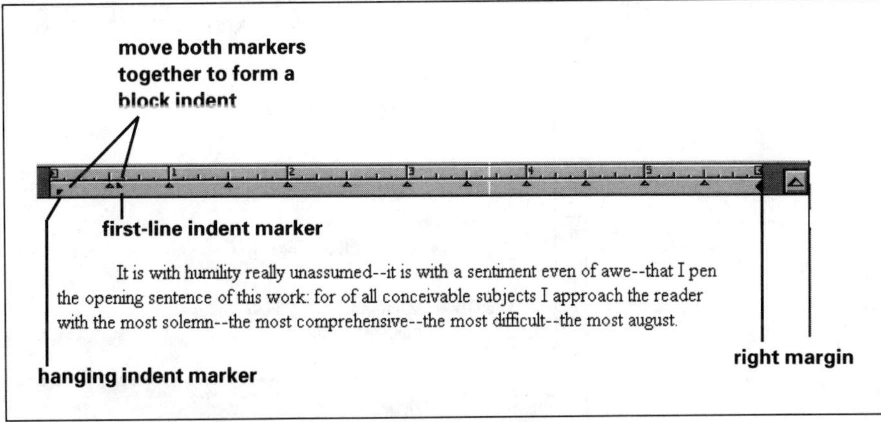

FIGURE 13.10

A first-line indent shown on the ruler and in a sample paragraph

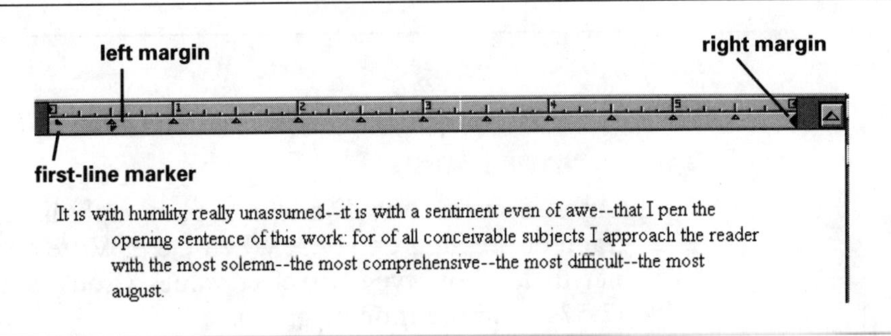

FIGURE 13.11

A hanging indent shown on the ruler and in a sample paragraph

FIGURE 13.12

A block indent shown on the ruler and in a sample paragraph. Notice that the paragraph is indented from both the left margin and the right margin.

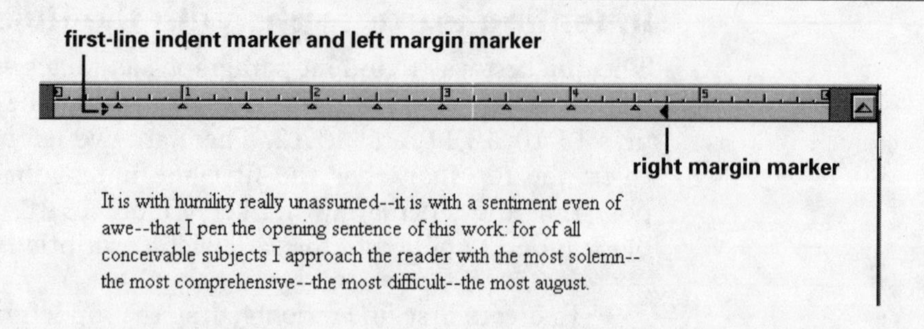

FIGURE 13.13

The sample sandwich menu with non-heading paragraphs indented from the left margin

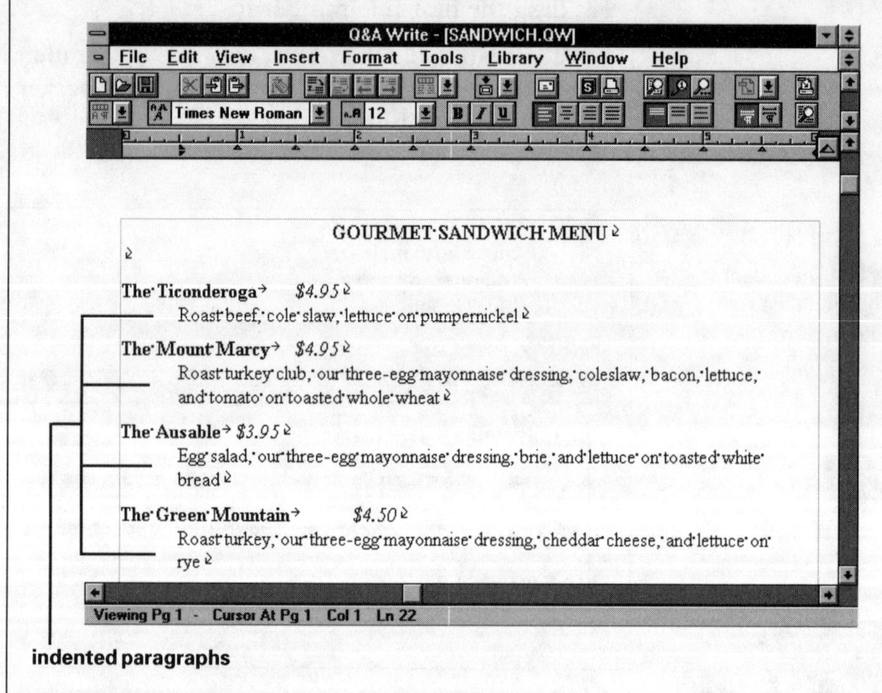

Indenting Paragraphs with the Format Menu

A more accurate way of indenting paragraphs is choosing Format ➤ Paragraph or pressing Ctrl+F5. When Q&A Write opens the Paragraph Format dialog box, type or select values (from 0" to 22.755" or 0 cm to 57.57cm) in the Indents group.

- To create a first-line indent, type or select a value in the <u>F</u>irst Line box in the Indents group. For example, to indent the first line by one-half inch, type or select 0.5", and leave 0" in both the <u>L</u>eft and <u>R</u>ight boxes.

- To create a hanging indent, type or select a value in the <u>L</u>eft box in the Indents group. For example, to indent all but the first line in a paragraph by one-half inch, type or select 0.5" in the Left box and leave 0" in both the <u>F</u>irst Line and <u>R</u>ight boxes.

- To create a block indent from both left and right margins, type or select a value in all three boxes in the Indent group. For example, to indent the paragraph by one-half inch, type or select 0.5" in all three boxes. To create a block indent from the left margin, type or select a value in the <u>F</u>irst Line and <u>L</u>eft boxes and leave 0" in the <u>R</u>ight box. To create a block indent from the right margin, leave 0" in the <u>F</u>irst Line and <u>L</u>eft boxes and type 0.5" in the <u>R</u>ight box.

T I P

Q&A Write uses the unit of measure that you have set in Windows Control Panel. You can select either English (inches), which is the default, or Metric (centimeters) in the International application. For greater accuracy, select Metric.

Setting and Using Tabs

In the previous section, you learned about indenting paragraphs. Now you'll learn about tabs, which also allow you to set first-line indents. In addition, tabs enable you to separate text within a line or paragraph (for example, to define columns in a table). You can set evenly-spaced or irregularly-spaced tabs in Q&A Write using either the ruler or by choosing Format ➤ Paragraph. To set a tab using the ruler, select a tab type from the tab drop-down list and then click on a location on the ruler. To set a tab using a menu command, choose For<u>m</u>at ➤ <u>P</u>aragraph (or press Ctrl+F5), click on the <u>T</u>abs button in the Paragraph Format dialog box, and start adding tabs in the Tabs dialog box (Figure 13.14).

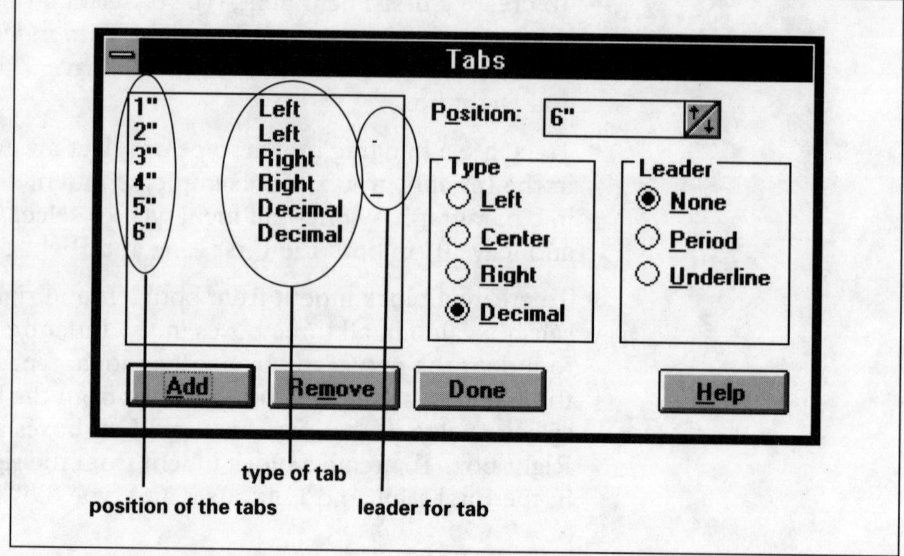

You can set four types of tabs and three types of *leaders* (for example, the dotted line between the item and page number in a table of contents) in Q&A Write. Table 13.5 lists each tab option found in the Tabs dialog box, shows its symbol on the ruler, and provides a description.

TABLE 13.5: Q&A Write Tab Options

BUTTON	NAME	DESCRIPTION	TABS DIALOG BOX OPTION
▲	Left Tab	Typed characters start at the tab mark; each additional character is added to the right side of the tab mark. This is the Q&A Write default tab setting.	Left
▲	Center Tab	Typed characters start at the tab mark; each additional character is added alternately to the left and to the right side of the tab mark.	Center

TABLE 13.5: Q&A Write Tab Options

BUTTON	NAME	DESCRIPTION	TABS DIALOG BOX OPTION
	Right Tab	Typed characters start at the tab mark; each additional character is added to the left side of the tab mark.	Right
	Decimal Tab	Typed characters start at the tab mark; each additional character is added to the left side of the tab mark. When you type a period, it remains at the tab mark; remaining characters are added to the right side.	Decimal
	No Leader	There are no leader characters in the place between two tab markers. This is the Q&A Write default.	None
	Dotted Leader	There is a line of dots between two tab markers.	Period
	Underline Leader	There is a solid underline between two tab markers.	Underline

You can indent paragraphs more quickly using tabs (especially the default of every half-inch) than by setting paragraph indents. Simply move the insertion point to the beginning of the paragraph to be indented and press the Tab key. If you have set Q&A Write to show hidden characters such as paragraph marks and tab marks, you'll see the tab symbol (a right-pointing arrow) on your computer screen.

Other than indenting paragraphs, the most common use for tabs is in creating tables. For example, to start a three-column table, type the first column, press Tab, type the second column, press Tab, and then finish by typing the third column. If you have to adjust the location of a tab stop, you can use the ruler or choose For__mat__ ➤ __P__aragraph.

You can change the default Q&A Write margins by choosing For__mat__ ➤ Page Setup or pressing Ctrl+F9. In the __D__efault Tab Stops text/list box of the Page Setup dialog box (Figure 13.15), either type or select a value from 0 to 22.755~".

The Page Setup dialog box in which you can change margins settings, the default tab stops, and the hyphen hot zone

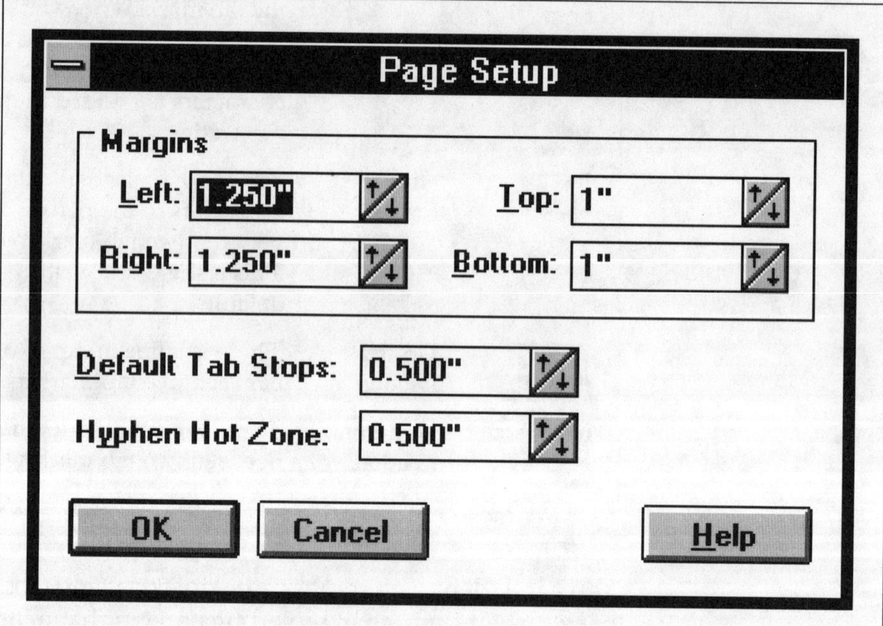

Setting Tabs with the Ruler

On the ruler (Figure 13.16), the default tab positions appear as small tri-angles. If you look carefully, you'll notice that the left side of the triangle is bold; this indicates that the tab is left-aligned. You can use the ruler to change tab alignment and to set and clear tab positions: Left, Right, Center, or Decimal. To choose tab alignment and set tab stops for the current

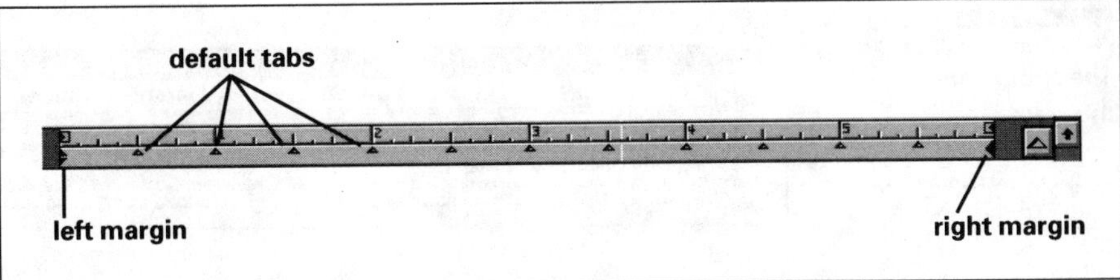

FIGURE 13.16

The Q&A Write ruler with icons showing its default tabs

document using the ruler, use these steps:

1. Move the mouse pointer to the Tab icon on the right side of the ruler. Press and hold down the left mouse button. Q&A Write opens the tab drop-down list box.

2. While holding down the mouse button, drag the mouse pointer down the list and select a tab button. Q&A Write highlights your selection.

3. Release the mouse button. Q&A Write closes the drop-down list box.

4. Move the mouse pointer to the desired tab location on the ruler and click the left mouse button on the button on the ruler. Q&A Write marks the position on the ruler with a triangle marking the proper alignment and removes all the default tab positions to the left of the new tab stop.

5. To set additional tab stops, repeat steps 1 to 4. Figure 13.17 shows the sample menu with added tabs.

TIP

To delete a user-set tab symbol, just drag it off toward the top of the ruler.

Setting Tabs with the Menu Bar

To set tab stops using specific measurements, it's probably best to choose Format ➤ Paragraph and then click on Tabs. In this way, you can set all the tab positions and select tab alignment for each for the current document. You can select from the four types of tab alignment described in

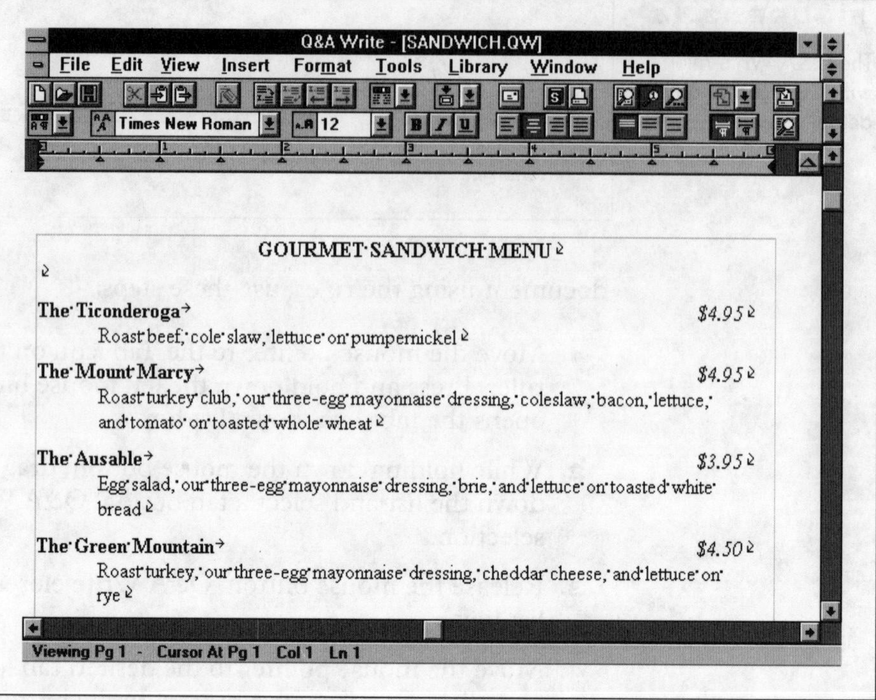

Table 13.5. To set tabs for the current document using the menu bar, follow these steps:

1. Choose Format ➤ Paragraph. Q&A Write displays the Format Paragraph dialog box.

2. Click on the Tabs button. Q&A Write displays the Tabs dialog box.

3. Select the tab alignment from the Type group.

4. Select a tab position by typing or selecting a value from 0" to 22.755" from the Position text box.

5. Click on the Add button.

6. Repeat steps 3, 4, and 5 to set other tab positions.

7. To remove a tab position, select it in the box on the left side of the dialog box. Then click on Remove.

8. When you have specified the desired tab positions, click on Done.

Leaders between two tab positions extend between one tab position and the one for which you selected leaders. For example, to have leaders run between a tab set at 1" and one set at 2", select leaders when you specify the 2" tab position.

Defining the Look of a Page

At this point, you have learned about all character and paragraph formats available in Q&A Write. Now you'll find out about dealing with the entire document as a whole. When you define the look of a page, you are actually defining the look of the document as a whole. For example, when you specify headers or footers (the next topic), be aware that they will appear on every page of the document. When you specify left, right, top, and bottom margins, you are changing margins for the entire document.

Adding Headers and Footers to a Document

To display identical information on every page of a document, you can define *headers* and *footers*, a few lines of text at the top and bottom of the page, respectively. For example, you can show the file name, today's date and time, your name, the document's title, and so on. The headers for this book show the chapter and page number, the chapter title, and the section title. This makes it easy to locate information quickly and easily.

To specify headers or footers for Q&A Write, choose View ➤ Header or View ➤ Footer. Q&A Write opens a *pane* (Figure 13.18), a small window within the document window. Type or stamp information in the pane and then click on the Close button to return to your document.

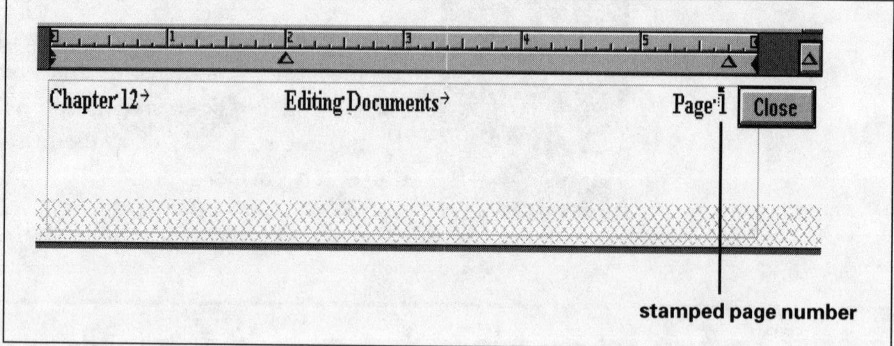

FIGURE 13.18

The Q&A Write header pane with some information already typed in

Stamping Information in a Header, Footer, or Elsewhere

You can insert the page, date, time, file name, and keep track of document statistics by inserting items such as document name and the person who created or edited the document. For example, if you prepare a daily report, you don't have to look at your calendar, just stamp the date. If every document header must contain the name of its author in the left corner, insert the Who – Current stamp. You can insert stamps by choosing Insert ▸ Stamp and selecting an entry from the cascading menu (Figure 13.19):

Document Name	The file name and extension (for example, SANDWICH.QW)
Full Document Name	The path, file name, and extension (for example, C:\QAWIN\SANDWICH.QW)
Page Number	The current page number
Total Pages	The total number of pages in the document
Time – Current	The current system time, formatted *hh*:*mm*:*ss*.
Time – Creation	The system time at which you first saved this document
Time – Last Saved	The system time at which you most recently saved this document

FIGURE 13.19

The Stamp cascading menu.

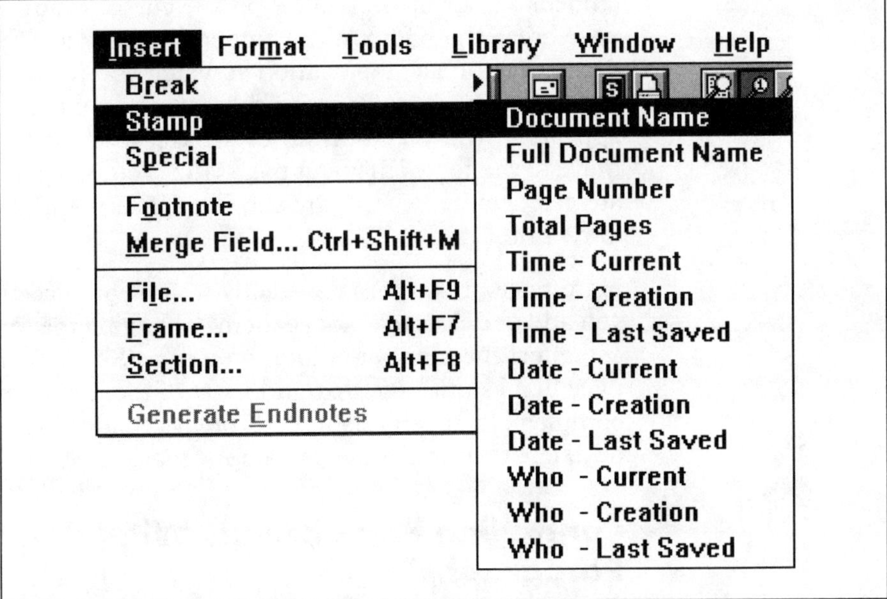

Date – Current	The current system date, using the Long Date Format, which is set in the Windows Control Panel
Date – Creation	The system date on which you first saved this document
Date – Last Saved	The system date on which you last saved this document
Who – Current	The user who is currently working on this document
Who – Creation	The user who first saved this document
Who – Last Saved	The user who last saved this document

Inserting Page Breaks

In most cases, you'll rely on Q&A Write to automatically insert page breaks. As you add text to a page, Q&A Write keeps track of the number of lines. When it reaches 45 lines (using the default margin settings), it embeds a page break and moves the cursor to the top of the next page. A page break that Q&A Write embeds is called a *soft page break*. You can insert a page break at a location at which you think there should be a separation between one line and the next. For example, if a section heading appears at the very bottom of a page, it's best to force that heading to move to the top of the next page. You'll embed a *hard page break* immediately above the heading by choosing Insert ➤ Break ➤ Page or pressing Ctrl+Enter.

Hard page breaks remain exactly where you place them--whether or not you add or delete text above them. Changing the font or point size or both can affect the number of lines on a page. So it's best to wait to insert hard page breaks until the text and most of the formatting in the document is complete. In contrast, soft page breaks change location whenever you add or delete text or change certain formats.

Controlling Page Breaks Within Paragraphs

You can use the page-break related options available in the Paragraph Format dialog box to control whether a line, page, or column break occurs within a paragraph, or outside the paragraph. You can determine whether part of a paragraph appears at the bottom of the page and the rest flows to the top of the next page or whether the entire paragraph stays together on one page. You can also control whether a particular paragraph (for example, a heading) always appears on the same page with the following paragraph (for example, the paragraph following the heading). For instance, if a term paper contains a short section consisting of a heading and one two- or three-sentence paragraph, it may be important to keep everything together on a single page—even though the text on the previous page may end halfway down the page. Here are the options:

Allow Break	Allows a page break to occur within the selected paragraph. Clearing this check box prevents a page break from occurring within the selected paragraph.
Keep With Next	Prevents a page break between the selected paragraph and the following paragraph. Clearing this check box allows each paragraph to appear on a separate page.

Specifying Margins for a Document

Margins are the borders extending from the four edges of the paper in to the text on the page. The Q&A Write default margins are 1.25" on the left and right sides and 1" at the top and bottom. You can change margin settings to fit more text on a page (for example, if you must produce a one-page memo containing more text than will fit on a typical page), make the margins smaller. Keep in mind that some printers will not print within the first half-inch from each edge of the paper. Valid values for Q&A Write margins are from 0" to 22.755". However, you cannot set overlapping margins.

You also might want to change the margins to fit pages in a binder without punching holes through text, or to emphasize the contents of a small poster by adding more white space around the borders. You can set margins by choosing Format ➤ Page Setup, or by pressing Ctrl+F9.

Adjusting Left and Right Margins with the Ruler

It's simple and quick to adjust the left and right margins with the ruler (Figure 13.20). Just select the area in which you want the margins to change and then drag the margin markers to the desired position. Q&A adjusts the text in the work area and removes any default tab markers to the left of the left margin and to the right of the right margin.

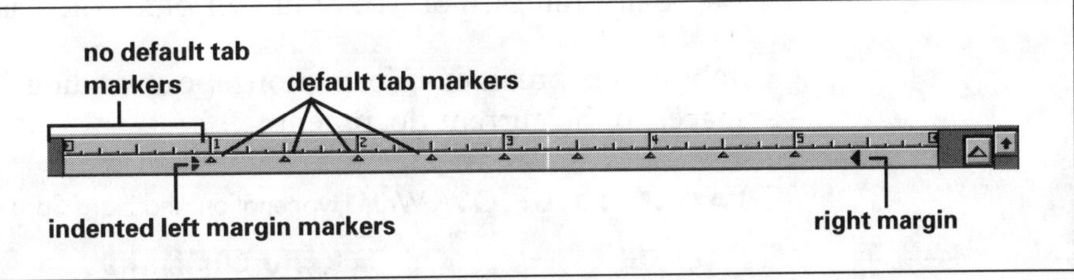

Adjusting Margins with the Format Menu

To adjust all four margins in the same dialog box and to be able to enter exact measurements, choose Format ➤ Page Setup or press Ctrl+F9. Either type or select a value from 0" to 22.755" in any of the text boxes in the Margins group. Then either click on OK or press Enter.

Setting Hyphenation

When you type text and a long word wraps to the next line, the result may be a right margin that looks very ragged. To smooth out the margins, Q&A Write can add hyphens where needed. Q&A Write provides four commands related to breaking words between two lines or ensuring that words stay together on the same line.

- You can enable soft hyphenation within a hyphenation zone. Q&A Write only inserts a *soft hyphen* when it is needed or if it occurs in the hyphenation dictionary; otherwise the word will remain unbroken on one line.

- You can determine the width of the *hyphen hot zone,* an area before the right margin. Whenever Q&A Write encounters a word that flows into the hyphen hot zone, it looks the word up in a hyphenation dictionary, which indicates the location at which a soft hyphen is inserted. The word is then broken at that location. Half the word stays on its original line, the other half moves to the beginning of the next line. The default hyphen hot zone is 0.5" wide but can range from 0" to 22.755" wide.

- You can insert a *hard hyphen* into a word to force it to break at the location that you choose (whether it is right or wrong).

- You can insert a *hard space* between two words to force them to stay together on the same line. Examples of words that look better if they remain tied together are proper names such as San Francisco or Mr. Smith, or dates such as May 1st.

Table 13.6 provides information about adding hyphenation and hard spaces to the current document.

TABLE 13.6: Q&A Write Hyphenation and Hard Space Commands

ACTION	MENU COMMAND	KEY COMBINATION
To insert a hard space at the cursor location	Insert ➤ Special ➤ Hard Space	Ctrl+Spacebar
To insert a hard hyphen at the cursor location	Insert ➤ Special ➤ Hard Hyphen	Ctrl+-

TABLE 13.6: Q&A Write Hyphenation and Hard Space Commands (continued)

ACTION	MENU COMMAND	KEY COMBINATION
To define the hyphen hot zone, set margins and tab stops for the current document	Format ➤ Page Setup	Ctrl+F9
Insert a soft hyphen at the cursor location	Insert ➤ Special ➤ Page	Ctrl+Shift+-
To open the Paragraph dialog box where you can enable soft hyphenation by checking Hyphenate	Format ➤ Paragraph	Ctrl+F5

To start soft hyphenation in the current document, choose Format ➤ Paragraph or press Ctrl+F5. In the Paragraph Format dialog box, make sure that there is a check mark in the Hyphenate check box.

To change the width of the hyphen hot zone, choose Format ➤ Page Setup or press Ctrl+F9. In the Page Setup dialog box, either type or select a value from 0" to 22.755". Then either click on OK or press Enter.

To insert a hard hyphen, move the cursor between two characters in a word, and choose Insert ➤ Special ➤ Hard Hyphen or press Ctrl+-. To insert a *hard space*, move the cursor to the space between two words, and choose Insert ➤ Special ➤ Hard Space or press Ctrl+Spacebar. You can also determine the location at which Q&A Write inserts a soft hyphen by moving the cursor to the location between two characters in a word, and choose Insert ➤ Special ➤ Soft Hyphen or press Ctrl+Shift+-.

Finding and Replacing Text

After you have some experience using Q&A Write, you'll start looking for shortcuts in document editing. Finding and replacing text automatically are features you'll probably use during every work session. If you have to make the same change several times in a document (for example, change your company name or replace a word or group of words on every page), the <u>F</u>ind and Re<u>p</u>lace commands are lifesavers. In this section, you'll discover how to use <u>F</u>ind and Replace to search for and optionally change characters. In the following section, you'll learn about finding and replacing character and paragraph formats.

Finding Text

Choose <u>E</u>dit ➤ <u>F</u>ind or press Shift+F7 and fill in the Find dialog box (Figure 13.21) to move to a specific word or phrase in the current document. For example, you can look for the word nepotism, or you can look for the sentence, "Nepotism runs in my family." The character, word, phrase, or sentence for which you are searching is the *search string*. You can refine a search by selecting restrictions from the menu bar on the Find dialog box:

<u>M</u>atch ➤ <u>W</u>hole Word	Searches for only complete words rather than parts of words that match the search string. For example, you can look for the word *auto* without finding *automatic* or *automobile*. A check mark preceding the menu item indicates that the command is active.

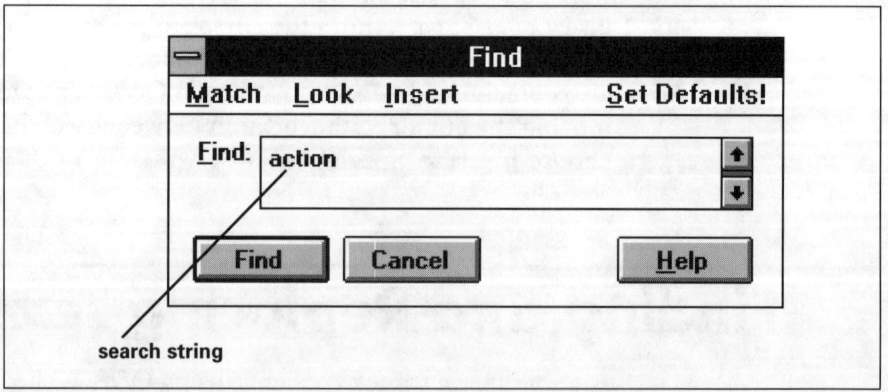

FIGURE 13.21

The Q&A Write Find dialog box

Match ➤ Case Sensitive	Searches for an exact match on uppercase and lowercase text. For example, you can look for the title *My Life* without finding *my life* or in *my lifetime*. A check mark preceding the command indicates that this command is active.
Match ➤ Character Formats	Allows you to restrict the search by looking for a particular font, point size, or color. You can also search for bold, italic, underline, strikethrough, and double underline emphasis. For example, you can search for Proposal in bold Helvetica 14 text and not find proposal in the body text of Times New Roman 12. To omit character formats, choose Match ➤ Character Formats and in the Find Format dialog box, select Any from the bottom of the Font, Size, and Color drop-down list boxes and clear any check boxes in the Emphasis group, including the Emphasis check box itself.
Look ➤ Within Frames	Searches only for text in frames. (For information about using frames in your documents, see your Q&A Write documentation.)
Look ➤ Backwards	Searches for the search string from the insertion point toward the top of the document. The default is to search from insertion point forward.
Insert ➤ Break	Inserts a break marker in the search string so that you can search for the next page, line, or column break in your document.
Insert ➤ Tab	Inserts a tab marker in the search string so you can search for the next tab marker in your document.

Insert ➤ Wildcard	Inserts a wildcard symbol in the search string so you can search for the characters that you have already specified followed by any characters.
Set Defaults!	Saves settings for case-sensitive, whole-word, and in-frame searches.

TIP

Remember that in order to start a search at the top of a document, press Ctrl+Home.

To search for text in a document, follow these steps:

1. Choose Edit ➤ Find or press Shift+F7. Q&A Write displays the Find dialog box (Figure 13.21).

2. In the Find text box, type the word or phrase that you would like to find. You can type approximately 128 characters. When you start typing, Q&A Write makes available the Find button.

3. Select restrictions from the Match, Look, and Insert menus. To save the restrictions, click on Set Defaults.

NOTE

If you are not sure of the spelling of the string for which you are searching but remember the first few characters, type those characters and then choose Insert ➤ Wildcard to insert a wildcard symbol. When you click on the Find button, Q&A Write will search for a string starting with the characters that you typed and ending with any characters. For example, you can type comp and a wildcard symbol to search for computer, compensation, companion, compartment, and so on.

4. Click on the Find button. If Q&A Write finds the search string, it moves to the correct page and highlights the search string. If you started the search from a location within the document and Q&A Write does not find the search string before it reaches the end of the document, it displays a message (Figure 13.22). If you started the search at the top of the document and Q&A Write does not find the search string, it displays another information box (Figure 13.23).

5. To find the next occurrence of the search string, either choose Edit ➤ Find Again or press F7.

If you did not start the search at the top of the document and Q&A Write does not find the search string, it asks you if you wish to search from the top of the document.

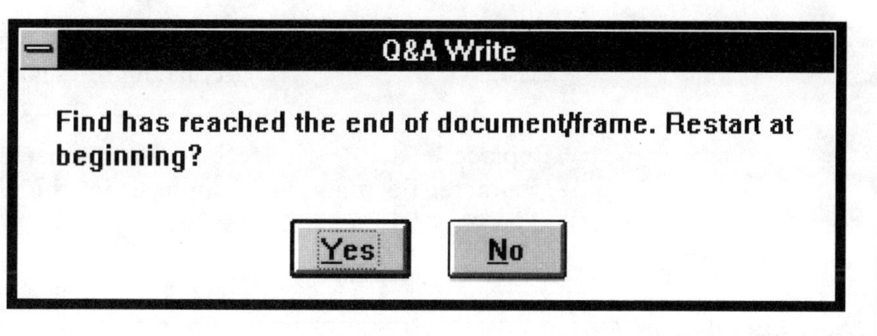

If you have started the search at the top of the document and Q&A Write does not find the search string, it informs you that the search string is not found.

Replacing Text

Most times when you search for text, you'll want to use a *replace string*. For example, if your company name changes, you'll have to go through every document you use as a template to replace the company name. You could do this in three ways: search every document page by page, deleting the old name, and typing the new name in its place; use the Find command to find the name and then type in the replacement; or automate the entire process by choosing Edit ➤ Replace and typing a search string and a replace string in the Find & Replace dialog box (Figure 13.24). Except for the addition of Replace menu, the options in the Find & Replace dialog box are the same as those in the Find dialog box. In the replace menu, you are introduced to new commands.

Replace ➤ Preserve Case	Maintains the original case when replacing the search string with the replace string.
Replace ➤ Character Formats	Specifies character formats and emphasis for the replacement string.

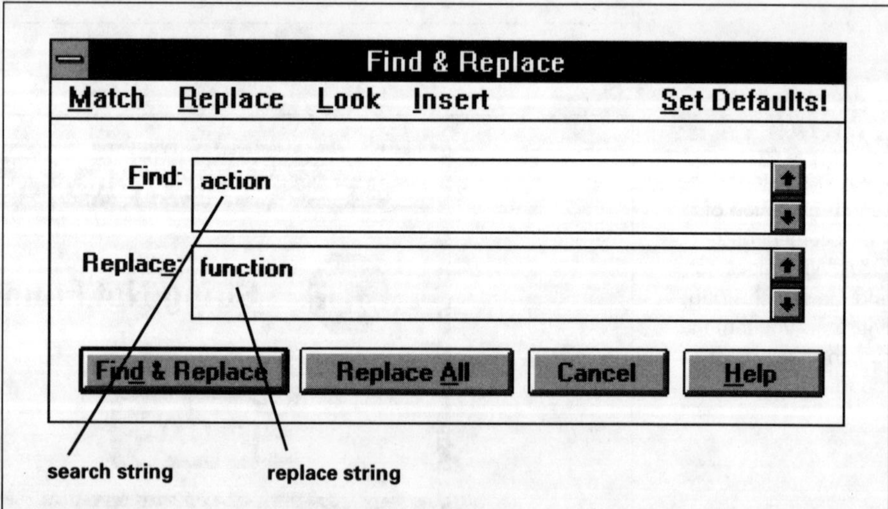

FIGURE 13.24

Q&A Write Find & Replace dialog box

To replace text, follow these steps:

1. Choose <u>E</u>dit ➤ Rep<u>l</u>ace or press Ctrl+F7. Q&A Write displays the Find & Replace dialog box. If you performed a search earlier in this Q&A Write session, the last search string you used appears in the <u>F</u>ind scroll box. If you replaced text earlier in this Q&A Write session, the last replace string appears in the Repla<u>c</u>e scroll box.

2. Type the search string in the <u>F</u>ind scroll box, and select restrictions and formats from the <u>M</u>atch, <u>L</u>ook, and <u>I</u>nsert menus. You can type up to 128 characters. Q&A Write makes available the Fin<u>d</u> & Replace and Replace <u>A</u>ll buttons.

3. Type the replace string in the Repla<u>c</u>e scroll box, and select restrictions and formats from the <u>M</u>atch, <u>R</u>eplace, <u>L</u>ook, and <u>I</u>nsert menus. You can type up to 128 characters.

4. To automatically replace all occurrences of the search string with the replace string, click on the Replace <u>A</u>ll button. After Q&A Write has finished the replace process, it displays an information box:

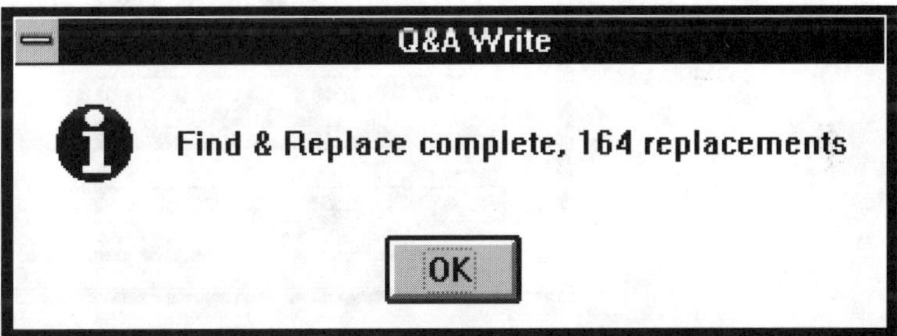

WARNING

You cannot undo a replace operation in Q&A Write. However, you can implicitly perform an undo by closing the document without saving it. Then open it to resume your work. Before starting a replace procedure, it's a good idea to save your document. Then if you have to undo, you'll still have the most recent version with which to work.

5. To find the first occurrence of the search string after the insertion point in order to decide whether to replace it, click on the Fin<u>d</u> & Replace button. Q&A Write highlights the first occurrence of the search string and opens the Replace? dialog box (Figure 13.25).

6. To replace the highlighted search string, click on <u>R</u>eplace & Continue. To continue to the next search string without replacing, click on Skip & <u>C</u>ontinue. To replace all search strings following the insertion point with the replace string, click on Replace <u>A</u>ll.

7. When you have completed the replacement process, click on <u>D</u>one. Q&A Write replaces the search string with the replace string and highlights the next occurrence of the search string. Q&A Write returns to the document.

FIGURE 13.25

The Replace? dialog box in which you can perform several replacement options

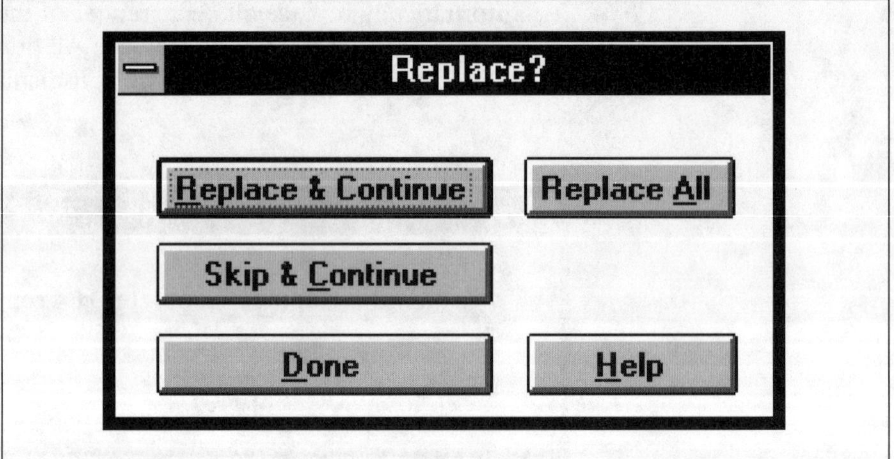

N O T E

When you need to type a long name or string of text that will be repeated over and over in your document, you might consider typing a symbolic piece of text (such as *xxx*) as a substitute. Then, when you are done typing your document, use Q&A's search and replace option to find *xxx* and replace it with what you really want.

Finding and Replacing Formats

Q&A Write also provides a find and replace feature for character and paragraph formats. Simply choose Edit ➤ Find & Replace Formats or press Ctrl+H. In the Find & Replace Formats dialog box (Figure 13.26), select the find format by choosing either Find ➤ Character Formats or Find ➤ Paragraph Formats. Then select the replace format by choosing either Replace ➤ Character Formats or Replace ➤ Paragraph Formats. Whether you choose a find or replace character format, Q&A Write displays the Character Format dialog box (Figure 13.27). If you choose to find or replace paragraph formats, you'll get the same result, the Paragraph Format dialog box (Figure 13.28).

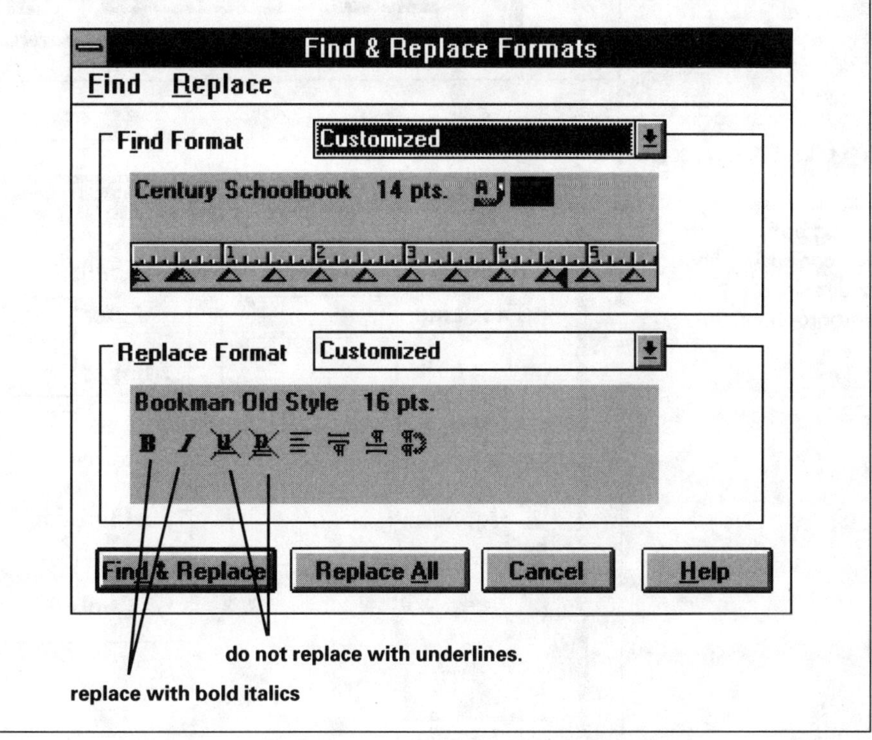

The Character Format dialog box in which you can specify find and replace character formats

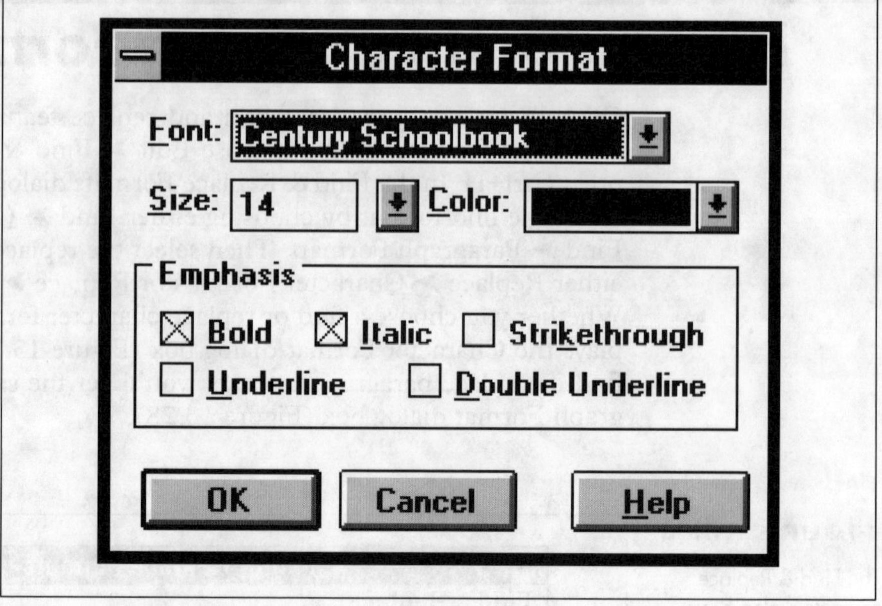

The Paragraph Format dialog box in which you can specify find and replace paragraph formats

The steps for finding and replacing formats is exactly the same as for simply finding formats. If you are looking for formats and don't want to replace them, just don't choose replace formats from the Replace menu. To search and optionally replace character and paragraph formats, follow these steps:

1. Choose Edit ➤ Find & Replace Formats or press Ctrl+H. Q&A Write opens the Find & Replace Formats dialog box.

2. To define character formats to be searched for, choose Find ➤ Character Formats. In the Character Format dialog box, open the drop-down list boxes. Then place check marks or clear the check boxes. Then click on OK or press Enter. Q&A Write adds text and symbols to the Find Format group.

3. To define paragraph formats to be searched for, choose Find ➤ Paragraph Formats. In the Paragraph Format dialog box, open the drop-down list boxes. Then place check marks or clear the check boxes. Then click on OK or press Enter. Q&A Write adds text and symbols to the Find Format group.

4. To define replacement character formats, choose Replace ➤ Character Formats. In the Character Format dialog box, open the drop-down list boxes. Then place check marks or clear the check boxes. Then click on OK or press Enter. Q&A Write adds text and symbols to the Replace Format group.

5. To define replacement paragraph formats, choose Replace ➤ Paragraph Formats. In the Paragraph Format dialog box, open the drop-down list boxes. Then place check marks or clear the check boxes. Then click on OK or press Enter. Q&A Write adds text and symbols to the Replace Format group.

6. To automatically replace all occurrences of the find format with the replace format, click on the Replace All button. Q&A informs you when it has replaced all the formats.

7. To find the first occurrence of the find format after the insertion point in order to decide whether to replace it, click on the Find & Replace button. Q&A Write highlights the first occurrence of the find format and opens the Replace? dialog box.

8. To replace the highlighted find format, click on Replace & Continue. To continue to the next find format without replacing, click on Skip & Continue. To replace all find formats following the insertion point with the replace format, click on Replace All.

9. When you have completed the replacement process, click on Done. Q&A Write replaces the search string with the replace string and highlights the next occurrence of the search string. Q&A Write returns to the document.

To Sum Up

In this chapter, you learned about editing a document: formatting characters, paragraphs, and the entire document. Finally you found out about finding and replacing both text and formats.

Starting with the next chapter, you'll start to learn about advanced Q&A operations. In the following chapter, you'll find out how Q&A interacts with other Windows applications. You'll learn about importing and exporting data and some of the Windows technologies that make working with other Windows applications possible. You'll also discover how closely Q&A for Windows and Q&A for DOS work together.

part three

Importing, Exporting, and Securing Data

chapter

14

Exchanging Data with Other Applications

WITH so many Windows applications in use in business today, it is almost inevitable that you will use Q&A's exporting and importing capabilities. These routines allow you to exchange information between Q&A databases and other application files. For instance, if you have a Q&A database of employees and salaries that you want to upload to a mainframe, you can use the Q&A's export function. If you have created a list of employees in an Excel spreadsheet, you easily can import that list into one of your Q&A databases.

Think of applications as people who speak different languages. If you write a letter in English and send it to someone who only reads French, the only way for the recipient to read and use the information in the letter is to have it translated into French. Q&A works similarly; it cannot read an Excel file, for example. However, if you use Q&A's import feature to translate the data using something called a *filter*, Q&A can read and use the information from the other application. Exporting information is very similar to importing but works in reverse. You can use filters to export data from Q&A into a new file with a different format. Then another application can open and use the file immediately.

Exporting Your Data into a Different Format

When you export data from a database, Q&A creates a new file that another program can use. The type of program that can use this file is determined by the translation filter that you use. Table 14.1 lists these filters and the programs for which they are used. Note that the data that you export is not removed from your database—it is just copied from it into a new file.

TABLE 14.1: Q&A Export and Import File Types

FILE TYPE	FILE EXTENSION	EXPORTS AND IMPORTS:
dBase II	.DBF	dBase II files
dbase III	.DBF	dBase III files
dBase IV	.DBF	dBase IV files
Excel 2.1	.XLS	Excel 2.1 files
Excel 3	.XLS	Excel 3 files
Excel 4	.XLS	Excel 4 files
Lotus 123 2.1	.WKS	Lotus 123 version 2.1 files
Lotus 123 3.x	.WK3	Lotus 123 version 3.0, 3.1, 3.1 plus, and other versions of the 3 series files
Paradox 2	.DB	Paradox 2 files
Paradox 3/3.5	.DB	Paradox 3 and Paradox 3.5 files
Text	.TXT	Text (ASCII) files
Text MAC	N/A	Macintosh text files

Creating a new export file involves several steps:

1. Open the desired database, and choose File ➤ Export. Q&A displays the Export dialog box (Figure 14.1).

2. In the Database Fields box, select the fields that contain the data that you want to export. For example, to export the names in the Last Name field, select that field.

3. Click on the Add button. Q&A places the field in the Export Order box.

4. To select all fields, click on Add All.

The order in which you add the fields to this box is the order in which the fields will appear in the exported file. You can sort the data as it is exported. Just click on the Sort button, and Q&A displays the standard Sort

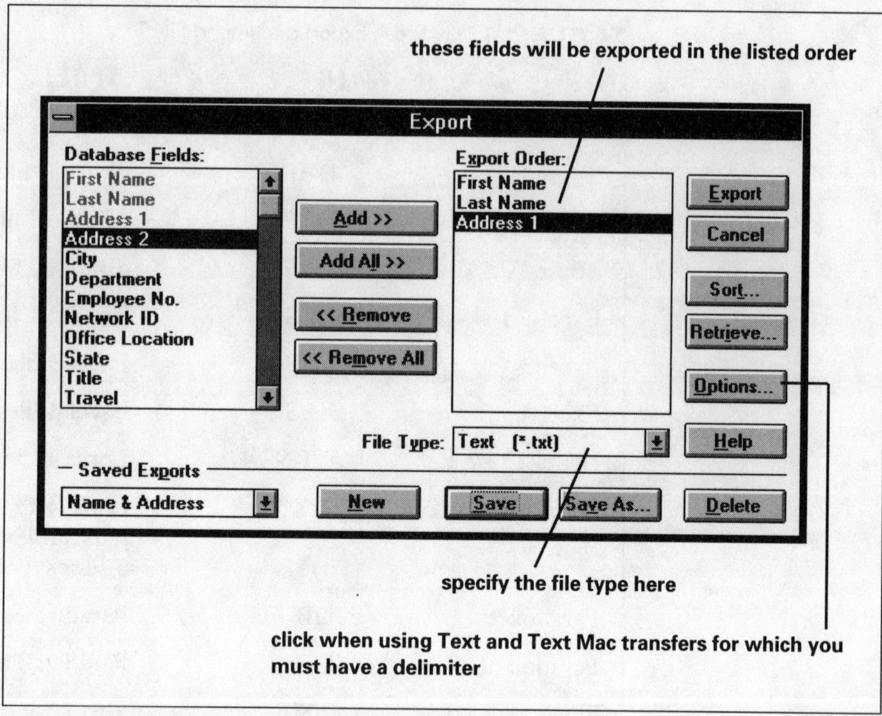

dialog box (Figure 14.2). Either create a new sort or select a saved one. Then click on Attach.

To attach a retrieval to this export, click on the Retrieve button. Q&A displays the Retrieve dialog box (Figure 14.3). Select the desired retrieval and click on Attach. Q&A returns to the Export dialog box.

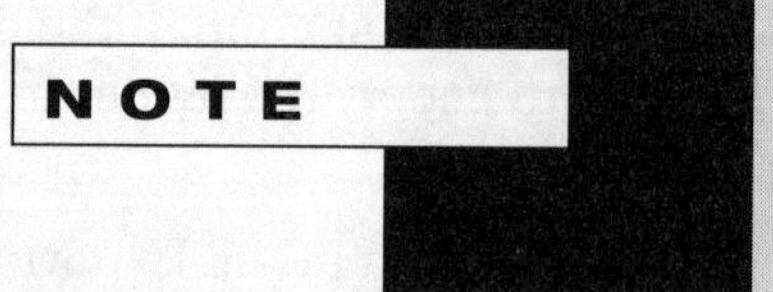

N O T E

Since you cannot create a retrieval during the export process, you must define and save a retrieval spec before you start exporting.

Use the File Type drop-down list box to select the file type for the export. Notice that the items in the drop-down list box are the filters described in Table 14.1. If you are exporting your data as a Text or Text Mac file type, you can choose Options to select the *field delimiters* used for the export. You'll learn about the Options button and field delimiters later in the

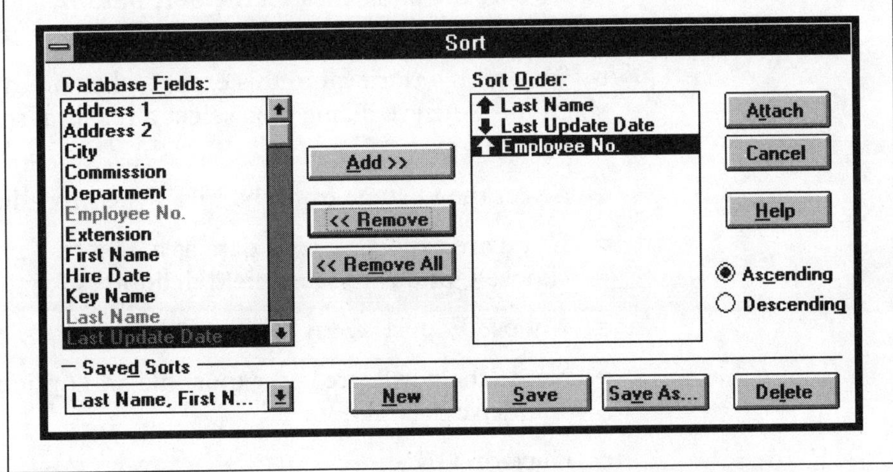

FIGURE 14.2

The Sort dialog box in which you can create or select a saved Sort spec to attach

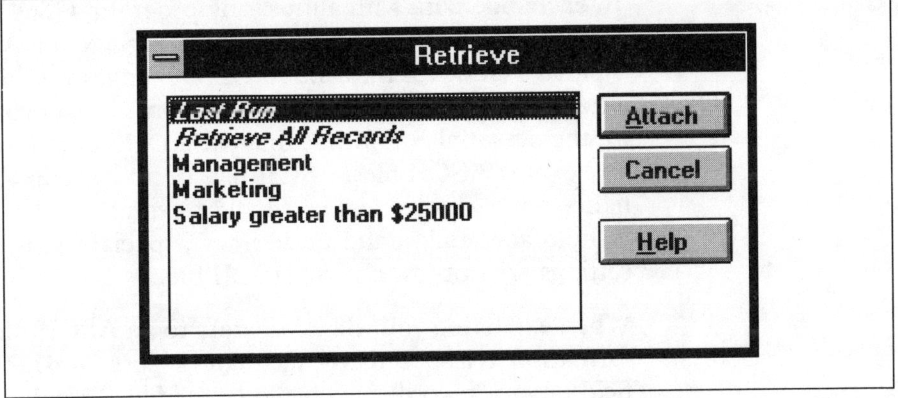

FIGURE 14.3

In the Retrieve dialog box, select a retrieve spec to attach to your export.

chapter. Choose Export. Q&A then displays the Export To dialog box, which lets you specify the name of the export file to be created and the drive and directory in which you will store it. To close the dialog box, click on OK. To create an export file, follow these steps:

1. Choose File ➤ Export. Q&A displays the Export dialog box.

2. From the Database Fields box, select a field that contains data to be exported and click on Add.

3. Repeat step 2 for additional fields.

4. To sort the data, click on the Sort button, and in the Sort dialog box, either create or select a sort. Click on Attach.

5. To attach a retrieval to this export, click on the Retrieve button. In the Retrieve dialog box, select a retrieval spec and click on Attach.

6. Select the file type from the File Type drop-down list box.

7. If you are exporting your data as a Text or Text Mac file type, choose Options to select field delimiters for the export.

8. Choose Export. Q&A displays the Export To dialog box.

9. Name the newly created export file and optionally select the disk and drive destination.

10. Click on OK.

Transferring Text Files

To exchange data with almost any program, Q&A provides Text or Text Mac filters. The format of the resulting text or ASCII files (American Standard Code for Information Interchange) was introduced years ago as a standard file format for all applications. Most programs (not only those for the personal computers that use a DOS operating system) can import and export ASCII files. ASCII files don't contain all the formats and enhancements of the original file. For example, character formatting (that is, boldface, italics, and underlines), special fonts, graphics, and margin settings are not saved in an ASCII file.

When exporting your database data to an ASCII file, Q&A places the information in a special arrangement (Figure 14.4). The data from the first field of your record is exported to the file. This data is followed by a *field delimiter* or *designator*—a single character that designates the beginning of the next field's data. Through Q&A, you have the choice of five designators: commas, carriage returns, semicolons, spaces, and tabs. (Designators are described in more detail later in this chapter.) Following the designator is the next field's contents. For each record, this arrangement of data and designators continues until all fields are listed. At the end of the record, Q&A inserts a carriage return and a line feed character which starts the next line where the next record begins.

FIGURE 14.4

An ASCII file with commas as the field delimiter. Notice that each record is on its own line and each field of that record is separated by commas.

McCue,Jim,12 Tree Rd.,San Jose
Rivas,Carl,14 Cox Ave.,Santa Clara
Vallez,Paul,325 Shaw Ave.,Saratoga
Howley,Scott,364 Reece Pl.,Cupertino
Nicoles,Jennifer,9 Kingman Ave.,Sunnyvale

When you choose Text or Text Mac from the File Type list box, the Options button becomes active. If you click on this button, Q&A opens the Text Export Options dialog box (Figure 14.5), which lists all the field delimiters you can use for exporting your data, allows you to export data for text fields enclosed in quotation marks, or use field templates for certain data (such as telephone numbers and zip codes).

To choose a field delimiter, just click on one of the five choices in the Field Separator group. The most commonly used field delimiter (and the Q&A default) is the comma.

FIGURE 14.5

The Text Export Options dialog box is available when you select either Text or Text Mac file type.

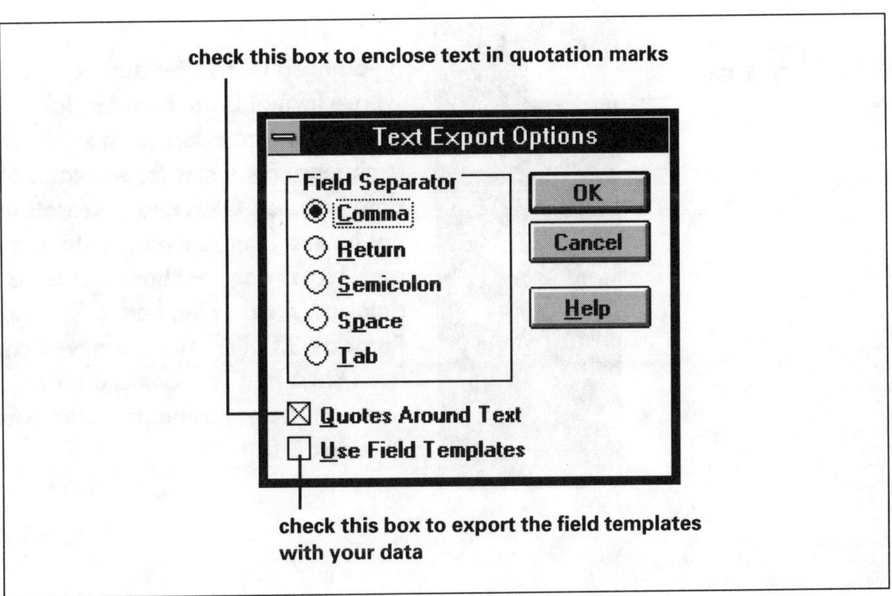

NOTE

When you choose a delimiter from the Field Separator box, make sure that you choose a character *not* found in your data. For example, if your data includes embedded spaces and is not enclosed in quotation marks, do not choose a space for your field delimiter. If you do, Q&A or any other application reading the ASCII file will read the data improperly. However, if you check Quotes Around Text, you can select a field delimiter in a text field. When data is enclosed within quotation marks, Q&A (and other programs) considers all the characters and spaces within quotes as part of the data.

Checking Quotes Around Text instructs Q&A to enclose the exported data from text fields with quotation marks. Many mainframes export and import data with quotation marks enclosing text information. Check the Use Field Templates check box if you want to export the field templates with your data. For instance, if you used a field template to format the telephone number 4085551212, checking the Use Field Templates check box exports the number as (408)555-1212.

TIP

If you need to transfer data to or from a program whose format is not found in Table 14.1, try to find another program format to serve as a medium of exchange. For instance, you cannot directly transfer data between Q&A and Microsoft Access; Q&A does not have a filter to export data to an Access file format, and Access does not have a filter to import Q&A databases. However, both Q&A and Access can read Paradox 3.0 files. Therefore, you can export your data from Q&A to a Paradox 3.0 format. Then import the data into Access using its import features for Paradox 3.0.

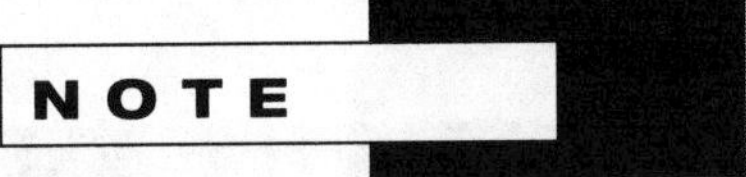

Importing Data into Your Database

Importing data is very similar to exporting data, except, of course, the process is reversed. When you import, Q&A reads information from a differently formatted file and adds it to either an existing or a new database. As you learned from Table 14.1, Q&A uses the same filters for both importing and exporting.

There are three ways to import data into a Q&A database: import data into an already open database; import data into a closed database; or have Q&A create a database as it imports information.

The first step in importing information into a database is to specify which database is to receive the imported data. The process of specifying the receiving database depends on whether you are importing to an open, closed, or new database. Once you specify which database to import into, the importation process is identical for all databases.

To import data into an opened database(while no databases are open), do the following:

1. Open the database into which you want to import data.

2. Choose File ➤ Import. This brings you to the Import From dialog box (Figure 14.6).

To import data into a closed database (while no databases are open), do the following:

1. Choose File ➤ Import. This brings you to the Import To dialog box (Figure 14.7).

2. Through the Directories list box, select the directory where the database to receive the data is located.

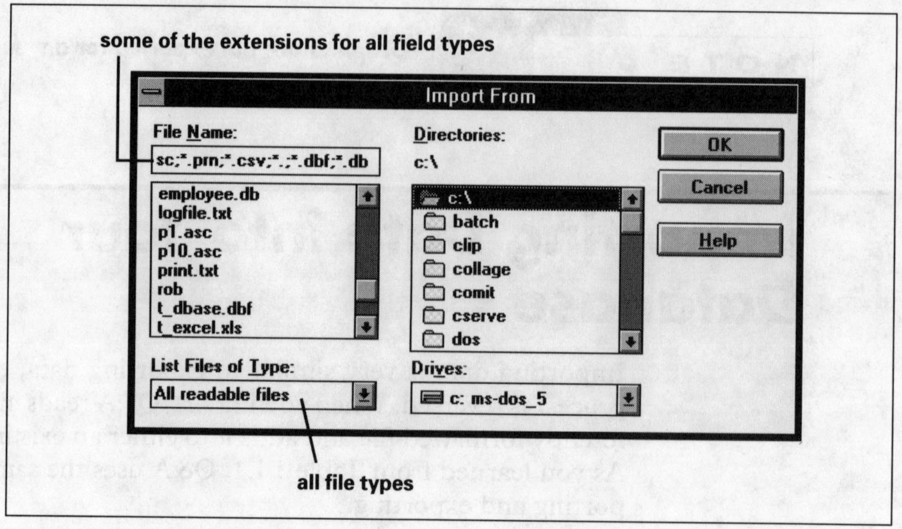

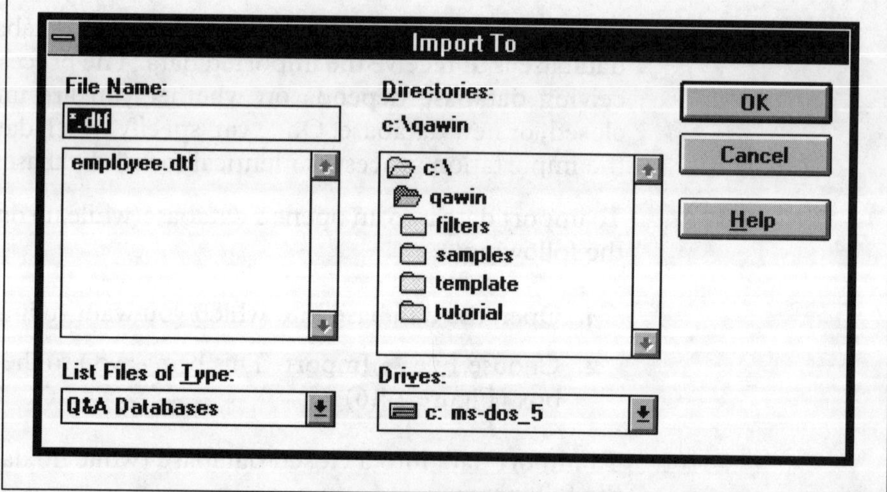

3. In the File **N**ame box type the name of the database to receive the
data. You may also select the database from the list box in the
lower left corner.

4. Click OK or press Enter. This brings you to the Import From dialog box.

To import data into a new database, follow these steps.

1. Choose File ➤ Import. This brings you to the Import To dialog box.

2. Through the Directories list box, select the directory where you want to create the database to receive the data.

3. In the File Name box type the name of the database you want Q&A to create for importing the data.

4. Click OK or press Enter. This brings you to the Import From dialog box.

After Q&A knows what database will receive the imported data, it displays the Import From dialog box in which you specify the file you wish to use for importing data into your database. (You also can choose the drive and subdirectory in which the file is saved.) From the File Name list box, choose the file to be imported. To narrow your choice, select a file type from the List Files of Type box. (The default is All readable files, which displays all the files in the current subdirectory.) After completing your selections, click on OK. In most cases, Q&A displays the Import dialog box (Figure 14.8). However, if you selected an ASCII file, Q&A displays the Text Import Options dialog box (Figure 14.9) first. From this dialog box can choose a field delimiter.

In the From list in the Import dialog box, click on the field name from which you want information imported, and in the To list, click on the field into which you want information imported. When you are ready to add a field to the To list, click on Add.

Q&A recognizes the information in the From list box as a table of information broken into rows and columns (Figure 14.10). However, the From list displays only one column of the table at a time. To scroll through the columns, use the Scan Data arrows at the bottom of the From list box. As you scan through the columns, notice that the Record indicator at the bottom of the dialog box changes accordingly. Q&A sees each column of the table as a different record. Think of the rows of the table as the fields of each record. All the rows may not be visible at one time. Therefore, use the scroll bar on the From list to view the other rows.

FIGURE 14.8

The Import dialog box lets you specify the data to be imported.

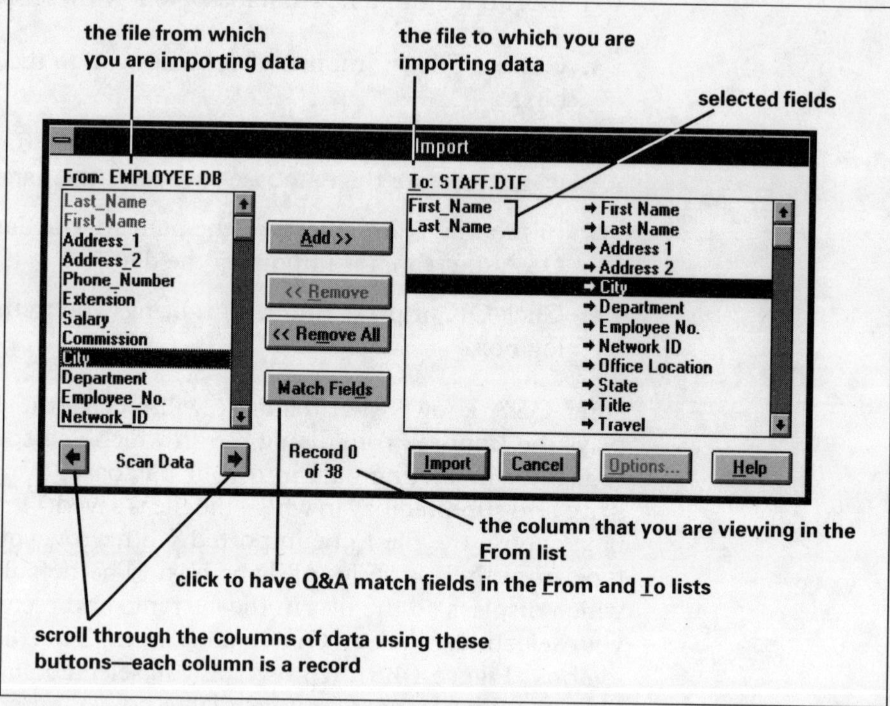

FIGURE 14.9

The Text Import Options dialog box

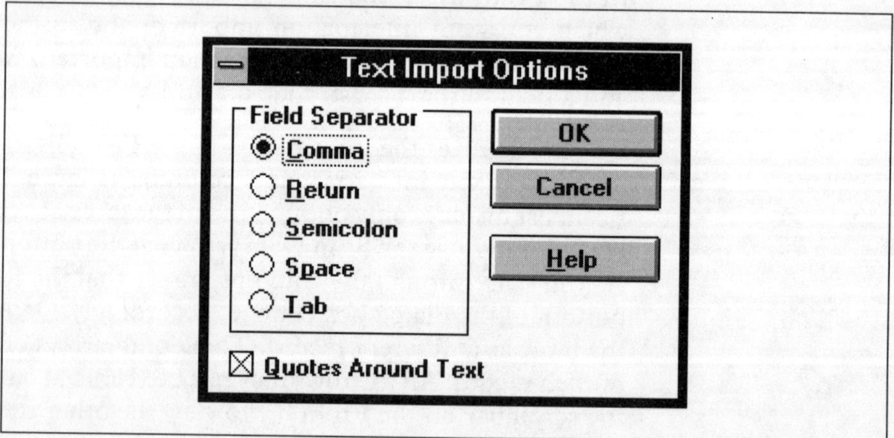

This is how Q&A views a Paradox or dBase file. The first column, recognized as Record 0, lists the field names of the database. The subsequent columns list the data of the different records.

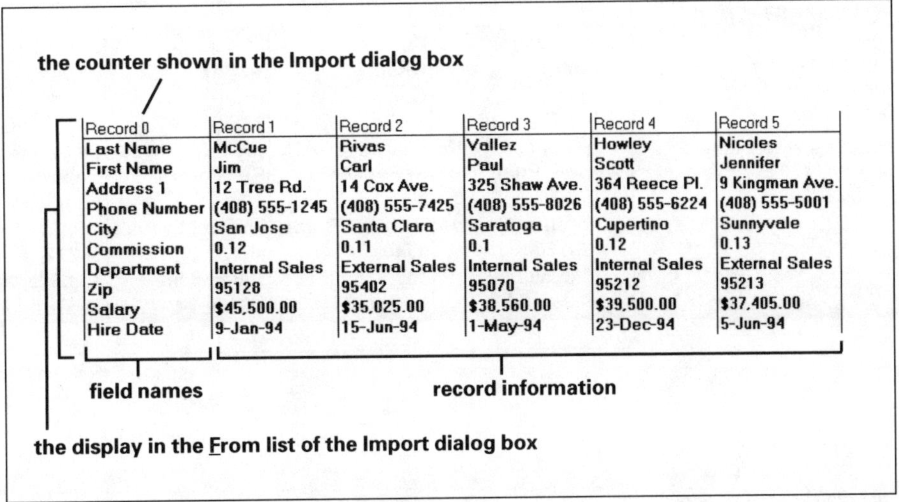

When you import information from a database file, the contents of the first column of the From list contains the names for the fields that can be imported. These can be matched with the field names in the To list and imported. However, if you are importing information from a spreadsheet, the first column in the From list displays the column letters of the spreadsheet, like A, B, or C (Figure 14.11). If you are importing an ASCII file (Figure 14.12), the From list just displays the data from the file. Figure 14.13 illustrates the spreadsheet used in Figure 14.11. Notice that the

This is how Q&A views an Excel or 1-2-3 spreadsheet file.

Record 0	Record 1	Record 2	Record 3	Record 4	Record 5
A	McCue	Rivas	Vallez	Howley	Nicoles
B	Jim	Carl	Paul	Scott	Jennifer
C	12 Tree Rd.	14 Cox Ave.	325 Shaw Ave.	364 Reece Pl.	9 Kingman Ave.
D	(408) 555-1245	(408) 555-7425	(408) 555-8026	(408) 555-6224	(408) 555-5001
E	San Jose	Santa Clara	Saratoga	Cupertino	Sunnyvale
F	0.12	0.11	0.1	0.12	0.13
G	Internal Sales	External Sales	Internal Sales	Internal Sales	External Sales
H	95128	95402	95070	95212	95213
I	$45,500.00	$35,025.00	$38,560.00	$39,500.00	$37,405.00
J	9-Jan-94	15-Jun-94	1-May-94	23-Dec-94	5-Jun-94

FIGURE 14.12

This is how Q&A views an ASCII file. All the columns in the table represent the data in the ASCII file.

Record 1	Record 2	Record 3	Record 4	Record 5
McCue	Rivas	Vallez	Howley	Nicoles
Jim	Carl	Paul	Scott	Jennifer
12 Tree Rd.	14 Cox Ave.	325 Shaw Ave.	364 Reece Pl.	9 Kingman Ave.
(408) 555-1245	(408) 555-7425	(408) 555-8026	(408) 555-6224	(408) 555-5001
San Jose	Santa Clara	Saratoga	Cupertino	Sunnyvale
0.12	0.11	0.1	0.12	0.13
Internal Sales	External Sales	Internal Sales	Internal Sales	External Sales
95128	95402	95070	95212	95213
$45,500.00	$35,025.00	$38,560.00	$39,500.00	$37,405.00
9-Jan-94	15-Jun-94	1-May-94	23-Dec-94	5-Jun-94

FIGURE 14.13

This is the spreadsheet used in Figure 14.11. Notice that the column headings go across the top of the spreadsheet in this figure while the same column headings are listed vertically within the first column of the table shown in Figure 14.11.

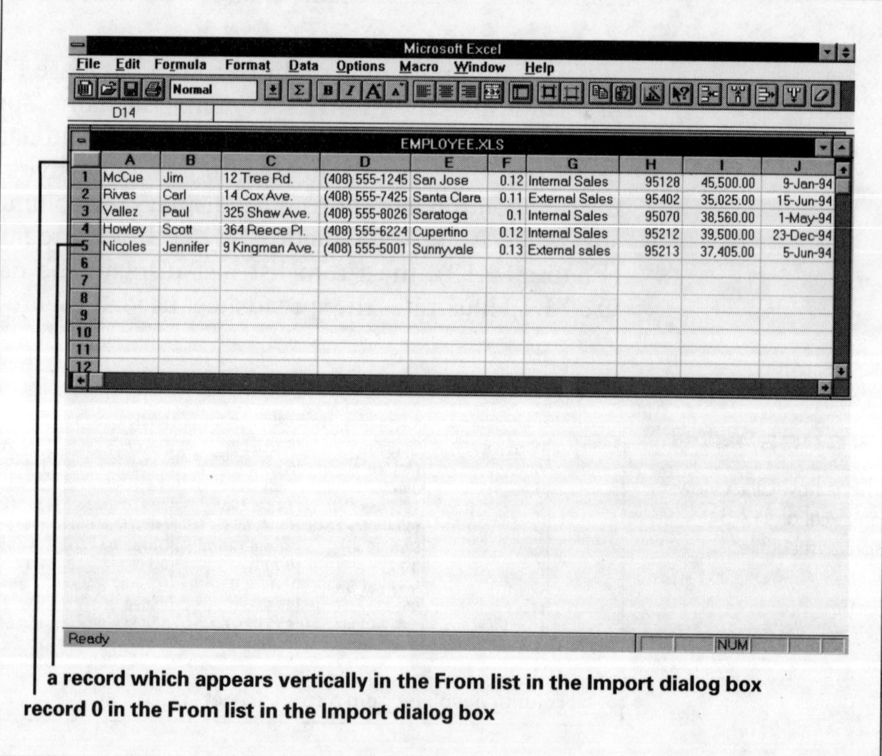

a record which appears vertically in the From list in the Import dialog box

record 0 in the From list in the Import dialog box

column headings go across the top of the spreadsheet in this figure while the same column headings are listed vertically within first column of the table shown in Figure 14.11. This happens because Q&A views each column of data in the spreadsheet as a different field to be imported into your database. The rows of the spreadsheet are viewed as different records.

When importing data from database files, you can use the Match Fields button in the Import dialog box. The Match button automatically matches fields in the From and To lists. For example, if you click this button when importing a Paradox database, if there is a Last Name field in both the From list and the To list, both fields are automatically matched. This can be very useful if you are constantly swapping information between like databases in different database programs.

Continue selecting fields from the To list and the From List, and then clicking on Add. After making your last selection, click on Import. Q&A imports the data into the database continuing from the Import From dialog box. To import data into a Q&A database, follow these steps:

1. In the Import From dialog box, specify the file that contains the data to be imported and click on OK.

   - If you selected any file but an ASCII file, Q&A displays the Import dialog box. Skip to step 2.

   - If you selected an ASCII file, Q&A displays the Text Import Options dialog box. Choose the delimiter that was used when creating the ASCII file. You then see the Import dialog box.

2. In the From list box in the Import dialog box, click on a field name to be imported.

3. In the To list box, select a field into which you want information imported.

4. Click on Add.

5. Repeat steps 2, 3, and 4 until you have specified all the fields to be imported.

6. Click on Import. Q&A imports the data into the specified database.

If you do not know the type of delimiter used in an ASCII import file, you can see it by opening the file using any word processor (for example, Q&A Write).

To Sum Up

This is the first chapter in which you saw how other Windows applications can work with the Q&A Database. In this chapter, you learned how to import and export data between Q&A and other applications. You found that you are not limited to importing and exporting data from other database programs—you can import spreadsheet data and text (ASCII) information as well.

In the next chapter, you'll find out how Q&A Database and Q&A Write work together to create and send form letters and envelopes.

chapter

15

Creating and Editing Mail Merge Documents and Envelopes with Q&A Write

To save a Q&A Write merge list   513

choose File ➤ Save (or press Ctrl+S) or choose File ➤ Save As (or press F12), select ASCII in Save Files of Type, type a file name, making sure that .TXT is the file extension, and either click on OK or press Enter.

To change to a new merge list for a merge document   513

choose Insert ➤ Merge Field or press Ctrl+Shift+M, click on the Change Database button, select a merge list or database, and either click on OK or press Enter.

To create programming statements for merge files   514

choose Insert ➤ Merge Field, choose a database, and either click on OK or press Enter. Click on the Programmed Field button, create a programming formula in the Formula box, and either click on OK or press Enter.

To define a return address   515

choose File ➤ Preferences ➤ Envelope, type your address in the Return Address for Envelopes box, and click on OK.

To create an envelope   516

choose Tools ➤ Create Envelope, and either type the information or choose Insert ➤ Merge Field (or press Ctrl+Shift+M), double-click on the desired field.

ONE of the many advantages of using Q&A is that the two applications—Q&A Database and Q&A Write—work so well together. Q&A Write and optionally Q&A Database allow you to create and send documents that are customized for individuals. By using the mail merge feature, you can automate—yet personalize—a large mailing. In this chapter, you'll learn how to produce form letters and envelopes. (You have already learned how to create mailing labels, another type of form document, in Chapter 9.)

Creating and Editing Mail Merge Documents

The basic components of mail merge are a *merge document* and a *merge list,* which are merged to produce form letters. For the most part, the merge document is like any other Q&A Write document. It contains text for your entire audience (for example, information about a sale or the move to a new office), but omits unique information, such as the name, address, city, state, and ZIP code of the recipient of the letter. You can create a merge document from scratch or by editing an existing document.

The *merge list* contains the unique information about the recipient of each letter. A merge list is all or part of the data in a database—either from Q&A Database, a table that you create in Q&A Write, or information from a different application. In addition to the name and address information previously mentioned, other typical fields in a merge list are amount owed, credit and sales history, date of last contact, and so on.

You can use Q&A programming to insert special messages into a letter, depending on the value in a field. For example, you can create a special mailing for customers who live in a particular area, work in one or two target corporations, or who meet certain criteria (for example, they are late in paying a bill or have spent over a certain amount within the last few months).

The process that Q&A uses to merge Q&A Database information or other data into Q&A Write form letters is known as *mail merge*. The mail merge operation involves retrieving and optionally sorting selected records from the merge list and inserting the information into the merge document. There are endless opportunities for using mail merge to your advantage—at home and in business. Now let's take a look at how this process works in Q&A.

Inserting Merge Fields from a Q&A Database

The first step in mail merge is to create a merge document. You can create a merge document in two ways. You can make room for and insert merge fields to an existing document, or you can create a new document, inserting the merge fields and typing the text as you go. However you create a merge document, there is just one method to insert merge fields.

To insert a merge field into the current merge document, choose Insert ➤ Merge Field or press Ctrl+Shift+M. In the Merge Database dialog box (Figure 15.1), select a database file. For example, to open STAFF.DTF,

The Merge Database dialog box

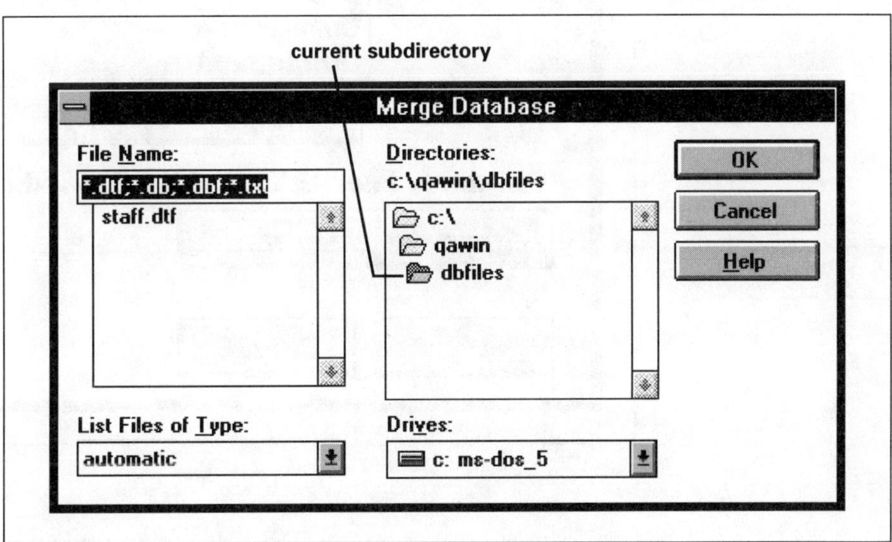

in the <u>D</u>irectories scroll box, double-click on the folder icon representing the subdirectory in which it is located. If you don't see the subdirectory for which you are looking, you may have to double-click on the root directory (in this instance, c:\), and double-click your way down the path until the name of the desired subdirectory is displayed. Double-click on the name of the database file to open it. Q&A opens the Insert Merge Field dialog box (Figure 15.2), which displays all the fields in the open database in the <u>F</u>ieldname scroll box. The Insert Merge Field dialog box contains these options:

<u>F</u>ieldname	Select a field for the merge document from this scroll box.
Programmed Field	Click on this button to write a programming statement for the selected field. You'll find out about mail merge programming later in this chapter.

The Insert Merge Field dialog box lets you select a field to be inserted into your merge document.

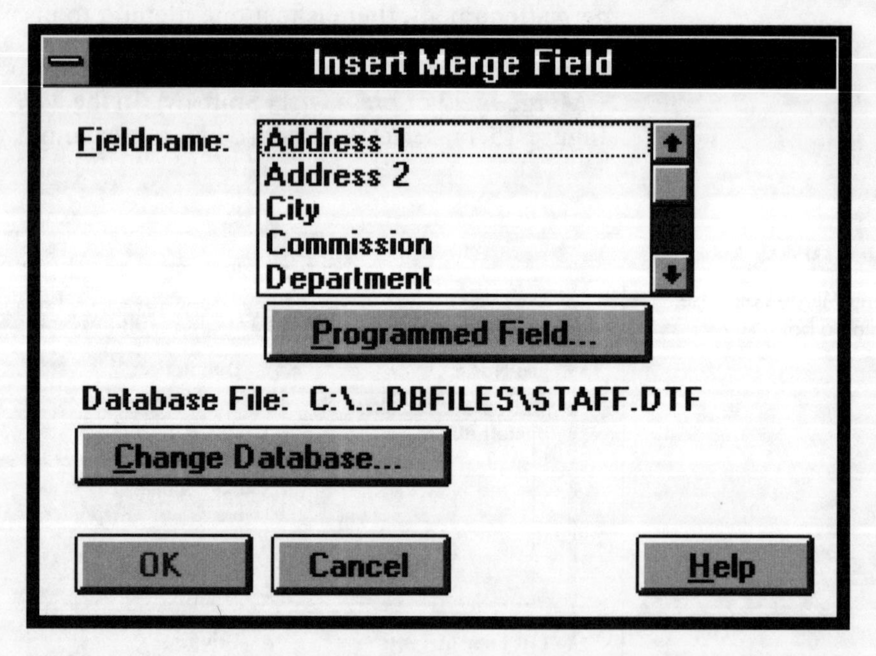

Change Database	Click on this button to open another database from which you can select merge fields.

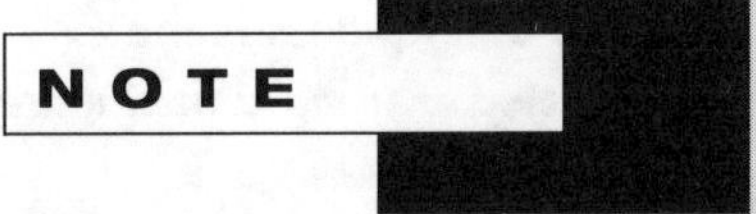

Q&A Database does not have to be open to perform merging and programming operations in Q&A Write.

You can edit the text before or after a merge field once it is inserted in the merge document. For example, you can insert spaces and punctuation between merge fields.

If you want Q&A Write to move the contents of the next field on the line to fill in a blank field, place a line break (press Shift+Enter or choose Insert ➤ Break ➤ Line) instead of pressing Enter at the end of a line. The most common reason for a blank field is the use of two address lines, one for the street address and the other for apartment number or post office box. When the street address is the only address, the second line is blank. To avoid any blank lines in the merge document, add line breaks instead of a carriage return.

To insert a merge field into the current merge document, simply follow these steps:

1. Move the cursor to the location of the merge field in the merge document, and choose Insert ➤ Merge Field or press Ctrl+ Shift+M. Q&A displays the Merge Database dialog box.

2. Select a database file. Q&A opens the Insert Merge Field dialog box.

3. Double-click on the desired field, or select the field and either click on OK or press Enter. Q&A inserts the name of the field surrounded by international quotation marks (» «) into the document at the cursor location.

4. To force Q&A Write to fill in the area representing a blank field, insert a line break rather than a carriage return at the end of each line.

5. Repeat steps 3 and 4 until you have added all the desired merge fields. Figure 15.3 shows a sample merge document.

TIP

Once you have added a merge field to a document, you can cut, copy, and paste it to other places in the document. You are not restricted to using a field more than once.

A merge document is saved like any other document. Choose File ➤ Save (or press Ctrl+S) or File ➤ Save As (or press F12). Name the file as you would any other document, and either click on OK or press Enter.

FIGURE 15.3

A sample merge document. Note that two fields are duplicated, and spaces and punctuation have been inserted between fields. Line breaks replace carriage returns at the end of the name and address merge fields.

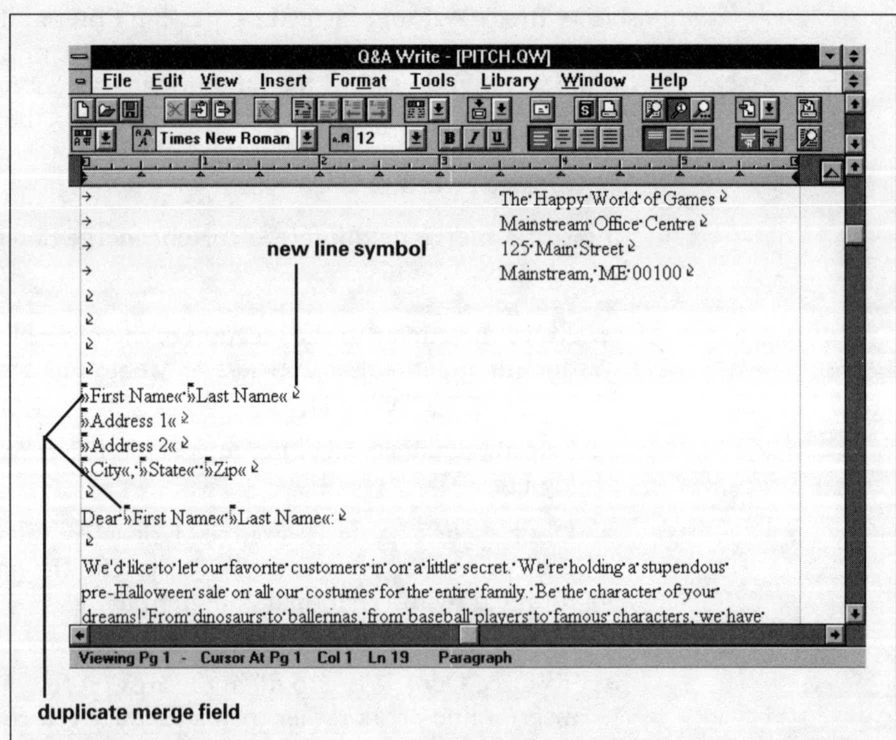

Merging and Printing a Merge Document

When you have finished creating the merge document and are ready to print, choose File ➤ Print Merge. Q&A Write displays the Print Merge dialog box (Figure 15.4), which contains these options:

Copies	Type or select from the text/list box the number of copies (from 1, the default, to 999) of each form letter to be printed.
Pages	Click on either All, the default, to print all pages of a form letter; or Envelope Only, to print envelopes.
Reverse Order	Check to print in reverse order, starting with the last form letter. A clear check box, the default, means that the form letter is printed in order of first to last.

FIGURE 15.4

The Print Merge dialog box

Co<u>l</u>late	Check to collate (print every copy of the first page of the form letter, then every copy of the second page of the form letter, and so on). The default is a clear check box.
<u>D</u>raft Quality	Check to print the merge documents in a draft (lower resolution) format. The default is a clear check box, which means that Q&A prints a higher resolution letter, ready for mailing.
Print <u>E</u>nvelope	Check to print envelopes along with the merge documents. When this check box is clear, the default, Q&A prints only the form letters.
Previe<u>w</u>	Click to see the merge documents on screen as they will print.
<u>P</u>rint	Click or press Enter to print all the merge documents for the records that you have retrieved.

To preview your merge documents before they print, click on Previe<u>w</u>. Before you see a preview (or even print a merge document), Q&A displays the Retrieve dialog box (Figure 15.5), which allows you to merge all records, merge records based on an existing retrieve or sort spec from the Q&A database, or create a retrieve or sort spec.

- To merge all records, either click on OK or press Enter.

- To use an existing retrieve spec, select it from the Save<u>d</u> Retrieves drop-down list box and then either click on OK or press Enter.

- To create a new retrieve spec, use the steps you learned in Chapter 8. Then either click on OK or press Enter.

After reviewing your merge documents, click on the Prin<u>t</u> button at the top of the Print Preview window.

The Retrieve
dialog box

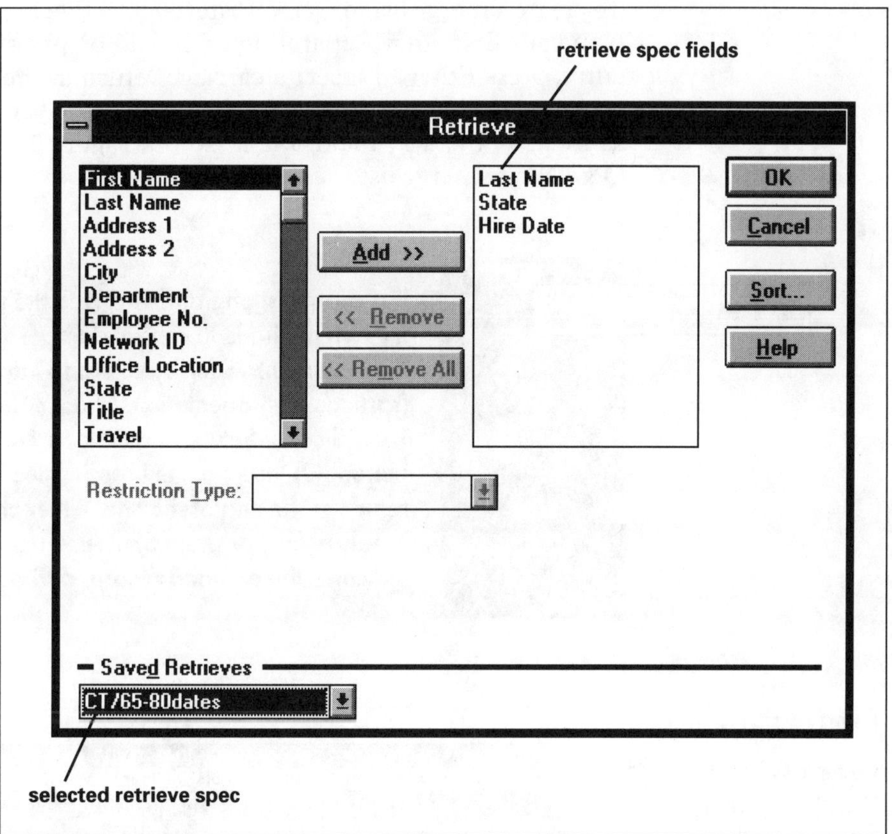

Creating a Merge List in Q&A Write

You don't even have to use a Q&A database to merge information into a document. Instead, on those rare occasions when you don't want to use records from or create a database with Q&A Database, you can create a merge list in Q&A Write. For example, you might want to send out five identical letters to people that you wish to contact one time only. Alternatively, you might have already accumulated the information you want to use for your merge in a Windows spreadsheet application. You can either create a merge list by typing in values or you can copy it from another application using the Windows clipboard feature. For instance, you can copy information from such applications as Excel, Quattro Pro, or Word for Windows. You can use Q&A Write to edit any information that you copy from another Windows application.

CREATING AND EDITING MAIL MERGE DOCUMENTS AND ENVELOPES WITH Q&A WRITE

To create a merge list in Q&A Write, choose File ➤ New. In the work area, type your first entry, separating each field by pressing Tab. After the last entry, press Enter to insert a carriage return at the end of the line. Type each succeeding record on a line by itself. Q&A Write identifies each field as Field 1, Field 2, Field 3, and so on. Figure 15.6 illustrates a sample Q&A Write merge list.

TIP

If a record is long and wraps to the next line, you can try two methods to control document format: (1) Make the document wider by selecting landscape (spreadsheet) orientation. Choose File ➤ Print Setup. Then click on Setup, and click on the Landscape radio button. (2) Insert a line break instead of a carriage return at the end of the line. Either choose Insert ➤ Break ➤ Line or press Shift+Enter. A carriage return indicates the end of a record, and a line break does not.

FIGURE 15.6

A sample Q&A Write merge list

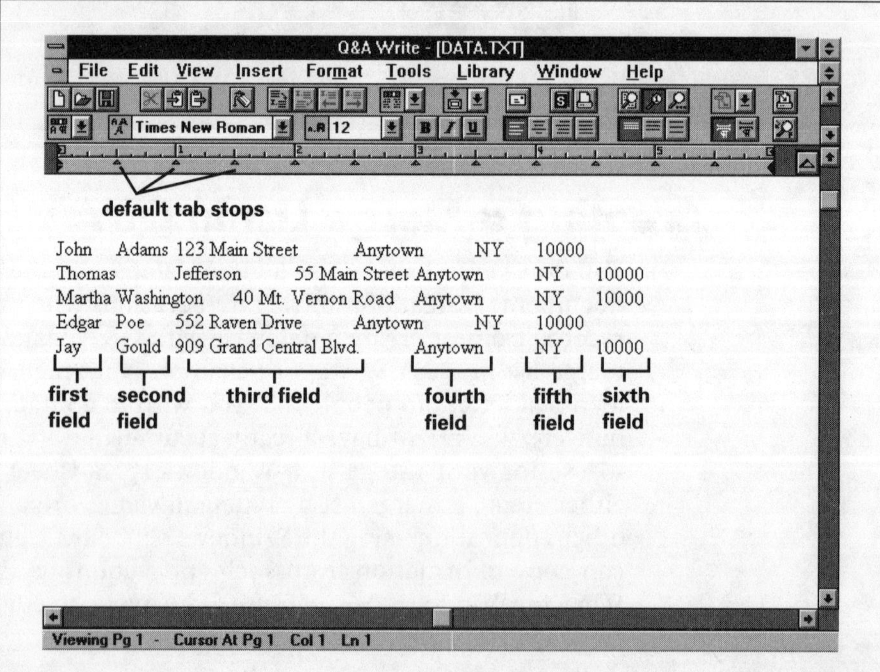

Save the merge list by choosing File ➤ Save (or pressing Ctrl+S) or choosing File ➤ Save As (or pressing F12). In the Save Document dialog box, select ASCII in Save Files of Type. This removes most Q&A Write formats from the merge list so that there is no possibility of inserting hidden symbols into the merge document during the merge. (This also removes tab stops that you inserted in the merge list leaving you with a merge list with Q&A's default tab stops.) Then type a file name in the File Name text box, making sure that .TXT is the file extension. Either click on OK or press Enter.

You can either create a new merge document or use an existing one, as you learned in the "Inserting Merge Fields from a Q&A Database" section earlier in this chapter.

If you use an existing merge document, you may have to change from the database file with which it is currently associated to your new merge list. To do this, choose Insert ➤ Merge Field or press Ctrl+Shift+M; in the Insert Merge Field dialog box, click on the Change Database button. In the Merge Database dialog box, in the List Files of Type drop-down list box, select ASCII, and from the File Name text/list box, select the merge list that you just created. Either click on OK or press Enter.

To merge and print, choose File ➤ Print Merge, following the instructions in "Merging and Printing a Mail Merge Document."

Mail Merge Programming

To take full advantage of mail merge, you can create programming statements for merge list that are based on Q&A Database databases. For complete information about writing Q&A programming statements, see Chapter 11.

When you create a mail merge programming formula, you can only use functions; IF THEN statements and commands are not allowed in Q&A Write programming. In addition, you cannot use field IDs as you can in Q&A database programming. Other than those restrictions, creating a Write programming formula is very similar to creating Q&A form programming statements. Table 15.1 provides two examples of mail merge programming. Notice that the statements in Figure 15.1 don't begin with a field ID or an equal sign. Also notice that the statements are not surrounded by brackets.

TABLE 15.1: Examples of Valid Write Programming Statements

PROGRAMMING STATEMENT	DESCRIPTION
@DATE-6	Merges the current date minus six days.
Commissionx1200	Merges the value of the commission field times a hypothetical twelve hundred dollar sale.

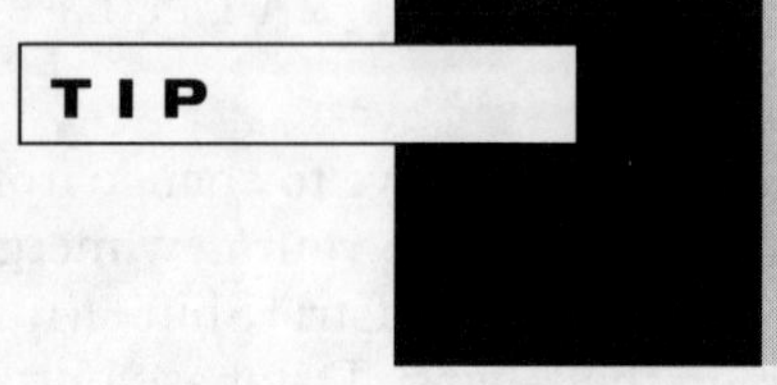

T I P   If you need to merge field values from multiple databases, use mail merge programming to create an @XLOOKUP to a field in another database. For information about @XLOOKUP, see Appendix D.

To create a mail merge programming statement, follow these steps:

1. Choose Insert ➤ Merge Field. Q&A displays the Merge Database dialog box.

2. Choose a Q&A Database file and either click on OK or press Enter. Q&A displays the Insert Merge Field dialog box.

3. Click on the Programmed Field button. (This feature is only available when merged from a Q&A database; if the button is dimmed, it's probably because the current merge list is not a Q&A Database file.) Q&A displays the Program Helper dialog box (Figure 15.7).

4. Create your programming formula in the Formula box.

5. Either click on OK or press Enter.

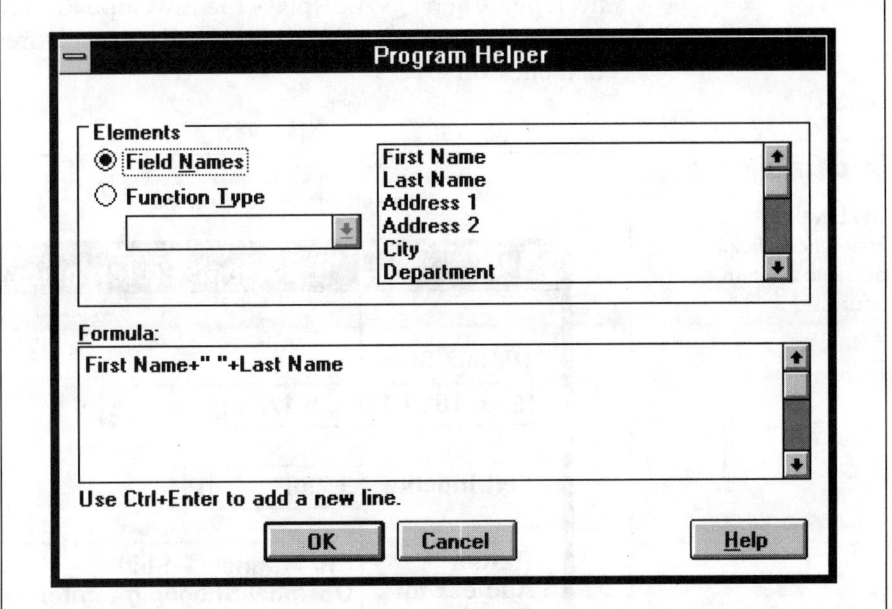

Creating and Printing Envelopes

In the age of typewriters, it was very easy to produce a single envelope for a letter. Now creating and printing envelopes on a computer frightens many people. But with Q&A Write, turning out envelopes is both quick and easy.

Q&A Write provides three options for creating and printing envelopes: single customized envelopes, merge envelopes associated with merge documents, and merge envelopes not associated with merge documents. Before you get started, you may want to specify a default return address.

Defining a Return Address

Unless you explicitly provide a return address, the upper left corner of envelopes are blank. This is acceptable if your stationery is preprinted. However, if you buy blank envelopes, Q&A Write allows you to add a default return address to your preferences. Simply choose File ➤ Preferences ➤

Envelope. When Q&A displays the Envelope Preferences dialog box (Figure 15.8), type your address in the Return Address for Envelopes box. Then click on OK.

The Envelope Preferences dialog box with a return address

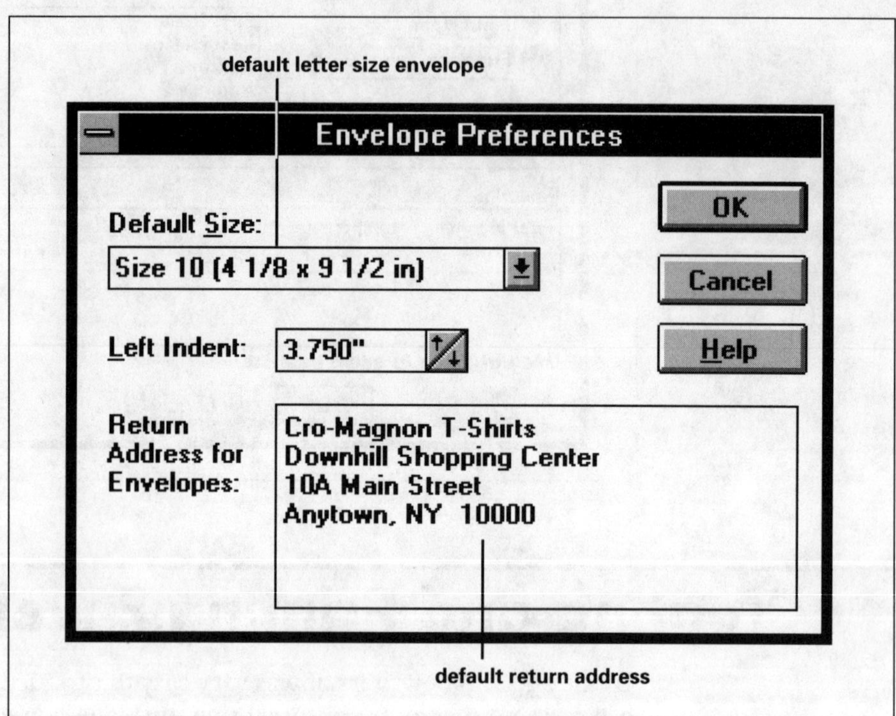

Creating an Individual Envelope

There are two ways to create an envelope in which to send a single letter: select the name and address from the current document, or type the name and address information on the envelope.

 If you typed a letter using Q&A Write, select the name and address on the letter (Figure 15.9), choose Tools ➤ Create Envelope or click on the Envelope

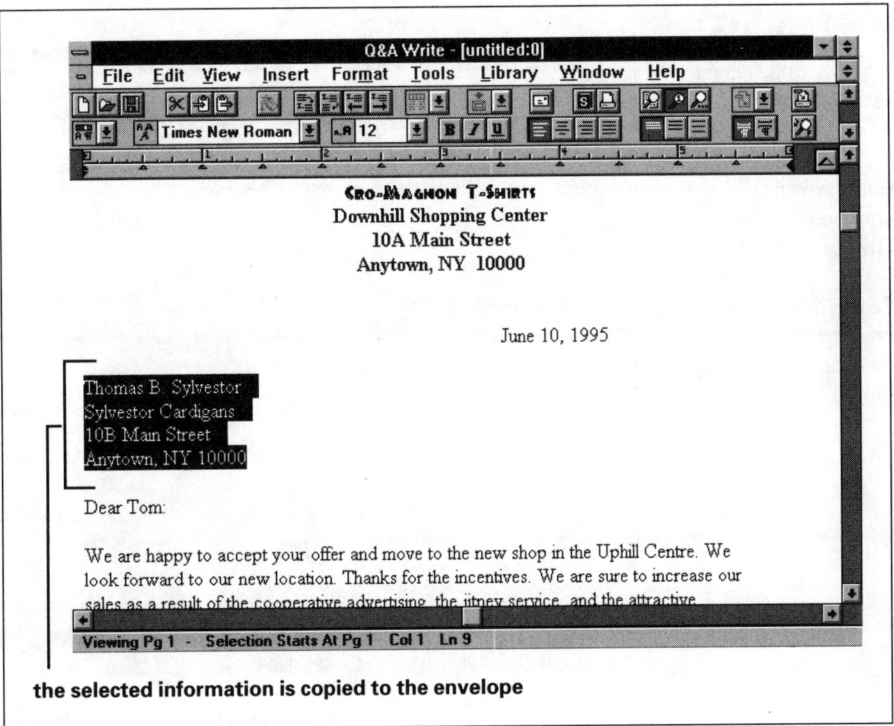

the selected information is copied to the envelope

button on the tool bar. Q&A Write attaches an envelope (Figure 15.10)
to the document.

> **N O T E**
>
> You can edit an envelope the same way you edit any
> other Q&A Write document. To edit an envelope
> associated with the current document, choose Tools ➤
> Edit Envelope.

Q&A does not allow you to create an envelope without having it attached
to a document. So when you wish to create an individual envelope without an associated letter, choose File ➤ New or press Ctrl+N to open a
new document. Then choose Tools ➤ Create Envelope or click on the
Envelope button on the tool bar, and type the name and address information on the envelope.

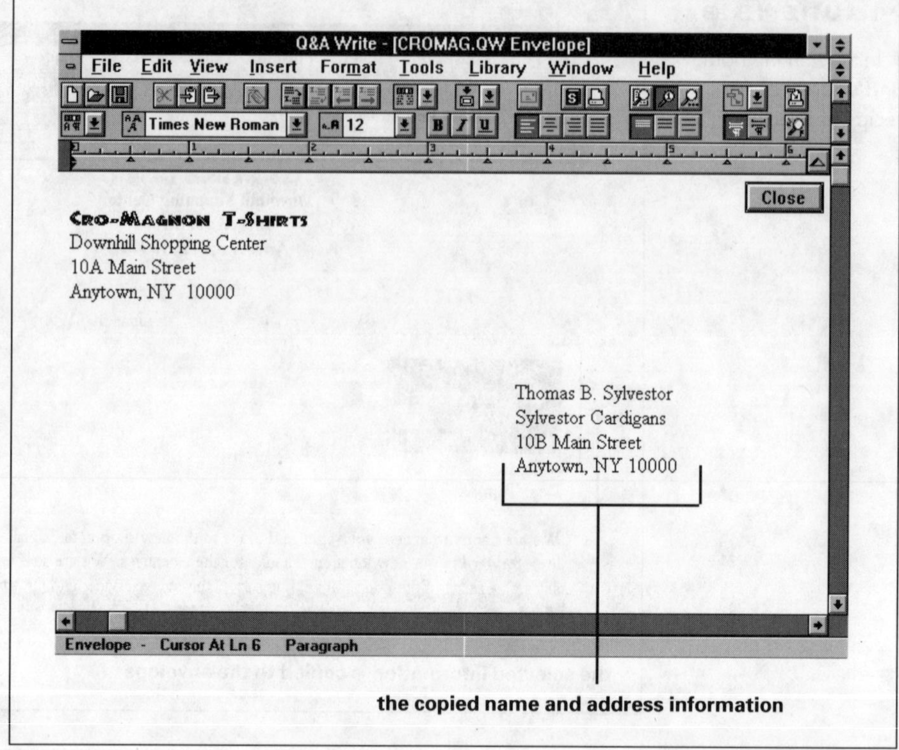

the copied name and address information

After you complete the envelope, return to the current document by clicking on the Close button. To remove an envelope, choose Tools ➤ Delete Envelope.

Creating a Merge Envelope for a Merge Document

Creating a merge envelope attached to a merge document is almost the same as creating a merge document. However, because a database is already associated with the merge document, there is no needed to select another one. To create a merge envelope for a merge document, open an existing merge document and follow these steps:

1. Choose Tools ➤ Create Envelope or click on the Envelope button on the tool bar. Q&A opens an envelope and places the cursor at

the first line of the recipient information area. If you have specified a return address, it appears in the upper left corner of the envelope.

2. If needed, move the cursor to the location of the merge field in the envelope, and choose Insert ➤ Merge Field or press Ctrl+Shift+M.

3. Double-click on the desired field, or select the field and either click on OK or press Enter. Q&A inserts the name of the field surrounded by international quotation marks (» «) into the document at the cursor location.

4. To force Q&A Write to fill in the area representing a blank field, insert a line break rather than a carriage return at the end of each line.

5. Repeat steps 3 and 4 until you have added all the desired merge fields. Figure 15.11 shows a sample merge envelope.

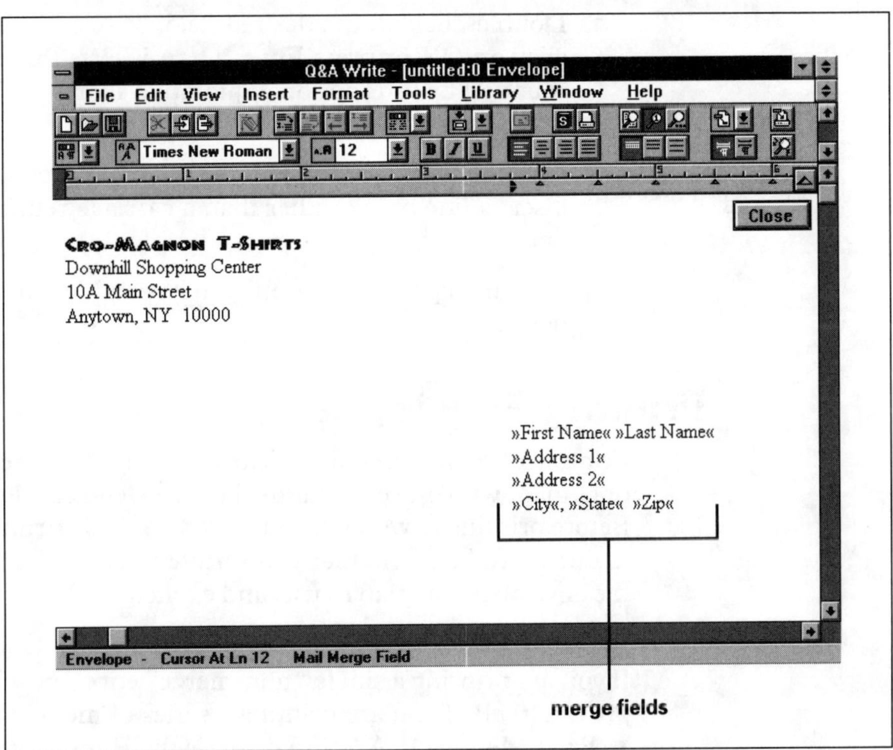

Creating a Merge Envelope Without a Merge Document

Creating a merge envelope without an associated merge document is similar to creating a new merge document. Remember that every envelope must be associated with a document, so open a new document and follow these steps:

1. Choose Tools ➤ Create Envelope or click on the Envelope button on the tool bar. Q&A opens an envelope and places the cursor at the first line of the recipient information area. If you specified a return address, it appears in the upper left corner of the envelope.

2. If needed, move the cursor to the location of the merge field in the envelope, and choose Insert ➤ Merge Field or press Ctrl+Shift+M. Q&A displays the Merge Database dialog box.

3. Select a database file. Q&A opens the Insert Merge Field dialog box.

4. Double-click on the desired field, or select the field and either click on OK or press Enter. Q&A inserts the name of the field surrounded by international quotation marks (» «) into the document at the cursor location.

5. To force Q&A Write to fill in the area representing a blank field, insert a line break rather than a carriage return at the end of each line.

6. Repeat steps 4 and 5 until you have added all the desired merge fields.

Printing Envelopes

Printing envelopes in Q&A Write is exactly the same as printing any other document with one exception—how you feed envelopes into your printer. Before printing envelopes, you *must* read the instructions in your printer's manual. Find out whether your printer can handle the size and weight of the envelopes you plan to use, and explicitly follow the directions for feeding and printing envelopes.

If you are printing a single "non-merge" envelope, choose File ➤ Print or press Ctrl+P. If you are printing a series of merge envelopes, choose File ➤ Print Merge. Q&A Write displays the Print Merge dialog box.

- To merge all records, either click on OK or press Enter.

- To use an existing retrieve spec, select it from the Saved Retrieves drop-down list box and then either click on OK or press Enter.

- To create a new retrieve spec, use the steps you learned in Chapter 8. Then either click on OK or press Enter.

After reviewing your merge envelopes, feed in an envelope and click on the Print button at the top of the Print Preview window.

To Sum Up

In this chapter, you learned how Q&A Database and Q&A Write work together to create merge letters, single envelopes, and merge envelopes.

In the next chapter, you will learn how important it is to secure a database, the types of security that Q&A provides, and how to use passwords, specify user IDs, and set access limits to secure a database.

chapter

16

Securing a Database

● **To create a user group**   **529**

choose <u>S</u>elect ➤ Database <u>S</u>tructure, if needed. Choose Secu-ri<u>t</u>y ➤ <u>U</u>sers and Groups. Click the <u>N</u>ew button. Type a group name in the <u>G</u>roup Name box. To change the access rights of a field, select that field from the <u>D</u>atabase Field Access list. Then, from the Field Access Rights box, click the radio button representing the type of access you want for that field. Click on OK.

● **To create a user ID**   **534**

choose Security ➤ <u>U</u>sers and Groups while in Database Structure mode. Choose the group in which you want to create a user ID. Click Ne<u>w</u>. In the <u>U</u>ser ID box, type the user identification. Enter the password for that user ID in the <u>P</u>ass-word box. Check the access rights for the user. Click <u>A</u>dd and click on Don<u>e</u>.

● **To find a user ID in all your groups**   **536**

open the Users & Groups dialog box by choosing Securi<u>t</u>y ➤ <u>U</u>sers and Groups while in Database Structure mode. Click on <u>F</u>ind. In the <u>F</u>ind User box, type the name of the user ID for which you are looking. Click on OK.

● **To move a user ID to a different group**   **538**

while in the Users & Groups dialog box, select the user ID to be moved and click on <u>M</u>ove. Select the group in which you want the user ID. Click on OK.

To copy a user ID   **539**

while in the Users & Groups dialog box, select the user ID to be copied. Click on <u>C</u>opy. Type a user ID for the new user. Click on OK.

To open a password-protected database   **541**

select <u>F</u>ile ➤ <u>O</u>pen. Select the database to be opened. In the User ID and Password dialog box, enter a valid user ID and password and click OK.

To set up an automatically assigned user ID and password   **542**

choose <u>F</u>ile ➤ Pre<u>f</u>erences. Click on the Database category. In the <u>U</u>ser ID text box, type the user ID for a user opening the database. In the <u>P</u>assword text box, type a password. Click on OK.

To set up a Xlookup Password   **545**

choose Securi<u>t</u>y ➤ <u>X</u>lookup Password while in Database Structure mode. In the <u>U</u>ser ID box, enter the user ID used to gain access to the external database. In the <u>P</u>assword box, type the password for that user ID. Click OK.

To add a database lock   **549**

choose Securi<u>t</u>y ➤ <u>D</u>atabase Lock from Database Structure mode. From the Allow Users To group, choose the access rights for database users. Type a password in the Database Lock <u>P</u>assword box. Check the <u>E</u>nable Lock check box to activate the database Lock for all users. Click on OK.

DATABASES are excellent for storing confidential data. To protect your data from being erased, altered, or viewed, Q&A provides a range of security options, such as preventing either entering a database or editing a lookup table. The passwords with which you lock your databases are encrypted and hidden within the database file. This makes malicious or mischievous attempts to break into a database almost impossible.

Q&A's Security Types

There are two different types of security for your databases: Users & Groups and Database Lock. Both of these security options are controlled from the Security menu in the Database Structures mode.

- The Users and Groups security option allows you to create groups of users who have access to a variety of features and modes in the database. You can limit each group and user ID in different ways. Use this type of security mainly for protecting the data in your database.

- The Database Lock security option prevents *all* users from using particular Q&A features and modes. With this feature, all users have the same limitations. Use a database lock to protect the design of your database.

Securing Your Database with Users & Groups

Use the Users & Groups security option to deny database access to certain users, create groups of users with a variety of access privileges, or set read-only and no access fields. This form of database security is used more than a database lock because it allows you to create passwords with a variety of limitations for different groups and individual users. For example, you can create a password-protected database that allows the managers in a single department to view all the fields in the database while hiding the salary field from users in other departments.

Creating User Groups

The first step toward protecting a database with the Users & Groups option is to create a *group*, which is a category that contains the identifications and passwords of different database users.

If, for example, you don't want a marketing employee to see a field named Employee Evaluation, you can create a group called Marketing and define that field as hidden. Therefore, anyone using a password and user ID contained in the Marketing group cannot see or access the Employee Evaluation field.

Table 16.1 describes the Field Access Rights you can define for a field.

TABLE 16.1: Q&A Field Access Levels

ACCESS RIGHT	ICON	CLICK ON THIS RADIO BUTTON TO:
Read/Write	🔒	Gives the group complete rights to the field; users can read and change information.
Read Only	✎	Allows users to read— but not change— information in the field.
No Access	✘	Prevents users from reading and changing information in the field in any mode.

The icon preceding each field name in the <u>D</u>atabase Field Access list specifies the field access rights for that field. When you select a field and change its access rights in the Field Access Rights group, the icon changes accordingly. You can also change the field access rights by double-clicking on the field name in the <u>D</u>atabase Field Access list box. Every time you double-click a field name in this list box, the field access rights change.

The Administrator and Unassigned Users Groups

The Administrator and Unassigned User groups are predefined groups in the <u>G</u>roups drop-down list box in the Users & Groups dialog box. Each of these groups has a special purpose:

- The Administrator group contains the access IDs of the users with complete rights to the database. You must check the box marked "Can assign password rights." You'll find out more about this when you learn how to create user IDs and passwords.

- The Unassigned Users group contains the user IDs that you do not want to assign to a particular group. This group can also serve as a temporary holding group until you decide where to place unassigned users.

Both these groups have Read/Write access to all fields. To create a group, follow these steps:

1. If you are not already in Database Structure view, choose Select ➤ Database Structure.

2. Choose Security ➤ Users and Groups. Q&A displays the Users & Groups dialog box (Figure 16.1).

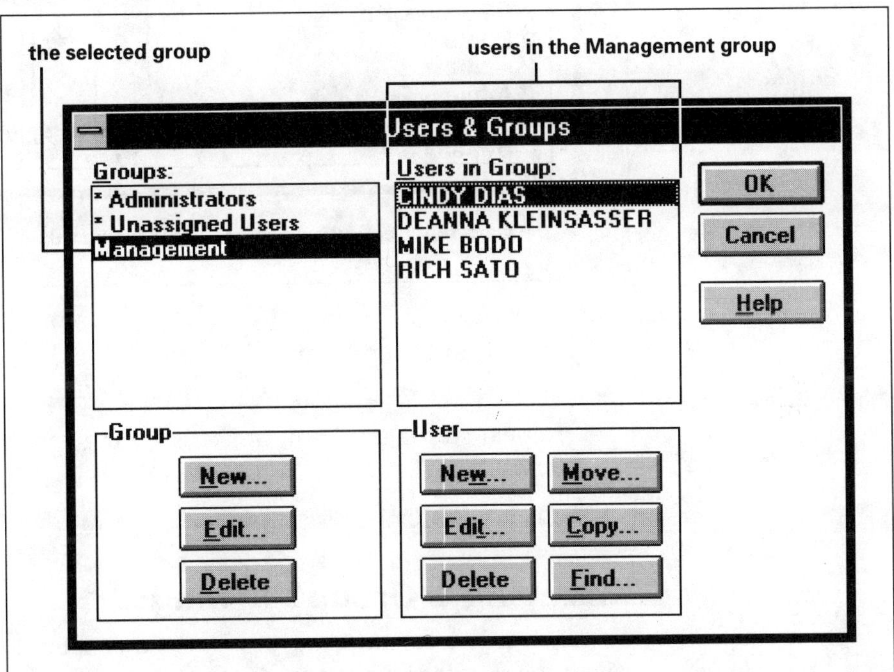

3. Click on the New button in the Group box. Q&A displays the New Group dialog box (Figure 16.2).

4. Type a group name in the Group Name box.

5. To give a field special access rights, select it from the Database Field Access list, and in the Field Access Rights box, click on the

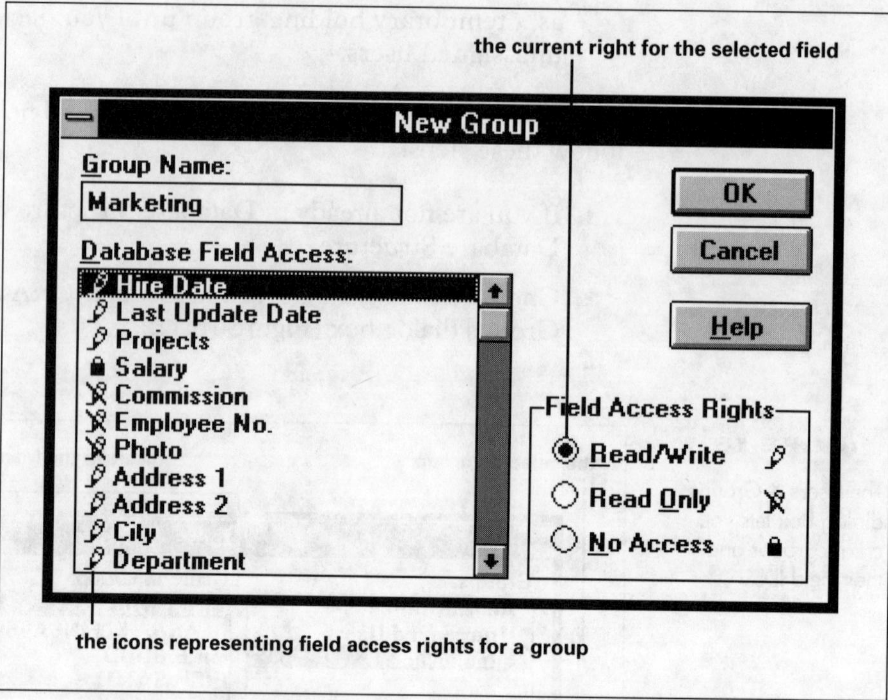

radio button representing the type of access you want for that field.

6. Repeat step 5 until you finish assigning access rights for your fields.

7. Click on OK or press Enter.

Changing a Group's Settings

If you decide to change a group's name or alter a group's access rights, select the group and click on the Edit button in the Group box in the Users & Groups dialog box. Q&A displays the Edit Group dialog box (Figure 16.3), which is almost identical to the New Group dialog box. However, this dialog box contains the group settings selected in the Groups list box. Make your changes in the Edit Group dialog box and either click on OK or press Enter.

FIGURE 16.3

The Edit Group dialog box, which is virtually identical to the New Group dialog box, contains the settings for an already created group.

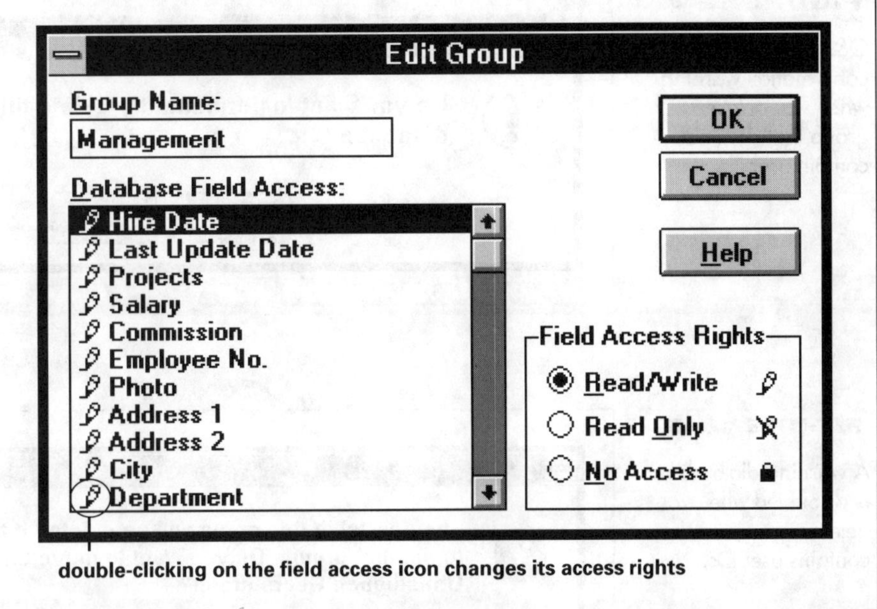

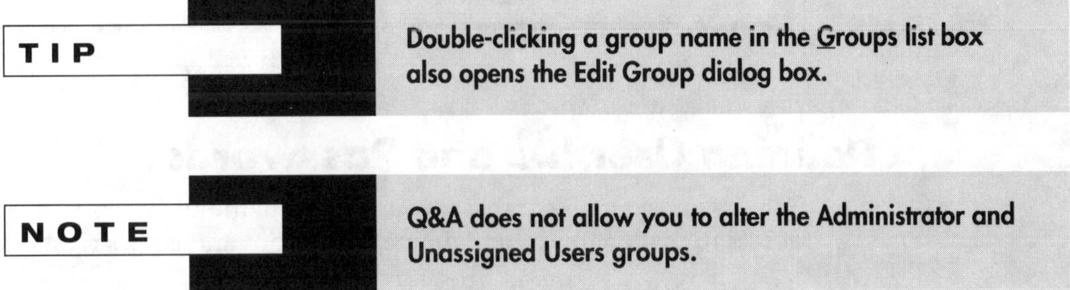

TIP

Double-clicking a group name in the Groups list box also opens the Edit Group dialog box.

NOTE

Q&A does not allow you to alter the Administrator and Unassigned Users groups.

Deleting a Group

To delete a group, select it from the Groups list box and click on the Delete button. Before Q&A performs the deletion, it prompts you (Figure 16.4). If the group contains user IDs, Q&A asks you if you want to keep them (Figure 16.5). If you click on Yes, Q&A places the user IDs in the Unassigned Users group. If you choose No, Q&A deletes both the user IDs and the group. Choose Cancel to stop the deletion.

FIGURE 16.4

Q&A displays a confirmation warning when you delete a group that does not contain user IDs.

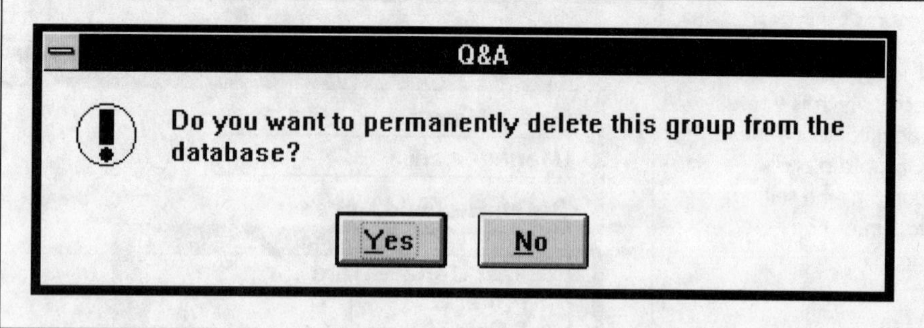

FIGURE 16.5

A warning dialog box is displayed when you delete a group that contains user IDs.

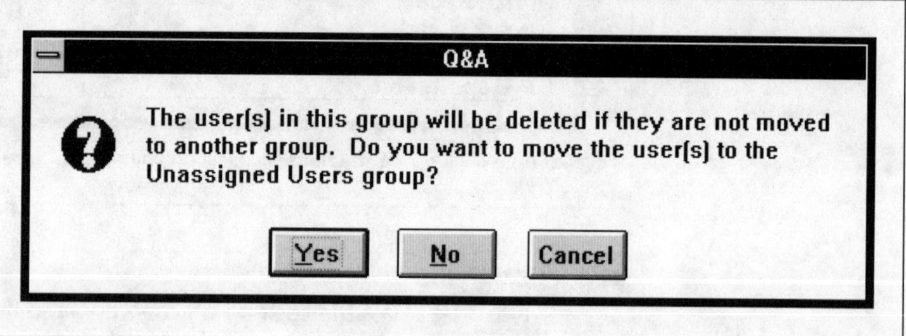

Defining User IDs and Passwords

When you secure a database, you need to name the users that can have access to that database, and define a password and access rights for each.

The *User ID* identifies the user. You can use a name, word, or any combination of characters as a user ID. For example, for a user named David Wyllie, assign a user ID of Dave Wyllie, DWyllie, Dave W, or some other unique name.

When someone enters his or her user ID, Q&A asks the user to enter a password. This avoids the situation in which an unauthorized user knows a user ID but not the password. The password, like the user ID, should be easy for the user to remember.

When you assign a password and user ID, you can also specify the access rights a user has for the database. Unlike the field access rights in the Edit

Group or New Group dialog boxes, the access rights defined when creating a user ID control whether the user can perform actions that affect the entire database, such as performing a mass update or designing a report.

Q&A access rights in the New User dialog box are:

- Checking the Can Assign Password Rights check box allows a user to access the Security menu from Database Structure view. If the check box is not checked for this user, Q&A removes the Security menu, making it inaccessible. Only a user ID in the Administrators group can access the Can Assign Password Rights option. If you try to assign this right to a user ID not in the Administrators group, Q&A moves the user ID there. If you remove this right from a user ID in the Administrators group, Q&A moves the user ID into the Unassigned User group. At least one user ID must have the Can Assign Password Rights check box checked, or Q&A will not let you leave the Users & Groups dialog box. Otherwise, once you exited the dialog box, nobody would be able to access the Security menu again.

- Checking the Can Change Design and Program box lets the user alter the database structure through the Database menu. If this check box is not checked, the user cannot access any Database menu commands and Q&A locks all the columns in Database Structure view. If both the Can Change Design and Program check box and the Can Assign Password Rights check box are unchecked, the user cannot access Database Structure mode.

- Checking the Can Mass Delete check box allows the user to perform a mass delete.

- Checking the Can Delete Individual Records check box allows a user to delete records from the database in Add/Edit mode.

- Checking the Can Mass Update check box allows the user to perform mass updates.

- Checking the Can Design Reports and Forms check box allows the user to create reports and input forms.

- Checking the Can Enter/Edit Data check box allows the user to add records to the database and to edit existing records.

When you create a user ID in a group, the user is limited to the access rights assigned to his or her user ID as well as the field access rights assigned to his or her group.

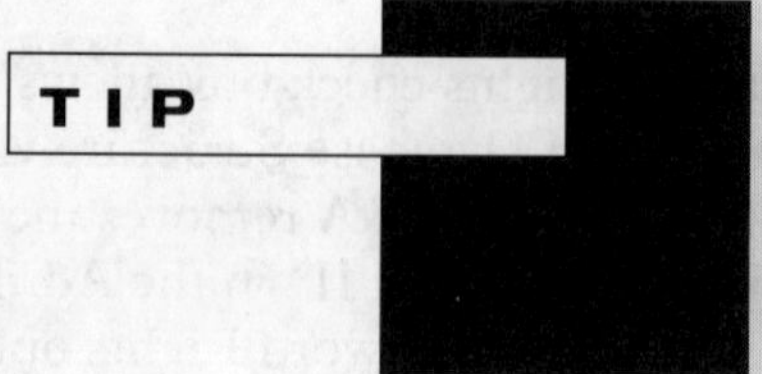

Since passwords are assigned to each user ID, users need not be concerned if someone knows his or her user ID. Therefore, we recommend that you standardize user IDs. This makes it easier for users to remember them.

Once you create a password in the Users & Groups dialog box, nobody can open that database unless they have a user ID and password. To create a user ID, follow these steps:

1. If you are not already in Database Structure view, choose <u>S</u>elect ➤ Database <u>S</u>tructure.

2. Choose Securi<u>t</u>y ➤ <u>U</u>sers and Groups. Q&A displays the Users & Groups dialog box.

3. Choose the group in which you want to create a user ID and password.

4. Click on Ne<u>w</u> from the User box. Q&A displays the New User dialog box (Figure 16.6).

5. In the <u>U</u>ser ID box, type the user ID, enter the password for that user ID in the <u>P</u>assword box, select the appropriate access rights, and click on <u>A</u>dd to add the user to the group.

6. Repeat steps 3, 4, and 5 until you have added all the users to the group.

7. When you have completed adding users, click on the Don<u>e</u> button.

FIGURE 16.6

The New User dialog box in which you define a new user and his or her password and access rights

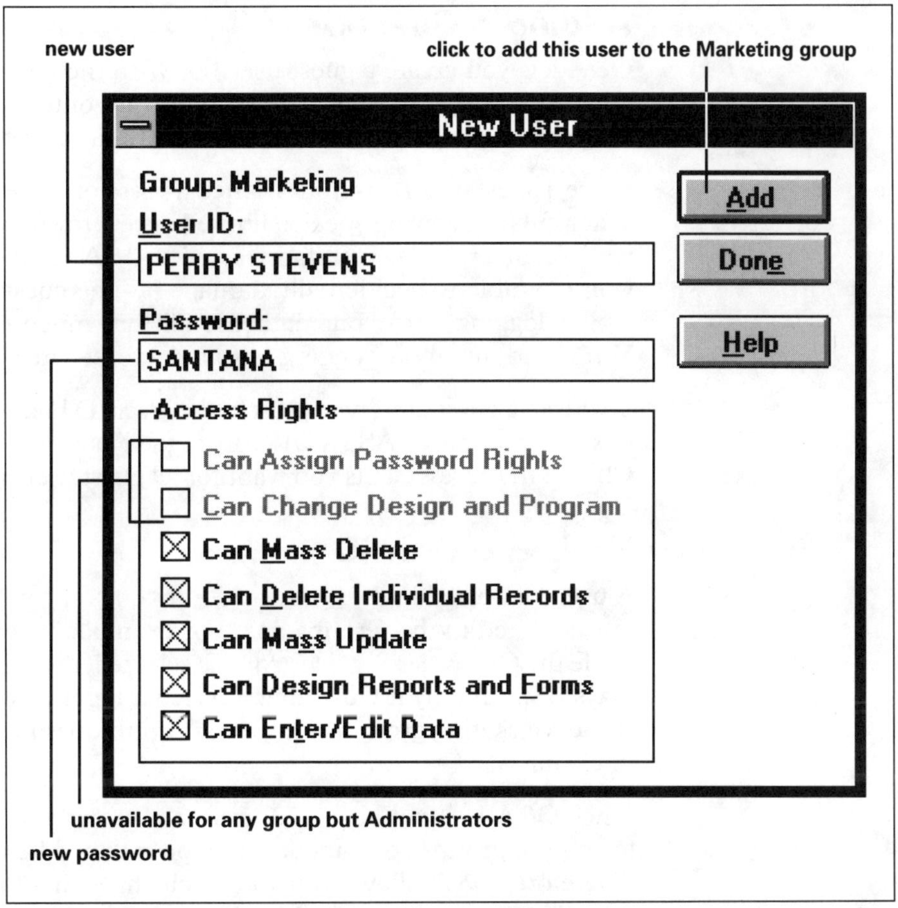

TIP

Users can accidentally lock themselves out of their databases by quickly defining a user ID and exiting the Users & Groups dialog box. The reason they are locked out is that they didn't assign their user ID a password. When you create a new user, Q&A sets the password to PASSWORD. If you ever lock yourself out of your database by defining a user ID and not a password, try *PASSWORD* as your password.

Adding a Guest User

Q&A lets you create a guest user ID. With the guest user ID, you do not need to assign a password, making logging onto a database easier. Logging onto a database is described later in this chapter.

Since a guest user ID is not assigned a password, the guest user ID feature is helpful for allowing special, limited access to your database. Therefore, when someone who is unfamiliar with Q&A views your data, he or she won't be able to accidentally damage it. The guest user ID feature also makes logging onto your database all that much easier for such users. You'll find out about logging onto a database later in this chapter.

To create a guest user, type guest in the User ID box of the New User dialog box. Then remove PASSWORD from the Password box and leave it blank. Choose the access rights you want for all guest users and click on OK.

Finding a User ID

A user is inserted in the Users in Group box only if the group it is defined in is selected in the Groups box. For example, if you add a user BSmith while the Customer Service group is selected, the Users in Group box displays BSmith only if Customer Service is highlighted in the Groups box. If the Marketing group is selected, BSmith does not appear in the Users in Group box.

Since Q&A lets you have 120 users per group and a total of 1000 users for all the groups combined, it can be rather difficult to find a user ID. Therefore, Q&A allows you to search through all groups looking for a user. When you click on the Find button, Q&A displays the Find User dialog box (Figure 16.7). In the Find User box, type the name of the user ID for which you are looking, and click on OK. If Q&A finds the user ID, it displays the Users & Groups dialog box with the user ID and group highlighted. If the user does not exist, Q&A issues a message and returns to the Find User dialog box (Figure 16.8).

FIGURE 16.7

The Find User dialog box lets you search for a user ID.

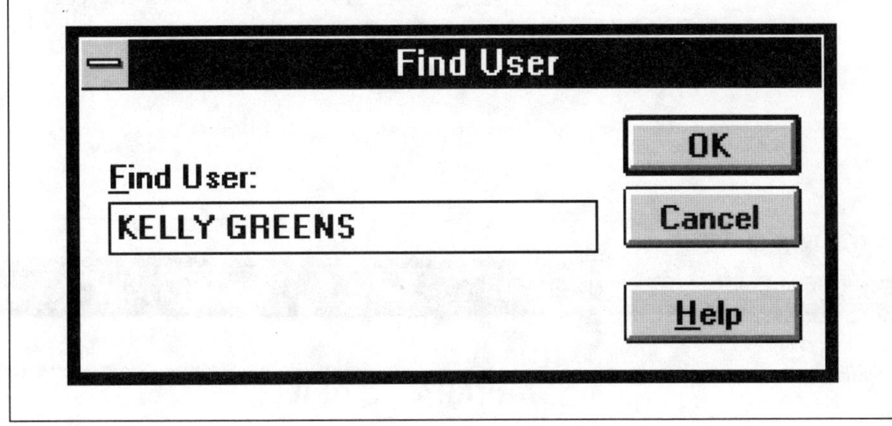

FIGURE 16.8

If Q&A does not find the user ID, it displays this warning.

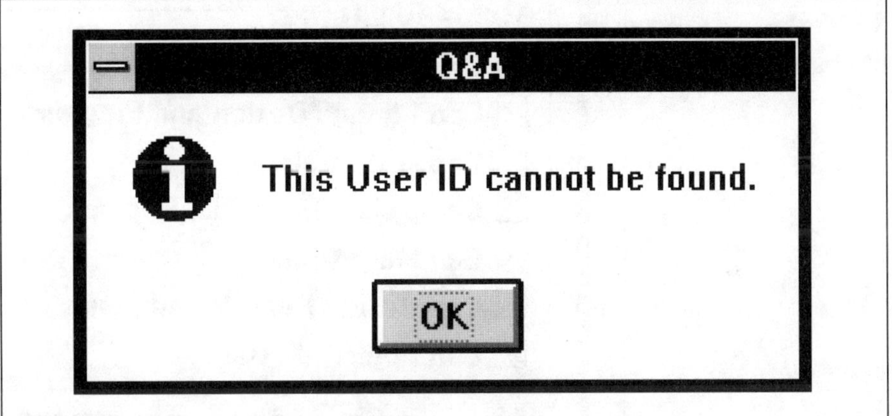

Editing a User ID's Security Settings

To change security settings (also referred to as access rights) for a user ID, use the Edit User dialog box (Figure 16.9). Follow these steps:

1. If you are not already in Database Structure view, choose <u>S</u>elect ➤ Database <u>S</u>tructure.

2. Choose Security ➤ <u>U</u>sers and Groups. Q&A displays the Users & Groups dialog box.

3. Choose the user ID to be edited in the Users in Group box.

4. Click on the Edit button from the User box. Q&A displays the Edit User dialog box (Figure 16.9).

5. Make your changes and click on OK.

Use the Edit User dialog box to change a user's security settings.

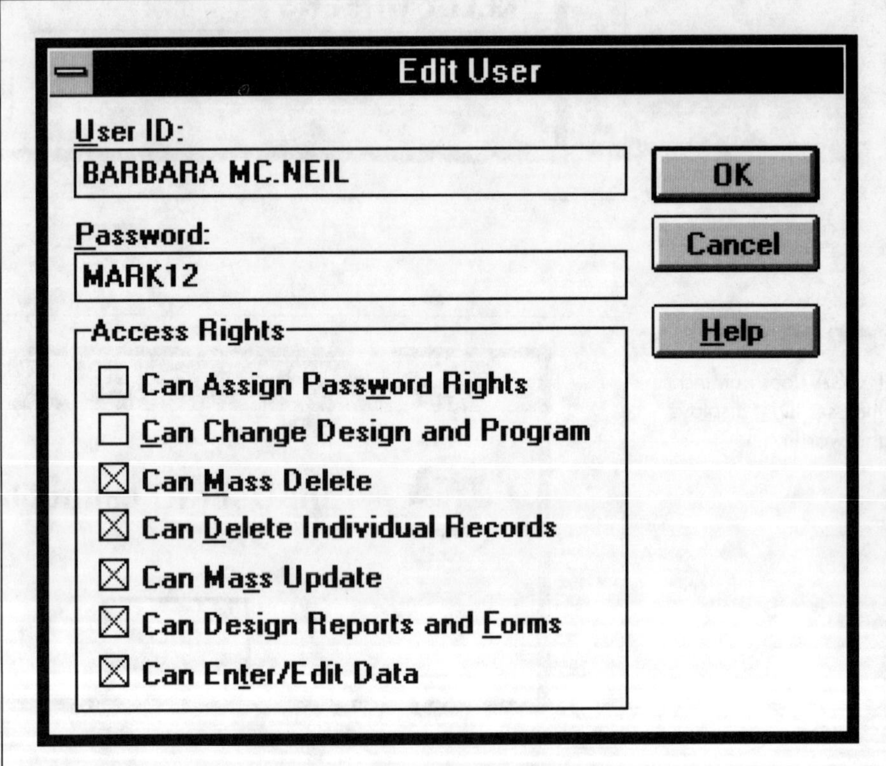

Moving a User ID to a Different Group

You have already learned how Q&A automatically moves users from one group to another. You can also move a user ID into a different group to change field access rights or to place the user ID with other, similar user IDs. In the Users & Groups dialog box, select the user ID you want to move and click Move. When Q&A displays the Move User dialog box (Figure 16.10), select the group to which you want to move the user ID, and click on OK.

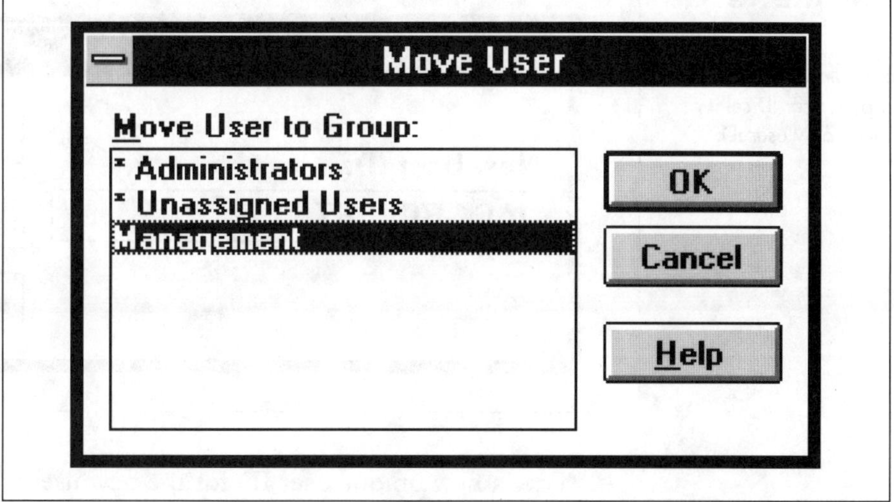

If you move a user ID out of the Administrators group, Q&A automatically removes the Can Assign Password Rights and Can Change Design and Program rights. If you move a user ID into the Administrators group, it automatically gains those rights.

Copying a User ID

To ease the task of creating multiple security settings for groups, Q&A lets you copy other user IDs. Since a group may contain many users with the same settings, this feature is very helpful in designing security for a widely used database.

When you copy a user ID, you are actually copying its security settings to a new user ID. To copy a user ID, follow these steps:

1. If you are not already in Database Structure view, choose Select ➤ Database Structure.

2. Choose Security ➤ Users and Groups. Q&A displays the Users & Groups dialog box.

3. Select the user ID to be copied.

4. Click on Copy. Q&A displays the Copy User dialog box (Figure 16.11).

The Copy User dialog box allows you to copy a user ID settings into a new user ID.

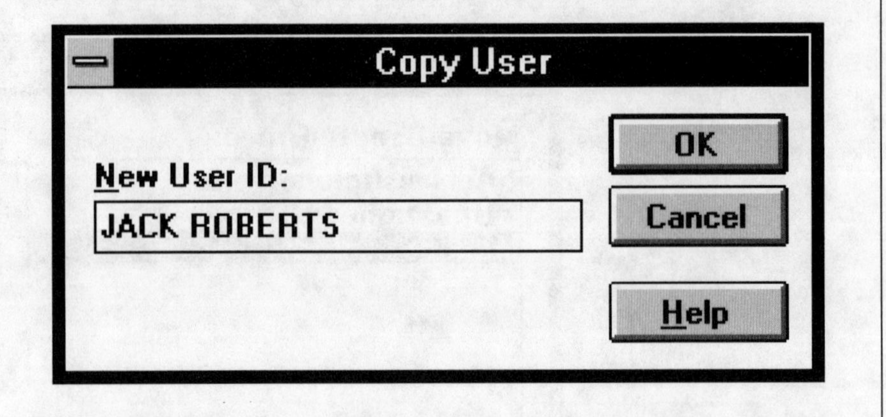

5. Type a new unique user ID for the new user.

6. Click OK or press Enter. Q&A displays the User & Groups dialog box containing the new user ID.

Deleting a User ID

If someone leaves your company or transfers to another department, you will need to delete the security settings for that user. To delete a user from a group, select the user ID from the Users in Group box and click on Delete. Q&A asks you if you want to delete the user ID (Figure 16.12). If you choose Yes, that user ID is removed.

Q&A displays this confirmation box when you delete a user ID.

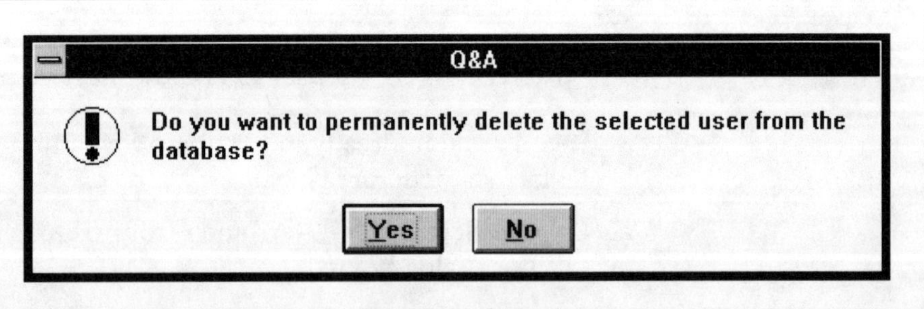

Logging onto a Database

When someone tries to open a password-protected database, he or she sees the User ID & Password dialog box (Figure 16.13), which prompts for the user ID and password. Using a user ID and password to enter a database is called *logging in*. If the user ID and password are valid, Q&A opens the database, giving you the access rights defined for that user ID.

If you created a guest user, someone can log in as a guest by clicking on the guest radio button, leaving the text boxes empty, and clicking on OK. After logging in, the guest uses the database with the guest access rights that you assigned. Another way of entering as a guest is to type GUEST in the User ID text box, leave the Password box empty, and click on OK.

FIGURE 16.13

The User ID &
Password dialog box

**click on this radio button to sign on a guest (if a guest
password has not been assigned to that database)**

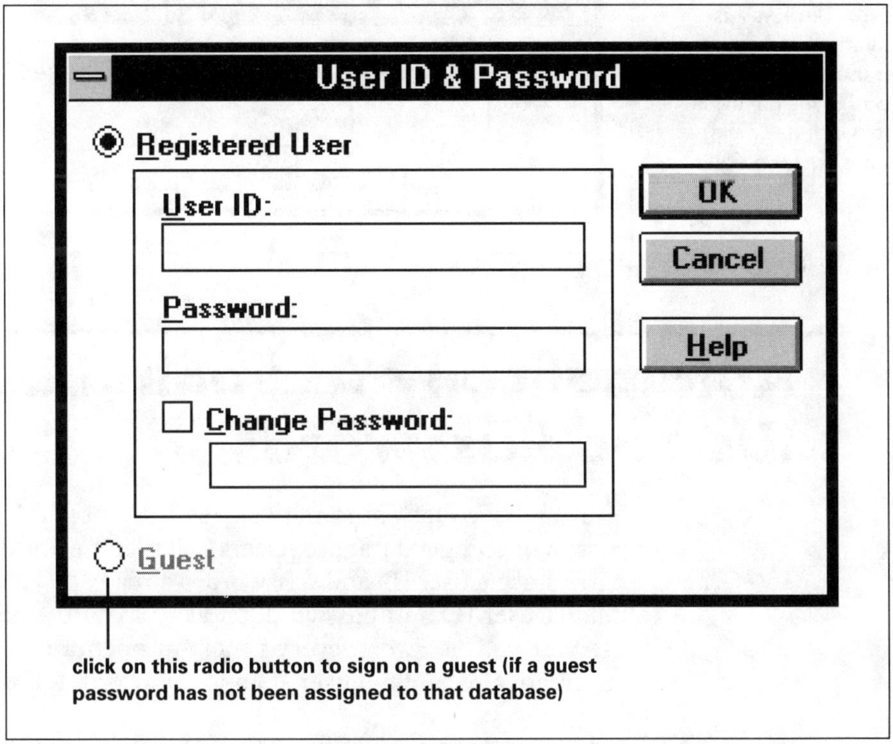

If a user tries to perform an action for which his or her user ID doesn't have rights, Q&A displays the information box shown in Figure 16.14. If the user chooses Yes, Q&A displays the User ID & Password dialog box again, allowing him or her to re-login as a user with sufficient access rights.

You can change a password in the User ID & Password dialog box. To change a password, type a user ID and password into the User ID and Password text boxes. Then check the Change Password check box and type the new password in the text box. When you click on OK to continue into the database, Q&A changes the password for that user ID. This allows you to change your own password without having to be in the Administrator group.

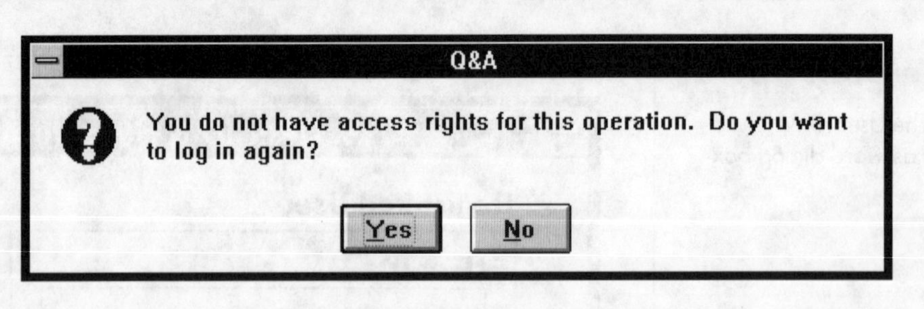

FIGURE 16.14

Q&A displays this information box when a user tries to access a part of the database to which he or she does not have rights.

Automatically Assigning User IDs and Passwords

You can have Q&A automatically assign a user ID and password to each person opening a database. Users will then be able to open secured databases since a user ID and password is already assigned. This is called your default user ID and password, and saves you the hassle of typing in your user ID and password every time you open a database. To set Q&A to automatically assign a user ID and password, follow these steps:

1. Choose File ➤ Preferences. Q&A displays the Preferences dialog box with the General category selected (Figure 16.15).

The Preferences dialog box with the General category selected

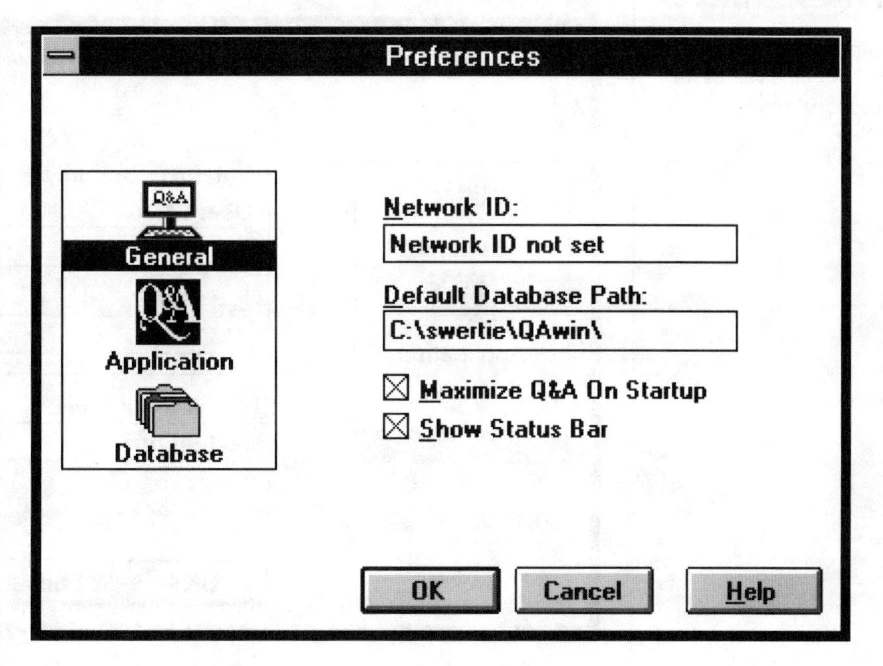

2. Click on the Database icon to display the Preferences dialog box for the Database category (Figure 16.16).

3. In the User ID box, type the user ID for a person opening the database, in the Password box, type the password for the user ID you entered in step 3, and click on OK or press Enter.

If the default user ID and password are valid for the database you opened, Q&A does not display the User ID & Password dialog box. However, if the automatically assigned user ID and password do not match any of the user IDs and passwords defined for the database being opened, Q&A opens the User ID & Password dialog box.

If a person using a default user ID and password needs to access a part of the database that he or she does not have rights for, Q&A will ask if he or she wants to switch to a user ID and password that has access rights to that part of the database. If he or she clicks yes, Q&A displays the User ID & Password dialog box. In this dialog box the user can change to a user ID and password with the necessary access rights. For more information about setting preferences, see Appendix C.

The Preferences dialog box with the Database category selected

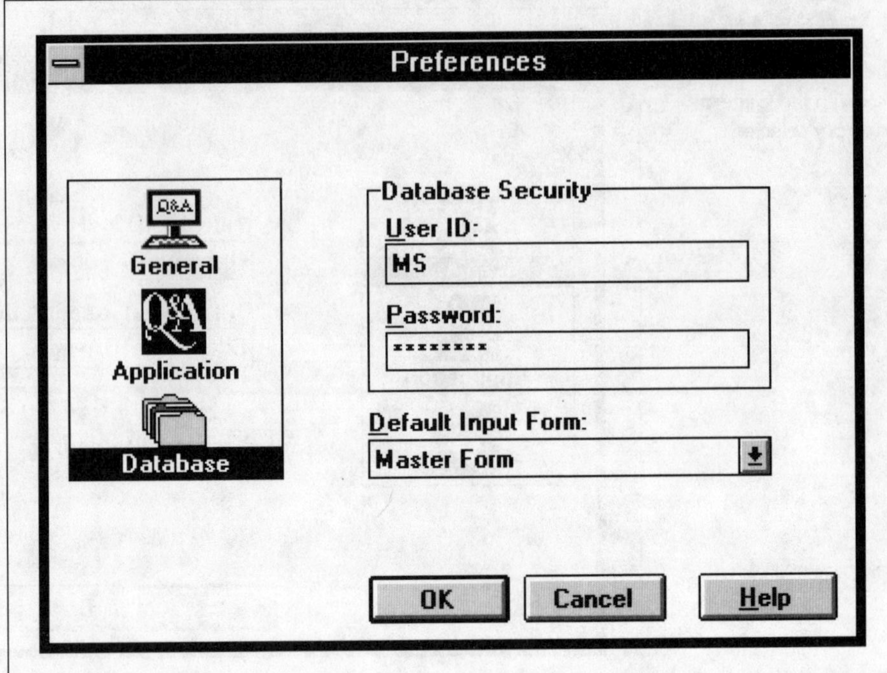

NOTE

The user ID and password in the Preferences dialog box are assigned to a person using a database only if that database is password-protected. Since an unsecured database does not require a user ID or password to open it, a person accessing an unsecured database is not automatically assigned a user ID and password.

Defining XLookup Passwords

In Appendix D, you'll find out how to use XLookup functions, which are used to extract data from a database while you are using another database. If the database from which you are extracting data is password-protected, you will not be able to get information from it unless you have a valid user ID and password.

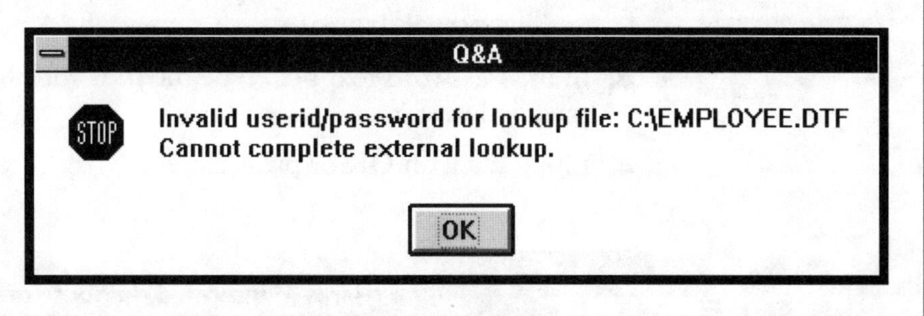

If you log in to a database using a user ID and password that are valid in the external database, the XLookup programming functions will retrieve the desired data. However, if you log in to a database using a user ID and password not valid for the external database, the XLookup programming statement will not work. Instead, Q&A display an information box (Figure 16.17) stating that your current user ID and password are invalid. In this case, a XLookup password comes in handy. Through the XLookup Password dialog box, you can set a special user ID and password for Q&A to use when attempting to retrieve data through an XLookup statement.

To set an XLookup password, change to Database Structure mode, and follow these steps:

1. Choose Security ➤ XLookup Password. Q&A displays the XLookup Password dialog box (Figure 16.18).

2. In the <u>U</u>ser ID text box, type the user ID to be used to gain access to the external database.

3. In the <u>P</u>assword text box, type the password for the user ID you specified in step 2.

4. Either click on OK or press Enter.

NOTE   If a user is in a secured database and the user ID and password in the Preferences dialog box are valid for the external database, you do not need to fill in the XLookup Password dialog box because the user ID and password are already set for that user. However, if the user is working in an unsecured database, it doesn't matter if the user ID and password in Preferences dialog box is valid for the external database. Since the person is in an unsecured database, the user ID and password from the Preferences dialog box was never assigned to that current user. Therefore, the user must fill in the XLookup Password dialog box to access an external password-protected database through the XLookup functions.

Protecting a Database Design with Database Locking

The second type of database security is a database lock. While Users & Groups security is focused on protecting your database data, the main purpose of a database lock is to protect the design of your database. Using database locking, you can protect your design by denying the user access to certain parts of Q&A.

Unlike the Users & Groups security option, there is no user ID and only one password for a database lock. Database locking is basically a security setup that you can turn on and off using an Enable box. To turn off or edit enabled database lock settings, you must use the database lock password, which you define in the Database Lock dialog box (Figure 16.19).

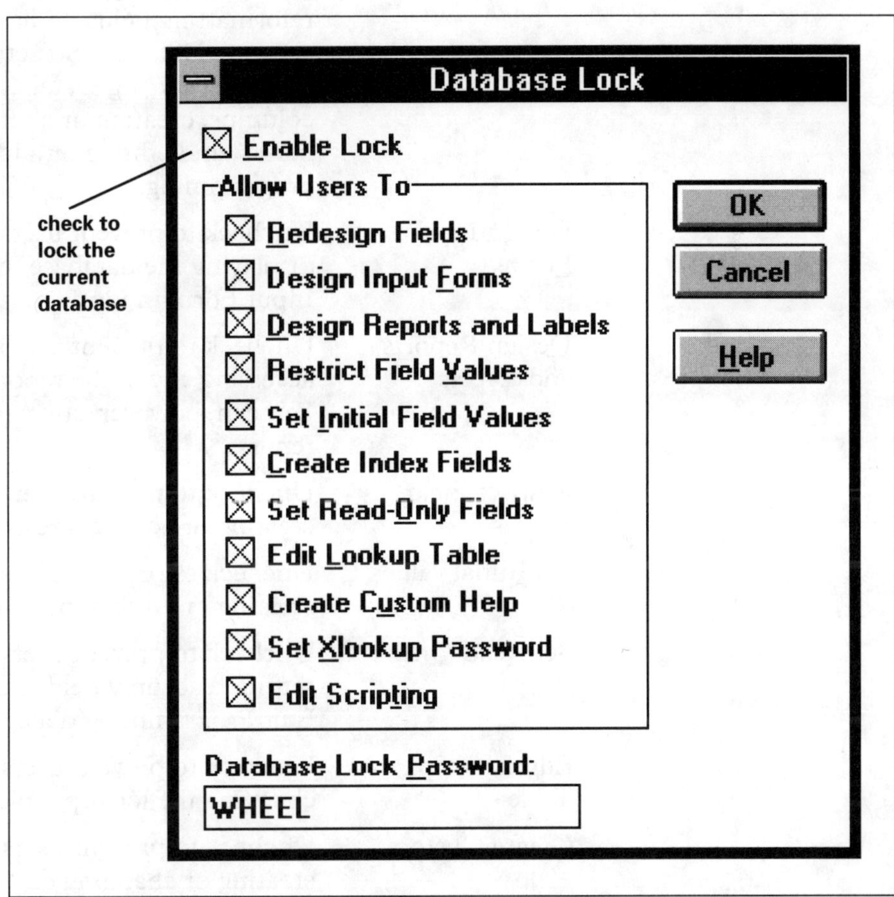

The following is a list of the database lock options with which you can regulate users. Note that the first time you open the Database Lock dialog box, all check boxes are checked.

<u>R</u>edesign Fields	Uncheck to prevent users from adding or deleting database fields, changing field types, renaming fields, reformatting fields, hiding and showing Database Structure columns, sorting Database Structure columns, creating or altering field masks, and editing or adding form programming.
Design Input <u>F</u>orms	Uncheck to prevent users from displaying the database in Design Input Form mode.
<u>D</u>esign Reports and Labels	Uncheck to prevent users from accessing any of the report modes. You can, however, still run existing reports.
Restrict Field <u>V</u>alues	Uncheck to prevent users from creating or editing a restriction spec.
Set <u>I</u>nitial Values	Uncheck to prevent users from creating or editing initial values.
Set Read-<u>O</u>nly Fields	Uncheck to prevent users from setting read-only fields through the Edit Programming dialog box.
Edit <u>L</u>ookup Table	Uncheck to prevent users from changing the lookup table.
Create C<u>u</u>stom Help	Uncheck to prevent users from creating or changing custom help boxes.
Set <u>X</u>Lookup Password	Uncheck to prevent users from setting or changing the XLookup password.

Edit Scripting	Uncheck to prevent users from using the <u>S</u>cripting Assistant. This prevents users from using scripts unless they are attached to a script button or appear on the <u>A</u>ssistant menu.

To create a database lock and enable it, display your database in Database Structure mode, and follow these steps:

1. Choose Securi<u>t</u>y ➤ <u>D</u>atabase Lock. Q&A displays the Database Lock dialog box.

2. From the Allow Users To group, choose the access rights for the database users. If a check box is checked, that feature is available.

3. Type a password in the Database Lock <u>P</u>assword box.

4. Place a check in the Enable Lock check box to activate the database lock for all users. If you need to turn off the database lock, clear this check box.

5. Click OK.

WARNING

Unlike the passwords for Users & Groups, if you forget a Database Lock password, there is no way to remove it. Even Symantec's technical support cannot remove the password for you.

To open the Database Lock dialog box once it has been enabled, choose Securi<u>t</u>y ➤ <u>D</u>atabase Lock while displaying the database in Database Structure mode. Q&A displays the Database Lock Password dialog box (Figure 16.20). Type the password that was set in the Database Lock dialog box, and click on OK.

To Sum Up

In this chapter, you learned how to create and use the two types of security systems: Users & Groups and Database Lock. For Users & Groups security, you found out how to create groups with field access rights and to add user IDs to those groups. For Database Lock security, you learned how to restrict access rights for all database users. In addition, you discovered how to open and use password-protected databases.

appendix

a

Installing Q&A for Windows

THIS appendix provides information and procedures for installing Q&A for Windows. Before installing Q&A for Windows, you should have already installed Windows 3.1 (or a more recent version) and printers and other peripheral devices using the Windows Control Panel applications. To ensure that you can reinstall Q&A if something happens to your original installation disks, you should also make copies of the disks and store them in an area away from your computer.

Minimum Hardware and Software Requirements

The minimum requirements for installing Q&A are:

- An IBM PC or 100% compatible personal computer with an 80386 or 80486 microprocessor

- PC DOS or MS-DOS 3.3 or a more recent version; DOS 5.0 or greater is recommended

- Windows 3.1 or a more recent version

- At least 4 megabytes of RAM (random access memory), your computer's main memory and temporary storage area. The more RAM you have, the better Q&A for Windows runs.

- At least 18 megabytes of hard disk drive space. The amount of space required depends on the files that you choose to install.

- Floppy disk drive—either 3.5-inch or 5.25-inch, double- or high-density, for installation and backups

- A VGA monitor. *VGA* (Video Graphics Array) shows characters, pictures, and other objects in high resolution and lets you have 16 colors at a time on your system.

- A mouse or other pointing device

Installing Q&A for Windows

Installing Q&A for Windows is easy. The installation program displays a series of dialog boxes that provide information on which you can base the options that you choose. Starting with the first dialog box, choose the type of installation you want:

Complete install	The recommended choice. The installation program installs both Q&A for Windows and Q&A Write, and selects the most appropriate options for you.
Q&A for Windows only	The installation program installs just the Q&A Database program and files.
Q&A Write only	The installation program installs just the Q&A Write program and files.
Custom installation	For experienced users. The installation program allows you to select the Q&A for Windows files that you wish to install.

N O T E   If you wish to reinstall Q&A for Windows at a later time and choose another installation type, just run the installation program again.

In the next dialog box, you can accept the suggested C:\QAWIN directory, or enter another directory name or select another drive identifier. The installation program displays the approximate amount of hard disk space Q&A for Windows requires.

To install Q&A for Windows, follow these steps:

1. Turn on your computer. If Windows does not load automatically, type win at the DOS prompt (C:\>).

2. Insert the first installation disk in the appropriate disk drive.

3. From the Program Manager window, choose File ➤ Run. Windows opens the Run dialog box.

4. In the Command Line box, type either a:install or b:install, depending on the disk drive in which you inserted the installation disk (see step 2). Press Enter. The Q&A for Windows Install Type dialog box appears.

5. Select an installation type. Then either click on OK or press Enter.

NOTE To stop the installation at any time, click on the Exit Install button.

6. Select the directory in which you wish the installation program to place the Q&A for Windows program files. Then either click on OK or press Enter. The installation begins.

7. After installing the contents of one disk, the installation program prompts you to insert the next one and either click on OK or press Enter. The installation program shows you how the installation is progressing and informs you when it is complete.

At the end of the installation, the installation program updates files, returns to Windows, and displays the Symantec program group window.

Removing Q&A for Windows from Your Computer

If you ever wish to delete Q&A for Windows from your computer, select the icon labeled Q&A/Q&A Write Uninstall from the Symantec program group window.

To uninstall Q&A for Windows, follow these steps:

1. Back up all your files onto disk and store the disks in an area away from your computer.

2. Double-click on the Q&A/Q&A Write Uninstall icon. The uninstall process deletes all program and associated files from the \QAWIN directory and subdirectories.

appendix

Overview of the Windows Environment

DESIGNED for the Windows novice, this appendix is devoted to Windows. In this appendix, you'll discover several ways of starting Windows, you'll find out about the basic elements of Windows, and you'll get an overview of how to use the Windows File Manager application, which can help you to run Q&A more efficiently. If you need more help or want more details about these or other Windows features, see the *Microsoft Windows User's Guide* or one of SYBEX's many fine books about Windows.

Windows is a graphical user interface (GUI—pronounced gooey), which emphasizes the use of graphics rather than typed commands to get the job done.

Starting Windows

The most common way of starting Windows is to type win at the DOS prompt and then press the Enter key. Windows automatically selects the appropriate mode (Standard or 386 Enhanced) for your computer system. Since a minimum requirement of running Q&A for Windows is an 80386 or 80486 microprocessor, you should be in 386 Enhanced mode. The following list provides some of the other ways that you can start Windows:

win :	Starts Windows without displaying the introductory logo
win/3	Starts Windows in 386 Enhanced mode
win qawin	Starts Windows and then starts Q&A Database
win qawrite	Starts Windows and then starts Q&A Write

The Basic Components of Windows

After starting Windows, the first window on the computer screen is the Program Manager (Figure B.1). The look and contents of this window depend on many factors, including the number and types of programs you have installed, the applications you use most often, how you like to plan and organize, your favorite colors, and so on. The three basic Windows elements are the desktop, the window, and the dialog box.

FIGURE B.1

A sample Program Manager window

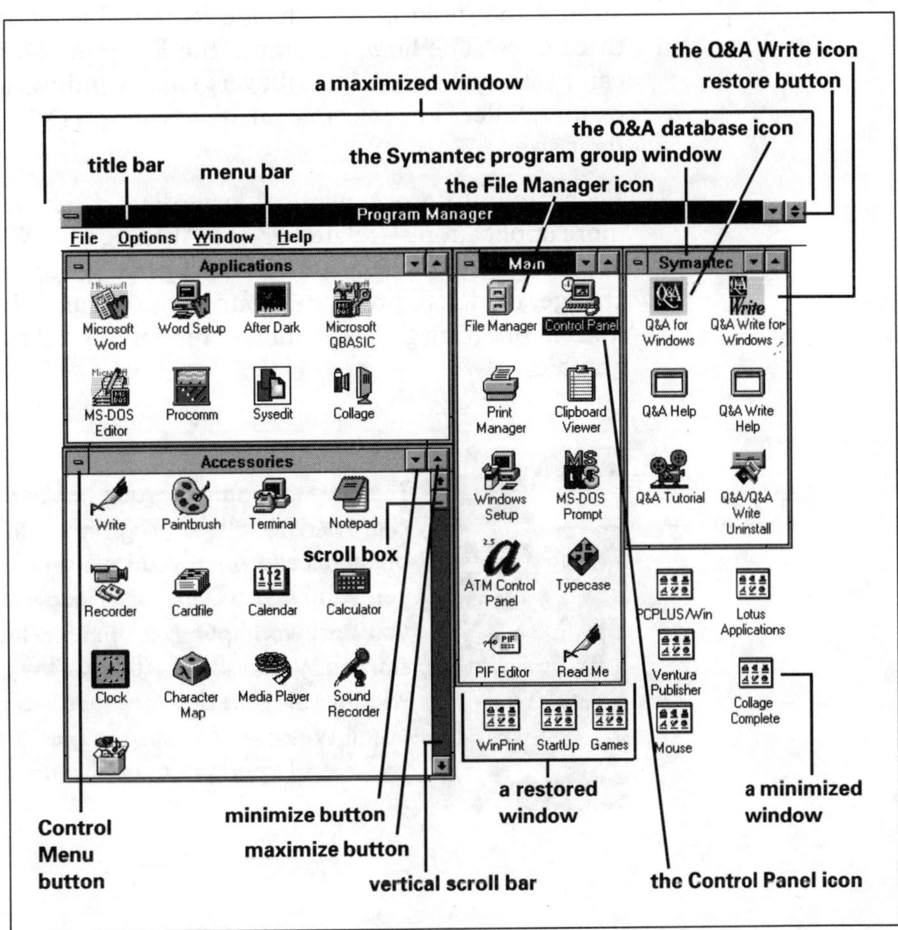

Desktop

The entire glass or plastic surface of your monitor is the desktop. The desktop contains all the objects displayed electronically on the screen, including program group windows, dialog boxes, icons, buttons, title bars, scroll bars, and menus.

Program Group Windows

A window is a large or small rectangular area within the desktop. You can change the size and location of a window, depending on its current size and location. Obviously, if a window takes up the entire desktop, it's impossible to move. However, once you decrease its size, you can move it around the desktop and change its size. Figure B.1 shows windows in three sizes. The largest window, the Program Manager, is *maximized*; it can't get any bigger. The eight very small windows are *minimized*; they can be no smaller. The four intermediate windows are *restored*; you can adjust their size.

Each program group window, regardless of its size, can contain one or more applications—related or not. Although the Windows Setup installation program sets up your initial program group windows, you can add, change, or delete program group windows and their contents. Applications in program group windows are represented by *icons*, which are small graphics.

TIP

The Startup program group has one special characteristic; all the programs in this group start automatically when you start Windows. For example, if you want to use Q&A for Windows immediately after you start work, put its icon in Startup. Then after starting Windows, you'll have the Q&A application window on your desktop, ready to go. When you first install Windows, the Startup group is empty. It's up to you to add appropriate applications.

Elements of a Window

At first glance, the Program Manager window seems cluttered with all sorts of objects. However, once you understand their function, you'll have a better idea of how Windows works.

Title Bar

The title bar, the topmost element, displays the name of the window or dialog box and contains one or more buttons.

Control Menu Button

The *Control Menu button* (which looks like a minus sign [-]) is located on the left side of the title bar of both windows and dialog boxes. The Control Menu button controls window size and position and allows you to either close the window or application or to switch to another Windows application. Click on the Control Menu button to open a menu from which you can select commands. Double-click to close the window (and therefore the application or document inside the window) or dialog box.

To move a window to a new location using the keyboard, choose the <u>M</u>ove command from the Control menu and press any combination of ←, →, ↓, and ↑. To move a window using the mouse, move the mouse pointer to the title bar, click and hold down the left mouse button, and drag the window.

To size a window using the keyboard, choose the <u>S</u>ize command from the Control menu and press any combination of ←, →, ↓, and ↑. To size a window using the mouse, move the mouse pointer to any border or corner of the window. When the mouse pointer changes to a double-pointing arrow, click and hold down the left mouse button, and drag the border or corner.

Minimize Button

Located on the right side of a window title bar, the *minimize button* allows you to reduce an active application to an icon. The application still runs in its minimized state but gives you room to view one or more other open windows.

Maximize Button

Located on the right side of a window title bar, the *maximize button* enables you to increase the size of a minimized or restored active window to the entire computer screen. If a window is already maximized, you'll see the restore button in place of the maximize button.

Restore Button

Located on the right side of a window title bar, the *restore button* decreases a maximized window so that its dimensions are the same as its last restored size. If a window is restored, you'll see the maximize button in place of the restore button.

Menu Bar

Immediately beneath Program Manager's title bar, the *menu bar* displays the main Windows commands. Move the mouse pointer to a word on the menu bar, click, and Windows opens a menu of commands. To open a menu using the keyboard, press the Alt key and then press the *hot key*, the underlined letter in the word (for example, the H in <u>H</u>elp).

Menu Commands

Once you open a menu, you can select a command by clicking on it. You can close the menu by clicking again at the top of the menu or anywhere on the desktop outside the list of menu commands. To select a command using the keyboard, press the letter that is underlined. To close a pull-down menu using the keyboard, press the Esc key.

Here are some general information about the commands in menus:

- Related commands on a menu are grouped together and separated from other groups of commands with a horizontal line.

- If a command looks grayed, it is unavailable. You'll have to perform some action before you can use the command. For example, to choose <u>E</u>dit ➤ <u>U</u>ndo, you must have performed an action that can be undone.

- If a command is preceded by a check mark, the command can be turned on or off. For example, in Windows if you choose <u>O</u>ptions

➤ <u>S</u>ave Settings on Exit, when you end this Windows session, all the changes that you have made are saved. However, if the <u>S</u>ave Settings on Exit command is not preceded by a check mark, any changes are not saved.

A novice Windows user can inadvertently cause some bizarre effects on the desktop. One way of quickly returning to your previous desktop settings is to choose <u>O</u>ptions ➤ <u>S</u>ave Settings on Exit, exit Windows, and start Windows again.

- If a command is followed by an *ellipsis* (…), selecting the command opens a dialog box in which you select choices and type text. Figure B.2 shows a typical dialog box and its options.

- If a command is followed by a right-pointing arrow, selecting the command opens a *cascading menu*, which is a submenu from which you can select another command.

- If a command is preceded by a check or a dot, the command function is the current selection.

Scroll Bars

There are two types of scroll bars—the vertical bar at the right side of some windows, lists, and work areas and the horizontal bar at the bottom of some windows, lists, and work areas. Pressing and holding down the left mouse button on the arrows at the ends of the scroll bar, and dragging the *scroll box* or *thumb* (the small box inside the scroll bar) allows you to move around the window, list, or work area. The scroll box also indicates your current location in a document. For example, the scroll box in Figure B.1 indicates that you are viewing the top of the window. The absence of a scroll bar indicates that you are viewing the entire contents of a window, list, or work area.

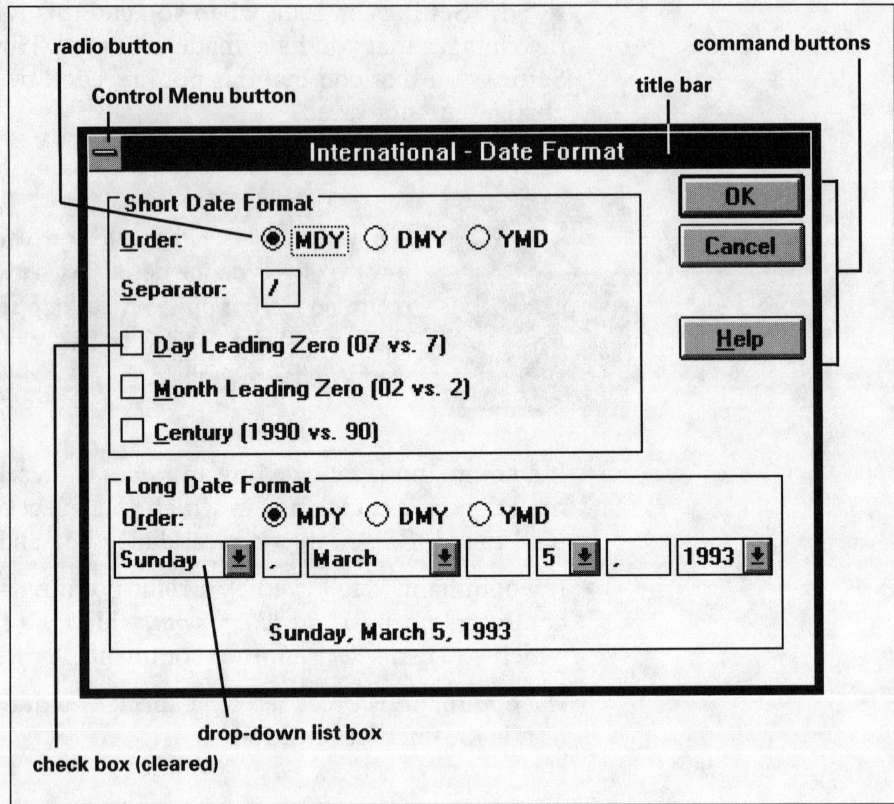

Dialog Boxes

Often Windows displays a dialog box, which is a small window, when you select a command. Dialog boxes contain elements that are both common to other windows and unique to the boxes themselves. You'll learn about these elements later in this appendix.

Elements of a Dialog Box

All dialog boxes have a title bar and most have a control menu button. Some even have their own menu bars from which you can open menus and select commands. Dialog boxes also have their own unique elements as shown in Table B.1.

TABLE B.1: Dialog Box Elements

ELEMENT	NAME	DESCRIPTION
	Text box	A box into which you type information, such as a file name or option name. A text box often is combined with a list box, forming a text/list box.
	Drop-down list box	When opened, this box displays a list of options from which you can choose
OK	Command button	When selected, this button implements a command. Clicking on OK performs an action using the options that you have selected in the dialog box. (A command button with a heavy border is the default command button and can be activated by pressing Enter.) Clicking on Cancel closes the dialog box without any other action being performed. Some command buttons contain selection letters. For example, press H to select the Help button. Another command button is Close, which closes a dialog box before completing the command. However, all settings that you have changed remain changed.

TABLE B.1: Dialog Box Elements (continued)

ELEMENT	NAME	DESCRIPTION
	Check box	A box in which you either place an X (check) or remove the X (clear). The third setting for a check box is shaded, which indicates that a selection includes a combination of both choices or has neither choice. In a group of check boxes, you can check or clear any combination.
Field Creation Order / Alphabetical	Radio button	Also known as an option button. When you select a radio button (think of tuning your car radio), all other radio buttons in the group are cleared.
	List box	A box that contains a list of options from which you can select. Just click on the up arrow or down arrow to move up or down through the list, respectively. A list box often is combined with a text box, forming a text/list box.
Keep With Next	Dotted box	A border that indicates your current position in the dialog box or the currently selected dialog box option.

Managing Files Using File Manager

You can use File Manager to manage your files in a more efficient way than if you try to manage them from within a Windows application, such as Q&A for Windows. For example, you can delete superfluous files, create a new Q&A subdirectory and then move a group of files to it, rename a group of files, and so on. Although you will only learn a few File Manager functions in this section, you can learn more by reading the *Microsoft Windows User's Guide* or another of SYBEX's Windows books.

To start File Manager, double-click on its icon (often found in the Main group). Windows displays the File Manager window (Figure B.3). On the left side of the window is the Tree pane, which displays icons representing directories and subdirectories for the current drive. On the right side of the window is the Contents pane, which lists the directories and files in the currently selected directory.

Finding Files

If you know the directory in which a file is located, you can click on the directory icon in the Tree pane and then, in the Contents pane, look for the icon representing the file.

To search for a file or group of files without knowing the directories in which they are located, File Manager provides the Search command on the File menu. To search through the current drive, display the top of the Tree pane and click on the root directory icon (for example, c: for a hard drive, or a: for a disk drive). Then choose File ➤ Search. In the Search For text box in the Search dialog box, type your search criteria. For example, type abc*.* to search for a file whose first three characters are *abc*, which ends with any number of characters, and which has any extension. For a successful search, File Manager displays a list of found files.

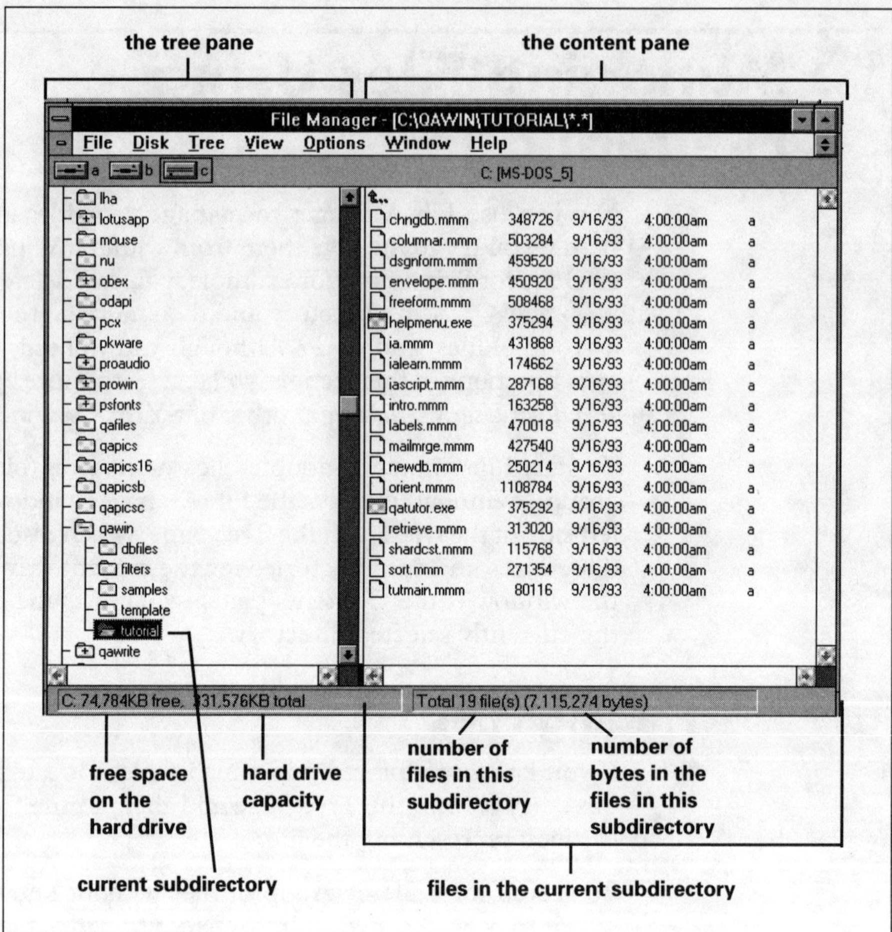

Deleting Files

The quickest way to delete one or more files is to select them in the Contents pane, press the Del key, and confirm, when asked.

Creating a Subdirectory

To create a subdirectory, click on the icon representing the directory under which the new subdirectory will reside. Then choose File ➤ Create Directory. In the Name text box in the Create Directory dialog box, type a directory name (which can't be longer than eight characters and follows other standard DOS conventions).

Moving Files

The fastest way to move files from one directory to another within the same drive is to use drag and drop. First adjust your view of the Tree pane so that you can see the icons for both the source directory (which currently holds the files) and the destination directory (to which you are moving the files). Then click on the icon for the source directory, select the files to be moved, and drag them to the target directory.

TIP

If you're only moving one file, all you have to do to select it is click on it. If you're moving more than one file, select the first one by clicking on it, and all subsequent files by holding down the Ctrl key as you click.

The other way to move files is to select them, choose File ➤ Move or press F7, and type the destination directory in the To text box in the Move dialog box. If you haven't selected one or more files to be moved, you will have to fill in the From text box as well. Then either click on OK or press Enter.

Copying Files

The copy operation is almost identical to the move operation. However, if you are copying files within the same drive, be aware that the drag and drop operation moves files; it doesn't copy them. The fastest way to copy files from one directory in one drive to another directory on another drive is to use drag and drop.

The other way to copy files is to select them, choose File ➤ Copy or press F8, and type the destination directory in the To text box in the Copy dialog box. If you haven't selected one or more files to be copied, you will have to fill in the From text box as well. Then either click on OK or press Enter.

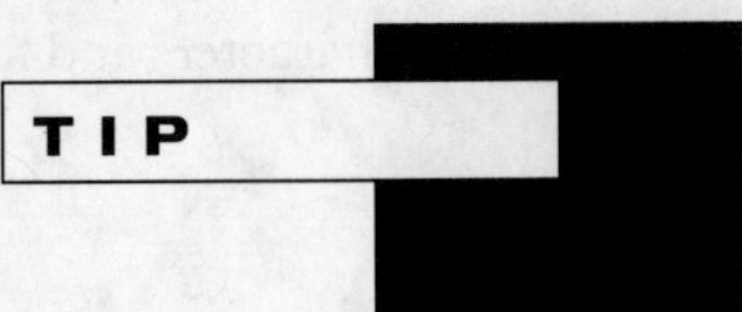

Copying files is a quick way of backing up. Just copy files to a disk and store the disk in an area away from your computer.

Renaming Files

If your company develops file naming conventions and you must rename your files, choosing File ➤ Rename is much more efficient than opening each file and opening the appropriate Windows application and file and then choosing File ➤ Save As. To rename a file, select it in the Contents window, choose File ➤ Rename, and fill in the From (if needed) and To text boxes in the Rename dialog box.

appendix

C

Changing Your Q&A Environment

BY choosing File ➤ Preferences in either Q&A Database or Q&A Write, you can customize your working environment. In Q&A Database, you can control three categories of program attributes: General, Application, and Database. In Q&A Write, you can customize user, file, tool bar, envelope, text, and table attributes. In this appendix, you'll learn about each of these preferences.

Customizing Your Q&A Database Environment

To customize your Q&A Database environment, simply choose File ➤ Preferences. In the Preferences dialog box (Figure C.1), click on either the General, Application, or Database icon.

Customizing Q&A Startup

Clicking on the General icon allows you to control the way Q&A looks when you start. It also automates other startup attributes.

Network ID	The network identifier is used to identify each person using Q&A. This is especially common when Q&A is being used by multiple users on a network.
Default Database Path	Q&A displays the name of the directory in which you wish Q&A database files to be stored and to appear in the Directories scroll box in the Open File dialog box. The default is C:\QAWIN\.

The Preferences dialog box, with General preferences shown

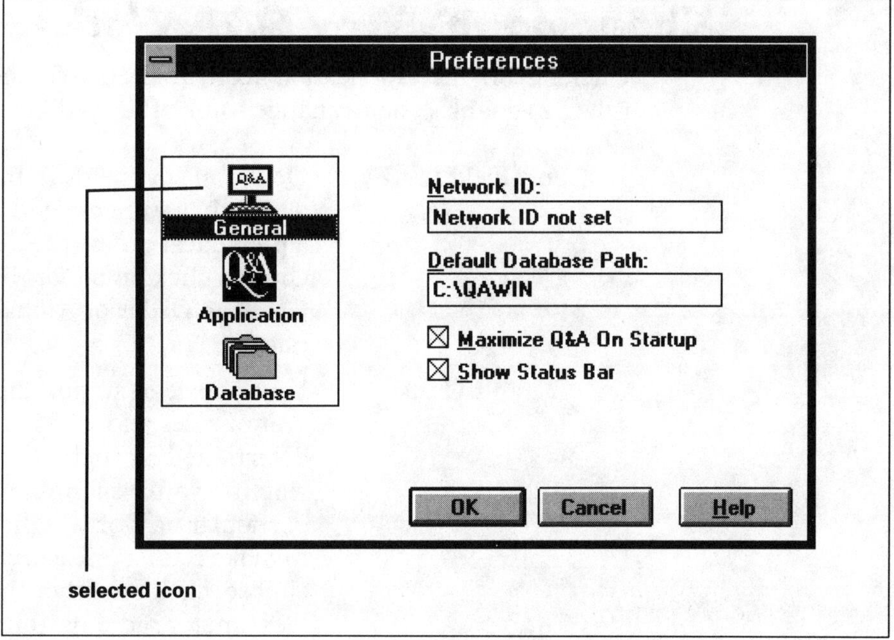

<u>M</u>aximize Q&A On Startup	Check this box if you wish to display the starting Q&A window in the full screen. Otherwise, the starting Q&A window is somewhat smaller than the full screen (it is restored). A restored window is the default.
<u>S</u>how Status Bar	As a default setting, the status bar is displayed at the bottom of the Q&A window. If you do not care about seeing the information in the status bar, remove the check from this check box.

Changing the Way Q&A Works

Clicking on the Application icon in the Preferences dialog box (Figure C.2) enables you to change some of the ways in which Q&A operates.

Sort Field List By
: Q&A can sort fields in the order in which they were created or in alphabetical order (the default). To choose, click on either the Field Creation Order or Alphabetical radio button.

Default Units
: Your choice in setting the default unit of ruler and grid measurement is determined by such factors as whether you are familiar with a particular unit or whether you need to make refined measurements. To choose, click on either the Inches or Centimeter radio button.

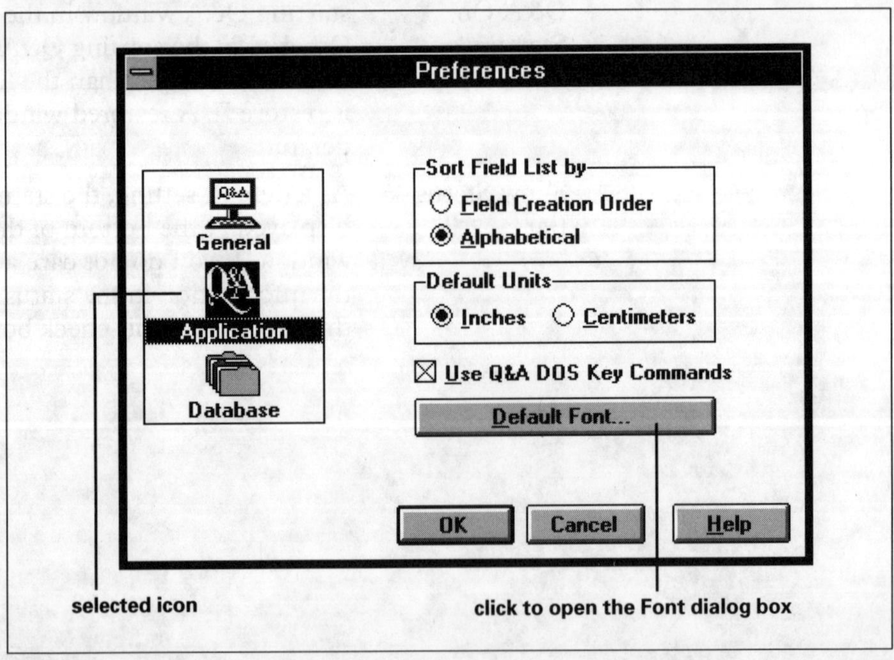

FIGURE C.2

The Preferences dialog box, with Application preferences shown

Use Q&A DOS Key Commands — Clicking on this button allows you to use Q&A for DOS keys and key combinations.

Default Font — Clicking on this button displays the Font dialog box (Figure C.3). In this dialog box, you can select a default font, font enhancement, point size, effects such as Strikeout and Underline, and colors.

NOTE Changing the default font does not affect already created databases, even a database you are running now; it only changes the default font for databases to be created in the future.

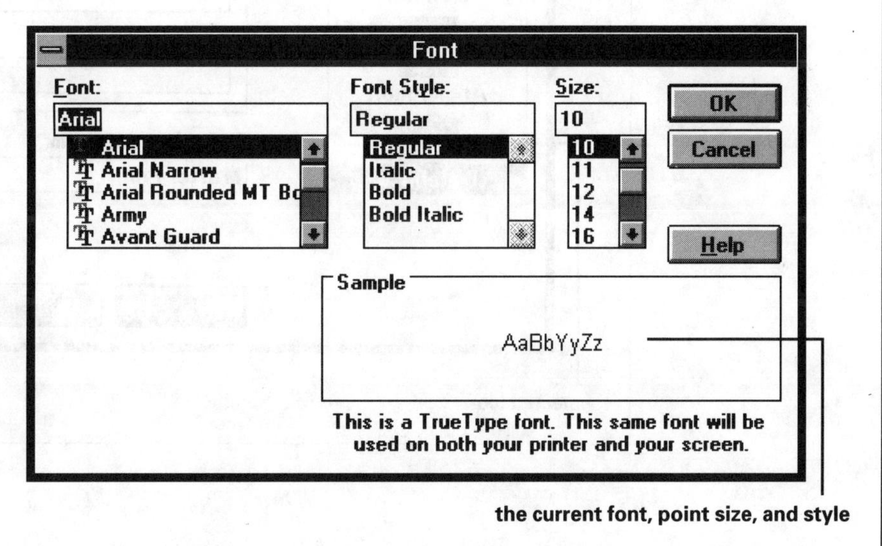

FIGURE C.3

The Font dialog box. You can also open this dialog box from within Q&A Database.

Setting Preferences for Databases

You also can set database preferences using the Preferences dialog box (Figure C.4). If your database administrator or network administrator has secured the current database, set a default user identification in the User ID text box and your password in the Password text box. This feature is covered in depth in Chapter 16.

You can select the input form that you use for a particular database by choosing from the Default Input Form drop-down box. For example, when you first use Q&A for Windows, the default input form is Master Form, which is associated with every database.

The Preferences dialog box with the database preferences displayed

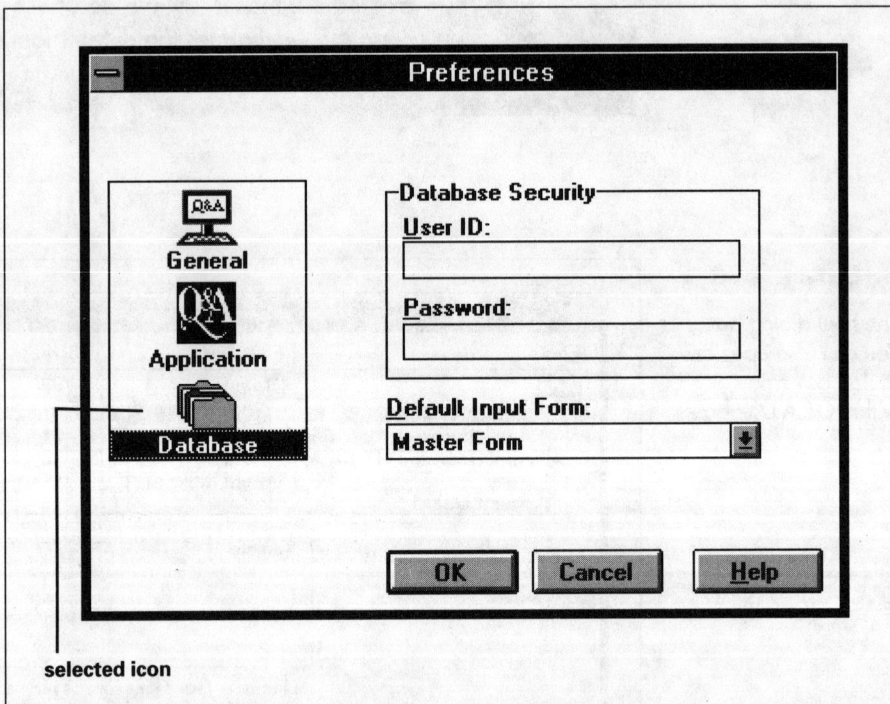

Customizing Your Q&A Write Environment

Customizing your Q&A Write environment involves choosing File ➤ Preferences and then choosing a command from the cascading menu. Table C.1 lists the Q&A Write preference commands, describes the options offered, and tells you whether you must open a document before being able to use the command.

TABLE C.1: Q&A Write Preferences

COMMAND	OPTIONS	NEED OPEN DOCUMENT?
File ➤ Preferences ➤ User	Furnishes your name for document statistics; displays or hide the status bar or tool bar; selects the default background color; increases the size of both the mouse pointer and I-beam cursor.	No
File ➤ Preferences ➤ File	Specifies the opening document; warns you when Q&A Write saves a "foreign" document in its original format; turns on and off automatic saves; tells you when auto-saving, opens a document using the quickest method; saves a backup copy of a document; prompts before saving a library	No
File ➤ Preferences ➤ Edit Tool Bar	Adds a tool bar button; increases the size of the tool bar; saves and opens tool bar files.	Yes
File ➤ Preferences ➤ Envelope	Selects an envelope size; indents the first line of recipient information; types a return address	Yes

TABLE C.1: Q&A Write Preferences (continued)

COMMAND	OPTIONS	NEED OPEN DOCUMENT?
File ➤ Preferences ➤ Text	Opens a document displaying or hiding non-printing symbols; specifies variations of Insert and Overtype mode; repaginates in the background; warns when deleting objects; displays, hides, or changes the position of the ruler; displays or hides the paragraph bar; enables or disables quick paste, smart delete & paste, and automatic spell checker lookup.	Yes
File ➤ Preferences ➤ Table	Specifies whether a table frame is displayed in Proof view (without showing the nonprinting symbols in the work area) or in Detail view (showing nonprinting symbols). Detail is the default. Specifies whether you type information By Row (from left to right) or By Column (from top to bottom). For more information, see the *Q&A Write User's Manual*.	Yes

Specifying User Preferences

In the User Preferences dialog box (Figure C.5), you can set these preferences:

Your Name	Type the name that Q&A Write uses for document statistics
Show Status Bar	Check this check box to display the status bar, or clear this box to hide the status bar.

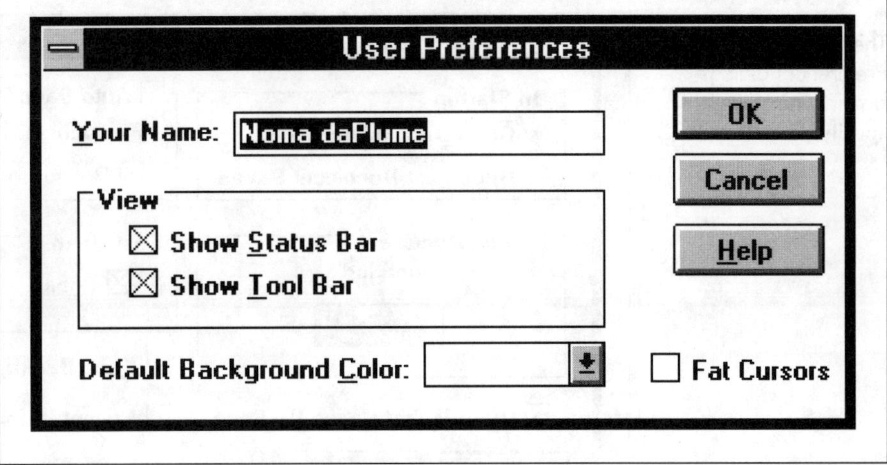

Show Tool Bar	Check this check box to display the tool bar, or clear this box to hide the tool bar.
Default Background Color	Open this drop-down list box to select the default background color for the work area.
Fat Cursors	Check this box to increase the size of both the mouse pointer and I-beam cursor. A cleared check box is the default.

Setting File Preferences

In the File Preferences dialog box (Figure C.6), you can define the document that opens when you start Q&A Write, how quickly a document opens, and specify several save preferences.

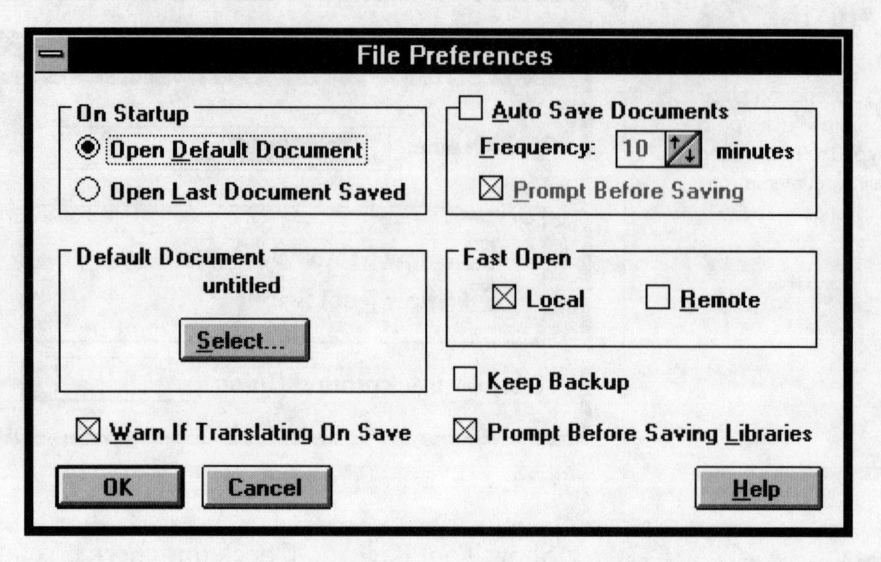

On Startup	You can choose from two opening documents when opening Q&A Write. You can click on either Open Default Document, which opens an empty, new document, or Open Last Document Saved, which opens the last document that you saved.
Default Document	To select a particular document to open as you start Q&A Write, click on the Select button. When Q&A Write displays the Select dialog box, choose a document.
Warn If Translating On Save	Check this check box to have Q&A Write issue a warning message when saving a "foreign" document. For example, if you open a Word for Windows document, edit it in Q&A Write, and save it back to Word for Windows format. This warning message just reminds you that you may lose some formatting.

Auto Save Documents	Check this box to automatically save documents. In the Frequency list box, set the number of minutes between automatic saves. In addition, Prompt Before Saving tells Q&A Write to display a message when autosaving a document.
Fast Open	You can display the first page of a document as Q&A Write opens the rest of the document. If you clear this check box, Q&A Write opens the entire document before displaying it in the work area. Either select Local or Remote to "fast open" a local or network file or both.
Keep Backup	Check this box to have Q&A Write save the last version of a file as a backup copy when you save a new version of the file. A clear check box, the default, means that no backup is saved.
Prompt Before Saving Libraries	Check this check box when you close a library after working on new documents. For information about Q&A Write libraries, see the *Q&A Write User's Manual.*

Customizing the Tool Bar

Using the Text Tool Bar dialog box (Figure C.7), you can customize the tool bar by increasing its size or adding buttons.

Available Controls	Select a new button from this scroll list
Number of Visible Tool Bar Lines	Select the number (from 1 to 4) of tool bar lines. The default is 2.

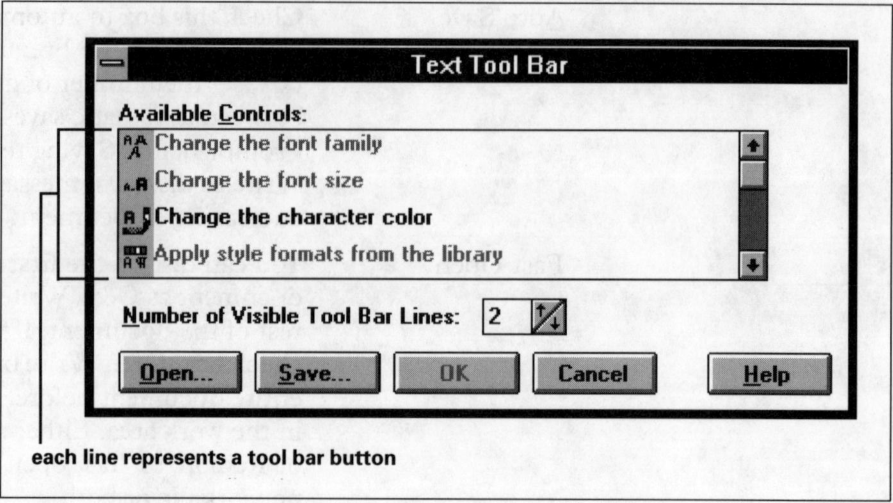

To place a button on the tool bar, follow these steps:

1. Double-click on an empty space on the tool bar. Q&A Write displays the Text Tool Bar dialog box.

2. Double-click on a button from the Available Controls scroll list. Q&A Write closes the dialog box.

3. Move the new button around the tool bar. To place the new button, move it to the desired place and click the left mouse button. Q&A Write reopens the Text Tool Bar dialog box.

4. Click on the Save button to save the custom tool bar settings to a file.

To open a tool bar file, double-click on an empty space on the tool bar, click on the Open button from the tool bar dialog box that is displayed, and select a file from the Open Tool Bar dialog box.

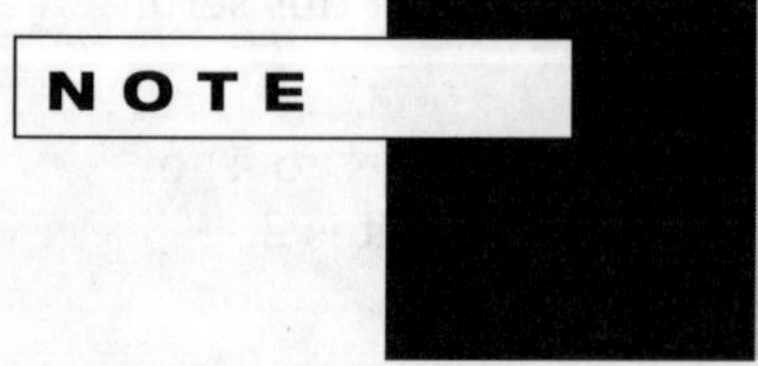

NOTE   If a custom tool bar consists of more lines than the current tool bar, select the appropriate number of lines from the Number of Visible Tool Bar Lines list box in the Text Tool Bar dialog box.

Setting Envelope Defaults

In the Envelope Preferences dialog box (Figure C.8), you can select one of 17 envelope sizes from the Default Size drop-down list box. A standard letter size envelope, Size 10 (4 1/8 x 9 1/2 in), is the default. You can set the Left Indent (from 0" to 9"); the default is 3.750." To regularly use a return address on envelopes, type a return address in the Return Address for Envelopes box.

FIGURE C.8

The Envelope Preferences dialog box

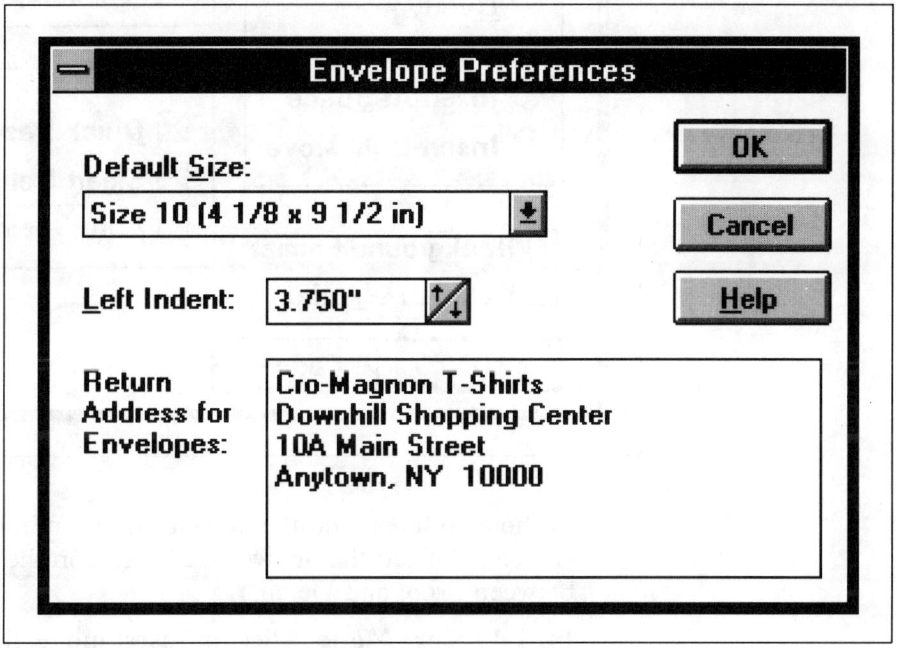

Defining Text Preferences

In the Text Preferences dialog box (Figure C.9), you can set a number of text preferences for Insert and Overtype modes, showing or hiding the ruler and paragraph bar, and specifying short cuts.

Initial View Click on the Proof radio button, the default, to display documents without non-printing symbols (such as spaces, tabs, new line and paragraph marks, and so on). Click on Detail

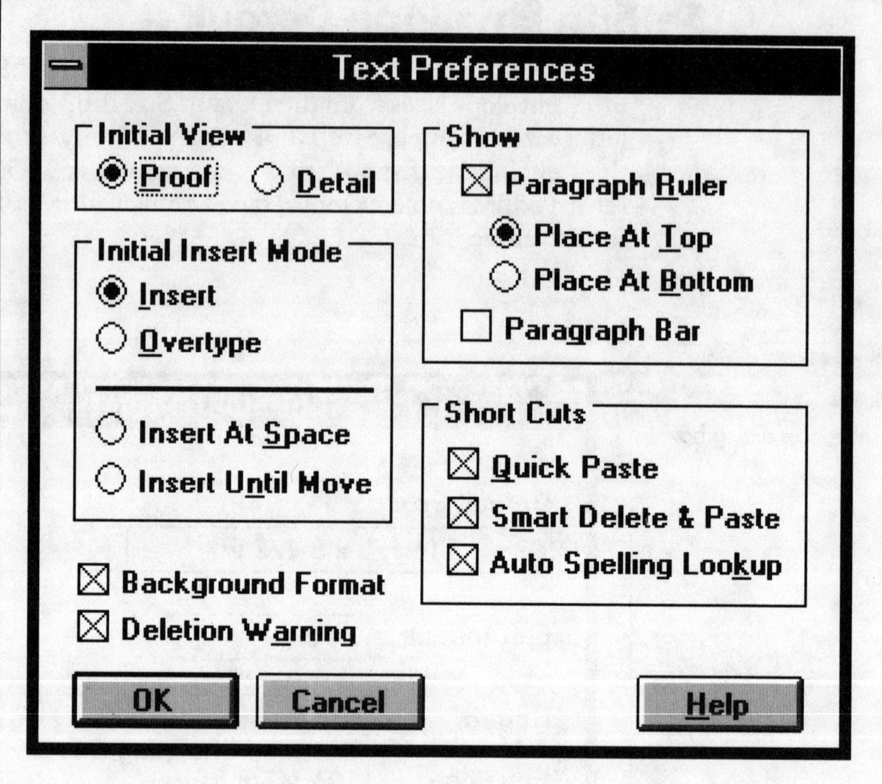

to show both text and the non-printing symbols. Remember that you can click on the Show/Hide button on the tool bar to switch between Proof and Detail.

Initial Insert Mode Click on Insert mode, the default, or Overtype mode to start working in insert mode or overtype mode, respectively. (See Chapter 12 for more information about Insert and Overtype modes.)

Clicking on the Insert At Space radio button allows you to work in a combination of Insert and Overtype modes. Whenever the cursor rests on a character, you are in Overtype mode, and whenever the cursor rests on a space, you are in Insert mode.

Insert Until Move is another combination of Insert and Overtype. When you open a document, you start in Insert mode, regardless of the cursor location. Then Q&A Write switches to Overtype mode when the cursor rests on a character and back to Insert mode when the cursor rests on a space.

Background Format Whenever you insert or delete a great deal of text, placing a check in this check box allows Q&A Write to repaginate your document as you continue to work. A checked check box is the default.

Deletion Warning Checking this check box tells Q&A Write to prompt you whenever you delete a frame, object, section (but not text) from a document. A checked check box is the default.

Show Check the Paragraph Ruler check box to hide the ruler when you start the next session of Q&A Write. (There is no effect on the current session.)

Click on the Place At Top or Place At Bottom radio button to display the ruler at either the top or bottom of the work area.

Check the Paragraph Bar check box to display the Paragraph Bar at the left side of the work area. To learn more about the paragraph bar, see the *Q&A Write User's Manual*.

Short Cuts Check Quick Paste to cut and paste by pressing the right mouse button:

- To cut text to the Clipboard and paste it in a new location, select the text to be cut. Then move to its new location and click the right mouse button. This cuts the selection for its original location and pastes it into its new location.

- To paste a selection from the Clipboard, move to the paste location and click the right mouse button.

- To copy text to the Clipboard and paste it in a new location, select the text to be copied. Then move to its new location, press Shift, and then click the right mouse button.

Check Smart Delete & Paste to remove extra spaces when cutting to the Clipboard or deleting.

Check Auto Spelling Lookup to have the spell checker automatically look up every misspelled word in the dictionary and show a list of possible replacement words. A cleared Auto Spelling Lookup check box results in the spell checker identifying misspelled words only.

Defining Table Preferences

In the Table Preferences dialog box (Figure C.10), you can specify whether you want the initial view of your table to be <u>P</u>roof or <u>D</u>etail. You can also specify whether you want the fill mode of the table to be by <u>R</u>ow or by <u>C</u>olumn.

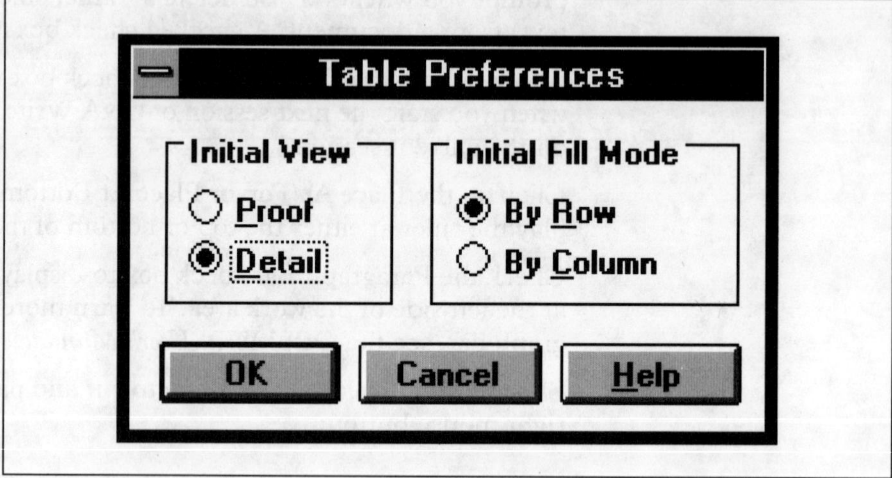

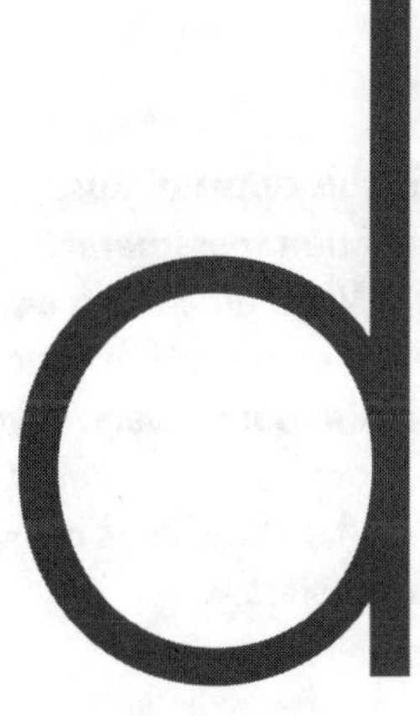

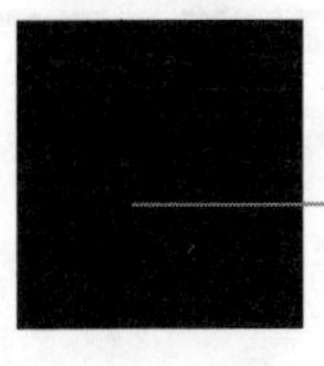

Q&A Programming Functions

THIS appendix describes all the Q&A field programming functions and commands. Before you read any further, we recommend that you read and thoroughly understand Chapter 11, which covers the basics of creating programming statements. Understanding these programming basics is necessary to comprehend the explanations and examples in this appendix.

Commands and functions in this appendix use this syntax: command *or* abbreviation (*parameter1, parameter2, …parameter3*). When entering a command or function, either type the full command or function *or* the abbreviation. Then fill in the parameters. If you use a programming function or command that can use multiple parameters (such as the statements above), you have a maximum of 50 parameters.

How Q&A Handles Data Internally

Q&A can show you database data in different formats. This makes the data more pleasing to view and sometimes more understandable. However, when calculating programming statements, Q&A uses the data as it is saved internally, which is sometimes different than it is displayed on your screen. Therefore, to use programming statements correctly, you need to understand how Q&A internally saves and uses data.

Saving Field Types Internally

Q&A internally saves various field types in special formats. For example, although you may see a date displayed as January 12, 1995, Q&A internally saves that date as 1995/01/12.

Q&A saves date, time, and Yes/No fields in special formats and calculates them in special ways. For instance, you can multiply a yes value in a Yes/No field type by a number.

Date Fields

Q&A saves dates in a YYYY/MM/DD format, where YYYY represents a four-digit year (such as 1995), MM represents a two-digit month (such as 01 for January), and DD represents the number of the day (such as 12).

When you use a date in a calculation, Q&A computes the date as a number of days. For example, the date January 12, 1995 is 728305, and the next day, January 13, 1995, is 728306. Since Q&A internally saves dates in this format, you can use them in calculations. For example, if you want to add four days to a date, you can enter something like this:

    #10=#20+4

In this example, if field #20 contains January 12, 1995, the date field #10 is set equal to January 16, 1995.

Time Fields

When you enter a time into a field, Q&A saves it internally in the 24-hour military format, HHMM. For instance, Q&A internally saves the time 3:00 PM as 1500. When you use a time in a calculation, Q&A computes the time as the number of minutes from midnight. For instance, Q&A recognizes the time 1:00 AM as 60. Therefore, if someone started work at 3:00 PM and continued for an hour and ten minutes, you can simply add 70 minutes to a time field containing 3:00 PM. Q&A then returns the time 4:10 PM.

Yes/No Fields

As you know, Yes/No formatted fields can contain the affirmative values YES, Y, TRUE, T, or 1, or the negative values NO, N, FALSE, F, or 0. However, Q&A internally saves these values as either YES or NO. When you use a value from a Yes/No field in a calculation, the negative values are represented by the number 0, and the affirmative values are represented by the number 1. For instance, if you multiply a NO value by the number 12, the result is 0.

Some functions return values of either YES or NO. You can use these values in IF THEN statements. For example, the @ERROR function in the following programming statement returns either a YES or NO value:

```
#10:IF @ERROR THEN @MSG("The XLOOKUP couldn't be found")
```

When the value returned by the @ERROR function equals YES, the condition of the IF THEN statement is considered to be true. Therefore, the expression following the THEN is executed. In this case, the statement The XLOOKUP couldn't be found is placed in the status bar of the Q&A window. If the returned value from the @ERROR function is NO, the condition of the IF THEN statement is considered to be false. Thus, the @MSG function is not executed.

String Functions and Commands

This section describes the programming functions and commands used with text values, also called string values or strings. String values are produced from text, keyword, and Yes/No field types.

@ASC or @AS(*text1*)

This function returns the ASCII value of the first character in *text1*, which can be a text string or a field ID number. If *text1* is a text string (rather than a field name or field id), you must enclose it in quotation marks.

NOTE   The @ASC function is case-sensitive. Therefore, "a" returns a different value than "A".

Examples

        #10=@ASC("$500")

In this example, *text1* equals $500. Since the @ASC function returns the ASCII value of only the first character of the variable, Q&A places 36, the value of the dollar sign, in field #10.

        #50=@ASC(#40)

If field #40 contains the word *Business*, field #50 contains 66, the ASCII value of the letter "B.".

@CHR or @CH(*number1*)

This function returns the ASCII character equivalent of *number1*, which can be a numeric value or a field ID. If the number specified is out of the range of acceptable ASCII numbers, Q&A will return nothing.

Examples

        #10=@CHR(36)

In this example, Q&A returns the character equivalent of the ASCII number 36, which is the dollar sign. Therefore, Q&A places $ in field #10.

        #50=@CHR(#40)

This statement returns the character that represents the ASCII value in field #40. For example, if field #40 contains the number 155, field #50 is equal to the cent character.

CLEAR(*field1, field2,...fieldn*)

This command clears the values from the field IDs or field names specified in the list. When entering the programming statement, be sure to separate each field with a comma.

Examples

        #20:CLEAR(Salary,#10,#5,Bonus,#30)

In the example, Q&A clears fields #10, #5, and #30 and the fields that are named "Salary" and "Bonus."

        #5:CLEAR(#10..#40)

The programming statement empties the values from all the fields in the range field #10 to field #40.

@DEL or @DE(*field,number1,number2*)

This function returns the value of *field* with text deleted. Q&A counts *number1* characters in *field* and then deletes *number2* characters.

Example

    #20=@DEL(#10,10,4)

This copies field #10, with the four characters immediately after the tenth character deleted. For example, if field #10 contains the value "Accounts 453, 345, and 5", Q&A places "Accounts 345, and 5" into field #20.

@DITTO or @DI(*#fn1, #fn2,...#fnn*)

This function copies the contents of one or more fields *#fn1, #fn2* to *#fnn* from one record to the next. This command only works when adding data. When entering the list of fields, separate each field with a comma. When Q&A executes this command, the data in specified fields in the last record you added is copied to the same fields in the new record.

Examples

    #10:@DITTO(#10,#20,#50)

This example copies the contents of fields #10, #20, and #50 from the last record added into fields #10, #20, and #50 of the current record.

    #10:@DITTO(#10..#45,#80)

This copies the range of fields #10 to #45 and field #80 from the last record added to the current record.

@FILENAME or @FN

This function returns the name and path of the database being used. @FILENAME is useful when creating XLOOKUP statements into the current database.

Examples

    #10=@FILENAME

This statement returns the path and filename of the current database (for example, C:\QAWIN\EMPLOYEE.DTF)

@HELP(*field1*) or @HP

For the @HELP function to produce a help box, define a custom help box using the Custom Help dialog box. Then use the @HELP function to refer to the help box in the Database Structure mode. Since you can specify a help box for a particular field (*field1*), you can choose to display a help box defined for a different field.

This function is used most often to prompt users with directions on data entry. Using help boxes with on-entry programming is a good way to guide someone through his or her data entry tasks. When you use @HELP with conditional programming, you can produce useful warning boxes.

Examples

    >#10:IF #10="PONY EXPRESS" THEN @HELP(#40)

When Q&A leaves field #10, the user sees the help box defined for field #40 only if field #10 contains "PONY EXPRESS".

@INSTR or @IN(*text1,text2*)

This function searches for *text2* within *text1*, a field or text string and returns the position of the first found occurrence of the text string. This function is not case-sensitive.

Examples

    #20=@INSTR(#10,"TAX")

In this example, Q&A returns the position of the first occurrence of the word "tax" in field #10. For example, if field #10 contains the text, "All taxes will be charged in full," field #20 now contains 5 because "tax" is located five characters from the beginning of field #10.

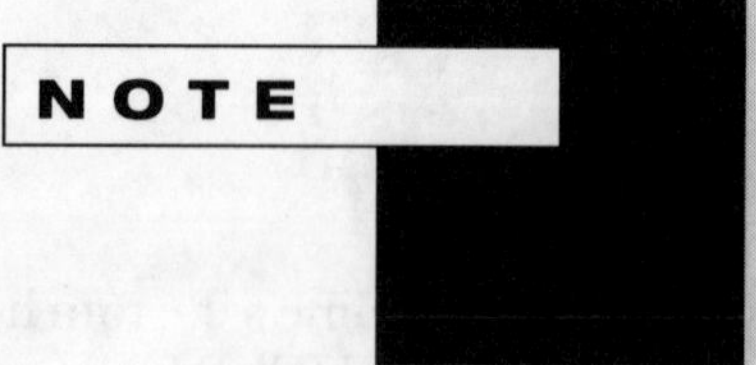

Q&A counts embedded spaces (such as the space between *income* and *tax* in the phrase *income tax* as characters. However, spaces ending a field (such as *expenses*   ) are not recognized.

@LEFT or @LT(*text1,number1*)

This function retrieves the *number1* leftmost characters in the text string or field *text1*. The @LEFT function starts counting from the leftmost position of *text1* and returns the characters from this position to the beginning of *text1*.

Example

    #20=@LEFT(#10,5)

In the example, field #20 is equal to the first five characters of field #10. If field #10 equals 88072-9000-878, field #20 is equal to 88072.

@LEN(*text1*)

This function returns the number of characters in the *text1* field or text. Don't confuse this function with the programming function @WIDTH, which returns the width of the field.

Example

    #20=@LEN(#10)

This statement returns the number of characters in field #10. For example, if field #10 contains the value "cash receipts," field #20 is equal to 13, including the space between cash and receipts.

This example was simple because field #10 is a text-formatted field. However, if the field is Yes/No, date, or time, Q&A calculates the number of characters a little differently.

Remember that Q&A saves Yes/No field values internally as either YES or NO. Dates are saved in YYYY/MM/DD format, and time is saved in a military time format. Therefore, the lengths of these values may be different than the characters on the screen. Table D.1 presents some examples of how Q&A recognizes date, time, and Yes/No values and these values are calculated in @LEN statements.

TABLE D.1: Q&A Date, Time and Yes/No Values in @LEN Statements

FORMAT	WHAT YOU SEE	HOW Q&A RECOGNIZES THE VALUE	@LEN
Date	November 13, 1972	1972/11/13	10
Date	January 1, 1967	1967/01/01	10
Time	3:00 PM	1500	5
Time	12:05 AM	105	4
Yes/No	Yes	Yes	3
Yes/No	No	No	2
Yes/No	True	Yes	3
Yes/No	False	No	2
Yes/No	1	Yes	3
Yes/No	0	No	2

@MID or
@MD(*text1,number1,number2*)

This function returns a text string, which is *number2* characters starting at *number1* position of *text1*. @MID is very similar to @LEFT; however, @MID can return a section of *text1* from the middle of a field, and @LEFT can only retrieve a range of text that begins at the leftmost part of a field.

Example

    #20=@MID(#10,5,8)

This example places the value "Analysis" in field #20 if field #10 contains "Cost Analysis Behavior." Q&A counts five characters into the value of field #10 and retrieves the next eight characters.

@MSG(*text1*)

This function displays *text1* in red characters on the status bar. This is in contrast to @HELP, which displays a field's custom help dialog box. *Text1* can be a text string, a field name, a field ID, or a combination of all. Enclose a text string within quotation marks.

Although more than 80 characters fit on the status bar, Symantec decided to limit the message length to 80. This aids in the interoperability between Q&A for Windows and Q&A for DOS.

Examples

    <#10:@MSG("Enter the client's ID number")

In the example, Q&A displays the message Enter the client's ID number in the status bar when you enter field #10.

    <#20:@MSG("The amount due from client ID "+#10)

If field #10 contains ZI737, the statement in field #20 returns, The amount due from client ID ZI737. This type of addition will only work if field #10 is a text field. If field #10 is *not* a text field, use the following programming statements which will change field #10's value to a text value as it is used in the computation:

<#20:@MSG("The amount due from client ID "@STR(#10))

@NUM(*text1*)

This function extracts the numeric values from the *text1* text string or a field.

Examples

#20=@NUM(#10)

If field #10 contains the value "Checking Account #0063251158," the programming statement puts 0063251158 into field #20.

#20=@NUM("DOB: 01/28/70 TOB: 730")

The example returns 012870730 from the multiple sets of numbers in *text1* and places it into field #20.

@REPLACE(*text1,text2,text3*)

This function replaces the text *text2* in field or text string *text1* with the different text *text3*.

The @REPLACE function replaces every occurrence of *text2*, unlike @REPLFIR and @REPLLAS, which replace only the first and last occurrences of the variable, respectively.

Examples

#30=@REPLACE(#20,"LIFO","FIFO")

If field #20 contains the value, "Their basis of inventory accounting is LIFO", field #30 returns the value, "Their basis of inventory accounting is FIFO".

#30=@REPLACE(#20,"LIFO",#10)

This statement replaces LIFO with the value in field #10 and returns the string to field #30.

@REPLACE is a great way to delete the occurrences of certain blocks of text. For instance, to delete the word "account" throughout a field, use 20=@REPLACE(#20,"account","").

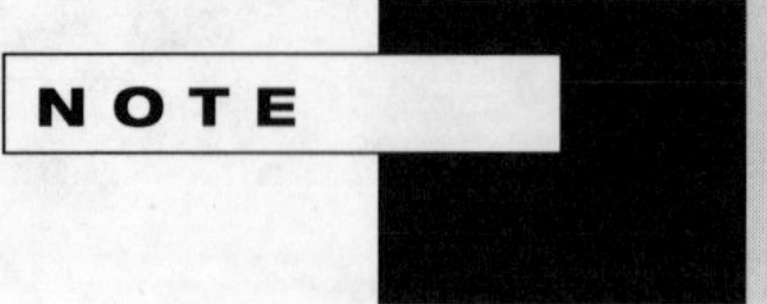

In field programming, you can specify blanks by putting two quotation marks ("") together. The logic behind this is that nothing (that is, blanks) is between the quotes.

@REPLFIR(*text1,text2,text3*)

This function replaces only the first occurrence of variable *text2* with variable *text3* in the field or text string *text1*.

Examples

#20=@REPLFIR(#20,"Wyllie","Mr. Wyllie")

This statement replaces the first occurrence of Wyllie with the value Mr. Wyllie. If field #20 equals, "Wyllie filed exempt and Wyllie is being investigated", this programming statement changes field #20 to "Mr. Wyllie filed exempt and Wyllie is being investigated".

@REPLLAS(*text1,text2,text3*)

This function replaces the last occurrence of *text2* with *text3* in the field or text string *text1*.

Example

#20=@REPLLAS(#20,"Mr. Wyllie","Wyllie")

If field #20 is equal to "Mr. Wyllie filed exempt and Mr. Wyllie is being investigated", this programming statement changes field #20 to equal "Mr. Wyllie filed exempt and Wyllie is being investigated".

@RIGHT or @RT(text1,number1)

This function retrieves the farthest right characters of *text1* specified by number 1. @RIGHT is very similar to the function @LEFT, which returns the leftmost characters of a field or text string.

Example

        #20=@RIGHT(#10,4)

In the example, Q&A copies the four rightmost characters in field #10 into field #20. For example, if field #10 contains "The company ID is DBE0023", field #20 is set equal to "0023".

@TEXT or @TXT(number1,text1)

This function repeats *text1 number1* times. @TEXT is most often used for conditional programming in reports. @TEXT is also commonly used in Q&A's Boolean programming.

Examples

        #10=@TEXT(12,"-")

The statement places 12 dashes in field #10.

        #20=@TEXT(#10>150,"You owe too much money")

This Boolean programming statement returns the value "You owe too much money" to field #20 if the value in field #10 is greater than 150. Otherwise, nothing is placed in field #20.

Q&A's Boolean programming works this way: the expression #10>150 is either true or false. When #10 is greater than 150, Q&A returns true for that expression. When #10 is not greater than 150, Q&A returns false for that expression. In essence, the programming statement is seen by Q&A as either:

        #20=@TEXT(true,"You owe too much money") or #20=@TEXT(false,"You
        owe too much money").

As explained at the beginning of this chapter, these affirmative or negative values are represented as the values 1 and 0. Therefore, Q&A views the programming statement as either:

    #20=@TEXT(1,"You owe too much money")

or

    #20=@TEXT(0,"You owe too much money")

Thus, if field #10 is greater than 150, then "You owe too much money" is repeated in field #20 once. Otherwise, if field #10 is not greater than 150, "You owe too much money" is repeated in field #20 zero times. In essence, nothing is put into field #20.

@WIDTH or @WTH(*field1*)

This function returns the length of the field *field1*. Don't confuse @WIDTH with @LEN, which returns the number of the characters in a field. This function is mainly used in Q&A for DOS. In Q&A for Windows, @WIDTH returns a 0 because the widths of the fields in Q&A for Windows is not measured in characters. However, if a Q&A for Windows database has been opened by Q&A for DOS, or a Q&A for DOS database is opened in Q&A for Windows, the @WIDTH function returns a field width.

Example

    #20=@WIDTH(#10)

In this statement, the value of field #20 is equal to the length of field #10.

Date and Time Functions

These functions are used to manipulate date and time values.

@D(*date1*)

This function translates the text value within the parentheses to a date. This allows you to use a date constant in an expression.

Examples

#10=#20-@D(January 1,1994)

In this example, January 1, 1994, is subtracted from the date in field #20, thereby calculating the number of days between the two dates.

#10=@DATE-@D(9/24/94)

This statement tells you the number of days the current date is from 9/24/94, which could be the number of days into the first quarter of the 1994 fiscal year.

@DATE or @DA

This function returns the current date based on your computer's internal clock.

Examples

#10=@DATE

This example places the current computer system date in field #10. For example, if today's date is February 17, 1995, then 2/17/95 appears in field #10. Note that your global format options might be set to display the date in a different format, such as 02/17/1995.

#10=@D(January 1, 1996)-@DATE

This example places the number of days from today's computer system date until January 1, 1996 into field #10.

@DOM or @DM(*date*)

This function returns the day of the month for the date within the parentheses.

Examples

#10=@DOM(#15)

Field #10 contains the day of month for the date in field #15. For example, if field #15 contains October 25, 1994, field number #10 contains 25.

#10=@DOM(@DATE)

Field #10 contains the day of month for today's date.

DOW$ or @DW$(*date*)

This function Returns the name of the week of the date within the parentheses.

Examples

        #10=@DOW$("6/17/95")

The example places the day of week for the date July 17, 1995, in field #10. Therefore, field #10 contains Saturday.

        #10=@DOW$(@DATE)

This statement returns the day of week for today's date and places it in field #10.

@MONTH or @MT(*date*)

This function returns the number representing the month of the date within the parentheses.

Examples

        #10=@MONTH("January 1, 1995")

Field #10 contains 1 because January is the first month of the year.

        #10=@MONTH(@DATE)

In this example, field #10 contains the integer representing the month of the current computer system date.

@MONTH$ or @MT$(*date*)

This function returns the name of the month for the date within the parentheses.

Examples

        #10=@MONTH("January 1, 1995")

The programming statement places January into field #10.

        #10=@MONTH(@DATE)

Field #10 contains the name of the month for the current date.

@T(*time*)

This function translates the string within the parentheses as a time. This lets you use a time constant in calculations.

Examples

    #10=@T(8:00 PM)+60

Field #10 equals 9:00 PM (8:00 PM plus 60 minutes).

    #10=(#20-@T(8:00 AM))/60

If field #20 contains the time you left work, field #10 equals the number of hours that you spent at work. In this example, the expression @T(8:00 AM) is the time the work day began. Dividing by 60 converts the answer into hours since Q&A internally calculates time as minutes.

@TIME or @TME

This function returns the current time based on your computer's internal clock.

Examples

    #10=@TIME

Field #10 contains the current time.

    #10=@TIME-#20

If field #20 contains the time you arrived at work, field #10 equals the number of minutes you have been at work.

@YEAR or @YR(*date*)

This function returns the year of the date within the parentheses. Q&A displays the year as a four-digit number.

Examples

    #10=@YEAR(@DATE)

In the example, Q&A places the year of the current date in field #10. For instance, if the date is January 28, 1995, then field #10 contains 1995.

    #10=@MONTH$(@DATE)+" "+@YEAR(@DATE)

If you don't want the whole date displayed in a field, use the @YEAR function to create the desired display. For example, if the current date is January 28, 1995, field #10 contains January 1995. @MONTH$ (@DATE) places January and ""+@YEAR(@DATE) adds a space and the year 1995 to field #10.

Mathematical Functions

@ABS or @AB(*number1*)

This function calculates the absolute value of the number *number1*.

Examples

    #10=ABS(-50)

The statement places 50, which is the absolute value of -50, in field #10.

    #10=ABS(#20-#15)

To measure the change in total sales, you can use the absolute value function. In this example, field #15 represents the sales of the previous fiscal quarter and field #20 contains the sales of the current quarter. The absolute value of the difference between field #20 and #15 is placed in field #10. So, if field #20=95,000 and field #15=105,000, field #10 equals 10,000.

@AVG or @AV(*value1,value2,...value n*)

This function averages the listed values. This list can be a series of numbers, fields, or a range of fields. Be sure to separate each item in the series with a comma. You cannot use field names in a range. If the field referred to in the list is empty, it is not included in the average.

Examples

    #10=@AVG(50,-12,.03)

This programming statement calculates the average of 50, -12, and .03. The result, 12.68, is placed in field #10.

    #10=@AVG(#20..#40)

Field #10 contains the average of the range of fields from #20 to #40. For this example, let's assume that your database has the following fields and values: #20=3, #25=8, #30=12, #35=2, #40=7, #80=6, and #245=9. The programming statement computes 3+8+12+2+7)/5 and places the result, 6.4 in field #10.

@EXP or @EX(*number1,exponent1*)

This function calculates a value to a certain power using the values within the parentheses. The number *number1* serves as the value that is raised to the *exponent1*.

Examples

    #10=@EXP(2,3)

This statement raises the number 2 to the third power, expressed mathematically as 2^3. Therefore, field #10 is set equal to 2*2*2, which is 8.

    #10=#20*@EXP(1+#30,#40)

You can use the exponent function to calculate the future value of an investment. If you set field #20 as your principal investment, field #30 as your interest rate per compounded period, and field #40 as the number of compounding periods, field #10 is equal to the future value of your investment by the time it has matured.

@INT or @IT(*number1*)

This function returns the integer portion of *number1*.

Examples

    #10=@INT(2.65)

Field #10 contains 2, the integer portion of 2.65.

    #10=@INT(#15/#25)

If you work in a manufacturing company and need to know how many units your company can afford to produce, you can use @INT to help in these calculations. To determine how many units your company can produce, divide the amount of money that your company can spend by the marginal cost, the additional cost per unit. In this example, field #15 equals 180,000, the total amount of cash available to spend. Field #25 equals the marginal cost, 43.5. Q&A sets field #10 to 4137, the number of complete units that your company can produce.

@MAX or @MX(*value1,value2,…value n*)

This function returns the maximum value of the list within the parentheses. Values in the list can be a series of numbers, fields, or a range. Be sure to separate each item on the list with a comma. Do not use field names in a range. If a field in the list is empty, Q&A ignores it when calculating.

Examples

#10=@MAX(15, 75, 16)

Q&A places 75, the maximum value in this list, in field #10.

#10=@MAX(#15..#30)

Q&A finds the maximum value in the range of fields #15 to #30 and places it in field #10.

@MIN or @MN(*value1,value2,value n*)

This function returns the minimum value of the list within the parentheses. Items in the list can be a series of numbers, fields, or a range. Be sure to separate each item in the series with a comma. Do not use field names in a range. If a field in the list is empty, Q&A ignores it when calculating.

Examples

#10=@MIN(3, -2, 12)

Q&A places -2, the minimum value in this list, in field #10.

#10=@MIN(#20..#50)

Q&A finds the minimum value from the range of fields #20 to #50 and places it in field #10.

@MOD or @MD(*number1,number2*)

This function returns the smallest nonnegative number that results from either repeatedly subtracting *number2* from *number1* or adding them together. In other words, the @MOD function divides *number1* by the absolute value of *number2*, and then multiplies the remainder by the absolute value of *number2*.

Examples

        #10=@MOD(7,2)

Field #10 equals 1 using one of these calculations: 7-2=5, 5-2=3, 3-2=1 *or* 7/2=3.5 .5*2=1

        #10=@MOD(11,-3)

Q&A places 2 in field #10 because 11+(-3)=8, 8+(-3)=5 5+(-3)=2 *or* 11/|-3|=3.66666 .666666*|-3|=2

        #10=@MOD(#20,#15)

If your company needs to manufacture as many complete units as possible and you need to know how much money you will have remaining, use the @MOD function to determine this number. To place the number of unused dollars in field #10, field #20 should contain the funds available for production to cover all variable costs, and field #15 should contain the marginal cost per unit.

@ROUND or @RND(*number1,decimal1*)

This function rounds a number up to the number of decimal points specified. You can set the decimal points from 15 to –15. A positive number in the decimal parameter instructs Q&A to round the number that many digits to the right of the decimal point. A negative number in the decimal parameter instructs Q&A to round the number that many digits to the left of the decimal point. When you round digits off left of the decimal point, Q&A replaces the rounded-off digits with zeros.

Examples

        #10=@ROUND(12785.453,2)

As a result of the statement, field #10 contains 12785.45.

        #10=@ROUND(45783.43,-3)

As a result of the statement, field #10 contains 46000.

@SGN(*number1*)

This function returns an integer representing the sign of the number. If *number1* is a positive number, Q&A returns the number 1. If *number1* is a negative number, Q&A returns the number -1. If *number1* is 0, Q&A returns 0.

Example

#10=@SGN(-20.4)

This statement places -1 in field #10.

@SQRT or @SQ(*number1*)

This function computes the square root of *number1*. If you use @SQRT on a negative number, Q&A calculates the absolute value of *number1*, and returns the square root of that number.

Examples

#10=@SQRT(25)

Field #10 equals to 5, the square root of 25.

#10=@SQRT(-9)

Field #10 equals 3. Q&A calculates the absolute value of -9, returning 9. Then Q&A computes the square root of 9.

@STD(*value1,value2,...value n*)

This function calculates the standard deviation of the list within the parentheses. The values in the list can be a series of numbers, fields, or a range. Be sure to separate each item in the series with a comma. You cannot use field names in a range. If a field in the list is empty, Q&A ignores it when calculating.

Examples

#10=@STD(40,50)

Field #10 equals 5, the standard deviation of 40 and 50.

#10=@STD(#20..#70)

In this example, field #10 contains the standard deviation of the range of fields #20 to #70.

@SUM(*value1,value2,...value n*)

This function returns the sum of the values, which can be a series of numbers, fields, or a range. Be sure to separate each item in the series with a comma. Do not use field names in a range. If a field in the list is empty, Q&A ignores it when calculating.

Examples

#10=@SUM(3.45,6.34,7.9)

Field #10 equals 17.69, which is 3.45+6.34+7.9.

#10=@SUM(#20..#45)

Field #10 equals the sum of all the fields ranging from #20 to #45.

@VAR(*value1,value2,...value n*)

This function returns the variance of the values in the list. This list can be a series of numbers, fields, or a range. Be sure to separate each item in the series with a comma. Do not use field names in a range. If a field in the list is empty, Q&A ignores it when calculating.

Examples

#10=VAR(12,45,8)

Field #10 equals 274.88, which is the variance of 12, 45, and 8.

#10–VAR(#15..#45)

Q&A calculates the variance of all the fields ranging from #15 to #45 and places it in field #10.

Financial Functions

The financial functions mainly concentrate on loans, bonds, and other investments dependent on interest rates.

@CGR(*pv,fv,np*)

This function calculates the compound growth rate, often called the rate of return. *Pv* is the present value or your principal. *Fv* is the future value of the investment. *Np* is the number of payment periods.

Example

    #10=@CGR(100,120,12)

This statement calculates the growth rate and places it in field #10. For example, if you have a $100 bond, which pays $120 in one year, the growth rate of your initial investment is .0153 per month. In essence, your investment increases 1.53% every month.

@FV(pa,i,np)

This function calculates the future value of an investment pa with a compounded interest rate i. np represents the number of payment periods. i is a percentage expressed in decimal form. For example, enter 6% as .06.

Examples

    #10=FV(500,.06,10)

In this example, $500 is deposited 10 times into an account gaining 6% per period. Q&A places the result, 6590.397, in field #10.

    #10=FV(#20,#30,#40)

Suppose every year for your newborn child's birthday, you deposit $550 in a special college account, which earns 6% annual interest. By the time the child is 18, you will have $16998.10 in that account (that is field #10). In this example, field #20=550, field #30=.06, and field #40=18.

@PMT(pv,i,np)

This function calculates the payments due on a loan where pv is present value, the amount loaned to you, i is the interest rate, and np is the number of payments.

Examples

    #10=@PMT(45000,.01014,120)

Field #10 contains 650, which is the result of making 120 payments on a $450,000 loan at a 1.014% monthly interest rate.

    #10=@PMT(6000,.098,4)

Field #10 contains 1884.64, which is the result of making four annual payments on a $6,000 loan at an annual interest rate of 9.8%.

@PV(*pa,i,np*)

This function calculates the present value, or principal, when you provide the payment amount (*pa*), interest(*i*), and number of payment periods(*np*).

Examples

    #10=@PV(650,.01014,120)

Field #10 contains 45,000, which is the present value for an annuity of 120 payments (10 years of monthly payments) of $650 at a 1.014% interest rate.

    #10=@PV(4000,.02,40)

This example calculates the present value of an annuity paying $4000 per quarter for 10 years at 8% a year, compounded quarterly. After calculating, Q&A places 109421.92 in field #10. Note that the annual interest of 8% was divided by 4 to get quarterly interest rates of 2%. Also, note that since there are 4 payments per year, the number of payments was 40.

@IR(*pv,pa,np*)

This function determines the interest rate of a loan based on the present value (*pv*), payment amount (*pa*), and number of payment periods (*np*).

Examples

    #10=@IR(45000,650,120)

If the present value of the loan is $45,000 and you make 120 payments (one payment every month for 10 years) at $650 each, your monthly interest rate is equal to 1.014%.

    #10=@IR(50000,800,120)

If you need a $50,000 loan and can make only $800 payments per month for the next 10 years, you need to look for a loan that offers an interest rate below 1.23% a month.

Typecast Functions

When using Q&A's programming capabilities to create complex calculations, you might need to change the value type.

Suppose you use the LOOKUP command to retrieve a date 10/25/94 from the lookup table and place it into a date field. The value that you retrieve may look like a date and may be placed in a date field. However, since you retrieved the date from the lookup table, which only contains text entries, you cannot use it as a date; special date retrievals will not work on this date, and you cannot add days to this date either. However, if you use the @TODATE typecast function, Q&A converts this text value into a date value. All the functions in this section, like @TODATE, change text values to other values. The one exception to this is @STR, which changes a value into a text value.

@TODATE or @TD(*text1*)

This function changes the *text1* text value to a date value.

Examples

```
#10=(@TODATE(#15))+7
```

This statement converts the text value in field #15 to a date value and adds seven days.

@TOTIME or @TT(*text1*)

This function changes the *text1* text value to a time value.

Examples

```
#10=@TOTIME(#15)+60
```

This statement changes the text value in field #15 to a time value and adds one hour.

@TOMONEY or @TM(*text1*)

This function changes the *text1* text value to a money value.

Examples

    #10=@TOMONEY(#15)

The text value in field #15 is converted to a money value.

    #10=@TOMONEY(@LOOKUP(#10,1))+250

After the @LOOKUP expression retrieves a text value from the lookup table, the @TOMONEY function converts it to a money value. $250 is added to this money value, which is placed in field #10.

@TONUMBER or @TN(*text1*)

This function changes the *text1* text value to a number value.

Examples

    #10=@TONUMBER(#15)

The example converts the text value in field #15 into a number value, which is then placed into field #10.

    #10=@TONUMBER(@LEFT(#10,3))+10

The @LEFT function returns a text value, which is converted into a number. Ten (10) is then added to the number and then placed into field #10.

@TOYESNO or @TY(*text1*)

This function changes the *text1* text value to a Yes/No value.

Examples

    #10=@TOYESNO(#15)

The example converts the text value in field #15 into a Yes/No value, which is placed into field #10.

    #10=@TOYESNO(Salary>25000)

In this example, Salary>25000 determines whether Salary is greater than 25000 and returns a 1 or a 0, depending on the result. This 1 or 0 is converted to a yes or no, which is placed in field #10. If field #10 is a YES/NO field, the result will be T or F.

Miscellaneous Functions

This section includes the functions that do not fall into any particular category.

@ERROR

This function returns a YES if the most recent XLOOKUP failed to retrieve a value, or NO if a value is retrieved. The value returned is actually a Yes/No value, which can be used as True and 1 or False and 0. In a programming statement, be sure to place the @ERROR function after the XLOOKUP statement or command.

Examples

    #20=@ERROR

If an XLOOKUP in a previous field retrieves a value from an external database, field #20 equals NO. Otherwise, the value YES is placed into field #20. If field #20 is a YES/NO field, the value placed in it will be either a F or a T.

    #20:IF @ERROR THEN @MSG("Cannot find that name")

Since the @ERROR function returns a value of YES(True) or NO(False), you can use it in calculations. If a value is not returned by a XLOOKUP, @ERROR returns YES, and the message "Cannot find that name" is displayed on the status bar. Otherwise, the IF THEN statement is not TRUE, and there is no further execution. This statement is a shortcut notation for the logic #20:IF @ERROR equals TRUE, perform @MSG ("Cannot find that name").

@REST(*text1,restriction*)

This function returns TRUE or FALSE depending on whether *text1* in the first parameter is equal to *restriction*. If *text1* equals *restriction*, a YES is returned. Otherwise, NO is returned.

Examples

    #10=@REST(#15,"Deanna")

This programming statement places a YES into field #10 if field #15 equals "Deanna."

    #10:IF @REST(#15,@DATE+7) THEN @MSG("1 week from now")

Since the @REST function returns a value of YES(True) or NO(False), you can use it in IF THEN calculations. This statement demonstrates the flexibility of the @REST function. When field #15 equals @DATE+7, "1 week from now" is displayed on the status bar.

@SELECT(*number1,selection1;selection2; …selectionn*)

This function returns the selection designated by *number1*. You must list at least two selections from which to choose. Since a selection might be a text string containing commas or semi-colons, Q&A allows you to separate the selections by using either commas or semi-colons. If the value in *number1* refers to a selection that does not exist (such as 0 or a value greater than the number of items in the list), the last selection is returned.

Examples

    #10=@SELECT(#15,"Paid","30 days","60 days")

If the value in field #15 equals 1, Paid is placed in field #10. If field #15 is 2, 30 days is returned. If field #15 is 3, 60 days is returned. If field #15 contains a value that is not 1, 2, or 3, 60 days is returned.

    #10=@SELECT(#15,#20;"Cupertino, CA";"Fresno, CA")

If the value in field #15 is 1, the value in field #20 is placed into field #10. If field #15 is 2, Cupertino, CA is returned. If field #15 equals 3, Fresno, CA is returned. If a value other than 1, 2, or 3 is in field #15, Fresno, CA is returned.

Context Functions

The context programming functions @ADD and @UPDATE are used to determine what routines in ADD/EDIT you are performing.

@ADD or @AD

This function returns a YES if you are adding a new record. If you are updating or editing existing records, the @ADD function returns NO.

Examples

        #10=@ADD

If you are adding a record the value YES is placed in field #10. Otherwise, field #10 contains NO.

        #10:IF @ADD THEN #50=@TIME

Since the @ADD function returns a value of YES(True) or NO(False), it can be used in calculations. If you are adding a new record, the time is placed into field #50.

@UPDATE or @UD

This function returns a YES if you are editing an already existing record. If you are adding a record, the @UPDATE function returns NO.

Examples

        #10=@UPDATE

If you are editing a record, the value YES is placed in field #10. Otherwise, field #10 contains NO.

        #10:IF @UPDATE THEN #50=@TIME

Since the @UPDATE function returns a value of YES(True) or NO(False), it can be used in calculations. If you are editing an already existing record, the time is placed into field #50.

Stage Functions

This section describes the functions that inform you about the Q&A setup and the current database.

@PLATFORM

Returns the platform you are using. Since you are using Q&A for Windows, you are operating in a Windows platform. Therefore, this function always returns WIN. However, if you are using your database in Q&A for DOS, this function returns DOS.

Example

    #10=@PLATFORM

Since you are using your database in Q&A for Windows, this function places WIN in field #10.

@LAYOUT

This function returns the name of the current input form.

Examples

    #10=@LAYOUT

If you are using the Master input form, Q&A places MASTER FORM in field #10.

    #10:@MSG("You are in input form: "+@LAYOUT)

If you are using an input form called MARKETING, this statement displays "You are in input form: MARKETING" in the status bar.

@GROUP

This function returns the name of the group to which the user is assigned. This function will not return a value if you are using a user ID from either the Administrator or Unassigned User group or if your database is not password-protected and you are not assigned a group.

Examples

    #10=@GROUP

If you are using a user ID that is part of the MANAGEMENT group, Q&A places MANAGEMENT in field #10.

    #10:@MSG("Your user ID is in group: "+@GROUP)

If you are logged in as a user ID in a group called 3rd Floor, Q&A displays "Your user ID is in group: 3rd Floor" in the status bar.

@USERID

This function returns the name of the user ID you are assigned. If your database is not password-protected and you are not assigned a user ID, this function will not return any value.

Examples

    #10=@USERID

If you are using a user ID called MWILLIAMS, Q&A places MWILLIAMS in field #10.

    #10:@MSG("Your user ID is "+@USERID)

If you are logged in as user ID GUEST, Q&A displays "Your user ID is GUEST" in the status bar.

Indirection

There might be times when you are in Add/Edit mode and you want to specify where the data from a particular field is to be placed. With *indirection*, you can program your database to accomplish this task. For example, if you had fields Amount, Placement, Credit, and Debit, you can enter the amount of a transaction in the Amount field. Then you type credit or debit in the Placement field. With indirection, you can have Q&A take the number in the Amount field and add it to whichever field you typed in Placement. Indirection statements are created with the @FIELD function, which is discussed next.

@FIELD(string) or @(string)

@FIELD takes the returned string and uses it as a field reference. The string can be a field and/or for calculation.

Examples

The following programming example places the value of the field amount into the field specified by the Transaction field. If you typed Checking in the Transaction field, the value in Amount field is placed into the field named Checking.

>#20:@FIELD(Transaction)=Amount

As seen below, you can also use calculations in the @FIELD string. The @MONTH$(Date Purchased) returns the month from the date in the Date Purchased field. The value in the Amount field is then placed in the field with the same name as the month returned. If you enter 10/25/95 in the Date Purchased field and 1500 in the Amount field, Q&A places 1500 into the field named October.

>#20:@FIELD(@MONTH$(Date Purchased))=Amount

Numbering Functions

For those who want to create different record numbers for each record, Q&A created the @NUMBER functions. The @NUMBER functions are based on an internal counter Q&A uses. The counter is used to stamp values into fields and expressions through the @NUMBER functions. Every time a counter stamps something with its value, it is incremented. This incrementing allows you to create record numbers.

@NUMBER or @NMB

This function increases the internal counter's value by one and returns the new value.

Examples

#10=@NUMBER

If the internal counter is set at 5, this statement and adds 1 to the counter making it 6, and places the number 6 into field #10.

@NUMBER(number) or @NMB(number)

This function with the number parameter increases the internal counter by the number specified and returns the new value.

Examples

#10=@NUMBER(5)

If the internal counter is set at 5, this statement adds 5 to the counter making it 10, and places the number 10 into field #10.

Resetting the Counter

If you need to reset the counter to a lower value, you can do so through the Calculation Options dialog box. To change the counter value, choose Edit ➤ Calculation Options. This displays the Calculation Options dialog box (see Figure D.1). Within the Reset @Number() box, you can see the internal counter value labeled From. In the To box you can change the internal counter value. Just type the value you want in the To box and click OK or press Enter.

FIGURE D.1

The Calculation Options dialog box lets you change the internal counter value. Here, the counter is set to 5 and is being changed back to 1.

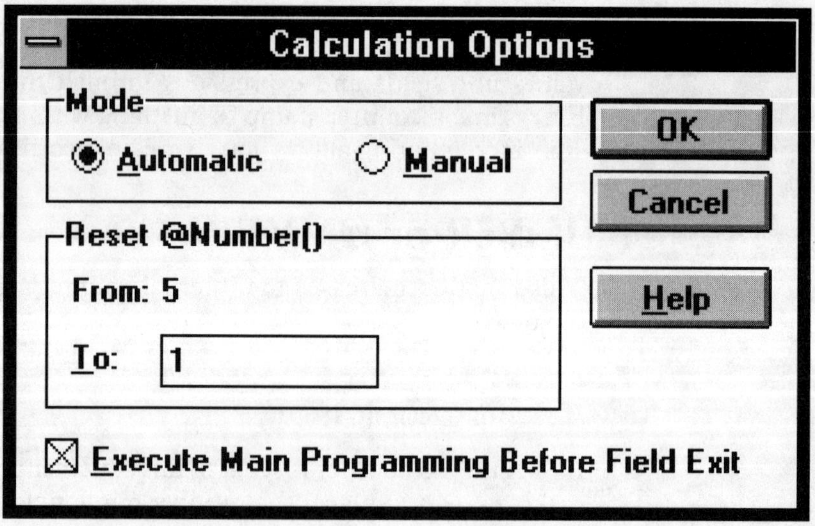

Lookup Table and Lookup Statements

Q&A allows your database to retrieve information from the *lookup table*, which is built into a Q&A database. The Edit Lookup table (Figure D.2) can store 64,000 characters of information from which it can retrieve. The lookup table is a matrix of five columns and as many rows as you need to use. However, since the number of characters the lookup table can contain is limited, your rows are also limited.

TIP

Unlike data from a record, you cannot transfer the data in a lookup table to other databases. You cannot transfer the entire lookup table either. However, since a lookup table is part of database's design, you can copy a lookup table by copying a database's design. Once you copy the design of the database, you can alter it to suit your needs.

FIGURE D.2

The lookup table is made up of a Key Column, four data columns and many rows.

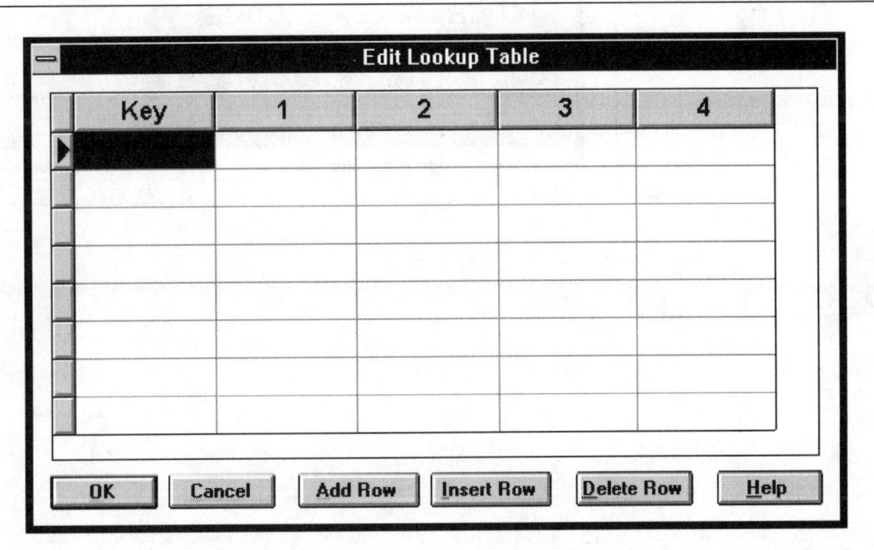

The first column of the lookup table, the *Key Column*, is a reference column. The remaining columns, *data columns*, are Column 1, Column 2, Column 3, and Column 4. The information stored in these data columns pertain to the information in the Key Column. To retrieve information in one of the four data columns, you need to specify the row in which the information lies. You can specify that row through the data in the Key column. Looking at Figure D.3, notice a list of different credit cards in the Key Column and their service charges in Column 1. If you need to get the service charge for a sale on a Visa card, instruct Q&A to retrieve the information in the first data column from the Visa row. To retrieve data from these tables, you can use LOOKUP, @LOOKUP, LOOKUPR, and @LOOKUPR functions and commands.

Use this lookup table to store credit card information and state abbreviations.

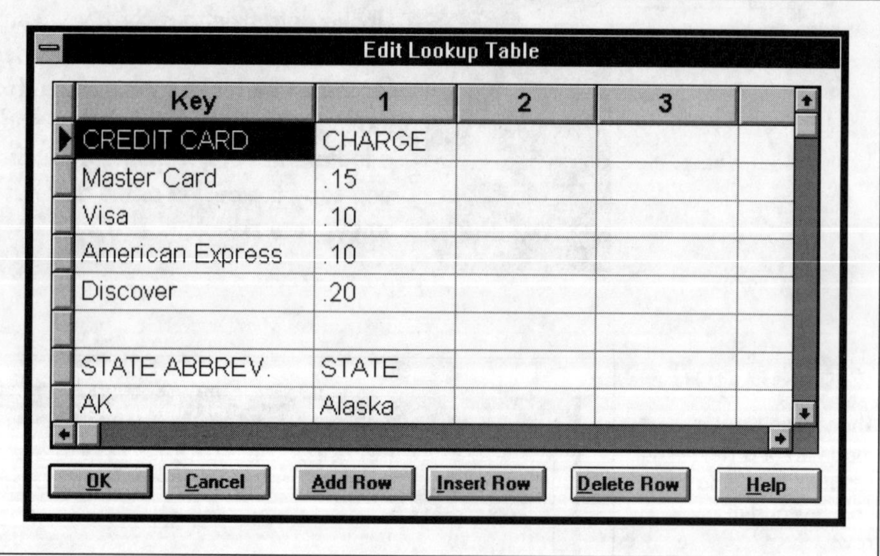

Key	1	2	3	
CREDIT CARD	CHARGE			
Master Card	.15			
Visa	.10			
American Express	.10			
Discover	.20			
STATE ABBREV.	STATE			
AK	Alaska			

If your database contains many items that can be represented by a code, the lookup table is an excellent way to reduce your data entry tasks. For example, if you have a field that requires the full name entry of a state, you can set up the lookup table to contain state abbreviations in the Key Column. Then type the full names of the states in a data column. You then can use the @LOOKUP function to retrieve the full name of the state by looking up its abbreviation.

Q&A saves the data entered in the lookup column as text despite its true type. Therefore, Q&A does not consider the lookup table entry 1995/12/01 as a date. Therefore, when you use the lookup commands and functions to retrieve a date from the lookup table, you can't use it as a date unless you convert it using the @TODATE typecast function. For instance, to add a week to a date retrieved through the @LOOKUP function, you can use a statement like this:

```
#10=@TODATE(@LOOKUP(#10,1))+7
```

Even though each database is only allowed one table, you can use this table to hold different sets of information. For instance, you can include various credit cards at the top of your lookup table and different state codes at the bottom.

When Q&A looks for information in the Key Column, it starts at the top of the table and reads down the column trying to find a match. So to make sure that Q&A retrieves the correct data, be careful not to repeat a value in the Key Column. However, if you do repeat a value, Q&A always returns the information pertaining to the first matching value found.

When you use a lookup function or command, don't worry about the case-sensitivity of the values in the lookup table. For example, if you are looking up the value visa in the Key Column, Q&A will find the value even if it is capitalized, like VISA or Visa.

Creating and Manipulating the Lookup Table

The lookup table is like any other table in Q&A. You can expand the widths of the columns by clicking on the right border of its heading. You can also change the order of the columns by clicking on a column's heading and dragging it to another position.

NOTE

When you move a column, it retains its original number as its header. Therefore, if you move Column 1 between Column 2 and Column 3, your columns are numbered across as 2,1,3,4. This rearrangement of your columns does not affect how the lookup functions and commands retrieve your data. If you construct a lookup function to retrieve data from Column 1 and move the column to a new location, your lookup function will still retrieve the data from Column 1, wherever it is located in the table.

To enter data into the lookup table, follow these steps:

1. In Database Structure mode, choose <u>D</u>atabase ➤ Edit <u>L</u>ookup Table. Q&A displays the lookup table.

2. To enter data into a row, double-click in the first cell of the row. Q&A puts the insertion point in the Key Column.

3. Type the key value in the cell.

4. Press Tab. Q&A moves the insertion point to the next column.

5. Repeat steps 3 and 4 until you run out of columns or you have completed that row.

6. To add information to the next row, repeat steps 2 to 5.

7. To add a row, add one to the bottom of the table by clicking on the <u>A</u>dd Row button.

8. To delete a row, click in any cell of that row and click the <u>D</u>elete Row button.

9. To insert an empty row in the table, move to the desired location and click on Insert Row. Q&A inserts an empty row.

10. When you have finished, click on OK.

Using the Lookup Functions and Commands

The Lookup functions @LOOKUP and @LOOKUPR use key and column parameters to locate the information to be retrieved. The retrieved information is then placed into the field that contains the programming statement.

The LOOKUP and LOOKUPR Lookup commands use key and column parameters to locate the information to be retrieved, and field parameters to indicate the location in which the retrieved information is placed.

key   LOOKUP searches through the Key Column for the row to be used in the lookup. If Q&A finds the value specified in the key parameter in the Key column of the lookup table, it retrieves information from that row. For instance, if you set this parameter to #15 and the value in field #15 equals visa, Q&A searches through the Key Column for the word visa. Then Q&A retrieves data from a column in the row containing visa.

       The key parameter can contain a field ID (such as #15), a field name (such as First Name), a text value (such as "Visa"), or a numeric value (such as 15). If you are using a text value in the key parameter, enclose it in quotation marks. Then, Q&A will not mistake it for a field name.

column   Specifies the column to use for extracting data from the lookup table. For instance, if the column parameter is set to 1, Q&A uses Column 1 as the column from which to retrieve data upon a successful match of the key parameter.

field   Specifies the destination field of the data that is retrieved from the lookup table.

If @LOOKUPR or LOOKUPR does not find a specified key value in the Key Column, it uses the next lower value. For example, if Q&A searches for and does not find the number 15 in the Key column, Q&A finds the row containing the next lower value, which might be 14. This also works with text values. For example, if @LOOKUPR or LOOKUPR cannot find the key value Peach, it returns the next lower value, which might be Peace.

This special feature in @LOOKUPR and LOOKUPR is perfect for finding items in a range. For instance, you can make a lookup table containing various tax brackets and use it to identify your tax for the year. If someone earns $33,167, Q&A can search the Key Column for that value. If that value is not found, Q&A finds the next lowest value which is 33,151 (the *low* end of the tax bracket). Q&A uses the information in this row, which contains the tax rates for the $33,151 to $33,200 tax bracket (Figure D.4).

FIGURE D.4

Use this lookup table to find tax rates within tax brackets.

Key	1	2	3	
Tax Bracket	Tax			
33001	6459			
33051	6473			
33101	6487			
33151	6501			
33201	6515			
33251	6529			
33301	6543			

As explained earlier, Q&A views the entries in the lookup table as text values only. Unfortunately, this means that Q&A looks at 5 as a greater value than 15 because the numbers are sorted alphanumerically rather than numerically. This can cause some problems when using @LOOKUPR and LOOKUPR.

T I P

To prevent any possible sorting and calculating problems, use the same number of digits for all number values in the Key Column. If a number has fewer digits than another, add leading zeros. For example, change the number 5 to 05 (Figure D.5).

FIGURE D.5

If you are listing numbers in a lookup table, make sure they all have the same number of digits. If a number does not have enough digits, add leading zeros.

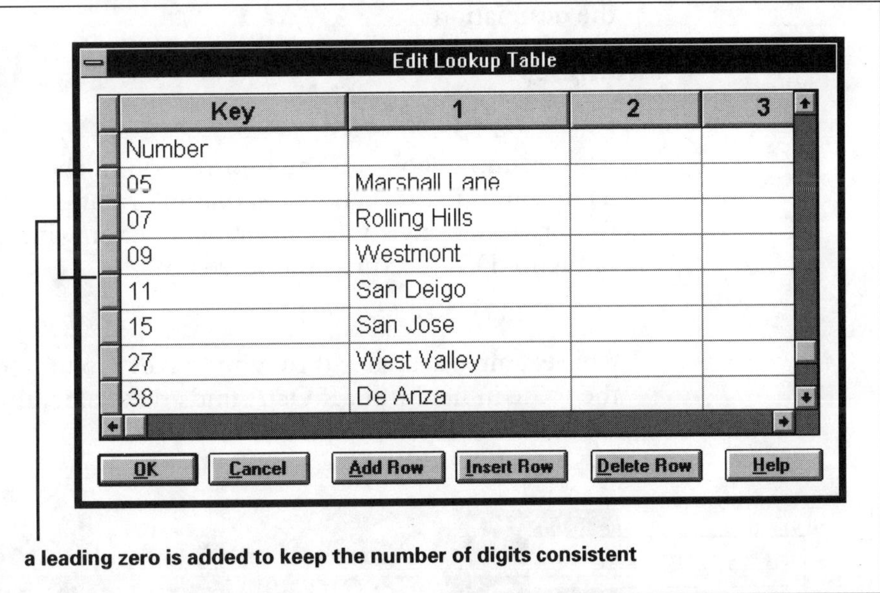

a leading zero is added to keep the number of digits consistent

@LOOKUP or @LU(*key,column*)

This function retrieves information from the lookup table and places it into the field in which the statement is located.

Examples

    #10=@LOOKUP("Visa",1)

This example looks up the information that lies in the row containing Visa and data column 1. It then places that information into field #10. If you use this programming statement in conjunction with the lookup table shown in Figure D.2, the result of the statement is the value .10.

    #10=@LOOKUP(#20,3)

This example searches through the Key Column of the lookup table for the value in field #20. If Q&A finds that value, the corresponding information in Column 3 is placed into field #10.

LOOKUP or LU(*key,column,field*)

This function retrieves information from the lookup table and places it at the destination.

Examples

    #10:LOOKUP("Visa",1,#50)

This example looks up the information in the row containing Visa and data Column 1. It then places that information into field #50. If you use this programming statement in conjunction with the lookup table shown in Figure D.2, it returns the value .10.

    #10:LOOKUP(#20,3,#25)

This example searches through the Key Column of the lookup table for the value in field #20. If Q&A finds that value, the corresponding information in Column 3 is placed in field #25.

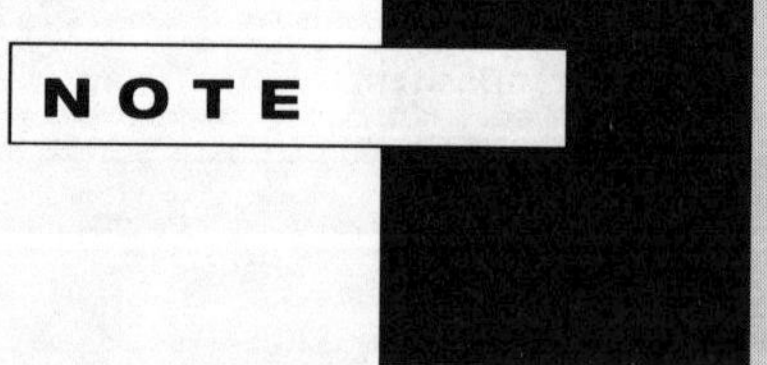

N O T E   You cannot set a field equal to a LOOKUP as you can for @LOOKUP. You must use the colon (:) with a LOOKUP. The same applies to LOOKUPR (described later).

@LOOKUPR or @LUR(*key,column*)

This function retrieves information from the lookup table and places the results in the field containing the statement. If Q&A does not find the key value, the @LOOKUPR function searches for the next lower value and returns it.

Examples

    #10=@LOOKUPR(33268,1)

This statement searches through the Key Column of the lookup table for the value 33268. If Q&A finds 33268, it retrieves the data at the intersection of that row and Column 1. Otherwise, Q&A uses the row containing the next lower value. If you use this statement with the lookup table shown in Figure D.3, Q&A uses the row containing 33251 and Column 1 to return 6529, and places the retrieved data in field #10.

    #10=@LOOKUPR(#15,#2)

This @LOOKUPR statement uses the values in field #15 to locate the row to use from the lookup table. Q&A uses the contents of field #2 to determine the column to be used.

LOOKUPR or LUR(*key,column,field*)

This function retrieves information from the lookup table and places it in another field. If Q&A does not find the key value, it searches for the next lower value.

Examples

    #10:LOOKUPR(33072,1,#40)

This statement searches through the Key Column lookup table for the value 33072. If Q&A finds 33072, it retrieves the data at the intersection of that row and Column 1. Otherwise, Q&A uses the row containing the next lower value. The retrieved data is placed in field #40. If this statement is used with the lookup table in Figure D.4, Q&A uses the row containing 33051 and Column 1 to return 6473.

    #10:LOOKUP(#20,2,#40)

Q&A finds the value in the lookup table by using the value in field #20 and Column 2 and places the retrieved data in field #40.

Using the XLookup Functions and Commands

XLookup functions and commands are extremely similar to the Lookup functions and commands. Both retrieve data from outside the records of your database. However, XLookup functions and commands retrieve data from an external database rather than from the lookup table. An XLookup uses a key parameter to find the correct record in the external database from which to retrieve information. Another parameter specifies the field on that record from which to retrieve the data. Once Q&A locates this value in the external file, it retrieves that data and places it in a field in the local database.

NOTE

If you think of the external database as being in Spreadsheet view, an XLookup is almost identical to a Lookup. Remember that Spreadsheet view of a database is made up of rows and columns. If you think of the records as rows in the database and the columns as the fields of those records, you'll retrieve the data at the intersection of the specified row and column (Figure D.6).

The construction of an XLookup requires various parameters (Figure D.7). The following list describes each of these parameters.

fn specifies the database to be used for retrieving data. In this parameter, type the database name from which you want to retrieve data. Enclose within quotation marks the information in the *fn* parameter. As a rule, you need to enclose all external references within quotation marks.

FIGURE D.6

It is easier to understand XLookups if you imagine that the external database is in the Spreadsheet view. The *xkf* parameter determines the row (record) from which to retrieve data. The *lf* parameter (described later) specifies the column from which to retrieve data.

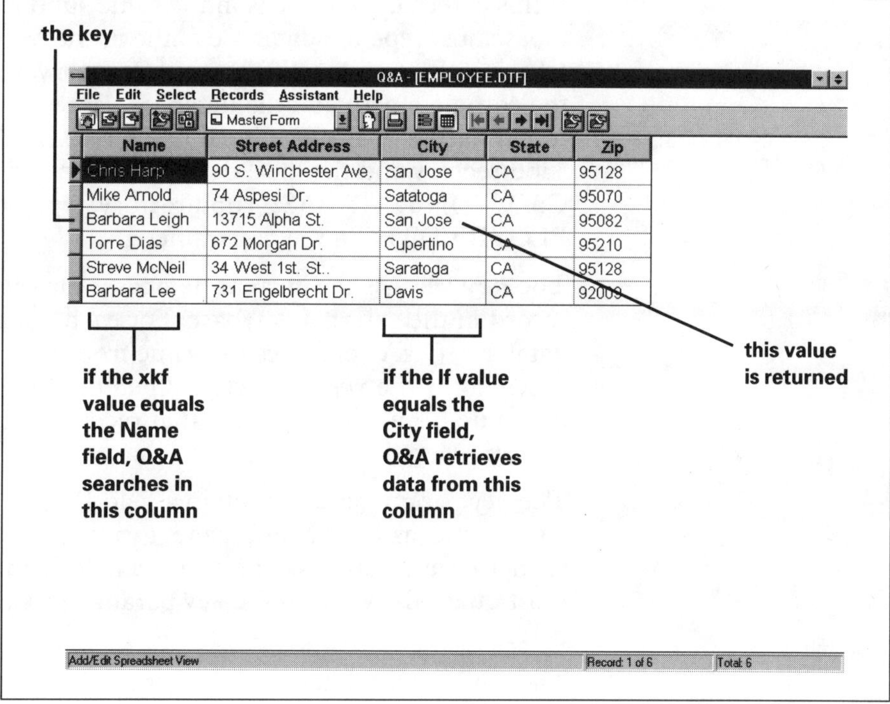

FIGURE D.7

The XLOOKUP statements consist of up to five parameters: *fn*, *key*, *xkf*, *lf*, and *df*.

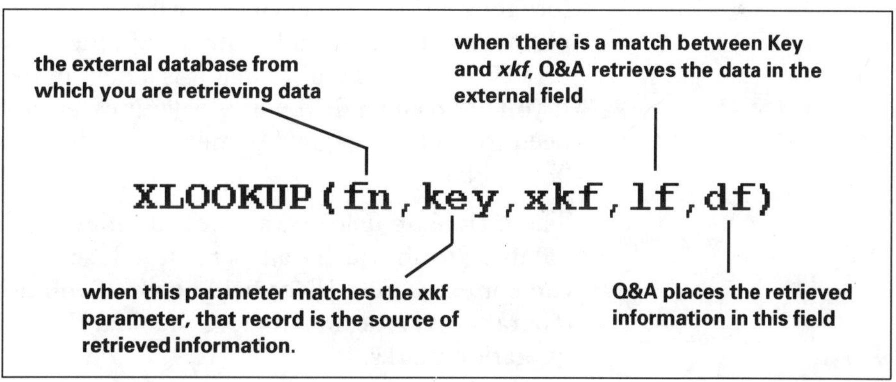

If this external database is in the same subdirectory as the local database, just type the database name in the *fn* parameter. If the database is located in a different subdirectory, you need to specify the complete path and the database name. For example, if the external database, EMPLOYEE.DTF, is located in the C:\QAWIN subdirectory and the local database is located in the C:\QAWIN\DATABASE subdirectory, type "C:\QAWIN\EMPLOYEE.DTF" in the *fn* parameter.

The ***key*** value is the current database value used to look up a record in the external database. For each record of the external database, Q&A compares the value from *key* to the external field specified by the *xkf* parameter. When the value from *key* matches the value from *xkf*, Q&A uses that record in the external database for retrieving data.

The *key* parameter can contain a field ID (such as #15), a field name (such as First Name), a text value (such as "Jones"), or a numeric value (such as 15). Since a field name or field ID is used most often, the value in the key parameter is often called the key field.

The ***xkf*** (external key field) parameter refers to the external database field used to match the value of the *key* parameter. *xkf* can contain a field ID (such as #15) or a field name (such as First Name). If you use a field ID as your *xkf* parameter, type an x before the field ID and enclose it within quotation marks. For example, to use the external key field #25, the *xkf* should look like "X#25". The X signifies that it is a field in the external database. If you are using a field name as your external key field, you only need to enclose the field name in quotation marks (for example, "First Name").

The ***lf*** (lookup field) parameter specifies the field of the external database from which data is retrieved. Like the *xkf* parameter, *lf* can contain a field ID or field name. If you use a field ID as your *lf* parameter, type an X before the field ID and enclose it within quotation marks.

The ***df*** (destination field) parameter specifies the current database field that receives the extracted data. Only use *df* with XLOOKUP and XLOOPUPR commands.

In order to find data quickly with an XLOOKUP search, the external key field (xkf) must be indexed. If it is not indexed, Q&A will not retrieve data. Indexing is covered in Chapter 11.

When performing an XLookup, Q&A scans through the records of the external database looking for a match between the *key* and *xkf* parameters. As soon as a match is found, Q&A stops and retrieves the information from that record. Even if there is another record in the external database that will match the key value, it is ignored. Therefore, we recommend that you make sure that the field that is to be used as the external key field contains unique values.

In today's business world, databases are filled with the addresses of friends, co-workers, contacts, and companies. This means that you will need to enter a lot of zip codes into your database. The @XLOOKUP function and XLOOKUP command are excellent for having Q&A enter zip codes for you. If you build a database containing the zip codes for every city in each state, you can simply have a XLookup retrieve the city and state for you when you enter a zip code. While creating a database of so much data might seem to be a finger-numbing experience, it really is not. You can acquire these zip codes in ASCII format through the United States Post Offices. So, if you read Chapter 15, you know everything needed to create a zip code XLookup system.

@XLOOKUP or @XLU(*fn,key,xkf,lf*)

This function returns a value from an external database to the field in which the statement is written.

Examples

    #10=@XLOOKUP("EMPLOYEE.DTF",F.Name,"First Name","Last
    Name")

This statement retrieves the value in the external field Last Name when the field F.Name matches the external field First Name. The database from which the information is being retrieved is EMPLOYEE.DTF. If field F.Name equals Jack and the external field First Name contains Jack, Q&A retrieves the data in the Last Name field and places it into field #10.

    #10=@XLOOKUP("C:\QAWIN\ZIPCODE.DTF",#40,"X#50","X#60")

In this example, the ZIPCODE.DTF database, which is located in another subdirectory, is the external database. If field #40 in the local database matches field #50 of the external database, the data in external field #60 is retrieved and placed into local field #10.

XLOOKUP or XLU(*fn,key,xkf,lf,df*)

This function returns a value from an external database and places it into another field.

Examples

    #10:XLOOKUP("EMPLOYEE.DTF",F.Name,"First Name","Last
    Name",L.Name)

Q&A places the value in the external field Last Name into local field L.Name when the external field First Name matches the local field F.Name. The external database from which the information is being retrieved is EMPLOYEE.DTF. For instance, if the field F.Name equals Rob and the external field First Name equals Rob, Q&A retrieves the data in the Last Name field and places it into the field L.Name.

    #10:XLOOKUP("C:\QAWIN\AREACODE.DTF"
    ,#40,"X#50","X#60",#60)

Q&A uses the AREACODE.DTF database, which is located in another subdirectory, as the external database. If the value in field #40 matches the value in external field #50, Q&A retrieves the data in external field #60 and places it into field #60.

Many people often use XLookups to fill in multiple fields in a record. For instance, imagine that you have two databases called Venture and Contacts. You have already filled the Contacts database with business acquaintances. However, sometimes you need to add a person, who already exists in Contacts, into Venture. Instead of manually retyping all of that person's information, you can use the XLOOKUP and XLOOKUPR command to retrieve all the data you need from the Contacts database. You can use a single XLOOKUP command to retrieve multiple sets of data. You only need to enter the *fn*, *key*, and *xkf* parameters once in the XLOOKUP command. However, you have to add multiple sets of *lf* and *df* fields to the fields to retrieve data (*lf*) and to place the information (*df*). Thus, the format for looking up data from multiple external fields is XLOOKUP(*fn,key,xkf,lf1,df1,lf2,df2,lf3,df3…lfn,dfn*).

@XLOOKUPR or @XLR(*fn,key,xkf,lf*)

This function returns a value from an external database and places it into the field in which the programming statement is located. If Q&A does not find the key, it returns the next lower value.

Examples

```
#10=@XLOOKUPR("TAXES.DTF",Income,"Income","Tax Rate")
```

This statement retrieves the value in the external field Tax Rate when the external field Income from the TAXES.DTF database matches the local field Income. If there is no match, Q&A returns the next lower value of the external field Income. For example, if the local field Income equals 56500, Q&A searches through the external database field Income for 56500. If it does not find a record with 56500, Q&A finds the next lower value, 56250. Q&A then retrieves the data (that is, 9.870) in the Tax Rate field and places it in local field #10.

```
#10=@XLOOKUPR("C:\QAWIN\LIBRARY.DTF",#40,"X#50","X#60")
```

If field #40 matches field #50 of the external database, LIBRARY.DTF, Q&A retrieves the data in external field #60 and places it in field #10. If Q&A does not find a match, it returns the next lower value in the external field #50.

XLOOKUPR or XLR(*fn,key,xkf,lf,df*)

This function returns a value from an external database and places it into another field. If Q&A does not find the key, it finds the next lower value.

Examples

    #10:XLOOKUPR("TAXES.DTF",Income,"Income","Tax Rate",Taxes)

When the external field Income matches the local field Income, Q&A retrieves the value from the external field Tax Rate. If there is no match, Q&A then uses the next lowest external key value. The retrieved value is placed into the local field Taxes. For example, if the local field Income equals 56500, Q&A searches through the external database field Income for 56500. If Q&A does not find a record with 56500, it finds the next lower value. In this example, Q&A finds 56250 and retrieves the data (that is, 9.870) in the Tax Rate field and places it in the local field Taxes.

    #10:XLOOKUPR("C:\QAWIN\LIBRARY.DTF",#40,"X#50","X#60",#70)

If local field #40 matches field #50 of the external database LI-BRARY.DTF, Q&A retrieves the data in external field #60 and places it in local field #10. If there is no match, Q&A finds the next lower value in external field #50 and places the retrieved data in local field #70.

Retrieving Data from dBASE Files Using XLookups

You can also use Q&A's XLOOKUP command to retrieve data from dBASE II, III, and IV files. While you use the command in the same way in which you use it for Q&A databases, consider these differences:

- The *fn* parameter must refer to the dBASE file that contains the extension .DBF.

- The *xkf* parameter can refer to two different parts of the dBASE database, depending on the version of dBASE (that is, dBASE II, dBASE III, dBASE IV). If you are using a dBASE II or dBASE III database in an XLOOKUP, use the dBASE.NDX file as your *xkf* parameter. This file must contain the .NDX extension. If you are using a dBASE IV file, use the field name as the *xkf* parameter.

- dBASE files are case-sensitive, therefore the value STEVE does not match the value Steve.

- Data cannot be returned from an encrypted dBASE file.

GOSUB and GOTO Programming

Q&A's GOSUB and GOTO programming features are powerful. However, they can be very complicated to understand. GOSUB programming lets you change the order of how fields are calculated as well as the order in which the expressions calculate. To help you understand the complexities of GOSUB programming, we use the following programming statements throughout this section.

```
Field A:    <#10:#50=#50+"A1,";#50=#50+"A2,"
Field B:    <#20:#50=#50+"B1,";#50=#50+"B2,"
Field C:    <#30:#50=#50+"C1,";#50=#50+"C2,"
Field D:    <#40:#50=#50+"D1,";#50=#50+"D2,"
Tracking: #50
```

Notice the way these statements are currently set up. If we leave the programming statements above as is, the Tracking field will contain the value A1,A2,B1,B2,C1,C2,D1,D2. However, we can change the order of calculation for these fields by using the GOSUB and GOTO commands, producing a variety of values in the Tracking field.

The commands involved in controlling GOSUB and GOTO programming are as follows:

The **GOSUB** command, when inserted anywhere within a programming statement, tells Q&A to stop calculating the expressions of that line and to calculate another line of programming. When Q&A is instructed through a GOSUB command to calculate a different section, Q&A's path of calculation is altered and does not stop or return to its original path until it executes a RETURN or STOP command. For instance, GOSUB #30 means continue calculating at the beginning of field #30 and finish calculating this programming statement when told to return. This altered path, the calculations between a GOSUB and its RETURN or STOP, is called a sub-routine. The command name GOSUB is derived from go do sub-routine.

The **RETURN** command instructs Q&A to stop a sub-routine and return to where it deviated from the standard programming path caused by the GOSUB command. When Q&A returns to the original programming statement it has strayed from with the GOSUB command, Q&A finishes calculating that statement.

The **STOP** command instructs Q&A to stop all sub-routines and calculations.

The **GOTO** command, when inserted anywhere within a programming statement, tells Q&A to go to the specified field. For instance, GOTO #30 means continue calculating at the beginning of field #30.

Here is an example of how these commands work.

```
Field A: <#10:#50=#50+"A1,";GOSUB #30;#50=#50+"A2,";GOTO
#40
Field B: <#20:#50=#50+"B1,";#50=#50+"B2,"
Field C: <#30:#50=#50+"C1,";RETURN;#50=#50+"C2,"
Field D: <#40:#50=#50+"D1,";STOP;#50=#50+"D2,"
Tracking: #50
```

The following paragraph is a step-by-step explanation of Q&A's calculation path for the preceding programming statements. Try to follow the flow of calculation. As Q&A calculates field #10 it adds "A1," to field #50 (#50=#50+"A1,"). Q&A then detours to field #30 through a GOSUB (GOSUB #30). Q&A begins calculating field #30, adding "C1," to field #50 (#50=#50+"C1,"). The sub-routine is halted by the RETURN command, telling Q&A to finish calculating field #10 where it left off (RETURN). Q&A then adds "A2," to field #50 (#50=#50+"A2,"). Once again the path of calculation is diverted. This time Q&A is instructed through a GOTO command to calculate field #40 (GOTO #40). Q&A begins calculating field #40, adding "D1" to field #50 (#50=#50+"D1,"). The calculation path is then stopped, using the STOP command (STOP).

If you plan to use these commands, there are a few conditions and factors of which you should be aware:

- A GOSUB must refer to a field that contains a RETURN, STOP, GOTO, or another GOSUB.

- Every GOSUB must have a RETURN or STOP to return or end the calculation path.

- Programming statements containing a GOSUB, GOTO, RE-TURN, or STOP must be on entry calculation fields; the programming statements must begin with a less than sign (<).

- If a programming statement containing a RETURN or STOP is executed while not in sub-routine, Q&A prompts you with an error dialog box, telling you that there is an unanticipated RE-TURN or STOP.

appendix

The Boundaries and Specifications of Q&A for Windows

This appendix lists the different boundaries and specifications for Q&A for Windows database.

AREA OF FUNCTION	ITEM	BOUNDARY
Installation	Q&A database portion only (hard disk space)	6.5 megabytes
	Q&A Write portion only (hard disk space)	8.8 megabytes
	Complete installation (hard disk space)	15.3 megabytes
System Settings	Operating System	Windows 3.1 or later (enhanced)
	RAM required	2 megabytes
	RAM recommended	4 megabytes
General Database	Fields (number per layout)	2045 fields
	Records (number per database)	520,000 records
	Field Names (number of characters per name)	78 characters
Add/Edit	Record (excluding pictures)	64,000 characters per record

AREA OF FUNCTION	ITEM	BOUNDARY
Add/Edit	Text (Amount of data per field)	32,000 characters per text field
	Number (Amount of data per field)	32.000 characters per number field
	Picture (Size of picture field)	16 megabytes
Retrieve	Spec Directory (number of saved specs)	300 specs
	Retrieve Spec (characters per spec)	1896 characters
	Fields (used per spec)	1896 fields
	Text Field (characters per field)	240 characters
	Multi-Line Text Field	1596 characters
	Number Field	240 characters
	Picture Field	0 characters
Sort	Spec Directory (number of saved specs)	300 specs
	Sort Levels	50 levels
	Sort Spec	64 characters
Mass Update	Spec Directory (number of saved specs)	300 specs
	Text Field (characters per field)	32,000 characters
	Number Field (characters per field)	32.000 characters
	Picture Field (characters per field)	32,000 characters

THE BOUNDARIES AND SPECIFICATIONS OF Q&A FOR WINDOWS

AREA OF FUNCTION	ITEM	BOUNDARY
Export	Spec Directory (number of saved specs)	300 specs
	Export Spec (characters per spec)	64,000 characters
Database Structure Programming	Program Spec (characters per spec)	64,000 characters
	Text Field (characters per field)	32,000 characters
	Number Field (characters per field)	32,000 characters
	Picture Field (characters per field)	32,000 characters
Restrictions	Restrict Spec (characters per spec)	64,000 characters
	Text Field (characters per field)	32,000 characters
	Number Field (characters per field)	32,000 characters
	Picture Field (characters per field)	0 characters
Indices	Index Spec (characters per spec)	no limit
	Fields used	115 fields
Initial Values	Initial Value Spec (characters per spec)	64,000 characters
	Text Field (characters per field)	2500 characters
	Multi-Line Text Field (characters per field)	1596 characters
	Number Field (characters per field)	32,000 characters

AREA OF FUNCTION	ITEM	BOUNDARY
	Picture Field (characters per field)	32,000 characters
Masking	Masking Spec (characters per spec)	64,000 characters
	Text Field (characters per field)	65 characters
	Number Field (characters per field)	0 characters
	Picture Field (characters per field)	0 characters
Custom Help	Help Spec (characters per spec)	64,000 characters
	Text Field (characters per field)	32,000 characters
	Number Field (characters per field)	32,000 characters
	Picture Field (characters per field)	32,000 characters
Security	Users	1000 users
	Groups	8 groups
	Users per group	120 users
Freeform Reports	Spec Directory (number of saved specs)	300 specs
	Fields (fields per report)	2195 fields
	Derived Fields (fields per report)	150 derived fields
Mailing Labels	Spec Directory (number of saved specs)	300 specs
	Fields (fields per report)	2195 fields
Columnar Reports	Spec Directory (number of saved specs)	300 specs

THE BOUNDARIES AND SPECIFICATIONS OF Q&A FOR WINDOWS

AREA OF FUNCTION	ITEM	BOUNDARY
	Columns (columns per report)	2195 columns
	Derived Columns	150 derived columns
Intelligent Assistant (DAVE)	Text Field (characters per query)	32,000 characters
	Number Field (characters per query)	78 characters
Scripting Assistant	Spec Directory (number of saved specs)	300 specs
	Scripting Spec (characters per script)	64,000 characters
	Menu	10 scripts
Input Form Design	Spec Directory (number of saved specs)	300 specs
	Input Form Spec (size of each input form)	16 megabytes
Navigation Programming	Navigation Spec (characters per spec)	64,000 characters
	Text Field (characters per field)	5000 characters
	Number Field (characters per field)	5000 characters
	Picture Field (characters per field)	5000 characters

INDEX

Note to the reader: Throughout this index, **boldfaced** page numbers indicate primary discussions of a topic. *Italicized* page numbers indicate illustrations.

D

I

GET A FREE CATALOG JUST FOR EXPRESSING YOUR OPINION.

Help us improve our books and get a *FREE* full-color catalog in the bargain. Please complete this form, pull out this page and send it in today. The address is on the reverse side.

Name ______________________________   Company ______________________________

Address ______________________________   City __________ State ____ Zip ________

Phone (____) ______________________

1. How would you rate the overall quality of this book?

- ❑ Excellent
- ❑ Very Good
- ❑ Good
- ❑ Fair
- ❑ Below Average
- ❑ Poor

2. What were the things you liked most about the book? (Check all that apply)

- ❑ Pace
- ❑ Format
- ❑ Writing Style
- ❑ Examples
- ❑ Table of Contents
- ❑ Index
- ❑ Price
- ❑ Illustrations
- ❑ Type Style
- ❑ Cover
- ❑ Depth of Coverage
- ❑ Fast Track Notes

3. What were the things you liked *least* about the book? (Check all that apply)

- ❑ Pace
- ❑ Format
- ❑ Writing Style
- ❑ Examples
- ❑ Table of Contents
- ❑ Index
- ❑ Price
- ❑ Illustrations
- ❑ Type Style
- ❑ Cover
- ❑ Depth of Coverage
- ❑ Fast Track Notes

4. Where did you buy this book?

- ❑ Bookstore chain
- ❑ Small independent bookstore
- ❑ Computer store
- ❑ Wholesale club
- ❑ College bookstore
- ❑ Technical bookstore
- ❑ Other __________________

5. How did you decide to buy this particular book?

- ❑ Recommended by friend
- ❑ Recommended by store personnel
- ❑ Author's reputation
- ❑ Sybex's reputation
- ❑ Read book review in __________
- ❑ Other __________________

6. How did you pay for this book?

- ❑ Used own funds
- ❑ Reimbursed by company
- ❑ Received book as a gift

7. What is your level of experience with the subject covered in this book?

- ❑ Beginner
- ❑ Intermediate
- ❑ Advanced

8. How long have you been using a computer?

years __________________

months __________________

9. Where do you most often use your computer?

- ❑ Home
- ❑ Work

- ❑ Both
- ❑ Other __________________

10. What kind of computer equipment do you have? (Check all that apply)

- ❑ PC Compatible Desktop Computer
- ❑ PC Compatible Laptop Computer
- ❑ Apple/Mac Computer
- ❑ Apple/Mac Laptop Computer
- ❑ CD ROM
- ❑ Fax Modem
- ❑ Data Modem
- ❑ Scanner
- ❑ Sound Card
- ❑ Other __________________

11. What other kinds of software packages do you ordinarily use?

- ❑ Accounting
- ❑ Databases
- ❑ Networks
- ❑ Apple/Mac
- ❑ Desktop Publishing
- ❑ Spreadsheets
- ❑ CAD
- ❑ Games
- ❑ Word Processing
- ❑ Communications
- ❑ Money Management
- ❑ Other __________________

12. What operating systems do you ordinarily use?

- ❑ DOS
- ❑ OS/2
- ❑ Windows
- ❑ Apple/Mac
- ❑ Windows NT
- ❑ Other __________________

13. On what computer-related subject(s) would you like to see more books?

____

____

____

____

14. Do you have any other comments about this book? (Please feel free to use a separate piece of paper if you need more room)

____

____

____

____

PLEASE FOLD, SEAL, AND MAIL TO SYBEX

SYBEX INC.
Department M
2021 Challenger Drive
Alameda, CA
94501

Common Q&A Database Shortcut Keys

SHORTCUT KEYS	EQUIVALENT COMMAND	DESCRIPTION
Alt+F4	File ➤ Exit	Exit this application
Ctrl+A	Edit ➤ Select All	Select the entire field
Ctrl+C	Edit ➤ Copy	Copy a selection into the Clipboard
Ctrl+E	Select ➤ Add/Edit	Add, modify, or delete information
Ctrl+F4	File ➤ Close	Close the file
Ctrl+I	Assistant ➤ Intelligent Assistant	Start the IA
Ctrl+J	Assistant ➤ Scripting Assistant	Start the Scripting Assistant
Ctrl+M	Select ➤ Design Input Forms	Work with input forms
Ctrl+O	File ➤ Open	Open a file
Ctrl+P	File ➤ Print	Prints records, reports, and input forms
Ctrl+Shift+D	Edit ➤ Paste Special ➤ Current Date	Paste the current date into this field
Ctrl+Shift+T	Edit ➤ Paste Special ➤ Current Time	Paste the current time into this field
Ctrl+V	Edit ➤ Paste	Paste a selection from the Clipboard into the file
Ctrl+W	File ➤ Q&A Write	Start Q&A Write from within Q&A Database
Ctrl+X	Edit ➤ Cut	Cut a selection into the Clipboard
Ctrl+Y	Select ➤ Design Reports/Labels	Work with reports and labels
Ctrl+Z	Edit ➤ Undo	Reverse the last deletion or action, if possible
Del	Edit ➤ Clear	Delete the selection